PERSIA AND THE BIBLE

PERSIA AND THE BIBLE

EDWIN M. YAMAUCHI

Foreword
by
Donald J. Wiseman

BakerBooks
A Division of Baker Book House Co.
Grand Rapids, Michigan 49516

Published by Baker Books
a division of Baker Book House Company
P.O. Box 6287, Grand Rapids, MI 49516-6287

First hardcover edition published 1990

First paperback edition published 1996
Second printing, May 2000

Printed in the United States of America

Library of Congress Cataloging-in-Publication Data

Yamauchi, Edwin M.
Persia and the Bible / Edwin M. Yamauchi
p. cm.
Includes bibliographical references
ISBN 0-8010-2108-1
1. Iran in the Bible. 2. Iran—History—To 640 A.D. 3. Iran—Antiquities. 4. Excavations (Archaeology)—Iran. 5. Bible—Antiquities. I. Title
BS680.I65Y35 1990
220.9'3'0935—dc20 89-48988

For information about academic books, resources for Christian leaders, and all new releases available from Baker Book House, visit our web site:
http://www.bakerbooks.com/

To
Bill and Enid Wilson
Cofounders of the Oxford Bible Fellowship

Contents

Foreword

Iran is once again a center of world attention. It is to be hoped that the interruption in archaeological work there is but temporary. It seems, therefore, an opportune moment to issue this book on Persia and the Bible, for that great and ancient people and civilization played a significant part in later Old Testament history. No authoritative and dependable survey of the whole subject has been written especially for students of the Bible in recent years, so Dr. Yamauchi's book is to be welcomed.

The author's writings on archaeology and the Bible always give a balanced presentation of the evidence, and he brings out clearly and fairly those controversial points where scholars differ in interpretation. For this Dr. Yamauchi has rightly earned an international reputation. Here he furnishes us with a carefully documented introduction to the peoples who made up the old cosmopolitan Persian confederation and to the rulers, with their great dynastic names of Cyrus, Darius, and Xerxes, who played a dominant role in the history of Achaemenian days.

Dr. Yamauchi has followed the methods outlined in his *The Stones and the Scriptures* (1972) and is fully aware of the limitation of the evidence at places in a history that has close links also with his *Greece and Babylon* (1967).

Archaeology provides vital, if sometimes scanty, clues that enable the reader and teacher to understand the background of the relevant biblical passages with their distinctive theological viewpoint. This book will enable us all to relate the appropriate and abiding message of the Bible to our own world with its similar problems.

DONALD J. WISEMAN
Emeritus Professor of Assyriology
University of London

Preface

Though the terms *Persia/Persians* occur only in Ezekiel, 2 Chronicles, Esther, Daniel, and Ezra, ancient Persia played an important role in all the exilic and postexilic Old Testament books, including at the least 2 Chronicles, Daniel, Esther, Ezra, Nehemiah, Haggai, Zechariah, and Malachi. Though we now have some excellent scholarly expositions of ancient Persian history, archaeology, and religion, it has been over thirty years since we have had a work such as Robert North's *Guide to Biblical Iran* (1956), which was specifically written to inform readers of the Bible about this important Persian background.

I have been interested in the subject of ancient Persia since 1961, when one of the first courses I taught was the Greek text of Herodotus. Since 1964 I have taught Persian history about once every three years, first at Rutgers University, and since 1969 at Miami University.

In 1974 and then again in 1975 I had the privilege of visiting Iran and viewing most of the important sites. On the second occasion I was one of about a dozen American scholars invited to participate in the Second International Congress of Mithraic Studies held at Tehran, under the sponsorship of the empress of Iran. It was a great privilege to meet leading Iranologists from many different nations.

Since the Islamic revolution of 1979, no further excavations have taken place. The spate of scholarly articles on ancient Persia has not diminished, however. This is an appropriate time to take stock of what we know about this fabled land and fascinating era.

It is my hope that in the future relations between Iran and the West may improve, so that travelers may view such important sites as Susa, Pasagardae, and Persepolis for themselves. The ancient Persian Empire was one of the grandest. Within this setting many important biblical events took place. It is my aim that readers of such books as Daniel, Esther, Ezra, and Nehemiah may better appreciate their historical and cultural backgrounds.

The writing of a full-scale study on ancient Persia is a formidable task as Professor R. N. Frye notes:

> In scholarship relating to ancient Iran one must strive to control all the sources as well as secondary literature, since in the field of ancient Iran the paucity of written sources is so great that all items of information, from the realms of art, archaeology, religion, and others, must be utilized to understand and to reconstruct the past. Because of the lack of sources in this area speculation is rife, and if two specialists on ancient Iran agree it is a rare occurrence. (R. N. Frye, "Remarks on Kingship in Ancient Iran," *Acta Antiqua* 25 [1977]: 101)

I am therefore grateful to the distinguished scholars who took the time to read parts of this manuscript and offered their critical comments: Jack Balcer (Persian and Greek History, Ohio State University), Robert Bianchi (Egyptology, Brooklyn Museum), James W. Boyd (Zoroastrianism, Colorado State University), David Graf (Persian History, University of Miami), Kenneth A. Kitchen (Egyptology, University of Liverpool), Alan R. Millard (Assyriology, University of Liverpool), Herbert Paper (Persian Languages, Hebrew Union College), William H. Shea (Persian History and the Old Testament, Biblical Research Institute), and Donald J. Wiseman (emeritus professor of Assyriology, University of London). These scholars do not necessarily agree with my views, and any errors and infelicities are my own.

I am also indebted to the following scholars for their generosity in sharing their publications and offprints: Kersey Antia (Zoroastrian Center), W. R. Darrow (Williams College), Pericles Georges (Harvard University), E. D. Francis (University of Texas), Ilya Gershevitch (Cambridge University), Jonas Greenfield (Hebrew University), John Hinnells (Manchester University), J. K. Hoffmeier (Wheaton College), Ken Hoglund (Duke University), Trudy Kawami (New York University), Bradley Lenz

(University of Wisconsin), Joseph Naveh (Hebrew University), Bezalel Porten (Hebrew University), Werner Sundermann (Akademie der Wissenschaften der D.D.R.), David Weisberg (Hebrew Union College), John Whitcomb (Grace Theological Seminary), and Hugh G. M. Williamson (Cambridge University).

Thanks are due to the many librarians who assisted my research, especially those at Miami University, Hebrew Union College, and the University of Cincinnati. I would like to single out Sarah Barr and Scott Van Dam of Miami's Interlibrary Service, and Jean Wellington and Michael Braunlin of the Classics Library at the University of Cincinnati.

For the maps I am indebted to the late Jerry Coltharp of the Audio-Visual Department of Miami University. Funds for research and for the acquisition of photos were provided by the Miami University Research Council, the Graduate School, and the College of Arts and Sciences. I wish to thank Dean Leonard Simutis and Dean Stephen Day for their support.

I am grateful to Robert North and to the Editrice Pontificio Istituto Biblico for permission to reproduce the map of Ecbatana, and to David Stronach and the British Institute of Persian Studies for permission to reproduce the map of Pasargadae.

Photos and illustrations were provided by: the American Numismatic Society (fig. 36), *Aramco World Magazine* (figs. 22, 23), Bodleian Library (fig. 116), the Boston Museum of Fine Arts (figs. 3, 119), Mary Boyce (figs. 115, 121), the British Museum (figs. 17, 24, 34, 37), the British School of Archaeology (fig. 12), the Brooklyn Museum (figs. 20, 21, 47, 52), the Cincinnati Art Museum (figs. 45, 49, 66, 120, 128), the Detroit Institute of Art (fig. 126), Andrew N. Gagg (fig. 25), Gebrüder Mann (figs. 86, 90, 91, 108), Holle Verlag (fig. 48), Istanbul Archaeological Museum (fig. 122), Museum of London (figs. 129, 133), Metropolitan Museum of New York (figs. 1, 2, 4, 10, 13, 15, 16, 43, 44, 50, 57, 60, 67, 68, 109), National Gallery of Art (fig. 127), Newcastle Museum of Antiquities (figs. 130, 132), the Oriental Institute of the University of Chicago (figs. 11, 26, 29, 51, 53, 55, 71, 92, 100, 111, 112, 114, 118), Palphot (fig. 125), Paul Popper (fig. 117), F. Vallat (figs. 61, 62), Vatican Museum (fig. 19), and the Yale University Gallery of Art (figs. 46, 134). Photos without attribution were taken by the author.

The author is indebted to the translator and the publisher for permission to cite from A. J. Podlecki, trans., *The Persians by Aeschylus* (Englewood Cliffs, N.J.: Prentice-Hall, 1970); also to McGill-Queen's University Press to cite from A. Podlecki, *The Life of Themistocles;* and to St. Martin's Press to cite from A. Burn, *Persia and the Greeks.*

Permission has been granted to adapt previous materials I have written by the following journals and publishers:

"The Achaemenid Capitals," *Near East Archaeological Society Bulletin*

"The Archaeological Background of Daniel," "The Archaeological Background of Esther," "The Archaeological Background of Ezra," "The Archaeological Background of Nehemiah," *Bibliotheca Sacra*

"Religions of the Biblical World: Persia," *The International Standard Bible Encyclopedia* (Eerdmans)

"Ezra, Nehemiah," *Expositor's Bible Commentary*; "Cyrus," "Darius," "Ecbatana," "Medes," "Nebuchadnezzar," "Pasargadae," "Susa," *The New International Dictionary of Biblical Archaeology* (Zondervan)

I am grateful for the patience of Dan Van't Kerkhoff and Allan Fisher of Baker Book House and for their helpful cooperation in seeing this manuscript into print.

Finally I am indebted to my wife, Kimie, for her patient endurance as a scholar's widow during the long gestation of this project.

I should like to call attention to three important reference works which have appeared recently:

J. Boardman, N. G. L. Hamond, D. M. Lewis and M. Ostwald, ed., *The Cambridge Ancient History* IV: *Persia, Greece and the Western Mediterranean c. 525 to 479* B.C.(2nd ed.; Cambridge: Cambridge University Press, 1988); M. A. Dandamaev and V. G. Lukonin, *The Culture and Social Institutions of Ancient Iran*, tr. P. L. Kohl (Cambridge: Cambridge University Press, 1989); M. A. Dandamaev, *A Political History of the Achaemenid Empire*, tr. W. J. Vogelsang (Leiden: E. J. Brill, 1990).

Abbreviations

AA	*Archäologischer Anzeiger des Jahrbuches des deutschen archäologischen Instituts*
AAH	*Acta Antiqua Academiae Scientiarum Hungaricae*
ABC	*Assyrian and Babylonian Chronicles* (see Grayson)
AfO	*Archiv für Orientforschung*
AHR	*American Historical Review*
AJA	*American Journal of Archaeology*
AJAH	*American Journal of Ancient History*
AJP	*American Journal of Philology*
AJSL	*American Journal of Semitic Languages*
AMI	*Archäologische Mitteilungen aus Iran*
ANET	*Ancient Near Eastern Texts* (see Pritchard)
ANRW	*Aufstieg und Niedergang der römischen Welt*
AO	*Archiv Orientální*
Arch	*Archaeology*
AS	*Anatolian Studies*
AUSS	*Andrews University Seminary Studies*
BA	*Biblical Archaeologist*
BAR	*Biblical Archaeology Review*
BASOR	*Bulletin of the American Schools of Oriental Research*

BCH	*Bulletin de correspondence hellenique*
BIFAO	*Bulletin de l'institut français d'archéologie orientale*
BJRL	*Bulletin of the John Rylands Library*
BMMA	*Bulletin of the Metropolitan Museum of Art*
BO	*Bibliotheca Orientalis*
BTS	*Bible et Terre Sainte*
BS	*Bibliotheca Sacra*
BSOAS	*Bulletin of the School of Oriental & African Studies*
BZ	*Biblische Zeitschrift*
CAH	*Cambridge Ancient History* (see Boardman)
CBQ	*Catholic Biblical Quarterly*
CDAFI	*Cahiers de la délégation archéologique française en Iran*
CHI	*Cambridge History of Iran* (see Gershevitch)
CHJ	*Cambridge History of Judaism* (see Davies)
CIMRM	*Corpus Inscriptionum et Monumentorum Religionis Mithriacae* (see Vermaseren)
CJ	*Classical Journal*
CP	*Classical Philology*
CQ	*Classical Quarterly*
CRAIBL	*Comptes-rendus de seances de l'Académie des Inscriptions et Belles-lettres*
CSCA	*California Studies in Classical Antiquity*
CW	*Classical World*
DB	Darius's Behistun inscription, taken from R. G. Kent, *Old Persian,* rev. ed. (New Haven: American Society, 1953)
DOTT	*Documents from Old Testament Times* (see Thomas)
EI	*Eretz Israel*
EM	*Etudes Mithriaques* (see Duchesne-Guillemin)
EQ	*Evangelical Quarterly*
EW	*East and West*
Exped	*Expedition*
GRBS	*Greek, Roman and Byzantine Studies*
HJ	*Hibbert Journal*
HR	*History of Religions*
HSCP	*Harvard Studies in Classical Philology*
HTR	*Harvard Theological Review*
HUCA	*Hebrew Union College Annual*
IA	*Iranica Antiqua*
IDBS	*The Interpreter's Dictionary of the Bible, Supplementary Volume* (see Crim)
IEJ	*Israel Exploration Journal*
IIJ	*Indo-Iranian Journal*
ILN	*Illustrated London News*
JA	*Journal asiatique*
JAC	*Jahrbuch für Antike und Christentum*
JAAR	*Journal of the American Academy of Religion*

JANE	*Journal of the Ancient Near Eastern Society of Columbia University*
JAOS	*Journal of the American Oriental Society*
JARCE	*Journal of the American Research Center in Egypt*
JBAChr	*Jahrbuch für Antike und Christentum*
JBL	*Journal of Biblical Literature*
JCS	*Journal of Cuneiform Studies*
JEA	*Journal of Egyptian Archaeology*
JESHO	*Journal of the Economic and Social History of the Orient*
JETS	*Journal of the Evangelical Theological Society*
JFA	*Journal of Field Archaeology*
JHS	*Journal of Hellenic Studies*
JMS	*Journal of Mithraic Studies*
JNES	*Journal of Near Eastern Studies*
JQR	*Jewish Quarterly Review*
JRAS	*Journal of the Royal Asiatic Society*
JRS	*Journal of Roman Studies*
JSJ	*Journal for the Study of Judaism*
JSOT	*Journal for the Study of the Old Testament*
JSS	*Journal of Semitic Studies*
JTS	*Journal of Theological Studies*
MDOG	*Mitteilungen der Deutschen Orient Gesellschaft zu Berlin*
MM	*Mysteria Mithrae* (see Bianchi)
MS	*Mithraic Studies* (see Hinnells)
NEASB	*Near Eastern Archaeological Society Bulletin*
NIDBA	*The New International Dictionary of Archaeology* (see Blaiklock)
NT	*Novum Testamentum*
OLZ	*Orientalische Literaturzeitung*
OP	*Old Persian* (see Kent)
Or	*Orientalia*
PAPS	*Proceedings of the American Philosophical Society*
PEQ	*Palestine Exploration Quarterly*
POT	*Peoples of Old Testament Times* (see Wiseman)
RA	*Revue archéologique*
RB	*Revue biblique*
REA	*Revue des études anciennes*
REG	*Revue des études grecques*
RhM	*Rheinisches Museum für Philologie*
RHR	*Revue de l'histoire des religions*
RQ	*Revue de Qumrân*
RSR	*Recherches de science religieuse*
RStR	*Religious Studies Review*
SCO	*La Soteriologia dei Culti Orientali nell'Impero Romano* (see Bianchi and Vermaseren)
SMSR	*Studi e Materiali de Storia delle Religioni*
TA	*Tel Aviv*

TAPA	*Transactions of the American Philological Association*
TB	*Tyndale Bulletin*
VT	*Vetus Testamentum*
WO	*Welt des Orients*
ZA	*Zeitschrift für Assyriologie und vorderasiatische Archäologie*
ZÄS	*Zeitschrift für ägyptische Sprache und Altertumskunde*
ZAW	*Zeitschrift für die alttestamentliche Wissenschaft*
ZDMG	*Zeitschrift der deutschen morgenländischen Gesellschaft*
ZNW	*Zeitschrift für die neutestamentliche Wissenschaft*
ZTK	*Zeitschrift für Theologie und Kirche*

Introduction

Nomenclature

Persia is the ancient name for the area found in the modern country of Iran, though at its height under the Achaemenid rulers (sixth–fifth centuries B.C.) the Persian Empire also included territories now found in Egypt, Israel, Jordan, Syria, Turkey, Russia, Iraq, Pakistan, and Afghanistan.

The name *Persia* is first encountered as *Parsua* in Assyrian texts of the ninth century B.C. It later came to designate especially the area around Persepolis north of the Persian Gulf, Pars (Fars). The name persists in the designation of the modern Persian language as Farsi.

Iran, which has been the official name of the country since 1935, is cognate with the name *Aryan.*[1] The Iranians are Indo-European speaking and not Arabic speaking like their Muslim neighbors in Iraq (ancient Mesopotamia) to the west. Modern Persian, though it is written in Ara-

1. See V. G. Childe, *The Aryans: A Story of Indo-European Origins* (New York: Knopf, 1926). On the background of Hitler's notion of a blue-eyed Nordic superior race, see Leon Poliakov, *The Aryan Myth* (London: Sussex University Press, 1974).

bic characters, is an Indo-European language related to Sanskrit, Greek, Latin, and English. Farsi is derived from Middle Persian (Pahlavi), which was written in a script developed from the Aramaic alphabet, and ultimately from Old Persian, which was written in a cuneiform syllabary.[2] Today related branches of the Iranian family of Indo-European languages include: Kurdish, spoken in Turkey, Iraq, and Iran; Balochi in the Baluchistan area of Pakistan and Iran; and Pashto in Afghanistan.

The Land

Modern Iran covers an area of 630,000 square miles. This is the equivalent of the United States east of the Mississippi without New England. It is six times the size of Great Britain or three times the size of France.[3] Its borders extend 2,750 miles, including 1,100 miles in the south along the Persian Gulf and the Gulf of Oman, and 400 miles in the north along the shore of the Caspian Sea. Disputes with the Russians over boundaries in the north were settled in the twentieth century.[4] But disputes about the control of the Shatt al-Arab, the single confluence into which the Euphrates and the Tigris merge, resulted in the war with Iraq, which broke out in 1980.

In ancient times the natural boundary with Mesopotamia was formed by the Zagros Mountains, which extend 750 miles from northwest to southeast. These parallel ridges, ranging from 6,500 to 13,100 feet in height, form numerous narrow but fertile valleys. These were the homes of fierce mountain tribes who periodically attacked the lowlands of Mesopotamia. Today in the northern areas of the Zagros, the stubbornly independent Kurds similarly provide the governments of Iraq and Iran with their most serious challenge.

At the southwest corner of Iran is the alluvial plain of Khuzistan, which was dominated in antiquity by the city of Susa. This area, known as Elam, was a region intimately linked with Sumer in southern Mesopotamia in the third millennium B.C. The region is drained by the Karun River, which is navigable seventy miles from its mouth.

In northwestern Iran there is a relatively large lake, Lake Urmia (Lake Reza'iyeh), which was in the heartland of the Urartians and Man-

2. R. G. Kent, *Old Persian*, 2d ed. (New Haven: American Oriental Society, 1953).

3. D. N. Wilber, *Iran: Past and Present*, 5th ed. (Princeton: Princeton University Press, 1963), p. 2; W. B. Fisher, ed., *The Cambridge History of Iran I: The Land of Iran* (Cambridge: Cambridge University Press, 1968), p. 3; R. N. Frye, *The History of Ancient Iran* (Munich: C. H. Beckische Verlag, 1984), chapter 1.

4. P. Avery, *Modern Iran* (New York: Praeger, 1965), p. 2. Compare F. S. Fatemi, *The USSR in Iran* (South Brunswick, N.J.: A. S. Barnes, 1980).

naeans. It is a shallow body of water, 90 by 30 miles, almost as saline as the Dead Sea. The area of Azerbaijan between Lake Urmia and the Caspian Sea is one of the few areas to receive abundant rainfall.

The northern part of Iran is dominated by the Alburz Mountains, ranging 600 miles from west to east but only 60 to 80 miles from north to south. Its highest peak, Mount Demavend (19,000 feet), is even higher than the noted Mount Ararat, just across the border in eastern Turkey. North of the Alburz is the Caspian Sea, 85 feet below sea level.

Eastern Iran is dominated in the north by the hills of Khorasan and in the south by the hills of Baluchistan. Just to the east the Badakhshan area of Afghanistan was noted in antiquity as the source of the highly prized blue lapis lazuli stone.[5] The climate in these regions is extremely forbidding, with hot and dusty summers and severe winters.

The southern coastal region of the Makran did not provide much of a naval advantage to the ancient Persians. It is extremely arid, as Alexander and his men discovered to their dismay on their long trip back to Mesopotamia. Only a few minor ports served the ancient seamen who made the long voyage between the Persian Gulf and India.[6]

The interior half of Iran, some 300,000 square miles, consists of uninhabitable and almost impassable desert regions, the Dasht-i-Kavir ("Barren Plain") to the north and the Dasht-i-Lut ("Salt Desert") to the south. Areas of the latter consist of salty crust or slimy mud, which are extremely treacherous to travelers.

Natural Resources

The Zagros Mountains were especially rich in minerals such as the copper used to produce the famous Luristan bronzes. This attracted the interest of the Sumerians and Babylonians who lacked such resources. Later the Assyrians coveted the horses raised by the Medes. Petroleum, which plays such a dominant role in the region today, was only valued in its asphalt form as pitch to waterproof boats.[7]

The Zagros Mountains served as a barrier to the rain-bearing winds from the west. As a result central Iran is extremely dry, receiving an

5. G. Herrmann, "Lapis Lazuli: The Early Phases of Its Trade," *Iraq* 30 (1968): 21–57; V. I. Sarianidi, "The Lapis Lazuli Route in the Ancient East," *Arch* 24 (1971): 12–15.

6. See G. Possehl, ed., *Ancient Cities of the Indus* (Durham, N.C.: Carolina Academic Press, 1979), part 5, "Mesopotamia and Persian Gulf Maritime Trade with India," pp. 153–75.

7. See Herodotus 6.119. L. Lockhart, "Iranian Petroleum in Ancient and Medieval Times," *Journal of the Institute of Petroleum* 25 (1939): 1–18; R. J. Forbes, "Petroleum and Bitumen in Antiquity," *Journal of the Institute of Petroleum* 25 (1939): 19–23.

average of less than twelve inches of rain per year. There have, therefore, been only a few regions capable of supporting sizable populations.

Most of the people in antiquity lived in the west in the valleys of the Zagros, in Azerbaijan, in Khuzistan, and along what has been called the shore of the inland desert. Today the major cities are located on the high plateau, such as Tehran at 3,800 feet above sea level, Isfahan at 5,400 feet, and Shiraz at 5,200 feet. The topographical features that separated enclaves of populations contributed to the variety and even disunity of the population in ancient times and do so even today.[8]

The technological discovery that enabled the ancient Iranians to conserve their limited water supply was their development of *qanats*, systems of underwater channels. These are dug into the water table at a depth of one hundred meters and extend great distances, commonly from six to ten miles. Their presence is betrayed on the surface by a series of air shafts. The system, which is first attested in the eighth century B.C., was extended throughout the Achaemenian Empire and is still in use today in the Near East.[9]

Historical Outline

In the early third millennium B.C. the first recorded history concerns the Elamites of Susa. The Elamites had their own form of writing known as Proto-Elamite, which has been found not only at Susa, Anshan, and Tepe Sialk but also far to the east at Tepe Yahya.[10] The fact that the kings of Susa were married to Sumerian princesses did not dissuade the Elamites from sacking Ur around 1950 B.C.

During the second millennium B.C. the Elamites continued as rivals of the Mesopotamians. From time to time they were dominated by the Babylonians. In other eras they swept into Mesopotamia and carried off such treasures as the Stele of Naram-Sin and the Code of Hammurabi from Babylon to Susa.

Toward the end of the second millennium B.C. tribes of Indo-

8. R. N. Frye, *The Heritage of Persia* (Cleveland: World, 1963), p. 13; M. E. L. Mallowan, *Early Mesopotamia and Iran* (London: Thames and Hudson, 1965), p. 16.

9. P. W. English, "The Origin and Spread of Qanats in the Old World," *Proceedings of the American Philosophical Society* 112 (1968): 170–81; H. Wulff, "The Qanats of Iran," *Scientific American* 218 (Apr. 1968): 94–105.

10. W. C. Brice, "The Writing System of the Proto-Elamite Account Tablets of Susa," *BJRL* 45 (1962): 15–57; W. Hinz, "Zur Entzifferung der Elamischen Strichschrift," *IA* 2 (1962): 1–17; C. C. Lamberg-Karlovsky, "The Proto-Elamite Settlement at Tepe Yahya," *Iran* 10 (1971): 87–94. For western Iran, especially Elam, during the fourth through second millennia B.C., see E. Carter and M. W. Stolper, *Elam: Surveys of Political History and Archaeology* (Berkeley: University of California Press, 1985); F. Hole, ed., *Archaeology of Western Iran* (Washington, D.C.: Smithsonian Institution, 1987).

Europeans from the steppes of Russia infiltrated Iran. They eventually settled in the west, where they were first reported by the Assyrians in the ninth century as the Madai (Medes) and as Parsua or Parsumash (Persians).

After a twenty-eight-year hegemony by the invading Scythians from Russia, the Medes became united in the seventh century. They dominated the Persians until the rise of Cyrus II (circa 550), who was himself half-Median and half-Persian.

The most brilliant period of Persian history was that under the Achaemenid rulers—Cyrus and his successors. They extended the Persian Empire to Egypt and Turkey to the west and Bactria and the Indus Valley to the east.[11] During this period the Persians under Darius and Xerxes were defeated by the heroic efforts of the Greeks in 490 at Marathon, in 480 at Salamis, and in 479 at Plataea and Mycale.[12] It was in this era that Darius and Xerxes built their monumental palaces at Persepolis.

Around 400 B.C. a former disciple of Socrates, Xenophon, accompanied a band of about ten thousand Greek mercenaries into the heart of the Persian Empire in a fruitless attempt to place Cyrus the Younger on the throne. Toward the end of the fourth century Alexander decisively defeated the Persian forces at Granicus in western Turkey, Issos in southeastern Turkey, and Gaugamela/Arbela in Mesopotamia. Not content with the capture of these Persian capitals, Alexander pushed his men to the farthest boundaries of the Persian realm, over the snow-capped Hindu-Kush mountains in the northeast and down the Indus River to the southeast.[13]

After Alexander's untimely death in 323, Mesopotamia and Persia were inherited by Seleucus, one of his generals. This area was, however, too vast for the Seleucids to control. In 260 B.C. descendants of the Macedonian soldiers established the independent kingdom of Bactria (in Afghanistan), which was to last until approximately 100 B.C.[14]

Of greater significance was the reestablishment of an independent

11. See W. Culican, *The Medes and Persians* (New York: Praeger, 1965); J. M. Cook, *The Persian Empire* (New York: Schocken, 1983); I. Gershevitch, ed., *The Cambridge History of Iran II: The Median and Achaemenian Periods* (Cambridge: Cambridge University Press, 1985).

12. See A. R. Burn, *Persia and the Greeks* (New York: St. Martin's, 1962); E. D. Francis, "Greeks and Persians," in *Ancient Persia*, ed. D. Schmandt-Besserat (Malibu: Undena, 1980), pp. 53–86.

13. M. Wheeler, *Flames over Persepolis* (New York: Reynal, 1968); C. Starr, "Greeks and Persians in the Fourth Century B.C.," *IA* 11 (1975): 39–99; 12 (1977): 49–116.

14. T. Rice, *Ancient Arts of Central Asia* (New York: Praeger, 1965), chapter 4, "Bactria and North-Western India from Achaemenid to Islamic Times"; E. Knauer, "Some Aspects of the Classical Heritage in Afghanistan," *Exped* 18/3 (1976): 14–25; F. R. Allchin and N. Hammond, *The Archaeology of Afghanistan* (London: Academy, 1978); E. Yamauchi, "Bactria," in *The New International Dictionary of Biblical Archaeology*, eds. E. M. Blaiklock and R. K. Harrison (Grand Rapids: Zondervan, 1983), pp. 87–90.

Persian kingdom by the Parthians (Arsacids) around 250 B.C. During their five-hundred-year history the Parthians proved to be among the most formidable enemies of the Romans. They ignominiously defeated Crassus at Carrhae (Harran) in 53 B.C. Only Trajan (A.D. 115) was able temporarily to seize Mesopotamia from the Parthians.[15]

A new Persian dynasty, the Sasanians, took control in A.D. 226. They established Zoroastrianism as the official state religion. The Sasanians were in constant conflict with the late Roman emperors (such as Julian) and the Byzantine rulers (such as Justinian).[16]

The Muslim Arabs defeated the Sasanians at Ctesiphon in 637 and annexed Persia to the Arab Empire in 642. The Iranians, unlike most Muslims, are Shiites, who do not recognize the legitimacy of the first three caliphs who succeeded Muhammad, but only the fourth caliph, Ali, and his descendants.[17]

After about 800 Iran was ruled in turn by a rapid succession of competing dynasties such as the Tahirids, the Samanids, the Saffarids, the Ziyarids, the Buyids, and the Ghaznavids. Iran was then invaded by the Seljuk Turks (eleventh–twelfth centuries), the Mongols (thirteenth–fourteenth centuries), and the Tartars (fourteenth–fifteenth centuries).

In spite of the political turmoil, the Iranian Middle Ages produced outstanding scholars and writers such as Ferdowsi, the author of the epic *Shah-Nama* ("Book of Kings"),[18] the Aristotelian polymath Avicenna (Ibn-Sina), Omar Khayyam (the author of the *Rubaiyat*), and Saʿadi (the author of the *Gulistan*).[19]

In the succeeding centuries Iran was ruled by the Safavids (sixteenth–eighteenth centuries), by the Zends (eighteenth century), and by the Qajars (nineteenth–early twentieth centuries). In 1925 General Reza Khan led a revolt and became the Shahanshah (king of kings). As the king was sympathetic to the Germans, the British forced him to abdicate in 1941 in favor of his son Reza Shah Pahlavi.

After he had dramatically westernized and modernized Iran's indus-

15. N. C. Debevoise, *A Political History of Parthia* (New York: Greenwood, 1968 reprint of 1938 edition); M. Colledge, *The Parthians* (New York: Praeger, 1967); R. Ghirshman, "L'Iran et Rome aux premiers siècles de notre ère," *Syria* 49 (1972): 161–65; E. Yarshater, ed., *The Cambridge History of Iran III: The Seleucid, Parthian and Sasanian Periods* (Cambridge: Cambridge University Press, 1983), part 1.

16. A. Christensen, *L'Iran sous les Sassanides* (New Rochelle: Caratzas Brothers, 1976 reprint of 1944 edition); R. Ghirshman, *Persian Art: The Parthian and Sassanian Dynasties* (New York: Golden, 1962); see Yarshater, *Cambridge History of Iran*, part 2.

17. B. Spuler, *Iran in früh-islamischer Zeit* (Wiesbaden: Steiner, 1952); C. E. Bosworth, ed., *Iran and Islam* (Edinburgh: University of Edinburgh Press, 1971); M. H. Tabatabai, *Shi'ite Islam* (Houston: Free Islamic Literatures, 1979).

18. R. Levy, trans., *The Epic of the Kings* (London: Routledge and Kegan Paul, 1967).

19. See A. J. Arberry, ed., *The Legacy of Persia* (Oxford: Clarendon, 1953); R. N. Frye, *The Golden Age of Persia* (New York: Barnes and Noble, 1975).

try and armed forces with funds derived from oil, the Shah celebrated his coronation on his forty-eighth birthday on October 26, 1967. Four years later the Shah celebrated the nation's 2500th birthday with unprecedented pomp and pageantry at Persepolis. Royal guests and emissaries from about seventy countries watched six thousand costumed marchers representing ten dynasties of Persian history pass in review.[20]

Less than a decade later the popular revolution inspired by the Ayatollah Khomeini succeeded in forcing the Shah into exile on January 16, 1979.[21] The Islamic revolution resulted not only in the prolonged captivity of American hostages from the embassy, but also in the persecution of Jews, Christians, and Bahais.[22] It has also meant the end of an era of government-sponsored conferences on the past glories of the Achaemenid Empire[23] and of archaeological investigations of the Iranian past.[24]

Iranian Archaeology

As the early Muslims believed that pre-Islamic texts were "bricks baked in Hell and written by the demons," there was little interest on their part in investigating or preserving such antiquities. There have been cases where texts such as the Harran inscriptions of Nabonidus have been deliberately used in the threshold of a mosque.[25] The ruins of Persepolis were already being plundered in Sasanian times. Three

20. "In Iran a Crown Well Earned," *Life* 63 (Nov. 10, 1967): 28–33; "The Shah's Princely Party," *Life* 71 (Oct. 29, 1971): 22–30; "Iran: The Show of Shows," *Time* (Oct. 25, 1971): 32–33.

21. H. Algar, *The Islamic Revolution in Iran* (London: Muslim Institute, 1980).

22. On Christianity in Iran, see R. E. Waterfield, *Christians in Persia* (New York: Barnes and Noble, 1973). On Bahais, see W. M. Miller, *What Is the Baha'i Faith?* (Grand Rapids: Eerdmans, 1977). On Jews in Persia, see G. Widengren, "Quelques rapports entre juifs et iraniens à l'époque des Parthes," *Supplement to VT* 4 (1957): 197–242; idem, "The Status of the Jews in the Sassanian Empire," *IA* 1 (1961): 117–62; J. Neusner, *A History of the Jews in Babylonia* (Leiden: Brill, 1965–1970), various volumes on the Parthian and Sasanian periods; idem, "Jews and Judaism under Iranian Rule: Bibliographical Reflections," *HR* 8 (1968): 159–77.

23. Numerous conferences and exhibitions were sponsored by the Shah's government, resulting in a number of publications: *7000 Years of Iranian Art* (Washington, D.C.: Smithsonian Institution, 1964–1965); W. Eilers, ed., *Iran 2500th: Festgabe deutscher Iranisten zur 2500 Jahrfeier Irans* (Stuttgart: Hochwacht, 1971); C. J. Adams, ed., *Iranian Civilization and Culture* (Montreal: McGill University Press, 1972); *Commémoration Cyrus,* 3 vols. (Tehran/Liège: Bibliothèque Pahlavi, 1974); J. Duchesne-Guillemin, ed., *Etudes Mithriaques, Textes et Mémoires,* 4 vols. (Tehran/Liège: Bibliothèque Pahlavi, 1978).

24. Because of political and military developments, 1978 was the last full year of archaeological activity. For when Westerners are again allowed to visit Iran, see S. Matheson, *Persia: An Archaeological Guide,* 2d ed. (London: Faber and Faber, 1976).

25. D. S. Rice, "From Sin to Saladin," *ILN* (Sept. 21, 1957): 466–69.

doorways were removed and set up at Qaṣr-i-Abu Naṣr, thirty-five miles from Persepolis.[26]

Muslims who saw the standing ruins of ancient Near Eastern sites misunderstood their significance. Ibn al-Balkhi, a writer of the twelfth century, commenting on the colossal winged bulls, remarked: "Further, there is to be seen here the figure of Buraq."[27] Buraq was the winged horse upon which Muhammad is said to have made his miraculous night journey to Jerusalem to the al-Aqsa mosque.[28]

One of the first Western travelers to the Near East was a Jewish merchant from Spain, Benjamin of Tudela (circa 1160). Benjamin visited various Jewish communities, saw the ruins of Nineveh and Babylon, and reported the tradition of Daniel's tomb at Susa. His reports, however, were not published until the sixteenth century.

In the seventeenth century Pietro della Valle spent twelve years in the Near East. He not only described the ruins of Ur, Babylon, and Persepolis, but was the first to send back to Europe copies of cuneiform texts from Persepolis. Carsten Niebuhr visited Persepolis in 1765. He correctly noted that there were three different systems of writing in an exposition published in 1788. In 1802 Georg Grotefend, a German school teacher, identified three royal names from tablets from Persepolis as those of Hystaspes, Darius, and Xerxes, and thereby established the values of thirteen Old Persian cuneiform signs.[29]

It was the daring of the Englishman, Henry Rawlinson, which was responsible for the complete decipherment of cuneiform. At the total disregard of life and limb he copied the trilingual inscription (Old Persian, Elamite, Akkadian) of Darius at Behistun (Bisitun) between 1837 and 1843. Elamite was the language of Susa, and Akkadian was the Semitic language used by the Assyrians and Babylonians. This inscription with reliefs of Darius and his defeated enemies is carved on the sheer face of a cliff. Rawlinson climbed up on the narrow ledge below the inscription.

> On reaching the recess which contains the Persian text of the record, ladders are indispensable in order to examine the upper portion of the table; and even with ladders there is considerable risk, for the foot-ledge is so narrow, about eighteen inches or at most two feet in breadth, that with a ladder long enough to reach the sculptures sufficient slope cannot be given to enable a person to ascend, and, if the ladder be shortened in

26. C. K. Wilkinson, "The Achaemenian Remains at Qaṣr-i-Abu Naṣr," *JNES* 24 (1965): 341–45.

27. Cited by D. Wilber, *Persepolis, Capital of Parsa* (New York: Thomas Y. Crowell, 1969), p. 105.

28. See J. Porter, "Muhammad's Journey to Heaven," *Numen* 21 (1974): 64–80.

29. C. W. Ceram, *Gods, Graves and Scholars* (New York: Knopf, 1953), chapter 16; C. H. Gordon, *Forgotten Scripts* (New York: Basic, 1968), chapter 3.

> order to increase the slope, the upper inscriptions can only be copied by standing on the topmost step of the ladder, with no other support than steadying the body against the rock with the left arm, while the left hand holds the notebook, and the right hand is employed with the pencil. In this position I copied all the upper inscriptions, and the interest of the occupation entirely did away with any sense of danger.[30]

Over a century later George Cameron rechecked Rawlinson's copies in a somewhat less precarious manner—by means of a boatswain's chair and a painter's scaffold.[31]

I shall describe in detail the excavation of key sites later, but let me briefly summarize key archaeological developments in the modern era. In 1894 the French secured a virtual monopoly on excavations in Persia from Nasr ed-Din Shah. They have sponsored excavations at Susa from 1897 to the present except for the periods of the two World Wars. In the 1901/1902 season they made one of the most famous discoveries ever—the eight-foot-high basalt stele of Hammurabi's Code, which is now one of the treasures of the Louvre Museum.

The career of the archaeologist Roman Ghirshman (1895–1979) dominated much of French activity in Iran. Among the sites that he helped to excavate were Tepe Sialk (1933–1938), Bishapour (1935–1941), and Begram in Afghanistan (1941–1943). He became the director of the French excavations at Susa in 1946. Then in nine campaigns from 1951 to 1962 he worked at the Elamite site of Choga-Zanbil with its great ziggurat.

Especially significant contributions have been made in modern times by David Stronach, director of the British Institute of Persian Studies. He undertook excavations at Pasargadae (1961–1963) and at the Median site of Tepe Nush-i Jan (1967–1977).

Key American contributions have been the University of Chicago expeditions at Persepolis, which were directed by two scholars originally from Germany—Ernst Herzfeld (1931–1934) and Erich Schmidt (1935–1939). George Cameron and Richard Hallock published some of the thousands of Elamite texts from Persepolis in 1948, 1965, and 1969.

Of great importance for the early Iron Age have been the excavations and surveys conducted by the University of Pennsylvania under Robert H. Dyson, Jr., T. Cuyler Young, Jr., and others in and around Hasanlu between 1957 and 1974. No fewer than eight projects in Iran have been directed by members of the Hasanlu team.[32] Another key American

30. Cited in L. Deuel, ed., *The Treasures of Time* (New York: Avon, 1961), p. 115.

31. G. Cameron, "Darius Carved History on Ageless Rock," *National Geographic* 98 (Dec. 1950): 825–44; idem, "The Monument of King Darius at Bisitun," *Arch* 13 (1960): 162–71.

32. L. D. Levine and T. C. Young, Jr., eds., *Mountains and Lowlands* (Malibu: Undena, 1977), p. vii.

expedition, directed by William Sumner (1971–1978), has led to the identification of a site in Fars (Malyan as ancient Anshan, long an unresolved problem).

Wolfram Kleiss of the Deutsches Archäologisches Institut has conducted eight campaigns (1968–1978) to uncover the important Urartian site of Bastam in northwestern Iran. L. Vanden Berghe of the Belgian University of Ghent has conducted key excavations in the Luristan district of the Zagros Mountains in the 1970s.

The Iranians themselves have played an increasingly more active role especially through their Centre for Archaeological Research. Ali Sami conducted excavations at Pasargadae for five years beginning in 1949. Ezat Negahban made spectacular discoveries of gold treasures at the Caspian site of Marlik in 1961 to 1962.

The respective contributions of the various national institutions are as follows:[33]

	1972–1973	**1977**	**1978**
Iranian	10	8	16
American	7	1	3
British	4	1	3
German	3	3	2
French	3	3	1
Belgian	2	1	1
Canadian	2		1
Austrian	1		1
Italian	1		1
Dutch	1		
Danish	1		
Swedish	1		
Japanese	1	1	
Totals	37	18	29

The great proliferation of excavations in the 1970s may be compared with the situation at the time the Hasanlu dig was begun in 1957; then there were but two excavations in the field.[34]

33. See *Proceedings of the IInd Annual Symposium on Archaeological Research in Iran* (Tehran: Iranian Centre for Archaeological Research, 1974), pp. viii–x; "Survey of Excavations in Iran—1977," *Iran* 16 (1978): 185ff.; "Survey of Excavations in Iran—1978," *Iran* 17 (1979): 143ff.

34. For general bibliographies, see J. D. Pearson, ed., *A Bibliography of Pre-Islamic Persia* (London: Mansell, 1975); J. P. Elwell-Sutton, ed., *Bibliographical Guide to Iran* (Totowa: Barnes and Noble, 1983). For Iranian texts, see L. de Meyer, "Elamitic," and "Ancient Persian," in *A Basic Bibliography for the Study of the Semitic Languages*, ed. J. H. Hospers (Leiden: Brill, 1973), 1: 118–22, 123–26. On excavations, see L. Vanden Berghe, *Archéologie de l'Iran ancien* (Leiden: Brill, 1959); idem, *Bibliographie analytique de l'Iran ancien* (Leiden: Brill, 1979); P. Calmeyer, "Archäologische Bibliographie," *AMI* 7 (1974): 251–58, and following issues; D. Stronach, ed., "Survey of Excava-

tions," *Iran* 5 (1967): 133–49. On art, see E. Porada, "Bibliography for the Art of Ancient Iran," *JANES* 9 (1977): 67–84; S. J. Pattullo, "Additions to the Selected Bibliography for the Art of Ancient Iran," *JANES* 10 (1978): 109–12. For a history of Iranian scholarship, see J. Duchesne-Guillemin, "L'étude de l'iranien ancien au vingtième siècle," *Kratylos* 7 (1962): 1–44; M. J. Dresden, "Survey of the History of Iranian Studies," *Handbuch der Orientalistik* 1, 4th Band (Leiden: Brill, 1968): 168–90. For Iranologists and their writings, see *Bio-Bibliographies de 134 Savants* (Leiden: Brill, 1978).

1

The Medes

Biblical References

According to the table of nations (Gen. 10)[1] the Medes (*Madai*) were descendants of Japheth. There are some references to the Medes in the preexilic prophets (Isa. 13:17; Jer. 25:25; 51:11, 28), and many more from the exilic period (2 Kings 17:6; Dan. 5:28; 6:8, 12, 15). The references to "Darius the Mede" in Daniel 5:31; 9:1; 11:1 have aroused considerable discussion. The sole New Testament reference to the Medes is found in the list of places represented by those who heard the gospel on the day of Pentecost (Acts 2:9).

1. J. Simons, "The 'Table of Nations' (Gen. X): Its General Structure and Meaning," *Oudtestamentische Studiën* 10 (1954): 155–84; D. J. Wiseman, "Genesis 10: Some Archaeological Considerations," *Journal of the Transactions of the Victoria Institute* 87 (1954): 14–25; E. Yamauchi, "Meshech, Tubal, and Company," *JETS* 19 (1976): 239–47; T. C. Mitchell, "Nations, Table of," in *The Illustrated Bible Dictionary*, ed. N. Hillyer (Leicester: Inter-Varsity, 1980), 2: 1055–59.

Iranian Languages

The Iranian languages are related to other ancient Indo-European languages such as Greek, Latin, and Sanskrit (which was brought into India by the Indo-Aryans around 1800 B.C.) as well as to modern German and English.[2]

Proto Indo-European	Old Persian	Sanskrit	Greek	Latin	English
**pətē[r]*	*pitar*	*pitár*	*patēr*	*pater*	father
**nōmn̥*	*nāman*	*nāman*	*onoma*	*nōmen*	name
**deivo*	*daiva*	*devá*	*theos*	*deus*	god
**ekᵘos*	*asa*	*áśva*	*hippos*	*equus*	horse

As there are no connected texts in the Median language,[3] we must rely on place- and personal-names and loan-words for our fragmentary knowledge of Median.[4] The evidence indicates that Median was close to Old Persian, both belonging to the Iranian branch of Indo-European languages. Among the differences between the two dialects, Median *s* corresponds with Old Persian *th,* Median *z* corresponds with Persian *d,* and so forth.[5] There are a number of important Median loan-words in Old Persian, for example, *xšāyathya* "king"[6] and *xšathra-pāvā,* which through Greek *satrapēs* became the English word *satrap.*[7] A number of Median personal-names have been preserved in the Greek text of Herodotus:

Greek	Median	Meaning
Megabatēs	Bagapāta	"protected by the god(s)"
Intaphernēs	Viⁿdafarnā	"finding fame"
Hystaspēs	Vištāspa	"with harnessed horses"
Mitrobatēs	Mithrapāta	"protected by Mithra"
Mitradatēs	Mithradāta	"given by Mithra"[8]

2. H. W. Bailey, "The Persian Language," in *The Legacy of Persia,* ed. A. J. Arberry (Oxford: Clarendon, 1953), p. 182.

3. I. M. Diakonoff, "Media," in *The Cambridge History of Iran II: The Median and Achaemenian Periods,* ed. I. Gershevitch (Cambridge: Cambridge University Press, 1985), p. 114. Diakonoff believes that the Medes must have had a system of writing although no texts have been discovered.

4. W. Brandenstein and M. Mayrhofer, *Handbuch des Altpersischen* (Wiesbaden: Harrassowitz, 1964), pp. 12–13; M. Mayrhofer, "Die Rekonstrucktion des Medischen," *Anzeiger der Österreichischen Akademie der Wissenschaften, Philosophisch-historische Klasse* 105 (1968): 1–23.

5. R. G. Kent, *Old Persian,* 2d ed. (New Haven: American Oriental Society, 1953), p. 8.

6. I. Gershevitch, "Dialect Variation in Early Persian," *Transactions of the Philological Society* (1965): 23, questions the usual Median explanation of this word and asserts that it is a Persian word.

7. G. Widengren, "The Persians," *Peoples of Old Testament Times,* ed. D. J. Wiseman (Oxford: Clarendon, 1973), p. 351, n. 97.

8. The name appears in Ezra 1:8 and 4:7. Mithradates was also the name of the king of Pontus in northern Turkey who warred against the Romans. For the name *Dat-Mithra,* see R. A. Bowman, *Ara-*

Indo-Europeans

Although the complex problems of the origins, routes, and dates of various Indo-European migrations cannot be fully treated here, we may briefly summarize certain points.[9] The original home of the Indo-Europeans has been located in the Austro-Hungarian plains[10] or in southwest Russia.[11] At an early stage they were in contact with speakers of Finno-Ugric.[12] The Indo-Iranian tribes separated from the Balts and the Slavs in the fifth millennium B.C., according to Harmatta.[13] Waves of Indo-European migrations filtered south and east especially at the end of the Early Bronze and during the Middle and Late Bronze Ages (between 2300 and 1200 B.C.).

Evidence for these migrations has been demonstrated by: the settling of the Greeks on the Greek mainland;[14] the arrival of the Luwians[15] and the Hittites in Anatolia;[16] the presence of an Indo-Aryan aristocracy of charioteers among the Hurrians of Mitanni;[17] and most notably the Indo-Aryan invasion, which may have destroyed the great centers of Harappa and Mohenjo-Daro in the Indus River Valley, events reflected in the Rig Veda.[18]

There are close parallels between the religious vocabulary of the

---

maic Ritual Texts from Persepolis (Chicago: University of Chicago Press, 1968), pp. 32, 73, 78. For other Median and Persian names in Herodotus, see R. Schmitt, "Medisches und persisches Sprachgut bei Herodot," *ZDMG* 117 (1967): 119–45; idem, "The Medo-Persian Names of Herodotus in the Light of the New Evidence from Persepolis," *AA* 24 (1976): 25–35.

9. See R. A. Crossland, "Indo-European Origins: The Linguistic Evidence," *Past and Present* 12 (1957): 16–45.

10. Favoring a Central European origin for the Indo-Europeans are Diakonoff, "Media," p. 49; W. H. Goodenough, "The Evolution of Pastoralism and Indo-European Origins," in *Indo-European and Indo Europeans,* eds. G. Cardona et al. (Philadelphia: University of Pennsylvania Press, 1970), pp. 254–62.

11. Favoring a South Russian origin for the Indo-Europeans are M. Gimbutas, "The Indo-Europeans: Archaeological Problems," *American Anthropologist* 65 (1963): 815–36; R. N. Frye, *The History of Ancient Iran* (Munich: C. H. Beckische, 1984), pp. 45, 47.

12. Crossland, "Indo-European Origins," p. 37.

13. J. Harmatta, "Migrations of the Indo-Iranian Tribes," *AA* 26 (1978): 186.

14. C. W. Blegen, "The Coming of the Greeks," *AJA* 32 (1928): 141–54; E. Grumach, "The Coming of the Greeks," *BJRL* 51 (1968): 73–103, 400–30.

15. J. Mellaart, "The End of the Early Bronze Age in Anatolia and the Aegean," *AJA* 62 (1958): 9–33.

16. H. A. Hoffner, "The Hittites and Hurrians," *POT,* ed. D. J. Wiseman (Oxford: Clarendon, 1973), chapter 9.

17. R. T. O'Callaghan, *Aram Naharaim* (Rome: Pontificium Institutum Biblicum, 1948), pp. 64–70; R. Ghirshman, *L'Iran et la migration des Indo-Aryens et des Iraniens* (Leiden: Brill, 1977). See M. Mayrhofer, *Die Arier in vordern Orient, ein Mythos?* (Vienna: Österreichische Akademie der Wissenschaften, 1974).

18. S. Pigott, *Prehistoric India* (Baltimore: Penguin, 1952); M. Wheeler, *Civilizations of the Indus Valley and Beyond* (London: Thames and Hudson, 1966); idem, *Early India and Pakistan,* rev. ed. (New York: Praeger, 1968); H. D. Sankalia, "New Light on the Indo-Iranians or Western Asiatic

Sanskrit texts of the Vedas of India and the Avestan Zoroastrian texts of Iran.[19] That the Iranians, like other Indo-Europeans, were divided into castes of warriors, priests, and peasants is a hypothesis proposed by Georges Dumézil.

Iranian Migrations

There are sharp disagreements as to the route and the date of the migrations of the Medes and the Persians into the Iranian plateau from the north. A western route over the Caucasus along the western shore of the Caspian Sea[20] and an eastern route from the Gurgan area southeast of the Caspian have been suggested. Dates spanning the second millennium B.C. have been proposed. Let us examine some of the leading proposals.

In the Gurgan area southeast of the Caspian and north of the Alburz Mountains there are over three hundred tells. Among these Tepe Hissar was excavated by Erich Schmidt in 1931/1932, Shar Tepe by T. J. Arne in 1932/1933, and Yarim Tepe by David Stronach in 1960/1961.

Tureng Tepe, excavated by F. Wulsin in 1931, was investigated in the 1960s by Jean Deshayes. The Gray Ware, which predominates on the Gorgan plain from period IIb dated by radiocarbon to 2375 ± 250 B.C., is attributed by Deshayes to the earliest Indo-Europeans in Iran, indeed to the ancestors of the Medes.[21]

There are as yet some unresolved problems with Deshayes' hypothesis. Gray Ware to the north in Soviet Turkestan is later than the Gray Ware in the Gorgan plain, which is the reverse of what one would expect.[22] There is also a considerable chronological gap between the

---

Relations Between 1700 B.C.–1200 B.C.," *Artibus Asiae* 26 (1963): 312–32; T. Barrow, "The Proto-Indoaryans," *JRAS* (1973): 123–40. The Aryan invasion of the Indus Valley had been dated circa 1500, but the recalibration of radiocarbon dates on the basis of the analysis of bristlecone pine tree rings has shifted many dates back two to three centuries. See G. F. Dales, "Archaeological and Radiocarbon Chronologies for Proto-historic South Asia," *South Asian Archaeology 1971* (London: Duckworth, 1972), pp. 157–69; E. Yamauchi, "Problems of Radiocarbon Dating . . .," *Journal of the American Scientific Affiliation* 27 (1975): 25–31.

19. See M. J. Dresden, "Indo-Iranian Notes," in *W. B. Henning Memorial Volume*, eds. M. Boyce and I. Gershevitch (London: Lund Humphries, 1970), pp. 134–39; S. Insler, *The Gathas of Zoroaster* (Tehran/Liège: Bibliothèque Pahlavi, 1975), pp. 335–37.

20. The western route has been favored by F. Altheim, K. Jettmar, M. Mayrhofer, E. Grantovsky, W. Brandenstein, and R. Ghirshman (see below). But as Diakonoff, "Media," p. 52, points out, it is the less likely route.

21. J. Deshayes, "Tureng Tepe and the Plain of Gorgan in the Bronze Age," *Archeologia* 24 (Sept.–Oct. 1968): 35–38; idem, "New Evidence for the Indo-Europeans from Tureng Tepe, Iran," *Arch* 22 (1969): 10–17; idem, "Tureng Tepe et la periode Hissar IIIC," *Ugaritica* 17 (1969): 139–63.

22. V. M. Masson and V. I. Sarianidi, *Central Asia: Turkmenia Before the Achaemenids* (London: Thames and Hudson, 1972), p. 105.

end of Tureng Tepe IIIC, which Deshayes dates to 1600 B.C., and the earliest Gray Ware in the west where the Medes settled. An even greater gap may be indicated by radiocarbon dates from the end of Hissar IIIC because they yield a date of 1841 ± 65 B.C.[23]

M. Winn would make a distinction because of this gap. He would ascribe the earlier Gray Ware to Indo-Europeans, and the later Gray Ware that appeared in the Iron Age in the west to the Iranians.[24] I. M. Diakonoff believes that the arrival of the Indo-Iranian tribes on the Iranian plateau took place in the first half of the second millennium B.C.[25] But the earliest archaeological evidence of newcomers seems to date to the early part of the second half of the second millennium B.C.[26]

23. C. H. Bovington et al., "The Radiocarbon Evidence for the Terminal Date of the Hissar III C Culture," *Iran* 12 (1974): 195–99.

24. M. Winn, "Thoughts on the Question of Indo-European Studies into Anatolia and Iran," *Journal of Indo-European Studies* 2 (1974): 117–42.

25. Diakonoff, "Media," p. 41.

26. O. W. Muscarella, "Excavations at Dinkha Tepe, 1966," *BMMA* 27 (1968): 187–96, notes that Gray Ware was brought to this site near Hasanlu in the thirteenth century, if not earlier.

Painted ware from Sialk. (Metropolitan Museum of Art, gift of the Tehran Museum, 1939 [39.60.9])

The beginning of the Iron I period in Iran has been dated as early as 1450 and as late as 1200 and its end at 1000.[27] The terminology is somewhat misleading since iron objects do not appear in significant numbers until the Iron II period (1000–800/750 B.C.), as Vincent Pigott has shown.[28]

In some seminal studies T. Cuyler Young, Jr., noted that during the Iron I period Gray Ware, related in form to that of the Gorgan region, spread rapidly over much of western Iran. It appeared in places such as Qazvin and Khorvin near Tehran, at Tepe Sialk, at numerous sites around Hamadan—sites that can be correlated to areas where the Assyrians encountered the Medes.[29] Young thus concludes that the Iranians came from the northeast.

On the other hand, Charles Burney and David Lang suggest that the Iranians came from the northwest. They link some of the Iron I materi-

27. T. C. Young, Jr., "The Search for Understanding: Excavating the Second Millennium," *Exped* 13/3–4 (1971): 24; V. Pigott, "The Question of the Presence of Iron in the Iron I Period in Western Iran," in *Mountains and Lowlands*, eds. L. D. Levine and T. C. Young, Jr. (Malibu: Undena, 1977), p. 211.

28. Only a single iron object at Hasanlu V and one at Giyan I are attested from Iron I. For an overview, see P. R. S. Moorey, "Archaeology and Pre-Achaemenid Metalworking in Iran: A Fifteen Year Retrospective," *Iran* 20 (1982): 81–101.

29. T. C. Young, Jr., "A Comparative Ceramic Chronology for Western Iran, 1500–500 B.C.," *Iran* 3 (1965): 53–85; idem, "The Iranian Migration into the Zagros," *Iran* 5 (1967): 11–34.

Spouted Gray Ware from Sialk. (Metropolitan Museum of Art, acquired by exchange, Tehran Museum, 1948 [48.98.6])

als with a Caucasian origin and cite parallels with objects from the Talysh Hills (circa 1450–1350 B.C.). They consider the possibility that the Iranians might have traveled from the Gorgan area north around the Caspian Sea before entering western Iran.[30] This seems to be an unnecessarily complex explanation.

Possible products of early Iranians south of the Caspian Sea are the rich treasures excavated at Marlik by Ezat Negahban in 1961/1962.[31] Dated about 1200 to 1000 B.C., these splendid finds are among the masterpieces in the Tehran Museum. From artistic links with objects found elsewhere, Negahban ventured to conclude that the Marlik culture dominated areas south of the Caspian Sea and Azerbaijan.

Ghirshman has opposed the theory that the Iranians came from the Gorgan area. He points out differences in the pottery and culture between the Gorgan and Median areas.[32] He argues that the discovery of

30. C. Burney and D. M. Lang, *The Peoples of the Hills: Ancient Ararat and Caucasus* (New York: Praeger, 1972), p. 116.

31. E. Negahban, "Notes on Some Objects from Marlik," *JNES* 24 (1965): 309–27; idem, *A Preliminary Report on the Marlik Expedition* (Tehran: Institute of Archeology, 1965).

32. Ghirshman, *L'Iran et la migration*, pp. 47–48.

Painted Sialk vessel with warrior. (J. H. and E. A. Payne Fund, courtesy, Museum of Fine Arts, Boston)

Iranian-type pottery from near Karakorum, which is Iron II or Iron III, undercuts the theory of an origin of the Gray Ware from the northeast.[33] For Ghirshman the obvious route of the Iranian tribes is from the Caucasus in the northwest, the same route followed centuries later by the Cimmerians and Scythians.[34]

Ghirshman has, however, modified his ideas about the date of the arrival of the early Iranians. He now agrees that they may have come as early as Iron I, which he dates from 1250 to 1000, and associates the Iranians with Hasanlu V and Necropolis A of Sialk.[35]

Tepe Sialk is an important site south of Tehran and on the western edge of the interior desert, which Ghirshman excavated.[36] In his earlier

33. Ibid., p. 45.

34. Ibid., p. 49.

35. Ibid., pp. 46–47, 72.

36. R. Ghirshman, *Fouilles de Sialk près de Kashan* (Paris: Geuthner, 1938–1939); E. Yamauchi, "Tepe Sialk," in *NIDBA*, eds. E. M. Blaiklock and R. K. Harrison (Grand Rapids: Zondervan, 1983), p. 447.

Gray Ware spouted pot from Solduz. (Metropolitan Museum of Art, acquired by exchange, Tehran Museum, 1948 [48.98.21])

publications Ghirshman had associated the coming of the Iranians with Cemetery B, which he dated to approximately 1000 B.C.[37] Robert Dyson would date the Sialk B assemblage later to the eighth century B.C.[38]

Though Young has asserted that there is no major cultural break with the inception of the Iron II period (1000–800/750), Dyson notes the following developments about 1000:

> The old settlement pattern of many villages was replaced by one made up of a series of fortified strong points. This dramatic shift indicates a major cultural change of some kind—either control by a foreign state, an influx of additional grey-ware-using people of related but not identical type, or the reorganization of the local political system into a kind of advanced hierarchy.[39]

37. R. Ghirshman, *Iran* (Baltimore: Penguin, 1954), chapter 2; idem, *The Art of Ancient Iran* (New York: Golden, 1964), pp. 3, 17, 280. This earlier view is still repeated by Widengren, "Persians," p. 313.

38. R. H. Dyson, Jr., "Problems of Protohistoric Iran as Seen from Hasanlu," *JNES* 24 (1965): 200–201.

39. Ibid., p. 197.

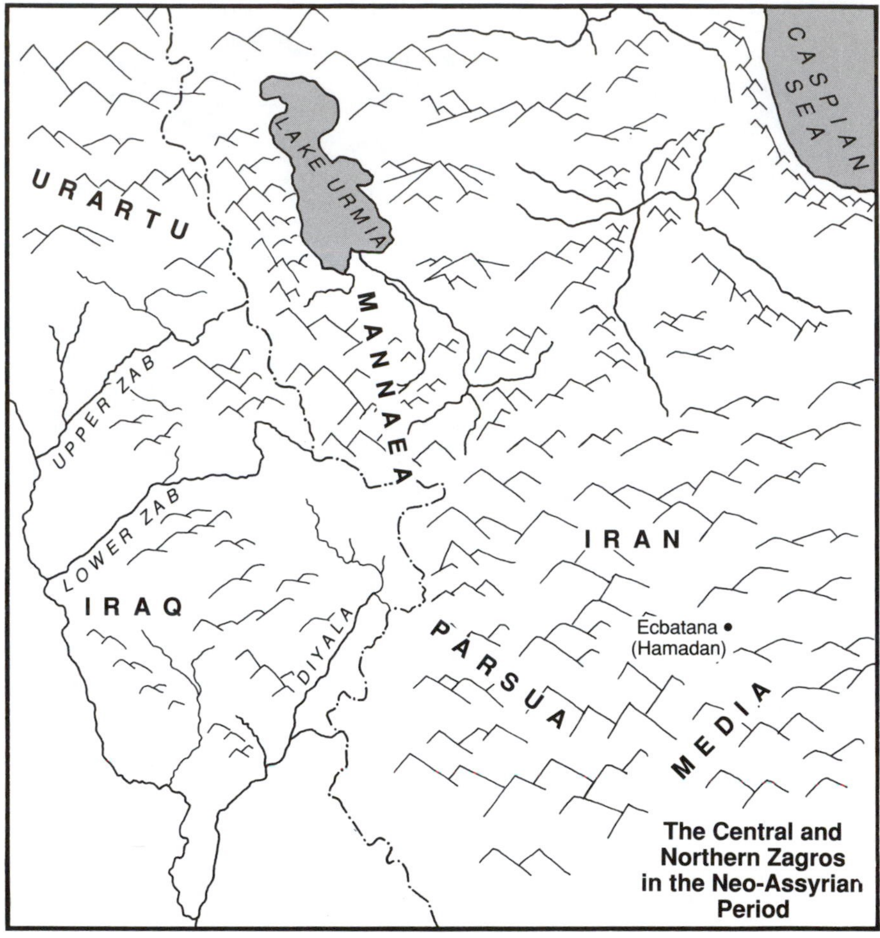

The Central and Northern Zagros in the Neo-Assyrian Period

Then, too, as Pigott has shown, there is a dramatic increase in the presence of iron objects in the tenth century.[40]

Although scholars are divided as to the date and the route of the earliest Iranian migrations, most agree that the widespread appearance of Iron III (800–550) culture in the Zagros is to be associated with the rise of the Medes to power.[41] Ghirshman postulates later invasions of Iranians in either the Iron II or the Iron III age to explain the origin of

40. Pigott, "Question of the Presence of Iron," pp. 227ff.

41. T. C. Young, Jr., "Persia," in *Encyclopedia of Ancient Civilizations*, ed. A. Cotterell (New York: Mayflower, 1980), p. 147.

the eastern Iranians (Hyrcanians, Parthians, Bactrians, Arians, Chorasmians, and Sogdians).[42]

The Median Homeland

The heartland of the Medes, once they were settled, was east of the Chaine Magistrale of the northern Zagros Mountains in modern Luristan. This is a highland region three to five thousand feet above sea level. An analysis of the Assyrian references leads Louis Levine to place the Medes more specifically in the Kermanshah and Assadabad valleys.[43] The capital of Media was Ecbatana (modern Hamadan; see chapter 8). This was located on the major route from Mesopotamia to the Iranian plateau known as the Khorasan Road, which in later centuries ran from Baghdad to Kermanshah, past Bisitun to Tehran, and ultimately to Khorasan in the east. Another Median site often mentioned by the Assyrians was Harhar, which also lay near this route.

The northern frontier of the Medes was the territory of Mannae (biblical Minni; see Jer. 51:27), just south of Lake Urmia.[44] Their southern border was the region of Ellipi in the southern Zagros. The eastern border has been associated with a Mount Bikni ("the lapis lazuli mountain"), that is, a site on the road to Badakhshan in the east, the source of lapis lazuli. This has usually been identified with the towering Mount Demavand east of Tehran. Levine, however, proposes to identify Mount Bikni with Mount Elvend (Alwand, 11,600 feet high) near Hamadan.[45]

The climate in Media is temperate during much of the year. Persian kings used Ecbatana as their summer capital. Winters, however, are severe. Though rainfall is sometimes negligible in the valleys, there is considerable precipitation in the form of snow.

Median Archaeology

In 1964 Ghirshman lamented, "we know next to nothing about the Median architecture."[46] A year later Edith Porada echoed his plaint:

42. Ghirshman, *L'Iran et la migration,* p. 46.

43. L. D. Levine, "Geographical Studies in the Neo-Assyrian Zagros—I and II," *Iran* 11 (1973): 1–28, 99–124. Diakonoff, "Media," p. 75, defines the basic territory of Media as the triangle between the present-day towns of Zanjan, Hamadan, and Qazvin or Tehran.

44. On the Minni, see E. Yamauchi, *Foes from the Northern Frontier* (Grand Rapids: Baker, 1982), chapter 2.

45. Levine, "Geographical Studies in the Neo-Assyrian Zagros—II," pp. 118–19.

46. Ghirshman, *Art of Ancient Iran,* p. 87.

"As yet it is impossible to give a survey of Median art because no unquestionably Median site has been excavated and no inscribed work of Median art has been found."[47]

In the late 1960s and in the 1970s this lacuna was filled at least partially by the excavations of three Median sites. Baba Jan Tepe, sixty miles southwest of Hamadan near the village of Nurabad, was excavated in a series of seasons from 1966 on by Clare L. Goff.[48] She uncovered a large fortified manor, 33 by 34 meters, built in the eighth to seventh centuries B.C. around a central courtyard and surrounded by nine towers. The building was later redesigned to include a colonnaded central hall with buttressed porticos. To the east was another fortified manor with a roof supported by wooden columns, surrounded by long rectangular living rooms and kitchens. The excavator assumed that there may have been some clerestory lighting (that is, lighting from highly placed windows) as is presumed for later Achaemenid buildings at Persepolis.

On the East Mound a fort with a spiral ramp similar to the one at Nush-i Jan was built. The most interesting discovery was a building with a colorful painted chamber. Not only were the walls and the columns painted red, but the ceiling had been elaborately decorated with painted tiles of different designs that lay strewn on the floor.[49] The excavator identified the chamber as a secular reception hall with a small domestic shrine in one corner.[50]

The forts were destroyed early in the seventh century. Squatters later turned their ruins into workshops and stables. An intrusive horse burial together with harness pieces and bronze objects was probably the sign of nomadic invaders.[51] Goff concluded:

> To sum up then: the culture of Baba Jan III is most probably Median. It derives from the Grey Ware Iron II cultures of the Elburz mountains and represents an Iranian penetration into the Central Zagros at the beginning of the ninth century. It was at its most prosperous in the late ninth and most of the eighth centuries. . . . The culture of Baba Jan II is also Median, introduced by a related Median tribe from further East, nearer Hamadan and Malayer. The newcomers probably moved into the vacuum created by the Assyrians but may just possibly have sacked Baba Jan

47. E. Porada, *The Art of Ancient Iran* (New York: Crown, 1965), p. 138.

48. C. Goff, *An Archaeologist in the Making* (London: Constable, 1980).

49. C. Goff, "Excavations at Baba Jan 1967," *Iran* 7 (1969): 115–30.

50. C. Goff, "The Architecture of the East Mound: Levels II and III.1," *Iran* 15 (1977): 125.

51. Goff, "Excavations at Baba Jan 1967," pp. 123–26. The horse was domesticated by the third millennium B.C. Evidence that the Iranians brought horses with them in the early first millennium B.C. has also been found at Hasanlu, Dinkha Tepe, and Sialk. See Muscarella, "Excavations at Dinkha Tepe, 1966," pp. 187–96; E. L. B. Terrace, "Some Recent Finds from Northwest Persia," *Syria* 39 (1962): 215.

Tepe Nush-i Jan, excavated mound.

> III themselves. The later burning of Level II and the change in culture between Levels II and I could represent further stages in Median unification, a Scythian raid, or a local disaster.[52]

The second important Median site is Godin Tepe, about thirty miles southwest of Hamadan. Excavated by T. Cuyler Young, Jr., from 1965 to 1973, Godin was a large fortified manor of the Median period. It was surrounded with towers and with walls provided with arrow slits. The most impressive room was a throne hall with five rows of six columns, which anticipated the later palace of Cyrus at Pasargadae. It had a throne seat, a hearth, and benches around the walls. A smaller columned hall also had benches by the walls. Numerous magazines or storerooms were situated to the east. Staircases led to an upper story.[53] Stuart Brown views the expansion of the Godin manor as evidence "that some strategically located chiefdoms in the central Zagros were capitalizing on a situation of economic intensification and competition and that social stratification and elite access to coercive power, trends toward state formation, were becoming entrenched."[54]

52. C. Goff, "Excavations at Baba Jan: The Pottery and Metal from Levels III and II," *Iran* 16 (1978): 42. O. W. Muscarella, "Median Art and Medizing Scholarship," *JNES* 46 (1987): 112, n. 12, questions whether Baba Jan Tepe is a Median site, but offers no rebuttal to the excavator's views. Frye, *History of Ancient Iran,* p. 65, accepts the site as Median. Moorey, "Archaeology and Pre-Achaemenid Metalworking," p. 96, is undecided: "Who the creators of the Baba Jan 'manors' were, perhaps a branch of the Medes as Clare Goff has suggested, remains an open question."

53. T. C. Young, Jr., *Excavations at Godin Tepe* (Toronto: Royal Ontario Museum, 1969), pp. 27–29; T. C. Young, Jr., "Survey of Excavations in Iran during 1970–1," *Iran* 10 (1972): 185.

54. S. C. Brown, "Media and Secondary State Formation in the Neo-Assyrian Zagros," *JCS* 38 (1986): 116.

Tepe Nush-i Jan, well-preserved outer walls.

The third and perhaps most interesting Median site is Tepe Nush-i Jan, forty miles south of Hamadan, which was excavated from 1967 to 1977 by David Stronach. Medes occupied the site from about 750 to 600; radiocarbon testing yielded a date of 723 ± 220. The excavator uncovered four well-preserved structures on top of a steep mound.

On the far western edge was a temple with a fire altar. Next to it was a columned hall, 20 by 16 meters, with three rows of four columns. Underneath this building a slanted corridor was dug, extending at least 18 meters, probably to secure water. On the eastern edge was a fort equipped with arrow slits and a spiral ramp leading to the roof. The fort included four parallel storerooms.[55]

55. D. Stronach, "Excavations at Tepe Nush-i Jan, 1967," *Iran* 7 (1969): 1–20; M. Roaf and D. Stronach, "Tepe Nush-i Jan, 1970," *Iran* 13 (1973): 129–40.

Tepe Nush-i Jan, arrow slits in the fort's wall.

The fourth and most significant structure was located in the center of the mound—the oldest fire temple yet uncovered. An antechamber was provided with a bench, a basin, and a deep niche probably used for preliminary ceremonies. The main room, 11 by 7 meters and 8 meters high, was decorated with blind windows and recessed windows that anticipated designs of the quadrangular towers at Naqsh-i Rustam near Persepolis and at Pasargadae. Behind a low wall was a square fire altar with extensive evidence of ash. The depth of the ashes indicated an occasional, rather than a perpetual, fire.[56]

When the site was abandoned, the structure was carefully filled in with shale and mud to a depth of 6 to 7 meters. Such a practice is without parallel in Iran, but was similar to the practice of Nebuchadnezzar's restoration of the temple of Ninmah. Nabonidus, the last Neo-Babylonian ruler, filled the harbor temple at Ur with clean sand. Stronach believes that the Medes adopted the practice after the Medo-Chaldean victory over the Assyrians in 612.[57] Peter Moorey notes that

56. D. Stronach, "Notes on Religion in Iran in the 7th and 6th Centuries," *Orientalia J. Duchesne-Guillemin Emerito Oblata* (Leiden: Brill, 1984), p. 480. See also idem, "Notes on Median and Early Achaemenian Religious Monuments," in *Temples and High Places in Biblical Times*, ed. A. Biran (Jerusalem: Hebrew Union College, Jewish Institute of Religion, 1984), pp. 123–30.

57. D. Stronach, "Tappeh Nuši Jan: A Case for Building Rites in 7th/6th Century B.C. Media," in *Proceedings of the IInd Annual Symposium on Archaeological Research in Iran*, ed. F. Bagherzadeh (Tehran: Iranian Centre for Archaeological Research, 1974), pp. 223–24.

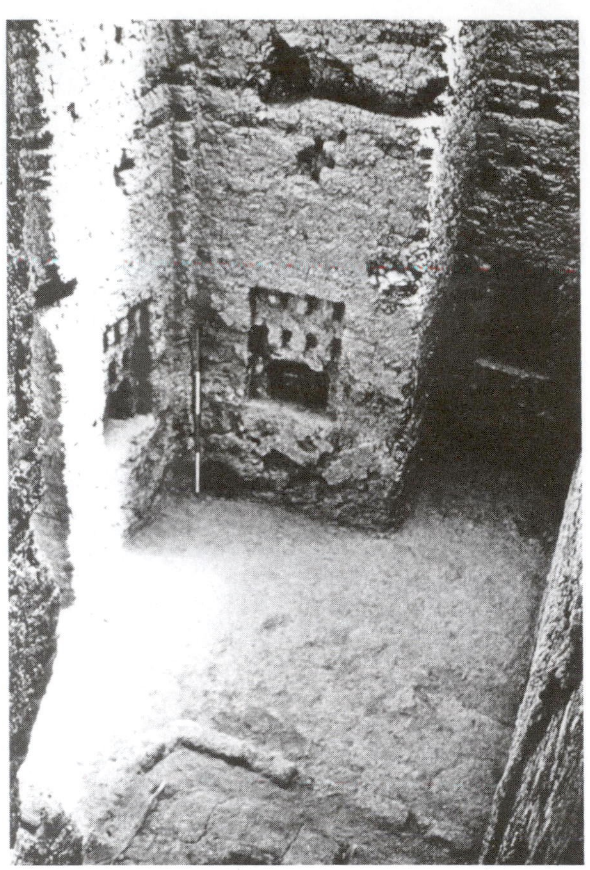
Tepe Nush-i Jan, blind windows in the central temple.

the sacred fire was ritually extinguished at the time of the king's death.[58]

The excavator found, in addition to pottery, some jewelry and other artifacts that may possibly include booty taken from the Assyrians. Some silver bars, cut pieces, and rings found in a hoard from the fort are interpreted by A. D. H. Bivar as an early kind of ingot currency used by the Medes.[59]

58. P. Moorey, *Ancient Iran* (Cambridge: Ashmolean Museum, n.d.), p. 33; Roaf and Stronach, "Tepe Nūsh-i Jān, 1970," p. 138, n. 23, citing Diodorus Siculus 17.114.4: "that they should sedulously quench what the Persians call the sacred fire, until such time as the funeral should be ended. This was the custom of the Persians when their kings died."

59. A. D. H. Bivar, "A Hoard of Ingot-Currency from Nush-i Jan, near Malayir," *Iran* 9 (1971): 97–107. See J. Curtis, *Nush-i Jan III: The Small Finds* (London: British Institute of Persian Studies, 1984), pp. 2–21. Curtis cites as a parallel the reference to Jehoiada the priest who collected silver in the house of the Lord (2 Kings 12:9–10).

David Stronach, excavator of Tepe Nush-i Jan.

The Assyrians and the Medes

The *Mādāia* are first mentioned in a text of Shalmaneser III (836 B.C.). The name *Parsua* also occurs first in this monarch's reign in 844 (see the following chapter). The Medes are mentioned in the texts of every Assyrian king thereafter until the time of Ashurbanipal, sometimes being called "the mighty Medes," "the distant Medes," or "the Medes by the Salt Desert."[60] The Assyrians under Shamshi-Adad V (823–811 B.C.) inflicted a severe defeat upon the Medes from Lake Urmia to the Salt Desert. During the reign of Adadnerari III (810–783 B.C.) eight campaigns were directed against the Mannaeans and the Medes.[61]

60. S. Parpola, *Neo-Assyrian Toponyms* (Kevalaer: Butzon and Bercker, 1970), pp. 230–31.
61. Diakonoff, "Media," pp. 67–68.

A Mede bringing horses to Sargon II. (Metropolitan Museum of Art, gift of John D. Rockefeller, Jr., 1933)

The Medes are mentioned frequently in the texts of Tiglath-pileser III (745–727) and Sargon II (721–705). We learn that the Assyrians were especially interested in obtaining horses from the Medes. A text of Tiglath-pileser III lists a total of at least 1,615 horses received as a tribute from the Medes.[62] A possible representation of a mounted Mede has been identified on a relief from Nimrud.[63]

Tiglath-pileser III invaded the Zagros region twice; Sargon invaded it six times. As Levine has demonstrated, the Assyrians were interested in controlling the "Khorasan" route through the Zagros.[64] There are eighteen references to Assyrian deportations from the area of Media.[65] What is of interest to students of the Bible is the fact that Sargon replaced some of these deportees with newcomers from the land of Hatti, that is, areas of Syria, Phoenicia, and Palestine (2 Kings 17:6).[66]

62. Brown, "Media and Secondary State Formation," p. 113, n. 4.

63. R. Ghirshman, "Un Mède sur les bas-reliefs de Nimrud," *Iraq* 36 (1974): 37–40.

64. L. D. Levine, "Sargon's Eighth Campaign," in *Mountains and Lowlands*, eds. Levine and Young, pp. 140–59.

65. B. Oded, *Mass Deportations and Deportees in the Neo-Assyrian Empire* (Wiesbaden: Ludwig Reichert, 1979), p. 26.

66. D. D. Luckenbill, *Ancient Records of Assyria and Babylonia* (Chicago: University of Chicago Press, 1927), 2: 183. See H. Hoffner, "The Hittites and Hurrians," in D. J. Wiseman, *Peoples of Old Testament Times* (Oxford: Clarendon, 1973), pp. 199–200; cf. D. J. Wiseman, *Chronicles of the Chaldean Kings* (London: British Museum, 1956).

In an essay published in 1973 Geo Widengren stated: "Sargon II made several expeditions to the east, but he scarcely penetrated Median territory."[67] He was unaware of an important discovery made by Levine and Young at Najafabad deep in Median territory. There they found a stele of Sargon II, which is the first Assyrian monument found on the Iranian plateau. Its text, published in 1972, describes Sargon's sixth campaign. According to the text the Assyrians followed the route of the modern road from Kirmanshah to the Assadabad Valley below Mount Alvand.[68]

Deioces

Sargon's texts, which list some fifty Median chieftains, indicate the highly decentralized situation of the Medes in the late eighth century B.C.[69] According to Herodotus (1.96–99) it was Deioces who united the Medes and established his capital at Ecbatana.[70] Deioces has been dated, according to the data given by Herodotus (1.102), between 700 and 647. Scholars have identified Deioces with Daiaukku, a ruler over the Mannai whom Sargon II exiled to Hamath in Syria in 715.[71] A. T. Olmstead concludes:

> Daiaukku is nothing but Deiokes, and it is quite possible that the prototype of the Median prince who founded, according to Herodotus, the Median kingdom at this very time, is to be seen in this underling. We should also note that the name is Iranian.[72]

Although the Greek name in Herodotus seems to be related to the Akkadian name, Herodotus's account may be questioned on three grounds: (1) the exile of Daiaukku in 715 does not correspond with his chronology for Deioces; (2) the Assyrian texts identify Daiaukku as a Mannaean; and (3) Assyrian texts indicate that the unification of the Medes did not take place until the reign of Phraortes at the earliest.[73]

67. Widengren, "Persians," p. 314.

68. L. D. Levine, "Prelude to Monarchy," in *Iranian Civilization and Culture*, ed. C. J. Adams (Montreal: McGill University Press, 1972), p. 42; idem, *Two Neo-Assyrian Stelae from Iran* (Toronto: Royal Ontario Museum, 1972).

69. Diakonoff, "Media," p. 86.

70. Diakonoff prefers to attribute the city's foundation to Cyaxares. On Ecbatana, see chapter 8.

71. Luckenbill, *ARAB*, 2: 56.

72. A. T. Olmstead, *Western Asia in the Days of Sargon of Assyria, 722–705 B.C.* (New York: H. Holt, 1908), p. 109.

73. Diakonoff, "Media," p. 83; Frye, *History of Ancient Iran*, p. 69; J. M. Cook, *The Persian Empire* (New York: Schocken, 1983), p. 8.

R. R. Helm points out that after exiling Daiaukku to Hamath, Sargon collected tribute from twenty-two Median chiefs.[74] This situation is indirectly corroborated by the Old Testament.[75]

Vassal Treaties

The Assyrian king Esarhaddon (681–669) sent his troops deep into Median territory to the edge of the Salt Desert in 676 B.C. Four years later when the king installed his son, Ashurbanipal, as the crown prince, he imposed vassal treaties on Median princes, which pledged them to support his son.[76] The bringing of tribute by Iranians, perhaps Medes, is depicted on ivory fragments of a throne found at Nimrud.[77]

The vassal treaties that were found at Nimrud in 1955 by Max Mallowan include some of the largest cuneiform tablets discovered (one measures 18 by 12 inches). Among the treaties published by D. J. Wiseman in 1958 was one with the Median Ramataia of Urukazaba(r)na. This tablet, which contains 675 lines of cuneiform script, is the longest extant Assyrian treaty. It is filled with a long list of dreadful imprecations upon any who might dare to breach the treaty:

> Like locusts devour . . . lice and caterpillars
> may they cause your towns, your land (and) your district to be devoured.
> May they treat you as a fly (caught) in the hand;
> may your enemy squash you.
> Just as urine stinks,
> just so may your smell be before
> god and king (and) mankind.
> As for you, may they strangle you, your women,
> your sons and your daughters with a cord.[78]

But sentiments of independence and hatred of the Assyrian overlords must have prevailed against any fear of the gods, because this tablet was found smashed to pieces in the throne room, no doubt by the Medes when they helped sack Nimrud in 612.

In retrospect an ironic consequence of the Assyrian oppression, according to Brown, was the stimulation of the Median economy and the

74. R. R. Helm, "Herodotus' *Medikos Logos* and Median History," *Iran* 19 (1981): 86.

75. Note that Jer. 25:25; 51:11, 28, refers to Median "kings."

76. Esarhaddon's brothers had killed their father Sennacherib in 681 (2 Kings 19:36–37; Isa. 37:38).

77. M. E. L. Mallowan, *Nimrud and Its Remains* (London: Collins, 1966), 1: 250–51.

78. D. J. Wiseman, *The Vassal-Treaties of Esarhaddon* (London: British Museum, 1958), pp. 74, 76.

centralization of the Median state: "In short, the Neo-Assyrian imposition of tribute and tax on vassal Median chiefdoms would have touched off a chain reaction of effects that would have encouraged hierarchical tendencies both within individual polities and among the various chiefdoms affected."[79]

Phraortes

The rise of a unified Median state in the early seventh century B.C. is attested in Assyrian texts.[80] During the last years of Esarhaddon's reign (681–669) liver omen texts refer to his concern about a Kashtariti (a personal name derived from the Assyrian form of the Median word, *khšathrita,* meaning kingship). He was a chief of the Kar-Kašši region in the central Zagros,[81] who sought to unite the Medes, Mannaeans, and Cimmerians in an anti-Assyrian coalition. So concerned were the Assyrians with the Medes that their king, Ashurbanipal, launched a major expedition around 659 in which he claimed to have captured seventy-five Median townships.[82]

Kashtariti has been identified with the Median king whom Herodotus names Phraortes (Persian *Fravartiš,* meaning "protector"). According to Herodotus (1.102) Phraortes subdued the Persians, who at this time were ruled by Teispes (*Chishpish*) the son of Achaemenes (*Hakhamanish*), the eponymous ancestor of the Achaemenid rulers.

The identification of Kashtariti is based upon the observation that over a century later a rebel against Darius I was described in the Behistun inscription (DB II, #24:2.13–17): "One man, Phraortes by name, a Median—he rose up in Media. To the people thus he said, 'I am Khshathrita, of the family of Cyaxares.' " It is assumed that this pretender was calling upon the glory of his distant ancestor, Khshathrita, father of Cyaxares (Phraortes), just as other rebels against Darius claimed to be Nebuchadnezzar redivivi.

This reasoning, however, has been challenged by René Labat. According to Herodotus, Phraortes died while fighting in a battle against the Assyrians. But Labat argues that there is no record of such a conflict in

79. Brown, "Media and Secondary State Formation," p. 114.

80. Diakonoff, "Media," p. 110.

81. G. Cameron, *History of Early Iran* (New York: Greenwood, 1968 reprint of 1936 edition), p. 178. L. Lockhart and J. A. Boyle, "The Beginnings: The Achaemenids," in *Persia: History and Heritage,* ed. J. A. Boyle (London: Henry Melland, 1978), p. 19, suggest that his town, Akessaia, was the future Ecbatana. The more natural reading is that his area was in Kassite territory. See E. Yamauchi, "Kassites," in *NIDBA,* eds. E. M. Blaiklock and R. K. Harrison (Grand Rapids: Zondervan, 1983), pp. 276–78.

82. Luckenbill, *ARAB,* 2: 328.

texts of Ashurbanipal (668–626) for the usual date for Phraortes' death (653).[83]

There is, furthermore, the complicated and vexing question of the domination of "Asia" by the Scythians, an invading nomadic tribe from the Russian steppes, for twenty-eight years (Herodotus 1.103; 4.1).[84] Most scholars would place such a Scythian interregnum after Phraortes and before Cyaxares, that is, between 653 and 625.[85]

Labat, citing variant readings of the Herodotus text, would propose to subsume almost wholly the Scythian period (625–597) as contemporary with the reign of Cyaxares (625–585), and lower the dates of Phraortes from 647 to 625.[86] This would make the equation with the Kashtariti mentioned around 670 unlikely.[87]

In a brief but important article, Alan R. Millard has proposed another solution to the problem of reconciling Herodotus with the Near Eastern evidence. He would accept Labat's dating of Phraortes from 647 to 625, but would divide the Scythian interregnum into two phases: (1) twenty years of dominance in Asia (645–625), that is, eastern Turkey; and (2) eight years of dominance in Media during the first years of Cyaxares (625–617). This interpretation would fit the Near Eastern data by placing the Scythian domination after the passing of the Cimmerian threat and before the attack of Cyaxares against the Assyrians in 615.[88]

Levine summarizes the possible catalytic influence of the temporary Scythian incursion in Media as follows:

> The effect of the Scythian presence in Iran, as transient as it may have been, was to radicalize the long standing alliances, as we have already noted. In political terms, it is perhaps here that we should seek the rise of the Median confederacy. Under pressure from the Assyrians from the west and from the Scythians from the north, the old loose structure of local principalities was no longer adequate.[89]

83. R. Labat, "Kaštariti, Phraorte, et les débuts de l'histoire Mède," *JA* 249 (1961): 2–4. Helm, "Herodotus' *Medikos Logos,*" p. 86, also doubts the identification.

84. On the Scythians, see T. Rice, *The Scythians,* 3d ed. (New York: Praeger, 1961); Yamauchi, *Foes;* Cook, *Persian Empire,* p. 4.

85. Helm, "Herodotus' *Medikos Logos,*" pp. 87, 90; R. Drews, "The Fall of Astyages and Herodotus' Chronology of the Eastern Kingdoms," *Historia* 18 (1969): 7, 9.

86. For the traditional chronology of Median kings derived from Herodotus, see Cook, *Persian Empire,* p. 4; Diakonoff, "Media," pp. 112–13; Frye, *History of Ancient Iran,* p. 75; Helm, "Herodotus' *Medikos Logos,*" p. 87.

87. Labat, "Kaštariti, Phraorte, et les débuts de l'histoire Mède," pp. 5–7.

88. A. R. Millard, "The Scythian Problem," in *Glimpses of Ancient Egypt,* eds. J. Ruffle et al. (Warminster: Aris and Phillips, 1979), pp. 119–22. E. Cavaignac, "A propos du début de l'histoire des Mèdes," *JA* 249 (1961): 158, dates the beginning of the Scythian domination from the foundation of Sinope in 630 B.C.

89. Levine, "Prelude to Monarchy," p. 43.

The impact of the Scythians was noted in the Old Testament, as Levine observes: "That they played an important role is reflected in as distant a source as the Book of Jeremiah, where they (Ashkenaz) are named along with Urartu, the Medes and Mannaeans as the wrath that emanates from the north (51:27ff.)."[90]

Cyaxares

All scholars agree upon the dates of Cyaxares, the son of Phraortes, whose long forty-year reign (625–585 B.C.) saw the ascendancy of the Medes to their greatest heights (Herodotus 1.106). In alliance with the Chaldeans or Neo-Babylonians, he extended the Median kingdom westward through Urartu to eastern Anatolia.

The Greek name *Cyaxares* reflects the Old Persian name *Huvakhštra;* in Akkadian texts he is called *Umakištar.* According to Herodotus (1.103) Cyaxares reorganized the Median army into three classes of mobile troops—spearmen, bowmen, and cavalry. Partly through a ruse, he was able to defeat the Scythians and expel them from Media—at any rate the greatest number of them.[91]

The climactic events that led to the welcomed toppling of the hitherto invincible Assyrian Empire (see the Book of Nahum) have been recorded in a series of relatively objective "Chaldaean Chronicles," published by C. J. Gadd in 1923 and by D. J. Wiseman in 1956.[92]

The Medes first appear in the Chronicles in the year 615, when they attacked the province of Arraphu, apparently in a move that was independent of the Chaldeans. During this same year the Chaldeans made an unsuccessful assault against Ashur.[93]

In 614 the Medes first attacked the city of Tarbiṣu, northwest of Ashur, then assaulted and took the great city of Ashur itself: "He inflicted a terrible massacre upon the greater part of the people, plundering it (the city) and carrying off [prisoners from it.]"[94] The chronicler

90. Ibid.

91. I have argued elsewhere (*Foes*) that some of the Scythians may have remained behind to serve as mercenaries in the Babylonian army. See T. Sulimirski, "Scythian Antiquities in Western Asia," *Artibus Asiae* 17 (1954): 282–318.

92. C. J. Gadd, *The Fall of Nineveh* (London: British Museum, 1923); D. J. Wiseman, *Chronicles of Chaldaean Kings (626–556 B.C.)* (London: British Museum, 1956); see also A. K. Grayson, *Assyrian and Babylonian Chronicles* (Locust Valley: J. J. Augustin, 1975), pp. 87–98.

93. E. Yamauchi, "Chaldea, Chaldeans," in *NIDBA*, eds. E. M. Blaiklock and R. K. Harrison (Grand Rapids: Zondervan, 1983), pp. 123–25.

94. Wiseman, *Chronicles*, p. 57.

emphasizes that the "King of Adad," that is, the Chaldean ruler Nabopolassar,[95] arrived after the city had fallen to the Medes.

Cyaxares, who is now mentioned for the first time in the Chronicles, and Nabopolassar then met by the captured city and established an alliance of "mutual friendship and peace" (Akkadian *sulummū;* compare Hebrew *shalōm,* Arabic *salām*). According to Greek sources the alliance was sealed by the marriage of a Median princess to the son of Nabopolassar, the great Nebuchadnezzar.[96] Tradition also relates that it was to please his Median wife that Nebuchadnezzar erected the Hanging Gardens of Babylon.[97]

The Fall of Nineveh

In 612 B.C. the Medes and Chaldeans launched a joint attack upon the Assyrian capital of Nineveh, against which Jonah had preached in the eighth century.[98] The Chronicles pinpoint the date of this crucial event to the month of Ab (July/August). Line 42 of the text (B.M. 21901) is unfortunately broken at a crucial juncture after the numeral "three." The lacuna has been variously restored by translators: by Gadd as "three [battles];" by Wiseman as "three [measures]," that is, of distance; by A. K. Grayson as "three [months]," that is, of the siege.

Although the text is broken it may be presumed that the Assyrian king, Sin-shar-ishkun, was killed. The Chronicle records: "The great spoil of the city and temple they carried off and [turned] the city into a ruin-mound and heaps of debri[s . . .]."[99] Thus were the prophecies of Nahum (2:10; 3:7) and Zephaniah (2:13–15) fulfilled. The latter predicted that the great Assyrian metropolis would be made a pasture for flocks. Today one of the two mounds of the ruins is Tell Kuyunjik ("Mound of Many Sheep"). The other mound is Tell Nebi Yunus, named after the traditional tomb of Jonah standing on top of it.[100]

95. E. Yamauchi, "Nabopolassar," in *NIDBA,* eds. E. M. Blaiklock and R. K. Harrison (Grand Rapids: Zondervan, 1983), pp. 326–27.

96. D. J. Wiseman, *Nebuchadrezzar and Babylon* (London: Oxford University Press, 1985); E. Yamauchi, "Nebuchadnezzar," in *NIDBA,* eds. E. M. Blaiklock and R. K. Harrison (Grand Rapids: Zondervan, 1983), pp. 332–34.

97. R. Koldewey, the excavator, located the Hanging Gardens near the Ishtar Gate. See E. Yamauchi, "Babylon," in *Major Cities of the Biblical World,* ed. R. K. Harrison (Nashville: Thomas Nelson, 1985), pp. 32–48; J. Oates, *Babylon* (London: Thames and Hudson, 1979). D. J. Wiseman, "Mesopotamian Gardens," *AS* 33 (1983): 137–44, has proposed a more probable site along the river. See W. Nagel, "Where Are the 'Hanging Gardens' Located in Babylon?" *Sumer* 35 (1979): 241–42.

98. D. J. Wiseman, "Jonah's Nineveh," *TB* 30 (1979): 29–51.

99. Wiseman, *Chronicles,* p. 61.

100. A. Parrot, *Nineveh and the Old Testament* (New York: Philosophical Library, 1955); E. Yamauchi, "Nineveh," in *Layman's Bible Dictionary,* ed. T. Butler (Nashville: Holman, forthcoming).

The Chronicles also refer to the participation in the fall of Nineveh of the *Ummanmanda*, a word that has the connotation of "hordes." A considerable controversy has raged over whether this word refers to the Scythians,[101] or whether it simply is another designation for the Medes. The fragmentary nature of the text makes a definite conclusion difficult. A thorough study of the term convinces G. Komoróczy that in the context the Ummanmanda are Medes.[102]

While this may be true, such a conclusion does not necessarily rule out Scythian participation in these events. I have argued elsewhere that Scythian-type arrowheads from Ashur and from Nimrud[103] may be evidence that some of the remaining Scythians turned against their erstwhile allies, the Assyrians, just as they did against the Urartians at Karmir Blur.[104]

A remnant of the Assyrians, led by Ashur-uballit, escaped to establish a rump government at the northwestern outpost of Harran (where Abraham had tarried on his journey to Palestine). But they were overcome there in 610 by Nabopolassar with the aid of the Ummanmanda. The usual view is that this area fell thereafter under the Medes, but Dieter Baltzer has argued that Harran fell to the Chaldeans.[105]

A half-century later the last of the Neo-Babylonian kings, Nabonidus (556–539 B.C.), who came from Harran, was urged by his god in a dream to rebuild the temple there that had been destroyed by the Ummanmanda:

> The Ummanmanda that you mention, they and their land, and the kings their allies no longer exist. In the third year coming I shall make Cyrus king of Anshan [*i.e.*, Persia] his petty servant, expel them. With his few troops he will sweep out the widespreading Ummanmanda.[106]

After the fall of Harran and before the conflict with the Lydians in western Turkey (590), the Medes must have annexed the territories to

101. Wiseman, *Chronicles*, pp. 16–17.

102. G. Komoróczy, "Ummān-Manda," *AAH* 25 (1977): 43–67.

103. Mallowan, *Nimrud*, p. 407, thinks that the arrowhead may be Median rather than Scythian. Though not every Scythian-type arrowhead can be associated with the Scythians, many can be attributed to either Scythian marauders or mercenaries. See note 84 above.

104. B. Piotrovsky, *The Ancient Civilization of Urartu* (New York: Cowles, 1969), p. 178.

105. D. Baltzer, "Harran nach 610 'medisch'? Kritische Überprüfung einer Hypothese," *WO* 7 (1973): 86–95.

106. D. W. Thomas, ed., *Documents from Old Testament Times* (New York: Harper, 1968), p. 90; A. L. Oppenheim, *The Interpretation of Dreams in the Ancient Near East* (Philadelphia: American Philosophical Society, 1956), pp. 189, 202–3, 250; see also C. J. Gadd, "The Harran Inscriptions of Nabonidus," *AS* 8 (1958): 35–92.

the north of the Mannaeans and the Urartians.[107] During the last five years of his reign Cyaxares fought with Alyattes of Lydia (Herodotus 1.73–74), a conflict that was ended by the prediction of an eclipse by Thales[108] and by the mediation of Labynetus (Herodotus 1.74), that is, Nabonidus. A Lydian princess was then married to Astyages, the son of Cyaxares. The boundary between the two powers was fixed at the Halys River.

Astyages

Astyages (585–550 B.C.) is the Greek for Old Persian *Arštivaiga,* "Brandishing a Lance," *Ištumēgu* in Akkadian. His daughter, Mandana, married a Persian, Cambyses I, and gave birth to the famous Cyrus the Great. Xenophon's propagandistic *Cyropaedia,* "The Education of Cyrus," describes Cyrus's perception of the Median garb as follows:

> Then he noticed that his grandfather was adorned with pencillings beneath his eyes, with rouge rubbed on his face, and with a wig of false hair—the common Median fashion. For all this is Median, and so are their purple tunics, and their mantles, the necklaces about their necks, and the bracelets on their wrists. (*Cyropaedia* 1.3.2)

According to Herodotus (1.135), the Persians admired and adopted Median dress.[109]

The Persians had developed into a kingdom subordinate to the Medes, probably during the reign of Cyaxares.[110] When Cyrus had come of age, he led the Persians in a revolt against his grandfather (550).[111] According to Herodotus (1.127–28) Cyrus overcame the Medes in two battles. Strabo (15.3.8) located the scene of the decisive battle in the plain where Cyrus was to build his new capital: "Cyrus held Pasargadae in honor because he there conquered Astyages the Mede in his last battle, transferred to himself the empire of Asia, founded a city, and constructed a palace as a memorial to his victory."

107. Dyson, "Problems," p. 212. The capital city Tušpa was captured about 609 B.C., probably by the Medes. Frye, *History of Ancient Iran,* p. 73.

108. This report, however, is questioned by O. Neugebauer, *The Exact Sciences in Antiquity,* 2d ed. (New York: Harper, 1957), pp. 142–43.

109. See A. Roes, "The Achaemenid Robe," *BO* 8/4 (1951): 137–41; G. Thompson, "Iranian Dress in the Achaemenian Period," *Iran* 3 (1965): 121–26; P. Roos, "An Achaemenian Sketch Slab and the Ornaments of the Royal Dress at Persepolis," *East and West* n.s. 20 (1970): 51–59; P. Beck, "A Note on the Reconstruction of the Achaemenid Robe," *Iran* 9 (1972): 116–22.

110. Diakonoff, "Media," p. 133.

111. Drews, "Fall of Astyages," has argued for the date 553 for the fall of Astyages instead of 550.

The Medes and Persians

The extent of a Median Empire before its absorption by the Persians under Cyrus is not clear.[112] Thereafter the Medes were to play a subordinate though important role under the Persians in the Achaemenid period (550–330 B.C.). The Medes did have to pay the annual tax (Herodotus 3.91–96).

The Medes were especially prominent at the Achaemenid court as attested in the reliefs at Persepolis.[113] They are depicted with short, curled beards and as wearing domed felt caps, knee-length leather tunics, and high-laced shoes. They are armed with rectangular shields and short swords carried in decorated scabbards. The Mede bowing before the king in the treasury reliefs from Persepolis is interpreted by Walter Hinz as the royal chamberlain.[114]

As Widengren notes, "both Medes and Persians were often called simply 'Medes' by the Greeks, and this usage evidently dates from the first contact between Greeks in Ionia and Iranians of the west."[115] The Persians were known as Medes down to the age of Demosthenes (fourth century B.C.).

In Hebrew sources the term *Mede* may sometimes include the Persians, as in prophetic passages (Isa. 13:17ff.; Jer. 51:11, 28).[116] Daniel refers to the laws of the "the Medes and Persians, which cannot be annuled" (Dan. 6:8, 12, 15). Esther (1:3, 14) reverses the order to "Persia and Media."[117]

Liberal scholars, who since the time of Porphyry (A.D. 233–305)[118] have regarded Daniel as a *vaticinium ex eventu* (a "prophecy after the event"), interpret the second of the four kingdoms of chapters 2 and 7 of Daniel as an erroneously conceived Median kingdom.[119] Conserva-

112. On the question of a Median Empire, see Diakonoff, "Media," p. 120, map 5, and his *Istoriya Midii* (Moscow: Akademii Nauk, 1956), chapter 5.

113. See Ghirshman, *Art of Ancient Iran*, pp. 157ff.

114. W. Hinz, "Medisches und Elamisches am Achämenidenhof," in *Altiranische Funde und Forschungen*, ed. W. Hinz (Berlin: W. de Gruyter, 1969), pp. 63ff.

115. Widengren, *POT*, p. 316.

116. John Bright, *Jeremiah* (Garden City: Doubleday, 1965), p. 360, suggests: "One might suppose from this that these poems reflect, at least in good part, the period prior to Cyrus' overthrow of the Median king Astyages (550), and the beginning of his spectacular career of conquest." That is, Jeremiah's prophecy was a prediction and not a *vaticinium ex eventu* after the fall of Babylon to the Persians in 539.

117. A. Millard, "Medes," in *The International Standard Bible Encyclopedia*, ed. G. W. Bromiley, rev. ed. (Grand Rapids: Eerdmans, 1986), 3: 297–99.

118. M. V. Anastos, "Porphyry's Attack on the Bible," *The Classical Tradition: Literary and Historical Studies in Honor of H. Caplan* (Ithaca: Cornell University Press, 1966), pp. 433–34; P. M. Casey, "Porphyry and the Origin of the Book of Daniel," *JTS* n.s. 27 (1976): 15–33.

119. H. H. Rowley, *Darius the Mede and the Four World Empires in the Book of Daniel* (Cardiff:

tive scholars, following ancient Jewish and patristic interpreters, believe that this second kingdom was the Medo-Persian Empire.[120]

Darius the Mede

The identification of Daniel's "Darius the Mede" (Dan. 5:31; 6:1–2; 9:1–2; 11:1) remains as contested as ever. Charles C. Torrey, who questioned the authenticity of almost all of the exilic books of the Bible, thought that it was but a confused name for the later Darius I.[121] Claus Schedl has also identified Darius the Mede with the great Persian Darius. He argues that the title came from the fact that Darius I marched into Media to quell the revolt of Fravartish.[122] This is hardly convincing.

There have been two major attempts to resolve the problem. The first, proposed by John Whitcomb, was that Darius the Mede is to be identified with Gubaru/Gobryas, the provincial governor of Babylon.[123] The second proposal, offered by D. J. Wiseman, was that Daniel 6:28 be translated, "Daniel prospered in the reign of Darius *even* the reign of Cyrus the Persian," that is, taking the former name as a throne name.[124]

An attempt has been made by James M. Bulman to add support to Wiseman's thesis. He notes the use of dual names, points to the Septuagint and Theodotion, which render Daniel 11:1 the "first year of Cyrus" rather than the "first year of Darius," and cites other parallels in what is attributed to Darius the Mede as compared to the career of Cyrus. He explains the use of the byname *Darius the Mede* for Cyrus in Daniel as follows:

> Unlike the authors of Chronicles and Ezra, however, he does not represent Cyrus as the agent of fulfilment of prophecy. But since Jeremiah,

---

University of Wales Press, 1935); N. Porteous, *Daniel* (Philadelphia: Westminster, 1965); D. Flusser, "The Four Empires in the Fourth Sibyl and in the Book of Daniel," *Israel Oriental Studies* 2 (1972): 148–75; L. F. Hartman and A. Di Lella, *The Book of Daniel* (Garden City: Doubleday, 1978); A. Lacocque, *Daniel* (Atlanta: John Knox, 1978).

120. E. J. Young, *The Prophecy of Daniel* (Grand Rapids: Eerdmans, 1949); J. F. Walvoord, *Daniel, The Key to Prophetic Revelation* (Chicago: Moody, 1971); L. Wood, *A Commentary on Daniel* (Grand Rapids: Zondervan, 1973); J. Baldwin, *Daniel* (Downers Grove: Inter-Varsity, 1978); G. F. Hasel, "The Four World Empires of Daniel 2 Against Its Near Eastern Environment," *JSOT* 12 (1979): 17–30.

121. C. C. Torrey, "Medes and Persians," *JAOS* 66 (1946): 1, 3.

122. C. Schedl, *History of the Old Testament* (Staten Island: Alba House, 1973), 5: 51–86.

123. J. Whitcomb, *Darius the Mede* (Grand Rapids: Eerdmans, 1959); idem, *Daniel* (Chicago: Moody, 1985), pp. 89–90.

124. D. J. Wiseman, "Some Historical Problems in the Book of Daniel," in *Notes on Some Problems in the Book of Daniel*, D. J. Wiseman et al. (London: Tyndale, 1965), pp. 12–16.

> who mentioned no name, emphasized the Medes as conquerors of Babylon, Daniel was led . . . to use the name which was associated with them.[125]

A new attempt to resolve the problem has been made by William H. Shea in a carefully argued article[126] that can be but briefly summarized here. Shea finds Wiseman's arguments unconvincing because of the problem of patronymics (fathers' names) and also the chronological notices (Dan. 10:1; 11:1). He applauds Whitcomb for making the distinction between two persons named Gubaru in the cuneiform texts: Gubaru I, the conqueror of Babylon, and Gubaru II, the governor of Babylon.[127] But whereas Whitcomb identifies Darius the Mede with Gubaru II, Shea identifies him with Gubaru I.

Shea concludes that there are six points in which the careers of Gubaru I and Darius the Mede match: (1) Gubaru led the Medo-Persian troops who captured Babylon (see Dan. 5:28). (2) He installed governors there (see Dan. 6:1–2). (3) He was probably quite old, since he died soon after the capture of Babylon (see Dan. 5:30). (4) According to cuneiform texts he died about a year after he conquered Babylon (see Dan. 9:1; 11:1). The explanation for the transition from the regnal reckoning of Darius the Mede to the "third year of Cyrus" (Dan. 10:1) would be the assumption that the former had passed from the scene. (5) The distinction between the kingdoms of Darius and of Cyrus in Daniel fits the evidence of the chronology and development of Cyrus's titularies. (6) Just as Darius was "made king," Gubaru served as a vassal under Cyrus.[128]

Median Objects

Prior to the excavations at Median sites in the late 1960s and 1970s, there were few tangible objects that could be ascribed to the Medes. One example of alleged Median craftsmanship is a decorated gold scabbard from the Oxus Treasure.[129] This is identical to the swords worn by the Medes in the Persepolis reliefs.

125. J. M. Bulman, "The Identification of Darius the Mede," *Westminster Theological Journal* 35 (1973): 247–67.

126. W. H. Shea, "Darius the Mede: An Update," *AUSS* 20 (1982): 229–48.

127. Grayson, *Assyrian and Babylonian Chronicles*, pp. 109–10.

128. L. L. Grabbe, "Another Look at the *Gestalt* of 'Darius the Mede,' " *CBQ* 50 (1988): 198–213, questions all of these proposed solutions to the enigma of "Darius the Mede."

129. O. M. Dalton, *The Treasure of the Oxus*, 2d ed. (London: British Museum, 1964), p. 9. On the nature of the treasure, see my review in *JAOS* 90 (1970): 340–43.

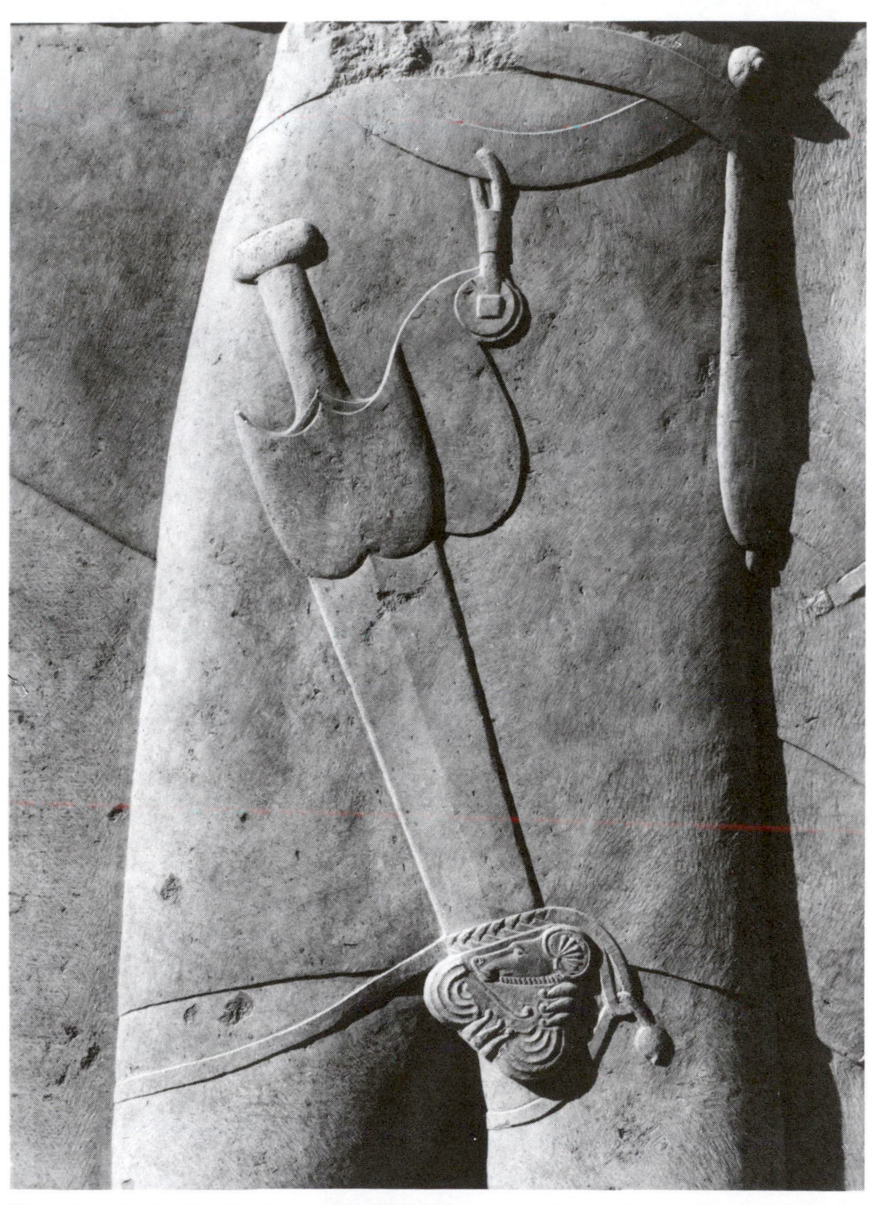

The sheath of a Median's sword. (The Oriental Institute, University of Chicago)

Richard D. Barnett, who made the identification, notes that the horseman depicted on the sheath wears an Assyrian-type crown and Iranian trousers. He then speculates: "I have also suggested that he can only be Astyages himself, the great king of the Medes (585–550 B.C.), for who else can have laid claim to the Assyrian crown, and also had himself depicted performing the symbolic central act of the Assyrian king's lion hunt?"[130] Barnett further believed that three swords from the Scythian burials at Kelermes, Chertomlyk, and Melgunov were also Median, although they also include a mixture of Urartian and Scythian elements.[131] The Median attribution of the sheath has been challenged by Oscar Muscarella.[132] His further contention that the Ziwiye Treasure (which includes a similar melange of elements) is Median has not been widely accepted.[133]

Charles Virolleaud and Charles Fossey made limited soundings at the Median capital of Ecbatana (Hamadan) in 1913 and recovered a number of objects, including a jug with a long spout, which Ghirshman identifies as Median.[134] Many other objects, including some magnificent gold masterworks, have been recovered from Hamadan and its vicinity.[135] (See chapter 8.) Recently Peter Calmeyer has listed as Median a cuneiform text on a bronze plate, inscribed cylinder seals, and bronze pitchers and fibulas.[136] The provenience of these objects and their identification as Median, however, have also been sharply questioned by Muscarella.[137]

Median Tombs

In 1964 Ghirshman, following Herzfeld, identified a number of tombs carved in cliffs as Median. The tomb at Kizkapan bears a relief with two men in Median dress holding Scythian-type bows, which Ghirshman would interpret as a ruler and his successor.[138] The relief at Dukkan-i Daud depicts a man holding the barsom, a bundle of sacred

130. R. D. Barnett, "Median Art," *IA* 2 (1962): 79.

131. Ibid., p. 90.

132. Porada, *Art of Ancient Iran*, p. 134.

133. Muscarella, "Median Art and Medizing Scholarship," p. 114, has challenged the Median attribution of many other objects, including a gold vessel in the Cincinnati Art Museum.

134. Ghirshman, *Art of Ancient Iran*, p. 94.

135. E. Herzfeld, *The Persian Empire* (Wiesbaden: Harrassowitz, 1968), p. 159.

136. P. Calmeyer, "Zu einiger vernachlässigten Aspekten Medischer Kunst," in Bagherzadeh, *Proceedings*, pp. 112–27.

137. O. W. Muscarella, "Excavated and Unexcavated Achaemenid Art," in *Ancient Persia: The Art of an Empire*, ed. D. Schmandt-Besserat (Malibu: Undena, 1980), pp. 31–35.

138. Ghirshman, *Art of Ancient Iran*, pp. 86–89.

Median tomb at Kizkapan. (Courtesy of the British School of Archaeology in Iraq)

twigs. Herzfeld thought that some of these tombs were the prototypes of the Achaemenid tombs at Naqsh-i Rustam. Ghirshman dated them to the seventh or sixth centuries (pre-Achaemenid).

H. Von Gall, however, argues that tombs at Dakkan-i Daud, Fakhraqah, Sahna, and Ishqavand can only date from the time of Darius I at the earliest.[139] According to Von Gall, the Ionian capitals of the columns at Kizkapan are not, as Herzfeld believed, the earliest examples of such columns in the sixth century, but are no earlier than the end of the fifth century.[140] The figure depicted on the Dukkan-i Daud tomb, holding the barsom, is in his view obviously a magus. The magi were originally a priestly caste of the Medes (see chapter 13). On the tomb at Ishqavand a relief depicts a man in a Persian garment praying before an incense vessel and a smaller figure in a Median garment before a fire altar, perhaps a magus.

According to Herodotus (1.140) the magi exposed their corpses to dogs or carrion birds, just as the Parsees (modern Zoroastrians) expose

139. H. Von Gall, "Zu den 'Medischen' Felsgräbern in Nordwestiran und Iraqi Kurdistan," *AA* (1966): 19–43.

140. Compare Porada, *Art of Ancient Iran*, p. 138.

their dead to vultures before disposing of the bones.[141] Because of the small size of some of the rock chambers, Von Gall interprets these as the repositories for the bones of the corpses of magi who had been thus exposed to excarnation.[142]

141. R. Masani, *Zoroastrianism* (New York: Collier, 1962), pp. 99–107.

142. H. Von Gall, "Neue Beobachtungen zu den sog. Medischen Felsgräbern," in Bagherzadeh, *Proceedings*, pp. 139–53.

2 Cyrus

Parsua/Persia

The Persians were Indo-European Iranians who were closely related to the Medes. Like the Medes they had migrated from the steppes of Russia into the western Iranian plateau. The name *Parsua* first occurs in inscriptions from the reign of Shalmaneser III in 844 B.C. Variants of the name—such as *Barsua, Parsuash,* and *Parsumash*—occur in the Neo-Assyrian texts.[1] The name *Barshua* appears in Urartian.[2]

The location of the earliest Parsua has been variously placed. In 1965 Robert H. Dyson, Jr., noted:

1. S. Parpola, *Neo-Assyrian Toponyms* (Kevalaer: Butzon and Bercker, 1970), pp. 274–75. J. Hansman, "Elamites, Achaemenians and Anshan," *Iran* 10 (1972): 109, drew the following conclusions: "The first (Parsuash) is to be located in Luristān and further north where the name possibly passed directly into Assyrian. The second (Parsuwash/Parsumash) is to be placed in south Iran where the name perhaps reached Assyria by way of a southern Mesopotamian form."

2. J. E. Reade, "Kassites and Assyrians in Iran," *Iran* 16 (1978): 139, notes that by this name the Urartians referred to a territory somewhere south of Lake Urmia.

> Parsua is sometimes placed in Solduz (Wright, 1943) and sometimes in the reaches of the upper Diyala (Diakonov, 1956; Ghirshman, 1964a, 398). The area of Parsua was close to the city of Meshta (Tash Tepe; modern Mianduab) and the province of Missi, according to both Urartian and Assyrian annals.[3]

Since Dyson wrote, the researches of Louis Levine have clarified the location of early Parsua. He summarizes his conclusions as follows:

> 1) From the time of Shalmaneser III to Sennacherib, all references to Parsua can be accommodated in a single location. There is no need for a theory of multiple Parsuas. 2) None of the texts can be shown to place Parsua in the north, around Lake Urmia. All of the texts which have clear geographical indicators place Parsua among the southernmost Zagros areas known to the Assyrians. 3) The best location that can be advanced at present for Parsua is in the Northern Mahidasht, around the town of Ravansar.[4]

That is, the early location of the Persians would be west of the Medes in the vicinity of the Great Khorasan Road, which led from the Mesopotamian plain past Ecbatana (Hamadan) to points east.

A Migration Southward?

Inasmuch as the heartland of the Persians from the sixth century on was the province of Pars (Fars) in the area around Persepolis north of the Persian Gulf, many scholars have assumed a migration of the Persians from their earlier Zagros location southward. This migration may have begun under pressure of the Scythian incursion (seventh century B.C.). Levine observes: "Parsua seems to disappear from the northern Māhīdasht, only to reappear in the reign of Ashurbanipal somewhere to the south, this time under a king named Cyrus (I)."[5]

The theory of the southward migration of the Persians has been most thoroughly developed by Roman Ghirshman. In his view the

3. R. H. Dyson, Jr., "Problems of Protohistoric Iran as Seen from Hasanlu," *JNES* 24 (1965): 199. R. M. Boehmer, "Zur Lage von Parsua im 9-Jahrhundert vor Christus," *Berliner Jahrbuch für Vor- und Frühgeschichte* 5 (1965): 199, located Parsua to the west of Lake Urmia in the ninth century, and then to the south of it in the eighth century.

4. L. D. Levine, "Sargon's Eighth Campaign," in *Mountains and Lowlands*, eds. L. D. Levine and T. C. Young, Jr. (Malibu: Undena, 1977), p. 138; idem, "Geographical Studies in the Neo-Assyrian Zagros II," *Iran* 12 (1974): 106–8.

5. L. D. Levine, "Prelude to Monarchy: Iran and the Neo-Assyrian Empire," in *Iranian Civilization and Culture*, ed. C. J. Adams (Montreal: McGill University Press, 1972), p. 43.

Persians migrated from the Zagros first into Khuzistan, settling at Susa, Masjid-i Sulaiman, and Bard-i Nishandeh, before they proceeded eastward to Pasargadae. There are great artificial terraces at the two latter sites, which Ghirshman compares with the terrace at Pasargadae, the capital of Cyrus II. He suggests that Masjid-i Sulaiman, which is about twenty-five miles southeast of Shushtar, may have been the capital of Cyrus I in the seventh century.[6] Ghirshman's reconstruction has been followed by numerous scholars, including Alessandro Bausani,[7] John Boyle,[8] André Godard,[9] and Walter Hinz.[10]

Other scholars have questioned the idea of a southward migration, postulating instead that the various names (Parsua/Parsumash/Parsa), though they may be etymologically related, are designations of different branches of the Persian tribes.[11] I. M. Diakonoff maintains that Parsua represents Iranian Parsava or "borderland." Though it is etymologically related to Parsuash/Parsumash, he does not believe that the former can designate the native land of the Persians.[12]

David Stronach, who at first followed Ghirshman,[13] has raised a number of objections to Ghirshman's theory and has proposed an alternative theory. Stronach points out that the path suggested by Ghirshman is highly improbable in view of the difficult terrain and the presence of Assyrians and Elamites along the way.[14] In opposition to Ghirshman, Stronach dates the Achaemenid village at Susa not from the eighth to seventh centuries but to around 600.[15] Instead of Ghirshman's early dates for Masjid-i Sulaiman and Bard-i Nishandeh—both east of Susa—Stronach suggests that their terraces are no earlier than the fifth century.[16] Finally, Stronach dates the great terrace of Pa-

6. R. Ghirshman, "Masjid-i-Solaiman résidence des premiers Achéménides," *Syria* 27 (1950): 204–20; idem, *Iran* (Baltimore: Penguin, 1954), pp. 122–23; idem, *The Art of Ancient Iran* (New York: Golden, 1964), pp. 129-31; idem, *Terasses sacrées de Bard-è Néchandeh et Masjid-i Solaiman* (Leiden: Brill, 1977), pp. 149–61.

7. A. Bausani, *The Persians* (New York: St. Martin's, 1971), p. 13.

8. L. Lockhart and J. A. Boyle, "The Beginnings: The Achaemenids," in *Persia: History and Heritage,* ed. J. A. Boyle (London: Allen and Unwin, 1978), p. 19.

9. A. Godard, *The Art of Iran* (New York: Praeger, 1965), p. 101.

10. W. Hinz, *Darius und die Perser* (Baden-Baden: Holle, 1976), p. 49. Hinz guesses that ten to twenty thousand were involved in such a trek.

11. Dyson, "Problems," pp. 203–4; R. N. Frye, *The Heritage of Persia* (Cleveland: World, 1963), pp. 45–46; E. Porada, *The Art of Ancient Iran* (New York: Crown, 1965), p. 137; J. M. Cook, *The Persian Empire* (New York: Schocken, 1983), p. 2.

12. I. M. Diakonoff, "Media," in *The Cambridge History of Iran II: The Median and Achaemenian Periods,* ed. I. Gershevitch (Cambridge: Cambridge University Press, 1985), pp. 62–63.

13. D. Stronach, "Excavations of Pasargadae: First Preliminary Report," *Iran* 1 (1963): 20–21.

14. D. Stronach, "Achaemenid Village I at Susa and the Persian Migration to Fars," *Iran* 12 (1974): 239.

15. Ibid., p. 244.

16. Ibid., p. 246.

sargadae not to the time of Cambyses I (circa 600) as Ghirshman proposed, but to the era of Cyrus II (559–530).[17]

Malyan/Anshan

One of the great puzzles of Iranian topography was the location of Anshan, a city second only to Susa in Elamite history. In a highly perceptive article published in 1972, John Hansman, following the lead of William Sumner, suggested that Anshan be identified with the site of Malyan (or Maliyūn) about twenty-eight miles north of Shiraz and twenty-six miles west of Persepolis.[18]

The mound, which rises some 4 to 6 meters above the plain and covers about five hundred acres, was subject to excavations between 1971 and 1978 directed by William Sumner.[19] The identification of Malyan as Anshan has now been established beyond doubt by the frequent appearance of the name in Middle Elamite texts found at the site.[20]

This new information has implications for the route of the Persians prior to their arrival in Fars. Stronach believes that the identification of Malyan, located west of Pasargadae, as the great Elamite city means that the Persians could not have approached from the west. He therefore concludes:

> With these considerations in mind it is probably necessary to assume that the Persian tribes approached the region of Fars directly from the north (if not from the east as well) and that they then pushed *westwards* at the expense of the Elamites. One other clue in this context lies in the title used by the rulers of the Neo-Elamite kingdom, for, as far as we know, Kudur-Nahunte (693–693 B.C.) was the last Elamite monarch to call himself king of "Anzan and Susa." In other words, an important part of the region of Anzan or Anšan may have been abandoned to the Persians soon after 700 B.C.[21]

The identification of Malyan as Anshan also has implications for the early history of the Achaemenid rulers of Persia. It was formerly thought that Anshan and Parsumash were quite distinct lands. We now

17. Ibid., p. 247.

18. Hansman, "Elamites," pp. 101–25.

19. W. Sumner, "Excavations at Tall-i-Malyan, 1971–72," *Iran* 12 (1974): 155–77; idem, "Excavations at Tall-i Malyan (Anshan), 1974," *Iran* 14 (1976): 103–13.

20. E. Reiner, "Tall-i Malyān, Epigraphic Finds, 1971–72," *Iran* 12 (1974): 176; E. Carter and M. Stolper, "Middle Elamite Malyan," *Exped* 18/2 (1976): 38–39. Although Anshan gave its name to the territory claimed in the title of the Achaemenians, the site of Anshan itself seems not to have been occupied by them.

21. Stronach, "Achaemenid Village," p. 247.

Achaemenian metalwork. (Metropolitan Museum of Art, Fletcher Fund, 1956)

know that Anshan, which was a name not known to the Greeks, was an archaic name for the province of Parsumash/Parsa.[22]

22. M. Dandamayev, "The Dynasty of the Achaemenids in the Early Period," *AAH* 25 (1977): 39–41. R. N. Frye, *The History of Ancient Iran* (Munich: C. H. Beckische, 1984), p. 66, comments: "From the time of Sennacherib (705–681 B.C.) until the rise of the Achaemenids we find reference to the Parsu-ma-aš or Parsu (both presumably for Parsua) only in the south."

Early Achaemenids

With the aid of data from Herodotus and from cuneiform texts such as the Cyrus Cylinder and the Behistun inscription, we can reconstruct the genealogy of the Achaemenids as follows:[23]

Chart 1 The Genealogy of the Achaemenids

Achaemenes (700–675?)

Teispes (675–640?)

Cyrus I (640–600?)	Ariaramnes (640–615?)
Cambyses I (600–559?)	Arsames (590–550?)[24]

In the Behistun inscription, Darius proclaims: "My father was Hystaspes; Hystaspes' father was Arsames; Arsames' father was Ariaramnes; Ariaramnes' father was Teispes; Teispes' father was Achaemenes."[25] We know nothing about the eponymous founder of the dynasty save his name (*Achaemenes;* Old Persian *Hakhamanish*).

The name of his son was *Teispēs* in Greek, which reflects the Old Persian *Chishpish.* Scholars have compared this with the name of the Hurrian god *Teshup* (compare Urartian *Teseba*), and to the name of a leader of the Cimmerians, *Teushpa.*[26] Hansman suggests that it was probably Teispes who established Achaemenid rule in Anshan/Parsumash as an ally of Elam against the Assyrians.[27]

Many scholars held the view that Teispes divided his kingdom between his two sons. Cyrus I inherited Anshan while his younger brother, Ariaramnes, inherited Parsa/Parsumash.[28] But this theory proves to be untenable in that Anshan and Parsa are names for the same region.[29] Ariaramnes and his son Arsames must, therefore, have been petty rulers of a small kingdom somewhere else.[30]

23. The early dates for the Achaemenids are those suggested by Ghirshman, *Art of Ancient Iran,* pp. 385–86.

24. This figure assumes that these kings lived very long lives. Note that Arsames, the father of Hystaspes and grandfather of Darius I, was still alive in 522. W. Eilers, "The Name of Cyrus," *Acta Iranica* 3 (1974): 9, following Herodotus (7.11), assumes additional kings, which would make Cyrus the Great Cyrus III rather than Cyrus II.

25. R. G. Kent, *Old Persian,* rev. ed. (New Haven: American Oriental Society, 1953), p. 119.

26. W. Eilers, "Kyros: Eine namenkundliche Studie," *Beiträge zur Namenforschung* 15 (1964): 205–6; E. Yamauchi, *Foes from the Northern Frontier* (Grand Rapids: Baker, 1982), p. 53.

27. Hansman, "Elamites," p. 109.

28. G. Cameron, *History of Early Iran* (Chicago: University of Chicago Press, 1936), pp. 212, 223.

29. Stronach, "Achaemenid Village," p. 248.

30. Dandamayev, "Dynasty of the Achaemenids," p. 42; Hinz, *Darius,* p. 59, suggests that they may have been kings of Yutiya in the eastern district of Anshan; Frye, *History of Ancient Iran,* p. 79, places them to the southwest of Pasargadae.

For the reign of Cyrus I we have a seal with the Elamite text, "Cyrus of Anshan, son of Teispes," depicting a mounted warrior spearing a victim.[31] Most significant is an Assyrian text from the thirtieth year of Ashurbanipal (639) which reads:

> Kurash, the king of the land of Parsumash, heard of the mighty victory which I obtained over Elam with the aid of Aššur, Bel, and Nebo, the great gods, my lords, (and that) I hurled over the whole of Elam as a flood. He sent Arukku, his oldest son, with his tribute to serve as a hostage in Nineveh, my residence, and to implore my lordship.[32]

As we never hear of Arukku again, we may presume that he perished in the overthrow of Nineveh by the Medes in 612.

In 1930 Ernst Herzfeld published two gold tablets from Hamadan that were texts of Ariaramnes and of his son Arsames in Old Persian.[33] The first text reads:

> Ariaramnes, the Great King, King of Kings, King in Persia, son of Teispes the King, grandson of Achaemenes. Saith Ariaramnes the King: This country Persia which I hold, which is possessed of good horses, of good men, upon me the Great God Ahuramazda bestowed (it). By the favor of Ahuramazda I am king in this country. Saith Ariaramnes the King: May Ahuramazda bear me aid.[34]

Although some scholars have accepted Herzfeld's contention that these are the earliest Achaemenid texts known,[35] others cite grammatical irregularities as an indication that these texts were composed only at a much later date, perhaps in the reign of Artaxerxes II.[36]

31. Hinz, *Darius*, p. 53. See R. T. Hallock, "The Use of Seals on the Persepolis Fortification Tablets," in *Seals and Sealing in the Ancient Near East*, eds. McG. Gibson and R. D. Biggs (Malibu: Undena, 1977), p. 127.

32. E. Weidner, "Die älteste Nachrichte über der persische Königshaus: Kyros I. ein Zeitgenosse Assurbānaplis," *AfO* 7 (1931–32): 3; A. R. Millard, "Fragments of Historical Texts from Nineveh: Ashurbanipal," *Iraq* 30 (1968): 106.

33. E. Herzfeld, "Āriyāramna, König der Könige," *AMI* 2 (1930): 113–27.

34. Kent, *Old Persian*, p. 116.

35. E. g., Ghirshman, *Iran*, p. 120; idem, *Art of Ancient Iran*, p. 268; W. Culican, *The Medes and Persians* (New York: Praeger, 1965), p. 49; P. Lecoq, "Le problème de l'écriture vieux-perse" in *Commémoration Cyrus*, Acta Iranica 3 (Tehran-Liège: Bibliothèque Pahlavi, 1974), 3: 52, comments: "De toute évidence, l'inauthenticité de ces deux textes restes à prouver." Also positive toward these texts is C. Herrenschmidt, "La Perse rien que la Perse: Essai sur la royauté d'Ariyaramnès et d'Arsamès," in *Pad Nām I Yazdān*, eds. P. Gignoux et al. (Paris: C. Klincksieck, 1979), pp. 5–22.

36. Dandamayev, "Dynasty of the Achaemenids," p. 41; R. G. Kent, "The Oldest Old Persian Inscriptions," *JAOS* 66 (1946): 206–12; W. Brandenstein and M. Mayrhofer, *Handbuch des Altpersischen* (Wiesbaden: Harrassowitz, 1964), p. 90; Diakonoff, "Media," p. 133.

Cyrus the Great

Cyrus II was the greatest of the Achaemenid kings and the founder of the Persian Empire. Prior to his accession we assume that the Persians had already developed a subordinate kingdom.[37] Reigning over the Persians from 559 to 530, Cyrus well deserves the epithet *the Great.*

The name *Cyrus* comes from the Greek *Kuros.* The Old Persian was *Kūrush,*[38] the Elamite *Kurash,* and the Akkadian *Kurash(u).* The Hebrew transliteration was *Kôresh,* the Egyptian *Kawarushu.*

Various etymologies have been proposed for the name. Wilhelm Eilers has suggested an association with the name given to certain rivers.[39] Herzfeld believed that the name was originally an ethnic adjective.[40] János Harmatta thinks that the root of *kuru* could be "young child" or "youth."[41]

Biblical References

There are a number of references to Cyrus the Great in the Old Testament. For instance, the Book of Daniel places the prophet in Babylon when Cyrus captured it in 539 (Dan. 1:21; 6:28; 10:1). The Persian king's generous edict (discussed in detail below), which permitted the Jews to return to their homeland from captivity in Babylonia, is also cited in 2 Chronicles 36:22–23 and Ezra 1:1–4 and 6:3–5.

The most controversial references to Cyrus are in the Book of Isaiah, a prophet who ministered during the reigns of Uzziah, Jotham, and Hezekiah (eighth and early seventh centuries). Cyrus is mentioned explicitly in Isaiah 44:28 and 45:1 as the Lord's "shepherd" and as his "anointed" (Hebrew *mašiaḥ,* or "messiah"). Additional passages, which seem to have Cyrus in mind, are Isaiah 41:2–3, 25–26; 45:13; and 46:11.[42]

Literary differences in the Book of Isaiah and the difficulty of accepting that the author could explicitly predict a king who would rule 150 years later, have troubled scholars for years. Since the time of J. C.

37. Diakonoff, "Media," p. 88; P. Briant, "La Perse avant l'Empire," *IA* 19 (1984): 71–118.

38. Eilers, "Name of Cyrus," p. 4, argues for a short initial vowel.

39. Eilers, "Kyros: Eine namenkundliche Studie," pp. 180–236.

40. E. Herzfeld, *The Persian Empire: Studies in the Geography and Ethnography of the Ancient Near East* (Wiesbaden: F. Steiner, 1968), p. 344.

41. J. Harmatta, "The Rise of the Old Persian Empire: Cyrus the Great," *AAH* 19 (1961): 6.

42. S. Smith, *Isaiah Chapters XL–LV* (London: Oxford University Press, 1944), pp. 183–93, suggests many other passages.

Doederlein (1745–1792), many have postulated for chapters 40 to 66 a Deutero-Isaiah, who prophesied in the sixth century *after* the rise of Cyrus.[43] Charles C. Torrey went so far as to reject the name of Cyrus in the Isaiah passages as interpolations. As G. H. Jones observes:

> His case for giving chapters xli and xlv an Abrahamic interpretation is but one shot in his volley against the presence of Cyrus-Babylonian allusions in Deutero-Isaiah. Consequently, he resorts to textual surgery and applies his scalpel ruthlessly to cut out all references to Babylon and Chaldea, and similarly all references to Cyrus.[44]

On the other hand, conservative Jewish and Christian scholars have sought to emphasize the unity of Isaiah as the product of an eighth- to seventh-century prophet, and the predictions of Cyrus as an extraordinary example of fulfilled prophecy.[45]

The ancient historian Josephus (*Antiquities* 11.1–18) declared that Cyrus was inspired to allow the Jewish exiles to return after he had

43. D. M. Beegle, *Prophecy and Prediction* (Ann Arbor: Pryor Pettengill, 1978), pp. 67–69; J. L. MacKenzie, *Second Isaiah* (Garden City: Doubleday, 1968), pp. 73–79; J. Morgenstern, "The Message of Deutero-Isaiah in Its Sequential Unfolding," *HUCA* 29 (1958): 1–67; idem, 30 (1959): 1–102; Y. T. Radday, *The Unity of Isaiah in the Light of Statistical Linguistics* (Gerstenberg: H. A. Hildesheim, 1973); C. E. Simcox, "The Role of Cyrus in Deutero-Isaiah," *JAOS* 57 (1937): 158–71; M. Smith, "II Isaiah and the Persians," *JAOS* 83 (1963): 415–20; C. Westermann, *Isaiah 40–66* (Philadelphia: Westminster, 1969), pp. 158–62; R. N. Whybray, *Isaiah 40–66* (London: Oliphants, 1975), pp. 104–6. This view has also been accepted by evangelical scholars such as F. F. Bruce, "My View: Faith vs. Scientific Study of the Bible," *Bible Review* 3/2 (1987): 4. See D. F. Payne, "Isaiah," in *The International Bible Commentary*, ed. F. F. Bruce (Grand Rapids: Zondervan, 1986), pp. 714–18.

44. G. H. Jones, "Abraham and Cyrus: Type and Anti-Type?" *VT* 22 (1972): 310. J. D. Smart, *History and Theology in Second Isaiah* (Philadelphia: Westminster, 1965), pp. 120–22, supports the theory of a gloss, though for different reasons. The idea of an insertion of the name *Cyrus* has also been accepted by R. K. Harrison, *Introduction to the Old Testament* (London: Tyndale, 1970), pp. 794–95. W. S. LaSor, D. A. Hubbard, and F. W. Bush, *Old Testament Survey* (Grand Rapids: Eerdmans, 1982), p. 376, conclude: "Taking the book at face value, one must assume that various prophesies (sic) were remembered, possibly written down, and preserved beginning *ca.* 740 and continuing through the Exile and return, until the canonical shape of the book was achieved. . . . Therefore, although there must be some degree of flexibility in considering various suggestions, no reason suffices to reject the view that Isaiah was the dominant personality for the entire prophecy that bears his name. The presence of later interpolations and explanatory glosses is not only a possibility but a demonstrable fact." J. D. W. Watts, *Isaiah 1–33* (Waco: Word, 1985), pp. xxvii–xxx, though accepting the view that much of the book is from the prophet and his followers, believes that these materials were first put into writing only in 435 B.C. For an extensive bibliography on Cyrus in Isaiah, see J. D. W. Watts, *Isaiah 34–66* (Waco: Word, 1987), pp. 148–49.

45. O. T. Allis, *The Unity of Isaiah* (London: Tyndale, 1951), chapter 4; G. L. Archer, Jr., *A Survey of Old Testament Introduction*, 2d ed. (Chicago: Moody, 1974), chapter 23; A. A. MacRae, *The Gospel of Isaiah* (Chicago: Moody, 1977), chapter 3; R. Margalioth, *The Indivisible Isaiah* (New York: Yeshiva University Press, 1964); J. Oswalt, *The Book of Isaiah, Chapters 1–39* (Grand Rapids: Eerdmans, 1986), pp. 23–28; J. B. Payne, *Encyclopedia of Biblical Prophecy* (New York: Harper and Row, 1973), p. 317; J. C. Whitcomb, Jr., "Cyrus in the Prophecies of Isaiah," in *The Law and the Prophets*, ed. J. Skilton (Philadelphia: Presbyterian and Reformed, 1974), pp. 388–401; E. J. Young, *The Book of Isaiah* (Grand Rapids: Eerdmans, 1972), 3: 190–93.

read Isaiah's prophecy. The Jewish rabbis of the Talmudic age, however, were embarrassed at the thought that Cyrus, a pagan king, should be so honored and used by Jehovah. They applied Isaiah 41:2 to Abraham rather than to Cyrus.[46] In interpreting Isaiah 45:1 the rabbis sought to construe the text as a conversation between Jehovah and the Messiah about Cyrus. In the tractate *Megillah* we read:

> Rabbi Nahman the son of Hamda inquired: Why does it say: Thus saith the Lord to His anointed, to Cyrus? Was Cyrus actually the anointed (the messiah)? The real meaning is this: The Lord addressed Himself to the messiah saying: I am dissatisfied with Cyrus: I said, He will rebuild My house and ingather My exiles, and what did he say? Whosoever there is among you of all His people . . . let him go up. I thought that he would rebuild the land of Israel and he satisfied himself with giving permission to the others to go up and build.[47]

Old Persian Sources

Although Old Persian is written in cuneiform script, its syllabary differs almost entirely from the Akkadian syllabary.[48] A heated scholarly controversy has raged over the question of whether the Old Persian script existed before Cyrus and was then first used by him for his royal monuments, or whether the script was invented at the time of Darius I (521–486). The latter position has been vigorously advocated by Hinz on the basis of his interpretation of paragraph 70 of Darius's Behistun inscription, which reads in Roland Kent's translation:

> By the favor of Ahuramazda this is the inscription which I made. Besides, it was in Aryan, and on clay tablets and on parchment it was composed.[49]

Hinz, however, would translate the text to read: "I have created the script of another kind, in Aryan, which did not exist heretofore, also on

46. Jones, "Abraham and Cyrus," p. 306.

47. Cited by F. Melzer, "The Attitude of 'Hazal' (Rabbis of the Talmud) to Cyrus," *Return to Zion* (Jerusalem: World Jewish Bible Society, 1964), p. 58.

48. H. H. Paper, "The Old Persian /L/ Phoneme," *JAOS* 76 (1956): 24–26; J. J. Jensen, "Behistun, Darius und die altpersische Keilschrift," *ZDMG* 125 (1975): 294–300; G. Cohen, "Origin of Persian Cuneiform," *Comments on Etymology* 6 (1976): 1–11; P. Lecoq, "Le problème," finds the closest similarities with the Aegean syllabaries.

49. Kent, *Old Persian*, p. 132. Unfortunately paragraph 70 is lacking in the Akkadian and Elamite versions of Darius's text.

Old Persian text from Pasargadae.

clay tablets and on leather."[50] This position has been endorsed by Wilhelm Brandenstein and Manfred Mayrhofer.[51]

On the other hand, other scholars would interpret paragraph 70 as referring simply to Darius's innovation of broadcasting his edict in copies on brick and translating it into Aramaic on parchment.[52] They would maintain either that the Old Persian script was extant before the time of Cyrus II, or that it was introduced by Cyrus II.[53] In any event

50. Hinz, *Darius,* p. 87; R. Borger and W. Hinz, "Eine Dareios-Inschrift aus Pasargadae," *ZDMG* 109 (1959): 119–27; W. Hinz, "Die Entstehung der altpersischen Keilschrift," *AMI* n.F. 1 (1968): 95–98. For a detailed account of the controversy, see M. A. Dandamayev, *Persien unter den ersten Achämeniden* (Wiesbaden: L. Reichert, 1976), pp. 23–52.

51. Brandenstein and Mayrhofer, *Handbuch des Altpersischen,* p. 17; M. Mayrhofer, "Überlegungen zur Enstehung der altpersischen Keilschrift," *BSOAS* 42 (1979): 290–96.

52. J. Lewy, "The Problems Inherent in Section 70 of the Bisitun Inscription," *HUCA* 25 (1954): 208.

53. Lecoq, "Le problème," p. 57; R. Ghirshman, "À propos de l'écriture cunéiforme vieux-perse," *JNES* 24 (1965): 244–50; I. M. Diakonoff, "The Origin of the 'Old Persian' Writing System and the Ancient Oriental Epigraphic and Annalistic Traditions," in *W. B. Henning Memorial Volume* (London: Lund Humphries, 1970), pp. 98–124; R. Hallock, "On the Old Persian Signs," *JNES* 29 (1970):

Barrel inscription of Nebuchadnezzar. (Metropolitan Museum of Art, funds from various donors, 1885 [85.15])

we have but three very short trilingual inscriptions from Pasargadae that are ascribed to Cyrus, which are not very informative:

(CMa) "I am Cyrus the King, an Achaemenian"

(CMb) "Cyrus the Great King, son of Cambyses the King, an Achaemenian. He says: When . . . made. . . "

(CMc) "Cyrus the Great King, an Achaemenian"[54]

Akkadian Sources

We do have some valuable contemporary inscriptions in the Semitic Akkadian language, which was used by the Neo-Babylonians. There are hundreds of Mesopotamian economic texts from the period of Cyrus's reign.[55] An inscribed brick from Uruk reads: "Cyrus, the rebuilder of Esagila and Ezida, the son of Cambyses, the mighty king, am I."[56] Quite invaluable is the Chaldean Chronicle of the Neo-

52–55; W. Eilers, "Der Keilschrifttext des Kyros-Zylinders," *Festgabe deutscher Iranisten zur 2500-Jahrfeier Irans,* ed. W. Eilers (Stuttgart: Hochwacht, 1971), p. 156; I. Gershevitch, preface to *The Evidence of the Persepolis Tablets,* by R. T. Hallock (Cambridge: Middle East Centre, 1971), p. 4; D. Stronach, *Pasargadae* (Oxford: Clarendon, 1978), pp. 102–3.

54. Kent, *Old Persian,* p. 116. For the Akkadian and Elamite versions, see Lecoq, "Le problème," p. 53. C. Nylander, "Bemerkungen zu einem Inschriftfragment in Pasargadae," *Orientalia Suecana* 11 (1962): 121–25; idem, "Who Wrote the Inscriptions at Pasargadae?" *Orientalia Suecana* 16 (1968): 135–78, has argued that Cyrus inscribed the Akkadian and Elamite versions, and that Darius added the Old Persian text. But Lecoq, "Le problème," pp. 54–56, notes that Nylander's comparisons are flawed.

55. H. G. Stigers, "Neo- and Late Babylonian Business Documents from the John Frederick Lewis Collection," *JCS* 28 (1976): 3–23; L. Cagni, G. Giovinazzo, and S. Grazini, "Typology and Structure of Mesopotamian Documentation during the Achaemenid Period," *Annali* 45 (1985): 547–83.

56. Eilers, "Der Keilschrifttext," p. 156; A. Tremayne, *Records from Erech, Time of Cyrus and Cambyses (538–21 BC)* (New Haven: Yale University Press, 1925).

Babylonian king Nabonidus.[57] The Chronicle is a relatively objective contemporary account. A so-called Verse Account describes the erratic behavior of Nabonidus in contrast with the reverential attitude of Cyrus.[58]

The famous Cyrus Cylinder, which was found by Hormuzd Rassam in the area of the Marduk Temple in Babylon in 1879, depicts the joyous welcome accorded to the king when he captured the city of Babylon.[59] It is twenty-three centimeters long and contains forty-five lines of text. The cylinder is one of the most prized objects in the British Museum. Recently a fragment of the Cyrus Cylinder, which somehow found its way into the Yale Babylonian Collection, has been identified and translated.[60] A literary analysis of the Cyrus Cylinder by Harmatta reveals that the Persian king was following the pattern of the edicts of the Assyrian king, Ashurbanipal (668–626), who is named in the fragment.[61] (See below for a fuller discussion.)

Greek Sources

Herodotus, "the father of history" (fifth century), is in many ways our most important narrative source for the Persians in general and for Cyrus in particular. After the Peace of Callias (449 B.C.), which brought an end to the hostilities between the Greeks and the Persians, Herodotus traveled widely throughout the Persian Empire, visiting Egypt and Babylon, but not Persia.

Herodotus was harshly criticized in the late nineteenth and early twentieth centuries, when archaeology was in its infancy and corroborative evidence from excavations was lacking.[62] Subsequent discoveries, however, have confirmed his reliability at many points, most notably in his description of the Scythians[63] and in his use of Persian sources.[64]

Richard N. Frye observes:

57. S. Smith, *Babylonian Historical Texts* (London: Methuen, 1924), pp. 98–123; *ANET*, pp. 305–7; A. K. Grayson, *Assyrian and Babylonian Chronicles* (Locust Valley: J. J. Augustin, 1975), pp. 104–11.

58. Smith, *Babylonian Historical Texts*, pp. 83ff.; *ANET*, pp. 312–15.

59. *ANET*, pp. 315–16; *DOTT*, pp. 92–94.

60. C. B. F. Walker, "A Recently Identified Fragment of the Cyrus Cylinder," *Iran* 10 (1972): 158–59; P.-R. Berger, "Der Kyros-Zylinder mit dem Zusatzfragment BIN II Nr. 32 . . . , " *ZA* 64 (1975): 192–234.

61. J. Harmatta, "The Literary Patterns of the Babylonian Edict of Cyrus," *AAH* 19 (1971): 217–31.

62. E. Yamauchi, *Composition and Corroboration in Classical and Biblical Studies* (Philadelphia: Presbyterian and Reformed, 1966), pp. 10, 16–19.

63. Yamauchi, *Foes*, chapter 6.

64. M. Miller, The Earlier Persian Dates in Herodotus," *Klio* 37 (1959): 32–37.

> On the whole, I believe one should follow the general rule that Herodotus generally reports what he heard and adds his own views in those matters where he moralizes, such as in the invasion of Greece by the Achaemenids, or the like. Whether his sources were reliable, of course, is another problem, but on the whole even if he reports stories which were current in his time, these stories are important for reconstructing ancient views.[65]

Herodotus was above all a raconteur of entertaining stories. The fact that he himself did not believe the account did not deter him from relating an interesting tale. At times he gives several contradictory stories. This was the case, for example, in his description of Cyrus's birth and youth, the variant versions of which contain patently legendary motifs.[66] On the other hand, scholars have been impressed with Herodotus's reliability in recounting the career of Cyrus. Stronach comments:

> At the same time, however, the final parts of Herodotus' story have the clear ring of a more factual account—the battles, defections, and the eventual surrender of Astyages, each finding an obvious echo in the contemporary Babylonian chronicle.[67]

Aeschylus, who fought against the Persians at Salamis, is an unimpeachable witness to the high regard in which Cyrus was held even among his enemies, when he writes in his play *The Persians* (performed in 472):

> Cyrus the Fortunate was third; who, while he governed, blessed the land with peace. He added to his empire Lydia and Phrygia; Ionia he subdued by force; and he incurred no anger of the gods, because his heart was wise.[68]

Xenophon, the disciple of Socrates, who accompanied ten thousand Greek mercenary soldiers (see his *Anabasis*) on a futile expedition into the heart of the Persian Empire around 400 to replace Artaxerxes II with his brother, Cyrus the Younger, has given us the *Cyropaedia* or "Education of Cyrus." This presents an idealized portrait of the king

65. Frye, *History of Ancient Iran*, p. ix.

66. R. Drews, "Sargon, Cyrus, and Mesopotamian Folk History," *JNES* 33 (1974): 387–93.

67. D. Stronach, "Cyrus the Great," *Revue d'archéologie et d'art iraniens* 7–8 (1971): 6. For other positive comments on Herodotus as a conscientious reporter and valuable source, see Diakonoff, "Media," pp. 110, 121; J. M. Cook, "The Rise of the Achaemenids and Establishment of Their Empire," *CHI* 2: 205.

68. Aeschylus, *Prometheus and Other Plays*, trans. P. Vellacott (Harmondsworth: Penguin, 1961), p. 144.

that reflects Xenophon's admiration for Cyrus the Younger. Among other errors is his assertion that Cyrus the Great conquered Egypt and that he passed away peacefully.

Finally, we have the account of Ctesias, the Greek physician of Artaxerxes II, who falsely depicted Cyrus as the son of a Persian bandit and a shepherdess. Ctesias, who should have had access to Persian documents, is a disappointingly unreliable source. Plutarch, who used Ctesias, comments: "It is not infrequent with him [Ctesias] to make excursions from truth into mere fiction and romance." Whereas Herodotus correctly named six of the seven conspirators led by Darius, Ctesias got only one of the names correct.[69]

His Parents and His Birth

Cyrus II was the son of Cambyses I, a Persian, and Mandane, the daughter of the Median king Astyages. This hybrid nature of Cyrus's parentage is reflected in a response from the Delphic oracle (Herodotus 1.91), which warned the Lydians to beware when a "mule" became king of the Medes:

> For that mule was in truth Cyrus; who was the son of two persons not of the same nation, of whom the mother was the nobler and the father of lesser estate; for she was a Median, daughter of Astyages king of the Medians.[70]

For chronological reasons Hinz doubts that Cyrus's mother was a Median.[71] Stronach, however, believes that Astyages may have had good reason to cement relations between the Medes and the Persians by such a marriage. He also points out that Cyrus's half-Median background may explain why the Medes never revolted against him.[72]

Stronach suggests a date for Cyrus's birth around 590. Hinz posits a specific date of 601, partly on his identification of "Darius the Mede,"

69. A. R. Burn, *Persia and the Greeks* (New York: St. Martin's, 1962), p. 12. Diakonoff, "Media," p. 142, comments: "Ctesias, even though he operated with names which may really have existed in Media, builds up a fantastic, completely imaginary dynasty; his main aim is to set upside down every fact given by Herodotus." See J. M. Bigwood, "Ctesias of Cnidus," unpublished Ph.D. diss. (Cambridge: Harvard University, 1964); idem, "Ctesias' Description of Babylon," *AJAH* 3 (1978): 32–53. See also A. Cizek, "The Life of Cyrus the Great Viewed by Herodotus, Ctesias and Xenophon," *Antiquité Classique* 44 (1975): 531–52.

70. R. Flacelière, *Greek Oracles* (New York: Norton, 1965), p. 55. J. Fontenrose, *The Delphic Oracle* (Berkeley: University of California Press, 1981), pp. 114, 303, doubts the authenticity of this and many other Delphic responses found in Herodotus.

71. Hinz, *Darius,* p. 90.

72. Stronach, "Cyrus the Great," p. 6; idem, *Pasargadae,* p. 285.

the conqueror of Babylon (Dan. 5:30) in 539, who was sixty-two years old then, with Cyrus.[73]

His Youth

Herodotus knew of four versions of Cyrus's youth (1.107–30). These legendary accounts have been compared with the stories of the rise of Sargon of Agade (twenty-third century B.C.) and with the account of Romulus, the founder of Rome (eighth century B.C.).[74] As in many other examples from Greek folklore, Herodotus tells about a dream that forewarned Astyages that his grandson, if allowed to live, would overshadow him (compare the story of Oedipus). Later Herodotus narrates the terrible vengeance Astyages took upon Harpagus, the man who failed to see to the death of the child Cyrus. In a story that recalls the myth of Tantalus and his son Pelops,[75] Astyages served Harpagus the flesh of his own son (1.119).

Xenophon's *Cyropaedia* (1.3.1ff.) tells charming tales about the visits of Cyrus as a child at his grandfather Astyages' court, where he played the role of a cupbearer. When asked by his mother why he wanted to stay in Media, Cyrus replied that this would enable him to become a better horseman (1.3.15).

Conquest of Media

We know that Cyrus began his thirty-year reign over the Persians around 559. The "Dream Text" from Sippar gives insight into when Cyrus began to challenge the Medes. In this text Nabonidus, the Neo-Babylonian king, is assured that Cyrus would liberate Harran from the Ummanmanda (Medes):

> At the beginning of my lasting kingship they (the great gods) showed me a vision in a dream. . . . Marduk said to me, "The Umman-manda of whom thou speakest, he, his land, and the kings who go at his side, will not exist for much longer. At the beginning of the third year, Cyrus, king of Anshan, his youthful servant, will come forth. With his few forces he

73. Hinz, *Darius*, p. 89.

74. B. Lewis, *The Sargon Legend* (Cambridge: American Schools of Oriental Research, 1980); D. Metzler, "Beobachtungen zum Geschichtsbild der frühen Achämeniden," *Klio* 57 (1975): 445, n. 16, citing G. Binder, *Die Aussetzung des Königskindes, Kyros und Romulus* (Meisenheim, 1964).

75. In the Greek myth Tantalus served the flesh of his own son to the gods. R. Graves, *The Greek Myths* (Baltimore: Penguin, 1955), 2: 25–27.

> will rout the numerous forces of the Umman-manda. He will capture Astyages, the king of the Umman-manda, and will take him prisoner to his country.[76]

This text, therefore, relates a dream that Nabonidus experienced in his first regnal year (556). The dream predicts that Cyrus would rebel against his Median grandfather during Nabonidus's third year (553).[77] Another text, the Nabonidus Chronicle, seems to indicate that it was in the sixth year of Nabonidus (550) that Cyrus decisively defeated the Medes.[78]

The final battle between the Persians and the Medes probably took place in the plain of Pasargadae, which was to be the site of Cyrus's capital built to commemorate his victory over the Medes (Strabo 15.3.8). The Nabonidus Chronicle confirms Herodotus's account (1.127ff.) that Cyrus was aided in his victory by the defection of Astyages' own men: "(Astyages) mustered (his army) and marched against Cyrus, king of Anshan, for conquest [. . . .] The army rebelled against Astyages and he was taken prisoner."[79] The text further indicates that Cyrus marched to Ecbatana, the Median capital, and carried its treasures back to the region of Anshan.

Ctesias suggests that Princess Amytis tried to hide her father in the palace.[80] Although he was captured, his life was spared according to Herodotus (1.130): "As for Astyages, Cyrus did him no further harm, and kept him in his own house till Astyages died."

Conquest of Lydia

After the Cimmerian invasion of Anatolia destroyed the Phrygian capital of Gordium in 676,[81] the most important kingdom in the area was Lydia. Lydia's capital at Sardis was some forty-five miles from

76. *DOTT*, pp. 89–90; A. L. Oppenheim, *The Interpretation of Dreams in the Ancient Near East* (Philadelphia: American Philosophical Society, 1956), p. 250.

77. H. Tadmor, "The Inscriptions of Nabunaid: Historical Arrangement," in *Studies in Honor of Benno Landsberger*, eds. H. Güterbock and T. Jacobsen (Chicago: University of Chicago Press, 1965), p. 352, suggests the possibility that Nabonidus may have seen the dream in his third year, which would then have been fulfilled three years later in his sixth year.

78. R. Drews, "The Fall of Astyages and Herodotus' Chronology of the Eastern Kingdoms," *Historia* 18 (1969): 1–11, argues that Cyrus's victory over Astyages should be dated 554 B.C.

79. Grayson, *ABC*, p. 106.

80. F. W. König, *Die Persika des Ktesias von Knidos* (Graz: Archiv für Orientforschung, 1972), p. 50. Although we know that Amytis was the daughter of Astyages, we have conflicting reports of her marital status. According to Berossus, she became Cyrus's wife; according to Berossus cited by Eusebius (*Chronicle* 29.35), she was married to Nebuchadnezzar.

81. Yamauchi, *Foes*, chapter 3.

the west coast of Turkey. From 560 B.C. Lydia was ruled by the legendary Croesus, who was famed for his gold[82] and for his lavish gifts to the Delphic oracle. When Croesus received the ambiguous response from Delphi ("after crossing the Halys [River] Croesus will destroy a great empire"), he was encouraged to march against the Persians.[83]

The beginning of the Lydo-Persian War is usually dated to 547.[84] The first encounter took place at Pteria in Cappadocia (Herodotus 1.76).[85] According to Herodotus (1.77) the battle took place in November. Because winter was approaching, Croesus retired to Sardis and asked his three powerful allies—Sparta, Egypt, and Mesopotamia—to send him aid in the following spring. He even dismissed his foreign mercenaries. Croesus had underestimated the cunning of Cyrus, who only pretended to withdraw but instead pursued the Lydians to Sardis.[86] In a battle in the plain of Sardis the Lydian horses were unsettled by the odor of the camels ridden by the Persians. The acropolis itself was taken when the Persians discovered an unguarded pathway (Herodotus 1.84). While archaeologists have failed to uncover the palace even after eighteen campaigns, [87] they have found burned levels and arrowheads from the Persian attack.[88]

A fragmentary passage in the Nabonidus Chronicle, dated to Cyrus's ninth year (547), has been interpreted as a reference to his campaign against Lydia. Sidney Smith, for example, declares:

> Since the name of the land probably begins *Lu . . .*, and Cyrus' campaign against Croesus of Sardis is to be dated 547–6, there need be no hesita-

82. E. Yamauchi, *New Testament Cities in Western Asia Minor* (Grand Rapids: Baker, 1980), p. 65. Though the tradition that the Lydian king Gyges (680–644 B.C.) was the first to invent coinage has been doubted by many scholars, it is quite credible. See E. Yamauchi, "Two Reformers Compared: Solon of Athens and Nehemiah of Jerusalem," in *The Bible World: Essays in Honor of Cyrus H. Gordon,* eds. G. Rendsburg et al. (New York: KTAV, 1980), pp. 274–76; D. Kagan, "The Dates of the Earliest Coins," *AJA* 86 (1982): 343–60.

83. See Herodotus 1.53; J. Pollard, *Seers, Shrines and Sirens* (New York: A. S. Barnes, 1965), p. 19; H. W. Parke, *Greek Oracles* (London: Hutchinson, 1967), p. 70. This also is questioned by Fontenrose, *Delphic Oracle,* pp. 113–14, 302.

84. Hinz, *Darius,* p. 98; M. Miller, "The Herodotean Croesus," *Klio* 41 (1963): 80; M. Mallowan, "Cyrus the Great (558–529 BC)," *Iran* 10 (1972): 7. J. Cargill, "The Nabonidus Chronicle and the Fall of Lydia," *AJAH* 2 (1977): 97–116, however, has questioned this date and has suggested 545; cf. J. Balcer, *Sparda by the Bitter Sea: Imperial Interaction in Western Anatolia* (Chico: Scholars, 1984), p. 33.

85. Hinz would place this battle at Kirşehir in central Turkey, just east of Lake Tuz.

86. On the city of Sardis, see Yamauchi, *New Testament Cities,* chapter 5; G. M. A. Hanfmann, *Letters from Sardis* (Cambridge: Harvard University Press, 1972).

87. G. M. A. Hanfmann, "On the Palace of Croesus," *Festschrift für Frank Brommer* (Mainz: Zabern, 1977), p. 154.

88. W. E. Mierse, "The Persian Period," in *Sardis from Prehistoric to Roman Times,* eds. G. M. A. Hanfmann and W. E. Mierse (Cambridge: Harvard University Press, 1983), p. 19.

> tion in identifying the campaign here described with that narrated in Herodotus, I, 75ff., and in Xenophon, Cyropaedia, VII, 1–2.[89]

As A. Leo Oppenheim translated the passage, it reads:

> In the month of Nisanu, Cyrus, king of Persia, called up his army and crossed the Tigris below the town Arbela. In the month Aiaru [he marched] against the country Ly[dia] . . . killed its king, took his possessions, put (there) a garrison of his own.[90]

The Chronicle speaks in terms of the months of Nisan (April) and Aiaru (May), whereas Herodotus speaks of the battle taking place in November. The Chronicle may, however, be referring to the beginning of the march from the area of Mesopotamia.[91] Max Mallowan and other scholars have questioned the restoration "Ly[dia]."[92] Moreover the statement that Cyrus killed the king would contradict the unanimous testimony of classical sources. The verb *idūk,* however, can be translated "defeated."[93] That Cyrus spared Croesus is maintained by Cargill and Diakonoff.[94]

Ctesias offers a number of fantastic details about the capture of Sardis. Wooden mannikins dressed like Persian soldiers when elevated over the walls caused panic among the inhabitants and led to the capture of the city. Croesus was chained in the temple of Apollo but mysteriously escaped three times. Cyrus then spared his life and granted him the city of Barene near Ecbatana.[95]

By the early fifth century the Greeks were familiar with the tradition that Croesus was spared a fiery death. A painted amphora of Myson (soon after 500) depicts Croesus on a pyre.[96] The poet Bacchylides (fl. 470) recounts:

> When he had come to that unlooked-for day he would not await the woeful lot of slavery, but had them build a pyre before his bronze-walled

89. Smith, *Babylonian Historical Texts,* p. 101. See Grayson, *ABC,* p. 282; Cargill, "Nabonidus Chronicle," pp. 104–5, also points out the difficulties in restoring the cuneiform text.

90. *ANET,* p. 306.

91. Stronach, *Pasargadae,* pp. 287–88; Miller, "Herodotean Croesus," p. 62: "We should suppose therefore that Cyrus proclaimed a levy in April, and began his march in May . . . arriving at the Halys in the later summer, perhaps not very long before Croesus' withdrawal."

92. Mallowan, "Cyrus the Great," p. 7, n. 34.

93. H. Tadmor, "Historical Implications of the Correct Rendering of Akkadian *dâku,*" *JNES* 17 (1985): 129; Grayson, *ABC,* p. 107.

94. Cargill, "Nabonidus Chronicle," p. 110; Diakonoff, "Media," p. 147.

95. König, *Die Persika,* pp. 52–53.

96. Hinz, *Darius,* p. 100.

hall and went up upon it . . . then Zeus sent a black veil of cloud and quenched the pale flame. (Ode 3)[97]

To stress the fragility of human happiness, Herodotus has Croesus reflect upon his conversation with Solon as he is lying on the pyre. When he shouts Solon's name, Cyrus has him explain and then spares his life (Herodotus 1.86ff.).

The Ionian and Aeolian Greeks along the west coast of Anatolia agreed to submit to Cyrus only if they could enjoy the same terms that they had under Croesus; but they were rebuffed (Herodotus 1.141). With the exception of Miletus, which had signed a treaty with Cyrus, the Greek cities were forcibly subdued, setting the stage for the Greco-Persian conflicts of the fifth century. The warning of the Spartans that Cyrus "must harm no city on Greek territory, else the Lacadaemonians would punish him," was contemptuously dismissed as an empty threat (Herodotus 1.151–53).

A stepped pyramidal tomb on a hillside in Sardis, which has parallels to Cyrus's own tomb, may have belonged to a Persian official stationed there. William E. Mierse comments: "The tomb, probably built around 540 B.C. for a Persian noble who fell in the battle for Sardis, could be the result of an experiment commissioned by an Iranian patron who wanted to apply the Lydian talent for stone work to a different type of structure."[98] Lydian and Ionian artisans were transported back to Pasargadae to work on the monuments there (see chapter 9).

Conquest of the East

Later evidence suggests that Cyrus spent the years between 546 and 540 B.C. consolidating his control over the eastern parts of his empire. The Behistun inscription of Darius lists the following areas as already under Achaemenid rule by 520: Parthia, Drangiana, Aria, Chorasmia, Bactria, Sogdiana, Gandara, Scythia, Sattagydia, Arachosia, and Maka. These were areas presumably won by Cyrus.[99] Classical sources refer

97. C. Segal, "Croesus on the Pyre: Herodotus and Bacchylides," *Wiener Zeitschrift für die Kunde des Morgenlandes* 84 (1971): 39–51. J. A. S. Evans, "What Happened to Croesus?" *CJ* 74 (1978): 34–40, believes that Bacchylides' version was correct, that is, that Croesus was allowed to commit suicide.

98. Mierse, "Persian Period," p. 103. See J. M. Cook and D. J. Blackman, "Archaeology in Western Asia Minor, 1965–70," *Archaeological Reports for 1970–71* (London: British School at Athens, 1971), p. 40; Hanfmann, *Letters from Sardis,* pp. 259–60. For another tomb in Ionia with Persian elements, see N. Cahill, "Taş Kule: A Persian-Period Tomb Near Phokaia," *AJA* 92 (1988): 481–50.

99. Stronach, *Pasargadae,* p. 290, n. 47.

Enameled brick lion from Babylon. (Metropolitan Museum of Art, Fletcher Fund, 1931 [31.13.2])

to an attempt to invade India through Gedrosia (Baluchistan), but such a route is improbable.

The Conquest of Babylon

Morale in Babylon had been depressed by the studied neglect of the god Marduk by the last Neo-Babylonian king, Nabonidus.[100] Quite unexpectedly, the king moved to Teima in Arabia for ten years, leaving Babylon in the hands of his son Belshazzar.[101]

Apparently in anticipation of the growing Persian threat, Nabonidus returned to Babylon in 543 and in a desperate measure gathered all the gods from the neighboring cities into Babylon. After years of neglect the king celebrated the New Year's rite once more in the spring of 539. But it was too late to win back the favor of the people and the priests.

The most important Babylonian who defected to the Persian side

100. E. Yamauchi, "Nabonidus," in *Wycliffe Bible Encyclopedia*, eds. C. F. Pfeiffer et al. (Chicago: Moody, 1975), pp. 1170–71; idem, "Nabonidus," in *The International Standard Bible Encyclopedia*, ed. G. W. Bromiley, rev. ed. (Grand Rapids: Eerdmans, 1986), 3: 468–70. W. von Soden, "Kyros und Nabonid: Propaganda und Gegenpropaganda," in *Kunst, Kultur und Geschichte der Achämenidenzeit und ihr Fortleben*, eds. H. Koch and D. N. MacKenzie (Berlin: Dietrich Reimer, 1983), pp. 61–68, argues that Nabonidus was maligned by Cyrus's propaganda.

101. This is why the Book of Daniel depicts Belshazzar as the de facto king rather than Nabonidus. For the resolution of alleged historical problems in Daniel including the issue of why Belshazzar rather than his father Nabonidus is featured, see G. F. Hasel, "The Book of Daniel: Evidences Relating to Persons and Chronology," *AUSS* 19 (1981): 37–49; W. H. Shea, "Nabonidus, Belshazzar, and the Book of Daniel: An Update," *AUSS* 20 (1982): 133–49; D. J. Wiseman, et al., *Notes on Some Problems in the Book of Daniel* (London: Tyndale, 1965); E. Yamauchi, "The Archaeological Background of Daniel," *BS* 137 (1980): 3–16.

was Ugbaru or Gubaru (Greek, Gobryas), the governor of Gutium in the Zagros.[102] In order to attack Babylon, Cyrus and his new ally had to outflank the Median Wall, which stretched twenty-four miles from Sippar on the Euphrates to Opis on the Tigris.[103]

Cyrus may have crossed the Tigris just south of Opis. Smith suggests that the Tigris was diverted before the attack upon Opis.[104] It was in September, according to the Nabonidus Chronicle, that Cyrus "did battle at Opis on the Tigris against the army of Akkad." By October 10 the Persians were able to capture Sippar "without a battle."

Herodotus (1.191) indicates that the Persians gained entrance into Babylon by diverting the Euphrates River. Some scholars find this difficult to accept.[105] But as Herodotus accurately described it,[106] and as the excavations of Robert Koldewey confirmed, the city of Babylon was not only bisected by the Euphrates but was also penetrated by many canals.[107] The height of the Euphrates would have been at its lowest level at this time of the year, normally about twelve feet deep. If the famine (mentioned in more than one text) was caused by a dry year, the level would have been even lower. The possibility that the Persians penetrated the walls through a water channel seems more credible than the suggestion by Hinz that the Babylonians left the gates open and allowed Gubaru to enter without realizing that he had defected to the enemy.[108]

According to Daniel 5 Belshazzar had been sacrilegiously using the vessels from the Jewish temple in celebrating a festival when Babylon fell. Herodotus (1.191) relates that at this time "they were dancing and making merry at a festival." Xenophon (*Cyropaedia* 7.5.15) states that the Persians chose to attack during a certain festival when "all Babylon was accustomed to drink and revel all night long."

The Nabonidus Chronicle confirms that Ugbaru (Gubaru) and his troops entered Babylon "without a battle" on October 12.[109] Cyrus

102. See chapter 1 on Darius the Mede; W. Röllig, "Gubaru," in *Reallexikon der Assyriologie und vorderasiatischen Archäologie,* ed. W. von Soden (Berlin: Walter de Gruyter, 1971), pp. 671–72.

103. Around 400 B.C. Xenophon saw the remains of this great wall, which was reputably 20 feet thick and 100 feet high. R. D. Barnett, "Xenophon and the Wall of Media," *JHS* 83 (1963): 13–15.

104. Smith, *Isaiah XL–LV,* p. 46; Burn, *Persia and the Greeks,* pp. 54–56.

105. For example, Stronach, *Pasargadae,* p. 291.

106. O. E. Ravn, *Herodotus' Description of Babylon* (Copenhagen: Busck, 1942).

107. R. Koldewey, *The Excavations at Babylon* (London: Macmillan, 1914); J. G. MacQueen, *Babylon* (London: Robert Hale, 1964), chapter 6; G. A. LaRue, *Babylon and the Bible* (Grand Rapids: Baker, 1969), pp. 51–53; D. J. Wiseman, *Nebuchadrezzar and Babylon* (London: Oxford University Press, 1985); E. Yamauchi, "Babylon," in *Major Cities of the Biblical World,* ed. R. K. Harrison (Nashville: Thomas Nelson, 1985), pp. 32–48. M. J. Mers, "Herodotus, Bible and Babylon," *NEASB* 17 (1981): 34, finds the diversion of the Euphrates quite plausible.

108. Hinz, *Darius,* p. 105; Briant, "La Perse avant l'Empire," p. 101.

109. Grayson, *ABC,* p. 110.

The Cyrus Cylinder. (Reproduced by courtesy of the trustees of the British Museum)

himself did not enter the city until October 29. The inhabitants of Babylon greeted Cyrus not as a conqueror but as a liberator, and spread green branches before him.[110] Belshazzar may have been killed, but Nabonidus was spared. He was sent into exile to Carmania in the east.

The Cyrus Cylinder

In 1879 Rassam discovered in Babylon a clay cylinder inscribed in Akkadian cuneiform. This document, called the Cyrus Cylinder, proclaims:

> When I, well-disposed, entered Babylon, I set up the seat of dominion in the royal palace amidst jubilation and rejoicing. Marduk the great god caused the big-hearted inhabitants of Babylon to . . . me. I sought daily to worship him. My numerous troops moved about undisturbed in the midst of Babylon. I did not allow any to terrorise the land of [Sumer] and Akkad. I kept in view the needs of Babylon and all its sanctuaries to promote their wellbeing.[111]

The cylinder also claims that Cyrus entered the city of Babylon "without fighting or battle." He showed his concern for the starving people

110. G. Cameron, "Cyrus the 'Father,' and Babylonia," in *Commémoration Cyrus* (Tehran/Liège: Bibliothèque Pahlavi, 1974), 3: 45–48, speculates that Cyrus occupied himself with irrigation projects in the Diyala region before attacking Babylonia.

111. *DOTT*, p. 93.

and restored their "dilapidated dwellings." In another cuneiform text Cyrus declares that he was the restorer of the Esagila and the Ezida.[112]

A fragment in the Yale Babylonian Collection was identified in 1970 by Paul-Richard Berger as part of the Cyrus Cylinder. This new piece informs us that Cyrus restored the city's inner wall and moats. Had these been damaged in the taking of the city? Cyrus also noted the works of an Assyrian king: "I saw inscribed the name of my predecessor King Ashurbanipal."[113]

Amelie Kuhrt has recently analyzed the Cyrus Cylinder in its original context, and has drawn some narrowly refined conclusions. She notes that the text is related to Marduk, that it is almost entirely concerned with the city of Babylon, that it is a typical Mesopotamian building text, and that it follows the example of the Assyrian Ashurbanipal. She sees it primarily as a propagandistic effort to manipulate public opinion and to legitimate Cyrus's authority over Babylon.[114]

We can conclude that Cyrus pleased the Babylonians by restoring to their cities the gods that had been removed by Nabonidus. Furthermore, Cyrus had his son, Cambyses II, observe the New Year's rite. This would have taken place on March 24, 538 (Nisan 1). On the fifth of Nisan Cambyses would have been subjected to a symbolic humiliation before the high priest of Marduk. The priest would pull Cambyses's ear and force him to kneel. Then Cambyses would have said, "I have not sinned, O Lord of the Lands. I have not destroyed Babylon, nor damaged the Esagila, or neglected the temple rites." The high priest would then slap Cambyses on the cheek. The appearance of tears would satisfy the god and conclude the ritual.[115]

The Persian takeover was conducted in such a manner that there was little disruption. The Nabonidus Chronicle claims that even after the city fell to Gubaru, "there was no interruption (of rites) in Esagil or the (other) temples and no date (for a performance) was missed."[116] An inventory of wool garments for the gods in Uruk is an important testimony to this continuity. John A. Brinkman observes: "Save that the volume of wool stuffs used for cult garments appears to drop off slightly during the critical years 539–538 (Nabonidus, Year 17 and Cyrus, Year 1), the cult at Uruk continues uninterrupted during the

112. The Esagila and Ezida were the principal temples in Babylon.

113. Walker, "Recently Identified Fragment," p. 158.

114. A. Kuhrt, "The Cyrus Cylinder and Achaemenid Imperial Policy," *JSOT* 25 (1983): 83–94. Compare H. W. A. M. Sancisi-Weerdenburg, "Colloquium (sic) Early Achaemenid History," *Persica* 10 (1981): 274.

115. Hinz, *Darius*, pp. 111–12; H. W. F. Saggs, *The Greatness That Was Babylon* (New York: Hawthorn, 1962), pp. 384–89. W. H. Shea (in a personal communication) prefers to date Cambyses's participation in the New Year's rite to March 537.

116. Grayson, *ABC*, p. 110.

change over from Babylonian independence to subjection under the Persian empire."[117]

The Titles of Cyrus

Cyrus was known by various titles, which have been preserved in a number of ancient texts. The Cyrus Cylinder, for instance, proclaims Cyrus "King of the World, Great King, Legitimate King, King of Babylon, King of Sumer and Akkad, King of the Four Quarters (of the Earth)."[118] William H. Shea's thorough study of the titularies of Cyrus and of Cambyses revealed that in 90 percent of the four hundred cases checked, the standard royal titulary in economic texts for Cyrus was "King of Babylon, King of Lands."[119] In carefully analyzing the chronology of these titles, Shea discovered that Cyrus was called "King of Lands" at the beginning of his first year (538) and "King of Babylon, King of Lands" at the end of this year. He concludes that the reason Cyrus did not carry the title *King of Babylon* during his first nine months was because Gubaru, the conqueror of Babylon, bore this title. He furthermore suggests that the latter be identified as the enigmatic "Darius the Mede" of the Book of Daniel (see chapter 1).[120]

Evidence of Cyrus's building was discovered by Leonard Woolley at Ur.[121] A brick from Ur is inscribed with the following title: "Cyrus the king of the world . . . the mighty gods have given into my hands all the kingdoms."

The Restoration of the Jews

Cyrus instituted the enlightened policy of placating the gods of his subject peoples instead of carrying off their cult statues and peoples as the Elamites, Hittites, Assyrians, and Babylonians before him had done.[122] His generosity in permitting the Jews to return to their home-

117. J. A. Brinkman, "Neo-Babylonian Texts in the Archaeological Museum at Florence," *JNES* 25 (1966): 209.

118. For the origin of such titles in Sumerian times, see W. W. Hallo, *Early Mesopotamian Royal Titles* (New Haven: American Oriental Society, 1957).

119. W. H. Shea, "An Unrecognized Vassal King of Babylon in the Early Achaemenid Period," *AUSS* 9 (1971): 113.

120. Ibid., pp. 120–23.

121. C. L. Woolley and M. E. L. Mallowan, *Ur Excavations IX: The Neo-Babylonian and Persian Periods* (London: British Museum, 1962).

122. As Kuhrt, "Cyrus Cylinder," p. 94, notes, later Achaemenids such as Darius I did deport populations, for example, moving inhabitants from Libya to Bactria (Herodotus 4.204; see also 5.13–16; 6.20).

The tomb of Cyrus at Pasargadae.

land was not unique but was paralleled by his benevolence to the Babylonians and others.

From the biblical view, however, it was ultimately Jehovah who had "stirred" Cyrus's heart. We have a Hebrew copy of Cyrus's edict to the Jews in Ezra 1:1–4 and an Aramaic memorandum of the same in Ezra 6:3–5.[123] The latter was found in the archives at Ecbatana during the reign of Darius I as the Jews were rebuilding their temple.

Earlier scholars (Julius Wellhausen, Willem H. Kosters, Maurice Vernes, Charles C. Torrey, Gustav Hölscher, Robert Pfeiffer, William O. E. Oesterley, Kurt Galling) had questioned the authenticity of the decree because of the Jewish phraseology of the document. But documents from the Persian period and archaeological discoveries have provided convincing evidence of its authenticity.[124] Especially impressive

123. See E. Yamauchi, "The Archaeological Background of Ezra," *BS* 137 (1980): 195–211; idem, "Ezra, Nehemiah," in *The Expositor's Bible Commentary,* ed. F. E. Gaebelein (Grand Rapids: Zondervan, 1988), 4: 563–771.

124. See especially E. J. Bickerman, "The Edict of Cyrus in Ezra 1," *JBL* 65 (1946): 249–75; C. G. Cameron, "Ancient Persia," in *The Idea of History in the Ancient Near East,* ed. R. C. Dentan (New Haven: American Oriental Society, 1955), p. 85; P. R. Ackroyd, *Exile and Restoration* (Philadelphia: Westminster, 1968), p. 131; M. Meuleau, "Mesopotamia under Persian Rule," in *The Greeks and the Persians,* eds. H. Bengston et al. (London: Weidenfeld and Nicolson, 1970), p. 378; R. de Vaux, "The Decrees of Cyrus and Darius on the Rebuilding of the Temple," in *The Bible and the Ancient Near East* (Garden City: Doubleday, 1971), pp. 63–96; C. Hensley, "The Official Persian Documents in the Book of Ezra," unpublished Ph.D. diss. (Liverpool: University of Liverpool, 1977), pp. 211–16; G. Widengren, "The Persian Period," in *Israelite and Judaean History,* eds. J. H. Hayes and J. M. Miller (Philadelphia: Westminster, 1977), p. 519. P. Ackroyd, "The Jewish Community in Palestine in the Persian Period," in *The Cambridge History of Judaism,* eds. W. D. Davies and L. Finkelstein (Cambridge: Cambridge University Press, 1984), 1: 138, concludes: "The general tenor of both forms is sufficiently credible when set alongside comparable material in Persian sources, particularly the Cyrus cylinder and the evidence regarding policy towards the Jewish community at Elephantine in the fifth century."

are the "Verse Account of Nabonidus" and the Cyrus Cylinder. The latter relates: "I (also) gathered their former inhabitants and returned (to them) their habitations."

According to Ezra 6:8 Cyrus not only permitted the Jews to return, but also gave them carte blanche authorization for funds from the imperial treasury. Because the accounts in Haggai and Zechariah do not mention support from the Persian treasury, some have questioned the promises made in this verse. Extrabiblical evidence, however, makes it quite clear that it was a consistent policy of Persian kings to help restore sanctuaries in their empire.

A memorandum concerning the rebuilding of the Jewish temple at Elephantine written by Bagoas, the Persian governor of Judah, and Delaiah, governor of Samaria, relates: "to build it on its site as it was before, and the meal-offering and incense to be made on the altar as it used to be."[125] Emil Kraeling interprets this passage to mean that this was "a directive presumably suggesting that the rebuilding be done at government expense," with a hint also of government subsidies for the offerings.[126]

Cyrus repaired the Eanna temple at Uruk, the Enunmah temple at Ur, and temples in Babylon, as we have noted above. Cambyses gave funds for the temple at Sais in Egypt.[127] The temple of Amon at Hibis in the Khargah Oasis was rebuilt from top to bottom by order of Darius.[128]

In 1973 French archaeologists discovered at Xanthos, on the Lycian coast in southwest Turkey, a cult foundation charter that provides striking parallels with the decree of Cyrus. It is a text in Greek, Lycian, and Aramaic, dated to 358 B.C.[129] This is still within the period when the area was controlled by a Persian satrap.

Among the parallels are these: it is a document issued in response to a local request, but one that would have received ratification from the Persian court; as in Ezra, amounts of sacrifices, names of priests, and the responsibility of the upkeep of the cult are specified; the gods which are invoked to curse those who disregard the decree are local deities. Alan Millard concludes:

125. *ANET*, p. 492.

126. E. Kraeling, *The Brooklyn Aramaic Papyri* (New Haven: Yale University Press, 1953), p. 107.

127. A. Gardiner, *Egypt of the Pharaohs* (London: Oxford University Press, 1961), pp. 366–67.

128. M. F. Gyles, *Pharaonic Policies and Administration 663–323 B.C.* (Chapel Hill, N.C.: University of North Carolina Press, 1959), p. 70.

129. T. R. Bryce, "A Recently Discovered Cult in Lycia," *Journal of Religious History* 10 (1978): 115–27; J. Teixidor, "The Aramaic Text in the Trilingual Stele from Xanthus," *JNES* 37 (1978): 181–86; H. Metzger, ed., *Fouilles de Xanthos VI: Le stèle bilingue de Létôon* (Paris: Klincksieck, 1979).

> Most obvious is the similarity of wording between Greek and Lycian requests and the satrap's Aramaic answer. Such resemblances in the Ezra passages, thought to show a forger's hand, are signs of normal practice. This practice explains how the Persian king or officer appears to know in detail about the cult in question; his information stems from its adherents. . . . The further objection that the Persians would have paid no attention to such details falls away.[130]

The Final Campaign

In 530, although nearly seventy years old, Cyrus campaigned in the distant northeastern part of his realm against the nomadic Massagetae (Herodotus 1.201–4), beyond the lower Oxus River by the Aral Sea. In this area Cyrus established an outpost on the Jaxartes River called Cyropolis (Cyreschata, modern Kurkath). Cyrus was killed in battle toward the end of July 530 B.C. On August 12 a text from Borsippa still bore the date "in the ninth year of Cyrus, of the King of the Lands," since news of the king's death had not yet reached Mesopotamia. But by August 31 the inscriptions at Babylon read, "year of the beginning of the rule of Cambyses, of the King of the Lands."[131]

According to Herodotus (1.205) Cyrus died campaigning against Tomyris, queen of the Massagetae.[132] The body of the great monarch was transported about a thousand miles to be placed in his tomb at Pasargadae. Arrian (6.29) reports that the tomb bore this inscription: "Mortal! I am Cyrus, son of Cambyses, who founded the Persian Empire, and was Lord of Asia. Grudge me not, then, my monument."[133]

130. A. R. Millard, "A Decree of a Persian Governor," *Buried History* (June 1974): 88.

131. Hinz, *Darius*, pp. 118–19.

132. Ctesias attributes Cyrus's death to a wound incurred in a battle against the Indian Derbicae. Berossus has Cyrus killed in a battle with the Scythian Dahern. Xenophon (*Cyropaedia* 8.7.5–28) depicts Cyrus giving his sons a philosophical dissertation on the art of ruling before dying a natural death. H. Sancisi-Weerdenberg, "The Death of Cyrus: Xenophon's *Cyropaedia* as a Source for Iranian History," in *Papers in Honour of Professor Mary Boyce* (Leiden: Brill, 1985), pp. 459–71, notes the parallels between Cyrus's speech in Xenophon and Darius's inscription at Naqsh-i Rustam.

133. Boyce, "Persian Religion," p. 286, explains the difference between the burial practices of the Achaemenids and the Magi and later Zoroastrians as follows: "The rulers of all three imperial dynasties were entombed at death; but Cyrus, who set the precedent, made a serious concession to orthopraxy in that he had his tomb built in such a way that no impurity from the embalmed body within could reach the good creations." See further, M. Boyce, *A History of Zoroastrianism* (Leiden: Brill, 1982), vol. 2, chapter 4. For Cyrus's buildings at Pasargadae and elsewhere in Persia, see chapter 9. For his religion, see chapter 12.

3

Cambyses

Sources

Cyrus's successor was his son Cambyses. The spelling of the name *Cambyses* is derived from the Greek *Kambusēs,* a transliteration of the Old Persian, which was *Ka^{m}būjiya.* The etymology of the name is disputed.[1] The Elamite form of his name was *Kanbuṣia,* and the Akkadian was *Kambuzia.*

Although Cambyses began ruling in 530 B.C., his accession year,[2] his first official regnal year began in the spring of 529 according to the postdating system used by the Persians. The greatest achievement of his eight-year reign was the conquest of Egypt in 525.

Cambyses left behind no inscriptions of his own in Persia. He is mentioned, however, in Darius's Behistun inscription (see the following chapter). We also have Akkadian inscriptions from Mesopotamia

1. R. G. Kent, *Old Persian,* 2d ed. (New Haven: American Oriental Society, 1953), p. 179. W. Eilers, "Kyros: Eine namenkundliche Studie," *Beiträge zur Namenforschung,* 15 (1964): 210–13, links Cambyses with Kamboja, an area north of Gandhara in India.

2. The first cuneiform text under his name is dated Aug. 31, 530 B.C. See M. A. Dandamayev, *Persien unter den ersten Achämeniden* (Wiesbaden: Ludwig Reichert, 1976), pp. 103–4.

that name him,[3] some very important Egyptian texts, and numerous classical references to him (above all, in Herodotus).

There are no biblical references to Cambyses because the Jews were unable to continue work on the temple during his reign.[4] The one place where he could have been mentioned is the history of the opposition to the Jews "down to the reign of Darius king of Persia" (Ezra 4:5). It has been argued by some scholars that the parallel account in Josephus (*Antiquities* 11.88), which substitutes Cambyses for Artaxerxes (I) of Ezra 4:7, gives the correct order. But it is more likely that Josephus has introduced some confusing ideas in his misguided attempt to correct this passage.[5]

In contrast to Cyrus, who had the reputation of a father, Cambyses was characterized as a willful tyrant. John Hart observes:

> He has suffered the fate of rulers who follow a long, successful and popular reign, "comparatio deterrima"—the invidious contrast that heightens the virtues of the first and magnifies the failings of the second. In fact Cambyses' reign was successful enough for its relatively short duration: every square mile of real estate acquired by Cyrus was retained, and to that already great empire were added Phoenicia by treaty and Egypt by conquest. But in the account of his reign truth and fiction have become inextricably intertwined. He emerges as a sort of cross between Caligula and Henry VIII (in his blacker moments).[6]

The Crown Prince in Babylon

Cambyses bore the name of his grandfather, Cambyses I, the father of Cyrus. His mother was Cassandane, the daughter of Pharnaspes. When she died, Cyrus mourned deeply for her (Herodotus 2.1).

3. One text involves a new scheme of rations for the temple servants of Ishtar at Uruk (compare Neh. 11:23). See E. J. Bickerman, "The Babylonian Captivity," in W. D. Davies and L. Finkelstein, eds., *The Cambridge History of Judaism I: The Persian Period* (Cambridge: Cambridge University Press, 1984), 1: 357. L. Cagni, G. Giovinazzo, and S. Graizni, "Typology and Structure of Mesopotamian Documentation during the Achaemenid Period," *Annali* 45 (1985): 582, note that the decline of commercial activities in Mesopotamia "can be historically explained by the Egyptian campaign which Cambyses undertook at the beginning of the 4th year of his reign (525 B.C.) and which had obvious repercussions on the economic sphere."

4. J. Prāšek, *Kambyses* (Leipzig: J. C. Hinrichs, 1912), p. 30, suggests that Cambyses may have been the enigmatic "Darius the Mede" of Daniel. See also C. Boutflower, *In and Around the Book of Daniel* (Grand Rapids: Zondervan, 1963 reprint of 1921 edition), pp. 144–46. But this is hardly possible. See W. H. Dubberstein, "The Chronology of Cyrus and Cambyses," *AJSL* 55 (1933): 419.

5. C. G. Tulland, "Josephus, *Antiquities*, Book XI: Correction or Confirmation of Biblical Post-Exilic Records?" *AUSS* 4 (1966): 178; H. G. M. Williamson, "The Historical Value of Josephus' Antiquities XI.297–301," *JTS* 28 (1977): 64; E. Yamauchi, "Josephus and the Scriptures," *Fides et Historia* 13 (1980): 50–51.

6. J. Hart, *Herodotus and Greek History* (New York: St. Martin's, 1982), p. 113.

We know nothing about Cambyses' youth. We do know that as the crown prince he accompanied his father during the conquest of Babylon in 539 B.C. The Cyrus Cylinder declares: "Marduk, the great lord, was well pleased with my deeds and sent friendly blessings to myself, Cyrus, the king who worships him, to Cambyses, my son. . . ."[7] Cambyses was entrusted by his father to participate in the all-important New Year's rite in Babylon on March 24, 538.

According to the badly damaged third column of the Nabonidus Chronicle, some three days after the New Year, Cambyses may have offended the priests of Nabu. Although we cannot be certain because of the fragmentary nature of the text, Cambyses may have offended the Babylonian priests by appearing in Elamite garb, armed with spears and quivers.[8]

We have twenty-nine texts that date to the first year of "Cyrus, King of Lands, Cambyses, King of Babylon," or variations of this formula. Most scholars have assumed that this coregency occurred during the first year of Cyrus. This conclusion was drawn because Cambyses may have had some difficulty in working with the Babylonian authorities; Cambyses was replaced after nine months by Gubaru.[9] On the other hand, William Shea has argued that the coregency, as was normally the case, should be dated to the very end of Cyrus's life.[10] That is, "the first year" of these inscriptions would refer not to Cyrus's first year over Babylon but to the first year of the coregency.

Reasons for the Invasion of Egypt

Cambyses invaded Egypt to annex the country that was the wealthiest area in the Near East. Herodotus sought the reason for the invasion in highly personal causes. He gives three accounts: (1) the Persians said that Cambyses was angry that Amasis had sent the daughter of his deposed predecessor, Apries, instead of his own daughter for his harem (3.1); (2) the Egyptian story, which Herodotus rejected, was that Cambyses was the son of the daughter of Apries (3.2); and (3) Herodotus tells the charming tale of Cambyses' mother becoming jealous of a new-

7. *ANET*, p. 316.

8. Grayson, *ABC*, p. 111. This is based on the interpretation of A. Leo Oppenheim, "The Babylonian Evidence of Achaemenian Rule in Mesopotamia," in *The Cambridge History of Iran II: The Median and Achaemenian Periods*, ed. I. Gershevitch (Cambridge: Cambridge University Press, 1985), pp. 554–55.

9. Prášek, *Kambyses*, p. 5; Dandamayev, *Persien*, p. 101; Oppenheim, "Babylonian Evidence," p. 558.

10. W. H. Shea, "An Unrecognized Vassal King of Babylon in the Early Achaemenid Period," *AUSS* 9 (1971): 99–128.

comer from Egypt, and her son as a young boy vowing, "Mother, when I am grown a man, I will turn all Egypt upside down" (3.3).

At the height of the Egyptian Empire the pharaohs married princesses from many countries but would not deign to send their own princesses abroad.[11] But in the postempire years (after 1200 B.C.) the Egyptians could not afford to be so particular. The fact that Solomon married a pharaoh's daughter is proof both of the prestige of the Israelite king and of the decline of Egypt in the tenth century.[12] We also have evidence that the pharaohs of the Twenty-first and Twenty-second Dynasties gave away their daughters in marriage to foreigners.[13]

The first story that Cambyses wanted to marry a daughter of Apries may have stemmed from Cambyses' attempt to lend an aura of legitimacy to his claim of being the heir to Apries.[14] This political fiction was also carried out in Cambyses' system of dating, which ignored the intervening reign of the usurper Amasis.

The Twenty-sixth (Saite) Dynasty

The dynasty that ruled Egypt at the time of the Persian invasion in 525 B.C. was the Twenty-sixth Dynasty from Sais in the Delta. Its six kings ruled during the momentous years that saw the collapse of the Assyrian Empire (612), the rise of the Neo-Babylonian Empire, the capture of Jerusalem (586), and the fall of Babylon to the Persians (539).

The years of their reigns, as listed by Herodotus, are remarkably close to those of the Egyptian texts.[15] The dates of the Saite kings are as follows:[16]

11. When the king of Babylonia, Kadašman-Harbe, was refused a daughter of the pharaoh Amenophis III, he wrote: "There are grown up daughters and beautiful women. If there is any beautiful woman . . . send her. Who shall say: 'She is not a king's daughter.' " S. Mercer, *The Tell El-Amarna Tablets* (Toronto: Toronto University Press, 1939), 1: 13. See J. A. Kundtzon, *Die El-Amarna Tafeln* (Leipzig: J. C. Hinrichs, 1915), p. 73.

12. The doubts of Y. Aharoni, *The Land of the Bible,* 2d ed. (Philadelphia: Westminster, 1979), p. 319, n. 42, that Solomon could have married a pharaoh's daughter are unfounded. See S. Horn, "Who Was Solomon's Egyptian Father-in-Law?" *Biblical Research* 12 (1967): 3–17; A. R. Green, "Solomon and Siamun," *JBL* 97 (1978): 353–67; E. Yamauchi, "Solomon," in *NIDBA,* pp. 419–22.

13. K. A. Kitchen, *The Third Intermediate Period in Egypt* (Warminster: Aris and Phillips, 1973), p. 282.

14. K. M. T. Atkinson, "The Legitimacy of Cambyses and Darius as Kings of Egypt," *JAOS* 76 (1956): 167–77. For a different analysis, see M. Lang, "War and the Rape-Motif or Why Did Cambyses Invade Egypt?" *PAPS* 116/5 (1972): 410–14.

15. A. B. Lloyd, *Herodotus Book II* (Leiden: Brill, 1976), p. 194. For the differences from an absolute chronology, see W. Kaiser, "Zu den Quellen der ägyptischen Geschichte Herodotus," *ZÄS* 94 (1967): 97.

16. These are the dates given by Kitchen, *Third Intermediate Period,* p. 468. Slightly different dates are given by K. S. Freedy and D. B. Redford, "The Dates in Ezekiel in Relation to Biblical,

Psammetichus I	664–610 B.C.
Necho II	610–595 B.C.
Psammetichus II	595–589 B.C.
Apries	589–570 B.C.
Amasis	570–526 B.C.
Psammetichus III	526–525 B.C.

Psammetichus I was the son of Necho I, whom Esarhaddon (680–669), the Assyrian conqueror of Egypt, had installed as his vassal. Psammetichus dated the beginning of his new dynasty to 664, but did not consolidate his power over all of Egypt until 656. This he did by shrewd diplomacy, installing his daughter as the future "God's Wife of Amun" at Thebes, thereby securing the allegiance of Upper Egypt.[17]

According to Herodotus (2.152) Psammetichus was aided by the fortuitous arrival of "men of bronze" from the sea, actually Ionian and Carian mercenaries, who had probably been sent to him by Gyges, the king of Lydia.[18] From Assyrian records we learn that around 639 B.C. Gyges stopped sending tribute to Assyria and sent aid to Tushamilki (that is, Psammetichus), which the Assyrians regarded as a treasonable act.[19]

The conventional view is that Psammetichus used these Greek mercenaries to liberate himself from the Assyrian yoke.[20] However, Anthony Spalinger, who has maintained that the Assyrian invasions were aimed not at the Egyptians but at the Nubians, has emphasized Psammetichus I's loyalty to the Assyrians.[21]

In any case, after the fall of Nineveh, Necho II in 609 rushed to the aid of the beleaguered Assyrians in Harran against the pursuing forces

---

Babylonian, and Egyptian Sources," *JAOS* 90 (1970): 474: Psammetichus II (594–588), Apries (588–569), and Amasis (569–526); and by the new edition of *The Cambridge Ancient History III.3: The Expansion of the Greek World,* eds. J. Boardman and N. G. L. Hammond, 2d ed. (Cambridge: Cambridge University Press, 1982), pp. 464–66: Necho II (610–594), Psammetichus II (594–589).

17. R. A. Caminos, "The Nitocris Adoption Stela," *JEA* 50 (1964): 71–101. Whether Psammetichus I invaded Nubia is debated. This is maintained by J. Yoyotte and S. Sauneron, "La campagne nubienne de Psammétique II et sa signification historique," *BIFAO* 30 (1952): 200, but is denied by A. Spalinger, "The Concept of the Monarchy during the Saite Epoch," *Or* 47 (1978): 18, n. 23.

18. Lloyd, *Herodotus Book II,* pp. 14ff; T. F. R. G. Braun, "The Greeks in Egypt," in *CAH* III.3, pp. 36–37.

19. M. Cogan and H. Tadmor, "Gyges and Assurbanipal," *Or* 46 (1977): 78; E. Yamauchi, *Foes from the Northern Frontier* (Grand Rapids: Baker, 1982), p. 24. A. Spalinger, "Psammetichus, King of Egypt II," *JARCE* 15 (1978): 49–58, would date the encounter between the Egyptians and the Scythians in his reign to 622–620 B.C. (compare Jer. 2:18, 36).

20. Braun, "Greeks in Egypt," p. 37; E. Yamauchi, *Greece and Babylon* (Grand Rapids: Baker, 1967), p. 64.

21. A. Spalinger, "Psammetichus, King of Egypt I," *JARCE* 13 (1976): 133; Kitchen, *Third Intermediate Period,* p. 406.

of the Medes and Chaldeans. It was in a vain attempt to block Necho's passage through the Megiddo Pass that Josiah, king of Judah, lost his life in 609 (2 Kings 23:29). According to Herodotus (2.159), Necho sent the clothes that he wore in this battle to the shrine of the Branchidae, that is, to Didyma near Miletus.[22] T. Braun observes: "This is the first official Egyptian dedication known to have been sent to a shrine in the Greek homeland."[23]

In 605 Necho was defeated in the famous Battle of Carchemish on the Euphrates by Nebuchadnezzar (Jer. 46:2). The excavations of C. Leonard Woolley and Thomas E. Lawrence (of Arabia) recovered a Greek shield, which is striking evidence of the presence of Greek mercenaries, who were fighting on both sides.[24] Scythian mercenaries may also have been involved.[25]

Psammetichus II is best known for his devastating campaign against Nubia in his third regnal year.[26] While the pharaoh himself probably went only as far south as the first cataract near Aswan, his troops may have reached the third or even the fourth cataract. Along the way his Greek and Carian mercenaries carved their version of "Kilroy was here" on the leg of one of the colossal statues of Ramesses II at Abu Simbel just north of the present border between Egypt and Sudan.[27]

It is possible that it was on this occasion that Jewish mercenaries were posted by the Egyptians on the island of Elephantine opposite Aswan.[28] Later, as Cambyses traveled to Nubia, he seems to have recruited them to serve the Persians.[29] From the Persian era (fifth century

22. See E. Yamauchi, "Didyma," in *New Testament Cities in Western Asia Minor* (Grand Rapids: Baker, 1980), chapter 9.

23. Braun, "Greeks in Egypt," p. 49.

24. Yamauchi, *Greece and Babylon*, p. 64; see also E. Yamauchi, "The Greek Words in Daniel in the Light of Greek Influence in the Near East," in *New Perspectives on the Old Testament*, ed. J. B. Payne (Waco: Word, 1970), pp. 186–88.

25. Yamauchi, *Foes*, pp. 96–97. Necho is also known for beginning a canal between the Nile and the Red Sea (Herodotus 2.158) and for the sponsorship of the circumnavigation of Africa by the Phoenicians (Herodotus 4.42). The latter feat is accepted by M. Cary and E. H. Warmington, *The Ancient Explorers* (Harmondsworth: Penguin, 1963), pp. 111–21, but questioned by A. B. Lloyd, "Necho and the Red Sea: Some Considerations," *JEA* 63 (1977): 142–55.

26. Yoyotte and Sauneron, "La campagne nubienne," pp. 157–207.

27. Braun, "Greeks in Egypt," pp. 50–51; Yamauchi, *Greece and Babylon*, pp. 64–66.

28. "The Letter of Aristeas 13," in *The Apocrypha and Pseudepigrapha of the Old Testament*, ed. R. H. Charles (Oxford: Clarendon, 1913), 2: 96: "And even before this time large numbers of Jews had come into Egypt with the Persians and in an earlier period still others had been sent *to Egypt* to help Psammetichus in his campaign against the king of the Ethiopians."

29. Some scholars associate the establishment of the Jewish garrison at Elephantine with Cambyses' expedition to Nubia. See Prāšek, *Kambyses*, p. 20; Dandamayev, *Persien*, p. 107. But the documents from Elephantine indicate that the colony was already established prior to Cambyses.

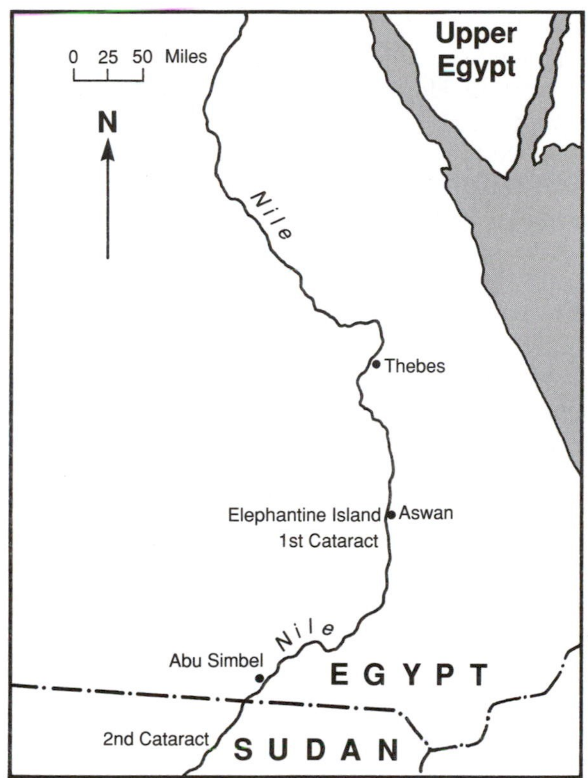

B.C.) have come numerous Aramaic documents from this Jewish garrison, which illuminate the background of the contemporary books of Ezra and Nehemiah.[30]

It was in the glow of his great victory over Nubia that Psammetichus II departed on a triumphal tour of Palestine in 593.[31] Unfortunately for the Jews of Palestine, this encouraged them to lean on the broken "reed of Egypt" against Jeremiah's advice, provoking the wrath of Nebuchadnezzar. Jeremiah, who was denounced as a traitor for his counsel, soon found himself involuntarily carried off to Egypt after the fall of Jerusalem to the Babylonians (Jer. 43).

Apries, who is called Hophra in the Old Testament, did send a

30. See chapter 6 on Artaxerxes I.

31. Freedy and Redford, "Dates in Ezekiel," pp. 476–79; Spalinger, "Concept of the Monarchy," p. 23.

small force around 588 B.C. to raise Nebuchadnezzar's siege of Jerusalem, but with little effect (Jer. 37:5; Ezek. 29:1–16). Jeremiah's reference to the defeat of Hophra (Jer. 44:30) is made credible by extrabiblical sources.[32]

In 571 Apries conducted a campaign against the Greek city of Cyrene in Libya. Resentful of the growing role played by Greek mercenaries in the army, Egyptian troops rebelled against Apries. The rebels were led by Amasis in a decisive victory at Momephis, a site in the northwest Delta.[33] At first Amasis gave Apries his freedom.[34] Three years later, however, Apries led a revolt in the area of Sais with a force of Greeks. This event is related in a granite stela found at Elephantine, which confirms Herodotus's narrative.[35] In spite of Apries' rebellion and consequent execution, he was given an honorable burial in the royal cemetery at Sais by Amasis.

It is ironic that Amasis, who first rose to power on the crest of nationalistic resentment against the Greek mercenaries of Apries, should later become famed as a *Philhellene* or "lover of the Greeks" (Herodotus 2.178). Amasis sent gifts to many Greek shrines including a major gift of alum for fireproofing the new temple at Delphi after the old one burned in 548 (Herodotus 2.180). His friendship with the Greek tyrant of Samos, Polycrates, was noteworthy. Amasis even married a Greek woman from Cyrene, Ladice.[36]

Herodotus (2.173–74) correctly describes Amasis as a bon vivant who enjoyed drinking and carousing. An Egyptian text is critical of the all too human behavior of this so-called divine pharaoh.

> In the morning Pharaoh could not rise, because he was completely beclouded, and he could not hold audience for anyone. And the people of the court moaned and said, "O good Lord! What kind of mess has Pharaoh got into?"[37]

32. J. K. Hoffmeier, "A New Insight on Pharaoh Apries from Herodotus, Diodorus and Jeremiah 46:17," *Journal of the Society for the Study of Egyptian Antiquities* 11 (1981): 165–70.

33. Herodotus 2.163–69. A. Wiedemann, *Herodots zweites Buch mit sachlichen Erläuterungen* (Milan: Cisalpino-Goliardica, 1971 reprint of 1890 edition), p. 581; F. K. Kienitz, *Die politische Geschichte Ägyptens vom 7. bis zum 4. Jahrhundert vor der Zeitwende* (Berlin: Akademie Verlag, 1953), pp. 161–62.

34. Even a share in the rule according to J. H. Breasted, *Ancient Records of Egypt* (Chicago: University of Chicago Press, 1906–1907), 4: 492.

35. Ibid., p. 509; Kienitz, *Die politische Geschichte*, p. 163; Spalinger, "Concept of the Monarchy," p. 25.

36. After the Persian invasion, Cambyses permitted Ladice to return to her home (Herodotus 2.181). See Ctesias #58; F. W. König, *Die Persika des Ktesias von Knidos* (Graz: Archiv für Orientforschung, 1972), p. 23.

37. Spalinger, "Concept of the Monarchy," p. 26; T. Säve-Söderbergh, *Pharaohs and Mortals* (Indianapolis: Bobbs-Merrill, 1961), p. 192.

After a long and relatively peaceful reign,[38] Amasis died late in 526, bequeathing his kingdom to his son, Psammetichus III.[39] The latter had but a half-year to reign before he had to face the Persian invasion. Cambyses at first spared the king but executed his son and sent his daughter into slavery (Herodotus 3.14).[40] Some time later, however, when Cambyses learned that Psammetichus was plotting an uprising, he had Psammetichus executed (Herodotus 3.15).

Naucratis

Archaeological confirmation of the Greek presence in Egypt during the Saite period comes from Naucratis in the northwest Delta. According to Herodotus (2.178) it was Amasis who gave the Greeks the city of Naucratis "where they might set altars and make holy places of their gods." Naucratis was to become the main point of contact for trade and cultural exchange between the Egyptians and Greeks during the Archaic Age.[41] The clever Greeks set up their own factory to manufacture "made in Egypt" scarabs for export to their homeland. The sight of monumental Egyptian statues seems to have influenced the Greeks in their rendering of their own statues.[42] It was the Greeks who called the Egyptian monuments "wheaten cake" *pyramidos* and "little spit" *obeliskos.*[43]

In the light of archaeological evidence we must not take Herodotus's statement to mean that Amasis founded the city of Naucratis *de novo.*[44] Corinthian pottery has been found at the site that dates as early as 630 to 620 B.C.,[45] that is, during the reign of Psammetichus I. What

38. The Babylonians invaded Egypt in the thirty-seventh year of Nebuchadnezzar (568/567 B.C.) during the reign of Amasis. D. J. Wiseman, *Chronicles of Chaldaean Kings* (London: British Museum, 1956), pp. 94–95; E. Edel, "Amasis und Nebukadrezar II," *Göttinger Miszellen* 29 (1978): 13–20.

39. Psammetichus III was the son of Amasis and Tent-Khata, not of Ladice.

40. Ctesias #9 erroneously names an Egyptian king who reigned about 450 B.C.: "Cambyses captured Amyrtaeus alive, but did him no harm beyond deporting him to Susa with 6,000 Egyptians of his own choice." C. J. Ogden, "The Story of Cambyses and the Magus, As Told in the Fragments of Ctesias," in *Sir Jamsetjee Jejeebhoy Madresssa Jubilee Volume,* ed. J. J. Modi (Bombay: Fort, 1914), pp. 235–36; König, *Die Persika,* p. 6.

41. R. M. Cook, "Amasis and the Greeks in Egypt," *JHS* 57 (1937): 227–37; J. G. Milne, "Trade between Greece and Egypt before Alexander the Great," *JEA* 25 (1939), 177–83; C. Roebuck, "The Organization of Naukratis," *Classical Philology* 46 (1951): 212–20; M. M. Austin, *Greece and Egypt in the Archaic Age* (Cambridge: Cambridge Philological Society, 1970); J. Boardman, *The Greeks Overseas,* 2d ed. (London: Thames and Hudson, 1973); Braun, "Greeks in Egypt," pp. 37–43.

42. R. Anthes, "Affinity and Difference between Egyptian and Greek Sculpture and Thought in the Seventh and Sixth Centuries B.C.," *PAPS* 107 (1963): 60–81; W. M. Davis, "Egypt, Samos, and the Archaic Style in Greek Sculpture," *JEA* 67 (1981): 61–81.

43. E. Yamauchi, "Obelisks and Pyramids," *NEASB* n.s. 24 (1985): 111–15.

44. See W. W. Hallo and W. K. Simpson, *The Ancient Near East* (New York: Harcourt, Brace, Jovanovich, 1971), p. 294.

45. Braun, "Greeks in Egypt," p. 38.

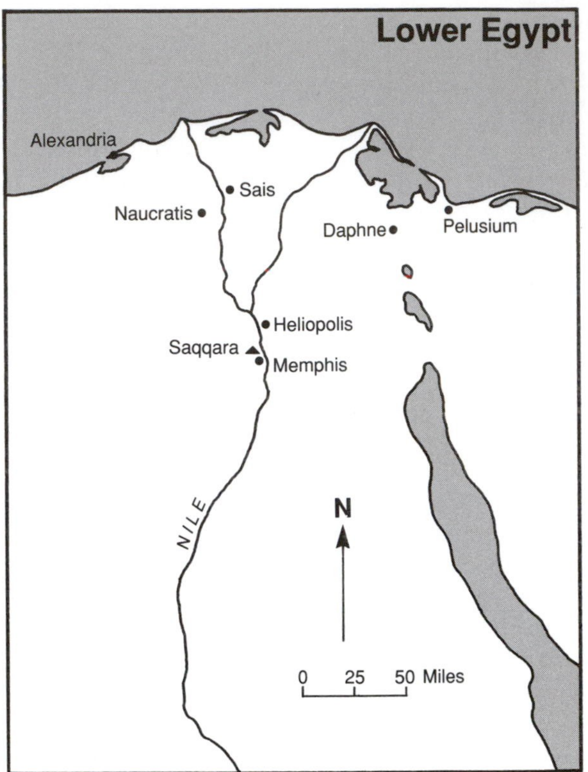

Amasis evidently provided was a new charter that made Naucratis a treaty port. It was probably in the reign of Amasis that the Hellenion, the common shrine of nine Greek cities, was erected. Herodotus himself visited the site and may have left the inscription that was recovered there in 1903.[46]

The site of Naucratis was excavated by Flinders Petrie in 1884/1885, by Ernest A. Gardner in 1886, and by David G. Hogarth in 1899 and 1903. They concentrated on uncovering five Greek temples in an area that is covered by a lake today. The Greek finds at Naucratis decline sharply around 525 B.C., presumably in the wake of the Persian invasion.[47]

Inasmuch as the stratigraphy of the earlier excavations was unsatisfactory and as major commercial and residential areas were not touched, a

46. W. D. E. Coulson and A. Leonard, Jr., *Cities of the Delta, Part I: Naukratis* (Malibu: Undena, 1982), p. 12.

47. Boardman, *Greeks Overseas*, p. 134.

new effort to excavate the site and to survey surrounding areas was mounted in 1977. Examination of surface pottery sherds indicates that the nearby site of Kom Firin may have been settled by Greeks as early as Naucratis.[48]

Guarding the northeastern Delta was the Greek fort at Daphnae (Tell Defenneh), which was also excavated by Petrie in 1886. This was the biblical Tahpanhes to which Jeremiah came in 582 (Jer. 43:6–7). The site could have supported twenty thousand soldiers, including not only Greek but also Scythian mercenaries.[49] The great majority of Greek wares from the site dates to the period from 570 to 525 B.C.[50] With the Persian invasion Daphnae was abandoned. Trade between Egypt and Greece was temporarily cut off until 500, but then flourished thereafter.[51]

Eliezer D. Oren uncovered a mudbrick fort some twelve miles east of Daphnae south of Pelusium. The large site of some ten acres contained many sixth-century amphorae from Chios, Samos, Lesbos, and Corinth. This may have been the biblical site of Migdol (Jer. 44:1; 46:14; Ezek. 29:10), which contained a community of Jews.[52]

The Persian Invasion

The Egyptians, who early in the sixth century had many allies, were gradually isolated by the rapid expansion of the Persians under Cyrus. They were cut off from Lydia in 547 and from Babylon in 539. Cyprus, which had been won over by Amasis, defected to the Persians. Even Amasis's friend, Polycrates of Samos, was compelled to send a contingent to the Persian fleet (Herodotus 3.44). Polycrates obliged by sending his foes, including his brother Syloson. Phanes, a mercenary from Halicarnassus (Herodotus's hometown), deserted the Egyptians (Herodotus 3.4) and advised Cambyses to seek the aid of the Arabs, who could supply camels and water (Herodotus 3.9). The Arabs controlled vast areas ranging from northeast Egypt to southern Palestine.[53]

48. Coulson and Leonard, *Naukratis*; idem, "A Preliminary Survey of the Naukratis Region in the Western Nile Delta," *JFA* 6 (1979): 151–68; idem, "Investigations at Naukratis and Environs, 1980 and 1981," *AJA* 86 (1982): 361–80.

49. Yamauchi, *Foes*, pp. 83–84.

50. Braun, "Greeks in Egypt," p. 44.

51. Boardman, *Greeks Overseas*, p. 141.

52. Herodotus 2.159; Boardman, *Greeks Overseas*, p. 134; Davis, "Egypt, Samos," p. 70.

53. H. Grimme, "Beziehungen zwischen dem Staate Liḥjān und dem Achämenidenreiche," *Orientalistische Literaturzeitung* 44 (1941): 337–43. For the importance of the Arabs, see M. Elat, "The Economic Relations of the Neo-Assyrian Empire with Egypt," *JAOS* 98 (1978): 28–30; I. Eph'al, *The Ancient Arabs* (Jerusalem: Hebrew University; Leiden: Brill, 1982).

Naophorous statue of Udjahorresnet. (Courtesy of the Vatican Museum)

The initial conflict between the Persians and the Egyptians took place at Pelusium in the northeast Delta, where years later Herodotus (3.12) was shown the skulls of the victims from the battle.[54] After the victory at Pelusium the Persians rapidly advanced to Memphis, the key city in Lower Egypt. With the capture of Memphis, open resistance subsided.

Cambyses now faced the task of establishing Persian control over a country that boasted one of the world's oldest civilizations. Our sources seem to be contradictory. On the one hand, Herodotus paints the picture of an erratic, willful conqueror who was determined to defy ancient conventions and to tread roughshod over religious sensibilities. On the other hand, some Egyptian sources depict Cambyses as accommodating himself to Egyptian customs.

While there may be no satisfactory solution to some of these contradictions, a key may be that Cambyses behaved differently with different elements in Egypt, favoring those who accepted the Persians and punishing those who did not. The stories about Cambyses' acts of desecration were probably derived from hostile sources—Egyptian or possibly Persian. On the other hand, some of the favorable accounts come from Egyptians who collaborated with the Persians.[55]

Udjahorresnet

One of the defectors to the Persian side is represented in a statue inscribed with forty-eight lines. Udjahorresnet's[56] statue, which is now in the Vatican Museum, is known as a *naophoros* figure because he holds in his hands a *naos* or shrine containing the image of Osiris. It is dated to the third year of Darius.

Udjahorresnet served Neith, the goddess of Sais in the western Delta.[57] She was the goddess of hunting and war, the mistress of the

54. In spite of his omissions, exaggerations, and errors, no one today doubts that Herodotus actually visited Egypt. See C. Sourdille, *La durée et l'étendue du voyage d'Hérodote en Egypte* (Paris: E. Leroux, 1910); W. Spiegelberg, *The Credibility of Herodotus' Account of Egypt in the Light of the Monuments* (Oxford: Blackwell, 1927); E. Lüddeckens, "Herodot und Ägypten," *ZDMG* 104 (1954): 330–46; T. W. Africa, "Herodotus and Diodorus on Egypt," *JNES* 22 (1963): 254–58; S. Benardette, *Herodotean Inquiries* (The Hague: M. Nijhoff, 1969), pp. 32–68; R. Drews, *The Greek Accounts of Eastern History* (Cambridge: Harvard University Press, 1973), p. 80. O. K. Armayor, "Did Herodotus Ever Go to Egypt?" *JARCE* 15 (1978): 59–74, while conceding that Herodotus visited Egypt, questions most of his information.

55. Kienitz, *Die politische Geschichte*, p. 56. One thinks of Josephus, who surrendered to the Romans and then attempted to absolve Titus from the blame for the burning of the Jewish temple. See H. Montefiore, "Sulpicius Severus and Titus' Council of War," *Historia* 11 (1962): 156–70.

56. The Egyptian reads *wd3-ḥr-rś-n.t.* As we are not sure of the vocalization of Egyptian, the name has been variously transcribed: Udjeharresnet, Udzahorresne, Wadjahoreresnet, etc.

57. Herodotus 2.170 identified Neith with Athena.

bow and arrow. Udjahorresnet's inscription lists a long catalogue of the titles so beloved of Egyptian nobility—"the Royal Chancellor, the Unique Companion, the True Acquaintance of the King. . . ." Most important is the revelation that Udjahorresnet was the admiral of the royal navy under Amasis and Psammetichus III.[58] He reports:

> There came into Egypt the great king of all the foreign countries Cambyses (Kambujet), while the foreigners of all the foreign countries were with him. When he had taken possession of this entire land, they established their residence, and he was the great sovereign of Egypt, great lord of all the foreign countries.[59]

Udjahorresnet boasts that he instructed Cambyses about the greatness of Neith and her residence at Sais.[60] The site of Sais (Sa el-Hagar) was at that time surrounded by a gigantic enclosure, filled with trees, sphinxes, and colossi.[61]

> I complained before the Majesty of the King of Upper and Lower Egypt, Cambyses, on the subject of all the foreigners, who had installed themselves in the temple of Neith, in order that they should be expelled from there, that the temple of Neith should appear in all its former splendor.[62]

Cambyses ordered the expulsion of these squatters,[63] destroying their dwellings and removing the rubble. Neith's temple was thus purified and its revenues and festivals restored.[64] Udjahorresnet claims that Cambyses not only visited the temple but prostrated himself before the goddess as every pharaoh had done before. He reports that Cambyses saved the residents of Sais from great calamity. Udjahorresnet may

58. The defection of Udjahorresnet may be reflected in the garbled tradition found in Ctesias #9: "He (Cambyses) overcame Amyrtaeus, for the eunuch Combapheus, who had great influence with the Egyptian king, surrendered the dikes and betrayed the Egyptian cause." Ogden, "Story of Cambyses," p. 235; König, *Die Persika,* p. 5.

59. G. Posener, *La première domination perse en Egypte* (Cairo: L'Institut Français d'Archéologie Orientale, 1936), p. 7; A. T. Olmstead, *History of the Persian Empire* (Chicago: University of Chicago Press, 1948), p. 90.

60. Some have taken this passage as an initiation of Cambyses into the so-called mysteries of Neith, but Posener, *La première domination,* p. 14, disagrees.

61. Davis, "Egypt, Samos," p. 79; P. Montet, *Lives of the Pharaohs* (Cleveland: World, 1968), p. 261.

62. Posener, *La première domination,* p. 15.

63. Who were these squatters? Some have suggested Greek mercenaries. Posener, *La première domination,* p. 16, believes they were Persian troops. P. G. Elgood, *The Later Dynasties of Egypt* (Oxford: Blackwell, 1951), p. 118, makes the unlikely suggestion that they were "the inhabitants of Sais too poor or too lazy to find accommodation elsewhere."

64. This parallels the expulsion of Tobiah from the temple in Jerusalem by Nehemiah (Neh. 13:8). For other parallels, see J. Blenkinsopp, "The Mission of Udjahorresnet and Those of Ezra and Nehemiah, *JBL* 106 (1987): 409–21.

Statue of Ptah-hotep from Memphis. (Courtesy of the Brooklyn Museum, Charles Edwin Wilbour Fund)

have considered it in the best interests of his district to cooperate with the Persians.[65]

As the chief physician, Udjahorresnet was empowered by the Persians to restore the medical colleges in Sais and throughout Egypt.[66] As

65. Posener, *La première domination*, p. 17. A. B. Lloyd, "The Inscription of Udjaḥorresnet: A Collaborator's Testament," *JEA* 68 (1982): 173, suggests that "Cambyses made a genuine attempt to reconcile the Egyptians to Persian rule by adopting the traditional role of Pharaoh with all its implications; Udjaḥorresnet was, therefore, able to accept the change of government much more easily than might otherwise have been the case simply by applying the eminently straightforward principle: 'The King is dead. Long live the King.' "

66. A. H. Gardiner, "The House of Life," *JEA* 24 (1938): 158.

Unguentarium from Leontopolis. (Courtesy of the Brooklyn Museum, Charles Edwin Wilbour Fund)

part of his service to the new pharaoh Udjahorresnet prepared the formal titulary whereby Cambyses was invested with the prenomen *Mesutre,* "Offspring of Re," emphasizing his legitimacy as the ruler of Egypt.[67]

There were other Egyptians who continued to hold office under the Persians.[68] A striking monument of such an Egyptian who served under the Persians is the statue of Ptah-hotep in the Brooklyn Museum. This is also a *naophoros* statue. Ptah-hotep's titles include: "The Prince and

67. See Posener, *La première domination,* p. 12. After Cambyses, Alexander the Great was depicted as the son of the last pharaoh, Nectanebo II. In the Temple of Dendur, which was sent by Egypt to the Metropolitan Museum in New York, we behold the pharaoh Augustus pouring a libation to the god Khnum of Elephantine. The Roman emperor received the Egyptian titles: "The King of Upper and Lower Egypt, Lord of the Two Lands, Autocrator, the Son of Re, Lord of Crowns, Caesar, living forever." C. Aldred, *The Temple of Dendur* (New York: Metropolitan Museum of Art, 1978), p. 27.

68. Dandamayev, *Persien,* p. 106. R. S. Bianchi, "Perser in Ägypten," in *Lexicon der Ägyptologie,* eds. W. Helck and W. Westendorf (Wiesbaden: Harrassowitz, 1982), columns 946, 950.

Count, Royal Treasurer and Sole Friend, . . . the Superintendent of all Royal Works, the Minister of Finance. . . ."[69] The only other material evidence from the century of Persian occupation in Egypt is a set of lion-figured unguentaria from Leontopolis, representing the lion-god Mahes in a style indicating they were probably made in Egypt for Persians.[70]

Cambyses inaugurated the Twenty-seventh Dynasty, which was to last from 525 to 402 B.C.[71] Although he entered Egypt in the middle of 525 and left about three years later, papyrus documents in demotic claim as many as eight years for his reign in Egypt. This must mean that Cambyses claimed jurisdiction over Egypt from the beginning of his reign in Persia in 529.[72]

The Desecration of Amasis's Body

An act that Herodotus (3.16) regarded as a senseless desecration may have been an attempt by Cambyses to strengthen his claim as the legitimate successor to Apries. Cambyses sought out the corpse of Amasis and attempted to mutilate it. But because the corpse had been embalmed, this proved to be in vain. He then had the corpse burned. To the Egyptians this was an especially terrible deed because they believed that the preservation of the body was necessary for the afterlife.[73]

Many scholars have questioned Cambyses' desecration of Amasis's body[74] but there may have been method in his madness. According to Manetho, Shabako, the first king of the new Cushite (Twenty-fifth)

69. J. D. Cooney, "The Portrait of an Egyptian Collaborator," *Bulletin of the Brooklyn Museum* 15 (1953): 5.

70. B. V. Bothmer, *Egyptian Sculpture of the Late Period, 700 B.C. to A.D. 100* (Brooklyn: Brooklyn Museum, 1960), p. 77. Compare J. D. Cooney, *Five Years of Collecting Egyptian Art (1951–1956)* (Brooklyn: Brooklyn Museum, 1956), p. 56. For possible linguistic remains, see K. Sethe, "Spuren der Perserherrschaft in der späteren ägyptischen Sprache," *Festgabe für Theodor Nöldeke* (Göttingen: König. Gesellschaft der Wissenschaften, 1916), pp. 112–33.

71. Some scholars date the end of the Twenty-seventh Dynasty to 401 or even 398 B.C. Just before the conquest by Alexander, the Persians briefly reoccupied Egypt from 343 to 332 under Artaxerxes III.

72. Atkinson, "Legitimacy of Cambyses," p. 168; M. F. Gyles, *Pharaonic Policies and Administration, 663–323 B.C.* (Chapel Hill: University of North Carolina Press, 1959), pp. 98–100; W. Culican, *The Medes and Persians* (New York: Praeger, 1965), p. 61.

73. J. Davis, *Mummies, Men and Madness* (Grand Rapids: Baker, 1972); R. S. Bianchi, "Egyptian Mummies: Myth and Reality," *Arch* 35/2 (1982): 18–25; E. F. Wente, "Funerary Beliefs of the Ancient Egyptians," *Exped* 24/2 (1982): 17–26. For a fuller bibliography on the subject, see E. Yamauchi, "Magic or Miracle? Diseases, Demons and Exorcisms," in *Gospel Perspectives* (Sheffield: JSOT, 1986), 6: 160, n. 125.

74. Kienitz, *Die politische Geschichte*, p. 57.

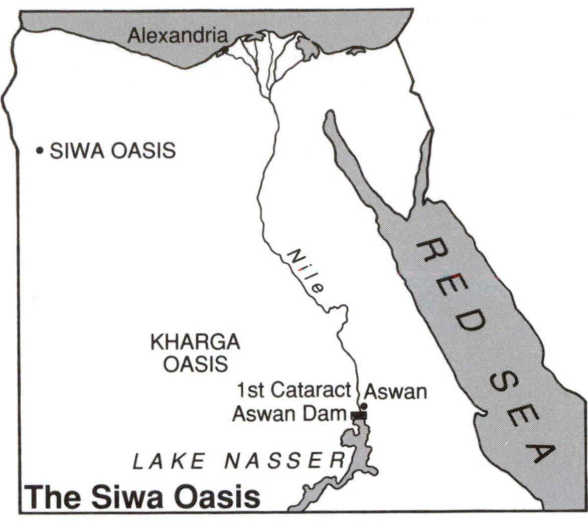

Dynasty, burned alive the preceding king (Bocchoris—the last king of the Twenty-fourth Dynasty). Kathleen Atkinson believes that Cambyses wanted to blacken the reputation of Amasis as a usurper.[75] Edda Bresciani observes:

> In reality Cambyses' action was in line with the Egyptian point of view; since he did not want to recognize Amasis as a legitimate Pharaoh, he saw to it that his memory was accursed in exactly the manner that he knew would be final and convincing to the Egyptian mentality.[76]

The Expedition to Siwa

Cambyses planned an expedition far to the west against the Phoenician colony of Carthage (in present-day Tunisia), but this plan was frustrated when the Phoenician seamen of his fleet balked at the prospect of fighting against their countrymen (Herodotus 3.17, 19). The Libyans to the west of Egypt submitted to the Persians and sent gifts, as did the Greek colony of Cyrene (Herodotus 3.13).[77] While

75. Atkinson, "Legitimacy of Cambyses," p. 171, cites the desecration of the corpse of Oliver Cromwell at the time of the Restoration. See *The Diary and Correspondence of Samuel Pepys* (London: George Bell and Sons, 1900), 1:128–29 (entry for Dec. 4, 1660).

76. E. Bresciani, "Egypt and the Persian Empire," in *The Greeks and the Persians*, ed. H. Bengtson (London: Weidenfeld and Nicolson, 1968), p. 336.

77. See B. M. Mitchell, "Cyrene and Persia," *JHS* 86 (1966): 99–113.

Ruins of the temple of Ammon at Siwa. (Courtesy of *Aramco World Magazine*; photo by John Feeney and Farouk El-Baz)

Cambyses sailed upstream to Thebes, he detached a contingent of fifty thousand men to burn the oracle of Zeus-Ammon at Siwa (Herodotus 3.25–26). After seven days of trekking through the desert they came to the city of Oasis, probably the El-Khargeh oasis, where some Greeks from Samos were settled.[78] Halfway between Oasis and Siwa the Persian troops were overwhelmed by a tremendous sandstorm (Herodotus 3.26).

Because Siwa was located about one hundred miles from the Mediterranean coast, the usual route to the shrine was from the north. Even then, because it was four hundred miles west of the Nile, it took an

78. J. A. S. Evans, *Herodotus* (Boston: Twayne, 1982), p. 50: "the story is without proof, but it may be true, for Samos was one of the first Greek states to interest itself in Egypt." See Davis, "Egypt, Samos," p. 69; U. Jantzen, "Ägyptische und orientalische Bronzen aus dem Heraion vom Samos," *Gnomon* 47 (1975): 392–402.

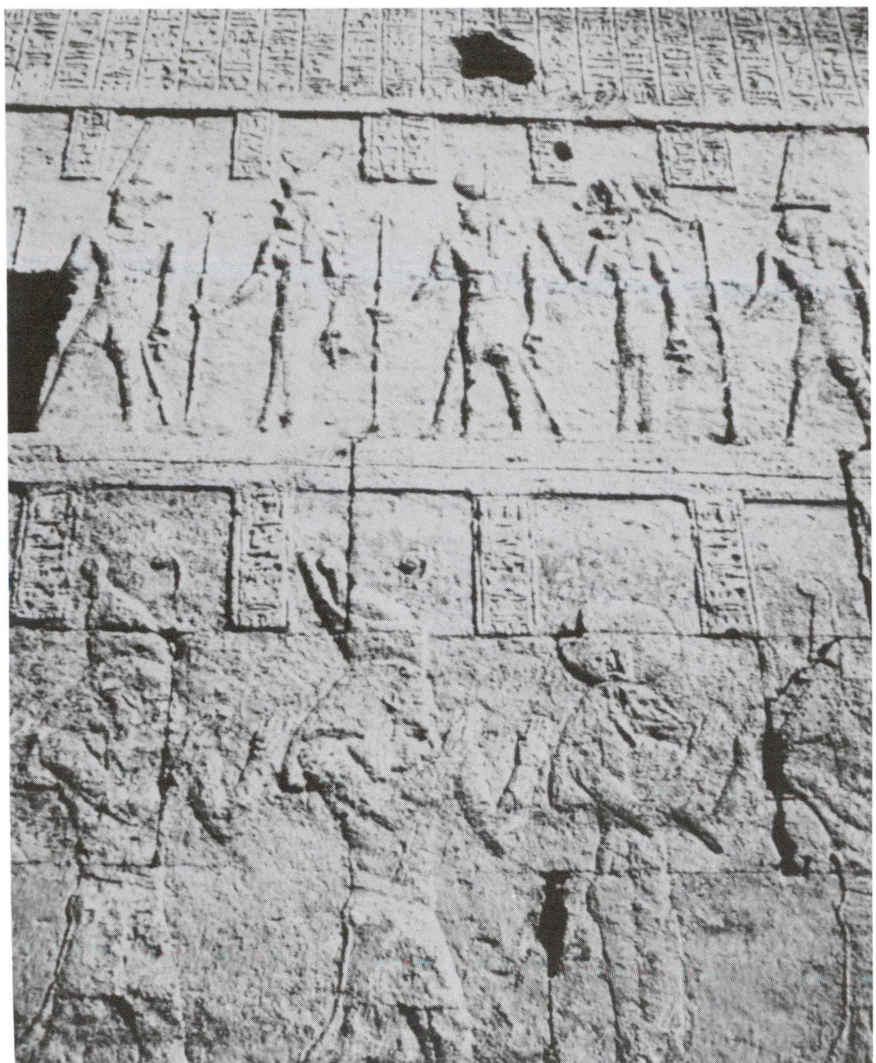

Wall of the temple of Ammon at Siwa. (Courtesy of *Aramco World Magazine*; photo by John Feeney and Farouk El-Baz)

arduous journey of at least fifteen days through vast stretches of treacherous deserts.[79]

79. Herodotus 4.181; Arrian, *Alexander* 3.4.1; Plutarch, *Alexander* 26–27. See G. Steindorff et al., "Der Orakeltempel in der Ammonsoase," *ZÄS* 69 (1933): 22; H. Kees, *Ancient Egypt* (Chicago: University of Chicago Press, 1961), p. 129.

Scholars have been sceptical about the expedition of Cambyses' army into the western desert,[80] but there are indications that such disasters are far from impossible. The Siwans themselves tell a story of a tribe of attacking Tibbu from the western Sudan, who were providentially buried in a sandstorm before they could attack.[81] According to Ahmed Fakhry, "in the year 1805, a caravan of 2,000 persons with their camels, en route from Dārfūr in the Western Sudan to Asyūt, was buried under the sands of the same Libyan desert."[82] A press report that some of the bones and weapons of the lost Persian army had been found, as cited by James Evans,[83] has proven to be unfounded.

Normally the Persian rulers were well disposed to foreign oracles, which tended to proffer favorable pronouncements.[84] We have reason to believe that Cambyses consulted the oracle at Buto (Herodotus 3.64), although he seems not to have believed its prophecy of his death. His wrath against the oracle at Siwa may have been aroused by an unfavorable prediction.

The Expedition to Ethiopia

Herodotus (3.17–20) informs us that Cambyses wanted to invade the land of the tall, long-living "Ethiopians," who lived south of Egypt. This was a continuation of the policy maintained by the preceding Saite Dynasty.[85]

The king of Ethiopia presented a bow to the Persian scouts (Herodotus 3.21–22), warning Cambyses not to invade unless the Persians could draw such a bow. B. G. Haycock comments:

> Whether or not this incident is historical, as it may well be, it illustrates

80. For example, K. H. Waters, *Herodotus on Tyrants and Despots* (Wiesbaden: F. Steiner, 1971), p. 54.

81. A. Fakhry, *The Oases of Egypt I: Siwa Oasis* (Cairo: American University in Cairo, 1973), p. 66.

82. Ibid.

83. Evans, *Herodotus*, p. 30.

84. On the Gadates inscription, see the following chapter. The Persians harshly treated the oracle at Didyma after the Ionian revolt was suppressed in 494, exiling the Branchidae and carrying off the bronze statue of Apollo to Ecbatana. For the key role of Delphi during the Persian conflict with the Greeks, see J. Elayi, "Le rôle de l'oracle de Delphes dans le conflit gréco-perse d'après 'Les Histoires' d'Hérodote," *IA* 13 (1978): 93–118; idem, "Le rôle de l'oracle," 14 (1979): 67–150.

85. Bresciani, "Egypt and the Persian Empire," p. 337.

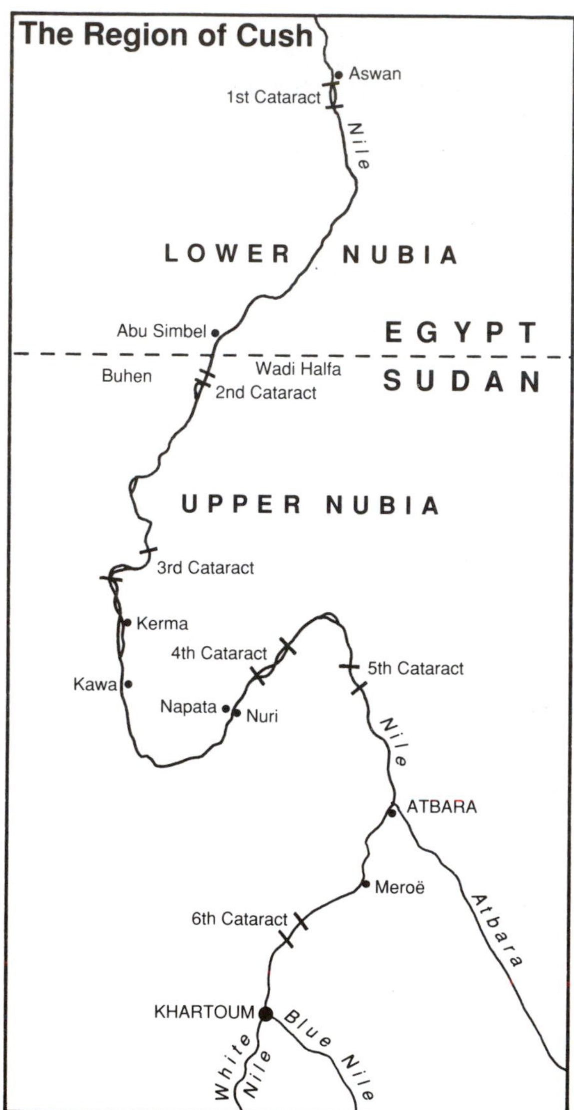

external attitudes and beliefs about Cush. The bow was indeed the weapon of the Nubians par excellence.[86]

86. B. G. Haycock, "The Place of the Napatan-Meroitic Culture in the History of the Sudan and Africa," *The Sudan in Africa* (Khartoum: Khartoum University Press, 1974), p. 38. I. Hofmann and A. Vorbichler, *Der Äthiopenlogos der Herodot* (Vienna: Institut für Afrikanistik und Ägyptologie, 1979), pp. 67, 172–77; idem, "Das Kambysesbild bei Herodot," *AfO* 27 (1980): 86–105, dismiss Cambyses' Ethiopian campaign as unhistorical. But their alternative explanation that Cambyses represents

For some time it was believed that confirmation of Cambyses' invasion existed in an inscription brought to Berlin in 1871, which mentions an enemy called KMBSWDN, who was identified as Cambyses by James Henry Breasted.[87] But this clashes with the chronology of the Meroitic kings established by George Reisner,[88] who dates the Nubian king of this inscription, Nastasen, to the fourth century B.C.[89] Fritz Hintze, who has reexamined the inscription, now reads the name as ḤMBSWTN, to be identified with Khabbash, a ruler of the first and second cataracts.[90] The king who would have been the contemporary of Cambyses would have been Amani-natake-lebte (538–519).[91]

Although the support from the Nastasen inscription proves to be illusory, there is no doubt that Cambyses invaded Nubia. We have an inscription of a Persian official from Cambyses' reign in the Wadi Hammamat in Upper Egypt, indicating that quarrying operations were conducted there.[92] Later Darius and Xerxes counted Cush (Kūša) as part of the Persian Empire. Cushite troops, wearing leopard and lion skins, served in Xerxes' army (Herodotus 7.69). Darius used ivory from Cush for his palace at Susa. Biennial gifts of gold, ebony, and ivory were sent by the Cushites to the Persians. On the Apadana stairway at Persepolis the Cushite delegation leads a long-necked animal, which looks like an okapi but which may have been intended to represent a giraffe—the tallest animal in the world and therefore a spectacular trophy.[93]

The Alleged Tauricide of the Apis

According to Herodotus (3.27), after the disastrous expedition to Siwa and the failure of the Ethiopian campaign, Cambyses returned to

---

among other legendary and mythological motifs Ahriman himself, the scion of the sun-god, and the mad Nabonidus, is wildly speculative.

87. J. H. Breasted, *A History of Egypt* (New York: Bantam, 1964 reprint of 1909 edition), p. 470.

88. G. A. Reisner, "The Meroitic Kingdom of Ethiopia: A Chronological Outline," *JEA* 9 (1923): 34–75.

89. J. M. Cook, "The Rise of the Achaemenids and Establishment of Their Empire," in *CHI* 2:214.

90. F. Hintze, *Studien zur Meroitischen Chronologie und zu den Opfertafeln aus den Pyramiden von Meroe* (Berlin: Akademie Verlag, 1959), pp. 17–20. See also A. Spalinger, "The Reign of King Chabbash: An Interpretation," *ZÄS* 105 (1978): 142–54.

91. *Africa in Antiquity I: The Essays*, eds. S. Hochfield and E. Riefstahl (Brooklyn: Brooklyn Museum, 1978), 2: 16.

92. Bianchi, "Perser in Ägypten," column 944; G. A. Wainwright, "The Date of the Rise of Meroë," *JEA* 38 (1952): 75.

93. A. Afshar, W. Dutz, and M. Taylor, "Giraffes at Persepolis," *Arch* 27/2 (1974): 114–17. By early dynastic times the giraffe was found only south of the first cataract. On the tomb of Rekhmire (1504–1450 B.C.) we see Nubians leading a giraffe. See *The Image of the Black in Western Art I: From the Pharaohs to the Fall of the Roman Empire* (New York: Menil Foundation, 1976), p. 48, fig. 14.

Memphis just as the Egyptians were celebrating the appearance of a new Apis bull. Cambyses misunderstood their festivities as exultation over his discomfiture. When he was shown the calf, Cambyses, who was nearly insane according to Herodotus (3.29), stabbed the Apis in the thigh, proclaiming: "Wretched wights, are these your gods, creatures of flesh and blood that can feel weapons of iron? that is a god worthy of the Egyptians."[94]

The Apis Bull

To understand the significance of Cambyses' act, we must examine the importance of the Apis bull in Egyptian religion.

The Apis (Egyptian *Hapi*) bull was regarded as the incarnation of Ptah, the creator god of Memphis.[95] It was held that Ptah inseminated Apis's mother with celestial fire. To qualify as the new Apis a calf had to have special characteristics according to Herodotus (3.28):

> The marks of this calf called Apis are these: he is black, and he has on his forehead a three-cornered white spot, and the likeness of an eagle on his back; the hairs of the tail are double, and there is a knot under the tongue.

John Ruffle comments: "They were selected by carefully observed signs, rather as a new Dalai Lama is chosen in Tibet, and taken to the temple where they were pampered throughout their life."[96]

After his ceremonious installation, the Apis would be extravagantly fed and cared for in the Apium (Greek *Apieion*), a special precinct opposite the temple of Ptah in Memphis. The Apis could be seen prancing in the courtyard each day at a fixed hour. Its movements were interpreted as oracular signs.[97]

Manetho claimed that the worship of the Apis went back to the Second Dynasty. Actually it was known in the First Dynasty, as shown

94. Diodorus Siculus (1.44.3) speaks of revolts by the Egyptians against the Persians because of "their lack of respect for the native gods." A later Persian king, Artaxerxes III (Ochus), was said by Plutarch (*De Iside et Osiride* 355B, #11) to have slain the Apis and to have eaten its flesh.

95. See H. Bonnet, "Apis," *Reallexikon der ägyptischen Religionsgeschichte* (Berlin: Walter de Gruyter, 1952), pp. 46–51. Other bulls include the Mnevis of Re at Heliopolis and the Buchis of Montu at Armant. Frankfort, *Ancient Egyptian Religion,* p. 10, argued that the Apis was the herald rather than the incarnation of Ptah. But see J. Vercoutter, "The Napatan Kings and Apis Worship," *Kush* 8 (1960): 64.

96. J. Ruffle, *The Egyptians* (Ithaca: Cornell University Press, 1977), p. 179; J. Vandier, *La religion égyptienne* (Paris: Presses Universitaires de France, 1949), pp. 234ff.

97. E. Kiessling, "Die Götter von Memphis . . . ," *Archiv für Papyrusforschung* 15 (1953): 26, n. 8.

Statue of the Apis bull. (Reproduced by courtesy of the trustees of the British Museum)

by archaeological evidence, and no doubt had its roots in prehistoric times.[98] It is from the reign of Amenophis III in the New Kingdom (fourteenth century B.C.) that we begin to find inscriptions regarding these bulls.[99] The first stage of the Serapeum, where the bulls were to be buried, was constructed around 1300 B.C., but the worship of the Apis reached its apogee from the Twenty-sixth Dynasty (650 B.C.) on.

A complete Apis inscription gave the bull's birthday, its accession date, the date of its death and burial (the latter was characteristically seventy days after the bull's death—compare Gen. 50:3), and then its length of life.[100] The average life span ranged from sixteen to nineteen years.[101]

The death of the Apis was announced in words similar to those used upon a pharaoh's demise: "the majesty of this god went forth to heaven"; or "the God was conducted in peace to the Beautiful West." A stele dated to Psammetichus I (612 B.C.) describes the embalming of the

98. W. B. Emery, *Archaic Egypt* (Baltimore: Penguin, 1961), p. 124.

99. Vandier, *La religion égyptienne*, p. 233.

100. See Breasted, *Ancient Records of Egypt*, vol. 4, nos. 974–79, 984.

101. Kitchen, *Third Intermediate Period*, p. 156; M. Malinine et al., *Catalogue des stèles du Sérapéum de Memphis I* (Paris: Imprimerie Nationale, 1968), p. xiii.

Apis: "every craftsman was occupied with his task, anointing the body with unguent, wrapping it in royal cloth of very god, his casket was of *ḥd*, *mr*-wood, and cedar, the choicest of every terrace."[102] In 1941 near the temple of Ptah at Memphis a number of objects associated with the Apis, dated to the reign of Shishak, were discovered.[103] These included four alabaster altars, a limestone manger, stands possibly used for an awning to shade the animal, and a large offering table (4 meters by 2 meters) used for washing or mummifying the bull.[104]

According to J. D. Ray,

> nothing in the Apis's life quite became him like the leaving of it; amid national mourning, often displayed hysterically, the bull was embalmed, encoffined and escorted out to the western desert, finally to lie in a massive granite sarcophagus in the catacomb known to modern visitors at Saqqâra as the Serapeum.[105]

The Serapeum

The bulls were carefully buried in mammoth sarcophagi carved from monolithic blocks of granite, measuring about 10 feet high and 13 feet long and weighing between 60 and 70 tons. One of the most spectacular discoveries in the history of Egyptology was the recovery of these sarcophagi by Auguste Mariette in 1851 at the so-called Serapeum (Greek *Sarapieion*) at Saqqarah, some twenty miles southwest of Cairo. They were found in underground galleries over one thousand feet long.[106] Mariette and his successors found only two of the sarcophagi intact; the others had been plundered at some unknown date.[107] Mariette found numerous bronze statuettes of the Apis, depicted with the sun disc and the uraeus (cobra) between its horns.[108]

Near the Serapeum spectacular discoveries were made by Walter B. Emery from 1964 until his death in 1971 and then by his successors,

102. Cited by Freedy and Redford, "Dates in Ezekiel," p. 477.

103. Kitchen, *Third Intermediate Period*, p. 189; I. E. S. Edwards et al., *Introductory Guide to the Egyptian Collection* (London: British Museum, 1969), p. 148. Ptolemy I donated over fifty silver talents and Ptolemy II gave one hundred talents of myrrh for the burials of Apis bulls.

104. M. el Amir, "The *sekos* of Apis at Memphis," *JEA* 34 (1948): 51–56; M. and A. M. Jones, "The Apis House Project at Mit Rahinah, First Season, 1982," *JARCE* 19 (1982): 51–58; idem, "The Apis House Project at Mit Rahinah: Preliminary Report of the Second and Third Seasons, 1982–1983," *JARCE* 20 (1983): 33–45.

105. J. D. Ray, "The World of North Saqqâra," *World Archaeology* 10/2 (1978): 151.

106. Malinine, *Catalogue*, p. vii. The so-called Petits Souterrains contained burials from the reign of Ramesses II to that of Psammetichus I; the Grands Souterrains contained the most spectacular sarcophagi, including those of the Persian era.

107. C. W. Ceram, *Gods, Graves, and Scholars* (New York: Knopf, 1953), p. 132.

108. G. Kater-Sibbes and M. J. Vermaseren, *Apis I–III* (Leiden: Brill, 1975–1977).

One of the gigantic sarcophagi for the Apis. (Courtesy of Andrew N. Gagg)

Geoffrey T. Martin and Harry S. Smith, until 1976.[109] They found a sacred animal necropolis with terraces, temples, ramps, and galleries dedicated to the gods, containing four million mummified ibises and five hundred baboons (both sacred to Thoth), five hundred thousand hawks (representing Horus), and a score of cows, representing Isis, the mother of the Apis bull.[110]

The Apis bull's mother had her Iseum built in the limestone cliffs on the desert edge north of the Serapeum perhaps as early as the sixth century B.C. Nearly a hundred inscriptions of people who took part in her burial have been recovered, the majority written in demotic, a late cursive form of Egyptian.[111]

Apis Inscriptions of the Persian Era

Two of the sarcophagi from the Serapeum have a direct bearing on

109. See W. B. Emery, "Preliminary Report on the Excavations at North Saqqara, 1969–70," *JEA* 57 (1971): 3–13; H. S. Smith, "Dates of the Obsequies of the Mothers of the Apis," *Revue d'Egyptologie* 24 (1972): 176–87.

110. Ray, "World," p. 151. Also recovered were a thousand documents in demotic, Greek, Aramaic, and Carian, primarily from the Ptolemaic period.

111. G. T. Martin et al., "The Excavations at North Saqqâra, 1969–70," *JEA* 57 (1971): 11–12.

the question of whether Herodotus was correct as to the tauricide by Cambyses.[112]

In the case of Apis A, we have the following data:

Birth: Twenty-seventh year (that is, of Amasis) = 543 B.C.

Death: Unknown, but by subtracting seventy days from the date of the burial, one could reach a date late in August 524 B.C.

Burial: Sixth year (of Cambyses) = November 6, 524 B.C.

Length of life: Nineteen years

For Apis B, we have the following data:

Birth: Fifth year (of Cambyses) = May 29, 525 B.C.

Death: Fourth year (of Darius) = August 31, 518 B.C.

Burial: Seventy days later

Length of life: Eight years

What is highly unusual is the overlap of a year and three months, from the birth of Apis B (May 525) to the death of Apis A (August 524), during which there were apparently two Apis bulls.[113] We do know that during the reign of Shoshenq III, around 798, one Apis died and another was installed in the same year.[114] Ideally a new Apis was found soon after the death of the old Apis, but during the Ptolemaic period there were often gaps of from one to three years between Apis bulls.[115]

Some have taken Apis A as the bull stabbed by Cambyses, and have explained the overlap by assigning the years of the profaned bull to Apis B.[116] A. Klasens holds that neither Apis A nor Apis B can be the bull killed by Cambyses.[117] He argues that the coexistence of two Apis

112. B. Porter and R. Moss, *Topographical Bibliography of Ancient Egyptian Hieroglyphic Texts . . . III: Memphis* (Oxford: Clarendon, 1931), p. 213. See Bresciani, "Egypt and the Persian Empire," p. 334; E. Drioton and J. Vandier, *L'Egypte* (Paris: Presses Universitaires de France, 1952), p. 624.

113. Such a situation is regarded as unthinkable by Atkinson, "Legitimacy of Cambyses," p. 170; and Evans, *Herodotus*, p. 52.

114. See Kitchen, *Third Intermediate Period*, p. 340.

115. Ideally the Apis should be found soon after the death of its predecessor. See Kitchen, *Third Intermediate Period*, p. 162. In A.D. 122, during the reign of Hadrian, a riot resulted upon the rediscovery of an Apis "after many years." C. Birley, *Lives of the Later Caesars* (Harmondsworth: Penguin, 1976), pp. 69–70.

116. This view was proposed by A. Wiedemann, *Der Tierkult der alten Ägypter* (Leipzig: J. C. Hinrichs, 1912), and accepted by H. R. Hall, *The Ancient History of the Near East* (London: Methuen, 1950), p. 312. See also Elgood, *Later Dynasties*, p. 122.

117. A. Klasens, "Cambyses en Egypte," *Ex Oriente Lux* (1945–1948): 347. I am indebted to Melani Howell for aid in translating this important Dutch article.

bulls was not inconceivable, citing one Apis bull who had to "wait in the wings" for three years before his predecessor died.

Klasens attempted to harmonize Herodotus's account with the inscriptional evidence of the two Apis sarcophagi by making the following assumptions: (1) Apis A died not in August 524, but rather at the end of May 525, just prior to Cambyses' invasion; (2) his burial was delayed because of the Persian invasion; (3) Herodotus (3.27) refers not to celebrating the birth but the accession of the Apis; (4) the bull killed by Cambyses was an Apis X, who was secretly interred; and (5) because we lack the accession date of Apis B, we do not know when he succeeded Apis A.[118]

While Klasens demonstrated that it was possible for two Apis bulls to coexist, and that it is remotely possible to insert an unknown Apis X into the sequence between Apis A and B, there is a flaw in his attempt to rehabilitate Herodotus on this crucial issue. It is clear that the sarcophagus of Apis A was dedicated by Cambyses himself.[119] As W. Culican points out,

> Cambyses takes the pharaonic titles "King of Upper and Lower Egypt, Son of Ra, Endowed with All Life" and is pictured wearing a pharaonic costume and kneeling before the Apis bull in an Egyptian posture of adoration.[120]

Thus the difficulty is not ultimately the chronological problem—although given the relative rarity of these animals and the short time involved this is also formidable—but rather the psychological improbability involved. It is difficult to believe that Cambyses would honor the Apis A by providing it with a sarcophagus in November 524, and then stab its successor a year later. He would certainly have been instructed in the significance of the rites by a counterpart of Udjahorresnet's in Memphis, and would not have misunderstood the rejoicing of the crowd at the acclamation of the new Apis.

The fact that we do not possess any Apis dedications for the reigns of Xerxes and of Artaxerxes I may be the result of a gap in our archaeological records or may indicate disruptions caused by periods of revolt.[121] (See the appendix on Serapis.)

As to the origin of Herodotus's account we can only speculate.

118. Ibid., pp. 346–48.

119. Kienitz, "Die politische Geschichte," p. 58; Bresciani, "Egypt and the Persian Empire," p. 334; A. Gardiner, *Egypt of the Pharaohs* (London: Oxford University Press, 1961), p. 364.

120. Culican, *Medes and Persians*, p. 60.

121. Kitchen, *Third Intermediate Period*, p. 162, n. 330.

Herodotus probably did not invent it. I would suggest the following scenario: If we assume that Cambyses stabbed himself accidentally in the thigh (see below), the rumor may have spread in Egypt that the Persian invader had been punished by the Egyptian gods. Later elaborations may have tailored the crime to fit the punishment by maintaining that Cambyses had stabbed the Apis in the thigh. Because such an Egyptian tale fit in so well with Herodotus's theme of *hubris* and avenging *nemesis,* Herodotus may have been happy to include it.[122]

We, therefore, have reason to believe that Cambyses, like Cyrus before him and Darius after him, tried to follow the general Persian policy of toleration and accommodation.[123] There is evidence of some negative actions, taken not from caprice, but to punish those segments of the religious establishment that failed to support him enthusiastically.

The Destruction of Temples

Although Cambyses did not murder the Apis bull, we need not doubt that the Persians destroyed some temples either to loot their contents or to punish resistance.[124] This is made clear by an explicit statement in a letter from the Jewish garrison in Elephantine to Bagohi, the Persian governor of Judah, on November 25, 407 B.C.:

> And during the days of the king(s) of Egypt our fathers had built that temple in Elephantine the fortress and when Cambyses (Aramaic KNBWZY) entered *Egypt* he found that temple built. And they overthrew the temples of the gods of Egypt, all (of them), but no one damaged anything in that temple.[125]

122. K. H. Waters, "The Purpose of Dramatisation in Herodotus," *Historia* 15 (1966): 157–71. See J. M. Balcer, *Herodotus & Bisitun* (Stuttgart: Franz Steiner, 1987), pp. 91–94.

123. Vercoutter, "Napatan Kings," p. 67: "One thing at least is certain, Shabaka did not interfere with the Apis cult, but on the contrary paid his tribute to the god as soon as he reached Memphis by seeing that his name was inscribed in the burial chamber of the animal god and so ensuring that he should benefit by the god's blessing."

124. Diodorus Siculus (1.46.4) speaks of the looting of silver, gold, and costly stones from the temples. See Klasens, "Cambyses en Egypte," p. 345. There is an interesting parallel in the dual policies of Piankhy (Twenty-fifth Dynasty), when he invaded Lower Egypt. According to Vercoutter, "Napatan Kings," p. 68: "On the one hand wrath against the people who had dared to resist him, with the result that most of them were taken captive and the treasuries of the town were carried off; on the other hand the desire to be recognized as legal ruler by the priesthood of the god Ptah. . . ."

125. B. Porten and J. C. Greenfield, *Jews of Elephantine and Arameans of Syene* (Jerusalem: Academon, 1976), p. 90; B. Porten, *Archives from Elephantine* (Berkeley: University of California Press, 1968), pp. 19–20.

The burned layer at Naucratis may have also resulted from the Persian invasion.

Later classical writers, including some who saw ruined temples in Egypt, ascribed their destruction to the great archfoe of Egypt, Cambyses. Strabo (17.1.27), who visited Egypt in 24 B.C., attributed many ruins to Cambyses:

> The city (Heliopolis) is now entirely deserted; it contains the ancient temple constructed in the Egyptian manner, which affords many evidences of the madness and sacrilege of Cambyses, who partly by fire and partly by iron sought to outrage the temples, mutilating them and burning them on every side, just as he did with the obelisks.[126]

Curtailment of Temple Donations

As Herodotus (2.37) observed, the Egyptian priests were well cared for:

> They neither consume nor spend aught of their own; sacred food is cooked for them, to each man is brought every day flesh of beeves and geese in great abundance, and wine of grapes too is given to them.

One measure of Cambyses, which certainly alienated many of the influential priests, was his act of drastically curtailing the donations to all but a few favored temples. Our evidence for this measure comes from the reverse side of Demotic Papyrus 215 of the Bibliothèque Nationale in Paris. Of the three temples that were exempted, we are certain only of the name of Memphis. Scholars have suggested "Babylon" near the later site of Cairo and Hermopolis Parva in the Delta as the other sites.[127] The decree stipulates:

> The cattle, which were given to the temples of the gods previously at the time of Pharaoh Amasis . . . with respect to them Cambyses commands, "Its half shall be given to them." As to the fowls, give them not to them. The priests themselves shall raise geese, and give (them) to their gods.

126. Pliny (*Natural History* 36.14.66–67) speaks of Cambyses storming a city and burning it. Justin (9) relates that Cambyses, "disgusted at the superstitions of the Egyptians, ordered the temple of Apis and the other gods to be demolished."

127. Kienitz, "Die politische Geschichte," p. 59; Klasens, "Cambyses en Egypte," p. 344, n. 37.

The text also mentions that the temples received gifts of grain, bread, wood, flax, incense, papyrus, and the equivalent of sixteen tons of silver.[128]

Many historians believe that the jaundiced portrait of Cambyses that emerges from the pages of Herodotus was probably the result of misinformation from hostile Egyptian priests, who resented Cambyses' curtailment of their provisions.[129] An example of such a prejudiced source is a late text from the Horus temple of Edfu, which associates the "Medes," that is, the Persians, with the villainous god Seth.

The Cambyses Legend

In 1899 a badly damaged Coptic manuscript was published that contained a highly garbled account of the invasion of Egypt by Cambyses. Cambyses is said to have sent a false letter in the name of the pharaoh to assemble the Egyptians at a festival for Apis. The Egyptian advisors, who are suspicious, have the people assemble, but also have them armed. The pharaoh at first believes that the people are armed against him, but is then informed of their true intent. Unfortunately the text breaks off at this point.

The text is hopelessly confused. Cambyses is identified with Nebuchadnezzar and the Persians with the Assyrians! Quite surprisingly the pharaoh places his trust in the Ammonites, Moabites, and Idumaeans. The references to the Gauls or Celts indicate that the text dates after the third century B.C.

H. L. Jansen believes that the text was originally composed in demotic by a native Egyptian in the second century B.C., and was then reworked by an Aramaic-speaking Jew. He maintains:

> It attempts to resolve existing points of conflict by referring to the common historical background and the faithfulness of the Jews toward their Egyptian lords and by showing indirectly that the Jewish contribution in Egyptian professional circles is recognized to be of high quality.[130]

128. W. Spiegelberg, *Die sog. demotisch Chronik des Pap. 215 der Bibliothèque National zu Paris* (Leipzig: J. C. Hinrichs, 1914), pp. 32–33; Olmstead, *History of the Persian Empire,* p. 91; Prášek, *Kambyses,* p. 12; W. Hinz, *Darius und die Perser* (Baden-Baden: Holle, 1976), p. 131.

129. Gardiner, *Egypt of the Pharaohs,* p. 364; Gyles, *Pharaonic Policies,* p. 39; Hinz, *Darius,* p. 131; Prášek, *Kambyses,* p. 30; R. N. Frye, *The Heritage of Persia* (Cleveland: World, 1963), p. 84; Posener, *La première domination,* pp. 164ff.

130. G. Müller, "Zu den Bruchstücken des kopt. Kambysesromans," *ZÄS* 39 (1901): 113–17; H. Grapow, "Untersuchungen über Stil und Sprache des kopt. Kambysesromans," *ZÄS* 74 (1938): 55–68; J. Schwartz, "Les conquérants perses et la littérature égyptienne," *BIFAO* 48 (1948): 65–80; H. L. Jansen, *The Coptic Story of Cambyses' Invasion of Egypt* (Oslo: I Kommisjon hos J. Dybwad, 1950);

The Death of Cambyses

In the spring of 522 Cambyses received bad news from Persia—he learned of a coup d'état and hastened home. According to Herodotus (3.64–66), Cambyses was traveling homeward in Syria, possibly in the area of Hamath,[131] when, jumping onto his horse, the cap fell off the sheath of his sword,[132] causing him to accidentally stab himself in the thigh. Gangrene developed and Cambyses died some three weeks later.[133] His death was viewed by the classical writers as a just punishment for his misdeeds.[134]

A controversy has arisen over whether Cambyses' death can be interpreted as a suicide. Darius's Behistun inscription, which is written in three languages, describes his death as follows:

> Old Persian: *uvāmaršiyuš amariyatā,* "he died his own death"
>
> Elamite: *hal-pi du-hi-e-ma hal-pi-ik,* "by his own death was dead"
>
> Akkadian: *mitūtu ramānišu mīti,*[135] "he died his own death"

Ernst Herzfeld interpreted this statement to mean that Cambyses committed suicide, an interpretation that has been accepted by many scholars.[136] On the other hand, Wilhelm Schulze cited parallels from twenty languages arguing that the phrase *he died his own death* can

---

L. S. B. MacCoull, "The Coptic Cambyses Narrative Reconsidered," *GRBS* 23 (1982): 185–88; E. Cruz-Uribe, "Notes on the Coptic Cambyses Romance," *Enchoria* 14 (1986): 51–56. Cambyses was the subject of a noted play, *Cambises* (1560–1561), by an English Renaissance scholar, Thomas Preston. See W. Armstrong, "The Background and Sources of Preston's *Cambises,*" *English Studies* 31 (1950): 129–35; W. D. Wolf, "Cambises," *English Literary Renaissance* 8 (1978): 116–19.

131. Herodotus (3.64) gives the name of the site as *Agbatana,* which was also the name of the Median capital Ecbatana (modern Hamadan). Josephus (*Antiquities* 11.30) places Cambyses' death at Damascus; Ctesias #12 has him die in Babylon. Olmstead, *History of the Persian Empire,* p. 92, places the site near Mount Carmel, but most guess that Agbatana reflects Akmatha (that is, Hamath).

132. Median and Persian scabbards had a tip that could fall off. See Yamauchi, *Foes,* p. 78, fig. 13; R. D. Barnett, "Median Arts," *IA* 2 (1962): 77–95.

133. According to Ctesias #12, Cambyses was carving a piece of wood with his knife when he accidentally stabbed himself. He died eleven days later.

134. Herodotus (3.64) has Cambyses struck in "the same part where he himself had once smitten the Egyptian god Apis." Justin (9) has the phrase *sponte evaginato* ("started out of its sheath") as though the sword was supernaturally moved against Cambyses.

135. Kent, *Old Persian,* pp. 117, 120; E. von Voigtlander, *The Bisitun Inscription of Darius the Great* (London: Lund Humphreys, 1978), p. 55; J. P. Asmussen, "Iranica, A: The Death of Cambyses . . . ," *Acta Orientalia* 31 (1968): 9–20.

136. E. Herzfeld, "Der Tod des Kambyses," *BSOAS* 8 (1935–1937): 589–97. Among those who have followed this interpretation are W. W. How and J. Wells, *A Commentary on Herodotus* (Oxford: Clarendon, 1928), 1: 396; Olmstead, *History of the Persian Empire,* p. 92; Kent, *Old Persian,* p. 177; H. S. Nyberg, *Der Reich der Achämeniden* (Bern: Francke Verlag, 1954), p. 75.

The unfinished tomb of Cambyses at Takht-i-Rustam. (Courtesy of The Oriental Institute, University of Chicago)

mean a natural death.[137] Muhammed Dandamayev points out that the phrase in Akkadian does not mean a normal death nor is it the usual expression for suicide. It is rather an unusual phrase that intimates a premature, unexpected, and violent death.[138]

The Tomb of Cambyses

We do not know whether the body of Cambyses was carried back to Persia for burial, though this is likely. It appears that Cambyses had begun to prepare a tomb for himself prior to his departure for Egypt. Some ruins on the south bank of the Pulvar River, six kilometers (3.6 miles) north of Persepolis, called today Takht-i-Rustam (The Throne of Rustam) were identified by Herzfeld in 1932 as the unfinished grave of Cambyses.[139] Herzfeld excavated in the center of the monument but failed to reach virgin soil.[140]

Other scholars have tried to interpret the structure as the foundation

137. W. Schulze, "Der Tod des Kambyses," *Sitzungsberichte der Preussischen Akademie der Wissenschaften* (1912): 685–703. See also J. Puhvel, "The 'Death of Cambyses' and Hittite Parallels," in *A. Pagliaro Festschrift* (Rome: Istituto di Glottologia di Roma, 1969), 3:169–75.

138. Dandamayev, *Persien*, pp. 146–48.

139. E. Herzfeld, *The Persian Empire* (Wiesbaden: F. Steiner, 1968), p. 36.

140. S. Matheson, *Persia: An Archaeological Guide*, 2d ed. (London: Faber and Faber, 1976), p. 223.

of a fire altar or shrine, but the striking similarities of the dimensions and orientation of the site with those of Cyrus's own grave are convincing proofs that this was also a tomb. The lower stage is 12.22 by 13.28 meters and 1.30 meters high. The second stage has a height of 1.06 meters; little remains of the third stage. The lack of evidence for the use of the toothed chisel, which became widespread after 515 B.C., indicates a date prior to this.[141]

Foundation slabs of limestone for twenty-three column bases in two parallel rows were discovered in 1973, located 170 meters east of Takht-i-Rustam at Dashti-i Gohar. The building, which has the same orientation as the Takht-i-Rustam, may very well have been an audience hall built by Cambyses.[142]

Cambyses' Survivors

Cambyses was survived by his three sisters, who were also his wives (Herodotus 3.31). Such consanguineous marriages had been a common practice in ancient Elam in southwest Persia.[143] The Egyptians, who also followed a matrilineal line of descent, married not only their sisters, but in the case of Akhnaton, even his own daughters![144]

Cambyses first married his sister Atossa, but did not take her with him to Egypt (Herodotus 3.31–32), a fact that may have become a source of tension. She later married the false Smerdis (Gaumata) and then Darius, by whom she became the mother of Xerxes.

Cambyses also married a sister, whose name is not given by Herodo-

141. W. Kleiss, "Der Takht-i Rustam bei Persepolis und das Kyros-grab in Pasargadae," *AA* (1971): 157–62; W. Kleiss and P. Calmeyer, "Das unvollendete achaemenidische Felsgrab bei Persepolis," *AMI* n.F. 8 (1975): 81–98.

142. A. B. Tilia, "Discovery of an Achaemenian Palace near Takht-i Rustam to the North of the Terrace of Persepolis," *Iran* 12 (1974): 200–204; idem, "Discoveries at Persepolis 1972–1973," in *Proceedings of the IInd Annual Symposium on Archaeological Research in Iran,* ed. F. Bagherzadeh (Tehran: Iranian Centre for Archaeological Research, 1974), pp. 243–44; E. Porada, "Classic Achaemenian Architecture and Sculpture," in *CHI* 2:801–802; W. Kleiss, "Zur Entwicklung der achaemenidischen Palastarchitektur," *IA* 15 (1980): 199–206.

143. W. Hinz, *Persia c. 2400–1800 B.C.* (Cambridge: Cambridge University Press, 1963), p. 24; idem, *Persia c. 1800–1550* (Cambridge: Cambridge University Press, 1964), p. 6; R. Labat, *Elam and Western Persia c. 1200–1000 B.C.* (Cambridge: Cambridge University Press, 1964), p. 21. Xanthus of Lydia, fragment 28, remarked: "The Magi think it permissible to have sexual intercourse with mothers and daughters and sisters." D. D. Sanjana, "The Alleged Practice of Consanguineous Marriages in Ancient Iran," *Zarathushtra in the Gathas,* 2d ed. (Leipzig: Harrassowitz, 1899), pp. 218–24, denies that the Iranians practiced such incestuous marriages.

144. J. Černy, "Consanguineous Marriages in Pharaonic Egypt," *JEA* 40 (1954): 23–29; H. Bell, "Brother and Sister Marriage in Graeco-Roman Egypt," *Revue internationale des droits de l'antiquité,* 2d ser. (1949): 83–92.

tus. Other sources give her the name of Roxane or Meroë.[145] She berated Cambyses for killing their brother, whereupon he kicked his pregnant wife and killed her (Herodotus 3.32). He was married to his youngest sister, Artystone, and also to Phaidime, a daughter of Otanes (Herodotus 3.68), an Achaemenid noble and one of the six who allied themselves with Darius.

It was Cambyses' misfortune that he left no progeny (Herodotus 3.66). According to the fertile imagination of Ctesias, Roxane bore him a stillborn child without a head.[146]

145. Josephus, *Antiquities* 2.249; Strabo 17.5.790.
146. Ctesias #14; König, *Die Persika,* p. 7.

Darius

Name

The name *Darius* comes from the Greek form, *Dareios,* used, for example, in the Septuagint. The transliteration of the name in Hebrew is *Dāryāwesh.* The original Old Persian was *Darayavaush* from *Dāraya-Vahu-Manah* ("he who sustains good thought"). The corresponding spelling in Elamite was *Dariamaush* and in Akkadian *Dariamush.* In Egyptian the king's name was spelled (*I*)*ntrywš.*

Darius was the name of three Persian kings: Darius I or Darius the Great (522–486 B.C.), whom we shall refer to simply as Darius; Darius II (423–405 B.C.), who was known as Nothus; and Darius III (335–330 B.C.), also known as Codomannus, the last Persian king, whose kingdom was conquered by Alexander.

Biblical References

Darius is mentioned prominently in Ezra 4–6 (compare Hag. 1:1, 15; 2:10; Zech. 1:1, 7; 7:1) as the Persian monarch under whom the temple at Jerusalem was finally reconstructed after the Jewish return from exile under Cyrus. "Darius the Persian" in Nehemiah 12:22 was probably Nothus, but Codomannus has also been suggested.[1]

Cuneiform Sources

The inscriptions of the Achaemenid kings were commonly written in trilingual cuneiform versions: Old Persian (OP);[2] Elamite, the agglutinative language of the area around Susa;[3] and Akkadian, the Semitic language of the Assyrians and Babylonians.[4]

As noted earlier (see chapter 2) Walter Hinz, following the suggestion of Franz H. Weissbach (1911), believes that Darius invented the OP script that must therefore be dated from Darius's time.[5] This theory is based on the observation that the Old Persian version was added only later at Behistun, and on Hinz's interpretation of paragraph 70 of the OP version of the Behistun inscription.

This view has been endorsed by Heinz Luschey, Manfred Mayrhofer, and Leo Trümpelmann, but it has been opposed, both in its earlier and later versions, by I. M. Diakonoff, Ilya Gershevitch, Roman Ghirshman, Richard Hallock, Ernst Herzfeld, Julius Lewy, Hans Schaeder, Vasilii Struve, and Ran Zadok, who believe that the OP script goes back at least to Cyrus. They would argue that paragraph 70 refers to the innovation of the writing of OP in Aramaic characters or on parchment.[6] This would seem to be the preferable interpretation.

1. See F. M. Cross, "The Discovery of the Samaria Papyri," *BA* 26 (1963): 121; idem, "Aspects of Samaritan and Jewish History in Late Persian and Hellenistic Times," *HTR* 59 (1966): 203ff.

2. See R. G. Kent, *Old Persian,* 2d ed. (New Haven: American Oriental Society, 1953); W. Brandenstein and M. Mayrhofer, *Handbuch des Altpersischen* (Wiesbaden: Harrassowitz, 1964).

3. See H. H. Paper, *The Phonology and Morphology of Royal Achaemenid Elamite* (Ann Arbor: University of Michigan Press, 1955); E. Reiner, "The Elamite Language," *Handbuch der Orientalistik* I Abt., 2 Band, 1–2 (Leiden: Brill, 1969), pp. 54–67. For the Elamite version of Darius's Behistun inscription, see G. Cameron, "The Elamite Version of the Bisitun Inscription," *JCS* 14 (1960): 59–68; W. Hinz, "Die Behistan-Inscrift des Darius in ihrer ursprünglichen Fassung," *AMI* 7 (1974): 121–34.

4. For Akkadian, see W. H. Ph. Römer, "Akkadian," in *A Basic Bibliography for the Study of the Semitic Languages,* I, ed. J. H. Hospers (Leiden: Brill, 1973), pp. 3–37. For the Akkadian version of Darius's Behistun inscription, see W. C. Benedict and E. von Voigtlander, "Darius' Bisitun Inscription, Babylonian Version, Lines 1–29," *JCS* 10 (1956): 1–10; E. von Voigtlander, *The Bisitun Inscription of Darius the Great* (London: Lund Humphries, 1978); R. Schmitt, "Zur Babylonischen Version der Bīsutūn Inschrift," *AfO* 27 (1980): 106–26. For the complex linguistic situation of written and unwritten languages and dialects in ancient Iran, see A. V. Rossi, "La varietà linguistica nell'Iran Achaemenide," *Aiōn* 3 (1981): 141–96.

5. R. Borger and W. Hinz, "Eine Dareios-Inschrift aus Pasargadae," *ZDMG* 109 (1959): 117–27; W. Hinz, *Darius und die Perser* (Baden-Baden: Holle, 1976), p. 170. See also chapter 2, notes 51–55.

6. J. Lewy, "The Problems Inherent in Section 70 of the Bisutun Inscription," *HUCA* 25 (1954): 184, appealed to an apocryphal letter of Themistocles, which reads: "Send me the four biggest of the silver kraters and gold censers that are inscribed in Old Assyrian letters (i.e. cuneiform) and not in the

In any case, OP seems to have been used almost exclusively for royal inscriptions. Gershevitch goes so far as to speculate that there may have been only one scribe needed in the entire realm for inscribing OP texts, and that there may have been no more than twenty who could read this script.[7] Against this extreme position we may note that there are some monolingual OP seals found in the foundations at Persepolis and five short OP inscriptions found in Egypt.[8]

We have about sixty different OP inscriptions of Darius (one hundred if we include duplicates). This is more than from all the other Achaemenid kings combined.[9] The inscriptions after Darius are often nothing more than imitations of the texts of Darius.

The Behistun Inscription

By far the longest and most informative text from the Achaemenid era is Darius's trilingual Behistun inscription (DB).[10] The site, known in Farsi or modern Persian as *Bīsītun* (Arabic *Beḥistūn*; OP **bagastāna,* "place of the God"), is located twenty miles east of Kermanshah on the key route that led from Mesopotamia to the Iranian plateau.

There around 518 B.C. on a sheer cliff 69 meters (225 feet) above the plain Darius had carved a monumental record of his rise to power.[11] One could get to only about 30 meters (100 feet) below the monument so that its meaning remained a puzzle to the ancients. Ctesias thought that the relief depicted Queen Semiramis. Persian Muslims held that it represented a teacher beating his pupils. Persian Christians maintained that it represented Christ and his twelve disciples. Robert Ker Porter, who visited the site in 1818, thought that it portrayed the Assyrian king Shalmaneser in his triumph over the ten tribes of Israel.

The relief actually features figures of a spearbearer, a bowbearer, then Darius treading upon the supine pretender Gaumata, followed by

---

script (i.e. Aramaic) recently used [or prescribed] by Darius, father of Xerxes, for the Persians." On the other hand, C. Nylander, "ΑΣΣΥΡΙΑ ΓΡΑΜΜΑΤΑ, Remarks on the 21st 'Letter of Themistokles,' " *Opuscula Atheniensia* 8 (1968): 119–36, interprets the "Old Assyrian letters" as Aramaic, and the script prescribed by Darius as Old Persian.

7. I. Gershevitch, preface to *The Evidence of the Persepolis Tablets,* by R. T. Hallock (Cambridge: Middle East Centre, 1971), pp. 4, 7.

8. M. A. Dandamayev, *Persien unter den ersten Achämeniden,* trans. H.-D. Pohl (Wiesbaden: Reichert, 1976), p. 35.

9. J. Harmatta, "A Recently Discovered Old Persian Inscription," *AAH* 2 (1952–54): 11–12; E. Yamauchi, "The Achaemenid Capitals," *NEASB* 8 (1976): 42–43.

10. All references to the DB will be to the Old Persian version found in Kent.

11. The last recorded event is dated to 519.

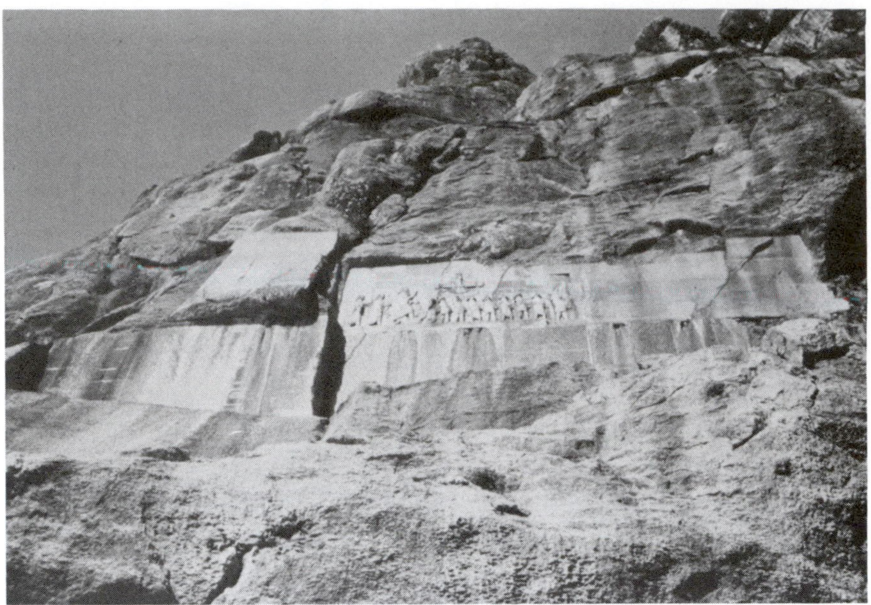

The Behistun relief.

nine other bound rebels including a Scythian wearing a pointed hat, who was added later. Hovering over the prisoners is a divine winged figure, which usually is interpreted as a representation of the god Ahuramazda.[12]

The texts are spread over an area 7 meters (23 feet) high and 18 meters (59 feet) wide. The relief panel is about 3 meters (10 feet) high and 5.5 meters (18 feet) wide. Darius is depicted as life-size, 1.73 meters (5 feet 8 inches), his companions are but 1.47 meters (4 feet 10 inches), and the rebels are on a diminutive scale of only 1.17 meters (3 feet 10 inches).

Darius's lancebearer was Gobryas (OP *Gaubaruva*), and his bowbearer was Intaphernes (OP *Vindafarnāh*). Short labels help to identify each of the defeated rebels. In addition to Gaumata the magos, who lies on his back, we have the bound figures of the following (with corresponding passages in the DB indicated):

1. Açina, professed king of Elam (DB #16)
2. Nidintu-Bel, rebel king in Babylon (DB #18)
3. Phraortes, king of Media (DB #24)
4. Martiya, a Persian who sought to be king in Elam (DB #22)

12. For example, by H. Luschey, "Studien zu dem Darius-Relief von Bisutun," *AMI* 1 (1968): 80. But see chapter 12, pp. 430–33.

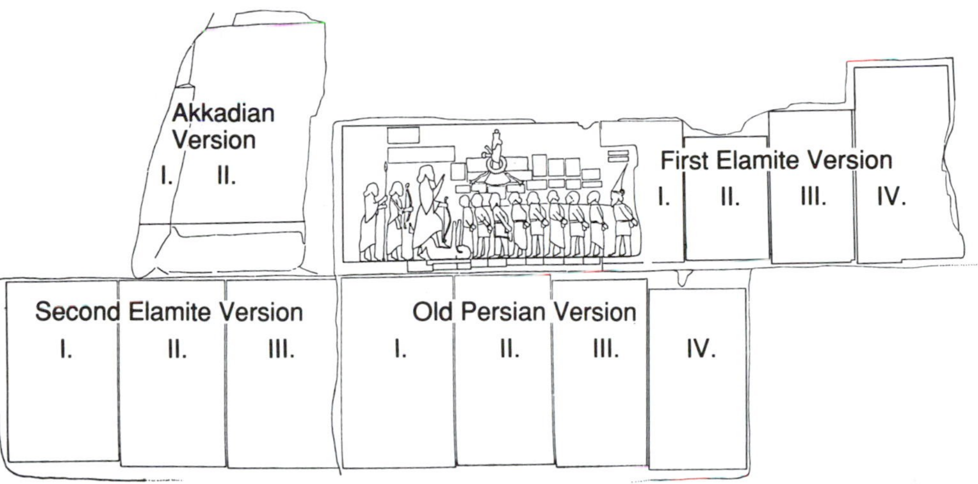

The Behistun Inscription (After L. Trümpelmann).

5. Ciçantakhma, a Sagartian (DB #33)
6. Vahyazdata, a Persian, who claimed to be the true Smerdis (DB #40)
7. Arkha, an Armenian, who claimed to be the son of Nabonidus (DB #49)
8. Frada from Margiana (DB #38)
9. Skunkha, the Scythian wearing a pointed cap (DB #74)[13]

According to the observations of Trümpelmann,[14] which have been accepted by Luschey[15] and Hinz,[16] the carving of the relief and the engraving of the trilingual inscription were accomplished in the following stages:

1. The relief.
2. The first Elamite version (DBelam) on four panels to the right.
3. The Akkadian version (DBbab) on the projecting rock to the left.
4. The Old Persian version in four panels below the relief.
5. A second copy of the Elamite version in three panels below the Akkadian version was added in 518, as the addition of the rebel Skunkha had damaged the first Elamite version.
6. A fifth panel of Old Persian after the insertion of Skunkha's figure.

13. Luschey, "Studien," pp. 77–79.

14. L. Trümpelmann, "Zur Enstehungsgeschichte des Monumentes Dareios' I. von Bisutun und zur Datierung der Einfuhrung der altpersischen Schrift," *AA* (1967): 281–98.

15. Luschey, "Studien," p. 91.

16. Hinz, "Die Behistan-Inschrift."

Darius also had the contents of this inscription widely distributed in the vernacular dialects throughout the empire (see Esther 1:22; 3:12; 8:9). We have a fragmentary Akkadian text from Babylon. Ursula Seidl believes that fragments from Babylon may indicate that not only the text but the relief was also reproduced.[17] Aramaic copies were also sent to the Persian outpost of Jewish mercenaries in distant Elephantine in Upper Egypt.[18]

Among the three versions, the Akkadian has been badly damaged while the Old Persian is the best preserved. In 1948 George Cameron was able to lower himself from the top of the mountain on a painter's scaffold to make latex squeezes of the inscription. In 1957 he made additional squeezes suspended in a boatswain's chair. It was then that he discovered that the text to the right of the relief was slavishly identical to the lower Elamite version.[19]

The Decipherment of Cuneiform

In 1621 Pietro della Valle had visited the ruins of Persepolis and made some copies of cuneiform signs. Carsten Niebuhr in 1765 discerned that three different writing systems were employed at Persepolis. By 1802 Georg Grotefend, a high school teacher in Göttingen, identified the signs for the names of Hystaspes, Darius, and Xerxes, although the signs were not alphabetic as he supposed, but syllabic. He reasoned correctly that the cuneiform texts contained the formula, "king of kings," preserved in later Sasanid formulas.[20] Unfortunately Grotefend's pioneer efforts made little impact at the time.[21]

17. U. Seidl, "Ein Relief Dareios' I. in Babylon," *AMI* 9 (1976): 125–30.

18. A. E. Cowley, *Aramaic Papyri of the Fifth Century* B.C. (Oxford: Clarendon, 1923), pp. 248–71; J. C. Greenfield and B. Porten, *The Bisitun Inscription of Darius the Great: Aramaic Version* (London: Humphries, 1982). An Akkadian charter for a guild from the reign of Cyrus implies that the craftsmen were addressed in Aramaic according to D. B. Weisberg, *Guild Structure and Political Alliance in Early Achaemenid Mesopotamia* (New Haven: Yale University Press, 1967), p. 15.

19. In 1904 L. W. King and R. Campbell Thompson had also used a kind of boatswain's chair to copy the inscription. See L. W. King and R. C. Thompson, *The Sculptures and Inscriptions of Darius the Great on the Rock of Behistun in Persia* (London: British Museum, 1907). This served as the standard edition until Cameron's improved readings. See G. Cameron, "Darius Carved History on Ageless Rock," *National Geographic* 98 (Dec. 1950): 825–44; idem, "The Monument of King Darius at Bisitun," *Arch* 13 (1960): 162–71; idem, "The Old Persian Text of the Bisitun Inscription," *JCS* 5 (1951): 47–54; R. G. Kent, "Cameron's Old Persian Readings at Bisitun Restorations and Notes," *JCS* 5 (1951): 55–57; M. W. Stolper, "George G. Cameron (1905–1979)," *BA* 43 (1980): 183–89.

20. The phrase is found as early as the reign of Tiglath-pileser I of Assyria (1116–1078 B.C.). See R. Frye, "The Charisma of Kingship in Ancient Iran," *IA* 4 (1964): 37. It appears in the New Testament (Rev. 17:14; 19:16) and was retained by the late Shah of Iran.

21. C. H. Gordon, *Forgotten Scripts* (New York: Basic, 1968), pp. 47–52.

We owe the full decipherment of Old Persian and ultimately all the cuneiform scripts to the perseverance and courage of the Englishman, Henry Rawlinson, who from 1835 to 1847 succeeded in copying almost all of the Behistun inscription, often working in total disregard for his life and limb. As he recounted:

> On reaching the recess which contains the Persian text of the record, ladders are indispensable in order to examine the upper portion of the table; and even with ladders there is considerable risk, for the foot-ledge is so narrow, about eighteen inches or at most two feet in breadth, that with a ladder long enough to reach the sculptures sufficient slope cannot be given to enable a person to ascend, and, if the ladder be shortened in order to increase the slope, the upper inscriptions can only be copied by standing on the topmost step of the ladder, with no other support than steadying the body against the rock with the left arm, while the left hand holds the notebook, and the right hand is employed with the pencil. In this position I copied all the upper inscriptions, and the interest of the occupation entirely did away with any sense of danger.[22]

Rawlinson's extraordinary dedication to this task is revealed by the fact that after the Afghan War he spurned a prestigious British post in India to complete his self-appointed mission of copying the inscription. As Rawlinson related:

> At the close of that war in 1843 I was offered, as a reward for my services, the highest political employment and an assured career in India; but I had not forgotten Behistun. It had become the ambition of my life to carry on my cuneiform researches, and especially to work out the Babylonian puzzle; and accordingly, to the astonishment of my friends, I deliberately declined the brilliant prospect opened out to me in India, and elected to return to what was called "exile" at Baghdad, where for twelve weary years . . . I resided, in an exhausting climate, cut off from all society, sparingly supplied with the comforts of civilization, and, in fact, doing penance in order to attain a great literary object.[23]

By 1847 Rawlinson had correctly identified all but two of the thirty-seven syllables of the Old Persian script.

22. H. Rawlinson, "Notes on Some Paper Casts of Cuneiform Inscriptions," *Archaeologia* 34 (1852), cited in *The Treasures of Time,* ed. L. Deuel (New York: Avon, 1961), p. 115.

23. H. Rawlinson, *The Athenaeum* (Nov. 8, 1884), p. 493, cited by A. V. W. Jackson, *Persia—Past and Present* (New York: Macmillan, 1906), p. 179, n. 1.

Classical Sources

The dramatist Aeschylus, who personally fought against the Persians at Marathon and Salamis, included important information in *The Persians,* first performed in 472. Aeschylus had the ghost of Darius appear to his wife to rebuke the folly of their son, Xerxes. Aeschylus misconstrued the act of *proskunēsis* by the Persians before their king as an act of worship rather than of obeisance, and hence called Darius *isotheos* ("equal to god") and *theos Persais* ("the Persians' god").[24]

Ctesias, the Greek physician who spent seventeen years at the court of Artaxerxes II (405–359), wrote in conscious opposition to Herodotus. He was followed by later writers such as Deinon, Plutarch, and Xenophon, but is a notoriously poor source. In marked contrast to Herodotus, Ctesias gets only one of the names of the six conspirators with Darius correct.[25]

Herodotus gives us the most complete account of the accession of Darius (3.66–88), his satrapies (3.89–96), his invasion of European Scythia (4.1–142), the Ionian revolt from 499 to 494 (5.23–6.27), the punitive expedition shipwrecked at Mount Athos in 492 (6.42–44), and the famous Battle of Marathon in 490 (6.112–17).[26]

There are some passages in Herodotus that classicists have rejected as entirely fabricated such as the celebrated "constitutional debate" (3.80–88), during which three conspirators discuss the relative merits of three forms of government: Otanes argues for democracy, Megabyzus for oligarchy, and Darius for monarchy.

Although these ideas and the mode of presentation have been appraised as thoroughly Greek,[27] some Iranologists have argued that there may be elements in the passage that go back to Persian traditions.[28] Soviet scholars Vasilii Struve and Muhammed Dandamayev

24. In Hebrew, Arabic, and Greek the verb *worship* also has the root meaning "to prostrate oneself" on the ground. See E. Yamauchi, "*ḥāwâ*" in *Theological Wordbook of the Old Testament,* eds. R. L. Harris, G. L. Archer, and B. K. Waltke (Chicago: Moody, 1981), 1: 267–69. There is a continuing controversy as to whether Alexander demanded "obeisance" or "worship" from his followers. See J. P. V. D. Balsdon, "The 'Divinity' of Alexander," *Historia* 1 (1950): 363–88; E. Fredericksmeyer, "Three Notes on Alexander's Deification," *AJAH* 4 (1979): 1–9.

25. Dandamayev, *Persien,* p. 110.

26. See R. Drews, *The Greek Accounts of Eastern History* (Cambridge: Harvard University Press, 1973), pp. 75ff.

27. K. Bringmann, "Die Verfassungsdebatte bei Herodot 3,80–82 und Dareios' Aufstieg zur Königsherrschaft," *Hermes* 104 (1976): 266–79.

28. F. Gschnitzer, *Die sieben Perser und das Königtum des Dareios* (Heidelberg: Carl Winter, 1977), p. 31, believes that Herodotus 3.83, about Otanes' refusal to be considered a candidate, rests on genuine tradition. Although Herodotus's account is thoroughly Greek, Gschnitzer calls attention to Judges 9:7–15 and 1 Samuel 8:11–18 to support the possibility of something like a *Verfassungsdebatte* in the ancient Near East.

believe that the debate may reflect some of the motifs found in Darius's inscriptions.[29] Impressed by the accuracy of Herodotus's knowledge of Persian names, Rudiger Schmitt also argues that the passage contains authentic material and should not be dismissed as entirely fabricated.[30] A classicist, Patrick T. Brannan, noting coincidences between Ctesias and Herodotus in the passage, has also concluded that the debate "may be prudently considered substantially historical."[31]

When it comes to the account of the overthrow of the usurper Gaumata/Bardiya/Pseudo-Smerdis by Darius and his six colleagues, Herodotus reveals an impressive correspondence with the information that can be derived from Darius's Behistun inscription.[32] His statement that the usurper reigned for seven months matches the exact interval of Gaumata's revolt, which lasted six months and twenty-seven days.[33] He transmitted with remarkable accuracy all but one of the six names of Darius's colleagues. And even in that one case he gave us a genuine Persian name that may be explained as a later substitution.[34] In other passages as well, he demonstrates a correct knowledge of Persian names as confirmed by new evidence from the publication of the tablets from Persepolis.[35] Delores Heygi concludes, "a comparison of the sources of Herodotus with other Greek and Persian evidence and an examination of the OP names equally point to the fact that Herodotus had here and there very good information."[36]

Among those who could have been able to supply Herodotus with such accurate information, passed down in their families, would have been the descendants of the six co-conspirators. For example, Zopyrus, the son of Megabyzus (Herodotus 3.70, 81) and the grandson of Zopyrus, one of the six, deserted to Athens from the Persians (Herodo-

29. Dandamayev, *Persien*, pp. 145, 163.

30. R. Schmitt, "Die Verfassungsdebatte bei Herodot 3, 80–82 und die Etymologie des Dareios-Namens," *Historia* 26 (1977): 243–44.

31. T. Brannan, "Herodotus and History: The Constitutional Debate Preceding Darius' Accession," *Traditio* 19 (1963): 438.

32. For a chronological integration of information from the DB and from Herodotus, see J. Wiesehöfer, *Der Aufstand Gaumātas und die Anfänge Dareios' I* (Bonn: Rudolf Habelt, 1978), pp. 96–97.

33. A. Poebel, "The Duration of the Reign of Smerdis, the Magian, and the Reigns of Nebuchadnezzar III, and Nebuchadnezzar IV," *AJSL* 56 (1939): 130. Poebel refutes the attempt of A. T. Olmstead, "Darius and His Behistun Inscription," *AJSL* 55 (1938): 392ff., to show that Bardiya reigned a year and seven months, instead of just seven months. Herodotus (3.66–67) is also correct in assigning seven years and five months to Cambyses.

34. See Schmitt, "Zur babylonischen Version der Bīsutūn-Inschrift," *AfO* 27 (1980): 125; idem, "Die Verfassungsdebatte," pp. 243–44.

35. On these tablets, see chapter 10 on Persepolis.

36. D. Hegyi, "Historical Authenticity of Herodotus in the Persian 'Logoi,' " *AAH* 21 (1973): 80.

tus 3.160).[37] Other descendants of these ruling families could have been contacted by Herodotus in western Asia Minor.[38]

Ancestry and Preaccession Years

Darius, born around 550, was about twenty-eight years old when he came to the throne.[39] He was not a member of the family of Cyrus and Cambyses but belonged to a collateral Achaemenid line. Both his grandfather Arsames, and his father Hystaspes, the satrap of Parthia, were still alive at the time of his accession in 522.

Darius served under Cambyses in Egypt as a spearbearer among the Immortals, an elite force of ten thousand royal soldiers. In the inscription engraved by his tomb at Naqsh-i Rustam (DNb) he boasted: "Trained am I both with hands and with feet. As a horseman I am a good horseman. As a bowman I am a good bowman both afoot and on horseback. As a spearman I am a good spearman both afoot and on horseback."[40]

The Usurpation of Gaumata

According to Darius (DB #10) Cambyses secretly murdered his full brother before he invaded Egypt in 525. Since Cambyses was away in Egypt for a number of years, the people in Persia became evil:

> Afterwards, there was one man, a Magian (*maguš*), Gaumata by name; he rose up from Paishiyauvada. A mountain by name Arakadri—from there 14 days of the month Viyakhna (March 11, 522) were past when he rose up. He lied to the people thus: "I am Smerdis (OP *Bardiya*), the son of Cyrus, brother of Cambyses." After that all the people became rebellious from Cambyses, (and) went over to him, both Persia and Media and the other provinces.[41]

The name of Cambyses' brother was *Bṛdiya* in Old Persian (Elamite *Birtiya*, Akkadian *Barziya*), which was rendered as *Smerdis* by Herodo-

37. Dandamayev, *Persien*, p. 145; J. Wells, "The Persian Friends of Herodotus," *JHS* 27 (1907): 37–47.

38. Drews, *Greek Accounts*, pp. 82–83.

39. A. T. Olmstead, *History of the Persian Empire* (Chicago: University of Chicago Press, 1948), p. 107; Hinz, *Darius*, p. 145.

40. Kent, *OP*, p. 140.

41. DB #11; Kent, *OP*, p. 120.

tus and *Mardos* by Aeschylus.[42] The usurper who pretended to be Smerdis was called Gaumata by Darius in the Behistun inscription. To avoid confusion we will use Bardiya as the name of Cambyses' brother and Gaumata for the usurper, avoiding the use of the name *Smerdis*, which could be used for either.

Conflict between princely brothers is well attested in the history of the Achaemenid house. Royal fratricide became well known in the west as Plato (*Laws* 3, 695B) and Plutarch (*Moralia* 490A) refer to it.

According to the Behistun inscription (and Ctesias), the murder of Bardiya by Cambyses took place before Cambyses invaded Egypt in 525. Herodotus (3.30) erred in placing the crime during Cambyses' stay in Egypt.

Gaumata began the revolt on March 11, 522. From contemporary texts we see that he was recognized by April 14 in Babylonia, although others acknowledged Cambyses as king as late as April 18. By July 1 Gaumata was widely recognized throughout the empire.[43]

The view that Gaumata as a magos was championing the cause of the Medes against the Persians has been suggested,[44] but the center of the revolt, Paishiyauvada, is considered to lie in the Persian heartland around Pasargadae.[45] Darius himself admitted that Gaumata had widespread support. Herodotus (3.67) says that upon his death, "all the Asiatics except the Persians wished him back."

On the other hand, Darius claimed that Gaumata terrorized those who would oppose him, and also took away pastures, herds, slaves, and houses from his enemies.[46] The Akkadian version (DBbab #12) is even stronger than the corresponding OP passage: "He was killing many people who had known Barziya previously." This may explain why even those who knew the imposture were afraid of denouncing it.

According to Herodotus (3.67) Gaumata proclaimed exemption from taxes and compulsory military service for three years.[47] On the basis of

42. Other variant spellings include: Nicolaus of Damascus *Merdis*, Pompeius Trogus *Mergid*, Aristotle *Smerdēs*, Ctesias *Tanyoxarkes*, Xenophon *Tanaozares*. See Wiesehöfer, *Der Aufstand*, p. 46; Dandamayev, *Persien*, p. 108, n. 444. According to Ctesias, Tanyoxarkes was made the satrap of Bactria, Chorasmia, Parthia, and Carmania; according to Xenophon, Tanaozares was the satrap of Media, Armenia, and Cadusia. If indeed Bardiya was a satrap, his murder would have been more difficult to conceal. But these late traditions are hardly reliable.

43. Dandamayev, *Persien*, pp. 126–27; Hinz, *Darius*, p. 132.

44. J. A. S. Evans, *Herodotus* (Boston: Twayne, 1982), p. 57. The OP version of the DB #36 calls Gaumata a *maguš*; the corresponding DBelam has *ma-ku-iš*; but the corresponding DBbab calls him *LU KUR ma-da-*[*a-a*], that is, "Median man."

45. Dandamayev, *Persien*, p. 133; Hinz, *Darius*, p. 133.

46. DB #11; Kent, *OP*, p. 120.

47. Such acts of generosity were commonly enacted by monarchs at the beginning of their reigns to curry favor. Compare Herodotus 6.59. Even the evil Gaius Caligula began his reign by the remission of some taxes and the granting of gifts (Suetonius, *Gaius Caligula* 16).

this text, Wiesehöfer has developed an elaborate theory of the religious and social aims of Gaumata. He was a disciple of Zoroaster who strove for the underprivileged against the nobility.[48] But first, in order to overthrow the tyranny of Cambyses, Gaumata had temporarily to win over the nobility by pretending to be Bardiya.[49] The Zoroastrian magi then exalted the god Ahuramazda to centralize the king's power.[50] All of this is quite speculative.

Whereas the Behistun inscription and Ctesias speak only of one magos, Herodotus (3.61) mentions a second magos, named Patizeithes. Trogus/Justin also mention two magi, Gometes and his brother Oropastes.[51]

Darius claimed that he restored the "sanctuaries"[52] that Gaumata destroyed. The exact nature of these structures is disputed. Wiesehöfer maintains that these could not be the sanctuaries of the Achaemenids or those of the common folk, but must be the ancestral shrines of the nobility, Gaumata's main rivals.[53]

The usurper Gaumata resembled Bardiya but with one difference—he had been punished by having his ears cut off. This fact was discovered by Phaedyme, the daughter of Otanes (Herodotus 3.69).

Such acts of mutilation were widely practiced in the ancient world. Darius reports that he mutilated his rebellious enemies. In the case of Phraortes, for example, he reported: "I cut off his nose and ears and tongue, and put out one eye; he was kept bound at my palace entrance, all the people saw him."[54] The Middle Assyrian Laws (circa 1100 B.C.) numbers 4 and 9 ordered the cutting off of the nose and ears of slaves who received a stolen object, and the cutting off of the ears of a female slave who dared to veil herself. The edict of the pharaoh Horemhab of the Eighteenth Dynasty (circa 1300 B.C.) prescribed the cutting off of the noses of those found guilty of extortion.[55] Conspirators under the Twentieth Dynasty (twelfth–eleventh centuries B.C.) had their noses and ears lopped off.

48. Wiesehöfer, *Der Aufstand,* p. 140.

49. Ibid., p. 166.

50. Ibid., p. 149.

51. Wiesehöfer (p. 142) analyzes the name *Oropastes* as OP **Ahura-upastā* ("possessing the help of Ahura") and uses this as evidence for the alleged Zoroastrianism of Gaumata.

52. OP *āyadanā;* Akkadian *bītāte ša ilāni.*

53. Wiesehöfer, *Der Aufstand,* pp. 133–34.

54. DB #32; Kent, *OP,* p. 124.

55. J. H. Breasted, ed., *Ancient Records of Egypt* (Chicago: University of Chicago Press, 1927), 2: 26–27.

The Six Co-Conspirators

As noted in the previous chapter, Cambyses was on his way home to suppress the revolt when he died. Once it was confirmed that the new king was not the true Bardiya but his look-alike, the magos Gaumata, Darius and six other nobles banded together in a conspiracy to overthrow the usurper. The trustworthiness of Herodotus as a transmitter of authentic Persian materials is most clearly seen in his accurate knowledge of the names of these co-conspirators:

Names Transcribed	Herodotus 3.70	OP DB #68[56]
Intaphrenes	'Intaphrenēs	Vi^{n}dafarnā
Otanes	'Otanēs	Utāna
Gobryas	Gōbruēs	Gaubaruva
Hydarnes	Hydarnēs	Vidarna
Megabyzus	Megabuxos	Bagabuxša
Aspathines	'Aspathinēs	Ardumaniš

Intaphrenes (or Intaphernes) stands beside Darius as his bowbearer on the relief at Behistun. In the hand-to-hand struggle with the magi he lost one of his eyes (Herodotus 3.78). Aeschylus, who calls him Artaphrenes, gives him the main credit for the overthrow of the usurper. Later, however, Intaphrenes insisted on his prerogative of direct access to the king, but was denied entrance because the king was with one of his wives. Infuriated by what he believed was the king's reluctance to see him, he cut off the noses and ears of the servants who blocked his path. Darius then had Intaphrenes and almost all of his family put to death (Herodotus 3.118–19).

Otanes was descended from the Achaemenid line. His sister Cassandane married Cyrus. He himself married Darius's sister. His daughter was wed to Cambyses, and his granddaughter to Xerxes. His son Smerdomenes served as a general under Xerxes. The family was given an estate in Cappadocia in eastern Turkey.

Gobryas was the lancebearer who is depicted both on the relief at Behistun and that at Naqsh-i Rustam. He was married to Darius's sister, and his daughter was one of Darius's wives. His son, Mardonius, was a major commander in Xerxes' army.

Hydarnes became the satrap of Armenia, where his descendants continued to live until the time of Antiochus III. His son, Hydarnes, was the commander of the Immortals.

56. Kent, *OP*, pp. 130–32.

Megabyzus's son Zopyrus served as the satrap in Babylon, and his grandson Megabyzus was a general (Herodotus 7.82). The latter's son, Zopyrus, however, deserted to the Athenians and probably served as one of Herodotus's major Persian informants (Herodotus 3.160).

Aspathines is the only name which differs in the lists of Herodotus and Darius. But even here Herodotus seems to have transmitted a genuine Persian name, which represents OP *Aspačanā,* Darius's bow-bearer who is portrayed in the Naqsh-i Rustam relief.[57] Of Ardumanish in Darius's list nothing is known. Dandamayev speculates that he may have lost his life in the conflict against the magi.[58] In any case his place among the six leading families seems to have been taken at some later date by Aspathines.

The Overthrow of Gaumata

Darius reported laconically, "I with a few men slew that Gaumata the Magian, and those who were his foremost followers. A fortress by name Sikayauvati, a district by name Nisaya, in Media—there I slew him."[59] The date was September 29, 522 B.C. Herodotus (3.76–79) describes a furious hand-to-hand fight between the conspirators and the two magi. As Gobyras and one magos struggled in the dark, Darius stood helplessly by, afraid to strike his friend. Gobryas cried out that he should strike anyway, and by good luck Darius stabbed the magos.[60]

Herodotus then reports the massacre of many magi, which was later commemorated by the festival of the *magophonia* (3.79). This tradition is also reported in other classical sources.[61] Walter Henning believes that a Sogdian word in a Manichaean-Sogdian manuscript, *mwgzt* (**magu-žati*), is support for Herodotus's *magophonia.*[62]

In any case the suppression of the magi was neither universal nor long-lasting for the magi retained their important role even in Darius's

57. DNd; Kent, *OP,* p. 140; Schmitt, "Zur babylonischen," p. 125; Hegyi, "Historical Authenticity," pp. 78–79.

58. Dandamayev, *Persien,* p. 161.

59. DB #13; Kent, *OP,* p. 120.

60. Ctesias #45 reports a similar struggle. E. Herzfeld, *Iran in the Ancient East* (Oxford: Oxford University Press, 1941), p. 206, maintained that the tomb in Sakawand (Eshqavand) was that of the magos Gaumata. But H. Von Gall dates this tomb no earlier than the end of the fifth century B.C.

61. Classical references to the *magophonia* include Ctesias #46; Strabo 15.3.24; Josephus, *Antiquities* 11.31.

62. W. B. Henning, "The Murder of the Magi," *JRAS* (1943): 133–36. Henning's argument that the Sogdian word that corresponds with *magophonia* (although it now refers to Alexander) originally dates back to Darius's reign, has been accepted by R. N. Frye, *The Heritage of Persia* (Cleveland: World, 1963), p. 88; and Wiesehöfer, *Der Aufstand,* p. 178. It has been questioned by Dandamayev, *Persien,* pp. 138–39.

own reign as shown by the evidence of the Persepolis texts, which list provisions given to magi.[63]

An Official Hoax?

Although the correspondence between Herodotus and Darius's Behistun inscription is undeniable, some scholars are suspicious of the latter account as an officially sponsored hoax. In their view, Herodotus's faithful recounting of that version simply indicates his gullibility in believing the king's propaganda.

This cynical view was propounded at the turn of the century by Hugo Winckler,[64] who held that Cambyses did *not* murder his brother Bardiya. Rather it was the real Bardiya who seized power and was then overthrown by Darius. Darius then invented the figure of a pseudo-Bardiya, the magos Gaumata.

The great historian Albert T. Olmstead adopted this position.[65] He pointed to the differences in the time, place, and manner of the murder of Bardiya in the classical sources to argue that the truth, despite Darius's repeated protestations, was different from the official version.[66] Dandamayev has also argued against the official account because of the difficulty of keeping the murder concealed for five years (that is, from 526 to 522).[67]

This sceptical position has gained considerable currency in recent historiography. For example, Andrew R. Burn comments, "altogether, there is much to be said for Beloch's and Olmstead's bold theory, that it really was Bardiya, the son of Cyrus, who rebelled successfully against his brother with the support of the Magi."[68] Most recently Jack Balcer

63. Dandamayev, *Persien,* p. 238.

64. H. Winckler, *Altorientalische Forschungen* (Leipzig: E. Pfeiffer, 1893–1906).

65. As late as 1916 Olmstead accused Herodotus of falsely claiming that he had been to Babylon. The publication of Koldewey's excavations at Babylon (1899–1913) did much to dispel such hyperscepticism. See O. E. Ravn, *Herodotus' Description of Babylon* (Copenhagen: A. Busck, 1942); E. Yamauchi, *Composition and Corroboration in Classical and Biblical Studies* (Philadelphia: Presbyterian and Reformed, 1966), pp. 10, 16–17.

66. Olmstead, *History of the Persian Empire,* pp. 108–9.

67. Dandamayev, *Persien,* pp. 116–21. Dandamayev's position is also followed by E. J. Bickerman and H. Tadmor, "Darius I, Pseudo-Smerdis and the Magi," *Athenaeum* 56 (1978): 239–61. See C. Herrenschmidt, "Les historiens de l'empire achéménide et l'inscription de Bisotun," *Annales* 37 (1982): 813–23, for a survey of some recent studies.

68. A. R. Burn, *Persia and the Greeks* (New York: St. Martin's, 1962), p. 92. See W. Culican, *The Medes and Persians* (New York: Praeger, 1965), pp. 64–65; Evans, *Herodotus,* p. 56. M. Boyce, *A History of Zoroastrianism* (Leiden: Brill, 1982), 2: 78–81, supports this view of a hoax, although she also insists that Darius was a sincere Zoroastrian. She draws the interesting parallel with Henry VII, who blackened the image of his predecessor, Richard III. But the analogy is not convincing. Henry denigrated Richard but did not invent him.

has espoused this position in a detailed monograph. He raises such questions as: "Why did Cambyses kill his full brother? Why did the four key regions of the Achaemenid Empire rally around Gaumata? Why did the people opposed to Gaumata not speak out?" These questions cast doubt on the official version presented by Darius and Herodotus.[69] While some of his questions cannot be answered, others are not so difficult. Many kings have killed rival brothers; certain groups in the key regions may have responded positively to Gaumata's policies; people in many countries even today are afraid to speak out against powerful dictators. Balcer's speculation that Darius even had Cambyses murdered is without evidence.[70]

In spite of some admitted problems with the official position (such as the concealment of the murder of Bardiya), which are difficult but not insurmountable,[71] it is more difficult to believe that Darius concocted such a hoax and brazenly foisted it upon his empire.[72] The Behistun inscription can be compared to the similarly self-laudatory *Res gestae* of Augustus, which we have reason to believe is essentially accurate, though, of course, slanted.[73] On this point, Richard Frye observes: "In general, I believe, one should accept inscriptions unless sufficient reason for doubting their veracity exists, for inscriptions are public and subject to continuing scrutiny."[74] Roland Kent defends the official version for several reasons. The account of Darius on the Behistun rock, and the account by Herodotus, agree in the essentials, though differing in details. Kent notes that if Darius had slain the true

69. J. M. Balcer, *Herodotus & Bisitun* (Stuttgart: Franz Steiner, 1987), p. 58.

70. Ibid., p. 100. J. M. Cook, *The Persian Empire* (New York: Schocken, 1983), p. 50, comments: "Some scholars have thought of a conspiracy of Persian nobles in the army, in which Darius could have been involved. . . . But there is no evidence to base theories on; and Herodotus' story of the accident, in which the chape of his sheath came off, agrees with the Persian wearing of daggers."

71. Burn, *Persia and the Greeks*, p. 92; Wiesehöfer, *Der Aufstand*, p. 67. For an exposition supporting Darius and Herodotus, see F. Altheim and R. Stiehl, *Die aramäische Sprache unter den Achämeniden* (Frankfurt: V. Klostermann, 1960), pp. 75–105. Other authors supporting the official version include E. Bresciani, E. Herzfeld, F. W. König, and W. Hinz. To the objection that it would be impossible for Bardiya to be undiscovered for five or more years, R. N. Frye, *The History of Ancient Iran* (Munich: C. H. Beckische, 1984), p. 99, responds: "The last argument is unconvincing, however, since no one claims that the Magian proclaimed himself to be Bardiya as soon as the latter was murdered. If he fooled people, it was only from the time of his revolt to his death, which we know from Akkadian documents was from March to 29 September 522 B.C." G. Gnoli, "Politique religieuse et conception de la royauté sous les Achéménides," in *Commémoration Cyrus* (Tehran/Liège: Bibliothèque Pahlavi, 1974), 3: 148–49, n. 199, comments: "La thèse d'Olmstead . . . n'a pas recontré un large consensus, parce qu'elle n'est réellement fondée sur aucun argument solide."

72. W. W. How and J. Wells, *A Commentary on Herodotus* (Oxford: Clarendon, 1961 reprint of 1912 edition), 1: 393, long ago remarked about such revisionism: "This 'critical' view has not a particle of evidence in its favour, and is not worth discussing."

73. See P. A. Brunt and J. M. Moore, eds., *Res Gestae Divi Augusti* (London: Oxford University Press, 1967).

74. Frye, *Heritage*, p. 86.

The treasury relief from Persepolis. (Courtesy of The Oriental Institute, University of Chicago)

Smerdis, son of Cyrus and brother of Cambyses II, and if the fact had been known widely enough to have resulted in the sundry uprisings related by Darius in his inscription, it is inconceivable that no hint of this should have come down in the literature. Especially noteworthy is that the inveterate gossip Herodotus, in all his lengthy account of the event, gave no indication that there was a differing version. Further, if Darius needed to justify his slaying of the real brother of Cambyses, he would have had a much better account to set before the world—a true account, better than a cock-and-bull story about his having slain an imposter.[75]

The Suppression of Rebellions

Since Darius was not the obvious heir to the throne, he had first to quell rebellions that arose throughout the empire. Darius proclaimed:

75. Cited in A. J. Toynbee, *A Study of History* (London: Oxford University Press, 1946), 7: 599, n. 2.

> This is what I did by the favor of Ahuramazda in one and the same year after that I became king. Nineteen battles I fought; by the favor of Ahuramazda I smote them and took prisoner nine kings.[76]

In four other passages (DB 56, 57, 59, 62) Darius repeats the claim that he accomplished all of this in "one and the same year." Scholars have made various attempts to reconcile this statement with the dates and the battles that are listed. Hinz begins with Açina's rebellion, which he dates to December 10, 522, and ends the series of nineteen battles with the victory of Dadarshi over Frada, December 28, 521. He maintains that this was a leap year, which was eighteen days longer than a regular year.[77] A. Shahpur Shahbazi, on the other hand, dates Açina's capture to November 10, 522, and ends the year of battles with the execution of Arkha on November 27, 521. We shall follow his chronological scheme.[78]

According to Darius, "these are the provinces that became rebellious from me: Persia, Elam, Media, Assyria, Egypt, Parthia, Margiana, Sattagydia, Scythia" (DB #21). Rebellions broke out three times in Elam and twice in Babylonia. Even Parthia, his father's own province, rebelled. Among the few areas to remain loyal to Darius were Bactria, under the satrap Dadarshi, and Arachosia, under the satrap Vivana.[79]

The nine defeated kings are portrayed in chronological order in the Behistun relief, but the battles are listed in geographical order in the Behistun inscription. We will discuss these areas from west to east.

Persia. A man called Vahyazdata from the district of Yautiya in Persia claimed to be Bardiya. He was suppressed in two battles (#12 and 17 in Shahbazi's sequence) on May 24 and July 15, 521.[80]

Media. Fravartish (compare Greek Phraortes) claimed to be the king of Media. He was defeated in two battles (##7, 9) on January 13 and May 5, 521. He was then mutilated and impaled at Ecbatana.[81]

Elam. The earliest rebellion was led by Açina, but the people surrendered him to Darius (victory #1) on November 10, 522.[82] There was a later rebellion led by Atamaita.

76. DB #52; Kent, *OP*, p. 131.

77. Hinz, *Darius*, pp. 145–55. In an earlier study, "Zur Behistun-Inschrift des Dareios," *ZDMG* 96 (1942): 326–31, Hinz had also dated the end of the series to the capture of Arkha on Nov. 27, 521. See also R. Borger, *Die Chronologie des Darius-Denkmals am Behistun-Felsen* (Göttingen: Vandenhoeck and Ruprecht, 1982), p. 123.

78. A. S. Shahbazi, "The 'One Year' of Darius Re-Examined," *BSOAS* 35 (1972): 609–14. See further, Cook, *Persian Empire*, p. 56; Borger, *Die Chronologie des Darius-Denkmals*, p. 3; W. Vogelsang, "Four Short Notes on the Bisutun Text and Monument," *IA* 21 (1986): 121–40.

79. For a general discussion of these rebellions, see Burn, *Persia and the Greeks*, pp. 96–103.

80. DB ##40–42; Kent, *OP*, p. 127.

81. DB ##25, 31–32; Kent, *OP*, pp. 124–25.

82. DB #16; Kent, *OP*, p. 120.

Babylonia. A dangerous revolt was led by Nidintu-Bel, who claimed to be "Nebuchadnezzar (III), the son of Nabonidus." He was defeated in a battle (#3) by the Tigris on December 13, 522, and in a battle (#4) by the Euphrates on December 18, 522. In the first battle Darius had his men cross the river using inflated animal skins, just as the Assyrians had done in the past.[83] The last battle (#19) in the series was also fought against a pretender to the Babylonian throne, an Armenian called *Arkha* who also claimed to be a "Nebuchadnezzar (IV), the son of Nabonidus."[84] He was defeated on November 27, 521.[85]

Armenia. No less than five battles were fought by Darius's two generals, Vaumisa and Dadarshi, in this area. Vaumisa won victories (##6, 14) on December 31, 522, and June 11, 521.[86] Dadarshi fought battles (##11, 13, and 15) on May 20, May 29, and June 21, 521.[87]

Parthia. Darius's father Hystaspes, the satrap of Parthia, had to put down rebellions in his province twice (##10 and 16) on May 8 and July 11, 521.[88]

Margiana. An early revolt (#2) in this area, led by Frada, was defeated on December 10, 522, by an army led by Dadarshi, Darius's loyal satrap over Bactria.[89]

Arachosia. The loyal satrap Vivana won two victories (##5, 8) on December 29, 522, and February 21, 521, over an army sent east by the Persian pretender Vahyazdata.[90]

Sagartia. A rebel named Ciçantakhma claimed to be a descendant of the Median royal line of Cyaxares. He was captured, mutilated, and then impaled at Arbela. This incident is undated; Shahbazi would number this as battle #18.[91]

83. DB ##16, 18–19; Kent, *OP,* p. 120.

84. Compare F. M. T. de Liagre Böhl, "Die babylonischen Prätendenten zur Anfangszeit des Darius (Dareios) I," *BO* 25 (1968): 150–53. That two pretenders claimed to be "Nebuchadnezzar, the son of Nabonidus," supports the tradition that these names alternated in the Neo-Babylonian dynasty, as in the statement in Dan. 5:2 that Belshazzar, the son of Nabonidus, was a son (or descendant) of Nebuchadnezzar. It is quite plausible to assume that Nabonidus married a daughter of Nebuchadnezzar as argued by R. Dougherty, *Nabonidus and Belshazzar* (New Haven: Yale University Press, 1929), pp. 63–80; A. R. Millard, "Daniel 1–6 and History," *Evangelical Quarterly* 49 (1977): 72.

85. DB #49; Kent, *OP,* p. 128. C. Schedl, "Nabuchodonosor, Arpakšad und Darius," *ZDMG* 115 (1965): 242–54, makes the unlikely suggestion that the Nebuchadnezzar of the book of Judith reflects Nebuchadnezzar IV. D. B. Weisberg, *Texts from the Time of Nebuchadnezzar* (New Haven: Yale University Press, 1980), p. xxiii, thinks it unlikely that there could be two kings with the name *Nebuchadnezzar* in the Achaemenid period.

86. DB ##29–30; Kent, *OP,* p. 124.

87. DB ##26–28; Kent, *OP,* pp. 123–24.

88. DB ##35–36; Kent, *OP,* pp. 124, 127.

89. DB #38; Kent, *OP,* p. 127.

90. DB #45–46; Kent, *OP,* pp. 127–28.

91. DB #33; Kent, *OP,* p. 124.

Scythia. After Darius completed the first phases of his Behistun monument, a leader of the eastern "pointed-hat" Scythians[92] named Skunkha, led an uprising in the northeast. He was suppressed in 519, some years after the series of nineteen battles.[93]

The DBbab and the Aramaic fragments give figures (not always legible) for the number of rebels killed and imprisoned. For example, Hystaspes in his second battle killed 6,520 subjects and captured 4,192 prisoners.[94] Hinz estimates that more than 60,000 were killed in these campaigns;[95] Dandamayev places the figure of casualties at about 100,000.[96]

Darius in Egypt

Darius invaded Egypt and spent six months there. Egypt had been among the provinces that rebelled against Darius (DB #21). Herodotus (4.166) reports that Aryandes, the satrap appointed by Cambyses, provoked Darius by minting his own silver coins in imitation of the king's gold darics. Polyaenus (7.11.7) contains a most interesting account:

> Darius, since the Egyptians would not endure the cruelty of the satrap Aryandes and rebelled on account of it, himself traveled through the Arabian Desert and came to Memphis. It happened that the Egyptians during those days were mourning for the Apis which had become invisible (i.e. had died). When Darius decreed that a hundred gold talents should be given the one leading the Apis, they observed with amazement his piety and no longer aligned themselves with the rebels but of their own accord handed themselves over to Darius.[97]

We know from an Apis inscription that a bull died in the fourth year of Darius's reign (518) on August 31.[98] The traditional period of seventy days of mourning would have extended from August 31 to November 8. Since this would have fallen during the period of the annual flooding of the Nile, Darius probably arrived earlier in the autumn of 519.[99] Al-

92. For a general discussion of the Scythians and their dress, see E. Yamauchi, *Foes from the Northern Frontier* (Grand Rapids: Baker, 1982).

93. DB #74; Kent, *OP*, p. 134. For an improved reading of the passage, see Cameron, "Old Persian Text."

94. DBbab #29; Voigtlander, *Bisitun Inscription*, p. 58.

95. Hinz, *Darius*, p. 166.

96. Dandamayev, *Persien*, p. 209.

97. Cited by G. Cameron, "Darius, Egypt and the 'Lands Beyond the Sea,' " *JNES* 2 (1943): 310.

98. See above, chapter 3 on Cambyses.

99. R. A. Parker, "Darius and His Egyptian Campaign," *AJSL* 58 (1941): 376. J. Yoyotte, "Les inscriptions hiéroglyphiques de Darius et l'Egypte," *JA* 260 (1972): 266, however, would associate the

though the sum supposedly offered by Darius is exaggerated, the inscription on the Apis sarcophagus confirms that Darius paid respect to the Egyptians' god: "Really His Majesty (Darius) has loved the Apis more than any king."[100]

This helps explain why there are no reports of Egyptian opposition. As noted in the previous chapter, Darius made good use of cooperative Egyptian officials like Udjahorresnet, whom he commissioned to reestablish medical training throughout Egypt: "His majesty has done this because he knew the usefulness of this art to make alive every sick person."[101]

During a later visit (497–496) Darius had a temple to Amon built at Hibis in the el-Khargeh oasis as indicated by an OP inscription. The structure of Nubian sandstone (44 by 19 meters or 144 by 62 feet) was excavated by Herbert E. Winlock.[102] Darius also granted donations to the temple of Horus at Edfu.[103]

A study of contemporary demotic documents indicates that Egypt enjoyed stable religious and economic practices during Darius's reign. Cruz-Uribe concludes: "The sale of various pieces of private property appears frequently . . . and the apparent stability of the reign of Darius I allowed many documents of a personal business nature to survive in contrast to the reign of the other Persian kings."[104]

The Codification of Egyptian Laws

After listing five lawgivers of the Egyptians (Mneves, probably Menes; Sasyshi [Sheshi?]; Sesonchois [Shishaq]; Bocchoris; and Amasis), Diodorus (1.954.4) related: "A sixth man to concern himself with the laws of the Egyptians, it is said was Darius the father of Xerxes; for he was incensed at the lawlessness which his predecessor, Cambyses, had

---

reference in Polyaenus with a later visit by Darius to Egypt in 492/491 during the search for the Apis bull of year 31 of Darius.

100. Cited by Hinz, *Darius*, p. 191.

101. G. Posener, *La première domination perse en Egypte* (Cairo: L'Institut Français d'Archéologie Orientale, 1936), pp. 22–26.

102. H. E. Winlock et al., *The Temple of Hibis in El Khârgeh Oasis* (New York: Metropolitan Museum of Art, 1938–1953); Hinz, *Darius*, pp. 214–16. See M. C. Root, *The King and Kingship in Achaemenid Art* (Leiden: Brill, 1979), pp. 125–28; E. Cruz-Uribe, "Oasis of the Spirit," *Arch* 42/5 (1989): 48–53.

103. E. Bresciani, "Egypt and the Persian Empire," in *The Greeks and the Persians*, ed. H. Bengtson (London: Weidenfeld and Nicolson, 1968), p. 169; Posener, *La première domination*, p. 179; Boyce, *History of Zoroastrianism*, p. 124.

104. E. Cruz-Uribe, "A Sale of Inherited Property from the Reign of Darius I," *JEA* 66 (1980): 125; see also M. F. Gyles, *Pharaonic Policies and Administration, 663 to 323* B.C. (Chapel Hill: University of North Carolina Press, 1959).

Statue of Darius found at Susa.

shown in his treatment of the sanctuaries of Egypt, and aspired to live a life of virtue and of piety towards the gods."[105]

Striking confirmation of this tradition is found in the Demotic Papyrus 215 of the Bibliothèque Nationale of Paris. This is a text written during the third century B.C., which on its verso side reports Darius's order given in 518: "Darius decrees that the wise men among the soldiers, the priests, and scribes, assemble and write down all Egyptian laws having been in force until the year 44 of Amasis (526 B.C.)."[106] It took over twenty years (until 495 B.C.) for the task to be completed.[107]

105. Few laws have been recovered from Egypt in contrast to those which have been found in Mesopotamia. Some have argued that this lack can be explained from the fact that the pharaoh in Egypt was regarded as divine; his word was the law. But in fact, this lack is due to our fragmentary evidence according to Lorton, who cites an unpublished Middle Kingdom papyri, and the implications of the use of the term *hpw,* which can only refer to written laws. See D. Lorton, "Towards a Constitutional Approach to Ancient Egyptian Kingship," *JAOS* 99/3 (1979): 460–66; idem, "The King and the Law," *Varia Aegyptiaca* 2 (1986): 53–62.

106. N. J. Reich, "The Codification of the Egyptian Laws by Darius and the Origin of the 'Demotic Chronicle,' " *Mizraim* 1 (1933): 180; compare W. Spiegelberg, *Die sog. demotische Chronik des Pap. 215 der Bibliothèque National zu Paris* (Leipzig: J. D. Hinrichs, 1914).

107. Hinz, *Darius,* p. 192. Bresciani, "Egypt and the Persian Empire," p. 338, speaks of sixteen years of labor on the laws until Darius's nineteenth year (503), but the mutilated text contains a further reference to his twenty-seventh year (495). The later Persians were happy to support Ezra's attempt to promulgate the Jewish Law, that is, the Torah. H. H. Schaeder, *Esra der Schreiber* (Tübingen: J. C. B. Mohr, 1930), however, goes too far in making Ezra a Persian official.

The results were recorded on a papyrus-roll in Aramaic writing and in epistolary writing (i.e., demotic).

The need for such laws and their enforcement is vividly illustrated by a petition written in the ninth year of Darius (513) by Peteese, who tells an appalling tale of graft, corruption, and violence.[108]

An Egyptian Statue of Darius

In December 1972, French excavators at Susa made an extraordinary discovery. They found a larger than life-size statue of Darius, which unfortunately was missing its head. When intact it probably stood about 3 meters (nearly 10 feet) tall.[109] It was found near the east court of the palace of Darius on the Apadana mound.[110]

This is the first, nearly complete Achaemenid statue recovered. Fragments of Achaemenid statues had been found before. These include part of a colossal head of Darius from Susa (which preserves only the base of the nose, the mouth, and part of a beard) and a magnificent head, possibly of Darius (.285 meters—nearly a foot high), recovered from the Hamadan area.[111]

Moreover, engraved in the folds of the garments of the new statue are inscriptions in four languages—Old Persian, Elamite, Akkadian, and Egyptian. The statue was originally painted, for traces of red paint were found on the shoe. Egyptian inscriptions on two sides of the base list twenty-four subject peoples.[112] The Egyptian text proclaims: "Atum, lord of Heliopolis, has chosen him [Darius] to be the master of all which the solar disc circumscribes, for he knows that he is his son."[113] Neith, the goddess of Sais, also chose Darius to be the master of the world.

The trilingual cuneiform texts record: "This is the statue of stone which Darius the King ordered made in Egypt in order that in the future whoever sees it will know that the Persian possesses Egypt."[114] On the assessment that the statue's limestone was quarried from the

108. A. H. Gardiner, *Egypt of the Pharaohs* (Oxford: Clarendon, 1961), p. 368. See F. L. Griffith, *Catalogue of the Demotic Papyri in the John Rylands Library* (Manchester: Manchester University Press, 1909), 1: 60–112, 218–53.

109. D. Stronach, "Description and Comment," *JA* 260 (1972): 241ff.

110. M. Kervran, "Une statue de Darius découverte à Suse," *JA* 260 (1972): 235.

111. A. Parrot, "Acquisitions et inédits du Musée de Louvre," *Syria* 44 (1967): 247–51; R. Ghirshman, *The Art of Ancient Iran* (New York: Golden, 1964), p. 140.

112. M. Roaf, "The Subject Peoples on the Base of the Statue of Darius," *CDAFI* 4 (1974): 73.

113. J. Yoyotte, "Les inscriptions hiéroglyphiques de Darius et l'Egypte," *JA* 260 (1972): 254; see idem, "Les inscriptions hiéroglyphiques de la statue de Darius à Suse," *CDAFI* 4 (1974): 181–209.

114. F. Vallat, "L'inscription cunéiforme trilingue (DSab)," *JA* 260 (1972): 249.

Egyptian inscription on the base of the statue.

Zagros Mountains, Jean Yoyotte suggests that this is a copy of the original statue set before the temple of Atum in Heliopolis.[115] On the other hand, Edith Porada comments:

> There are ten short inscriptions at various points of the Wadi [Hamamat], carved between the years 496 to 492 B.C. by the chief of all workers of the king. Although it is conceivable that a stone such as that from which the statue was made existed also in Iran in the region between Hamadan and Burujird, the Egyptian derivation, which agrees with the style of the figure, seems more probable.[116]

François Vallat also believes that the statue was made in Egypt as the text proclaims, and notes the prominence of the Egyptian texts. He suggests that the statue was transferred to Susa by Xerxes after a revolt by the Egyptians.[117]

The Canal Inscriptions

Darius had a canal completed between the Nile and the Red Sea. Middle Kingdom inscriptions already referred to a canal dug by the

115. Yoyotte, "Les inscriptions hiéroglyphiques," 263–64; J. Perrot and D. Ladiray, "La porte de Darius à Suse," *CDAFI* 4 (1974): 43–56.

116. E. Porada, "Classic Achaemenian Architecture and Sculpture," in Gershevitch, *CHI*, p. 816.

117. F. Vallat, "Les textes cunéiformes de la statue de Darius," *CDAFI* 4 (1974): 165–68; idem, "La triple inscription cunéiforme de la statue de Darius Ier," *RA* 68 (1974): 157–66. See also H. Luschey, "Archäologische Bemerkungen zu der Darius-Statue von Susa," in *Akten des VII. Internationalen Kongresses für Iranische Kunst und Archäologie* (Berlin: Dietrich Reimer, 1979), pp. 207–17; Root, *King and Kingship*, pp. 68–72.

Egyptians between the Pelusiac branch of the Nile and the Red Sea. Recent satellite photos have revealed the location of this early canal.[118]

In the Saite period Necho II (610–595) attempted unsuccessfully to dig another canal, no doubt because the earlier canal had become unusable.[119] According to Herodotus (2.158):

> It was he [Necho] who began the making of the canal into the Red Sea, which was finished by Darius the Persian. This is four days' voyage in length, and it was dug wide enough for two triremes to move in it rowed abreast.

The canal extended some 50 miles, and was perhaps 45 meters (148 feet) wide and 3 meters (10 feet) deep. The project took about a dozen years to complete.[120]

Herodotus's report has been directly confirmed by the discovery of four fragmentary stelae of red granite inscribed in cuneiform and hieroglyphs, which commemorated the digging of the canal by Darius. These include: the Maskhuta stele found in 1864; the so-called Serapeum stele found by Napoleon's soldiers between Lake Timsa and the Bitter Lakes in 1799; the Shallūfa stele discovered twenty miles north of Suez by Charles de Lesseps, brother of the engineer who built the modern Suez Canal (this is the best-preserved text); and the Kubri or Suez stele, found about twenty miles north of Suez and first published in 1908.

Because these inscriptions proclaim Darius as the son of Neith, one may consider Udjahorresnet, the priest of Neith who had helped Cambyses, as the Egyptian advisor who helped compose these texts.[121] According to the OP text on these stelae Darius proclaimed:

> I am Persian; from Persia I seized Egypt; I gave order to dig this canal from a river by name Nile which flows in Egypt, to the sea which goes from Persia. Afterward this canal was dug thus as I had ordered and ships went from Egypt through this canal to Persia thus as was my desire.[122]

118. W. H. Shea, "A Date for the Recently Discovered Eastern Canal of Egypt," *BASOR* 226 (1977): 31–38; compare G. Posener, "Le canal du Nil à la Mer Rouge avant les Ptolemées," *Chronique d'Egypte* 13 (1938): 258–73.

119. Necho sponsored the most remarkable feat of ancient exploration, the circumnavigation of Africa by Phoenician seamen (Herodotus 4.42). See, however, A. B. Lloyd, "Necho and the Red Sea: Some Considerations," *JEA* 63 (1977): 148–55, who expresses scepticism about this feat.

120. Hinz, *Darius*, p. 206.

121. G. Lanczkowski, "Zur Entstehung des antiken Synkretismus Darius als Sohn der Neith von Sais," *Saeculum* 6 (1955): 227–43.

122. Kent, *OP*, p. 147.

It was not true, of course, that Darius was the first to conquer Egypt; here he is claiming credit for that which was accomplished by his predecessor.[123] The corresponding Egyptian text speaks of "twenty-four ships with tribute for Persia." Darius's purpose in completing the canal was to facilitate traffic between Egypt through the Red Sea, around the Arabian peninsula, and into the Persian Gulf.

India

We may conjecture that after suppressing the rebellious provinces, Darius proceeded eastward, perhaps in 516/515, to conquer the region that would become the satrapy of Hindush, the area along the Indus River south of the Punjab (today in Pakistan).[124] This area provided the Persian coffers with the greatest treasures, some 360 talents of gold dust annually (Herodotus 3.94).

About the year 510 B.C. Darius commissioned Scylax, a Carian seaman from Caryanda, to explore the Indus River to its mouth and then to sail westwards into the Red Sea (Herodotus 4.44).[125] Scylax and his companion set forth from Caspatyrus, perhaps near the modern Attock (33 degrees north, 72 degrees east).[126] Scylax's account, perhaps through the mediation of Hecataeus, may have served as the basis for Herodotus's (3.98–106) description of India.[127] His journey took unusually long, two and a half years. Max Cary and Eric Warmington speculate that he may have been delayed by adverse monsoons.[128]

123. In a similar fashion Sargon II claimed credit for the capture of Samaria in 722, although this occurred at the end of the reign of his predecessor, Shalmaneser V. See W. W. Hallo, "From Qarqar to Carchemish," *BA* 23 (1960): 51.

124. Hinz, *Darius*, pp. 192–97; E. Herzfeld, *The Persian Empire: Studies in the Geography and Ethnography of the Ancient Near East*, ed. G. Walser (Wiesbaden: F. Steiner, 1968), pp. 346–47. The suggestion of S. Chattopadhyaya, *The Achaemenids and India* (New Delhi: Munshiram Manoharlal, 1974), p. 16, that the conquest took place between 521 and 519 B.C., is improbable. The word *hindu* originally meant "river." The Assyrians had imported wood circa 700 B.C. from *Sind* (later Akkadian *Indu*; Elamite *Hintus*; OP *Hindush*; Greek *Indoi*; compare Aramaic *Hoddū* in Esther 1:1; 8:9).

125. M. Cary and E. H. Warmington, *Ancient Explorers* (Baltimore: Penguin, 1963), p. 78.

126. Caspatyrus is the Greek form of Kāsyapapura ("City of the Kāsyapa"), a name that may be cognate with Kashmir. The city is also mentioned in the first-century A.D. work, *The Periplus of the Erythraean Sea*, ed. W. H. Schoff (London: Longmans, Green, 1912), pp. 42, 189.

127. Herzfeld, *Persian Empire*, p. 316.

128. The southwest monsoon blows from the end of April to mid-October from the Red Sea toward India; the northeast monsoon blows from November to March from India toward the Red Sea. The secret of the monsoons was discovered by the Greek seaman Hippalus (Pliny, *Natural History*, 6.100–106), whose date has been variously placed between the second century B.C. and the first century A.D. By taking advantage of the monsoons, ships could make the round trip between India and Egypt in a year. See Cary and Warmington, *Ancient Explorers*, pp. 95–96, 265.

The Rebuilding of the Jewish Temple

Solomon's temple was destroyed by Nebuchadnezzar in 587 or 586 B.C.[129] Although the Jews who had returned under Cyrus had laid the foundation of a second temple in 536, work was halted during the next twenty years in the face of opposition (Ezra 4:1–5). The Lord then raised up two prophets to stir the people to action (Ezra 5:1).[130]

Beginning on August 29, 520 (Hag. 1:1), and continuing until December 18 (Hag. 2:1–9, 20ff.), Haggai delivered a series of three messages to provoke the people into recommencing work on the temple. Two months after Haggai's first message, Zechariah joined him (Zech. 1:1).

The renewed work was led by Zerubbabel, the son of Shealtiel and therefore from the Davidic line, and Jeshua the high priest. Some scholars have held that there is an "irreconcilable difference" between Ezra 3:10 and the references in Haggai 2:18; Zechariah 4:9; 8:9, as the former speaks of the foundation of the temple in 536 and the latter sources imply a second foundation in 520. We have evidence, however, that it was possible to have more than one foundation ceremony for a particular building. J. Stafford Wright notes a Hittite ritual that speaks of the refoundation of a building and Akkadian rituals that speak of "founding anew" particular temples.[131] Therefore a second foundation of the Jerusalem temple in 520 is conceivable.

Reports of the Jewish construction efforts were carried by their enemies to the Persian authorities. According to Ezra 5:3:

> At that time Tattenai, governor of Trans-Euphrates, and Shethar-Bozenai and their associates went to them and asked "Who authorized you to rebuild this temple and restore this structure?"

Judah was in the province of Trans-Euphrates, literally "across the

129. Scholars such as Albright, Freedman, Tadmor, and Wiseman, who believe that the Jews used a calendar, beginning in Nisan (April), date the fall of Jerusalem to the summer of 587. Others such as Horn, Malamat, Redford, Saggs, and Thiele, who believe that the Jews used a calendar beginning in Tishri (September), date the fall of Jerusalem to the summer of 586. See H. Tadmor, "Chronology of the Last Kings of Judah," *JNES* 15 (1956): 226–30; S. Horn, "The Babylonian Chronicle and the Ancient Calendar of the Kingdom of Judah," *AUSS* 5 (1967): 12–27; K. Freedy and D. Redford, "The Dates in Ezekiel in Relation to Biblical, Babylonian and Egyptian Sources," *JAOS* 90 (1970): 462–85.

130. See further E. Yamauchi's commentary on "Ezra" in *The Expositor's Bible Commentary*, ed. F. E. Gaebelein (Grand Rapids: Zondervan, 1988), 4: 563–771.

131. See J. S. Wright, *The Building of the Second Temple* (London: Tyndale, 1958), p. 17; F. I. Andersen, "Who Built the Second Temple?" *Australian Biblical Review* 6 (1958): 1–35; A. Gelston, "The Foundation of the Second Temple," *VT* 16 (1966): 232–35; J. Baldwin, *Haggai, Zechariah, Malachi* (London: Inter-Varsity, 1972), pp. 52–53.

river."[132] The governor Tattenai was at first mistakenly identified by scholars with Ushtannu, the satrap over Babylon and Trans-Euphrates, until Olmstead pointed out the correct identification in 1944. In a document dated June 5, 502, we have attested a Ta-at-tan-ni the *pahat* or governor subordinate to the satrap.[133] Shethar-Bozenai may have functioned as a Persian official known as the *patifrasa* or *frasaka* (inquisitor or investigator).[134]

The Aramaic word (*'uššarnā*) in Ezra 5:3 translated by the New International Version as "structure" (KJV "wall") also occurs in the Aramaic papyri (Cowley #26:5, 9, 21; #27:1, 18; #30:1, 11), where it indicates "material" or "equipment." Carl G. Tuland therefore suggests that Tattenai's investigations were made at a very early stage when the Jews were still gathering building materials.[135]

It is noteworthy that the Persian governor gave the Jews the benefit of the doubt by not stopping the work while inquiries were being made (Ezra 5:5). This indicates that he did not consider their activities to be rebellious.

Some scholars have speculated, however, that Zechariah was promoting Zerubbabel as a messianic figure who might lead a revolt against the Persians. According to one scenario "the two sons of oil" of Zechariah 4:10–14 are references to Zerubbabel and to Jeshua as messianic figures.[136] Olmstead held that the Jewish nationalists flirted with the idea of revolt until Darius passed through Palestine in 518 and had Zerubbabel executed. Zechariah then toned down his pronouncements.[137]

We have later references to Zerubbabel in Nehemiah 7:7; 12:1, 47. However, these are retrospective and yield no further information about his activities after the rededication of the temple. Although there is no evidence for his "execution," the Persians may have removed him.[138] Hayim Tadmor suggests that Zerubbabel was probably sum-

132. Aramaic *ᵃbar-nahᵃrā* from Akkadian *eber nāri.* See A. F. Rainey, "The Satrapy 'Beyond the River,' " *Australian Journal of Biblical Archaeology* 1 (1969): 51–58.

133. A. T. Olmstead, "Tattenai, Governor of 'Across the River,' " *JNES* 3 (1944): 46.

134. Cowley #37.5; B. Porten, *Archives from Elephantine* (Berkeley: University of California Press, 1968), p. 54.

135. C. G. Tuland, "*Uššayā'* and *'Uššarnā*," *JNES* 17 (1958): 269–75.

136. L. Waterman, "The Camouflaged Purge of Three Messianic Conspirators," *JNES* 13 (1954): 73–78; P. R. Ackroyd, *Exile and Restoration* (Philadelphia: Westminster, 1968), pp. 192–94; K.-M. Beyse, *Serubbabel und die Königserwartungen der Propheten Haggai und Sacharja* (Stuttgart: Calwer, 1972).

137. Olmstead, *History of the Persian Empire,* pp. 138–41. Olmstead makes uncritical use of the apocryphal 1 Esdras in his reconstruction. See Parker, "Darius and His Egyptian Campaign," p. 375.

138. J. Bright, *A History of Israel,* 2d ed. (Philadelphia: Westminster, 1972), p. 373.

moned back east as one of his descendants, Hattush, returned with Ezra (Ezra 8:2; 1 Chron. 3:19–22).[139]

Ezra 5:6–17 contains a report of the letter which Tattenai and his associates sent to Darius. The text, which contains a number of Persian loan-words,[140] reads in part:

> The king should know that we went to the district of Judah, to the temple of the great God. The people are building it with large stones and placing the timbers in the walls. The work is being carried on with diligence and is making rapid progress under their direction.

Tattenai then reports that he asked the Jews who had given them the authority to do this, and they had replied that Cyrus had issued such a decree to Sheshbazzar. He then continues:

> Now if it pleases the king, let a search be made in the royal archives of Babylon to see if King Cyrus did in fact issue a decree to rebuild this house of God in Jerusalem. Then let the king send us his decision in this matter.[141]

That such inquiries were sent directly to the king himself has been vividly confirmed by the Aramaic letters from Elephantine. These texts reveal the close attention paid to minute details by the king. Cameron concludes:

> Thus, too, the governor of the province "Across the River," Tattenai, . . . appealed directly to Darius I, and Darius II curtly intervened in the religious affairs of an obscure settlement of Jews in Egypt.[142]

According to Ezra 6:1–4, the king responded to the request:

139. H. Tadmor, "The Period of the First Temple, the Babylonian Exile and the Restoration," in *A History of the Jewish People,* ed. H. Ben-Sasson (Cambridge: Harvard University Press, 1976), p. 172.

140. For example, v. 6, Aramaic *'ᵃparsᵉkāyē'* from OP *frasaka* "investigator"; v. 8, Aramaic *'āsparnā'* from **asp̣rnā* "exactly"; v. 17, *ginzayyā'* from *ganza* "treasury." See F. Rosenthal, *A Grammar of Biblical Aramaic* (Wiesbaden: Harrassowitz, 1961), pp. 58–59; K. A. Kitchen, "The Aramaic of Daniel," in *Notes on Some Problems in the Book of Daniel,* D. J. Wiseman et al., eds. (London: Tyndale, 1965), pp. 35–43; I. Jerusalmi, *The Aramaic Sections of Ezra and Daniel* (Cincinnati: Hebrew Union College, 1970), pp. 19–29. Captain Hensley, "The Official Persian Documents in the Book of Ezra," unpublished Ph.D. diss. (Liverpool University, 1977), has demonstrated the authenticity of the numerous so-called Persian documents utilized in Ezra.

141. Sheshbazzar, who was older, was probably viewed as the official governor, while Zerubbabel served as the popular leader.

142. G. Cameron, *Persepolis Treasury Tablets* (Chicago: University of Chicago Press, 1948), p. 12.

> King Darius then issued an order, and they searched in the archives stored in the treasury at Babylon. A scroll was found in the citadel of Ecbatana in the province of Media, and this was written on it:
>
> "Memorandum: In the first year of King Cyrus, the king issued a decree concerning the temple of God in Jerusalem:
>
> 'Let the temple be rebuilt as a place to present sacrifices, and let its foundation be laid. . . . The costs are to be paid by the royal treasury.' "

We know that Persian officials wrote on scrolls of leather and papyrus from the remains of clay bullae found in the east and discoveries made in Egypt. Diodorus (2.32.4) informs us that the Persians had "royal parchments" recording events of the past (compare Esther 6:1). The fact that the scroll in question was found in the fortress is regarded as significant by Geo Widengren:

> This was a tradition which continued for many centuries, for in the Sasanian period, documents were still kept in the so-called *diz in nipišt,* "the fortress of the archives." Such a detail adds to the reliability of the story as to how the document was found.[143]

The fact that the search was made in Babylon and then in Ecbatana conforms to the fact that Cyrus left Babylon in the spring of 538 to spend the summer in Ecbatana.[144]

Because the accounts in Haggai and Zechariah do not speak of support from the Persian treasury, some have questioned the promise of aid made in Ezra 6:4. We have already seen, however, that it was the consistent policy of Persian kings to help restore the sanctuaries of their subjects. Bagoas, the Persian governor of Judah, and Delaiah, governor of Samaria, issued a memorandum concerning the rebuilding of the Jewish temple at Elephantine, "to rebuild it on its site as it was before, and the meal-offering and incense to be made on that altar as it used to be." Kraeling interprets this passage to mean that this was "a directive presumably suggesting that the rebuilding be done at government expense" with a hint of government subsidies for the offerings.[145] That the Persian kings were interested in the details of foreign cults is demonstrated by a letter sent by Darius II in 419 to

143. G. Widengren, "The Persian Period," in *Israelite and Judaean History,* eds. J. H. Hayes and J. M. Miller (Philadelphia: Westminster, 1977), p. 499.

144. R. de Vaux, "The Decrees of Cyrus," in *The Bible and the Ancient Near East* (Garden City: Doubleday, 1971), p. 89.

145. Cowley #32; *ANET,* p. 492; E. Kraeling, *The Brooklyn Museum Aramaic Papyri* (New Haven: Yale University Press, 1953), p. 107.

the Jews of Elephantine concerning the keeping of their feast of unleavened bread.[146]

The motives of the Persian kings in providing for the rebuilding of their subjects' temples were not altogether altruistic. They wanted both their political support and also their prayers, "so that they may offer sacrifices pleasing to the God of heaven and pray for the well-being of the king and his sons" (Ezra 6:10). The Jews of Elephantine wrote to the Persian governor of Judah that if he helped them get their temple rebuilt, "the meal-offering, incense, and burnt offering will be offered in your name, and we shall pray for you at all times, we, and our wives, and our children."

Darius solemnly warned the enemies of the Jews against interfering with the rebuilding of the temple: "Furthermore, I decree that if anyone changes this edict, a beam is to be pulled from his house and he is to be lifted up and impaled on it" (Ezra 6:11). Herodotus (3:159) relates that Darius impaled three thousand Babylonians when he took the rebellious city. According to the Behistun inscription Darius impaled numerous rebels, oftentimes after mutilating them.

With the support of the Persian crown the Jews were finally able to complete the second temple.

> They finished building the temple according to the command of the God of Israel and the decrees of Cyrus, Darius and Artaxerxes,[147] kings of Persia. The temple was completed on the third day of the month Adar, in the sixth year of the reign of King Darius. (Ezra 6:14–15)

The temple was thus finished on March 12, 515, a little over seventy years after its destruction. As the renewed work on the temple had begun September 21, 520 (Hag. 1:4–15), sustained effort had been expended for four years and three months by the inspired community.

Because Herod the Great completely rebuilt Zerubbabel's second temple and Titus then destroyed it in A.D. 70, no trace of this building remains. Kathleen Kenyon identified as the only visible remains of Zerubbabel's construction a straight joint of stones with heavy bosses about 33 meters (108 feet) north of the southeast corner of the temple platform, which Maurice Dunand confirmed as similar to Persian masonry found in Phoenicia.[148]

146. On the Aramaic papyri from Elephantine, see B. Porten, *Archives;* B. Porten and J. C. Greenfield, *Jews of Elephantine and Arameans of Syene* (Jerusalem: Akademon, 1974); B. Porten, "Aramaic Papyri and Parchments: A New Look," *BA* 42 (1979): 74–104.

147. The reference to Artaxerxes I may have been inserted here because he contributed to the work of the temple at a later date under Ezra (Ezra 7:21ff.).

148. See M. Dunand, "Byblos, Sidon, Jerusalem," *Vetus Testamentum Supplement* 17 (1969): 64–

The Invasion of European Scythia

The Persians distinguished among three groups of *Saka* (Scythians).[149] The first group was known as *Saka tyaiy paradraya,* "Beyond-the-sea Scythians." Most scholars place this group in Europe—to the north of the Black Sea in the Ukraine and to the west in Thrace (Bulgaria).[150]

The second group was the *Saka haumavarga.* This name has usually been explained as a description of those Scythians who consumed the hallucinogenic "haoma" plant, although some recent studies derive the designation from a leader named **Hu-marga,* "he who has good plains."[151] These Scythians have been located in Central Asia between the Jaxartes and the Oxus Rivers, which flow into the Aral Sea.[152]

The last group was the *Saka tigrachauda* or "pointed-hat Scythians." Most scholars place these Scythians in the east just west of the *Saka haumavarga.*[153] The key indication is a reference in the Behistun inscription to the Araxša River, which should be identified with the Araxes (Oxus) River.[154] Their defeated leader Skunkha is depicted as the last of the defeated rebels on the Behistun relief.

Herodotus devotes half a book to the strange and savage Scythians and their customs, an account whose accuracy has been confirmed by

---

70; K. Kenyon, *Royal Cities of the Old Testament* (New York: Schocken, 1971), pp. 38–41; idem, *Digging up Jerusalem* (London: Benn, 1974), pp. 111–12, 177–78.

149. See Yamauchi, *Foes,* pp. 100ff.

150. Kent, *OP,* p. 195; Cook, *Persian Empire,* p. 59; C. Herrenschmidt, "Désignation de l'empire et concepts politiques de Darius Ier d'après ses inscriptions en vieux-perse," *Studia Iranica* 5 (1976): 33–65; S. Parlato, "La cosidetta campagna scitica di Dario," *Annali Istituto Orientale di Napoli* 41 (1981): 246. On the other hand, V. V. Struve, *Etyudy po Istorii Severnogo Prichernomor'ya Kaukaza i Srednei Azii* [*Studies on the History of the Northern Black Sea Coast, the Caucasus, and Central Asia*] (Leningrad: Nauka, 1968), pp. 103–14, places them east of the Aral Sea. R. Schmitt, "Die achaimenidische Satrapie *Tayaiy Drayahya,*" *Historia* 21 (1972): 522–27, believes that the sea in question is not the Black Sea but the Propontis (Sea of Marmara) leading into the Black Sea.

151. Parlato, "La cosidetta campagna," pp. 222–24; H. Kothe, "Der Skythenbegriff bei Herodot," *Klio* 51 (1969): 75.

152. Herzfeld, *Persian Empire,* pp. 327–29.

153. In an attempt to argue that Darius made but one expedition against the Scythians in the west in 519, rather than an earlier campaign in the east in 519 and a later one in the west, Balcer had placed these Scythians in the area between the Crimea and the Caspian Sea. J. M. Balcer's proposal, "The Date of *Herodotus* IV.1, Darius' Scythian Expedition," *HSCP* 76 (1972): 99–132, was supported by G. Cameron, "Darius the Great and His Scythian (Saka) Campaign," in *Monumentum H. S. Nyberg* (Leiden: Brill, 1975), 1: 77–88. Balcer was opposed by J. Harmatta, "Darius' Expedition against the Sakā Tigraxauda," *AAH* 24 (1976): 15–24 and by W. Nagel, "Frada, Skuncha und der Saken-Feldzug des Darius I," *Kunst, Kultur und Geshichte der Achämenidenzeit und ihr Fortleben,* eds. H. Koch and D. N. MacKenzie (Berlin: Dietrich Reimer, 1983), pp. 169–89. Balcer, *Herodotus & Bisitun,* p. 154, n. 3, has now retracted this proposal.

154. Harmatta, "Darius' Expedition," p. 23.

archaeological discoveries.[155] Darius crossed the Bosporus into Scythian territory in 514 on a bridge built by a Greek engineer. At the site he set up stelae and "engraved on the one in Assyrian (i.e. cuneiform) and on the other in Greek characters the names of all the nations that were in his army" (Herodotus 4.87) as he had done along his canal in Egypt. The Scythians, however, frustrated the king by their mobility and their refusal to stand and fight (Herodotus 4.134).

According to Balcer Darius's motive in invading European Scythia may have been his desire to gain the gold that the Scythians controlled.[156] On the other hand, Georges has linked Herodotus's statement that Darius planned to erect eight forts about fifty miles apart (4.124) with varied archaeological evidence to conclude that Darius engaged in a grand strategy of stemming the tide of the Scythians in the northwest as Cyrus had fought against the Massagetae in the northeast.[157]

The archaeological evidence for the Persian penetration into these areas is scanty but tantalizing. A Persian cuneiform tablet was discovered in 1937 in a vegetable garden in Gerla beyond the Transylvania Alps in Romania by the uncle of the Iranologist János Harmatta.[158] The base of a stele inscribed by Darius was discovered by Eckhard Unger near Buar Hisar in Turkish Thrace.[159] There was no doubt an invasion of Scythia by Darius, although Herodotus's details are unreliable.[160]

The Ionian Revolt

The Greek cities of Ionia in western Turkey were subjected to the Persians shortly after the conquest of Lydia by Cyrus in 547. Under the benevolent reign of the Persians the Greeks should not have found their existence intolerable. A famous example of Persian concern for their subjects' religious affairs is Darius's celebrated letter to Gadates

155. See Yamauchi, *Foes.*

156. See Balcer, "Date of *Herodotus*," p. 132; J. Balcer, *Sparda by the Bitter Sea* (Chico: Scholars, 1984), p. 184.

157. P. Georges, "Darius in Scythia: New Evidence and a New Hypothesis," paper delivered at the annual meeting of the Association of Ancient Historians, Madison, Wis., May 1983. H.-J. Schnitzler, "Der Sakenfeldzug Dareios' des Grossen," in *Antike und Universalgeschicte* [Hans Erich Stier Festschrift] (Münster: Aschendorff, 1972), pp. 64, 66, posits a crossing of the Caspian Sea by the Persian army and maintains that Darius's campaigns against the western and eastern Scyths had the common aim of securing the northern border on either side of the Caspian.

158. J. Harmatta, "A Recently Discovered Old Persian Inscription," *AAH* 2 (1952–1954): 1–16.

159. Hinz, *Darius,* p. 205.

160. See T. Sulimirski, "The Scyths," in *The Cambridge History of Iran II: The Median and Achaemenian Periods,* ed. I. Gershevitch (Cambridge: Cambridge University Press, 1985), p. 190; and T. Nowak, "Darius' Invasion into Scythia: Geographical and Logistical Perspectives," unpublished M.A. thesis (Miami University, 1988), which makes full use of Soviet scholarship on this subject.

in reference to the "gardeners."[161] Gadates was a Persian governor in Ionia who had disregarded Darius's orders. The text reads:

> King of Kings, Darius, son of Hystaspes, to his servant Gadates thus says:
> "I hear that you are not in all things obeying my orders; for in that you are cultivating my land, introducing food-crops from beyond Euphrates into lower Asia, I commend your policy, and for this great credit will be given to you in the house of the King. But in that you are causing my intention on behalf of the gods to be forgotten, I shall give you, if you do not change your course, cause to know that I am angered; for you have levied tribute from the sacred gardeners of Apollo, and ordered them to dig unhallowed soil, not knowing my feelings towards the god, who spoke all truth to the Persians."[162]

In 507 Athenian envoys traveled to Sardis to see the Persian satrap Artaphernes. Probably as a hedge against their bitter rivals, the Spartans, the Athenian envoys offered the elements of "earth and water" to obtain a treaty with Darius (Herodotus 5.73).[163] Their actions, however, were disavowed by the Athenians when they returned.

The Persians found it convenient to rule the Ionian cities through the use of Greek tyrants.[164] Miletus, for example, was ruled for the Persians by the tyrant Aristagoras. In 499, for personal rather than patriotic reasons, Aristagoras raised the banner of revolt against the Persians among the Ionian cities. Sparta refused to help since she was loath to send her troops far away from her restive helots or state slaves (Herodotus 5.50). Athens agreed to send twenty ships and Eretria on the island of Euboea agreed to send five ships to aid the rebels.[165]

The Persian satrap over Ionia resided in Sardis. One striking monument from the Persian occupation of this city is a pyramid tomb, the base of which bears a striking resemblance to the base of the tomb of Cyrus.[166] In 498 the Ionian rebels and their allies managed to burn the lower city of Sardis. Excavations under George Hanfmann have un-

161. F. W. Schehl, "Darius' Letter to Gadatas," *AJA* 54 (1950): 265.

162. Cited by Burn, *Persia and the Greeks,* p. 114. Compare F. Lochner-Hüttenbach, "Brief des König Darius an den Satrapen Gadatas," in Brandenstein and Mayrhofer, *Handbuch der Orientalistik,* pp. 91–98; *Archaic Times to the End of the Peloponnesian War,* ed. C. W. Fornara (Baltimore: Johns Hopkins University Press, 1977), pp. 36–37.

163. See A. E. Raubitschek, "The Treaties between Persia and Athens," *GRBS* 5 (1964): 151–59.

164. D. Gillis, *Collaboration with the Persians* (Wiesbaden: Franz Steiner, 1979).

165. For a critical analysis of Herodotus's account of the Ionian revolt, see M. Lang, "Herodotus and the Ionian Revolt," *Historia* 17 (1968): 24–36. For studies more sympathetic to Herodotus, see L. Solmsen, "Speeches in Herodotus' Account of the Ionian Revolt," *AJP* 64 (1942): 194–207; K. H. Waters, "Herodotus and the Ionian Revolt," *Historia* 19 (1970): 504–8.

166. G. M. A. Hanfmann, *Letters from Sardis* (Cambridge: Harvard University Press, 1972), pp. 259–60.

covered evidence of this attack in a burned level along the Pactolus River.[167]

In the wake of the Ionian revolt the island of Cyprus also revolted against the Persians. In 1971 German archaeologists discovered striking evidence of the siege of Old Paphos by the Persian army in 498 B.C. They uncovered about 450 arrowheads and javelin points, 400 stone missiles, tunnels, and siege ramps. The Persians had ransacked nearby sanctuaries to construct the ramps with numerous statues, sphinxes, stelae, and incense altars.[168]

The decisive battle that crushed the revolt took place off the island of Lade near Miletus in 494,[169] during which the Persian fleet capitalized on dissension in the Ionian ranks (Herodotus 6.11–17). Miletus was severely punished. It has only been recently near the Delphinion that evidence of the Persian destruction of Miletus has been brought to light.[170]

The Persians also destroyed the famous oracular temple of Apollo at Didyma near Miletus (Herodotus 6.19). The Persians banished the Branchidae priest of Didyma to the eastern part of their empire and carried off the bronze statue of Apollo to Ecbatana.[171] In 1962 the German Archaeological Institute at Istanbul discovered the first evidence of the Persian destruction of this site.[172]

In light of the earlier treaty of 507, the Persians may have regarded Athenian participation in the Ionian revolt as treason and a violation of her status as a so-called vassal. According to Louis Orlin this casts a different light on the wars between the Persians and the Greeks that resulted from the Ionian revolt:

> [W]e should strive to understand that the Persians were not the essentially greedy, rapacious, tyrannical, even insane individuals that Herodotus has portrayed, nor were their subjects slaves. On the contrary they were believers in law, order, tolerance and fairness.[173]

167. D. G. Mitten, "A New Look at Sardis," *BA* 29 (1966): 57, had suggested that the numerous "puppy" burials may have been desperate sacrifices made before the siege of Sardis. But detailed study now dates these to the period between 575 and 525 B.C. and indicates that these are the remains of ritual meals dedicated probably to Kandaulas. See C. H. Greenwalt, "Ritual Dinners in Early Historic Sardis," *University of California Classical Studies* 17 (1978): 1–82.

168. K. Nicolaou, "Archaeological News from Cyprus, 1971," *AJA* 77 (1973): 56.

169. See the maps in E. Yamauchi, *New Testament Cities in Western Asia Minor* (Grand Rapids: Baker, 1980), pp. 116–17.

170. M. J. Mellink, "Archaeology in Asia Minor," *AJA* 78 (1974): 123.

171. See chapter 9, "Didyma," in Yamauchi, *New Testament Cities.*

172. R. Naumann, "Didyma," *AS* 13 (1963): 24.

173. L. L. Orlin, "Athens and Persia ca. 507 B.C.: A Neglected Perspective," in *Michigan Oriental Studies in Honor of George G. Cameron*, ed. L. L. Orlin (Ann Arbor: University of Michigan Press, 1976), p. 265 .

Enraged by the Athenian role in the attack on Sardis, Darius charged one of his servants to remind him thrice at each dinner: "Master, remember the Athenians" (Herodotus 5.105).

Marathon

In 492 Darius sent an expedition led by his son-in-law Mardonius to punish the Greeks. Unfortunately for the Persians their fleet was wrecked off the peninsula of Mount Athos in the northern Aegean. The expedition, however, was not a total loss. The Persians gained a foothold in Europe with the submission of Thrace and Macedonia. Many other Greek city-states were cowed into "Medizing."

A second expedition was sent in 490, this time directly across the Aegean. It was led by Datis a Mede and Artaphernes the younger, Darius's nephew. The Persians headed first for Eretria, which was betrayed to them after a siege of a week. Some of the Eretrians were transported back to "Kissian" country about twenty miles from Susa,[174] where Herodotus learned they still dwelt in his day "keeping the ancient language" (6.119). Plato (*Anthologia Palatina* 7.259) reports their lament:

> Leaving the rough Aegean's surge and swell,
> Afar in inland plains lie we.
> Farewell, Eretria famed, our home; farewell
> Athens, our neighbor there; farewell, dear sea.[175]

News of the Persian invasion and the fall of Eretria was carried by the runner Phidippides (or Phillippides) to Sparta 150 miles away.[176] He reached his destination "on the day after he left Athens" (Herodotus 6.106). The Spartans responded that they could not march until the moon was full. Most believe this was in observance of the Carneian Festival of Apollo, but William Pritchett would associate their reluctance with a general lunar superstition.[177]

The Persians were led to land at the Bay of Marathon by the exiled Athenian tyrant Hippias (Herodotus 6.107), whose father Pisistratus had once made a successful invasion there. This set the stage for one of the

174. Herzfeld, *Persian Empire,* pp. 11–13.

175. Cited by Burn, *Persia and the Greeks,* p. 253.

176. It was much later that Lucian (A.D. 180) added the detail of the same runner racing from Marathon to announce the Athenian victory just before he expired. See F. J. Frost, "The Dubious Origins of the 'Marathon,' " *AJAH* 4 (1979): 159–63; E. Badian, "The Name of the Runner," *AJAH* 4 (1979): 163–66.

177. W. K. Pritchett, "Phases of the Moon and Festivals," in *The Greek State at War I* (Berkeley: University of California Press, 1971), chapter 9.

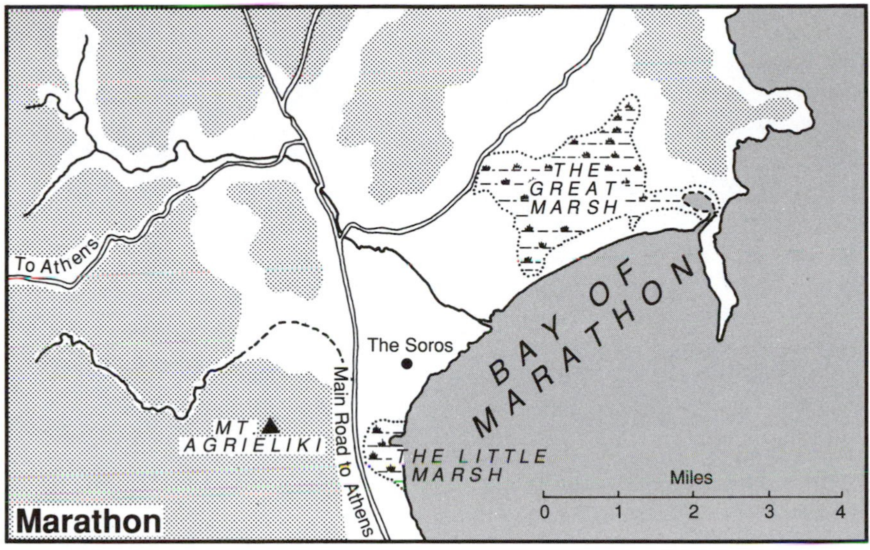

most significant battles in history, although most would not agree with John Stuart Mill, who wrote: "The battle of Marathon, even as an event of English history, is more important than the battle of Hastings."[178]

Although the main locations of the Battle of Marathon, fought in the fall of 490, are clearly indicated from Herodotus and from topographical and archaeological considerations,[179] the details of the conflict have provoked a battle among scholars. As Nicholas Hammond observes, "many studies of the campaign and the battle of Marathon have suffered from conflicts between scholars in the field of hypothesis."[180]

The ten Athenian generals (*stratēgoi*) were evenly divided as to whether they should remain behind to defend Athens or take the offensive at Marathon. The *polemarch* or military archon, Callimachos, broke the tie in favor of the latter strategy.[181] Even if the polemarch was

178. Cited by V. Ehrenberg, *From Solon to Socrates* (New York: Barnes and Noble, 1973), p. xvi.

179. W. K. Pritchett, *Marathon* (Berkeley: University of California Press, 1960); idem, "Deme of Marathon," in *Studies in Ancient Greek Topography: Part II, Battlefields* (Berkeley: University of California Press, 1969), chapter 1.

180. N. G. L. Hammond, "The Campaign and the Battle of Marathon," *JHS* 88 (1968): 13. Compare A. R. Burn, "Hammond on Marathon: A Few Notes," *JHS* 89 (1969): 118–19; J. A. S. Evans, "Herodotus and Marathon," *Florilegium* 6 (1984): 1–26. For a popular account, see Alan Lloyd, *Marathon* (New York: Mentor, 1973).

181. There is still a dispute as to whether the generals were subordinate to the polemarch, or vice versa. See C. Hignett, *History of the Athenian Constitution* (New York: Oxford University Press, 1953), p. 170; P. Bicknell, "The Command Structure and Generals of the Marathon Campaign," *L'Antiquité Classique* 39 (1970): 427–42.

The Plain and Bay of Marathon.

nominally in control, all recognized that Miltiades was the decisive leader.

Once the opposing armies had taken their positions, there was a delay of five or six days before the battle began. The Athenians may have been waiting for the promised Spartan reinforcements. The Persians may have been waiting for some aid from pro-Persian sympathizers such as members of the Alcmaeonid clan.[182] Rumor had it that they used a shield to send a signal to the Persians (Herodotus 6.115).[183]

The Athenians had a force of about nine thousand hoplites (heavily armed infantrymen who fought in a phalanx formation, usually eight men deep).[184] They carried shields in their left hand and spears in their right. There was also a contingent of about one thousand men from Plataea, a city to the northwest of Athens.

The Persians, who may have been two or three times as numerous, were not heavily armored but relied chiefly on their archers. These

182. D. Gillis, "Marathon and the Alcmaeonids," *GRBS* 10 (1969): 133–45, believes that the Alcmaeonid clan was sympathetic to the Persians. On the other hand, M. F. McGregor, "The Pro-Persian Party at Athens from 510 to 480 B.C.," *HSCP* Supplementary Volume 1 (1940): 71–95, agrees with Herodotus in absolving the Alcmaeonids of such treasonable sentiments. The Peisistratids would have welcomed the restoration of the tyrant Hippias. See D. Graf, "Medism: Greek Collaboration with Achaemenid Persia," unpublished Ph.D. diss. (Ann Arbor: University of Michigan, 1979).

183. A. T. Hodge and L. A. Losada, "The Time of the Shield Signal at Marathon," *AJA* 74 (1970): 31–36, determined by experiments that the signal could have been given at almost any time during the day.

184. Plutarch (*Moralia* 305B) mentions nine thousand hoplites; Justin-Trogus (2.9) ten thousand. At Plataea in 479 B.C. Athens mustered eight thousand hoplites (Herodotus 9.28). See A. Snodgrass, "The Hoplite Reform and History," *JHS* 85 (1965): 110–22; idem, *Arms and Armour of the Greeks* (London: Thames and Hudson, 1967); Pritchett, "Depth of Phalanx," *The Greek State at War I*, chapter 11.

may have had a range of 150 meters (about 500 feet) or more.[185] To take advantage of these differences Miltiades devised the brilliant tactic of charging at a run.[186]

> When the Persians saw them come running they prepared to receive them, deeming the Athenians frenzied to their utter destruction, who being (as they saw) so few were yet charging them at speed, albeit they had no horsemen nor archers. . . . They were the first Greeks, within my knowledge, who charged their enemies at a run, and the first who endured the sight of Median garments and the men clad therein; till then, the Greeks were affrighted by the very name of the Medes [that is, Persians]. (Herodotus 6.112)

The Athenians deliberately made their center weak and their wings strong (Herodotus 6.111). The Persians therefore broke through their center, but the Greeks then swung their wings around and caught the Persians in a pincers movement. At that moment the Persians fled toward the great marsh in the north to scramble on board their ships anchored in the bay.

A painting of the battle by Panainos, the nephew of Phidias, once hung in the *Stoa Poikile* (the painted porch) in the Agora at Athens.[187] According to Pausanias's (1.15.1) description of the painting, we see that "in the center of the battle . . . the barbarians are fleeing and are pushing one another into the marsh."[188] Kynegeiros, the brother of Aeschylus, reaches an enemy ship only to have his arm hacked off by a Persian axe. The southern frieze of the Nike temple also depicts the Battle of Marathon.[189]

One puzzling aspect of the battle, for which Herodotus has often

185. See W. McLeod, "The Bowshot and Marathon," *JHS* 90 (1970): 197–98. At Plataea two stades (about 200 meters) was beyond bowshot (Herodotus 9.23).

186. Herodotus's account that the Athenians ran with their armor the full distance of eight stades was an exaggeration. On the basis of experiments with Penn State athletes, W. Donlan and J. Thompson, "The Charge at Marathon: Herodotus 6.112," *CJ* 71 (1970): 342, conclude "with some confidence that the maximum distance for a phalanx-charge at double time, maintaining formation and arriving fit for close engagement was no more than one stade, approximately 200 yards."

187. As Zeno lectured in this portico, his followers became known as Stoics. The American School of Classical Studies recently recovered evidence of the Stoa Poikile in the northwest corner of the Agora. See T. L. Shear, Jr., "The Athenian Agora: Excavations of 1980–1982," *Hesperia* 53 (1984): 1–19. R. E. Wycherley, "The Painted Stoa," *Phoenix* 7 (1953): 20, comments: "By far the best known monument of Athens was the Stoa Poikile, the Painted Colonnade, if one may judge from ancient authors. . . . Of all works of art at Athens, none was more famous than the painting of the battle of Marathon in the Poikile, in which the Athenians took a peculiar pride."

188. See J. J. Pollitt, ed., *The Art of Greece 1400–31 B.C.* (Englewood Cliffs, N.J.: Prentice-Hall, 1965), p. 108.

189. E. B. Harrison, "The South Frieze of the Nike Temple and the Marathon Painting in the Painted Stoa," *AJA* 76 (1972): 353–78.

been criticized, is his failure to mention any involvement of the Persian cavalry, after having stressed their presence several times. Hammond believes that the horses may have been grazing in the north; Andrew Burn holds they may have been on board ship. Arnold Gomme suggests that the Persians may have been embarking their horses at night to attack Athens. When the Athenians discovered this fact, they chose to attack.[190] Pritchett believes that a gloss in the Byzantine lexicon, the *Suda,* can be integrated with Herodotus:

> The horsemen are away. After Datis had invaded Attika, they say that the Ionians, when he had withdrawn, climbing trees, signaled to the Athenians that the horsemen were away; and Miltiades, having become aware of their departure, in this way joined battle and conquered.[191]

In light of possible explanations about the absence of the Persian cavalry and other matters, Nicholas G. L. Whatley concludes that Herodotus's account of the battle is not as defective as some critics have charged.[192]

Herodotus (6.117) recounts that the Persians lost 6,400 men and the Athenians only 192.[193] While some scholars are suspicious of these figures, such lopsided casualties were typical of ancient battles recorded in classical, biblical, and Near Eastern sources. As Mardonios comments (Herodotus 7.9), "the victors come not off without great harm; and of the vanquished I say not so much as a word, for they are utterly destroyed." That is, the greatest number of casualties were inflicted when the other side was routed from the field of battle.

Bones, which were turned up near the great marsh by a German military surveyor in the nineteenth century, may possibly have belonged to the Persian dead.[194] We can be certain of the 192 Athenian dead, because their names were inscribed on stelae, their bodies were cremated, and their remains were buried in the Soros mound. Some six centuries later Athenians were still making offerings to these heroes (Pausanias 1.32.4).

190. A. W. Gomme, "Herodotus and Marathon," *Phoenix* 6 (1952): 80–83; J. A. S. Evans, "Cavalry about the Time of the Persian Wars: A Speculative Essay," *CJ* 82 (1987): 339–43.

191. Cited by Pritchett, *Marathon,* p. 170; compare Fornara, *Archaic Times,* pp. 48–49. Against the majority of scholars, G. Shrimpton, "The Persian Cavalry at Marathon," *Phoenix* 34 (1980): 20–37, maintains that the cavalry were there but fled in the face of the hoplite charge.

192. N. Whatley, "On the Possibility of Reconstructing Marathon and Other Ancient Battles," *JHS* 84 (1964): 119–39.

193. J. Boardman, "The Parthenon Frieze—Another View," in *Festschrift für Frank Brommer,* eds. U. Hockmann and A. Krug (Mainz: Philipp von Zabern, 1977), pp. 39–49, suggests that the famous Parthenon frieze, which has 192 figures, was designed as a monument to the Athenian dead at Marathon.

194. E. Vanderpool, "A Monument to the Battle of Marathon," *Hesperia* 35 (1966): 101, n. 15.

The Soros or monument to the Athenian dead at Marathon.

The Soros still stands in the Plain of Marathon 9 meters (30 feet) high and 150 meters (164 feet) in diameter. Heinrich Schliemann, the famous excavator of Troy, dug at the mound in 1884 but found only Mycenaean remains. But Balerios Staes in excavations in 1890 and 1893 found a thick layer of ashes, burnt bones, early fifth-century B.C. vessels, and a sacrificial pit with animal remains.[195] Numerous Persian arrowheads, some of them possibly shot by Scythian archers,[196] were recovered from the mound. A Greek sword was also found on the battlefield.[197] The Soros probably marks the center of the heaviest fighting.[198]

Recently Spyridon Marinatos found what he interpreted as remains of the Plataean allies (see Pausanias 1.32) 1.25 miles southwest of the Soros in a low mound only 3.35 meters (11 feet) high with a diameter measuring 30 to 35 meters (95 to 114 feet). The location of the mound persuaded Marinatos that the battle line may have been longer than previously estimated. Remains of eleven individuals have been identified, most between twenty and twenty-five years old. There was even a ten-year-old boy who may have served as a scout.[199] Other scholars, however, doubt that the tomb was that of the Plataeans, and suggest that it covered the remains of some scouts.[200]

195. Pritchett, *Marathon*, pp. 141–44.

196. See Yamauchi, *Foes*, pp. 102–3; E. Erdmann, "Die sogenannten Marathonpfeilspitzen in Karlsruhe," *AA* 88 (1973): 30–58.

197. Pritchett, *Marathon*, p. 174.

198. Also commemorating the battle was a tall column, whose Ionic capital has been recovered. See Vanderpool, "Monument"; W. C. West, III, "The Trophies of the Persian Wars," *CP* 64 (1969): 7–19; W. K. Pritchett, "The Battlefield Trophy" in *The Greek State at War II* (Berkeley: University of California Press, 1974), chapter 13; Fornara, *Archaic Times*, pp. 50–51.

199. S. Marinatos, "Further News from Marathon," *Athens Annals of Archaeology* 3 (1970): 153–66; idem, "New Light on Marathon," *Illustrated London News* 260 (Jan. 1972): 54–55.

200. K.-W. Welwei, "Das sog. Grab der Plataier im Vranatal bei Marathon," *Historia* 28 (1979): 101–6; J. A. G. Van der Veer, "The Battle of Marathon, A Topographical Survey," *Mnemosyne* 35 (1982): 302; W. K. Pritchett, *The Greek State at War IV* (Berkeley: University of California Press, 1985), pp. 126–29.

Dagger and arrowheads from Marathon. (Reproduced by courtesy of the trustees of the British Museum)

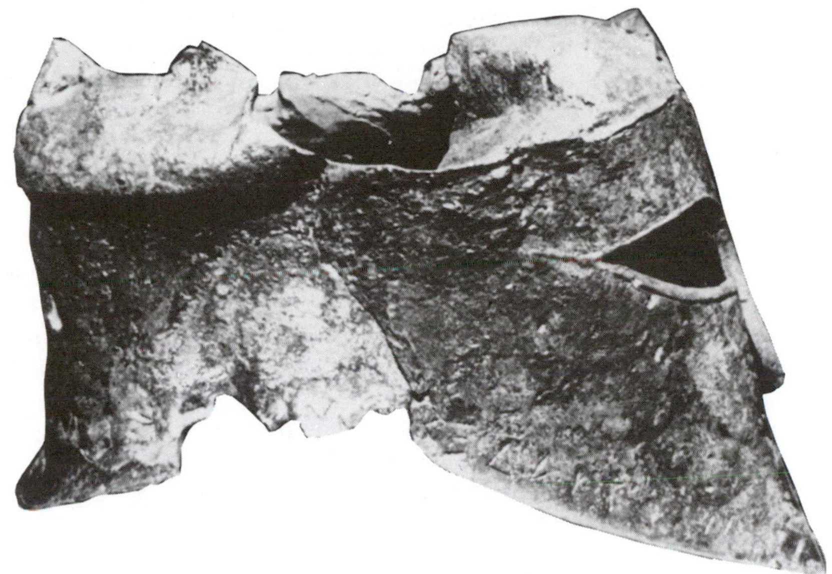

The helmet of Miltiades dedicated at Olympia.

Victory at Marathon had still not averted danger from Athens, located twenty-five miles away (twenty-two miles by the direct route over Mount Pentelicus).[201] Hammond calculates that the battle may have begun about 6 A.M. and have been over by 10 A.M. From his own experience in traversing the route on foot, he estimates that the Athenians had to march rapidly for eight hours to arrive back in Athens before the Persian fleet could round Cape Sunium at 6 P.M.[202] Thus thwarted, the Persians sailed away.

Two days later a force of 2,000 Spartans arrived, having covered 150 miles in three days. Although informed that their help was no longer needed, they still marched to Marathon to view the battlefield.

Miltiades was the hero of the day. German excavators at Olympia in 1961 recovered a helmet, which was dedicated by Miltiades, and also

201. The marathon race was not a part of the ancient Olympic games. It was included in the revived Olympic games in 1896 to commemorate the legendary effort of Phidippides, who ran to Athens to announce the victory and then dropped dead. The current distance of 26 miles and 385 yards in races like the Boston Marathon was the distance from Windsor Castle to the stadium at London in the 1908 Olympics. It became the standard distance after the 1924 Olympics.

202. N. G. L. Hammond, *A History of Greece to 322 B.C.* (Oxford: Clarendon, 1959), p. 216, n. 2. Hammond's estimate of a relatively swift voyage by the Persian fleet from Marathon to Phaleron (off the coast of Athens) is questioned by A. T. Hodge, "Marathon to Phaleron," *JHS* 95 (1975): 169–71; idem, "Marathon: The Persians' Voyage," *TAPA* 104 (1975): 155–73. Experiments with a trireme built under the supervision of John Morrison indicate that swift speeds could have been achieved. See A. Toufexis, "The Glory That Was Greece," *Time* (Aug. 17, 1987): 73.

another helmet with the inscription, "Athenians took (this) of the Medes." But then Miltiades tragically became a victim of what the Greeks called *hubris*, excessive pride that leads to a fall. He commandeered a fleet to punish the island of Paros, which had Medized. The expedition turned out to be a fiasco. Miltiades was tried by the Athenians, fined a crushing sum of fifty talents, and died from gangrene contracted during the unsuccessful siege.

Marathon was a great victory for the Greeks, but one that only initiated further hostilities. The Persians sailed away to sail back another day. If John Stuart Mill exaggerated the significance of Marathon, Robert Graves goes to the other extreme in minimizing its importance:

> Truth-loving Persians do not dwell upon
> The trivial skirmish fought near Marathon.
> As for the Greek theatrical tradition
> Which represents that summer's expedition
> Not as a mere reconnaissance in force
> By three brigades of foot and one of horse
> (Their left flank covered by some obsolete
> Light craft detached from the main Persian fleet)
> But as a grandiose, ill-starred attempt
> To conquer Greece—they treat it with contempt;
> And only incidentally refute
> Major Greek claims, by stressing what repute
> The Persian monarch and the Persian nation
> Won by this salutary demonstration:
> Despite a strong defense and adverse weather
> All arms combined magnificently together.[203]

Babylon

Although Darius was less than successful in the west, he was quite enterprising in the east. (For his new capital, see chapter 10 on Persepolis.) Early in his reign two pretenders, the so-called Nebuchadnezzar III and Nebuchadnezzar IV, led the Babylonians to rebel against Darius. Babylon was recaptured for the king by a remarkable act of self-mutilation by Zopyrus, the son of Megabyzus, who cut off his own

203. Compare Balcer, *Herodotus & Bisitun*, p. 155: "Only the Persian failure at Marathon, a trivial event for the Persians yet in retrospect monumental for the Athenians, drove Xerxes' armies to defeat, reorganization and withdrawal from the Aegean basin." In a serious attempt to understand Marathon from the Persian point of view, F. Schachermeyr, "Marathon und die persische Politik," *Historische Zeitschrift* 172 (1951): 30, suggests that the Persian aim in 490 was not the military conquest of Athens but the peaceful restoration of Hippias with the cooperation of Alcmaeonids.

nose and ears (Herodotus 3.154–57) to gain entrance into the city as one who had supposedly been punished by Darius. Darius impaled about three thousand rebels, but hardly destroyed their walls and their gates as Herodotus asserts (3.159). In the first place, this would not have been necessary. Second, Darius continued to use the city. And finally, Herodotus describes an intact city on his visit (1.178–200) less than a century later.

After the capture of Babylon by Cyrus in 539, the city served as a favorite residence of the Achaemenid kings for at least part of the year. According to Xenophon (*Cyropaedia* 8.6.22): "Cyrus himself made his home in the center of his domain, and in the winter season he spent seven months in Babylon, for there the climate is warm; in the spring he spent three months in Susa, and in the height of summer two months in Ecbatana."

The Achaemenid kings made good use of the great palace built by Nebuchadnezzar, which was excavated by Robert Koldewey between 1899 and 1913.[204] The major palace was located on the east bank of the Euphrates River at the northern edge of the city next to the Ishtar Gate. It occupied a trapezoidal area 300 meters (984 feet) west to east, and between 120 and 200 meters (394 and 656 feet) north to south, enclosing five major courts. The central court, 52 by 17 meters (170 by 56 feet), was the most important because the king's throne room was located at its southern end. This room was decorated with enameled bricks in the form of Proto-Aeolic columns, probably inspired by Greek artisans. This court was no doubt the setting for Belshazzar's feast (Dan. 5).

Just to the north of the main palace area was the northern palace. Nearby was an area that functioned as a museum down to the Persian era. It was here that diorite fragments of Darius's Behistun inscription were found. A further inscription indicates that Darius began a "House of the King's Son" in the year 498.

To the west of Nebuchadnezzar's palace, Darius erected a small palace, measuring 35 meters (115 feet) by 20.5 meters (68 feet). Its colonnaded forehall and rectangular hall with two rows of four columns bear a striking resemblance to the Achaemenid buildings at

204. See R. Koldewey, *The Excavations at Babylon* (London: Macmillan, 1914); E. Unger, *Babylon* (Berlin: W. de Gruyter, 1970 reprint of the 1930 edition); A. Parrot, *Babylon and the Old Testament* (New York: Philosophical Library, 1958); J. G. MacQueen, *Babylon* (London: Robert Hale, 1964); G. A. Larue, *Babylon and the Bible* (Grand Rapids: Baker, 1969); J. Oates, *Babylon* (London: Thames and Hudson, 1979); Wiseman, *Nebuchadrezzar and Babylon*; see also E. Yamauchi, "Babylon," in *Major Cities of Bible Times*, ed. R. K. Harrison (Nashville: Nelson, 1985), pp. 32–48.

Pasargadae and Persepolis. Column bases, variously colored tiles, as well as clay tablets and a limestone fragment with the name of Darius have been recovered from the site.[205] (For Darius's buildings at Susa, see chapter 7.)

The Royal Road

The motto engraved on the U.S. Post Office building in New York City is taken from Herodotus's (8.98) description of the couriers on the Royal Road that Darius established to link Susa in southwestern Persia to Sardis in western Anatolia:

> It is said that as many days as there are in the whole journey, so many are the men and horses that stand along the road, each horse and man at the interval of a day's journey; and *these are stayed neither by snow nor rain nor heat nor darkness from accomplishing their appointed course with all speed.*

Elsewhere in connection with Aristagoras's futile effort to get the Spartans to join the Ionian revolt, Herodotus (5.52–53) gives further details about the Royal Road:

> Its course through Lydia and Phrygia is of the length of 20 stages and 94½ parasangs. Next after Phrygia it comes to the river Halys, where there is a defile which must be passed ere the river can be crossed, and a great fortress to guard it. After the passage into Cappadocia the road in that land as far as the borders of Cilicia is of 28 stages and 104 parasangs. On this frontier you must ride through two defiles and pass two fortresses. . . . Thus the whole tale of stages is 111. . . . there are 13,500 furlongs, the number of parasangs being 450; and if each day's journey be 150 furlongs, then the sum of days spent is 90, neither more nor less.[206]

That is, the route of 1,700 miles was covered by ordinary travelers in 90 days, averaging 19 miles per day. But the royal couriers covered the

205. Although some scholars would attribute the building in Babylon to Artaxerxes II, F. Haerinck, "Le palais achéménide de Babylone," *IA* 10 (1973): 108–32, ascribes it to Darius. See Oates, *Babylon*, pp. 138, 159.

206. The parasang was a Persian measure equal to 30 Greek stadia or about 3.4 miles. The furlong is an English measure of 220 yards used to translate the Greek *stadion,* which meant: a distance of about 200 yards; a race of that distance; the place to view such a race. We derive our word *stadium* from the Latin form of this word.

same distance in a week or 243 miles per day by changing horses, perhaps every 20 miles or so.[207]

We are certain only of the ends of the route, Susa and Sardis.[208] There are two suggested courses of the Royal Road through Anatolia (Turkey): the northern route following Herodotus's account that the road crossed the Halys River and the southern route following the more customary line used in later periods.

The northern route was advocated by William Ramsay, the greatest archaeologist of Anatolia,[209] and is still followed by many today.[210] Ramsay had the road pass from Sardis to Satala to Acmonia then northeast to avoid the central salt desert, to Pessinus, to the ancient Phrygian capital of Gordium, to Ancyra (modern Ankara),[211] then across the Halys River to Tavium near Pteria. Opinions differ as to the continuation of the route east: Heinrich Kiepert drew the route from Pteria northeast to Comana then south to Sebasteia and southeast to Melitene; David Hogarth had the road leading south from Pteria to Caesareia Mazaca and then east to Melitene; still others believe that Herodotus meant the road to lead directly south of Caesareia Mazaca through the Cilician Gates to Tarsus.[212] The northern route probably crossed the Euphrates near Melitene, the southern route near Zeugma. It probably continued east of the Tigris to Arbela and then southeast to Susa.

Ramsay's northern placement of the Royal Road in Anatolia was rejected by William Calder as improbable: "But any Postmaster General who organized a post-road along this route from Sardis to the

207. The famous Pony Express, which ran 1,800 miles between St. Joseph, Mo., and Sacramento, Calif., during the nineteenth century, was covered in 10 days with posts between 7 and 20 miles apart.

208. W. Kleiss, "Ein Abschnitt der Achaemenidischen Königsstrasse von Pasargadae und Persepolis nach Susa, bei Naqsh-i Rustam," *AMI* 14 (1981): 45–53.

209. W. Ramsay, *Historical Geography of Asia Minor* (London: John Murray, 1890; Amsterdam: A. M. Hakkert reprint, 1962), pp. 27–31. On William Ramsay, see W. W. Gasque, *Sir William M. Ramsay* (Grand Rapids: Baker, 1966); see also E. Yamauchi, "Ramsay's Views on Archaeology in Asia Minor Reviewed," *New Testament Student V* (Phillipsburg: Presbyterian and Reformed, 1982), pp. 27–40.

210. A. A. M. van der Heyden and H. H. Scullard, eds., *Atlas of the Classical World* (London: Thomas Nelson, 1959), p. 38; C. G. Starr, "Greeks and Persians in the Fourth Century B.C.," *IA* 11 (1975): 47; C. Foss and G. M. A. Hanfmann, in *A Survey of Sardis and Major Monuments Outside the City Walls*, eds. G. M. A. Hanfmann and J. C. Waldbaum (Cambridge: Harvard University Press, 1975), pp. 25, 34, believe that the Royal Road followed the route of the modern Izmir (Smyrna) to Ankara highway; B. Dicks, *Ancient Persians* (North Pomfret: David and Charles, 1979), p. 73.

211. For the sites, see W. M. Calder and G. E. Bean, *A Classical Map of Asia Minor* (London: British Institute of Archaeology, 1958); B. Levick, *Roman Colonies in Southern Asia Minor* (Oxford: Clarendon, 1967), end map; E. Akurgal, *Ancient Civilizations and Ruins of Turkey* (Istanbul: Mobil Oil Türk, 1970); N. G. L. Hammond, *Atlas of the Greek and Roman World in Antiquity* (Park Ridge: Noyes, 1981), map 26a; T. Cornell and J. Matthews, *Atlas of the Roman World* (Oxford: Phaidon, 1982), pp. 150–51.

212. Levick, *Roman Colonies*, end map.

Cilician Gates would have serious risk, under the Persian Empire, of losing his ears."[213] Calder placed the Royal Road south of the great salt desert linking Philomelium, Laodiceia (in Lycaonia), to Cybistra north of the Taurus Mountains and then through the Cilician Gates to Tarsus. His main argument was that this routing would agree more closely to the distance of 750 miles indicated by Herodotus to the Euphrates than the northern route that would be one hundred miles longer.

Barbara Levick supports this southern route, which was close to the one chosen by Cyrus the Younger and his ten thousand Greek mercenaries about 400 B.C.[214] She believes that Herodotus was mistaken in his conception of the Halys River, imagining that the river flowed north and south to divide Anatolia. In fact, the southern route misses the Halys entirely.[215]

A related question concerns the route of Xerxes' great army from Cappadocia in eastern Turkey to Sardis. Herodotus (7.26) indicates that the army crossed the Halys, which would support a northern route.

After some discoveries were made east of Lake Caralis, Ramsay in 1920 changed his mind, and concluded that Xerxes' army had followed a southern route through Isaurian territory east of Lake Trogitis and south of the Sultan Dagh mountain range.[216]

Yet in spite of the difficulty of the northern routing, there is evidence to support it. At the ancient Phrygian capital of Gordium, fifty miles southwest of Ankara, Rodney Young found what he believes is part of the Royal Road, a section of which extends 6 meters (20 feet) in width. He comments:

> The road itself, which winds its way among the grave mounds, was evidently later than Phrygian times; indications are that it was part of the Royal Road of the Persian Empire, organized by King Darius in the late sixth or the early fifth century B.C. No doubt the Royal Road fol-

213. W. M. Calder, "The Royal Road in Herodotus," *Classical Review* 39 (1925): 9. C. H. E. Haspels, *The Highlands of Phrygia, Sites and Monuments* (Princeton: Princeton University Press, 1972), p. 22, also objects to Ramsay's routing: "From the above it is clear that Ramsay's idea that the Persian Royal Road passed through the highlands is unfounded. He made this ancient highway . . . enter the Phrygian mountains at the valley of Midas City, and continue westward through the Kümbet Valley. A highway meant for speedy and easy traveling, if necessary by an army, would not deliberately choose a route over difficult rocky country, when, as in this case it could be avoided without any complications." But a closer reading of Ramsay's reference to Midas City in his *Historical Geography*, p. 31, reveals that he was writing about a pre-Persian route and not the Royal Road itself.

214. Levick, *Roman Colonies*, pp. 12–13.

215. Ibid., p. 10. One difficulty with the northern route is Herodotus' (5.52ff.) statement that it passed for three days through Cilicia in the southeast.

216. W. M. Ramsay, "Military Operations on the North Front of Mount Taurus," *JHS* 40 (1920): 89–107. Levick, *Roman Colonies*, p. 12, doubts such a route through hostile Isaurian territory; she favors Calder's proposed southern route.

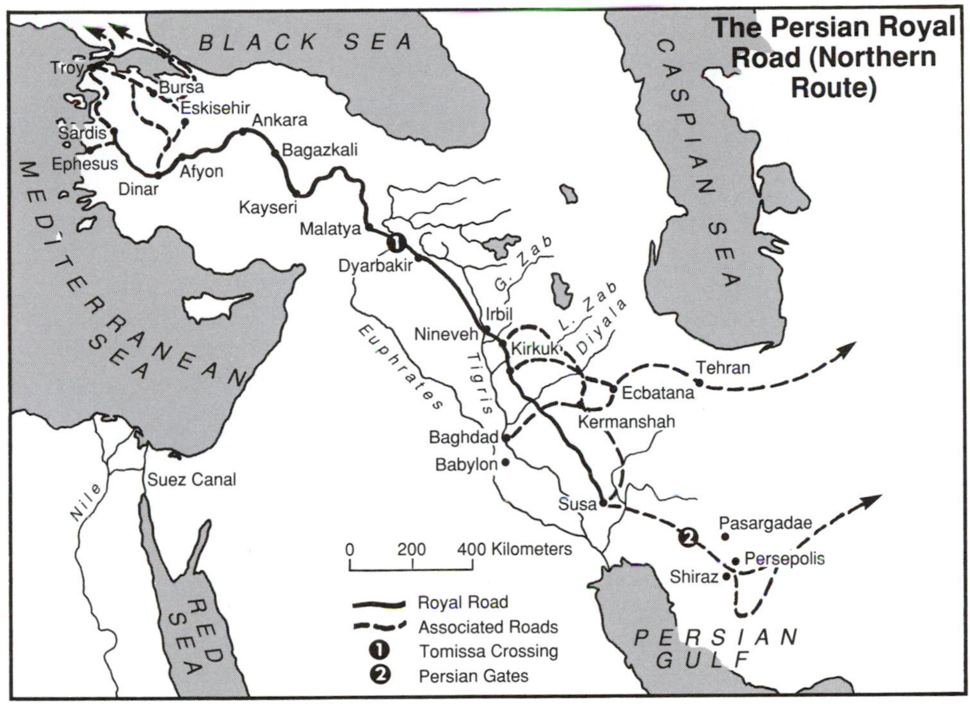

lowed the course of a still earlier route which dated back perhaps to Hittite times.[217]

In 1961 an expedition of three Yale undergraduates discovered evidence that they believe favors the northern route: "grave tumuli of both pre-Persian and post-Persian civilizations exist throughout the length of the northern route."[218] Herodotus (5.52) mentioned natural "defiles" through which one must pass before crossing the Halys. Such a narrow gorge through which the road must have passed was found north of Elmadağ.[219]

It was such a northern route that Cyrus must have taken to engage

217. R. S. Young, *Gordion, A Guide to the Excavations* (Ankara: Ankara Turizmi, 1968), p. 304. The northern route is favored by E. Cavaignac, "Les deux routes d'Asie Mineure," *JA* 244 (1956): 342–48.

218. S. F. Starr, "Mapping Ancient Roads in Anatolia," *Arch* 16 (1963): 162–63.

219. Other scholars have associated one of Herodotus's "gates" with the famous Cilician pass through the Taurus Mountains north of Tarsus.

Croesus at Pteria (near Tavium), and then devastate Gordium[220] on his pursuit of the Lydian army all the way to Sardis (Herodotus 1.75–79).

Satraps, Taxes, and Coins

Darius was responsible for the major organization of the empire into districts governed by satraps (Greek *satrapēs,* Median *xšathrapā[n],* OP *xšaçapāvan,* Elamite *šakčapawana,* Aramaic *'aḥašdarpān*).[221] The satrap was in charge of all aspects of provincial rule. He levied the funds necessary for his administration and provided troops for the king. But the imperial troops in the satrapies were commanded by royal officers independent of the satrap. Royal inspectors, called by the Greeks "the king's eyes" and "the king's ears," checked up on the satraps periodically.[222]

Among Achaemenid texts we have seven lists of peoples, six from the reign of Darius and one from the reign of Xerxes:

1. *DB* #6, the earliest list, contains twenty-three names.[223]
2. *DPe* #2 on the southern wall of Darius's palace at Persepolis.[224]
3. *DZ,* the Suez inscriptions. The Old Persian versions are fragmentary,[225] but a list of twenty-four names can be recovered from the Egyptian version.[226]
4. *DSe* ##14–30. The fragmentary Old Persian version[227] can be restored from the Akkadian version.
5. *DNa* #3, the inscription on Darius's tomb.[228]
6. *DSab,* the Egyptian inscription on the base of Darius's statue, gives a list of twenty-four nations identical to that on *DZ.*[229]
7. *Xph* #3, the so-called Daiva inscription of Xerxes at Persepolis.[230]

220. In the early seventh century B.C. the Cimmerians followed this general route westwards as they devastated Gordium. See Yamauchi, *Foes,* pp. 53–54.

221. I. M. Diakonoff, "Media," in Gershevitch, *CHI,* p. 137.

222. M. Ehtécham, *L'Iran sous les Achéménides* (Fribourg: St. Paul, 1946), pp. 56–58; C. Autran, " 'L'oeil du Roi,' " *Humanitas* 3 (1950–1951): 287–91; J. M. Balcer, "The Athenian Episkopos and the Achaemenid 'King's Eye,' " *AJP* 98 (1977): 258; idem, *Sparda,* pp. 178–79. In spite of the innumerable classical references to this institution, S. W. Hirsch, "The King's Eye," in *The Friendship of the Barbarians: Xenophon and the Persian Empire* (Hanover: Tufts University Press, 1985), chapter 5, wonders if all of these were based on a misunderstanding on the part of the Greeks.

223. Kent, *OP,* p. 119.

224. Ibid., p. 136.

225. Ibid., p. 147.

226. Roaf, "Subject Peoples," pp. 79–84.

227. Kent, *OP,* p. 142.

228. Ibid., p. 138.

229. See references cited in notes 109–17.

230. Kent, *OP,* p. 151.

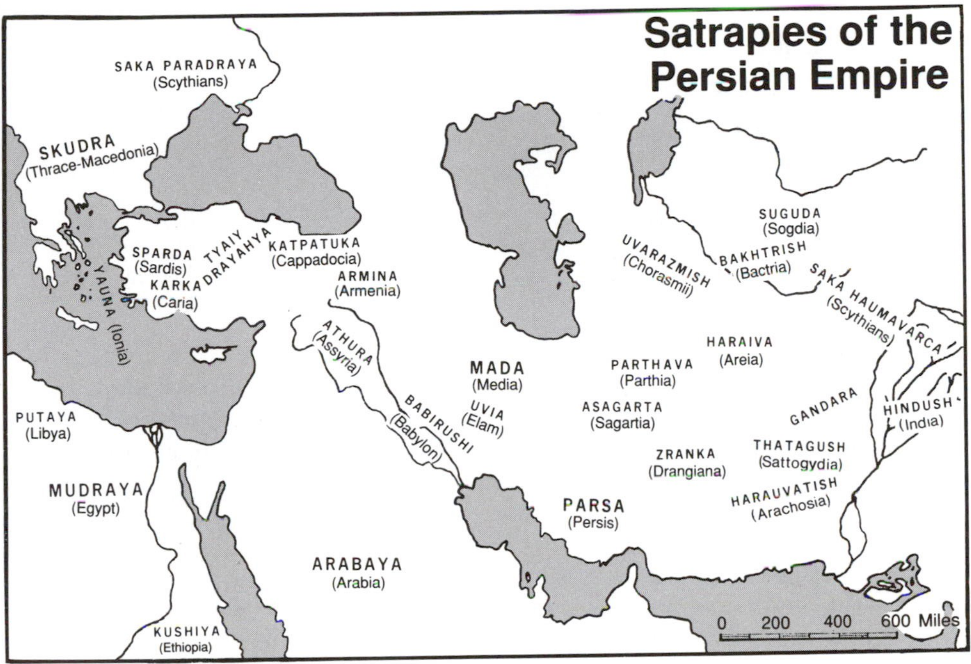

Herodotus (3.89) speaks of the organization of the empire by Darius into twenty satrapies, among whom are mentioned sixty-seven different tribes and nations. Herzfeld summarizes the data from our various sources as follows:

> The OP inscriptions all together contain 40 names of nations, of which 20 coincide with the names in the Greek list. The total of all nations from both the Greek and Persian lists is thereby raised to 80. The "catalogue of Xerxes' army" at Doriscus, 480 B.C. (Her. 7, 61–94) gives 46 names among the foot alone, and at Marathon Herodotus (9.27) says, "The Greeks all alone fought 46 nations." The books of Esther (1:1) and Daniel (6:1) speak of 127 (and 120) nations, and the original lists, kept in the offices of the tax collectors, may have contained that number.[231]

Various attempts, for example by Arnold Toynbee,[232] have been made to correlate the names from the Greek and the Old Persian

231. Herzfeld, *Persian Empire*, p. 288. See O. K. Armayor, "Herodotus' Catalogues of the Persian Empire in the Light of the Monuments and the Greek Literary Tradition," *TAPA* 108 (1978): 1–9.
232. Toynbee, *Study of History*, chapter 7, pp. 580–689.

The daric gold coin. (Courtesy of the American Numismatic Society, New York)

sources, but Cameron concluded that with the possible exception of XPh the Old Persian lists are not of satrapies but of various groups of peoples.[233] Their intent was not for bureaucratic or tax purposes, but to impress their readers with the great varieties of peoples represented in the Persian Empire. As Darius (DNa #4) proclaimed:

> If now thou shalt think that "How many are the countries which King Darius held?" look at the sculptures (of those) who bear the throne, then shalt thou know, then shall it become known to thee: the spear of a Persian man has gone forth far; then shall it become known to thee: a Persian man has delivered battle far indeed from Persia.[234]

On the basis of Herodotus's statement (3.97), scholars have concluded that the Persians themselves were exempt from taxation.[235] Although some of the privileged nobility may have been exempt, the Elamite tablets from Persepolis make plain that farmers from the Persian heartland had to pay one-tenth of their sesame, one-tenth of their wine, one-thirtieth of their grain, and so on, as taxes.[236]

Darius standardized weights and measures, and began the minting of coins:[237] silver coins known as *sigloi* (the Greek derivative from *shekel*), weighing about .2 ounces, and the famous gold *darics* (from the Greek *dareikoi* probably derived from Darius's name), weighing about

233. G. Cameron, "The Persian Satrapies and Related Matters," *JNES* 32 (1973): 47–56.

234. Kent, *OP*, p. 138.

235. For example, Dandamayev, *Persien unter den ersten Achämeniden*, pp. 184–85, 213.

236. H. Koch, "Steuern in der achämenidischen Persis?" *ZA* 70 (1981): 105–37.

237. Sixth-century bimetallic Lydian coins were found at Persepolis. See W. E. Mierse, "The Persian Period," in *Sardis: From Prehistoric to Roman Times*, ed. G. Hanfmann (Cambridge: Harvard University Press, 1983), p. 102. The tradition that Gyges of Lydia (seventh century B.C.) invented coins has been doubted by many numismatists and classical scholars, but has recently been defended by D. Kagan, "The Dates of the Earliest Coins," *AJA* 86 (1982): 343–60. See E. Yamauchi, *Greece and Babylon* (Grand Rapids: Baker, 1967), pp. 59–60; idem, "Two Reformers Compared: Solon of Athens and Nehemiah of Jerusalem," in *The Bible World: Essays in Honor of Cyrus H. Gordon*, eds. G. Rendsburg et al. (New York: KTAV, 1980), pp. 278–81.

Darius's cylinder seal with trilingual text. (Reproduced by courtesy of the trustees of the British Museum)

.3 ounces, which were 98 percent pure.[238] These latter bore images of the king kneeling with a strung bow in his left hand and a spear or a dagger in his right hand, or the king shooting with the bow. A famous seal found in Egypt depicts Darius with a bow and arrow in a chariot pursuing a lion.[239]

At Persepolis, in addition to grants of commodities, silver was also disbursed as supplementary payments from one-fourth shekel up to nine shekels.[240] A sheep cost three shekels and ten quarts of wine could be bought with a shekel. While it has been suggested that the payments in fractions of shekels indicate weights of silver rather than coins,[241] some payments may have been made with coins.

Because of these economic measures, Darius acquired the reputation of a "huckster" (Greek *kapēlos*) according to Herodotus (3.89):

> It is by reason of this fixing of tribute, and other like ordinances, that the Persians called Darius the huckster, Cambyses the master, and Cyrus the father; for Darius made petty profit out of everything, Cambyses was

238. G. F. Hill, "Notes on the Imperial Persian Coinage," *JHS* 39 (1919): 116–29; A. S. Hemmy, "The Weight-Standards of Ancient Greece and Persia," *Iraq* 5 (1938): 65–81; E. S. G. Robinson, "The Beginnings of Achaemenid Coinage," *Numismatic Chronicle* 18 (1958): 187–93; G. F. Hill, *Imperial Persian Coinage* (Chicago: Obol International, 1977 reprint of the 1919 article). The view that the name *daric* comes from an OP word for gold is now in disfavor. See A. D. H. Bivar, "Achaemenid Coins, Weights and Measures," in *CHI*, 2:621.

239. See G. F. Hill, "Notes on the Imperial Persian Coinage," *JHS* 39 (1919): 116–29. On royal seals, see A. Millard, "Königssiegel," in *Reallexicon der Assyriologie und Vorderasiatischen Archäologie*, ed. D. O. Edzard (Berlin: Walter de Gruyter, 1980–1983), chapter 6, pp. 135–40.

240. See Cameron, *Persepolis Treasury Tablets*.

241. P. Naster, "Were the Labourers of Persepolis Paid by Means of Coined Money?" *Ancient Society* 1 (1970): 129–34.

> harsh and arrogant, Cyrus was merciful and ever wrought for their well-being.[242]

This was hardly the impression that Darius wished to give. Rather, he presented himself as a god-fearing champion of justice as his epitaph relates:

> By the favor of Ahuramazda I am of such a sort that I am a friend to right, I am not a friend to wrong. It is not my desire that the weak man should have wrong done to him by the mighty; nor is that my desire, that the mighty man should have wrong done to him by the weak.[243]

Death and Burial

After an illness of a month, Darius died at Persepolis in November 486. He was sixty-four years old and had reigned thirty-six years. His tomb had already been prepared earlier in his reign.[244] This was carved in a rock cliff at Naqsh-i Rustam, "The Picture of Rustam," three and a half miles north of Persepolis, where there are four royal tombs. Only the third tomb from the left is explicitly identified by an inscription as that of Darius.[245] It is supposed that the other tombs are, from left to right, those of Darius II, Artaxerxes I, and on the extreme right, Xerxes. Carved on the cliff are earlier Elamite bas reliefs as well as later Sasanian reliefs of Ardashir and Shapur I (third century A.D.).

Like the other tombs the facade of Darius's tomb is cut in the form of a large cross, 22 meters (72 feet) high and 11 meters (36 feet) wide.[246] The top section bears a relief, originally painted, which depicts the king standing on a platform upheld by two tiers of representatives from thirty nations whose identities are given in a trilingual inscription.[247] Forming the left and right borders are six figures, among whom are

242. Polyaenos (7.11.13) also held that Darius kept the financial interests of the empire foremost in his thinking.

243. DNb #8a; Kent, *OP*, p. 140. See W. Hinz, "Die untere Grabinschrift des Dareios," *ZDMG* 115 (1965): 136–73. We now have evidence that copies of this inscription, like those of the Behistun inscription, circulated. See N. Sims-Williams, "The Final Paragraph of the Tomb-Inscription of Darius I (DNb, 50–60): The Old Persian Text in the Light of an Aramaic Version," *BSOAS* 44 (1981): 1–7.

244. Roaf, "Subject Peoples," p. 90.

245. DN series; see Kent, *OP*, pp. 137–41.

246. See F. Schmidt, *Persepolis III: The Royal Tombs and Other Monuments* (Chicago: University of Chicago Press, 1970). On the significance of the Ka'aba-i Zardusht structure in front of the tomb, see chapter 9 on Pasargadae.

247. DNa #3; Kent, *OP*, p. 138.

Gobryas and Aspathines.[248] Within are three vaults with three burial cists each.[249]

Darius is depicted standing on a three-stepped pedestal with his right hand upraised in an act of worship before an altar with the sacred fire.[250] Hovering above and between Darius and the altar is a winged figure that usually is interpreted as the god Ahuramazda. Recent study, however, has shown that the headdresses of the winged figure differ in various reliefs and from the crowns worn by the kings themselves. Some scholars have therefore concluded that the winged figure either represents the divine *Farnah* ("God-given Fortune"), a manifestation of the divine grace, or an ancestral spirit. In the reliefs of Darius this would probably be Achaemenes, the eponymous ancestor of the royal family; in later reliefs the figure may possibly represent Darius himself.[251] (See chapter 12 for a critique of this revisionist interpretation.)

His burial inscription reads:

> King Darius states: King, whoever you are, who may arise after me, protect yourself well from lies. Do not trust the man who lies. . . . Believe what I did and tell the truth to the people. Do not conceal (it). If you do not conceal these matters, but you do tell the people, may Ahura Mazda protect you. . . .[252]

Wives and Children of Darius

According to Greek sources we know the names of six wives, twelve sons, and six daughters of Darius. But even this roster may be incom-

248. See R. Borger, "Die Waffenträger des Königs Darius," *VT* 22 (1972): 385–98.

249. Boyce, *History*, 2: 110–11, comments: "Which of the nine cists was that of Darius himself is unknown, for they are hardly differentiated. It appears that the dead were laid in the stone cists in coffins of another material—probably gold, or plated with gold." It is likely that the inspiration for the tombs of Darius and his successors came from Urartu. See P. Calmeyer, "Zur Genese altiranischer Motive: III. Felsgräber," *AMI* 8 (1975): 99–113.

250. See Boyce, *History*, 2: 113. In later Zoroastrian practice a *patidana* or cloth mask had to be worn by those approaching the sacred fire.

251. H. von Gall, "Die Grosskönigliche Kopfbedeckung bei den Achämeniden," in *Proceedings of the IIIrd Annual Symposium on Archaeological Research in Iran* (Tehran: Iranian Centre for Archaeological Research, 1975), pp. 233–42; P. Calmeyer, "The Subject of the Achaemenid Tomb Reliefs," in *Proceedings of the IIIrd Annual Symposium on Archaeological Research in Iran* (Tehran: Iranian Centre for Archaeological Research, 1975), pp. 233–42; A. S. Shahbazi, "An Achaemenid Symbol," *AMI* 7 (1974): 135–44; idem, "An Achaemenid Symbol: II. Farnah '(God given) Fortune,' " *AMI* 13 (1980): 119–47; Boyce, *History*, 2: 100–105.

252. Sims-Williams, "Final Paragraph," 1–7. E. Badian, "Alexander in Iran," in *CHI*, 2: 494, n. 3, notes: "The three cuneiform versions at the tomb of Darius I in Naqsh-i-Rustam (NRb) were accompanied by an Aramaic version, no longer legible. . . ." On the question of Darius as a follower of Zoroaster, see chapter 12.

plete as we learn of a wife, Rtabāma, from the Elamite Treasury tablets, who is not accounted for by these sources.[253]

Daughter of Gobryas (OP *Gaubaruva*). Before his accession around 527, Darius married the daughter of Gobryas, who later served as his lancebearer. Darius took his wife with him during the invasion of Egypt by Cambyses. She bore him three sons: *Artabazanes* challenged the claim of his half-brother Xerxes to succeed Darius (Herodotus 7.2); *Ariabignes* commanded the Ionian and Carian ships of Xerxes' navy at Salamis (Herodotus 7.97; 8.89); and *Arsamenes* commanded the Mysians in Xerxes' army (Herodotus 7.68).

Atossa (OP *Hutauthā*), a daughter of Cyrus, had been married to her brother Cambyses, and then to the usurper Gaumata.[254] To solidify his claim to the throne, Darius took over the harem of his predecessor (Herodotus 3.88). Atossa was to become a powerful force at the court (Herodotus 7.3). Balcer remarks, "in the history of western civilization, Atossa ranks with Queen Eleanor of Aquitaine."[255] She bore Darius four distinguished sons: *Xerxes,* who was to succeed Darius (see the following chapter); *Achaemenes* was the satrap of Egypt, who also served as the admiral of the Egyptian navy (Herodotus 7.7, 97); *Hystaspes* was the commander of the Bactrians and the Scythians in Xerxes' army (Herodotus 7.64); and *Masistes* was the satrap of Bactria and one of Xerxes' six generals (Herodotus 7.82, 121). Masistes' wife and daughter became the objects of Xerxes' lust (Herodotus 9.110–13).

Artystone (OP *Rtastunā*), a younger unmarried daughter of Cyrus, became Darius's favorite wife (Herodotus 3.88). Darius had a golden image of her fashioned (Herodotus 7.69). Cameron has published a tablet, dated April 506, which contains Darius's order that one hundred sheep be granted to Cyrus's daughter Artystone, no doubt a namesake of his wife Artystone.[256] Darius's wife Artystone also bore two sons: *Arames,* the commander of the Arabians and Ethiopians (Herodotus 7.69), and *Gobryas,* the commander of the Cappadocians and Syrians (Herodotus 7.72).

Parmys (OP *Parmush*) was the only child of the true Bardiya, the

253. Hinz, *Darius,* p. 223. The *Persiaca* of Helleanicus of Lesbos reported that Darius had eleven sons.

254. Boyce, *History,* 2: 82, and others object that surely Atossa would have quickly discovered the imposture of Gaumata, when he married her after Cambyses' death, and publicized it. But Herodotus (3.68–69) notes that Gaumata took specific steps to isolate himself from all but a few, and kept the wives incommunicado from each other.

255. Balcer, *Sparda,* p. 155.

256. G. Cameron, "Darius' Daughter and the Persepolis Inscriptions," *JNES* 1 (1942): 214–18.

brother whom Cambyses had murdered secretly (Herodotus 3.88).[257] Her son *Ariomardus* commanded the Moschi and Tibareni (biblical Meshech and Tubal) of central and western Turkey (Herodotus 7.78).[258]

Phaedyme (OP *Faidumā*) was the daughter of Otanes, one of Darius's co-conspirators. She had been married to Cambyses. It was she who discovered the imposture of Gaumata (Herodotus 3.68–69).

Phratagune (OP *Frāta-gauna*) was the daughter of Darius's brother Artanes. Two of her sons fell at Thermopylae in 480 (Herodotus 7.224).[259]

257. Frye, *Heritage*, p. 87, notes that this would have been "a most unlikely act if Gaumata had really been the true Bardiya," that is, she would then be marrying her brother's murderer.

258. See E. Yamauchi, "Meshech, Tubal, and Company," *JETS* 19 (1976): 239–47; Yamauchi, *Foes*, chapter 1.

259. On the etymology of these names, see E. Benveniste, *Titres et noms propres en Iranien ancien* (Paris: Klincksieck, 1966).

5

Xerxes

Name

The name *Xerxes* comes from the Greek *Xerxēs,* which represents Old Persian *Khšayāršan,* meaning "ruling over heroes" or "he who rules over men." In Elamite his name was *Ikšerša;* in Akkadian *Aḫši'aršu.* In Hebrew his name was rendered *'aḥašweroš,* the Ahasuerus of Esther. Ahasuerus was identified in the Septuagint, Josephus, Jewish Midrash, and the Peshitta with Artaxerxes.[1] But there is no doubt that Ahasuerus was Xerxes (485–465 B.C.), the son of Darius I.

Biblical References

Apart from the Book of Esther, Xerxes is mentioned only in Ezra 4:6 in relation to the accusation that was lodged against the Jews in his reign. In a series of articles, Julian Morgenstern postulated a destruc-

1. B. Grossfield, *The First Targum to Esther* (New York: Sepher-Hermon, 1983), p. 75.

tion of Jerusalem in 485 B.C. at the beginning of Xerxes' reign as the immediate background of Ezra and Nehemiah.[2] With a rare exception,[3] most scholars would agree with the judgment of Martin Leesberg that "the arguments for this position rest upon an exegesis of many passages of the Old Testament which is highly subjective and in some cases is simply the piling of one assumption upon a previous one."[4]

There seems to be a clear allusion to Xerxes in Daniel 11:2, if one interprets the first three kings as Cambyses, Gaumata, and Darius: "then a fourth [that is, Xerxes], who will be far richer than all the others. When he has gained power by his wealth, he will stir up everyone against the kingdom of Greece."[5]

Cuneiform Sources

We have twenty-one Old Persian inscriptions of Xerxes with corresponding Elamite and Akkadian versions. However, with the notable exception of his Daiva inscription, which was found in 1935 at Persepolis[6] (see chapter 12), they are not very informative. As a whole they are but word-for-word adoptions of the texts of Darius. For example, a text discovered by a farmer in 1967 1,700 meters (about a mile) northwest of the terrace of Persepolis (XPl) reads in part:

> I am not hot-tempered . . . I hold firmly under control by my will. I am ruling over myself.
>
> The man who cooperates, according to his cooperation thus I protect, who does harm according to his damage thus I punish. It is not my desire

2. J. Morgenstern, "Jerusalem—485 B.C.," *HUCA* 27 (1956): 101–79; ibid., 28 (1957): 15–47; ibid., 31 (1960): 1–29; idem, "Further Light from the Book of Isaiah upon the Catastrophe of 485 B.C.," *HUCA* 27 (1966): 1–28.

3. J. Balcer, *Sparda by the Bitter Sea* (Chico: Scholars, 1984), p. 252.

4. M. W. Leesberg, "Ezra and Nehemiah," *Concordia Theological Monthly* 33 (1962): 82. Compare P. Ackroyd, "The Jewish Community in Palestine in the Persian Period," in *The Cambridge History of Judaism I: Introduction; The Persian Period*, eds. W. D. Davies and L. Finkelstein (Cambridge: Cambridge University Press, 1984), p. 153: "The theme has been worked out with great elaboration and increasing improbability by J. Morgenstern."

5. R. D. Culver, *The Histories and Prophecies of Daniel* (Winona Lake: BMH, 1980), p. 172; H. C. Leupold, *Exposition of Daniel* (Grand Rapids: Baker, 1969), p. 477; N. W. Porteous, *Daniel* (Philadelphia: Westminster, 1965), p. 158; J. F. Walvoord, *Daniel* (Chicago: Moody, 1971), p. 256; J. C. Whitcomb, *Daniel* (Chicago: Moody, 1985), pp. 145–46; L. Wood, *A Commentary on Daniel* (Grand Rapids: Zondervan, 1973), pp. 281–82; E. J. Young, *The Prophecy of Daniel* (Grand Rapids: Eerdmans, 1949), p. 232. The suggestion by L. F. Hartman and A. A. Di Lella, *The Book of Daniel* (Garden City: Doubleday, 1978), pp. 287–88, and W. S. Towner, *Daniel* (Atlanta: John Knox, 1984), p. 154, that the fourth king was Darius II, or Darius III, who opposed Alexander, is hardly persuasive.

6. A copy was later found at Pasargadae. See D. Stronach, "Excavation at Pasargadae: A Third Preliminary Report," *Iran* 3 (1965): 19.

> that a man should do harm, nor is that my desire if he should do harm, he should not be punished.
>
> What a man says against a man, that does not convince me, until I hear the solemn testimony of both.[7]

But this is a virtual doublet of Darius's tomb inscription at Naqsh-i Rustam (DNb). Rather than being a paragon of patience, Xerxes, according to both classical and biblical sources (Esther 1:12; 7:7), had a nasty and at times irrational temper,[8] although he could on occasion be magnanimous (Herodotus 7.136).

A striking example of Xerxes co-opting his father's inscription and changing it by the addition of his name is found on a rock on Mount Alvand near Hamadan, where his inscription was placed side by side with his father's.[9] Hinz believes that this slavish imitation reveals the dominating influence of Darius's example upon his son.

Indeed most of the inscriptions after the time of Xerxes are but stereotyped imitations of the inscriptions of Darius. According to Ilya Gershevitch, "the brief inscriptions of Xerxes's successors—which are only thirteen, dictated over a period of about one hundred years—are merely correctly written impersonal stereotypes modelled on brief inscriptions of Darius."[10]

Short inscriptions of Xerxes on bullae or seal impressions were found at Daskyleion, the capital of the Hellespontine satrapy, in excavations by Ekrem Akurgal in 1952 to 1955. They bear the image of a hero fighting a winged lion accompanied by the text "I am Xerxes, the King."[11] These seals must have accompanied letters sent from the king to the satrap while he was on his campaign against Greece.

Quite informative on social and economic matters are the thirty thousand Elamite tablets and fragments found in 1933 and 1934 in the northeast fortification walls, the so-called Persepolis Fortification texts (PF). They were inscribed from the thirteenth to the twenty-eighth year of Darius (509–494 B.C.) by Elamite accountants from Susa. In 1969 Richard Hallock published slightly over two thousand of these tablets,

7. B. A. Gharib, "A Newly Found Old Persian Inscription," *IA* 8 (1968): 60; W. Hinz, "Eine neue Xerxes-Inschrift aus Persepolis," in *Altiranische Funde und Forschungen* (Berlin: W. de Gruyter, 1969), pp. 45–52; M. Mayrhofer, "Xerxes König der Könige," *Almanach der Österreichischen Akademie der Wissenschaften* 119 (1969): 158ff.; idem, "Medismen in der 1967 gefunden Xerxes-Inschrift," *Linguistica* 13 (1973): 97–101; idem, "Xerxès, Roi des Rois," in *Commémoration Cyrus I,* Acta Iranica I (Leiden: Brill, 1974), pp. 108–16.

8. C. A. Moore, "Archaeology and the Book of Esther," *BA* 38 (1975): 69.

9. W. Hinz, *Darius und die Perser* (Baden-Baden: Holle, 1979) 2: 11.

10. I. Gershevitch, preface to *The Evidence of the Persepolis Tablets* by R. T. Hallock (Cambridge: Middle East Centre, 1971), pp. 8–9.

11. K. Balkan, "Inscribed Bullae from Daskyleion-Ergili," *Anatolia* 4 (1959): 123–28.

dealing with the payment of commodities and silver to workmen and couriers.[12]

Erich F. Schmidt found about 750 Elamite tablets and fragments in the Treasury, the so-called Persepolis Treasury tablets (PT). These date from the thirtieth year of Darius I to the seventh year of Artaxerxes I (492–458 B.C.). George Cameron published about a hundred of these texts between 1948 and 1965. Sixty-six PT tablets date from the reign of Xerxes.[13]

Classical Sources

Our most important classical source is unquestionably Herodotus. While he is not an infallible source, particularly in respect to statistics, he is nevertheless our best source. Firsthand investigations of Greece by scholars such as Nicholas G. L. Hammond and William K. Pritchett have vindicated his topographical accuracy. Pritchett writes: "That Herodotus visited Therme, Potidaia, Tempe, Thermopylai, and Thessaly, seems to be the opinion of all who have written on the subject."[14]

On political matters Herodotus has been suspected of various biases; in antiquity he was accused of an anti-Theban bias by Plutarch. But in general Herodotus seems to have been an earnest investigator. According to Frank J. Frost, "first of all, I think, we must agree that Herodotus does not willingly distort the truth about recent history. . . . After hearing all sides, he put down what he believed really happened."[15] There have been, of course, many scholars who have rejected this or that account of Herodotus in favor of an alternative reconstruction. In Charles Hignett's view some scholars "remain undaunted by the results of their speculations, and after destroying the available ancient evidence settle down happily amid the ruins to write what can only be called historical

12. R. T. Hallock, *Persepolis Fortification Tablets* (Chicago: University of Chicago Press, 1969); idem, "The Persepolis Fortification Archive," *Or* 42 (1973): 320–23; idem, "The Use of Seals on the Persepolis Fortification Tablets," in *Seals and Sealing in the Ancient Near East*, eds. McG. Gibson and R. D. Biggs (Malibu: Undena, 1977), pp. 127–33; idem, "Selected Fortification Texts," *CDAFI* 8 (1978): 109–35; idem, "The Evidence of the Persepolis Tablets," in *The Cambridge History of Iran II: The Median and Achaemenian Periods*, ed. I. Gershevitch (Cambridge: Cambridge University Press, 1985), chapter 11.

13. G. Cameron, *Persepolis Treasury Tablets* (Chicago: University of Chicago Press, 1948); idem, "Persepolis Treasury Tablets Old and New," *JNES* 17 (1958): 161–76; idem, "New Tablets fom the Persepolis Treasury," *JNES* 24 (1965): 167–92. For economic tablets in Akkadian, see S. Graziani, *I testi Mesopotamici datati al regno di Serse (485–465 a.C.)* (Rome: Herder, 1986). I owe this reference to M. Heltzer.

14. W. K. Pritchett, *Studies in Ancient Greek Topography II: Battlefields* (Berkeley: University of California Press, 1969), p. 18.

15. F. J. Frost, *Plutarch's Themistocles: A Historical Commentary* (Princeton: Princeton University Press, 1980), p. 10.

fiction."[16] As opposed to the view that Herodotus's depiction of the Persian kings are but conventional portraits,[17] K. H. Waters avers:

> We may conclude from the foregoing that Herodotus' portraits of the Persian kings are neither character-studies in a dramatic or novelistic sense, nor components of an over-riding theme of Hubris (arrogance) and Tisis (punishment); still less are they mere representatives of a type, as one view has it. They are factual, composed of scores of items of information more or less directly relevant to the History, and more or less consistent with the inconsistency of human beings.[18]

We have numerous Greek inscriptions from the period of the Persian invasions. The most controversial text is a late copy of the purported decree of Themistocles, preparing the Athenians to evacuate their city and to man their fleet before Salamis (see below, "The Themistocles Decree"). Inasmuch as this inscription seems to differ with Herodotus, scholars are divided on its authenticity. Many scholars seem to prefer Herodotus and to question the inscription. Pritchett, for example, argues: "Herodotus has in fact been proved to be correct in so many cases where he had earlier been doubted, that when a late document is found which flatly contradicts him, this document has to be considered *a priori* suspect."[19] Unfortunately for a history of Xerxes, Herodotus provides little information on the king after the battles of 479 B.C.

Thucydides, the historian of the Peloponnesian War (431–404 B.C.), gives us some valuable information on the relations between the Greeks and the Persians in the fifty-year interval between 480 and 430.

A unique source, especially for the Battle of Salamis, is the play *Persai*, that is, *The Persians*, by Aeschylus, which was performed in 472—but eight years after the battle.[20] Because Aeschylus himself was a participant in the battle, this is an eyewitness, if dramatized, account.[21]

According to the play, Xerxes led the expedition in order to surpass the achievements of his father Darius (11.753–58). The *Persai* reports the Battle of Salamis as it must have appeared to the Persians themselves. The queen grieves at the tragic defeat of her son. The ghost of

16. C. Hignett, *Xerxes' Invasion of Greece* (Oxford: Clarendon, 1963), p. 4.

17. J. G. Gammie, "Herodotus on Kings and Tyrants," *JNES* 45 (1986): 171–95.

18. K. H. Waters, *Herodotus on Tyrants and Despots* (Wiesbaden: F. Steiner, 1971), p. 85.

19. W. K. Pritchett, "Herodotus and the Themistokles Decree," *AJA* 66 (1962): 43.

20. In 476 Phrynichus's *Phoenician Women* was performed. From it we have only such fragments as: "This is the watery abode of the Persians" and "Abandoning the Sidonian ship." We have but the titles of several comedies about the Persians. See R. Schmitt, "Perser und Persisches in der Attischen Komödie," in *Orientalia J. Duchesne-Guillemin Emerito Oblata* (Leiden: Brill, 1984), pp. 459–72.

21. H. D. Broadhead, *The Persae of Aeschylus* (Cambridge: Cambridge University Press, 1960), p. 322; Frost, *Plutarch's Themistocles*, p. 134. For a literary analysis of the play, see A. N. Michelini, *Tradition and Dramatic Form in the PERSIANS of Aeschylus* (Leiden: Brill, 1982).

Xerxes' father, Darius, arises to rebuke his son's youthful folly (11.782–83).

The *Persai* contains numerous Persian names. Richmond Lattimore thought that this prosopography was to "a great extent fictitious, or at least historically insignificant and misleading."[22] A recent study by Iranologist Rudiger Schmitt, concludes: "On the whole one gains the impression that the first group of Iranian names in the Parodos (21–51) is much more trustworthy and exact than the last in the lament of the king and choir (958–99), among which are many non-Iranian names with lambda."[23]

Aeschylus also fought at Marathon, where his brother was slain. The dramatist's epitaph at Gela in Sicily referred not to his plays, but only to his patriotic endeavors against the Medes, that is the Persians: "The glorious sacred field of Marathon could tell of his valor, and so also could the long-haired Mede, who had good cause to know."

Ctesias, a Greek physician at the court of Artaxerxes II, wrote his *Persica* between 398 and 390, or about thirty years after Herodotus. He wrote to discredit his predecessor, and is in general very untrustworthy.[24]

Plutarch, a Greek writer of the second century A.D., is an important source for the leaders of fifth-century Greece, particularly his lives of Themistocles and Aristides, who were the leaders of the Greek resistance against Xerxes. Athenaeus, a Greek grammarian who lived in Alexandria and Rome in the third century A.D., has left us a melange of anecdotes in his *Deipnosophistae* ("Banquet of the Learned"), which contains many interesting tidbits about the Persians.

Parents and Siblings

As noted at the end of the last chapter, Xerxes was the son of Darius I and Atossa, the daughter of Cyrus, whom Herodotus called "all-powerful." He was born about 518 B.C. after Darius had gained the crown. Darius's oldest son was Artobarzanes, who had been born to an unnamed wife before Darius's accession (Herodotus 7.3). According to an inscription, "says Xerxes the king: Darius had also other sons; [but] as was the will of Ahuramazdā, Darius my father made me the greatest after himself."[25]

22. R. Lattimore, "Aeschylus on the Defeat of Xerxes," *Classical Studies in Honor of W. A. Oldfather* (Urbana: University of Illinois Press, 1943), p. 87.

23. R. Schmitt, *Die Iranier-Namen bei Aischylos* (Vienna: Österreichische Akademie der Wissenschaften, 1978), p. 71.

24. J. M. Bigwood, "Ctesias as Historian of the Persian Wars," *Phoenix* 32 (1978): 19–34.

25. E. E. Herzfeld, *A New Inscription of Xerxes from Persepolis* (Chicago: University of Chicago Press, 1932), p. 4.

Xerxes was the eldest of the four sons of Atossa. Many of his brothers and half-brothers served as generals and officers in his army; three of them were killed during the invasion of Greece.[26]

Preaccession and Accession

According to Herodotus (7.187), Xerxes was tall and handsome: "Of all those tens of thousands of men, for goodliness and stature there was not one worthier than Xerxes himself to hold that command." Although he was not an active soldier as his father had been, he was no doubt trained in military skills. Prior to his accession, Xerxes served as the viceroy over Babylonia for about a dozen years. As early as 498 B.C. we have a reference to the building of a palace at Babylon for "the king's son."

After Darius's death in November 486, Xerxes succeeded him as king.[27] He was about thirty-two years old. The only opposition he seems to have faced was from his brother Ariamenes, the satrap of Bactria, who was mollified by Xerxes and was made an admiral of the fleet.

Revolt in Egypt

Before Darius died a revolt broke out in Egypt. In 485 Xerxes went to suppress this revolt. By January 484, quarrying in the name of Xerxes was done in the Wadi Hammamat. According to Herodotus (7.7) Xerxes "laid Egypt under a much harder slavery than in the time of Darius; and he committed the governance of it to Achaemenes, his own brother, Darius' son." Xerxes confiscated materials from temples and imposed new taxes. Unlike his predecessors he did not pose as the pharaoh.

Revolt in Babylon

There were two short-lived revolts in Babylon, which were harshly repressed. We have three texts of the first and nine of the second

26. A. R. Burn, *Persia and the Greeks* (New York: St. Martin's, 1962), p. 333.

27. There is no warrant for Herzfeld's contention that Darius abdicated. See E. Herzfeld, "Xerxes' Charta von Persepolis," *AMI* 4 (1932): 117–39; idem, *New Inscription*, pp. 6–7. The verb that Herzfeld translated "went (away from)" is rendered "passed away" by other scholars. See A. T. Olmstead, *History of the Persian Empire* (Chicago: University of Chicago Press, 1948), p. 214.

usurper.[28] In the summer of 484 B.C. Belshimmani killed the Persian satrap in Babylon and proclaimed himself king. He was in power for no more than two months. More serious was the revolt in August 482 by Shamash-Eriba, who proclaimed himself "king of Babylon and the lands." His revolt was ended before the spring of 481. These revolts were crushed by Megabyzus, grandson of the Megabyzus who was one of the original six colleagues of Darius.[29]

In Babylon the great ziggurat (the Etemenanki) and the temple of Marduk (the Esagila) were destroyed. Arrian (3.16) reported, "Alexander entering Babylon bade the Babylonians build up again the temples which Xerxes destroyed, and especially the temple of Bel (i.e. Marduk), whom the Babylonians honor before all gods." Strabo (*Geography* 16.1.5) noted that Alexander was not able to rebuild the ziggurat. Herodotus (1.183) wrote that an eighteen-foot, solid gold statue of Marduk, which weighed about eight hundred talents, was carried off by Xerxes (compare Dan. 3:1–12). The priest who protested was killed.

All of this was a direct reversal of the conciliatory policy that Cyrus had established. From his long residence in Babylon before his accession, Xerxes must have been quite well acquainted with Babylonian religion and its rituals.[30] He knew that the statue of Marduk was essential for the vital New Year's festival.

Babylon lost its independent status when it was merged with Assyria (Herodotus 7.63). After the fifth year of Xerxes' reign the title "king of Babylon" was rarely used.[31]

The Persian Army and Navy

After the suppression of the revolts in Egypt and Babylon, Xerxes was ready for his massive invasion of Greece. He wished to extend the borders of the empire westward and to avenge the defeat of his father by the Athenians (Herodotus 7.8). He was urged on by Mardonius, the commander of an earlier expedition against the Greeks (Herodotus (7.9). Xerxes was also encouraged both by Demaratos, an exiled Spartan

28. F. M. Th. de Liagre Böhl, "Die babylonischen Prätendenten zur Zeit des Xerxes," *BO* 19 (1962): 110.

29. G. Cameron, "Darius and Xerxes in Babylonia," *AJSL* 58 (1941): 319; S. A. Pallis, "The History of Babylon, 538–93 B.C.," in *Studia Ioanni Pedersen* (Copenhagen: Einer Munskgaard, 1953), pp. 277–78.

30. G. Bermain, "Le songe de Xerxès et le rite babylonien du substitut royal," *REG* 69 (1956): 303–13, offers the unlikely suggestion that Xerxes' command to Artabanus to don the royal garments (Herodotus 7.15) was a reflection of the ancient Mesopotamian substitute king ritual.

31. According to D. Graf, "Greek Tyrants and Achaemenid Politics," in *The Craft of the Ancient Historian*, eds. J. W. Eadie and J. Ober (Lanham: University Press of America, 1985), p. 110, n. 39: "Unpublished texts in the Asmolean [sic] and British Museums indicate the title was used intermittently as late as the 14th year of his reign."

king, and by Hippias, an exiled Athenian tyrant. On the other hand, Artabanus, Xerxes' uncle, urged restraint (Herodotus 7.10).

As Xerxes organized the army he appointed eight brothers and half-brothers as leading officers. There were six major commanders (*archons*), including Mardonius, Tritantaechmes, Smerdomenes, Masistes, Gergis, and Megabyzus (Herodotus 7.82). The cavalry was commanded by three hipparchs: Harmamithres, Tithaeus, and Pharnuches (Herodotus 7.88). The lower officers were arranged on a decimal basis: captains of ten thousand men (*myriarchs*), of one thousand men (*chiliarchs*), of one hundred men (*hecatontarchs*) and of ten men (*decarchs*) (Herodotus 7.81).

Although there is little doubt that Xerxes was able to amass the largest army and navy ever mustered in antiquity, the enormous numbers listed by Herodotus have aroused the greatest scepticism. He reports that the Persian army contained 1,700,000 infantry (7.60), 80,000 cavalry (7.87), 20,000 Arabian camel and Libyan chariot corps (7.184), and 300,000 Thracians and Greeks (7.185). Including naval forces the Persian fighting men totaled 2,317,610 (7.184). As there were almost as many noncombatants who followed in the train, Herodotus arrives at the staggering total of 5,283,220 (8.186) as the sum of those who accompanied Xerxes.

The Greeks believed that they were fighting millions, as an epitaph from Thermopylae boasted:

> Four thousand warriors, flower of Pelops' land,
> Did here against three hundred myriads (i.e., three million) stand.
> (Herodotus 7.228)

The difficulties of accepting such figures are the logistical impossibilities of space and of supply. Theodore Cuyler Young, Jr., by assuming an infantry marching ten abreast and cavalry five abreast, calculates that such a vast host would have extended 1,320 miles: "By modern road it is approximately 608 miles from where the Persians crossed the Hellespont to Athens. Thus on Herodotus' count, half of the Persian column would still not have crossed the Hellespont when the head of the column was setting fire to the Acropolis."[32]

32. T. C. Young, Jr., "480/479 B.C.—A Persian Perspective," *IA* 15 (1980): 217, n. 8. To defend the literal reading of the numbers involved in the exodus (Exod. 12:37; Num. 11:21)—six hundred thousand men, which implies a multitude of about two million—G. L. Archer, Jr., cites the figures of Herodotus uncritically, without noting that no historian accepts these figures at face value. See G. L. Archer, *Encyclopedia of Bible Difficulties* (Grand Rapids: Zondervan, 1982), pp. 133–34. In view of the fact that the Hebrew Old Testament was written originally only with consonants, J. W. Wenham, "Large Numbers in the Old Testament," *TB* 18 (1967): 19–53, has proposed a different vocalization for the consonants in the word for thousand (*'eleph*) to read it as the word for clan and thus obtain more credible figures. See also R. A. Cole, *Exodus* (Downers Grove: Inter-Varsity, 1973), p. 112.

Ancient authors such as Ctesias, Isocrates, and Ephorus lowered the figures for Xerxes' army from Herodotus's millions to 700,000 to 800,000. Modern scholars have variously reduced the figures to: 500,000 (George B. Grundy), 360,000 (Reginald Macan, John M. Cook),[33] 300,000 (John B. Bury), 210,000 (Frederick Maurice), 180,000 (John Munro), 100,000 (Eduard Meyer, Charles Hignett),[34] 80,000 (Walter Hinz),[35] 65 to 75,000 (Hans Delbrück), 71,000 (Rodney Young),[36] down to 50,000 (E. von Fischer).

There are two rational methods for reducing Herodotus's figures. The first is to assume that Herodotus confused the figures of a chiliarch (1,000) for those of a myriarch (10,000).[37] As Ernle Bradford explains: "If one removes a nought from all of Herodotus's figures one comes up with an army of 170,000 infantrymen, 8000 cavalry, 2000 camel corps and charioteers, and 30,000 Greeks and Thracians."[38] Munro estimated a similar number by assuming that the total Persian army was 360,000, of which Xerxes only took half or 180,000 with him.[39] Munro's figures have been accepted by Albert T. Olmstead, Andrew Burn, and Jack Balcer.[40]

The second method of arriving at a rational figure is to consider factors of food, water, distance, and topography. Maurice, who was a British officer familiar with the region, traversed the route and concluded that Xerxes' army may have been about 150,500, but no more than 210,000.[41]

Herodotus lists contingents from forty-six different peoples from the vast reaches of the Persian Empire (7.61–88). These included such exotically accoutered soldiers like the Indians who wore garments of "tree-wool" (that is, cotton), and Ethiopians (or Nubians) who were wrapped in skins of leopards and lions.

The best troops were the Persians, Medes, and Elamites who served as the so-called Immortals (Herodotus 7.83). These soldiers,

33. J. M. Cook, *The Persian Empire* (New York: Schocken, 1983), p. 115.

34. Hignett, *Xerxes' Invasion*, p. 355.

35. Hinz, *Darius II*, p. 18.

36. Young, "480–479 B.C.," p. 227, suggests that Xerxes' army may have been similar to Alexander's army of 65,000 infantry plus 6,000 cavalry, equalling 71,000.

37. Burn, *Persia and the Greeks*, p. 327.

38. E. Bradford, *The Year of Thermopylae* (London: Macmillan, 1980), pp. 33–34.

39. J. A. R. Munro, "Some Observations on the Persian Wars," *JHS* 22 (1902): 294–98.

40. Olmstead, *History of the Persian Empire*, p. 248; Burn, *Persia and the Greeks*, pp. 326–32; Balcer, *Sparda*, p. 253.

41. F. Maurice, "The Size of the Army of Xerxes in the Invasion of Greece, 480 B.C.," *JHS* 50 (1930): 227. See also R. J. Lenardon, *Saga of Themistocles* (London: Thames and Hudson, 1978), p. 59, who posits a force of at most 200,000. The Persian army of Darius III, which opposed Alexander at Arbela, consisted of 200,000 infantry and 45,000 cavalry.

who were gorgeously clad, were so named because their numbers were always maintained at ten thousand. They were armed with bows, daggers, spears, and wicker shields. Most of the soldiers were lightly armed; the heavily armed infantry served mainly as marines on board ships.

The Persian cavalry was supplemented by the defection of the Greeks' best cavalry, those of Thessaly and of Boeotia. The Persians also had an excellent corps of engineers and other specialists, many of them from Ionia, the Greek settlements in western Asia Minor.

The Persian fleet included 1,207 triremes and 3,000 penteconters (Herodotus 7.184). The penteconters were smaller ships with fifty oars. The triremes, with three banks of oars on each side, were the main fighting ships.

The contingents of triremes came from the following regions (Herodotus 7.89–95):

Phoenicia	300
Greeks of Asia	290
Egypt	200
Cyprus	150
Cilicia	100
Caria	70
Lycia	50
Pamphylia	30
Cyclades	17
Total	1207

Later the Persians suffered considerable losses: four hundred ships in a storm off the coast of Magnesia (Herodotus 7.190) and two hundred in an attempt to sail around the windward side of the island of Euboea (Herodotus 8.13). Herodotus felt that the gods intended the Persians to be reduced to near equality with the Greeks. The Persians still had a two-to-one advantage at the Battle of Salamis.

Aeschylus (*Persai* 342–45) also gives us a similar number for the Persian fleet (1,000):

> Were numbers all, be well assured the barbarians [that is, the Persians] would have gained the victory with their fleet. For the whole number of the ships of Hellas amounted to ten times thirty, and, apart from these, there was a chosen squadron of ten. But Xerxes, this I know, had under his command a thousand, while those excelling in speed were twice a hundred, and seven more.

Aeschylus' reference to 207 fast ships is probably to be included in his total of 1,000. (If they were to be added, the total [1,207] would be exactly the same as Herodotus's figure.) Many scholars have accepted the figures of ships given by Aeschylus and Herodotus as accurate.[42] Other scholars, however, have sought to reduce these numbers. For example, Munro placed the paper strength of the fleet at 800, and the fleet at Salamis at about 660.[43] William Tarn speculated that the Persian navy was organized in five territorial fleets of 120 ships for a total of 600, plus 400 supply ships.[44]

The most important ships were those of the Phoenician cities of Sidon and Tyre.[45] The black basalt sarcophagus of Eshmunazar of Sidon (first half of the fifth century B.C.) has the following text: "And furthermore the Lord of Kings gave us Dor and Jaffa . . . in accordance with the mighty deeds that I did." This may refer to Sidon's participation in Xerxes' navy.[46]

The admiral-in-chief was Achaemenes, Xerxes' brother. Under him were three other admirals, Megabazus, Prexaspes, and Ariabignes, son of Darius and Xerxes' half-brother (Herodotus 7.97).[47]

The Greek Army and Navy

In the *Persai* (239–40) we read:

> *Queen:* Does their prowess show itself in archer combat, using bows?
> *Chorus:* Not at all. They stand and fight in close array with spear and shield.

In contrast with the Persian army, which relied primarily on its ar-

42. W. W. How and J. Wells, *A Commentary on Herodotus* (Oxford: Clarendon, 1928), 2: 364: "Indeed, the traditional number of the king's navy (1000 or 1207) has been accepted by the majority of modern critics as probable or at least possible"; Broadhead, *Persae*, p. 339: "it is clear that the poet has wished to stress the numerical superiority of the Persians (cf. 337, 352) and I find it difficult to believe that in so doing he has gone clean contrary to the facts." Cook, *Persian Empire*, p. 116: "But even with some scaling down of the Levantine figures the total of triremes in the Persian fleet cannot have been much less than 1,000." See also N. G. L. Hammond, "The Battle of Salamis," *JHS* 76 (1956): 40–41; J. F. Lazenby, "The Strategy of the Greeks in the Opening Campaign of the Persian War," *Hermes* 92 (1964): 283.

43. Munro, "Some Observations," p. 299.

44. W. W. Tarn, "The Fleet of Xerxes," *JHS* 28 (1908): 206; Hignett, *Xerxes' Invasion*, pp. 345–48.

45. J. Elayi, "The Phoenician Cities in the Persian Period," *JANE* 12 (1980): 13–28; idem, "Studies in the Phoenician Geography in the Persian Period," *JNES* 41 (1982): 83–110.

46. H. Bengtson, *The Greeks and the Persians* (London: Weidenfeld and Nicolson, 1970), p. 405.

47. H. Hauben, "The Chief Commanders of the Persian Fleet in 480 B.C.," *Ancient Society* 4 (1973): 24–25.

chers, the Greek army consisted of heavily armored infantrymen known as hoplites. Walter How comments as follows: "The Greek army admits of a simple description; it was throughout a hoplite-phalanx composed of infantry heavily armed with helmet, shield, cuirass and greaves, having short swords, but trusting for offensive purposes most to the thrusting spear (seven to eight feet long) and to the weight and solidity of their serried ranks of shields and breastplates."[48]

The phalanx was normally eight ranks deep. On an open plain the phalanx was often invincible. On broken ground, however, it was difficult to maintain a tight formation. The phalanx was vulnerable in the rear and on its right flank, as the shields were on the left arms.

By the sixth century B.C. the Greeks had developed the trireme for its naval force.[49] The trireme required an intricate system of three banks of oars: the *thranites,* oarsmen at the top level, worked their oars through an outrigger; the *zygites* pulled their oars either over a gunwale or through oarports; and the *thalamites* worked at the lowest level no more than eighteen inches above the waterline.[50] The captains were known as *trierarchs.* The *kubernētēs* (or pilot) steered the ship from the stern. At the bow was the *prorates* who served as the eyes of the ship. The *keleustēs* called out the beat of the oarsmen accompanied by the *aulētēs,* playing on his flute.[51]

The remains of ship sheds in the Zea harbor of Athens averaged 37 meters (121 feet, 5 inches), with a further extension underwater, indicating that the ships were at least this long, perhaps up to 140 feet. They measured about 18 to 20 feet wide, with a draught of 4 to 6 feet. The oars would have extended an additional 14 feet on each side.

Each trireme carried a crew of about 200 with 10 to 30 *epibatai* or marines, and a few archers who were recruited from Crete. The main tactic would be to attempt to ram the enemy ship with the *embolos* or bronze ram at the prow of the ship.[52]

Triremes could make 115 to 146 nautical miles a day, and could reach a maximum speed of 11 to 12 knots (about 14 miles) per hour. Recently a modern replica of an ancient trireme was made by the

48. W. W. How, "Arms, Tactics and Strategy in the Persian War," *JHS* 43 (1923): 120; see A. M. Snodgrass, *Arms and Armour of the Greeks* (London: Thames and Hudson, 1967).

49. J. A. Davison, "The First Greek Triremes," *CQ* 41 (1947): 18–24.

50. Bradford, *Year of Thermopylae,* p. 75.

51. B. Jordan, *The Athenian Navy in the Classical Period* (Berkeley: University of California Press, 1974), pp. 144–50.

52. J. S. Morrison and R. T. Williams, *Greek Oared Ships, 900–322 B.C.* (Cambridge: Cambridge University Press, 1968), pp. 169, 181, 254. See also F. Meijer, *A History of Seafaring in the Classical World* (New York: St. Martin's, 1986).

Greeks under the direction of British scholars John S. Morrison and John F. Coates. After some practice, a volunteer crew of 140 men and 40 women from England was able to reach top speeds of 9 to 10 knots for short bursts.[53]

At Salamis Aeschylus reported that the Greek fleet numbered 300 (or possibly 310).[54] The largest number (200) was provided by Athens. Corinth provided the next largest number (40). Aegina, Megara, and Sparta provided the remainder.

Advantages and Disadvantages

The Persians had several significant advantages. They had the advantage of numbers, both in the army and in the navy. When Greek spies were caught at Sardis, Xerxes had them released so they could inform their countrymen of the huge numbers the Persians had mustered (Herodotus 7.146–47). The Persian ships were not only more numerous, but were swifter. They not only had their own cavalry, but the best cavalry contingents of Greece "Medized" served on the Persian side. Persian soldiers had no lack of courage (Herodotus 9.62). And they had a unified command. Their primary difficulty was the task of supplying food and water in a hostile land.

The Greeks had their own advantages and disadvantages. They were fighting on their own turf, according to Aeschylus (*Persai* 794): "The land itself is their ally." They were defending their land, their families, their temples, and their tombs (*Persai* 403–4). The Greeks did not have supply problems. Their citizen soldiers were in excellent physical shape. Their outstanding leaders were able to overcome rivalries. Even the agonistic competition between city-states could spur soldiers to greater effort. At Mycale we read of Athenians exhorting each other that they, and not the Lacedemonians (the Spartans), might win the victory (Herodotus 9.102).

But the Greeks were divided into fractious *poleis* or individual city-states; there was no concept of a unified Greece. Many of the city-states in the north and central areas had "Medized."[55] According to Herodotus (7.138):

53. P. Lipke, "Trials of the Trireme," *Arch* 41 (1988): 28. The average speed for a trireme in a hurry was eight knots.

54. Herodotus (8.48) gives the number as 378, Thucydides (1.71) as 400, and Demosthenes (*De Corona* 297) as 300.

55. D. Gillis, *Collaboration with the Persians* (Wiesbaden: F. Steiner, 1979); D. Graf, "Medism: The Origin and Significance of the Term," *JHS* 104 (1984): 15–30.

> Those of them that had paid tribute of earth and water to the Persian were of good courage, thinking that the foreigner would do them no harm; but they who had refused tribute were sore afraid, since there were not in Hellas ships enough to do battle with their invader, and the greater part of them had no stomach for grappling with the war, but were making haste to side with the Persian.

Other city-states such as Corcyra, which had a considerable fleet of sixty triremes, temporized, waiting to see which side would win (Herodotus 7.168). Between the chief allies, the Athenians and the Spartans, there was constant tension. The Peloponnesians wished to abandon mainland Greece and make their stand at the Isthmus of Corinth.

On the March

We may assume that Xerxes left Susa perhaps in April 481 B.C., and mustered his army at Critalla (Herodotus 7.26) in eastern Turkey in the fall of that year. The Persians then followed the proposed northern route of the Royal Road to a point and then turned south, passing near Colossae (Herodotus 7.30) and reaching Sardis about October. After spending the winter there, they left Sardis about March 480 (Herodotus 7.37), and marched northward. At Troy Xerxes sacrificed a thousand cattle to the Trojan Athena (Herodotus 7.43).

After their arrival at the Hellespont in April Xerxes reviewed his troops at Abydos (Herodotus 7.44). According to Maurice, "what probably happened was that Xerxes watched the royal troops below him march towards the bridges, but it would, I suggest, have exhausted his patience to have seen more than that body defile past him."[56]

Xerxes ordered two pontoon bridges built across the Hellespont from Abydos to a point near Sestos. These were constructed with two flax and four papyrus cables. The northern bridge was formed with 360 ships and was 4,220 yards long; the southern bridge was made with 314 ships and was 3,700 yards long. When a storm destroyed these bridges, Xerxes was furious and executed those who built them. He ordered the Hellespont to be scourged with 300 lashes and branded with hot irons (Herodotus 7.35).

After new bridges were built, a thousand horsemen and a thousand

56. Maurice, "Size of the Army," p. 215.

infantry crossed, followed by the sacred chariot of Ahuramazda and the chariot of Xerxes (Herodotus 7.40–41). The rest of the host took seven days and seven nights to cross the bridges (Herodotus 7.56).

Maurice, who investigated Xerxes' route from northwestern Anatolia across the Hellespont to Thrace (Bulgaria), concluded:

> But my examination of the story of the march from the Scamander to the Hebrus on the ground, with Herodotus in my hand, has impressed me with the fact that he must have been at great pains to examine eye-witnesses. The difficulties of the water supply, the time taken in the crossing, the use of one bridge for troops and the other for transport, the use of the lash at the European end of the bridge, and even the apparently fantastic story of the numbering, all turn out to have had some foundation and to be in accordance with what the conditions of ground made probable from the military point of view.[57]

In the light of the storm which destroyed the earlier Persian expedition of 492, the Persians worked for three years to cut a canal, which was wide enough for two triremes, through the Akte peninsula (Herodotus 7.23–24). A hoard of 300 gold darics was found at the site of the canal.[58] Magazines of grain had been stored ahead of time at Doriskos on the Thracian coast. Following a route similar to that later taken by Paul from Philippi westward, Xerxes and the army arrived at Therma (Thessalonica), 250 miles from Doriscus, around July 24.

Before the Persian host approached the area of Thessaly, the Greek allies in the spring of 480 B.C. had sent a force of ten thousand hoplites to the Vale of Tempe under the command of the Spartans. After a short time they decided to withdraw because they could not guard all the passes southward (Herodotus 7.173) and because the Aleuadai of Larissos in Thessaly were sympathetic to the Persians.[59] The Persians passed from Macedonia over Mount Olympos into Thessaly. Of the route described in Herodotus, Pritchett writes:

> In conclusion, the route assigned to Xerxes by Herodotus is a much more feasible military way than any of the possible alternatives. The topographical accuracy of the historian need never have been called into question.[60]

57. Ibid., p. 234.
58. A. A. M. van der Heyden and H. H. Scullard, eds., *Atlas of the Classical World* (London: Nelson, 1959), p. 54, fig. 100.
59. H. D. Westlake, "The Medism of Thessaly," *JHS* 56 (1936): 12–24.
60. W. K. Pritchett, "Xerxes' Route over Mount Olympos," *AJA* 65 (1961): 375.

The pass at Thermopylae.

Thermopylae

The Greeks now decided to make a stand with the navy at Artemision, on the northern end of the island of Euboea, and with the army at the pass of Thermopylae, between the mountains and the Gulf of Malis, four days' march from Athens. In the fifth century the pass was but 15 meters (about 50 feet) wide.[61] The fifth-century level was probably 20 meters (65 feet) below the present surface.

The pass at Thermopylae was guarded by six to seven thousand Greeks, including four thousand Peloponnesians, of which the core were the three hundred Spartans commanded by a Spartan king, Leonidas.[62] The three hundred were chosen from men with sons (Herodotus 7.205). There were also one thousand other Lacedemonians, seven hundred Thespians, four hundred Thebans, as well as some Phocians and Locrians. The bulk of the Spartan army was not prepared to march until after the Carneian Festival during the full moon, proba-

61. Herodotus's account of the site is accurate. See W. K. Pritchett, *Studies in Ancient Greek Topography, Part IV (Passes)* (Berkeley: University of California Press, 1982), chapter 9.

62. The Spartans had a unique dyarchy or system of two kings at a time. H. Mitchell, *Sparta* (New York: Cambridge University Press, 1964); W. G. Forrest, *A History of Sparta 950–192 B.C.* (New York: W. W. Norton, 1968).

Thermopylae and the former Bay of Malis.

bly of August 19 to 20.[63] Other Greeks were delayed because of their participation in the Olympic games (Herodotus 7.206).

For several days the Persian forces could not dislodge the Greeks because the narrow space nullified the advantage of their numbers. Not even the Immortals were able to force their way through. The courageous Greeks stood their ground. When a Spartan was told that the Persian arrows would be so numerous that they would blot out the sun, he quipped, "We shall fight them in the shade and not in the sunshine" (Herodotus 7.226).

Xerxes was frustrated by the lack of progress, until a local traitor, Epialtes, informed the Persians of a path called the Anopaea (or "Upper Way") on top of a mountain ridge that outflanked the Greek position (Herodotus 7.213–18). Leonidas had been aware of this contingency and had posted one thousand Phocians to stand guard over this route.

Hydarnes led the Immortals over the Anopaea, which not only wound at least ten miles through wooded hills but involved about 1,400 meters (4,600 feet) of ascent.[64] Paul Wallace recently hiked what

63. H. Popp, *Die Einwirkung von Vorzeichen, Opfern und Festen auf die Kriegführung der Griechen im 5. und 4. Jahrhundert vor Chr.* (Werzburg: Erlange, 1959), p. 91; Lazenby, "Strategy of the Greeks," p. 271.

64. A. R. Burn, "Thermopylai Revisited and Some Topographical Notes on Marathon and Plataiai," in *Greece and the Eastern Mediterranean in Ancient History and Prehistory*, ed. K. H. Kinzl (Berlin: Walter de Gruyter, 1977), p. 98.

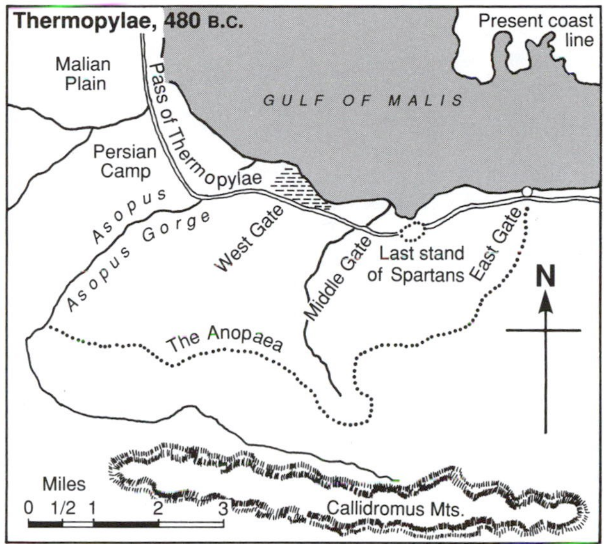

he deems is its probable course at night and as a result he suggests the following timetable:

> The march was begun at nightfall, probably in August with the full moon, and it must have taken about 12 hours to accomplish. The Persians left at the time of the lighting of the lamps (i.e. about 9:00 P.M.); they reached the top of the mountain at daybreak (i.e. about 5:30 A.M.); they reached Thermopylai around mid-morning (perhaps about 10:00 A.M.), sometime during the process of the battle there, which was begun at about the time when the "market-place is wont to fill" (i.e. about 8:00 or 9:00 A.M.).[65]

The final battle took place on August 28. When Leonidas learned that the Phocians had been bypassed, he was faced with three possibilities: he could try to fight on two fronts, he could withdraw completely, or he could stay with part of his forces to fight a rear guard action.[66] He chose to do the latter, allowing most of the allies to leave.

Leonidas made his gallant stand on a hill (on which today a monument stands), between the so-called Middle Gate and the East Gate. Spyridon Marinatos in 1939 found numerous arrowheads there. All of

65. P. W. Wallace, "The Anopaia Path at Thermopylai," *AJA* 84 (1980): 17–18. For an alternative view of the route, see W. K. Pritchett, "New Light on Thermopylae," *AJA* 62 (1958): 202–13.

66. A. V. Dascalakis, "Les raisons réelles du sacrifice de Léonidas et l'importance historique de la bataille des Thermopyles," *Studii Clasice* 6 (1964): 57–82; J. A. S. Evans, "The Final Problem at Thermopylae," *GRBS* 5 (1964): 235; R. H. Simpson, "Leonidas' Decision," *Phoenix* 26 (1972): 3; J. F. Lazenby, *The Spartan Army* (Chicago: Bolchazy-Carducci, 1986), pp. 92–93.

Statue of a Spartan warrior.

the three hundred Spartans died at Thermopylae save one who had been sent with a message to Thessaly. But among Spartans this was regarded not as a deliverance but a disgrace, so he committed suicide (Herodotus 7.232).

Herodotus reports that twenty thousand Persians were killed in the fray. In the ferocious fighting two half-brothers of Xerxes were killed. In his rage Xerxes had the corpse of Leonidas decapitated. Forty years later the Spartans recovered his remains and took them back to Sparta.[67] A famous Greek memorial to the dead Spartans reads: "Oh stranger, tell the Lacedaemonians that here we lie, obedient to their traditions" (Herodotus 7.228).[68]

Artemision

The Greeks were able to make a naval stand at Artemision because it blocked the entrance to the Euripus, the narrow sheltered channel between the island of Euboea and the mainland, normally taken by shipping. The Persians learned the reason for this by bitter experience when they tried to sail on the windward side of the island and wrecked their ships.

The Greek fleet sent to Artemision originally consisted of 271 triremes, of which the Athenians contributed 147. A later contingent of 53 triremes joined this force. Although the Spartans brought only ten ships, the fleet was under the nominal leadership of the Spartan Eurybiades. This was a concession made by Themistocles for the sake of unity. After an initial withdrawal back to Chalcis because of fright,

67. Pritchett, *Greek State at War, Part IV*, p. 168.

68. D. L. Page, *Further Greek Epigrams* (Cambridge: Cambridge University Press, 1981), pp. 233–34; see also H. T. Wade-Gery, "Classical Epigrams and Epitaphs," *JHS* 53 (1933): 72.

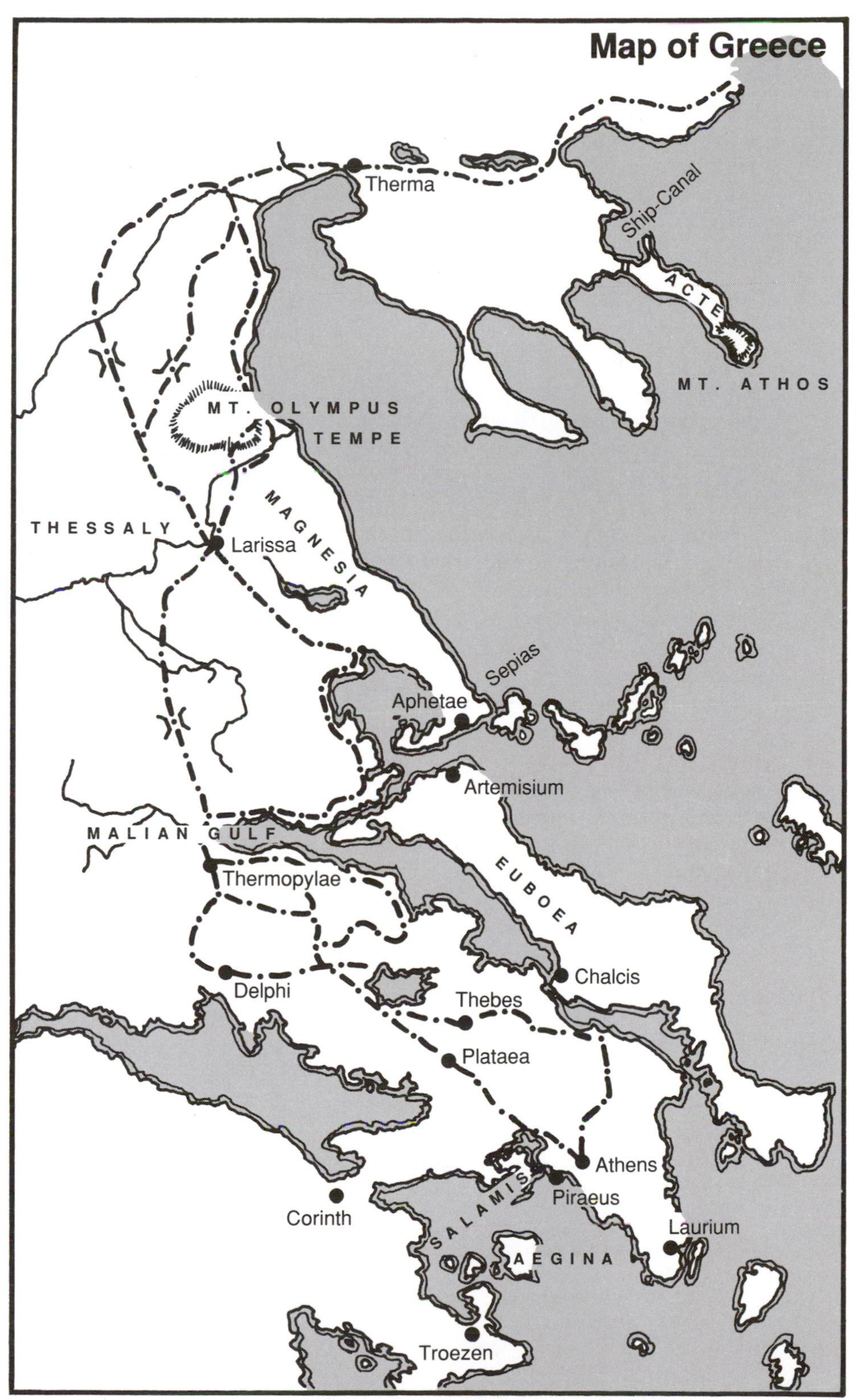
Map of Greece
Therma
Ship-Canal
ACTE
MT. ATHOS
MT. OLYMPUS
TEMPE
MAGNESIA
THESSALY
Larissa
Sepias
Aphetae
Artemisium
MALIAN GULF
Thermopylae
EUBOEA
Chalcis
Delphi
Thebes
Plataea
Athens
Piraeus
SALAMIS
Corinth
Laurium
AEGINA
Troezen

the allies were persuaded by bribes from the Euboeans to make a stand at Artemision (Herodotus 8.4–5).

The site of Artemision has been located at Pevki Bay. This was a site that gave the Greeks a favorable advantage.[69] The battle itself was a draw, but with the fall of Thermopylae to the rear, the Greeks had to withdraw.[70]

The Delphic Oracle

The most famous oracle in Greece was the temple of Apollo at Delphi.[71] Greeks seeking advice came to the shrine and received their answers in the inspired utterances of a priestess, seated on a tripod. These responses were rendered in poetic statements. The importance of the Delphic oracle is highlighted in thirty-three of the chapters that Herodotus devotes to the Persian War.[72]

While most of the twelve-member amphictyony (the league that was to guard the Delphic oracle) were on the Persian side, the disposition of the oracle itself is a matter of controversy.[73] Some scholars have accused the Delphic oracle of being sympathetic to the Persian cause.[74] But this is an unnecessary interpretation of what might appear to be defeatist advice.

Henry Immerwahr observed, "the idea that Delphi medized during the Persian War is un-Herodotean and in fact modern."[75] J. Elayi also concluded, "far from suspecting the Pythian Apollo of treason, he [Herodotus] ascribed to him the merit of the victory."[76] That this is the correct interpretation is shown in the continued high regard for Delphi even after the Persians were defeated, since the Greeks dedicated trophies of war to Apollo's shrine.[77]

69. A. W. Gomme, "A Forgotten Factor of Greek Naval Strategy," *JHS* 53 (1933): 20.

70. Pritchett, "Battle of Artemision in 480 B.C.," *Studies, Part II,* pp. 12–18.

71. The etymology of the Greek word for the spirit of divination in the slave girl exorcised by Paul (Acts 16:16) is related to *pythōn,* the snake that guarded the Delphic shrine.

72. J. Elayi, "Le rôle de l'oracle de Delphes dans le conflit gréco-Perse d'après 'Les Histoires' d'Hérodote," *IA* 14 (1979): 94.

73. P. Roussel, "Hérodote et l'expéditions des Perses contre Delphes," *REA* 29 (1927): 337.

74. For example, How and Wells, *Commentary,* 2: 246; Olmstead, *History of the Persian Empire,* p. 253; Balcer, *Sparda,* p. 256; J. V. A. Fine, *The Ancient Greeks: A Critical History* (Cambridge: Harvard University Press, 1983), p. 297.

75. H. Immerwahr, *Form and Thought in Herodotus* (Cleveland: Western Reserve University Press, 1966), p. 236; J. Fontenrose, *The Delphic Oracle* (Berkeley: University of California Press, 1978), p. 5.

76. Elayi, "Le rôle," p. 142.

77. In gratitude for their victory at Salamis, the Greeks dedicated at Delphi a colossal statue of Apollo holding in his hand the bow of a trireme.

At some point before the invasion the Athenians sought advice from Apollo.[78] The first oracle given to the Athenians was terrifying:

> Do not stay; fly to the ends of the earth, leaving your houses and city.
> For the whole body is unsound; nothing is left.
> Fire and war destroy it.
> Many fortresses will be destroyed, not yours alone.
> Many temples will burn, and blood drips upon their roofs, presaging inevitable evil.
> Leave the adyton [sanctuary] and be ready for woes. (Herodotus 7.140)

Alarmed by this dismaying response, the Athenians pled for a second oracle. The priestess then responded:

> Pallas [Athena] cannot appease Zeus with her many prayers.
> But I shall tell you this immovable decree:
> All Attica will be taken, but Zeus grants Athena *a wooden wall* that shall alone be untaken and will help you and your children.
> Do not await the onset of cavalry and infantry from the continent at your ease, but turn about and leave.
> You will face them sometime again.
> O divine Salamis, you will lose many children of men either at sowing time or at harvest. (Herodotus 7.141, emphasis added)

The key phrase, *a wooden wall,* was variously interpreted in antiquity. Noel Robertson has argued that it may have originally meant the wall at the Isthmus in support of the preferred Spartan policy.[79] Some Athenians thought that the oracle meant the wooden palisade about the Acropolis. Themistocles persuaded the Athenians that the wooden wall was their newly built fleet of triremes.

Some scholars have dismissed the second oracle as a "prophecy after the event" because of the reference to Salamis.[80] But Frost counters this scepticism by declaring:

78. The oracles have been dated either to 481 or 480 B.C.

79. N. Robertson, "The True Meaning of the 'Wooden Wall,' " *CP* 82 (1987): 10. Robertson, ibid., p. 18, reports: "Among the isthmus walls that can still be traced on the ground, there is a considerable stretch of mixed ashlar and polygonal masonry, with square protruding towers, on a ridge northwest of Cenchreae, which may well go back to this occasion."

80. Most scholars have accepted the oracles as genuine, but P. Georges has argued that these were manufactured after the fall of Thermopylae to induce the Athenians to fight at Salamis. See P. Georges, "Saving Herodotus' Phenomena: The Oracles and the Events of 480 B.C.," *CSCA* 5 (1986): 15. Fontenrose, *Delphic Oracle,* p. 128, questions the oracles on literary grounds: "So we must conclude that these two responses are dubious at best; if authentic they are extraordinary and unusual pronouncements of the Delphic Oracle."

> The assumption implicit in these statements is that the priests at Delphi had not the slightest belief in Apollo's power of prophecy, that they ignored the Pythia completely and made up oracles out of whole cloth, based on purely rational political and strategic considerations. I find this cynical notion inconceivable. . . . I have no idea why the priestess mentioned Salamis—but this is the exact point. If oracular responses could easily be explained, who would go to oracles?[81]

Robert Lenardon also accepts the authenticity of the oracles: "It seems to me preferable to believe that the clever and political Delphic priesthood did make their ambiguous utterances as Herodotus has recorded; that the ingenious and unscrupulous Themistocles, by whatever means, manipulated the whole proceedings for his own ends also appears not unlikely."[82]

Themistocles

The dominating figure in Athens at the time of Xerxes' invasion was Themistocles. He had arisen from an obscure background by clever political actions. He learned every citizen's name and had famous musicians practice at his home. Themistocles, notwithstanding his notorious avarice and calculation, did have several characteristics that made him an outstanding leader in Athens' gravest crisis. He could immediately evaluate the situation, decide quickly what needed to be done, and clearly explain his plan to others.[83] He has been compared to Winston Churchill:

> Both possessed the unpopular gift of being right when their more intellectual contemporaries were wrong. Both had a streak of that dazzling yet suspect histrionic genius which can transcend and transform a national emergency. Both were voted out of office with uncommon speed when

81. Frost, *Plutarch's Themistocles*, p. 100.

82. Lenardon, *Saga of Themistocles*, p. 66. H. W. Parke, *Greek Oracles* (London: Hutchinson University Library, 1967), p. 104, comments: "Also the double consultation is highly exceptional, but can be accepted as fully authentic, not merely because of such details as the name of the Pythia and the name of Timon, but also because no one after the event would have been likely to invent such peculiar happenings and those so little to the credit of the Delphic authorities." For others who support the authenticity of the oracles, see P. Green, *Xerxes at Salamis* (New York: Praeger, 1970), p. 96; N. G. L. Hammond, *A History of Greece to 322 B.C.* (Oxford: Clarendon, 1959), p. 223; How and Wells, *Commentary*, 2: 181–82; Hignett, *Xerxes' Invasion*, pp. 441–45. See further, A. R. Hands, "On Strategy and Oracles, 480/79," *JHS* 85 (1965): 56–61.

83. Frost, *Plutarch's Themistocles*, pp. 9, 12.

the crisis they surmounted was over. Under Themistocles' leadership the Athenians, too, lived through their finest hour.[84]

In 483 B.C. the Athenian state mines at Laurium yielded a bonanza of silver. The silver ore was extracted by state slaves, including children, who worked in narrow, cramped galleries. Themistocles persuaded the Athenians to use the one hundred talents (two and a half tons) of silver to finance the building of a fleet of two hundred triremes, ostensibly to be used against Athens' enemy Aegina (Herodotus 7.144), but probably with the eventual return of the Persians in mind.[85] Working at top speed, the Athenians could launch from six to eight new triremes a month.[86]

It was Themistocles who "acted on behalf of unity and sound strategy throughout in the face of the defeatism, stupidity and shortsightedness of those in command."[87] It was he who masterminded the brilliant strategy of the Battle of Salamis.

The Themistocles Decree

The most controversial of all Greek inscriptions is the so-called Themistocles decree, discovered in a coffee shop at Troizen by Michael Jameson in 1959.[88] The marble slab had originally been found by a farmer nearly thirty years earlier. Jameson published the text in 1960.[89]

The stele is 2 feet high, 15 inches wide, and 3 inches thick. The left side of the inscription is badly damaged. The present text was incised in the late fourth or early third century. It reads as follows:

> The temple-treasurers and priestesses shall stay on the Acropolis to protect the property of the gods. All the other Athenians and aliens who are of age shall embark on the 200 ships which have been prepared and shall fight the barbarian both for their own freedom and for that of the rest of the Greeks, with the aid of the Spartans and Corinthians and Aeginetans

84. Green, *Xerxes at Salamis,* p. 24.

85. Lenardon, *Saga of Themistocles,* p. 53. Themistocles also persuaded the Athenians to fortify the harbor of Piraeus.

86. Green, *Xerxes at Salamis,* p. 57.

87. F. J. Frost, "Themistocles' Place in Athenian Politics," *CSCA* 1 (1968): 119.

88. M. H. Jameson, "How Themistocles Planned the Battle of Salamis," *Scientific American* 204 (1961): 111–18, 120.

89. M. H. Jameson, "A Decree of Themistokles from Troizen," *Hesperia* 29 (1960): 198–223; idem, "A Revised Text of the Decree of Themistokles from Troizen," *Hesperia* 31 (1962): 310–15. See also his "Waiting for the Barbarian," *Greece and Rome,* 8 (1961): 5–18, and "The Provisions for Mobilization in the Decree of Themistokles," *Historia* 12 (1963): 385–404.

> and any others who are willing to share the danger.[90] The generals shall also appoint 200 trierarchs, one for each ship, beginning tomorrow, from those who possess land and a house at Athens and who have legitimate children and are not more than 50 years of age, and shall allot the ships to them. They shall also enrol 10 marines[91] for each ship from those above 20 and below 30 years of age, and four archers; and they shall assign the petty officers among the ships at the same time as they allot the trierarchs. The generals shall also post up the other crew members, ship-by-ship on the white notice-boards. . . .[92]

Women and children were to go to Troizen. The old men and movable possessions were to be removed to Salamis. Sacrifices were to be offered to Zeus, Athena, Nike (Victory), and Poseidon. Half of the ships were to be sent to Artemision and the other half were to remain near Salamis. Those who had been ostracized and recalled were to go to Salamis until further notice.[93]

Scholars are equally divided as to whether this text is a copy of an authentic decree of Themistocles from the fifth century or whether it is a forgery of the fourth century.[94] Among those who have argued for its authenticity are Jameson himself, and David Lewis, who avers: "There are arguments which lead one to suspect an editor. I see no reason to suspect forgery. There are too many traces of official and archaic language."[95] Hammond has also concluded: "It seems highly improbable that this is the work of a late-fourth-century forger."[96] Mortimer Chambers is willing to accept the first eighteen lines of the text as genuine.[97]

Hammond suggested September 481 as a date for the decree;[98] Jameson preferred June 480;[99] and Morrison and R. T. Williams opted for a date in August 480, just before the Persian army's arrival at Thermopylae.[100]

90. Jordan, *Athenian Navy,* p. 263: "It is entirely possible, even probable, that slaves were present on the ships which fought at Salamis."

91. In his original publication, Jameson had restored line 24 as "/[*ei*]*k*[*osin*]/" or twenty; he subsequently corrected the reading to "[*d*]*eka*/" or ten.

92. A. J. Podlecki, *The Life of Themistocles* (Montreal: McGill-Queens University Press, 1975), pp. 147–48.

93. S. M. Burstein, "The Recall of the Ostracized and the Themistocles Decree," *CSCA* 4 (1971): 93–110.

94. Podlecki, *Life of Themistocles,* p. 154: "The match must be declared a draw."

95. D. M. Lewis, "Notes on the Decree of Themistocles," *CQ* n.s. 11 (1961): 66.

96. N. G. L. Hammond, "The Narrative of Herodotus VII and the Decree of Themistocles at Troezen," *JHS* 102 (1982): 91.

97. M. H. Chambers, "The Authenticity of the Themistocles Decree," *AHR* 67 (1961–1962): 306–16.

98. Hammond, "Narrative," p. 91.

99. Jameson, "Decree of Themistokles," p. 203.

100. Morrison and Williams, *Greek Oared Ships,* p. 123.

On the other hand, many scholars believe that the text is a forgery, especially because of differences with Herodotus.[101] For example, the decree assigns 100 triremes to Artemision and 100 to Salamis, whereas Herodotus has 147 triremes at Artemision joined by 53 arriving later. The Themistocles decree proposes the evacuation of Athens before the battles of Thermopylae and Artemision, whereas Herodotus implies that the evacuation was the result of last-minute panic. The decree sends the Athenians to Troizen and Salamis; Herodotus also has them fleeing to Aegina. Hermann Bengtson expresses this sceptical point of view:

> How could one expect Leonidas and his soldiers to fight to the last man at Thermopylae while in Athens everyone was preparing to flee? The inscription, moreover, directly contradicts Herodotus, whom there is no reason at all to mistrust on this point. Allegedly a decree initiated on a motion by Themistocles, the inscription is obviously a later work, not deserving of credence; it cannot be dated earlier than about the middle of the fourth century B.C.[102]

If one keeps in mind the difference between a decree that makes certain proposals of planned action and a history that recounts what actually happened, there may not be a necessary conflict between Herodotus and the decree.[103] According to Russell Meiggs and David Lewis: "That the evacuation of civilians is ordered so early is not necessarily incompatible with the fact that, according to Herodotus, it happened later, nor is it entirely surprising that, at the time of the decree, Athens was not yet prepared to commit all her forces to Artemision."[104] Frost also suggests that "it is entirely in human character that an evacuation be ordered and yet not carried out until the last moment, when the attendant confusion would make observers and participants forget that a plan had been made months before."[105]

101. C. Habicht, "Falsche Urkunden zur Geschichte Athens im Zeitalter der Perserkriege," *Hermes* 89 (1961): 1–35; B. Jordan, *Servant of the Gods* (Göttingen: Vandenhoeck and Ruprecht, 1979), pp. vii, 79–80; Hignett, *Xerxes' Invasion*, pp. 458–68; Georges, "Saving Herodotus' Phenomena," p. 14. According to M. Chambers, "The Significance of the Themistocles Decree," *Philologus* 111 (1967): 160: "The credibility of Herodotus has been upheld time and again in the recent studies of Greek topography by Professor Pritchett and in the microscopically thorough study of the second Persian War by Mr. Hignett. So far as concerns the general course of the war and the unfolding of the campaigns, Herodotus is largely unshakeable." See S. Dow, "Bibliography of the Purported Themistokles Inscription from Troizen," *CW* 55 (1962): 105–8.

102. Bengtson, *Greeks and the Persians*, p. 56.

103. Lazenby, "Strategy," p. 264, n. 1.

104. R. Meiggs and D. Lewis, eds., *A Selection of Greek Historical Inscriptions to the End of the Fifth Century B.C.* (Oxford: Clarendon, 1969), p. 52. See also Frost, *Plutarch's Themistocles*, p. 119.

105. Frost, *Plutarch's Themistocles*, p. 103. See also Podlecki, *Life of Themistocles*, p. 167. C. W. Fornara, "The Value of the Themistocles Decree," *AHR* 73 (1967): 425–33, believes that the decree is consistent with at least some of the traditions in Herodotus.

Salamis

The Persian army arrived about September 5 in Attica, the region around Athens. After a brief siege they captured the Acropolis and destroyed the Old Parthenon, built under Peisistratus in the sixth century. Xerxes removed works of art including the famous statue of the tyrannicides, Harmodios and Aristogeiton, the work of Antenor. This was sent to Susa where Alexander found it in 331 B.C., and sent it back to Athens.

The Persian navy closed in on the Greek fleet, which had taken up a position in the Bay of Salamis between the island of Salamis and the mainland of Attica. Thus the stage was set for one of the greatest battles in Western civilization. We are relatively sure that the battle took place at the end of September inasmuch as the Spartans were celebrating the victory of Salamis by October 2, the date of a partial solar eclipse (Herodotus 9.10).[106] Most scholars prefer a date between September 27 and 29 for the battle.[107]

Prior to the battle Themistocles sent a secret message by his servant to Xerxes, informing him of the position of the Greek fleet (Herodotus 8.75).[108] Although this was couched as a secret betrayal to Xerxes, Themistocles wanted to coax the Persians into fighting a battle in the narrow straits of Salamis. He knew that the Greek ships were inferior to Persian ships in the open sea, because they were heavier and less maneuverable (Herodotus 8.60; Thucydides 1.74.1; *Persai* 413ff.) and because at Thermopylae the narrow space would nullify the numerical advantage of the Persians. He also wanted to keep the Peloponnesian ships from retreating south below the Isthmus.

Xerxes swallowed the bait for, as Balcer points out, "Xerxes believed Themistokles' message because it was not only plausible but also what he wanted to believe."[109] Xerxes sent his Egyptian fleet of two hundred ships to blockade the western exit of the Bay of Salamis, while his main fleet of Phoenician, Cypriote, and Ionian ships patrolled the eastern

106. This eclipse prevented Cleombrotos, king of the Spartans, from leading his army further north. Popp, *Die Einwirkung,* pp. 19–20, notes that this is another striking example of how religious, some would say superstitious, scruples affected the Greeks.

107. Sept. 22 is favored by Olmstead, *History of the Persian Empire,* p. 253; Sept. 27/28 is followed by most commentators according to Frost, *Plutarch's Themistocles,* p. 124; Sept. 28/29 is favored by Hignett, *Xerxes' Invasion,* p. 233, and Robertson, "True Meaning," p. 16, n. 30; Sept. 29 by Georges, "Saving Herodotus' Phenomena," p. 54.

108. Podlecki, *Life of Themistocles,* p. 23, comments: "It seems certain that, the uneasiness of some modern historians notwithstanding, a private communication of some sort was sent by Themistocles via his slave, although details of its exact content and some of the circumstances of its delivery may be uncertain."

109. Balcer, *Sparda,* p. 257; See also Frost, *Plutarch's Themistocles,* p. 141.

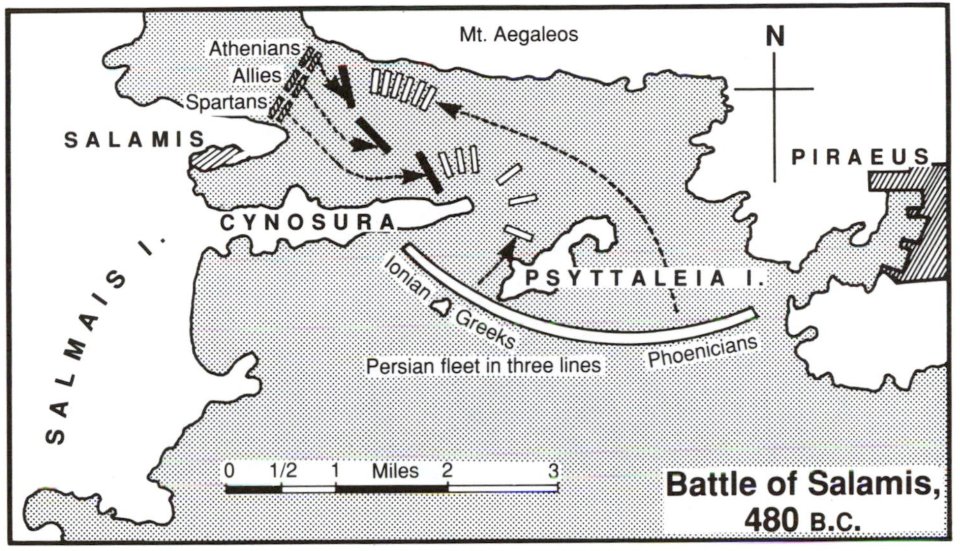

exit. The Persian sailors rowed all night long to make sure the Greek ships did not escape their so-called trap.

The Greek fleet of about three hundred triremes was divided into three squadrons: the Spartans (led by Eurybiades) held the Greek right, while the Athenians maintained the left and the center together with other allies. The Phoenicians held the Persian right, and the Ionian Greeks the left.

The battle began soon after dawn. According to Plutarch (*Themistocles* 14), Themistocles "chose the exact time at which a sea breeze would begin to blow and waves would throw the Persian ships into confusion." The Greeks feigned retreat by backing water (Herodotus 8.84–85) to lure the Persians into the narrowest part of the bay. Here the channel is reduced to but 1,300 yards, where not more than 100 to 120 ships could operate in a line. As Peter Green describes the action: "The Greek line, in fact, had become a noose; and the Persians were now energetically hanging themselves in it."[110]

The Persians fought bravely under the eyes of their king, but the very crush of their numbers proved to be a handicap. The Greeks fought in better order and with less confusion (Herodotus 8.86). Although the Spartan ships were battered by the Ionians, the Athenians and Aeginetans were able to ram many of the Phoenician and Cypriote

110. Green, *Xerxes at Salamis*, p. 194. For a detailed study of the topography, see W. K. Pritchett, "Towards a Restudy of the Battle of Salamis," *AJA* 63 (1959): 251–62.

The Bay of Salamis.

ships. They then attacked the Cilician, Pamphylian, and Lycian ships in the Persian right center. A most vivid eyewitness account of the battle is given to us by Aeschylus in the words of a Persian sailor:

> But when the white-horsed chariot of dawn appeared
> And filled the entire earth with radiance to behold,
> The first thing was a sound, a shouting from the Greeks,
> A joyful song, and to it, making shrill response,
> From the island rocks about there came an antiphony
> Of echoes; fear stood next to each one of our men,
> Tripped up in their hopes: for not as if in flight
> Were the Greeks raising then a solemn paean-strain,
> But rushing into battle with daring confidence;
> A trumpet, too, blazed over everything its sound.
> At once, with measured stroke of surging, sea-dipped oar,
> They struck the brine and made it roar from one command,
> And quickly all of them were visible to sight.
> Their right wing first, in order just as they had been
> Arranged, led off, and next the whole remaining force
> Came out to the attack, and with the sight we heard
> A loud voice of command: "O sons of Greeks, go on,
> Bring freedom to your fatherland, bring freedom to
> Your children, wives, and seats of your ancestral gods,
> And your forbears' graves; now the struggle is for all."
> Of course, on our side, too, a roar of Persian tongues
> Went forth in answer; the moment would not brook delay.
> Immediately ship struck its brazen-plated beak

On ship. The ramming was begun by a Greek ship
And it snapped off from one of the Phoenicians the whole
Curving stern, and men of both sides shot their spears.
At first the streaming Persian force withstood the shocks;
But when their crowd of ships was gathered in the straits,
And no assistance could be given one to another,
But they were being struck by their own brazen rams,
They kept on breaking all their equipage of oars,
And the ships of the Greeks with perfect plan and order, came
Around them in a circle and struck, and hulls of ships
Were overturned; and the sea no longer was visible,
Filled as it was with shipwrecks and the slaughter of men.
The beaches, too, and the reefs around were filled with corpses.
Now every ship that came with the Persian armament
Was being rowed for quick escape, no order left.
And they kept striking us, deboning us, like tunnies
Or a catch of fish, with broken fragments of oars, or bits
Of flotsam from the wrecks; and all this time, moaning
And wailing held control of that area of sea,
Until the eye of black night took it away.
So great a crowd of ills, not even if I took
Ten days in order to tell, could I tell the tale in full.
For be assured of this, that never in one day
Did such a huge number of men go to their deaths. (*Persai* 386–432)[111]

According to Herodotus (8.76), Xerxes had placed four hundred Persian soldiers on the island of Psyttaleia between Salamis and the mainland.[112] He had hoped that these could rescue some of their men and kill the Greeks who might be washed ashore. But Aristides, a political rival of Themistocles who had been recalled in 481 from his ostracism, led a force of hoplites who captured the island.[113]

Xerxes had been seated on a golden *diphros* on the slopes of Mount Aegaleos, observing the battle with secretaries at hand to make a rec-

111. A. J. Podlecki, trans., *The Persians by Aeschylus* (Englewood Cliffs, N.J.: Prentice-Hall, 1970), pp. 61–63.

112. The identification of this island has been a matter of some debate. A few scholars (K. J. Beloch, N. G. L. Hammond, H. D. Broadhead) have identified Psyttaleia with St. George's, a small island deep within the bay and close to the mainland. But most favor the large island of Leipsokoutali at the eastern approach to the bay. Wallace expresses the majority position: "The cumulative evidence, however, of the island's position according to the ancient authors, the persistence of the name Psyttaleia, the possible corruption of the name into Leipsokoutali, the descriptive phrases used of the island, the position of the island in the battle, and the physical remains found there and on the Cynosoura, forces us to conclude that Psyttaleia is Leipsokoutali, the island laying between the mouth of the Piraeus and the Cynosoura peninsula of Salamis." P. W. Wallace, "Psyttaleia and the Trophies of the Battle of Salamis," *AJA* 73 (1969): 303.

113. See also Aeschylus (*Persai* 447–64); C. W. Fornara, "The Hoplite Achievement at Psyttaleia," *JHS* 86 (1966): 51–55.

ord (Herodotus 8.90).[114] According to Aeschylus, (*Persai* 465–67): "Xerxes groaned aloud when he beheld the depth of the disaster; for he occupied a seat commanding a clear view of all the armament—a lofty eminence hard by the open sea."[115]

The Greeks lost but forty vessels, whereas the Persians suffered staggering losses, perhaps a third of their fleet. Many of the Persian sailors drowned because few of them could swim. Among the casualties was Xerxes' half-brother, Ariabignes.

Xerxes was responsible for the debacle. He had conquered almost all of Greece. If he had been more patient and had been content with a blockade, the fractious Greek allies may well have splintered. But, according to Walter How and Joseph Wells, "like the Czar Alexander at Austerlitz, he threw away the advantages gained by sound and cautious strategy in the vain hope of a brilliant victory."[116]

Afraid that the Greeks might cut off his avenue of retreat, Xerxes made a hasty withdrawal. He was accompanied by most of his troops. They reached the Hellespont after a hurried march of forty-five days. They found the bridges no longer intact, so Xerxes crossed over into Asia Minor in a ship.[117] Xerxes himself spent the year in Sardis (Herodotus 8.117).

The triumphant Greeks celebrated by voting the *aristeia* (awards of valor).[118] The Aeginetans won first prize and the Athenians won second prize. We have a clear example of the bias of Herodotus's Athenian source in the tale that the Corinthians fled, a story that the Corinthians denied. Herodotus indicated the Athenians allowed the Corinthians to erect a memorial to their dead on the island of Salamis. An

114. F. Frost, "A Note on Xerxes at Salamis," *Historia* 22 (1973): 118–19, and idem, *Plutarch's Themistocles,* p. 149, argues that a *diphros* was not so much a throne as a chair or stool. When the Persians left, this was left behind, and was displayed by the Greeks upon the acropolis. But according to D. B. Thompson, "The Persian Spoils in Athens," in *The Aegean and the Near East,* ed. S. S. Weinberg (Locust Valley: J. J. Augustin, 1956), pp. 287, 289: "It is most probable that Xerxes, as the great Persian king, sat on a high-backed throne, even at the battle of Salamis. . . . We should probably think of it as of wood, possibly with a little bronze decoration, and with silver feet."

115. Byron's Don Juan declared:

A king sate on the rocky brow
Which looks o'er sea-born Salamis;
And ships, by thousands, lay below,
And men in nations;—all were his!
He counted them at break of day—
And when the sun set where were they?

Cited from *The Complete Poetical Works of Byron* [Boston: Houghton Mifflin, 1933], p. 812.

116. How and Wells, *Commentary,* 2: 381.

117. Later the Athenians took some of the remaining cables of the bridges from Sestos, and displayed them as prize booty.

118. See W. K. Pritchett, "Aristeia in Greek Warfare," in *The Greek State at War, Part II* (Berkeley: University of California Press, 1974), chapter 14.

Plataea, looking toward Mount Cithaeron.

epitaph for Adeimantos, commander of the Corinthians, supports the Corinthians' claim: "Through Adeimantos all Hellas put on the wreath of freedom."[119]

As for individual honors, every general voted for himself, but at least each voted for Themistocles second (Plutarch, *Themistocles* 17.1–2.)! The Spartans did give Themistocles unprecedented honors for a non-Spartan.

Plataea

Xerxes left Mardonius in Greece with considerable troops—three hundred thousand according to Herodotus (8.100, 113). Scholars believe the true figure was closer to one hundred thousand or even sixty thousand.[120] The Persians made their base at Thebes and chose the level plains at Plataea north of the Cithaeron Mountain for the final confrontation. The battle probably took place in mid-August 479.[121]

Prior to the battle the Greeks swore an oath (Herodotus 7.132). The text of the oath reads as follows:

> I will fight to the death, and I will not count my life more precious than freedom. I will not leave my officer, the commander of my Regiment or

119. Page, *Further Greek Epigrams*, pp. 200–201.

120. Lazenby, *Spartan Army*, p. 102; Bengtson, *Greeks and the Persians*, p. 61; Burn, *Persia and the Greeks*, p. 511.

121. Ctesias erroneously places Plataea before Salamis (Bigwood, "Ctesias as Historian," p. 29).

> Company, either alive or dead. I will not withdraw unless my commanders lead me back, and I will do whatsoever the Generals order. I will bury the dead of those who have fought as my allies, on the field, and will not leave one of them unburied. After defeating the barbarians in battle, I will tithe the city of the Thebans; and I will never destroy Athens or Sparta or Plataia or any of the cities which have fought as our allies, nor will I consent to their being starved, nor cut them off from running water, whether we be friends or at war.
>
> And if I keep well the oath, as it is written, may my city have good health; but if not, may it have sickness; and may my city never be sacked; but if not, may it be sacked; and may my land give increase; but if not, may it be barren; and may the women bring forth children like their fathers; but if not, monsters; and may the cattle bring forth after their kind; but if not, monsters.[122]

The Spartans came in full strength (11,500) and occupied the right wing, the position of honor. The Athenians (8,000) occupied the left wing.[123] Herodotus (9.29) gives the total figure of 38,700 hoplites. Pritchett, who accepts these figures, believes that the hoplite line would have extended 4,837 yards or 2.75 miles.[124]

At first the Greeks occupied an advanced position. But the Persians used their cavalry to harass the Greek supply trains. The Greeks then decided to withdraw at night to await further reinforcements.

The central section, which was composed of contingents from twenty states, withdrew in good order and reached the temple of Hera within the town. These troops were so far removed that they did not play a role in the ensuing battle until the very end.[125] The withdrawal of the Spartans on the right wing, however, was hampered by the obstinance

122. Burn, *Persia and the Greeks*, p. 513. A stele with the text of the oath was first published in 1938. Those who regard the oath as inauthentic include V. Ehrenberg, M. Guarducci, C. Hignett, L. Robert, R. Sealy, H. Wade-Gery, and F. W. Walbank. Those who have accepted its authenticity include H. Berve, A. R. Burn, N. G. L. Hammond, H. W. Parke, A. E. Raubitschek, and C. B. Welles. See especially J. Shriver, "Documents from the Persian Wars," unpublished Ph.D. diss. (Cincinnati: University of Cincinnati, 1964), and P. Siewert, *Der Eid von Plataia* (Munich: Beck, 1972), who defend the oath's authenticity. For oaths in the biblical world, see E. Yamauchi, "Oaths," in *The New International Dictionary of Biblical Archaeology*, eds. E. M. Blaiklock and R. K. Harrison (Grand Rapids: Zondervan, 1983), pp. 343–44.

123. See Hignett, *Xerxes' Invasion*, appendix 12, for the Greek army at Plataea.

124. W. K. Pritchett, "New Light on Plataia," *AJA* 61 (1957): 24. Ctesias has but 300 Spartans, 1,000 Perioikoi, and 6,000 other Greeks face an army of 120,000 Persians!

125. The accuracy of these complicated maneuverings described by Herodotus is defended by W. K. Pritchett, "New Light on Plataia," p. 28: "We may conclude our study by stating that given the premise that Herodotus is using a point to describe the position of the Greek army, and that his point is the Spartan right wing, or Pausanias' headquarters, we believe that what emerges is a coherent and understandable topographical and strategic picture." See also Lazenby, *Spartan Army*, pp. 106–7.

Greek warrior attacking a Persian. (Courtesy of the Metropolitan Museum of Art, Rogers Fund, 1906 [06.1021.117])

of an officer.[126] The Athenians, noting that the Spartans were being delayed, also slowed their withdrawal.

As the dawning light (about 5 A.M.) revealed the situation to Mardonius, he launched a full-scale attack. The Spartans held back until they received the propitious omens.[127] But when they received the desired auspices, the Spartans fought furiously and killed Mardonius himself.

According to Plutarch (*Aristides* 19.5–6): "Of those who struggled on behalf of Hellas there fell in all 1,360 men. Fifty-two of these were

126. Modern scholars have sometimes rationalized this action, for example, A. R. Burn, "Persia and the Greeks," in *The Cambridge History of Iran II. Median and Achaemenian Periods*, ed. I. Gershevitch (Cambridge: Cambridge University Press, 1985), p. 329, who suggests that the Spartans left one battalion "probably deliberately, as bait."

127. Herodotus notes that the Greeks offered *sphagia* sacrifice at several stages of the battle (9.36, 41, 61, 62). See Popp, *Die Einwirkung*, pp. 51, 53. Pritchett, "Sacrifice before Battle," in *The Greek State at War, Part I* (Berkeley: University of California Press, 1971), chapter 8.

Achaemenian gold bowl. (Metropolitan Museum of Art, Harris Brisbane Dick Fund, 1954)

Athenians." The Spartans had only 92 men slain. But 600 from the left center were killed by the Theban cavalry. On the other hand, thousands of Persians were killed as they attempted to flee.[128]

Artabazos, the other Persian commander, was delayed (Herodotus 9.66). As he saw Mardonius's forces being pushed back by the Spartans, instead of attacking he withdrew his forces. Artabazos must have created a good story, for far from being punished by Xerxes, he was awarded the satrapy of Daskyleion in northwest Turkey.

After the victory the Greeks dedicated a tithe of the plunder at Delphi. According to Herodotus (9.80), Pausanias proclaimed that no one should touch the spoil: "They, scattering all about the camp, found there tents adorned with gold and silver, and couches gilded and silver-plated, and golden bowls and cups and other drinking-vessels." The spoil included the spars of the Persian ships, the cuirass of Macistius, the dagger of Mardonius, and the king's tent.[129] The total treasure left behind was worth about five hundred talents or three million days' wages of that time.[130] The names of thirty-one Greek allies were inscribed on a serpent column, which was later removed to Constantinople.[131] In celebration of the victory, the Plataeans established a quadrennial celebration that was still commemorated during Roman times.

128. W. K. Pritchett, *The Greek State at War, Part IV* (Berkeley: University of California Press, 1985), p. 6, notes: "As with many ancient battles, the loss of life was predominantly among the defeated."

129. It has been suggested that Xerxes' tent (*skēnē*) was the model for the dressing room of the theater in Athens, which was painted and formed the "scene" or backdrop of the play. H. von Gall, "Das persische Königszelt und die Hallen-architektur in Iran und Griechenland," in *Festschrift für Frank Brommer,* eds. U. Hockmann and A. Krug (Mainz: Phillip von Zabern, 1977), pp. 123–25.

130. Thompson, "Persian Spoils in Athens," p. 282.

131. Meiggs and Lewis, *Selection,* pp. 57–60. See W. C. West, "The Trophies of the Persian Wars," *CP* 64 (1969): 7–19.

Achaemenian gold bowl. (Cincinnati Art Museum, purchase)

Mycale

The last major battle between the Persians and the Greeks was fought at Mycale on the western coast of Asia Minor in 479 B.C. According to Herodotus (9.100), both the battles of Plataea and Mycale were fought on the same day. Scholars believe that while both were fought in August, Mycale must have followed Plataea.[132]

After Salamis the Persian fleet withdrew across the Aegean. A Greek fleet of 110 ships pursued under the leadership of Xanthippus (the father of the famous Pericles) and under the Spartan, Leotychidas. The Persians, having lost confidence in their fleet and suspicious of their Ionian allies, beached their ships and took a stand behind a palisade.

The Ionians did turn against their Persian masters, as the allies launched their attack. With the Greek victory at Mycale, Ionia was liberated from Persia. Leotychidas and the Spartans retired to the Peloponnese, but the Athenians under Xanthippus went on to capture the city of Sestos.

132. Cook, *Persian Empire,* p. 124: "But on balance it seems more likely that Plataea released man-power for Mykale." See also Hignett, *Xerxes' Invasion,* p. 249; Green, *Xerxes at Salamis,* p. 181.

Pausanias

The Spartan commander at Plataea was Pausanias, the nephew of Leonidas and a young man only in his twenties. He was hailed as a hero, but became a tragic case of *hubris* (arrogant pride). He made a personal dedication at Delphi for the national victory at Plataea, boasting: "After destroying the Median host, Pausanias, Captain General of the Hellenes, set up this memorial to Apollo."[133]

Pausanias had been raised in the stark simplicity of Spartan regimen. After the Battle of Plataea, he contrasted the spare meal of the Spartans with the gourmet repast of the Persians, remarking: "Men of Hellas, I have brought you hither because I desired to show you the foolishness of the leader of the Medes; who, with such provision for life as you see, came hither to take away from us ours, that is so pitiful" (Herodotus 9.82). But Pausanias must have been overcome by the splendor of the Persian booty to seek a more luxurious life. When he was at Byzantium he dressed in Persian garb and dined in Persian style.

Pausanias also entered into treasonable correspondence with the Persians, offering to bring the Greeks under Persian subjection if he could marry Xerxes' daughter (Thucydides 1.128). The king delivered the following response through Artabazus:

> So King Xerxes speaks to Pausanias. For the men whom you saved from Byzantium beyond the sea for me, a record of gratitude will be stored up for you in our house forever; and I am pleased with your words. Let neither night nor day keep you from accomplishing any of your promises to me and do not be hindered by any lack of gold or silver to spend or number of troops, if they be required anywhere. But with Artabazus, a good man whom I have sent to you, confidently fulfil my interests and yours in whatever way will be finest and best for us both. (Thucydides 1.129)[134]

It is noteworthy that the letter makes no reference to a marriage proposal. Herodotus (5.32) reports a different story, that Pausanias was engaged to Megabates' daughter "if the story is true."

While this dramatic devolution of the victor of Plataea may strike some as incredible, it is more understandable when one considers the tremendous impression made on the Greeks by Xerxes and the opulence of his court. According to Lenardon:

133. C. W. Fornara, *Archaic Times to the Peloponnesian War* (Baltimore: Johns Hopkins University Press, 1977), 61.

134. A. T. Olmstead, "A Persian Letter in Thucydides," *AJSL* 49 (1933): 154; A. Lippold, "Pausanias von Sparta und die Perser," *RhM* 108 (1965): 334.

> There is hardly anything in this account of Pausanias' career that has not been challenged by one scholar or another. . . . But after reviewing (at times with amazement!) the plethora of fanciful modern theories, one returns to Thucydides' account with renewed confidence. . . . The essentials of the story seem feasible—that Pausanias negotiated with Xerxes, i.e. Medized; that upon being evicted from Byzantium a second time he attempted once again to further his ambition for power, this time by fostering a revolt in Sparta and threatening the powerful office of the ephorate.[135]

When Pausanias' treachery was discovered, he was recalled to Sparta and accused of fomenting a revolution with the helots or the state slaves (Thucydides 1.132). After Pausanias fled into a temple, the Spartans, including his mother, walled the temple in and starved him to death.

The Exile of Themistocles

The Athenian citizens, who owed so much to Themistocles, proved to have a short-lived gratitude. According to Plutarch (*Themistocles* 22): "at last, when even his fellow-citizens were led by their jealousy of his greatness to welcome such slanders against him, he was forced to allude to his own achievements when he addressed the Assembly, till he became tiresome thereby." After Plataea his rival Aristides became the dominant leader.

Themistocles was ostracized from Athens in 471/470.[136] Ostracism was a temporary exile for ten years, after which the individual could take up his residence in Athens again. The word *ostracism* is derived from the Greek word for a piece of broken pottery (*ostrakon*, plural *ostraka*), a handy writing surface for letters, receipts, and the like. It is still uncertain whether for an effective ostracism to take place a quorum of six thousand citizens had to vote for an ostracism, or whether six thousand had to vote for a particular individual to be ostracized.[137] The practice of ostracism was first instituted by Cleisthenes, who was an archon in 508, but the first actual procedure was dated by Aristotle to 487.[138]

135. Lenardon, *Saga*, p. 113; A. Blamire, "Pausanias and Persia," *GRBS* 11 (1970): 305, also accepts Thucydides' account, remarking: "It is possible, indeed, that Thucydides *is* wrong, but those who reject his account must not at the same time ask us to accept an alternative version of their own." See also Frost, *Plutarch's Themistocles*, p. 196.

136. The date for his ostracism is disputed. See Lenardon, *Saga*, p. 138; Frost, *Plutarch's Themistocles*, p. 189; Fornara, *Archaic Times*, 65.

137. A. R. Hands, "Ostraka and the Law of Ostracism," *JHS* 79 (1959): 72.

138. Meiggs and Lewis, *Selection*, 21, pp. 40ff.

Archaeologists have recovered thousands of ostraka, most from the Athenian Agora excavations, the remainder mainly from the Kerameikos (potter's field), which was used as a cemetery. By far the largest number were inscribed with Themistocles' name. Once the most popular of men, he became the most rejected. According to Frost, "unofficial counts by H. B. Mattingly, Rudi Thomsen, and others, at this date show well over 2,250 ostraca for Themistocles."[139] Of these, 191 were found in a well on the north slope of the Acropolis. Analysis shows that this lot had been preinscribed by only fourteen hands for the voters.[140] In other words, the effort to ostracize Themistocles was well organized.

The disgrace of Pausanias also had grave implications for his friend, Themistocles. Although the latter did not agree with Pausanias' plans, he had not denounced them either. When Spartan ambassadors sought his condemnation, Themistocles fled for his life from Argos, where he was living since his ostracism. He then had a series of harrowing escapes, fleeing to Corcyra, to Epirus, to Macedonia, and then to Ephesus, before he ended his odyssey at the Persian court.

Although Plutarch (*Themistocles* 27.1) claimed that Themistocles came before Xerxes, Thucydides (1.137) is most likely correct in asserting that it was Xerxes' successor, Artaxerxes I, before whom Themistocles appeared.[141] Some members of the court harbored resentment against their great Athenian adversary,[142] but the king treated Themistocles with courtesy and generosity. He gave Themistocles the towns of Magnesia on the Maeander, Lampsacus, and Myos in western Asia Minor. Themistocles was even allowed to issue his personal coinage. It is ironic that the greatest Athenian leader in the war against the Persians ended his life as a Persian subject, married to a Persian wife and speaking the Persian language.

The Book of Esther

In view of Esther's setting in Susa (see chapter 7), its Persian background, its Aramaisms, and its lack of reference to Palestine, there is widespread agreement that Esther was composed in the eastern Diaspora, quite probably at Susa itself.[143] Scholars, however, disagree

139. Frost, *Plutarch's Themistocles,* p. 187.

140. Meiggs and Lewis, *Selection,* pp. 43, 46.

141. Lenardon, *Saga,* p. 137.

142. Diodorus (11.69) recounts that Mandane, the sister of Xerxes, was especially bent on vengeance because she had lost three of her sons at Salamis.

143. S. B. Berg, *The Book of Esther* (Missoula: Scholars, 1979), p. 10; J. Lewy, "The Feast of the 14th Day of Adar," *HUCA* 14 (1939): 130; F. Altheim and R. Stiehl, *Die aramäische Sprache unter den Achämeniden* (Frankfort am Main: Vittorio Klostermann, 1963), p. 207.

widely on the probable date of the composition of Esther, depending on their views of the purpose and nature of the book.[144]

Since the reference to Mordecai in 2 Maccabees 15:36 comes from late in the second century B.C., Esther must be dated before this. Charles Torrey, who generally advocated very late dates for the post-exilic books, argues that the most probable date is the middle of the second century B.C.[145] Franz Altheim and Ruth Stiehl, by relating Esther to certain events in Hellenistic history, advocate a date of 140 B.C.[146] Because of the absence of Esther and Mordecai from the roll call of heroes in Ben Sirah, Alfred Morris suggested that Esther was written between 175 and 172 B.C. to encourage Jewish cooperation with Antiochus IV before he became a tyrant.[147] This is a specious argument, however, since Ben Sirah was primarily concerned with builders such as Nehemiah. Ben Sirah had certain biases which led him to omit, for example, Ezra.[148]

Hans Bardtke favors a date between 250 and 200 B.C.[149] Sandra Berg, who believes that there may be references to the *proskynesis* (prostration) controversy of Alexander in Mordecai's refusal to bow to Haman, dates Esther in the Hellenistic period despite its strong Persian traditions and lack of Greek words.[150]

Carey Moore prefers to date Esther in the late Persian period, that is, the early fourth century.[151] Robert Gordis favors a similar date:

> The style indicates a date of composition of approximately 400 B.C.E., only a few decades after the reign of King Xerxes. . . . There is a considerable number of Persian and Aramaic words and idioms. There are, however, no Greek words, a fact which clearly points to a pre-Hellenistic date.[152]

Shemaryahu Talmon argues for a still earlier date. Noting that Je-

144. On the literary form of Esther, see E. M. Yamauchi, "The Archaeological Background of Esther," *BS* 137 (1980): 99–100; C. A. Moore, "Esther Revisited Again," *Hebrew Annual Review* 7 (1983): 169–86. On the association of Esther with the feast of Purim, see W. W. Hallo, "The First Purim," *BA* 46 (1983): 19–27.

145. C. C. Torrey, "The Older Book of Esther," *Harvard Theological Review* 37 (1944): 40.

146. Altheim and Stiehl, *Die aramäische Sprache,* p. 212; compare R. Stiehl, "Das Buch Esther," *Wiener Zeitschrift für die Kunde des Morgenlandes* 53 (1956): 4–22.

147. A. E. Morris, "The Purpose of the Book of Ezra," *Expository Times* 42 (1930): 124–28.

148. See P. Höffken, "Warum schwieg Jesus Sirach über Esra," *ZAW* 87 (1975): 184–201.

149. H. Bardtke, "Der Mardochäustag," in *Tradition und Glaube,* eds. G. Jeremias, H.-W. Kuhn, and H. Stegemann (Göttingen: Vandenhoeck and Ruprechte, 1971), p. 97.

150. Berg, *Book of Esther,* pp. 170–73.

151. C. A. Moore, *Esther* (Garden City: Doubleday, 1971), p. iii.

152. R. Gordis, *Megillat Esther: The Masoretic Hebrew Text* (New York: KTAV, 1974), p. 8.

hushua Grintz has made a strong case for the dating of Judith, which was patterned after Esther, in the reign of Artaxerxes II (404–359 B.C.), he concludes: "This conflux constitutes a strong argument in favour of dating the composition of the Esther-story in the beginning of the Persian era. The traditional setting of the book in the days of Xerxes I (485–465 B.C.) cannot be wide off the mark."[153] I would agree with his position.

Ahasuerus

As was noted at the beginning of this chapter, the Ahasuerus of the Book of Esther is the Hebrew name for Xerxes. According to André Barucq, the role that Ahasuerus holds in Esther "conforms perfectly to Xerxes as we know from Herodotus."[154] Moore agrees: "Much of what the author of Esther says about King Xerxes corresponds fairly well with what the classical writer had to say about such things."[155]

How were Persian kings such as Ahasuerus/Xerxes regarded? We might think Persian kings were regarded as gods if we took literally some of the epithets used, for example, by Aeschylus, such as "god born in Susa" or *isotheos*, "equal to god" (see *Persai* 157, 620, 634, 642, 654–55, 771, 857).[156] Henry Broadhead, however, has suggested that the terms should not be considered literally: "That Darius is called *daimōn* does not mean that Aeschylus ascribes king-worship to the Persians."[157]

The act of prostration (*Persai* 152) before the king was offensive to the Greeks. Although it is not true that the Persian kings were wor-

153. S. Talmon, " 'Wisdom' in the Book of Esther," *VT* 13 (1963): 449. Berg, *Book of Esther,* p. 2, concedes: "The number of Persian words in Esther and its numerous Aramaisms suggests the story's composition during a period not far removed from the events it describes."

154. A. Barucq, "Esther et la cour de Suse," *Bible et Terre Sainte* 39 (1961): 3.

155. Moore, "Archaeology and the Book of Esther," p. 69.

156. J. Lembke and C. J. Herington, trans., *Aeschylus Persians* (New York: Oxford University Press, 1981), p. 22, note: "The dead Darius is *daimōn* in the Greek text of 1030, but *theos* in 1031." Olmstead seems to have been misled by these references. Olmstead, *History of the Persian Empire,* p. 283: "At the royal entrance all must prostrate themselves in adoration, for by ancient oriental custom the king is in a very real sense a divinity"; "The use of frankincense . . . before the king's presence is one more hint that in Persia the monarch was reverenced as something more than human" (ibid., p. 217). See L. R. Taylor, *The Divinity of the Roman Empire* (Middletown: American Philological Association, 1931), appendix, in which the author discusses the so-called divinity of the Persian kings.

157. Broadhead, *Persae,* p. 163. See also A. S. F. Gow, "Notes on the *Persae* of Aeschylus," *JHS* 48 (1928): 136; P. Calmeyer, "Zur bedingten Göttlichkeit des Grosskönigs," *AMI* 14 (1981): 55–60.

shiped,[158] they were greatly venerated. The king normally lived in seclusion and dined in an inner room separated by curtains from others. According to Herakleides of Kyme, quoted by Athenaeus (4.145–46):

> Of the King's guests some dine outside in full view of the public, others indoors with the King. But even the latter do not dine with the King. . . . The King can see them through the curtain in the doorway, but they cannot see him. . . . The King generally breakfasts and dines alone, though on occasion his wife and some of his sons dine with him.

On festive occasions the king hosted large banquets.[159] The same passage in Athenaeus relates: "Occasionally however on a feast-day they all dine in one room with the King in the great hall. If, as often happens, the King has a drinking party, up to a dozen guests may be called into his presence by a eunuch after the meal is finished" (compare Esther 1–2:18). The Persians' predilection for drinking wine from sumptuous vessels is well attested in classical sources (Herodotus 1.126, 9.80; Xenophon, *Cyropaedia* 8.8.10; Strabo 15.3.20).

The celebrated Esther panel of the synagogue at Dura Europos depicts Ahasuerus, dressed in Parthian trousers, seated on a throne. Dalia Levit-Tawil suggests: "In conclusion, it is proposed that the 'enthroned' scene of Ahasuerus symbolizes the legitimate divine right of kingship of the Iranian monarch, as it was propagated through his role as the promoter of law and justice."[160]

158. R. N. Frye, *The History of Ancient Iran* (Munich: C. H. Beckische, 1984), p. 106, n. 68: "The kings were not divinised, as some have thought." Cook, *Persian Empire,* p. 133: "But there is in fact no evidence that they were even deified after death." Hinz, *Darius II,* p. 9: "die achämenidischen Iraner haben ihre Herrscher nie vergöttlicht." See J. Duchesne-Guillemin, "La Royauté iranienne et le x^{v}aranah," in *Iranica,* eds. G. Gnoli and A. V. Rossi (Napoli: Istituto Universitario Orientale, 1979), pp. 375–86.

159. According to Ctesias, who is admittedly a questionable source, the Persian kings would host as many as 15,000 guests. See F. W. König, *Die Persika des Ktesias von Knidos* (Leiden: Brill, 1972), p. 129. Compare Athenaeus 4.27. For a description of a Persian banquet, see Xenophon, *Cyropaedia* 8.4.1–27. See also M. Heltzer, "A propos des banquets des rois achéménides et du retour d'exil sous Zorobabel," *RB* 86 (1979): 102–6. The Assyrian king Ashurnasirpal (ninth century B.C.) once feted 69,574 guests for ten days at Nimrud. See D. J. Wiseman, "A New Stela of Aššur-Naṣir-Pal II," *Iraq* 14 (1952): 24 – 44.

160. D. Levit-Tawil, "The Enthroned King Ahasuerus at Dura," *BASOR* 250 (1983): 74. For illustrations of the mural and discussions, see M. Avi-Yonah, "Goodenough's Evaluation of the Dura Paintings," in *The Dura-Europos Synagogue: A Re-evaluation (1932–1972)*, ed. J. Gutmann (Missoula: Scholars, 1973), p. 123; D. Levit-Tawil, "The Purim Panel in Dura in the Light of Parthian and Sasanian Art," *JNES* 38 (1979): 93–109.

King Ahasuerus and Queen Esther. (Courtesy of the Yale University Art Gallery)

Vashti

One of the most serious discrepancies cited by scholars to discredit the historicity of Esther is the fact that Herodotus (7.61) indicates that Xerxes' queen was Amestris,[161] rather than the biblical Vashti (Esther 1:9ff.).

Amestris was a very vengeful, powerful, and influential woman, as may be seen in her reaction to an affair that took place when Xerxes was in Sardis after the Greek expedition. He first fell in love with the wife of his brother Masistes, but when she repulsed him, he fell in love with her daughter Artaynta. The king gave this woman a robe, which Amestris herself had woven. When Amestris discovered this affair, she was furious but bided her time until the king's birthday. Like Herod Antipas at his birthday (Mark 6:21–26),[162] Xerxes reluctantly acceded to his wife's request: "Nevertheless, Amestris being instant, and the law constrain-

161. Moore, *Esther*, pp. xivi, 73. W. Hinz, " 'Glückwunsch' aus Persepolis," in *Mémorial Jean de Menasce*, eds. P. Gignoux and A. Tafazzoli (Louvain: Imprimerie Orientaliste, 1974), p. 126, suggests that Amestris's name may reflect **hammis-srï* (joined with beauty).

162. Both Xerxes (Esther 5:3) and Herod Antipas (Mark 6:23) offered up to half their kingdoms.

ing him (for at this royal banquet in Persia every boon asked must of necessity be granted), he did very unwillingly consent" (Herodotus 9.111). Amestris then took dreadful vengeance upon Artaynta's mother and had her mutilated.

J. Stafford Wright has suggested that by assuming certain phonetic modifications, an identification of Vashti with Amestris can be made[163]—a conclusion accepted also by William Shea.[164] Shea has worked out a detailed synchronism to show how the events in Esther, which has a gap between the third year (Esther 1:3) and the seventh year (Esther 2:16), can be harmonized with Xerxes' absence in Greece from 480 to 479 B.C.[165] David Clines also notes: "The four years between the deposition of Vashti and the installation of Esther as queen (in the seventh year, 2:1b) coincide with the four years Xerxes was absent from Persia on the expedition against the Greeks."[166]

As to the objection that Esther could not have become the queen, because Amestris/Vashti certainly wielded power when her son Artaxerxes I came to the throne in 464, Shea responds:

> In essence, Herodotus breaks off his account of Xerxes' reign at this point (479 B.C.), after the description of these events that took place in Xerxes' 7th year subsequent to the king's return from the Greek campaign. Thus it is an overstatement of the case to say that Amestris was Xerxes' queen between his 7th and 12th years, since we have no further information about her until the time her son Artaxerxes I occupied the Persian throne. In view of this silence of our sources, there is no specific evidence to indicate whether or not Amestris was Xerxes' chief wife from his 7th year to the end of his reign.[167]

The biblical account simply implies that Vashti was demoted in the royal harem, not killed or divorced.[168] Shea suggests that if Amestris/

163. J. S. Wright, "The Historicity of the Book of Esther," in *New Perspectives on the Old Testament,* ed. J. Barton Payne (Waco: Word, 1970), pp. 40–41. D. J. Clines, *Ezra, Nehemiah, Esther* (Grand Rapids: Eerdmans, 1984), p. 258, objects to the identification of Amestris and Vashti: "The difficulty with Wright's view is that the Amestris/Vashti who in Esther is deposed in Xerxes' third year (484/3) is according to Herodotus accompanying Xerxes during part at least of his campaign against Greece (481–479 BC)." But this is a misreading of Herodotus (7.114), where Herodotus mentions that Amestris once buried Persians just as a number of boys and girls were buried by the Strymon River in Thrace. Herodotus does not imply that Amestris was with Xerxes; he clearly states that this incident occurred when Amestris "attained to old age." See How and Wells, *Commentary,* 2: 169; W. H. Shea, "Esther and History," *AUSS* 14 (1976): 240, n. 44.

164. Shea, "Esther and History," p. 235.

165. Ibid., pp. 231–40.

166. Clines, *Ezra, Nehemiah, Esther,* p. 261.

167. Shea, "Esther and History," p. 240.

168. Persian kings had a large harem in addition to their chief wife. Cook, *Persian Empire,* p. 136: "The fourth-century Greek writers spoke of 360 concubines in the King's harem—one for each day of

Vashti's brutality had occurred in Susa just after Xerxes' return from the west, it would have provided the king with a further reason to find another chief wife.

The Persepolis Fortification tablets shed new light on the activities of the Persian queens, especially of Artystone (Elamite *Irtašduna*), one of the wives of Darius. She possessed a large estate in the village of Matannan (PF 1857), and another at Kuknaka (PF 1837). She had charge of considerable amounts of grain (PF 166), and had her own servants (PF 1236, 1454). The king ordered 1,940 liters of wine for her (PF 1795), possibly for a great banquet. She also had some food supplied on one occasion when the king came to Kuknaka (PF 718).[169]

Later Jewish tradition would embellish the account of Vashti. According to the Talmud the queen refused to come because Gabriel had smitten her with leprosy![170] The Targum maintained:

> It happened during the days of the evil Xerxes, the Xerxes in whose days the work of [rebuilding] the house of our great God ceased, and remained idle until the second year of Darius upon the advice of the wicked Vashti, daughter of Evil Merodakh son of Nebukhadnezzar. Because she did not permit the [re]building of the Temple, it was decreed concerning her that she be executed unclad.[171]

Haman

The high official Haman (Esther 3:1ff.),[172] who even had access to the royal seal,[173] was determined to annihilate the Jews because of

---

the year; and Darius III was reported to have lost 329 when he fled from Alexander in Syria." See Plutarch, *Artaxerxes* 27.2, 5.

169. W. Hinz, "Achämenidische Hofverwaltung," *ZA* 61 (1971): 298–99.

170. J. M. Brown, "Rabbinic Interpretations of the Characters and Plot of the Book of Esther," unpublished Ph.D. diss. (Cincinnati: Hebrew Union College, 1976), p. 22; M. Zlotowitz, *The Megillah: The Book of Esther* (New York: Art Scroll Studios, 1976), p. 46.

171. Grossfeld, *First Targum*, p. 40. The Targum also adds: "The King then ordered these seven princes to bring Queen Vashti unclad. Since she used to make Israelite girls work unclad and made them beat wool and flax for her on the Sabbath day, therefore, it was decreed upon her to be brought unclad."

172. Haman could not have been the Hofmarshall or chamberlain of Xerxes because we have the names of the individuals who filled that office according to Hinz, "Achämenidische Hofverwaltung," p. 308. R. Zadok, "On the Historical Background of the Book of Esther," *Biblische Notizen* 24 (1984): 18–19, analyzes Haman's name as derived from the Elamite divine name *Humpan* and his father's name, Hamdata, as derived from **Hauma-dāta* (created by Hauma). Zadok (p. 23) makes the improbable suggestion that Haman's dislike "might very well have been determined and motivated by the protracted conflict between the Judean repatriates and the Susian element among the elite of Samaria."

173. On the use of the royal seal by officials, see Hinz, "Achämenidische Hofverwaltung," p. 262. See also M. C. Root, *The King and Kingship in Achaemenid Art* (Leiden: Brill, 1979), pp. 118–22.

Mordecai's insult to him. His suggestion to the king as to how he should honor a benefactor (Esther 6:6–9), who, much to his chagrin, turned out to be Mordecai rather than himself, is illustrated by the request of the exiled Spartan king Demaratus. "When Demaratus was commanded to choose a gift for himself, he asked to be permitted to ride in state through Sardis, wearing his tiara upright just like the Persian Kings" (Plutarch, *Themistocles* 29).

According to Esther (2:23; 5:14; 9:14), Haman and his sons were hung on high gallows. Many extrabiblical inscriptions and reliefs depict this form of disgraceful execution. According to Herodotus (3.159), Darius I impaled three thousand Babylonians when he took the city of Babylon, an act that Darius mentions on his Behistun inscription.[174]

Jewish tradition added further ignominy to Haman's disgrace. When the daughter of Haman mistook her father for Mordecai, because he was leading the latter on horseback, she dropped a chamberpot on her father's head. When she learned that it was her father whom she had struck, she was overcome with shame and leaped to her death.[175]

Queen Esther

Esther's name is derived from the name of the Babylonian god Ishtar.[176] Her Hebrew name *Hadassah* (Esther 2:7) is usually derived from the word for myrtle, but other etymologies have been suggested.[177]

Herodotus's (3.84) statement that the queen could come only from the seven leading Persian families is often cited as an obstacle to accepting the biblical record of Esther as the queen. But as Wright perceptively notes, Herodotus is contradicted by the fact that Amestris was the daughter of an Otanes, who was not from one of these families. Darius also married outside of these families.[178]

The process by which Esther beautified herself is discussed in one of Albright's last articles. He suggested that an incense burner found at Lachish should be compared with cosmetic burners from Arabia,

174. R. G. Kent, *Old Persian* (New Haven: American Oriental Society, 1953), pp. 127–28.

175. Brown, "Rabbinic Interpretations," p. 63; Grossfeld, *First Targum*, p. 63.

176. The "Pan-Babylonian" scholars of the early twentieth century tried to interpret Mordecai and Esther as reflections of Marduk and Ishtar. See E. M. Yamauchi, "Tammuz and the Bible," *JBL* 81 (1965): 283–90. On the other hand, W. Eilers, "Iran and Mesopotamia," in *The Cambridge History of Iran III.1: The Seleucid, Parthian and Sasanian Periods*, ed. E. Yarshater (Cambridge: Cambridge University Press, 1983), p. 498, derives Esther's name from Iranian *stāra* (star).

177. R. Lemosin, "Estudios filológico-derásicos acerca de Ester y el Irán antiguo I," *Aula Orientalis* 1 (1983): 93–96.

178. Wright, "Historicity of the Book of Esther," p. 38.

which impregnated not only the women but also their clothes with the fragrance of the incense (cf. Esther 2:12; Ps. 45:8).[179]

Both Josephus and the Jewish rabbis exaggerated the beauty of Esther and elaborated on her virtues and piety.[180] The rabbis held that Esther was one of the four most beautiful women in history along with Sarah, Rahab, and Abigail (*Megillah* 15a). Josephus (*Antiquities* 11.205) maintained that Esther "surpassed all women in beauty" in the entire habitable world. Esther's courage is heightened by Josephus's remark that around Ahasuerus's throne stood men with axes ready to punish those who approached the throne without being summoned.

One of the additions to the canonical Esther in the Greek version is a "Prayer of Esther."[181] According to the rabbis, Esther, in her prayer, reminded God that she was but a poor orphan. According to Josephus, "Esther prays for two things, for eloquence and for greater beauty than she had ever had before, so that she may by both these means turn aside the king's anger; the Septuagint omits the request for additional beauty and mentions merely her desire for eloquence."[182]

In the center of Hamadan (ancient Ecbatana) stands the Synagogue of Esther and Mordecai, containing sarcophagi covered with brocaded cloth. It has been suggested that one of the tombs may be that of the Jewish queen of the Sasanian ruler Yazdegird (A.D. 399–421).[183]

Mordecai

Mordecai's name is derived from Marduk, the god of Babylon. In the past a number of scholars doubted the historicity of Mordecai. Elias Bickerman remarked: "But the name, which means 'man of Marduk' or 'worshiper of Marduk,' . . . is not Jewish at all. We may wonder whether the hero of the original tale was a Jew."[184] As one of the objections to

179. W. F. Albright, "The Lachish Cosmetic Burner and Esther 2:12," in *A Light unto My Path*, eds. H. N. Bream et al. (Philadelphia: Temple University Press, 1974), pp. 25–32; H. Shanks, "Albright, The Beautician Reveals Secrets of Queen Esther's Cosmetic Aids," *BAR* 2 (1976): 1, 5–6.

The apocryphal addition to Esther (14:2) describes the reaction of Esther when she became alarmed at Haman's plan: "She took off her splendid apparel and put on the garments of distress and mourning, and instead of costly perfumes she covered her head with ashes and dung, and she utterly humbled her body, and every part that she loved to adorn she covered with her tangled hair."

180. See E. Yamauchi, "Josephus and the Scriptures," *Fides et Historia* 13 (1980): 42–63, for how this Jewish historian used and expanded Scriptures.

181. On these apocryphal additions to Esther, see C. A. Moore, *Daniel, Esther and Jeremiah: The Additions* (Garden City: Doubleday, 1977).

182. L. H. Feldman, "Hellenization in Josephus' Version of Esther," *TAPA* 101 (1970): 149.

183. S. Matheson, *Persia: An Archaeological Guide* (London: Faber and Faber, 1972), pp. 108–12.

184. E. Bickerman, *Four Strange Books of the Bible: Jonah, Daniel, Koheleth, Esther* (New York: Schocken, 1967), p. 181.

the historicity of Esther, Theodor Gaster noted that "there is no mention anywhere but in the Book of Esther of . . . a courtier named Mordecai who eventually replaced Haman."[185] Even Jacob Hoschander, who attempted to support the historicity of Esther albeit by dating it nearly a century too late, despaired of finding attestation for Mordecai: "It is exceedingly doubtful whether the name of Mordecai ever occurred in the Persian annals, as there is scarcely room for doubt that among the Persians he had a pure Persian name."[186]

The name does appear in Aramaic letters, but more significant is the occurrence of the name *Mardukā* in a tablet from Borsippa in Mesopotamia. The tablet was first noted in 1904 in the Amherst collection in England, but was not published until 1942 by Arthur Ungnad[187] after it had been sold to the Berlin Museum. *Mardukā* is listed as a *sipīr* (accountant) who made an inspection tour of Susa during the last years of Darius or early years of Xerxes. It was Ungnad's conviction that "it is improbable that there were two Mardukas serving as high officials in Susa."[188] He, therefore, concluded that this individual is none other than Esther's uncle. This conclusion has been widely accepted.[189] According to Gordis it is "the strongest support thus far for the historical character of the book."[190]

The case for the historical identification of Mordecai with Marduka, attested as a royal Persian official, has been complicated by the publication of the Elamite tablets from Persepolis. We now have more than thirty texts (for example, PF 81, 412, 489, 790, 863, 941, 942, 991, 1183, 1236, 1581, 1858; PT 1, 84), dated between 505 and 499, with the name *Marduka* or *Marduku*, which may refer to up to four individuals.[191] Although we cannot be certain, it is possible that one of these may have been the biblical Mordecai.

Gordis notes that the fact that Mordecai sat "in the gate" indicates

185. T. H. Gaster, *Purim and Hanukkah in Custom and Tradition* (New York: Henry Schuman, 1950), p. 4.

186. J. Hoschander, *The Book of Esther in the Light of History* (Philadelphia: Dropsie College, 1923), p. 297.

187. A Ungnad, "Keilinschriftliche Beiträge zum Buch Esra und Esther," *ZAW* 58 (1940/1941): 240–44.

188. A. Ungnad, "Keilinschriftliche Beiträge zum Buch Esra und Esther," *ZAW* 59 (1942/1943): 219.

189. S. H. Horn, "Mordecai: A Historical Problem," *Biblical Research* 9 (1954): 1425; Berg, *Book of Esther*, p. 20; Moore, *Esther*, p. 1; Moore, "Archaeology and the Book of Esther," p. 74.

190. Gordis, *Megillat Esther*, p. 6.

191. J. A. Delaunay, "Remarques sur quelques noms de personne des archives élamites de Persépolis," *Studia Iranica* 5 (1976): 17. Hallo, "First Purim," p. 24, doubts the identification with Mordecai because "this official probably did not serve during the reign of Xerxes." But though the Persepolis Fortification texts date only to the reign of Darius, the treasury texts extend into the reign of Xerxes.

his high official status (Esther 2:19, 21; 5:9, 13). It was this elevation of Mordecai through Esther that infuriated Haman: "The verses mean not that the mere sight of Mordecai arouses Haman's wrath, but rather that the spectacle of Mordecai as a royal official, obstinately refusing to pay deference to his superior, infuriates Haman."[192]

Esther 2:6 is sometimes thought to present a problem since it seems to state that Mordecai was deported by Nebuchadnezzar in 597 B.C.[193] This would mean that Mordecai would have been about 120 years old in the time of Xerxes. Even more improbable, Esther would have been about seventy-five years old—a situation that the rabbis accepted! But as a number of scholars have pointed out, the relative pronoun *'ašer* should be taken not with Mordecai (the first name in the series) but rather with Kish, the great-grandfather of Mordecai (the last name in the series).[194]

While it is true that the Spartans refused to bow down before Xerxes (Herodotus 7.136),[195] the Jews regularly bowed down to kings (1 Sam. 24:8–9) and to other superiors (Gen. 23:7; 27:29). Mordecai's refusal to bow down before Haman has, therefore, puzzled commentators. It is possible, as Clines suggests, that Mordecai was refusing to bow down to Haman because as a Jew he did not wish to bow down to the descendant of Agag, the ancient enemy of Israel.[196] The Targum explained Mordecai's refusal to bow before Haman by the following assumption:

> Now all the king's servants who were at the king's palace gate used to bow down to the image which Haman placed within his chest and worshipped Haman, for that is what the king had commanded concerning him; Mordekhai, however, would not bow down to his image, because it was forbidden for the Jews to bow down to and worship idolatry.[197]

192. R. Gordis, "Studies in the Esther Narrative," *JBL* 95 (1976): 47.

193. Moore, *Esther,* p. xiv; G. Widengren, "Persian Period," in *Israelite and Judaean History,* eds. J. H. Hayes and J. M. Miller (Philadelphia: Westminster, 1977), pp. 492–93.

194. Wright, "Historicity of the Book of Esther," p. 38; E. J. Young, *An Introduction to the Old Testament,* 2d ed. (Grand Rapids: Eerdmans, 1958), p. 376.

195. The exact meaning of the Greek *proskynesis* as practiced in Iran, and as later demanded by Alexander, is greatly controverted. It may have meant anything from abject prostration to bowing and the kissing of the hand. Themistocles, when he sought refuge among the Persians, was willing to offer *proskynesis* to Artaxerxes I according to Plutarch (*Themistocles* 27). See F. Von Sachsen-Meiningen, "Proskynesis in Iran," in *Geschichte der Hunnen,* eds. F. Altheim and R. Stiehl (Berlin: W. de Gruyter, 1960), 2: 125–66; E. V. Groningen, "Griechen am Perserhof und die Proskynesis," in *Festschrift zum 150 jährigen Bestehen der Berliner ägyptischen Museums* (Berlin: Akademie, 1974), pp. 453–57.

196. Clines, *Esther Scroll,* p. 45.

197. Grossfeld, *First Targum,* p. 49.

The Persian Background of Esther

Even scholars who regard Esther as a historical novel because of alleged difficulties concede that the author is intimately acquainted with the Persian background of the purported period. Berg notes:

> The author's familiarity with both general and specific features of Persian life during the Achaemenian period also lends credence to his story. . . . The story's intimate knowledge of Persian court-etiquette and public administration strengthens impressions of its accuracy.[198]

Gordis also states, "Esther has an excellent familiarity with Persian law, custom, and language in the Achaemenid period."[199] Rudolf Mayer observes that Esther betrays an accurate knowledge of chronological data, the topography of Susa, palace protocol, court intrigues, and the like.[200] Lewis Paton[201] and Moore[202] list in their commentaries an impressive array of items and customs that lend verisimilitude to the story. Talmon concludes:

> On the other hand there is a fairly universal agreement among scholars that the author of the Esther-story generally shows an intimate knowledge of Persian court-etiquette and public administration. . . . If his tale does not mirror historical reality, it is indeed well imagined.[203]

Especially striking are the thirty or more personal names of Persian and Elamite origin and twelve Persian loan-words in the text of Esther.[204] In contrast to the confusion that reigns in the spelling of these names in the Greek and Latin versions,[205] the Masoretic Text has preserved the Persian names with remarkable accuracy.[206]

Of special significance is the observation that the names of Haman's sons can be analyzed as daiva names.[207] The word *daiva,* which meant

198. Berg, *Book of Esther,* p. 2.

199. Gordis, "Studies in the Esther Narrative," p. 44.

200. R. Mayer, "Iranischer Beitrag zu Problemen des Daniel- und Esther-Buches," *Lex tua Veritas* (*Festschrift für Hubert Junker*) (Trier: Paulinus Verlag, 1961), p. 130.

201. L. B. Paton, *The Book of Esther* (New York: Charles Scribner's Sons, 1916), p. 65.

202. Moore, *Esther,* p. xli.

203. Talmon, " 'Wisdom' in the Book of Esther," p. 422.

204. Gordis, *Megillat Esther,* p. 44; H. S. Gehman, "Notes on the Persian Words in the Book of Esther," *JBL* 43 (1924): 321–28.

205. Moore, *Esther,* pp. xlii–xliii.

206. A. R. Millard, "The Persian Names in Esther and the Reliability of the Hebrew Text," *JBL* (1977): 481–88. Millard elsewhere shows that the Hebrew text had also preserved accurately Assyrian royal names; see his "Assyrian Royal Names in Biblical Hebrew," *JSS* 21 (1976): 1–14.

207. J. Duchesne-Guillemin, "Les nom des eunuques d'Assuérus," *Le Muséon* 66 (1953): 108.

god in early Iranian and Avestan (early Hindu) texts,[208] became degraded to the status of demon in Zoroastrian and magical texts of the Sasanian period.[209] This implies that these Iranian names came from an early period.

Also of great importance is the fact that one of Haman's sons is named *Vaizatha* (Esther 9:9; *AV,* Vajezatha) since as Mayer observes, the diphthong *ai* shifted to *e* between the reigns of Xerxes and Artaxerxes I. This indicates that the name transmitted in Esther is strikingly "old and authentic."[210] Many other parallels to the Persian names in Esther have now been provided by the Elamite Persepolis texts. For example:

The Eunuchs (Esther 1:10)	**Elamite Parallel**
Mehuman	Mihimana (PF 455)
Bigtha	Bakatanna (PF 1793)
Carcas	Karkiš (PF 10)
Hathach (Esther 4:5)	Hitikka (PF 973)
The Princely Advisors (Esther 1:14)	
Meres	Maraza (PF 760)
Marsena	Maršena (PF 522)
Memukan	Mamakka (PF 1344)
Haman's Father (Esther 3:1)	
Hammedatha	Hamadadda (PF 1459)
Sons of Haman (Esther 9:7–9)	
Aridai	Irdaya (PF 1475)
Aridatha	Hardadda (PF 390)[211]

The care that the Hebrew scribes exercised in transmitting such foreign names stands in marked contrast with the practice of Josephus, who did not wish to bore his readers with long lists of unpronounceable names. Louis Feldman notes: "He likewise omits ([*Antiquities*] 11.190 and 192) . . . the names of King Ahasuerus' seven chamberlains (Esther 1.10) and of his seven counsellors (Esther 1.14), as well as (*Ant.* 11.289) the names of Haman's ten sons (Esther 9.7–9)."[212]

208. G. Widengren, *Les religions de l'Iran* (Paris: Payot, 1968), pp. 137–39, 162–66.

209. E. M. Yamauchi, *Mandaic Incantation Texts* (New Haven: American Oriental Society, 1967), p. 31.

210. Mayer, "Iranischer Beitrag," p. 135.

211. I owe these parallels to an unpublished paper, which William Shea generously shared with me.

212. Feldman, "Hellenization," p. 150.

Gordis summarizes the various lines in favor of the historicity of Esther by concluding, "all in all, the case for the historical basis for the book is impressive."[213] Moore admits, "on the face of it, the story seems to be true. . . . Nothing in the book seems improbable, let alone unbelievable."[214] If this is the case, and if the alleged historical problems are not insoluble, then it would seem preferable to take the book at face value as a historical narrative rather than to resort to subjective and highly speculative reconstructions. Scholars such as Wright, Shea, and Claus Schedl have indeed argued for such a view.[215]

Xerxes' Death and Tomb

After his return from the west, in addition to his involvement with Esther, Xerxes was mainly preoccupied with completing the work of his father at Persepolis (see chapter 10). Having reigned for twenty years, Xerxes was killed in a palace plot in early August 465. He was assassinated by the captain of the bodyguard, Artabanus, who plotted to take over the throne. Diodorus (11.69) reports: "And Artabanus, being led at night by Mithridates (the king's chamberlain) into the king's bed-chamber, slew Xerxes and then set out after the king's (three) sons."

Xerxes' tomb is believed to be the one on the extreme right of the four tombs at Naqsh-i Rustam. Like the others, it has a facade designed like a recessed cross.

213. Gordis, *Megillat Esther,* p. 8.

214. Moore, *Esther,* p. xxxv.

215. C. Schedl, "Das Buch Esther und das Mysterium Israel," *Kairos* 5 (1963): "das Buch ist tatsächlich das, als was es sich ausgibt: *Geschichte!*" The Book of Esther does not mention God. R. Gordis, "Religion, Wisdom and History in the Book of Esther—A New Solution to an Ancient Crux," *JBL* 100 (1981): 359–88, explains this omission by suggesting that Esther was written in the form of a Persian chronicle. Either by chance or by design Esther is the one book of the Old Testament that has not been recovered from Qumran. On questions of its canonicity and spiritual message, see Yamauchi, "Archaeological Background of Esther," pp. 110–12; J. G. Baldwin, *Esther* (Downers Grove: Inter-Varsity, 1984); J. C. Whitcomb, *Esther: Triumph of God's Sovereignty* (Chicago: Moody, 1979). For a detailed discussion of the controversy over Esther among Jews, see Roger Beckwith, *The Old Testament Canon of the New Testament Church* (Grand Rapids: Eerdmans, 1985), pp. 283–95.

6

Artaxerxes I

Name

Artaxerxes is the Greek form of the Old Persian *Artaxšaçā*, derived from *arta* (justice) plus *khshatra* (kingdom), that is, "having a kingdom of justice" or "having just rule." In Thucydides the name was spelled *Artoxerxēs*. In Akkadian it was spelled *Artakšatsu*, in Elamite *Irtakšašša*, in Hebrew and Aramaic *'Artaḥšaste'*, and in Egyptian *3rtḥššš*.[1] It is possible that this was a throne name; it was to be borne by two others.[2] According to Josephus (*Antiquities* 11.6) Artaxerxes' name before his accession was Cyrus.

Artaxerxes I was nicknamed by the Greeks "long-armed" (Greek *markocheir;* Latin *Longimanus*). According to Plutarch (*Artaxerxes* 1), "the first Artaxerxes, among all the kings of Persia the most remarkable for a gentle and noble spirit, was surnamed the Long-handed, his right hand being longer than his left, and was the son of Xerxes."

1. W. H. Shea, "Esther and History," *AUSS* 14 (1976): 228.

2. R. Schmitt, "Thronnamen bei den Achaemeniden," *Beiträge zur Namenforschung* 12 (1977): 422–25; idem, "Achaemenid Throne-Names," *Annali Istituto Orientale di Napoli* 42 (1982): 83–95.

Biblical References

The traditional view holds that Ezra preceded Nehemiah and was commissioned by Artaxerxes I in his seventh year (458 B.C.). Some, however, have argued that Ezra served under Artaxerxes II (see below).[3]

It is certain that Nehemiah (Neh. 1:1; 2:1) served as the cupbearer of Artaxerxes I, who ruled from 464 to 424 B.C., because an Elephantine papyrus (Cowley #30), dated to 407, mentions the sons of Sanballat, the governor of Samaria and adversary of Nehemiah.

It is widely accepted that Malachi also prophesied during the reign of Artaxerxes I. According to Gunther Wanke:

> Malachi was therefore very probably active shortly before the appearance of Ezra in Jerusalem, perhaps even at the same time as Ezra, so that he might in fact have been supporting the latter's campaign for reform. At the very least Malachi helped to prepare the way for Ezra's reforms and therefore belongs to the period around 455 B.C.E.[4]

Other scholars would date books like Isaiah 56–66 (the so-called Trito-Isaiah), Jonah, many of the psalms, Proverbs, and Ecclesiastes to the Persian era.[5] But such dating of many of these books cannot be accepted without question.[6]

Cuneiform Sources

A text in Old Persian and Akkadian indicates that Artaxerxes I completed the great throne hall begun by Xerxes.[7] The Akkadian version reads: "Artaxerxes the Great King says: By the protection of Ahuramazda this house Xerxes my father began, and I finished; me may Ahuramazda along with the gods protect, and my kingdom, and what I

3. There were three kings named Artaxerxes: I (464–424), II (403–359), and III (358–337).

4. G. Wanke, "Prophecy and Psalms in the Persian Period," in *The Cambridge History of Judaism I: Introduction; The Persian Period,* eds. W. D. Davies and L. Finkelstein (Cambridge: Cambridge University Press, 1984), p. 173. See also W. J. Dumbrell, "Malachi and the Ezra–Nehemiah Reforms," *Reformed Theological Review* 35 (1976): 42–52.

5. M. Smith, "Jewish Religious Life in the Persian Period," in *CHJ,* p. 244.

6. P. R. Ackroyd, "Some Historical Problems of the Early Achaemenian Period," *Proceedings, Eastern Great Lakes and Midwest Biblical Societies* 4 (1984): 38. H. Williamson, commenting on the chapters of G. Wanke and H. Gese in *CHJ* in his review in *VT* 35 (1985), p. 233, remarks: "It is doubtful, however, whether it is possible to date much of this literature so precisely, and indeed the two distinguished authors are fully aware of this and so have to waste a good deal of their valuable space justifying their choices."

7. R. G. Kent, *Old Persian* [*OP*], rev. ed. (New Haven: American Oriental Society, 1953), pp. 113, 153.

built."[8] Another Old Persian inscription of this king is an identical one-line text found on four silver dishes.[9] In 1971 an alabaster vase with a quadrilingual inscription of Artaxerxes I was brought to light in Russia. The Egyptian version of the text declared him to be "the great pharaoh."[10]

The most important corpus of cuneiform texts from the late Achaemenid period are the Murashu texts discovered in 1893 at Nippur.[11] In 1898 Hermann V. Hilprecht and Albert T. Clay published 480 of a reported 730 tablets; other scholars published an additional 22 texts. In 1974 Matthew W. Stolper wrote a dissertation using 179 hitherto unpublished Murashu texts from the University Museum in Pennsylvania and 4 from the British Museum.[12] The archive dates from the reigns of Artaxerxes I, Darius II, and Artaxerxes II, that is, from 454 to 404 B.C. Stolper reports that there are an additional 194 unpublished tablets and fragments in the Istanbul Museum, of which 80 date from the reign of Artaxerxes I.[13]

Murashu and Sons were wealthy bankers and brokers who loaned almost everything for a price. One might call the House of Murashu an institution of agricultural credit. Among 2,500 individuals mentioned in the texts, about 70 (approximately 3 percent) can be identified as Jews.[14] Theophoric names with various forms of the name *Yahweh* (Yah, Yeho, Yahu, Ia, Iama) may be recognized as Jewish.[15] According to Ran Zadok, "36 out of 70 or 51.4% bore Yahwistic names, lower than Elephantine, but about the same as in Judea."[16] Jews were found in 28 of 200 settlements in the region around Nippur.

8. R. G. Kent, "Old Persian Texts: VII. Artaxerxes I, Persepolis A," *JNES* 4 (1945): 228.

9. Kent, *OP*, pp. 114, 153.

10. See A. S. Strelkov, "The Moscow Artaxerxes Cylinder Seal," *Bulletin of the American Institute for Iranian Art and Archaeology* 5 (1937): 17–21; M. Mayrhofer, *Supplement zur Sammlung der altpersischen Inschriften* (Vienna: Österreichischen Akademie der Wissenschaften, 1978), p. 28.

11. See E. Yamauchi, "Nippur," in *The New International Dictionary of Biblical Archaeology*, eds. E. M. Blaiklock and R. K. Harrison (Grand Rapids: Zondervan, 1983), pp. 339–42.

12. M. W. Stolper, "Achaemenid Babylonia: New Texts from the Murašû Archive," unpublished Ph.D. diss. (Ann Arbor: University of Michigan, 1974).

13. M. W. Stolper, *Entrepreneurs and Empire* (Leiden: Nederlands Historisch-Archaeologisch Instituut te Instanbul, 1985), pp. 13–14.

14. R. Zadok, *The Jews in Babylonia during the Chaldean and Achaemenian Periods* (Haifa: University of Haifa Press, 1979), p. 78. The earlier study by S. Daiches, *The Jews in Babylonia in the Time of Ezra and Nehemiah According to Babylonian Inscriptions* (London: Jews' College, 1910) had claimed the identification of about one hundred Jewish names.

15. M. W. Stolper, "A Note on Yahwistic Personal Names in the Murašû Texts," *BASOR* 222 (1976): 25–28; M. D. Coogan, "Patterns in the Jewish Personal Names in the Diaspora," *JSJ* 4 (1973): 184–91; idem, *West Semitic Personal Names in the Murašū Documents* (Missoula: Scholars, 1975); idem, "More Yahwistic Names in the Murashu Documents," *JSJ* 7 (1976): 199–200; G. Wallis, "Jüdische Bürger in Babylonien während der Achämeniden-Zeit," *Persica* 9 (1980): 129–88.

16. Zadok, *Jews in Babylonia*, p. 78.

The Jews appear as contracting parties, agents, witnesses, collectors of taxes, and royal officials. A person named Hanani was in charge "over the birds of the King," that is, Darius II. Eleven of some two hundred officials in these texts were Jewish.[17] Apparently no social or commercial barriers existed between the Jews and the Babylonians. Their relative prosperity may explain why some chose to remain in Mesopotamia.[18]

Apart from the Murashu texts there are only approximately two hundred economic and legal cuneiform texts from Babylonia that date to the late Achaemenid period.[19]

Aramaic Sources

Aramaic, a Semitic dialect from Syria, became the international language of the Persian Empire in the fifth century B.C. because it was written in an efficient alphabetic script rather than in the cumbersome cuneiform.[20] The Aramaic of the Persian era is sometimes called Royal Aramaic because the Persian kings used it in their communications.

Five important groups of Aramaic documents have been discovered in Egypt: the Elephantine Papyri, the Brooklyn Museum Papyri (also from Elephantine), the Elephantine Ostraca, the Letters of Arsames (the satrap of Egypt), and the Hermopolis Papyri. A sixth corpus of documents, the Samaria Papyri, was discovered in Palestine.

Aramaic papryi were first discovered in 1898 on the Elephantine Island near Aswan in Upper Egypt. After initial publications in the early 1900s, a definitive edition of these texts was published by Arthur Cowley in 1923.[21] These were communications (dating between 495 and 398 B.C.) from a Jewish military garrison, which was probably

17. Ibid., p. 87; E. J. Bickerman, "The Babylonian Captivity," in *CHJ*, p. 347.

18. M. D. Coogan, "Life in the Diaspora: Jews at Nippur in the Fifth Century B.C.," *BA* 37 (1974): 6–12. For other expatriate groups in Mesopotamia, see D. J. Wiseman, "Some Egyptians in Babylonia," *Iran* 28 (1966): 154–58; R. Zadok, "Phoenicians, Philistines, and Moabites in Mesopotamia," *BASOR* 230 (1979): 57–66; idem, "On Some Foreign Population Groups in First-Millennium Babylonia," *Tel Aviv* 6 (1979): 164–81.

19. J. Oelsner, "Zwischen Xerxes und Alexander," *WO* 8 (1976): 313–14.

20. See E. Yamauchi, "Aramaic," in *NIDBA*, pp. 38–41; J. C. Greenfield, "Aramaic," in *The Interpreter's Dictionary of the Bible, Supplementary Volume*, eds. K. Crim et al. (Nashville: Abingdon, 1976), pp. 39–44; F. Rosenthal, *A Grammar of Biblical Aramaic* (Wiesbaden: Otto Harrassowitz, 1961). For the significance of Aramaic as the language of Jesus and the early Christians, see J. A. Fitzmyer, *A Wandering Aramean* (Missoula: Scholars, 1979).

21. A. E. Cowley, *Aramaic Papyri of the Fifth Century B.C.* (Oxford: Clarendon, 1923). These texts together with the Brooklyn Museum Aramaic Papyri and the Hermopolis Papyri have been retranslated by B. Porten in collaboration with J. C. Greenfield, *Jews of Elephantine and Arameans of Syene: Aramaic Texts with Translation* (Jerusalem: Hebrew University, 1976). See also P. Grelot, *Documents araméens d'Egypte* (Paris: Les Editions du Cerf, 1972).

established during Cambyses' occupation of Egypt.[22] About forty of the ninety-five Jewish names from Elephantine contain some form of the name *Yahweh.*[23]

These texts reveal that the Jews built a temple to Yaho (Yahweh), which was destroyed in 411 B.C. by fanatical Egyptians. It is believed that the sacrifice of sheep by the Jews may have been offensive to the priests of the ram-god Khnub (or Khnum), as a letter specifies that "sheep, ox, and goat are not to be offered" (Cowley #33). The so-called Passover Papyrus (Cowley #21), written in 419 by Hananiah, seems to refer to the Feast of Unleavened Bread.

One controversial text (Cowley #22) records offerings not only of 126 shekels for Yaho, but of 70 and 120 shekels, respectively, for deities called Ashim Bethel and Anat Bethel. The offerings were collected from 122 persons, including more than 30 women. Umberto Cassuto argues that the offerings to Ashim Bethel and Anat Bethel were not from the Jews but from the Arameans.[24] This interpretation is favored also by Bezalel Porten, who comments: "While the evidence for a syncretistic communal cult of the Jewish deity at Elephantine dissipates upon close inspection, that for individual Jewish contact with paganism remains."[25] The papyri do reveal the incidence of mixed marriages, which led to syncretistic practices. For example, one document has the salutation, "I bless you by Yaho [Yahweh] and by Khnub [the Eygptian god]."

Another lot of Aramaic papyri from Elephantine was acquired by Charles Wilbour in 1893. After his death these passed to his daughter, who eventually turned them over to the Brooklyn Museum. Emil Kraeling published them in 1953—sixty years after their acquisition.[26] They include records of loans, sales, and gifts of a temple servitor, Ananiah (451–401 B.C.).

Some three hundred ostraca have been found at Elephantine, about fifty of which have been published by André Dupont-Sommer. These ostraca mention the Sabbath, the Sabbath eve, and the date of the Passover. A Jew of Elephantine wrote on one ostracon that he would not send a jar the following day because it would be the Sabbath (com-

22. E. Bresciani, "Egypt, Persian Satrapy," in *CHJ*, p. 368.

23. See M. H. Silverman, "Aramean Name-Types in the Elephantine Documents," *JAOS* 89 (1969): 691–709; idem, "Hebrew Name-Types in the Elephantine Documents," *Or* 39 (1970): 465–91. The best summary of the material from Elephantine is B. Porten, *Archives from Elephantine* (Berkeley: University of California Press, 1968).

24. U. Cassuto, "The God of the Jews of Elephantine," in *Biblical and Oriental Studies* (Jerusalem: Magnes, 1975), p. 248.

25. B. Porten, "The Jews in Egypt," in *CHJ*, p. 392.

26. E. Kraeling, *The Brooklyn Museum Aramaic Papryi* (New Haven: Yale University Press, 1953).

Aramaic papyrus. (Brooklyn Museum, bequest of Miss Theodora Wilbour from the collection of her father, Charles Edwin Wilbour)

pare Neh. 13:15–21). The name *Shabbetai* occurs in these ostraca five times.[27]

Arsames, the satrap of Egypt, was in Susa from 411 to 408 B.C. Thirteen of his letters to his agents in Egypt were published by Geoffrey Driver in 1954. These letters written on leather were found in their original leather pouch.[28] The documents reveal Arsames as a typical governor, greedy for wealth and power. Jonas Greenfield observes: "The peremptory tone of the letters in Ezra are matched by that of the Arsham correspondence."[29]

In 1945 eight Aramaic letters were discovered at Hermopolis in Mid-

27. A. Dupont-Sommer, "L'ostracon araméen du Sabbat," *Semitica* 2 (1949): 29–39.

28. G. R. Driver, *Aramaic Documents of the Fifth Century B.C.* (Oxford: Clarendon, 1954).

29. J. C. Greenfield, "Aramaic Studies and the Bible," in *Vetus Testamentum 10th Congress Volume,* ed. J. Emerton (Leiden: Brill, 1980), p. 127.

dle Egypt near Amarna. The Hermopolis letters come from Arameans settled in Egypt. They are addressed to Syene (Aswan), the city on the mainland across from Elephantine Island, and are dated to the late sixth century B.C. We learn there were temples at Syene to the Queen of Heaven, to Nabu, and to Bethel (compare Jer. 48:13). It is clear from these letters that the Arameans had adopted the Mesopotamian gods Nabu and Baniu, and the Egyptian god Ptah, whom they worshiped along with their own gods Eshem, Hadad, Attar, and the Queen of Heaven (Jer. 7:18; 44:17–19).[30]

The Samaria Papyri were found in 1962 in a cave in Wadi Daliyeh (about nine miles north of Jericho) by the same Taʿamireh Bedouin who discovered the Dead Sea Scrolls. The papyri are dated from 375 to 335 B.C. They were found with the remains of about two hundred Samarians who vainly sought to escape from the soldiers of Alexander the Great.[31] The texts, which have not yet been published by Frank Moore Cross, reveal the highly syncretistic background of the Samarians. Names of such non-Israelite gods as Baal, Qos, Kemosh, Nabu, and Sahar appear in the papyri. Most significant is the evidence for a Sanballat, who was probably the grandson of the famous adversary of Nehemiah.

Classical Sources

Since Herodotus did not cover the reign of Artaxerxes I, and the latter passed away before the arrival of Ctesias at the Persian court, we are ill informed about much of this king's reign.

Ctesias (44–51) is our major source for the events following the death of Artaxerxes I and the accession of Darius II. Where his account overlaps with Thucydides, Ctesias's work is clearly inferior.[32]

Thucydides, the famous Athenian historian, was a general at the beginning of the Peloponnesian War (431–404), but was dismissed

30. E. Bresciani and M. Kamil, "Le lettere aramaiche di Hermopoli," in *Atti della Accademia Nazionale dei Lincei* Ser. VIII, 12/5 (1966), pp. 356–428; B. Porten, "The Religion of the Jews of Elephantine in Light of the Hermopolis Papyri," *JNES* 28 (1969): 116–21.

31. F. M. Cross, "The Discovery of the Samaria Papyri," *BA* 26 (1963): 110–20; P. W. Lapp and N. L. Lapp, eds., *Discoveries in the Wâdī ed-Dâliyeh* (Cambridge: American Schools of Oriental Research, 1974); N. L. Lapp, ed., *The Tale of the Tell* (Pittsburgh: Pickwick, 1975), pp. 66–76; P. W. Lapp, "Bedouin Find Papyri Three Centuries Older than Dead Sea Scrolls," *BAR* 4 (1978): 16–24; F. M. Cross, "The Historical Importance of the Samaria Papyri," *BAR* 4 (1978): 25–27.

32. J. M. Bigwood, "Ctesias' Account of the Revolt of Inarus," *Phoenix* 30 (1976): 1–25. See also R. Drews, *The Greek Accounts of Eastern History* (Cambridge: Harvard University Press, 1973), pp. 103–16.

when he failed to prevent the capture of Amphipolis.[33] In the section dealing with the so-called Pentecontaetia (the fifty-year [477–432] interval between the Persian invasions and the Peloponnesian War), Thucydides mentions Artaxerxes I in four passages (1.104.1; 1.137.3; 4.50.3; 8.5.4). He provides accurate but limited information on the Athenian intervention in Persian affairs.

Diodorus Siculus (first century B.C.) describes many events of this period in an annalistic fashion. But his attempt to assign different events to a single year (for example, the events of Themistocles' later years) is both misguided and misleading.[34]

Accession

Longimanus was the third son of Xerxes and Amestris. His older brothers were Darius and Hystaspes. Darius was the eldest; Hystaspes was a satrap in Bactria (Diodorus 11.69.2). Their father was assassinated in his bedchamber in August 465, by Artabanus, a powerful courtier.

According to Ctesias (29–30), Artabanus deceived Artaxerxes into believing that Xerxes was killed by his brother Darius, the crown prince. After some months, Artaxerxes, who was but eighteen years old, managed to kill his brother Darius (Diodorus 11.69.1–5). Artabanus then tried to kill Artaxerxes, but was killed by Artaxerxes instead. Artaxerxes then defeated his brother Hystaspes in Bactria. The fact that he was the new king was known in far-off Elephantine in Egypt by January 2/3, 464 (Cowley #6). His first regnal year is reckoned from April 13, 464. He was to reign for a little over forty years until 424.[35]

The Delian League

After the defeat of the Persians at Plataea and Mycale in 478 B.C., the Athenians and their allies formed the Delian League to harry Medizing states and to fight against the Persians. The league's treasury was located on the island of Delos. Gradually the voluntary nature of the

33. On Thucydides, see A. Andrewes, "Thucydides and the Persians," *Historia* 10 (1961): 1–18; D. Proctor, *The Experience of Thucydides* (Warminster: Aris and Phillips, 1980); R. Schmitt, "Achaimenidisches bei Thukydides," *Kunst, Kultur und Geschichte der Achämenidenzeit und ihr Fortleben,* eds. H. Koch and D. N. MacKenzie (Berlin: Dietrich Reimer, 1983), pp. 69–86.

34. R. K. Unz, "The Chronology of the Pentekontaetia," *CQ* 36 (1986): 68.

35. J. Neuffer, "The Accession of Artaxerxes I," *AUSS* 6 (1968): 81.

league evolved into an Athenian Empire.[36] Cities such as Naxos, which rebelled in 465,[37] were harshly repressed by Athens (Thucydides 1.98.4). Citing the threat of the Persian navy, the Athenians moved the treasury to their city in 454. From this later period we have tribute lists, which indicate that over two hundred cities in the league contributed an annual sum of approximately five hundred talents.

After the ostracism of Themistocles in 471, the dominant political and military Athenian leader was Cimon, the son of Miltiades. He carried out an aggressive policy against Persian forces in the eastern Mediterranean. His greatest victory was achieved at the mouth of the Eurymedon River in Pamphylia on the south coast of Asia Minor, where he defeated two hundred ships of the combined Phoenician, Cypriote, and Cilician forces of the Persian fleet in 466 (Thucydides 1.100.1).[38] This victory meant the liberation of Caria and Lycia in southwest Asia Minor from the Persians—at least for the time being.

When an earthquake in 464 incited the Messenians to revolt against the Spartans, the latter appealed to the Athenians for aid (Thucydides 1.101.2; 1.102.1). Cimon, who was favorably disposed to the Spartans, acceded to their request. But at the last minute the Spartans rejected the Athenians, a development that led to Cimon's ostracism in 461.

The Revolt in Egypt and Athenian Intervention

Soon after Artaxerxes I came to the throne, he was faced with a major revolt in Egypt that was to last a decade. The rebellion, which broke out in the winter of 461/460, was led by Inarus, a Libyan, and Amyrtaeus of Sais (Thucydides 1.104.1). They defeated the Persian satrap Achaemenes, the brother of Xerxes, and gained control of much of the Delta region.

At this time the Athenians had a fleet of two hundred triremes in the eastern Mediterranean in an effort to liberate Cyprus from the Persians. When the Athenians heard of the Egyptian revolt against the

36. The date at which this change took place is disputed. N. D. Robertson, "The True Nature of the 'Delian League' 478–461 B.C.," *AJAH* 5 (1980): 119, concludes: "In sum, the most decisive change in Athens' conduct came not in c. 450 but in the late 460s, and the change was that she resolved to play her own hand 'contrary to the agreements' of the Delian League."

37. The date of the revolt of Naxos is disputed. It has been dated to 470, 467, and 465. The latter date is suggested by Unz, in "Chronology," p. 83.

38. A. R. Burn, "Persia and the Greeks," in *The Cambridge History of Iran II: The Median and Achaemenian Periods* (Cambridge: Cambridge University Press, 1985), p. 334. The date is again disputed. B. D. Meritt, H. T. Wade-Gery, and M. F. McGregor, *The Athenian Tribute Lists* (Princeton: American School of Classical Studies at Athens, 1950), 3: 175, date Eurymedon to 469, as does R. Meiggs, *The Athenian Empire* (Oxford: Clarendon, 1972), p. 81.

Persians, their fleet sailed to Egypt (Thucydides 1.104.1–2). In 459 they helped capture Memphis, the capital of Lower Egypt. Andrew Burn comments: "The Egyptian war was the sternest struggle ever fought between the (Persian) empire and the Delian League."[39]

These Greek interventions took a tremendous toll in casualties. A casualty list of the year 459 includes 177 soldiers and 2 generals from a single tribe, for Athenian armies fought the Persians in Cyprus, Phoenicia, and Egypt, and fought fellow Greeks in Aegina and Megara.[40]

Megabyzus

In 456 Megabyzus, the satrap of Syria, advanced against Egypt with a huge fleet and army (Thucydides 1.109.3; Diodorus 11.77.1–5). Megabyzus managed to suppress the revolt in nineteen months. When his men drained a Nile channel to take the island of Prosopitis, the Greek stronghold, the Greeks were decisively defeated. The Greeks also lost their fleet of two hundred ships and six thousand men. An additional fleet of fifty Athenian ships sailed into a Persian trap in the summer of 454 (Thucydides 1.110.4). Only a few Greeks escaped through the desert to Cyrene on the Libyan coast. The Persian victory was depicted on engraved cylinder seals that portray Megabyzus triumphing over the defeated Egyptian rebels.[41]

In spite of promises made by Megabyzus, Inarus was impaled in 454 B.C. (Thucydides 1.110.3) at the instigation of Amestris, the mother of Artaxerxes I.[42] Angered at this betrayal, Megabyzus revolted against Artaxerxes, and defeated two expeditions sent against him.

Megabyzus was later reconciled to the king, until on a hunting expedition he shot at a lion before Artaxerxes, a breach of behavior that resulted in his being exiled. Once again Megabyzus was restored to favor and died at court at the age of seventy-six.

39. Burn, "Persia and the Greeks," p. 335. It was against the background of the problems in Egypt that the Persians may have found it expedient to support Ezra's return in 458 to secure a loyal buffer state in Palestine.

40. R. Meiggs and D. Lewis, *A Selection of Greek Historical Inscriptions to the End of the Fifth Century B.C.* (Oxford: Clarendon, 1969), pp. 73ff.; C. W. Fornara, ed., *Archaic Times to the End of the Peloponnesian War* (Baltimore: Johns Hopkins University Press, 1977), #72. See also D. Bradeen, "Athenian Casualty Lists," *Hesperia* 33 (1964): 16–62.

41. See W. Culican, *The Medes and the Persians* (New York: Praeger, 1965), p. 157.

42. Ctesias (33–36) gives a different chronology, and has Inarus killed five years later. For the contradictions between Thucydides and Ctesias on the Athenian campaign in Egypt, see Bigwood, "Ctesias' Account." Meritt, Wade-Gery, and McGregor, *Athenian Tribute Lists*, p. 180, comment: "The account of Ktesias is very circumstantial, and it would have more weight than it has if his historical credit were better and especially if he were not patently wrong in much of the story about the Egyptian disaster."

Cylinder seal of Artaxerxes I. (W. Hinz, *Darius II,* Bild 10, courtesy of Holle Verlag and Druckhaus Nonntal)

If the events of Ezra 4:7–23 took place during the Egyptian revolt, Artaxerxes would probably have been suspicious of the building activities in Jerusalem. How then could the same king have commissioned Nehemiah to rebuild the walls of the city in 445? By then both the Egyptian revolt and the rebellion of Megabyzus had been resolved.[43]

The Peace of Callias

Cimon, who commanded the league's fleet after being recalled from his ostracism, campaigned in Cyprus in 450, where the Greeks won both land and sea victories (Thucydides 1.112.2). Diodorus (11.62.3) quotes an epitaph in commemoration of this victory at Cyprus:

> Ever since the sea parted Europe from Asia and grim Ares stalks the cities of mortals, no deed such as this was ever done by men on this earth on land and sea together. For these men destroyed many Medes in Cyprus and a hundred ships they captured at sea with their crews, and Asia groaned mightily, stricken by them with both arms in the violent forces of war.

Cimon himself died that summer. Both the Greeks and the Persians were now weary from the fighting that had continued between them

43. D. L. Emery, "Ezra 4—Is Josephus Right after All?" *Journal of Northwest Semitic Languages* 13 (1987): 33–43, argues implausibly that the Ahasuerus and Axtaxerxes of Ezra 4 were correctly identified by Josephus as Cambyses!

for some forty years. Accordingly the Peace of Callias was arranged in 449 negotiated by the wealthy brother-in-law of Cimon.

The Peace of Callias is one of the most controversial issues in Greek history. While it is well attested by several sources (Isocrates, *Panegyricus;* Demosthenes 15.29; Diodorus 12.26.2), it is not explicitly mentioned by our two major sources, Herodotus and Thucydides. (There may be an allusion to it, however, in Herodotus 7.151.[44]) In antiquity the authenticity of the peace attributed to Callias was questioned by Theopompus because its Attic copy was written in the Ionic script, which was not used before the end of the fifth century B.C.[45]

Modern scholars are also divided about its authenticity.[46] Some scholars believe there was a peace treaty between the Persians and the Greeks but hold that it should be dated much later (to 434/433 or 422/421).[47] But the overwhelming majority are convinced of its authenticity.[48] Since 1940 almost all scholars who have written on the subject have regarded it as authentic.[49]

Most recently Ernst Badian has accepted the peace, commenting: "That the peace is, in some form, authentic, seems to me to be not too difficult to prove, with a degree of assurance that matches most of what can be established in the history of the fifth century B.C."[50] He believes that the peace was negotiated by Callias, but proposes that it was arranged with Xerxes before his death rather than with Artaxerxes I.[51]

The provisions of the Peace of Callias required the Greeks to stop trying to liberate Cyprus and to stop intervening in Egypt. The Persians agreed to the following provisions: to recognize the supremacy of Athens over those in the Delian League; not to send their ships west of the Bosporus into the Propontis or west of Phaselis into the Aegean; and

44. On the basis of textual evidence, M. S. Goldstein, "Athenian-Persian Peace Treaties," *CSCA* 7 (1975): 155–64, discounts Thucydides 8.56.4 and 8.58.2 as references to the treaty.

45. A. E. Raubitschek, "The Treaties between Persia and Athens," *GRBS* 5 (1964): 151.

46. D. L. Stockton, "The Peace of Callias," *Historia* 8 (1959): 73: "But *could* such a public forgery as this be committed in fourth century Athens? Some have thought not, decidedly. Yet Andocides, as we have seen could expect to get away with a whole parcel of lies. . . . As Plato appreciated, you can do a lot with a lie if it is a really big one."

47. H. Mattingly, "The Peace of Kallias," *Historia* 14 (1965): 273–81.

48. K. Meister, *Die ungeschichtlichkeit des Kalliasfriedens und deren historische Folge* (Wiesbaden: F. Steiner, 1982), p. 124, who questions the Peace of Callias, notes that of previous scholars 114 (76 percent) favor its authenticity.

49. See, for example, Andrewes, "Thucydides and the Persians," p. 15; J. M. Cook, *The Persian Empire* (New York: Schocken, 1983), p. 128; A. W. Gomme, *A Historical Commentary on Thucydides* (Oxford: Clarendon, 1959), 1: 332: "Most modern scholars, however, agree that Theopompos was wrong"; D. M. Lewis, *Sparta and Persia* (Leiden: Brill, 1977), pp. 50–51; R. Lonis, *Les usages de la guerre entre Grecs et Barbares* (Paris: Les Belles Lettres, 1969), pp. 102ff.; Meritt, Wade-Gery, and McGregor, *Athenian Tribute Lists*, pp. 275, 299.

50. E. Badian, "The Peace of Callias," *JHS* 107 (1987): 1.

51. Ibid., p. 7.

not to send satrapal troops within three days' march or one day's ride of the Ionian coast.[52]

The Order of Ezra and Nehemiah

The most important controversy that has arisen over Ezra and Nehemiah is the question of their order. Traditionally, Ezra arrived in the seventh year of Artaxerxes I (458—Ezra 7:7), and Nehemiah arrived in the same king's twentieth year (445—Neh. 2:1), some thirteen years later.

Some scholars, however, have adopted a reverse order of Nehemiah arriving in 445, and Ezra arriving in the seventh year of Artaxerxes II (398 B.C.). Other scholars, by adopting a textual emendation, have favored an intermediate position that maintains the contemporaneity of the men but places Ezra later than the traditional view in the twenty-seventh or the thirty-seventh year of Artaxerxes I, that is, in 438 or 428.

There are many arguments in favor of the reverse order. Only a few of these arguments will be considered here.[53]

As the text stands, Nehemiah and Ezra are noted together in Nehemiah 8:9 at the reading of the Law and in Nehemiah 12:26 and 36, at the dedication of the wall. Since the name *Nehemiah* is lacking in the 1 Esdras 9:49 parallel to Nehemiah 8:9, it has been argued that Nehemiah's name was inserted in the latter passage as a gloss. It has also been argued that Nehemiah 12:26 and 36, were added to the original text. John Emerton has asserted: "No meeting between them is recorded and they never both play active parts in the same action, one is active, and at most, the other's name is mentioned in passing."[54]

But it is not the case that one can delete either Ezra or Nehemiah from Nehemiah 12:26 without consequence, for to do so would leave one of the processions without a leader.

The fact that the references to the contemporaneity of Ezra and Nehemiah are few is readily explicable. John Bright points out:

> The Chronicler's interests were predominantly ecclesiastical, and to these Nehemiah was peripheral. Nehemiah, on the other hand, intended his memoirs as a personal *apologia* not as a history of the contemporary

52. Burn, "Persia and the Greeks," p. 337.

53. For a fuller exposition, see E. Yamauchi, "The Reverse Order of Ezra/Nehemiah Reconsidered," *Themelios* 5 (1980): 7–13; idem, "Ezra, Nehemiah," in *The Expositor's Bible Commentary*, by F. E. Gaebelein (Grand Rapids: Zondervan, 1988), 4: 583–86.

54. J. A. Emerton, "Did Ezra Go to Jerusalem in 428 B.C.?" *JTS* 17 (1966): 16; compare N. H. Snaith, "The Date of Ezra's Arrival in Jerusalem," *ZAW* 63 (1952): 63.

> Jewish community; he was concerned exclusively with what he himself had done.[55]

We have other examples of contemporary Old Testament figures who do not refer to each other (Jeremiah and Ezekiel, Haggai and Zechariah).[56]

The text as it now stands presents Ezra's priority over Nehemiah. If in fact Ezra came afterwards, the biblical writer's confusion must have arisen at a date removed from the events, which some believe was the third century B.C. Peter Ackroyd writes: "But if, as seems more probable, the Chronicler was active in about the middle of the fourth century, not more than a generation after this late dating for Ezra (in 398), then the disorder would be very difficult to explain."[57]

But other scholars are convinced that the evidence points to an even earlier date for the work of the so-called Chronicler. Cross concludes, "the fact that all genealogies in Chr_3 end shortly before 400 B.C. virtually eliminates the popular view that Ezra followed Nehemiah in the seventh year of the reign of Artaxerxes II, 398 B.C."[58]

Since the early years of Artaxerxes I were troubled by a major revolt in Egypt, some have questioned whether Ezra would have been sent on an unprotected journey in 458. In the year 458 the king sent an army of three hundred thousand men against Egypt. The roads would have been so filled with troop caravans, it has been argued, that there would have been no room for Ezra's caravan.[59]

On the other hand, the presence of troops would have protected the caravan from robbers. Indeed the precarious situation in Egypt probably made it desirable for the Persians to have a friendly agent in Palestine. Fritz Heichelheim, noting that Dor on the Palestinian coast is found on the Athenian tribute list for 454, concluded: "If we are right the new strength which Ezra was authorized to give . . . was urgently needed from the point of view of the Persian government to make defections in Palestine to the Athenians less dangerous."[60] Another classical scholar,

55. J. Bright, "The Date of Ezra's Mission to Jerusalem," in *Yehezkel Kaufmann Jubilee Volume*, ed. M. Haran (Jerusalem: Magnes, 1960), p. 86; compare M. W. Leesberg, "Ezra and Nehemiah: A Review of the Return and Reform," *Concordia Theological Monthly* 33 (1962): 85.

56. Josephus (*Antiquities* 11.158) has Ezra passing away before the arrival of Nehemiah, a state of affairs that has not been taken seriously by scholars.

57. P. R. Ackroyd, *Israel under Babylon* (London: Oxford University Press, 1970), p. 194; compare L. H. Brockington, *Ezra, Nehemiah and Esther* (London: Nelson, 1969), p. 32.

58. F. M. Cross, "A Reconstruction of the Judean Restoration," *JBL* 94 (1975): 14, n. 60. Others favoring a date of circa 400 for the work of the Chronicler, including Ezra and Nehemiah, are W. Rudolph, *Esdra und Nehemiah* (Tübingen: J. C. B. Mohr, 1949), p. 25; J. M. Myers, *Ezra–Nehemiah* (Garden City: Doubleday, 1965), p. lxx. H. G. M. Williamson, *Israel in the Book of Chronicles* (Cambridge: Cambridge University Press, 1977), p. 86, also favors the Persian period.

59. V. Pavlovský, "Die Chronologie der Tätigkeit Esdras," *Biblica* 38 (1957): 284–85.

60. F. Heichelheim, "Ezra's Palestine and Periclean Athens," *Zeitschrift für Religions- und*

John Myres, concurs: "In particular, the very wide authority given to Ezra in 458 reflects the general uneasiness and the anxieties of the Persian government, during the revolt of Inaros in the Delta."[61]

At the same time, Bo Reicke notes that the political situation in Palestine in 398 would have made Ezra's mission most unlikely. When Johanan, the high priest, killed his brother (Josephus, *Antiquities* 11.297–301), the Persian governor Bagoas imposed a penalty on Jerusalem for seven years. According to Reicke: "This temple crisis under Bagoas can simply not be squared wth Ezra's mission to restore the Temple, supported juridically and monetarily by the Persian throne (Ezra 7:6, 11–28)."[62]

Up to the 1960s there had been a growing consensus among critical scholars in favor of the reverse order. In 1970 William F. Stinespring went so far as to affirm:

> Indeed, the placing of Ezra after Nehemiah may now be spoken of as part of "critical orthodoxy," having been incorporated into such works as *The International Critical Commentary, The Interpreter's Bible, The Interpreter's Dictionary of the Bible, The Oxford Annotated Bible,* and into much of the church-school literature of the leading Protestant churches in North America.[63]

Yet the traditional order has never lacked defenders. In 1948 Harold Rowley wrote: "Despite this impressive support [for the reverse order], this view has never been unchallenged, and there have always been scholars of eminence—even more numerous than its supporters—who have refused to adopt it, but have adhered to the traditional view."[64] In 1965 Rowley listed twenty-six scholars who supported the traditional order.[65] In 1968 Ulrich Kellermann defended the traditional position by seeking to refute the arguments for the reverse order.[66]

Geistesgeschichte 3 (1951): 251–53. Compare also M. Smith, "Ezra," in *Ex Orbe Religionum,* eds. C. J. Bleeker et al. (Leiden: Brill, 1972), 1: 141–43; Meritt, Wade-Gery, and McGregor, *Athenian Tribute Lists,* pp. 10–11. On Dor, see G. Foerster, "Dor," in *Encyclopedia of Archaeological Excavations in the Holy Land,* ed. M. Avi-Yonah (London: Oxford University Press, 1975), 1: 334–37; A. Raban, "The Harbor of the Sea Peoples at Dor," *BA* 50 (1987): 118–26.

61. J. L. Myres, "Persia, Greece and Israel," *PEQ* 85 (1953): 13.

62. B. Reicke, *The New Testament Era* (Philadelphia: Fortress, 1968), p. 16.

63. W. F. Stinespring, prolegomenon to *Ezra Studies,* by C. C. Torrey (New York: KTAV, 1970 reprint), p. xiv. A scholar who still holds to the reverse order is Hinz, *Darius* 2: 43.

64. H. H. Rowley, "The Chronological Order of Ezra and Nehemiah," in *Ignace Goldziher Memorial Volume,* eds. S. Löwinger and J. Somogyi (Budapest, 1948), pp. 117–49.

65. Rowley's essay was reprinted in his *Servant of the Lord* (London: Lutterworth, 1952), which was reissued with some revisions (Naperville: Allenson, 1965), pp. 135–68.

66. U. Kellermann, "Erwägungen zum Problem der Esradatierung," *ZAW* 80 (1968): 55–87. See also I. H. Eybers, "Chronological Problems in Ezra–Nehemiah," in *Oud-Testamentiese Werkgemeeskap in Suider-Africa,* ed. W. C. van Wyck (Pretoria: University of Pretoria Press, 1976), pp. 10–29.

In the 1970s and 1980s there has been growing support for the traditional position. Many important scholars have voiced dissatisfaction with the arguments for the reverse order. Morton Smith, for example, comments: "The minor reasons commonly given for dating Ezra after Nehemiah are all of them trivial and have been disposed of by Kellermann."[67] Cross also writes: "Of the many arguments brought forward to support the position that Ezra followed Nehemiah to Jerusalem, most are without weight."[68] Shemaryahu Talmon suggests: "Such tenuous argumentation does not warrant a reordering of the biblical presentation. . . . Today a more optimistic appreciation of the biblical presentation seems to be gaining ground."[69] Hayim Tadmor notes: "Actually, more methodological problems are posed by assuming that Ezra came after Nehemiah than by accepting the view that he preceded Nehemiah."[70]

In summary, while the reverse order of Nehemiah before Ezra still has a few supporters, there has been renewed support among most scholars in recent years for the traditional order of Ezra before Nehemiah.

Ezra and the Renewal of the Law

The fact that Artaxerxes I commissioned Ezra the scribe[71] to administer the Law to his people has troubled some critics. But this fits in perfectly with Persian policy. A very close parallel is a similar commission given by Darius I to Udjahorresnet, an Egyptian priest and scholar. Joseph Blenkinsopp comments: "In the light of the preceding, we can now see that the two goals of Ezra's mission correspond to the two phases of Udjahorresnet's activity: the restoration of the cult at the national and dynastic shrine of Sais; the reorganization of judicial insti-

67. Smith, "Ezra," p. 143; idem, *Palestinian Parties and Politics That Shaped the Old Testament* (New York: Columbia University Press, 1971), p. 122.

68. Cross, "Reconstruction," p. 14, n. 60.

69. S. Talmon, "Ezra and Nehemiah," in *IDBS*, p. 320.

70. H. Tadmor, "The Babylonian Exile and the Restoration," in *A History of the Jewish People*, ed. H. Ben-Sasson (Cambridge: Harvard University Press, 1976–), p. 174. Among other scholars who subscribe to the traditional order of Ezra's coming under Artaxerxes I are E. Stern, "The Province of Yehud: The Vision and the Reality," in *Jerusalem Cathedra I* (Detroit: Wayne State University Press, 1981), p. 10; idem, "The Persian Empire," in *CHJ*, p. 73; H. G. M. Williamson, "Nehemiah's Walls Revisited," *PEQ* 116 (1982): 82; idem, *Ezra, Nehemiah* (Waco: Word, 1985), p. xliv.

71. On the role of scribes, see A. L. Oppenheim, "A Note on the Scribes in Mesopotamia," in *Studies in Honor of Benno Landsberger*, eds. H. G. Güterbock and T. Jacobsen (Chicago: University of Chicago Press, 1965), pp. 253–57; A. F. Rainey, *The Scribe at Ugarit: His Position and Influence* (Jerusalem: Israel Academy of Sciences and Humanities, 1968).

tutions, for which the smooth functioning of the Houses of Life was a necessary precondition."[72]

Darius commanded the codification of the Egyptian laws in demotic and Aramaic by the chief men of Egypt—a task that took from 518 to 503. On the reverse side of the Demotic Chronicle, we are told that Darius ordered "the wise men be assembled . . . from among the warriors, the priests and the scribes of Egypt so that they may set down in writing the ancient Laws of Egypt."[73]

Richard Frye places the commission to Ezra in its broader historical context:

> Darius was actively concerned not only with his own "imperial" laws, to be promulgated throughout the empire, but also with the local laws and traditional practices in various provinces. . . . Darius wrote to his satrap in Egypt Aryandes to collect the wise men of the realm to make a new code of laws. Although the work was not finished before his death, the successors of Darius continued to be interested in the codification of the Laws of their subject peoples. It is in this light that one must understand the efforts of Ezra (7,11) and Nehemiah (8,1) to codify the Mosaic law, which was not accomplished until the reign of Artaxerxes I.[74]

At least four different views exist on the contents of "The Book of the Law of Moses" that Ezra read (Neh. 8:2–15) to the assembled multitude for about five hours. Ranging from the minimal to the maximal they are:

A collection of legal materials: Rudolph Kittel, Gerhard von Rad, Martin Noth

The Priestly Code: Abraham Kuenen, Bernhard Stade, W. H. Koster, Eduard Meyer, W. O. E. Oesterly, Adolphe Lods, Hans-J. Kraus

Deuteronomic laws: Laurence Browne, Raymond Bowman, M. F. Scott, Ulrich Kellermann

The Pentateuch: Julius Wellhausen, Ernest Sellin, Hans Schaeder, Otto Eissfeldt, Wilhelm Rudolph, Kurt Galling, Sigmund Mowinckel, William F. Albright, John Bright, Frank Cross, and James Sanders[75]

72. J. Blenkinsopp, "The Mission of Udjahorresnet and Those of Ezra and Nehemiah," *JBL* 106 (1987): 419. See chapter 3 for Udjahorresnet's role under Cambyses.

73. Gardiner, *Egypt of the Pharaohs,* pp. 366ff.

74. R. N. Frye, "Institutions," in *Beiträge zur Achämenidengeschichte,* ed. G. Walser (Wiesbaden: Franz Steiner, 1972), p. 92.

75. S. Mowinckel, *Studien zu dem Buche Ezra-Nehemiah III: Die Ezrageschichte und das Gesetz Moses* (Oslo: Universitetsforlaget, 1965); U. Kellermann, "Erwägungen zum Esragesetz," *ZAW* 80

There is no reason to doubt that Ezra could have brought back with him the Torah. Bruce Waltke, who has made an important study of the Samaritan Pentateuch in an unpublished Harvard dissertation, writes: "Finally, the Pentateuch itself must be older than the fifth century. If the scribal scholars of the second Jewish commonwealth found it necessary to modernize the Pentateuch to make it intelligible to the people (cf. Neh. 8) in the fifth century, then obviously the original Pentateuch antedates this period by many years."[76]

The key part played by Ezra in promoting obedience to the Torah is underscored by Menahem Haran:

> In the interest of clarity let it be added that no one will deny Ezra's decisive role in the formation of Judaism. The solemn ceremony performed under his inspiration and leadership, that is, the declaration of the *'ᵃmānāh,* "pact," and the public undertaking of the duty to fulfil all the Law's commandments from that time on (Neh. 8–10), is certainly a watershed in the history of Israel and even overshadows its forerunner, the covenant-making in the time of Josiah (2 Kings 22:3–23:24). As a result of Ezra's activity the Law, in its entirety, becomes the normative document in the life of Israel, and the first phase of Judaism as a denominational community, as an *ecclesia,* begins.[77]

Nehemiah the Cupbearer of Artaxerxes I

The name *Nehemiah* means "Yahweh has comforted." It contains the same verbal root that is found in the names *Nahum* and *Menahem.* The name appears as *Neḥemyahu* on an ostracon from Arad dated to

(1968): 373–85; J. A. Sanders, "Adaptable for Life: The Nature and Function of Canon," in *Magnalia Dei,* eds. F. M. Cross et al. (Garden City: Doubleday, 1976), p. 550.

76. B. K. Waltke, "The Samaritan Pentateuch and the Text of the Old Testament," in *New Perspectives on the Old Testament,* ed. J. B. Payne (Waco: Word, 1970), p. 234.

77. M. Haran, *Temples and Temple-Service in Ancient Israel* (Oxford: Clarendon, 1978), p. 9. For postbiblical traditions about Ezra, see R. A. Kraft, " 'Ezra' Materials in Judaism and Christianity," *ANRW* (1979): II.19.1, pp. 119–36; E. Yamauchi, "Postbiblical Traditions about Ezra and Nehemiah," in *A Tribute to Gleason Archer,* eds. W. Kaiser and R. Youngblood (Chicago: Moody, 1986), pp. 167–76.

Ezra's exposition of the Torah in Neh. 8 and the assembly's confession in Neh. 9 are viewed by some as the basis of the postexilic development of the synagogue. The first inscriptional evidence for synagogues, however, comes from Ptolemaic Egypt. See M. Hengel, "Proseuche und Synagogue," in *Tradition und Glaube,* eds. G. Jeremias et al. (Göttingen: Vandenhoeck and Ruprecht, 1971), pp. 157–84; J. Gutman, "The Origin of the Synagogue," *AA* 87 (1972): 36–40; J. Koenig, "L'origine exilique de la synagogue," in *Mélanges d'Histoire des Religions* (Paris: Presses Universitaires de France, 1974), pp. 33–55; J. G. Griffiths, "Egypt and the Rise of the Synagogue," *JTS* n.s. 38 (1987): 1–15.

the seventh century B.C.[78] It also appears as the name of a slave on a fourth-century-B.C. Aramaic papyrus.[79]

Nehemiah was the cupbearer of Artaxerxes I (Neh. 1:11). "Cupbearer" (Hebrew *mašqeh*) is a hiphil participle of the verb *šaqā* and literally means "one who gives (someone) something to drink." It occurs twelve times in the Old Testament in the sense of "cupbearer," for example, in 1 Kings 10:5 and 2 Chronicles 9:4 of Solomon's attendants. In the Joseph story it occurs nine times (Gen. 40:1, 2, 5, 9, 13, 20, 21, 23; 41:9), but its significance is obscured by the King James Version and the Revised Standard Version which translate the word "butler." The English word *butler* comes from the Middle English *boteler*, that is, one who attends to bottles.

Classical sources give us detailed descriptions of cupbearers at the Persian court. Xenophon's *Cyropaedia* (1.3.9) describes one of his main duties as follows: "Now, it is a well known fact that the cupbearers, when they proffer the cup, draw off some of it with the ladle, pour it into their left hand, and swallow it down—so that, if they should put poison in, they may not profit by it." That the cupbearer could have other responsibilities as well is indicated by Tobit 1:22: "Now Ahikar was cupbearer, keeper of the signet, and in charge of administration of the accounts, for Esarhaddon had appointed him second to himself."

Various sources indicate that Nehemiah as a royal cupbearer probably had the following traits: He would have been well trained in court etiquette (compare Dan. 1:4ff.).[80] He was probably a handsome individual (compare Dan. 1:4, 13, 15; Josephus, *Antiquities* 16.230).[81] He would certainly have known how to select the wines to set before the king. A proverb in the Babylonian Talmud (Baba Qamma 92b) states: "The wine belongs to the master but credit for it is due to his cupbearer." He would have been a convivial companion with a willingness to lend an ear at all times. Robert North is reminded of Saki, the companion of Omar Khayyam, who served wine to him and listened to his discourses.[82] Nehemiah would have been a man of great influence as one with the closest access to the king, and one who could well determine who got to see the king (Xenophon, *Cyropaedia* 1.3.8–9).

78. Y. Aharoni, "Three Hebrew Ostraca from Arad," *EI* 9 (1969): 10–21; idem, "The 'Nehemiah' Ostracon from Arad," *EI* 12 (1975): 72–76; Israel Museum, *Inscriptions Reveal*, 2d ed. (Jerusalem: Israel Museum, 1973), #61, pp. 36–37.

79. F. M. Cross, "The Discovery of the Samaria Papyri," *BA* 26 (1963): 111.

80. See E. Weidner, "Hof- und Harems-Erlasse assyrischer Könige aus dem 2. Jahrtausend v. Chr.," *AfO* 17 (1954–1955): 257–93.

81. Hinz, *Darius*, 2: 30.

82. R. North, "Civil Authority in Ezra," in *Studi in onore di Edoardo Volterra* (Milan: Casa Editrice Dott. A. Giuffrè, 1971), 6: 397.

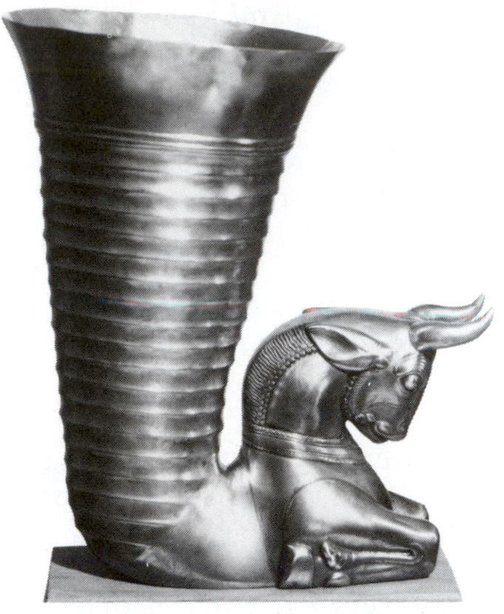

Silver rhyton. (Cincinnati Art Museum, purchase)

Above all Nehemiah would have enjoyed the unreserved confidence of the king. The great need for trustworthy attendants is underscored by the intrigues that were endemic to the Achaemenid court. According to Ilya Gershevitch: "If we are to believe the Greek writers, four—and if we count Bardiya, five—of the thirteen Kings seem to have been murdered, and at least half a dozen of them to have reached the throne through intrigues of their own or of others."[83]

Nehemiah a Eunuch?[84]

Eunuchs were widely used at royal courts,[85] sometimes as cupbearers.[86] The Rabshakeh of Sennacherib's army (2 Kings 18:17; Isa. 36:2), a high-ranking officer, may have been the chief cupbearer. Max Mallowan thinks that he was a eunuch.[87] Many scholars have, there-

83. Gershevitch, *CHI*, p. 227. The eunuch Halotus, who was the official "taster" for Claudius, was used by Agrippina to poison the emperor (Suetonius, *Claudius* #44). See J. P. V. D. Balsdon, *Romans and Aliens* (London: Duckworth, 1977), p. 228.

84. For a more detailed exposition of this issue, see E. Yamauchi, "Was Nehemiah the Cupbearer a Eunuch?" *ZAW* 92 (1980): 132–42.

85. Cook, *CHI*, p. 137, notes that at the Urartian court of Rusa II, out of 5,507 retainees, 3,892 were eunuchs.

86. Herod the Great had a eunuch cupbearer. See Josephus, *Antiquities* 16.230.

87. The Akkadian word for cupbearer was *šāqiu;* compare Sumerian *sagi.* See M. Mallowan's foreword to J. V. Kinnier Wilson, *The Nimrud Wine Lists* (London: British School of Archaeology in Iraq, 1972), p. x. Mallowan notes that "sons" are listed in the Nimrud wine lists after the royal cupbearers, but explains these references as "adopted" sons. D. J. Wiseman, "Rabshakeh," *The International Standard Bible Encyclopedia,* eds. G. W. Bromiley et al., rev. ed. (Grand Rapids: Eerdmans,

Ashurnasirpal II and his eunuch cupbearer. (Metropolitan Museum of Art, gift of John D. Rockefeller, 1932)

fore, assumed as certain or as probable the thesis that Nehemiah was a eunuch. Those who have maintained this position include such influential and diverse scholars as William F. Albright, Loring W. Batten, John Bright, John M. Cook, Balmer H. Kelly, Jacob M. Myers, Albert T. Olmstead, and Samuel Schultz.

It should be noted that the Hebrew text does not call Nehemiah a eunuch. The Hebrew word for eunuch is *sārîs,* which is a loan-word from the Akkadian phrase *ša rēš šarri* (or simply *ša rēši*), which literally

1988), 4: 30–31, is more cautious in explaining the etymology of the name and does not identify the officer as a eunuch. R. A. Henshaw, "Late Neo-Assyrian Officialdom," *JAOS* 100 (1980): 290, n. 115, also questions Kinnier Wilson's interpretation of the *rab šaqē* as a "grand eunuch."

means "one who (stands) at the head of the king." By the late second millennium B.C. the Akkadian phrase, in many cases, had the connotation of "eunuch."[88] The word occurs twelve times in Esther and seven times in Daniel, but not in Nehemiah.

In place of the *oinochoos* (cupbearer) of the Septuagint Codex Alexandrinus, both the Codex Vaticanus and the Codex Sinaiticus have *eunouchos* (eunuch). But this is simply an error for the former word.[89]

Eduard Meyer explained the Hebrew word *tirshāthā'* (which the KJV merely transliterates as Tirshatha) as a word designating palace eunuch from the New Persian word *tărash* (to cut).[90] But this word, which is used in the Old Testament but five times (Ezra 2:63; Neh. 7:65, 70; 8:9; 10:1), seems to be a title of honor for the governor of the province. The best explanation of the word still remains that advocated by Wilhelm Rudolph, who explained it as a term meaning "the one to be feared or respected," that is, "Excellency" from Old Persian *tarsa*.[91]

Another argument that has been used to identify Nehemiah as a eunuch is the reference to the queen's presence (Neh. 2:6). Not every high official who stood in the presence of the queen, however, was necessarily a eunuch. The Book of Esther nowhere indicates that Haman was a eunuch. On the contrary, the villain's downfall came when the king suspected him of trying to seduce the queen in her own chamber (Esther 7:8).

One of the edicts on harem conduct published by Ernst Weidner reads:

> A courtier or a eunuch when he would speak with a woman of the palace should not approach closer than seven steps. He may not speak with her if she is insufficiently clothed, nor may he remain standing and listening when two palace women are gossiping.[92]

88. See G. R. Driver and J. C. Miles, *The Assyrian Laws* (Oxford: Oxford University Press, 1935), p. 463; K. A. Kitchen, *Ancient Orient and Old Testament* (Chicago: Inter-Varsity, 1967), p. 165. A. L. Oppenheim, "A Note on *ša rēši*," *JANE* 5 (1973): 326–27, points out that the word does not always mean eunuch.

89. Lewis, *Sparta and Persian*, p. 20, cites as his only evidence for the view that Nehemiah was a eunuch the "tradition" represented in this Septuagint variant and the comment of Origen on Matt. 19:12.

90. E. Meyer, *Die Entstehung des Judenthums* (Halle: M. Niemeyer, 1896), p. 194; compare J. Theis, *Geschichtliche und literarkritische Fragen in Esra 1–6* (Münster: Aschendorff, 1910), pp. 66–67. U. Kellermann, *Nehemia Quellen Überlieferung und Geschichte* (Berlin: A. Töpelmann, 1967), p. 155, n. 17, declares such an etymology obsolete. W. T. in der Smitten, "Der Tirschātā' in Esra–Nehemiah," *VT* 21 (1971): 618–20, suggests that the word *tirshata* means "the circumcised one"—a most improbable suggestion.

91. W. Rudolph, *Esra und Nehemiah* (Tübingen: J. C. B. Mohr, 1949), in loc.; compare K. Galling, *Studien zur Geschichte Israels im persischen Zeitalter* (Tübingen: J. C. B. Mohr, 1964), pp. 57, 81.

92. Weidner, "Hof- und Harems-Erlasse," p. 261.

Beardless attendant with bottle and towel. (The Oriental Institute, University of Chicago)

The point is that courtiers (known in Akkadian as *manzaz pāni* or *mazia pāni*), who served as pages and bodyguards, were permitted to enter the harem even though they were not eunuchs.

Beardless officials in artistic representations have ordinarily been interpreted as eunuchs. Those portrayed with flabby cheeks, such as the cupbearer of Ashurnasirpal, may indeed have been eunuchs.[93] But it would be incorrect to interpret all beardless servants or officials as eunuchs; some may have simply been youths.[94] Moreover, there is no convincing iconographic evidence that Achaemenian cupbearers were eunuchs.[95]

Perhaps the strongest extrabiblical evidence that Nehemiah may

93. See E. Strommenger, *5000 Years of the Art of Mesopotamia* (New York: Harry N. Abrams, 1964), fig. 194, and p. 440. For possible eunuch cupbearers of Sargon II, see C. C. Smith, "The Birth of Bureaucracy," *BA* 40 (1977): 28, fig. 5.

94. J. E. Reade, "The Neo-Assyrian Court and Army: Evidence from the Sculptures," *Iraq* 34 (1972): 91; Oppenheim, "Notes," p. 333: "Consequently, I would like to suggest that many of the males shown on reliefs, etc., without beards are meant to represent youths, that is, young, beardless males."

95. See Yamauchi, "Was Nehemiah the Cupbearer a Eunuch?" pp. 138–39.

have been a eunuch cupbearer is the account of Ctesias, which notes that this was the case in his day. Ctesias was a Greek physician at the court of Artaxerxes II (404–359 B.C.). Unfortunately Ctesias is notorious as an unreliable historical source. In a key passage Ctesias describes the chief cupbearer of Astyages as a eunuch named Artembares. But Herodotus indicates that Artembares was not a eunuch. In the same passage Ctesias has Cyrus succeeding Artembares as cupbearer, and Cyrus was certainly not a eunuch.[96]

In conclusion, no firm evidence exists that Nehemiah was a eunuch. Dogmatic statements that he was are based on a web of arguments that in many cases are untenable and in other cases are less than convincing.

Nehemiah the Governor

Nehemiah was sent as the governor of Judah. The province of Judah was greatly reduced in the Persian era. The archaeological evidence of Yehud (Judah) coins and seals confirms the biblical boundaries.[97] According to Ephraim Stern:

> One criterion is the distribution of the *Yehud* stamps and coins which . . . were found to range from Beth-Zur in the south, Tell en-Nasbeh in the north, Jericho and Engedi in the east, and Gezer in the west. The distribution of these stamps and coins, which are imprinted with the official stamp of the Jewish province in the Persian period, corresponds exactly with the boundaries as recorded in the various lists in Ezra and Nehemiah.[98]

Stern also points out that the discovery of border fortresses revealed by surveys of the Adullam region by Levi Rahmani and the Hebron hills by Moshe Kochavi also "coincide with the borders indicated by the biblical lists and seal impression."[99]

In Nehemiah 5:15 Nehemiah refers to previous governors (plural of the Hebrew *peḥâ*).[100] Kurt Galling believes that Judah did not have governors, and therefore suggests that the reference here is to governors

96. F. W. König, *Die Persika des Ktesias von Knidos* (Graz: Archiv für Orientforschung, 1972), pp. 176–77.

97. See L. Mildenburg, "Yehud: A Preliminary Study of the Provincial Coinage of Judaea," in *Essays in Honor of Margaret Thompson,* eds. O. Mørkholm and N. M. Waggoner (Wetteren: Editions NB, 1979), pp. 183–96. Fourth-century coins from Judah are discussed by J. W. Betlyon, "The Provincial Government of Persian Period Judea and the Yehud Coins," *JBL* 105 (1986): 633–42.

98. Stern, *CHJ,* p. 86; see also E. Stern, *Material Culture of the Land of the Bible in the Persian Period 538–332 B.C.* (Warminster: Aris and Phillips, 1982), chapters 7 and 8.

99. Stern, "Province of Yehud," p. 20.

100. F. C. Fensham, "Peḥâ in the Old Testament and the Ancient Near East," in van Wyck, *Oud-Testamentiese Werkgemeenskap,* pp. 44–52.

of Samaria. New archaeological evidence, however, confirms the reference refers to previous governors of Judah.

In 1974 a collection of about seventy bullae (clay seal impressions) and two seals from an unknown provenience were shown to Nahman Avigad. One of the seals is the first to bear the inscription *YHD,* which was the Persian designation of the province of Judah. Avigad dates the seals and bullae to the sixth and early fifth centuries B.C.

On the basis of this new evidence, together with data from other sources, Avigad proposes the following list of the governors of Judah:[101]

Name	Source	Date
Sheshbazzar	Ezra 1:8; 5:14	538 B.C.
Zerubbabel	Haggai 1:1, 14	515 B.C.
Elnathan	bulla and seal	late sixth century B.C.
Yehoʿezer	jar impression	early fifth century B.C.
Ahzai	jar impression	early fifth century B.C.
Nehemiah	Nehemiah 5:14; 12:26	445–432 B.C.[102]
Bahohi (Bagoas)	Cowley #30:1	407 B.C.
Yeḥezqiyah	coins	330 B.C.

Nehemiah's Opponents

The exiles returned to a tiny enclave surrounded by hostile neighbors: Samaritans to the north, Ammonites to the east, Arabs and Edomites[103] to the south, and Phoenicians to the west.[104]

101. N. Avigad, *Bullae and Seals from a Post-Exilic Judean Archive* (Jerusalem: Hebrew University Press, 1976); Talmon, "Ezra and Nehemiah," pp. 325–27. P. R. Ackroyd, "Archaeology, Politics and Religion: The Persian Period," *Iliff Review* 39 (1982): 12–13, expresses some reservation about this reconstructed list of governors. See now H. G. M. Williamson, "The Governors of Judah under the Persians," *TB* 39 (1988): 59–82.

102. Stern believes that although there may have been some governors prior to Nehemiah, the use of the Yehud stamps and minting privileges attested in the mid-fifth century are evidences of Judah's independence from Samaria only at this date. See Stern, *CHJ,* p. 83.

103. Although Edomites are not mentioned by name in Ezra–Nehemiah, it is apparent from the harsh condemnation of the Edomites in Scripture (2 Chron. 25:11; Ezek. 25:12–14; Ps. 137:7; Obad.; Mal. 1:4) that the Edomites took advantage of the Babylonian conquest of Judah. An important confirmation of this enmity comes from an inscription from Arad (early sixth century B.C.), which reads: "Behold, I have sent to warn you today: (Get) the men to Elisha! Lest Edom should come thither. Send reinforcements to Ramoth-Negeb." See *Inscriptions Reveal,* #37; Y. Aharoni, "Three Hebrew Ostraca from Arad," *BASOR* 197 (1970): 16–42.

On the names found in Persian-period ostraca from Beersheba, one-third were Arabic while another one-third were compounded with the name of the Edomite god Qaus (compare Barkos in Ezra 2:35/Neh. 7:55). See J. Naveh, "The Aramaic Ostraca from Tel Beersheba (Seasons 1975–76)," *TA* 6 (1979): 182–98. Of forty-five ostraca from Arad, five have Yahweh names and four have Qos names. See also T. C. Vriezen, "The Edomitic Deity Qaus," *Oudtestamentische Studien* 14 (1965): 330–53;

There had been opposition to the rebuilding of the temple during the reign of Darius. There was now even greater concern about the attempt to rebuild the walls as Judah's neighbors learned of Nehemiah's plans.

An interesting parallel exists from Greek history. After the city of Athens had its walls destroyed by the Persians in 480 B.C., the Athenians wished to rebuild their walls. The Spartans tried to oppose this with the specious reason that if the Persians came back and took Athens, they would have a walled city to hold. According to Thucydides (1.90): "The Lacedaemonians, perceiving what was in prospect, came on an embassy, partly because they themselves would have preferred to see neither the Athenians nor anyone else have a wall."

Sanballat the Samaritan

After the fall of Samaria in 722, the Assyrian kings imported inhabitants from Mesopotamia and Syria "who feared the LORD and served their own gods" (2 Kings 17:24–33). The newcomers' influence served to dilute further the faith of the northerners who had already apostasized from the sole worship of Yahweh.

The opposition of the Samarians was not primarily motivated by religious differences but by political considerations. The appearance of a vigorous governor of Judah threatened the authority of the governor of Samaria. The satraps of neighboring provinces, especially in Anatolia, were constantly in opposition to each other.[105]

The New International Version translates the Hebrew phrase *lᵉkissēʾ*, in Nehemiah 3:7 as "authority" of the governor. It literally means "to the chair" or "throne." Fragments of a lion's paw and a bronze cylinder that belonged to the foot of a Persian throne similar to those depicted at Persepolis have recently been discovered in Sa-

B. Obed, "Egyptian Deferences to the Edomite Deity Qaus," *AUSS* 9 (1971): 47–50; M. Rose, "Yahweh in Israel, Qaus in Edom?" *JSOT* 1 (1977): 28–34.

By the fourth century B.C. the Edomites were pushed westward to the region south of Hebron, later known as Idumaea, by the Arab Nabataeans, who settled in the area around Petra in Jordan. See J. M. Myers, "Edom and Judah in the Sixth–Fifth Centuries B.C., in *Near Eastern Studies in Honor of William Foxwell Albright*, ed. H. Goedicke (Baltimore: Johns Hopkins University Press, 1971), pp. 377–92; J. Lindsay, "The Babylonian Kings and Edom, 605–550 B.C.," *PEQ* 108 (1976): 23–39; J. R. Bartlett, "The Rise and Fall of the Kingdom of Edom," *PEQ* 104 (1972): 26–37; idem, "The Moabites and Edomites," in *Peoples of the Old Testament Times* [*POT*], ed. D. J. Wiseman (Oxford: Clarendon, 1973), pp. 229–58; idem, "From Edomites to Nabataeans," *PEQ* 111 (1979): 53–66.

104. In the Persian period the Palestinian coast was occupied by the descendants of the Philistines and by Phoenicians. Ashkelon was under the Tyrians. From Ashdod (Neh. 13:23) has come an ostracon with a Phoenician name. See F. M. Cross, "An Ostracon from Nebī Yūnis," *IEJ* 14 (1964): 185.

105. See O. Leuze, *Die Satrapieneinteilung in Syrien und im Zweistromlande* (Halle: Königsberger Gelehrten Gesellschaft, 1935) for the situation in Syria and Mesopotamia.

maria. Miriam Tadmor remarks: "A throne so similar to that of the Achaemenid kings might have belonged to their representative, the governor of Samaria."[106]

A distinction must be made between the syncretistic and polytheistic "Samarians" of Nehemiah's day and the monotheistic "Samaritans" of Jesus' day. John MacDonald notes that "the word *translated* 'the Samaritans' occurs [in 2 Kings 17:29] for the first and only time in the Old Testament."[107] In this context it means the inhabitants of Samaria, that is, Samarians, and not the Jewish sect of the Samaritans.

Tobiah the Ammonite

Tobiah (Neh. 2:10) means "Yahweh is good"; the name appears in the Murashu documents as *Ṭūbiāma*. He may have been a Judaizing Ammonite, but was more probably a Yahwist Jew as indicated not only by his own name but also by that of his son, Jehohanan (Neh. 6:18).

Some scholars suggest that Tobiah was descended from an aristocratic family who owned estates in Gilead and was influential in Transjordan and in Jerusalem even as early as the eighth century B.C.[108] Benjamin Mazar has correlated varying lines of evidence to reconstruct the history of the Tobiad family to cover nine generations as follows:[109]

106. M. Tadmor, "Fragments of an Achaemenid Throne from Samaria," *IEJ* 24 (1974): 42.

107. J. MacDonald, "The Discovery of Samaritan Religion," *Religion* 2 (1972): 143. The recent trend in Samaritan studies is to lower the date of the Samaritan schism from the time of Nehemiah to the fourth century B.C. or even later. See J. A. Montgomery, *The Samaritans* (Philadelphia: John Winston, 1907); H. H. Rowley, "The Samaritan Schism in Legend and History," in *Israel's Prophetic Heritage*, eds. B. W. Anderson and W. Harrelson (New York: Harper and Bros., 1962), pp. 208–22; M. Delcor, "Hinweise auf das Samaritanische Schisma im AT," *ZAW* 74 (1962): 281–91; H. H. Rowley, "Sanballat and the Samaritan Temple," *Men of God* (London: Thomas Nelson, 1963), pp. 246–76; J. MacDonald, *Theology of the Samaritans* (Philadelphia: Westminster, 1964); L. A. Mayer, *Bibliography of the Samaritans*, ed. D. Broadribb (Leiden: Brill, 1964); R. Tournay, "Quelques relectures bibliques antisamaritaines," *RB* 71 (1964): 504–36; F. M. Cross, "Aspects of Samaritan and Jewish History in Later Persian and Hellenistic Times," *HTR* 59 (1966): 201–11; J. D. Purvis, *The Samaritan Pentateuch and the Origin of the Samaritan Sect* (Cambridge: Harvard University Press, 1968); H. G. Kippenberg, *Garizim und Synagogue* (Berlin: W. de Gruyter, 1971); R. J. Coggins, *Samaritans and Jews* (Atlanta: John Knox, 1975); J. D. Purvis, "Samaritans," in *IDBS*, pp. 776–77; S. Talmon, "The Samaritans," *Scientific American* 236 (Jan. 1977): 100–108; R. Pummer, "The Present State of Samaritan Studies," *JSS* 21 (1976): 39–61; ibid., 22 (1977): 27–47; J. Bowman, "The History of the Samaritans," *Abr-Nahrain* 18 (1978–1979): 100–15; H. Tadmor, "Some Aspects of the History of Samaria during the Biblical Period," in *Jerusalem Cathedra* (Detroit: Wayne State University Press, 1983), 3: 1–11; W. A. Brindle, "The Origin and History of Samaritans," *Grace Theological Journal* 5 (1984): 47–75.

108. B. Obed, "The Historical Background of the Syro-Ephraimite War Reconsidered," *CBQ* 34 (1972): 161.

109. B. Mazar, "The Tobiads," *IEJ* 7 (1957): 137–45, 229–38.

Generation	Tobiad	Contemporary of	Flourished
1	Tobiah, the king's arm	Zedekiah	590 B.C.
2	his son		
3	Tobiah, noble of Judah	Jeshua	520 B.C.
4	his son		
5	Tobiah, Ammonite official	Nehemiah	440 B.C.
6	Jehohanan	Nehemiah	420 B.C.
7	Tobiah, prince	Ptolemy II	270 B.C.
8	Joseph	Ptolemy III	230 B.C.
9	Tobiah/Hyrcanus	Antiochus III	200 B.C.

The region of Ammon was located in Transjordan around the modern capital of Amman. Tobiah is called *ʿebed* (literally "slave" or "servant"). The Revised Standard Version renders the term literally as a derisive epithet, "Tobias, the Ammonite, the slave." But *ʿebed* was often used of high officials both in biblical and extrabiblical texts. Tobiah was probably the governor of Ammon under the Persians. His grandson, Tobiah (#7), was explicitly called "the governor of Ammon." We learn from Josephus (*Antiquities* 12.160ff.) that the latter was the leader of the Jewish Hellenizers under Ptolemy II, a relationship that is also illumined by the Zenon Papyri.

ʿArâq el-Emîr (Caverns of the Prince), about eleven miles west of Amman, was the center of the Tobiads. The visible remains of a large building on top of the hill (Qaṣr el-ʿAbd, "castle of the slave," measuring 60 by 120 feet) have been interpreted as a Jewish temple built by Hyrcanus (#9).

On two halls are inscriptions with the name *Tobiah* in Aramaic characters. The date of the inscriptions is much disputed. Mazar favors the sixth to fifth centuries B.C., Joseph Naveh prefers the fourth century, Cross the fourth to third centuries, and Paul Lapp, who reexcavated the site in 1961 to 1962, dates it to the third to second centuries.[110]

Geshem the Arab

Geshem (Neh. 2:19), one of Nehemiah's opponents, is also called Gashmu in Nehemiah 6:1, a variant that is closer to the original Arabic name. *Jasuma,* which means "bulky" or "stout," is found in

110. C. C. McCown, "The ʿAraq el-Emir and the Tobiads," *BA* 20 (1957): 63–76; P. W. Lapp, "Soundings at ʿArâq el-Emîr (Jordan)," *BASOR* 165 (1962): 16–34; idem, "The Second and Third Campaigns at ʿArâq el-Emîr," *BASOR* 171 (1963): 8–39; J. Naveh, *The Development of the Aramaic Script* (Jerusalem: Israel Academy of Sciences and Humanities, 1970), pp. 62–64; M. Hengel, *Judaism and Hellenism* (Philadelphia: Fortress, 1974), 1: 49, 267–77.

Silver dish with Aramaic inscription. (Brooklyn Museum, Charles E. Wilbour Fund)

various Arabic inscriptions including Safaitic, Lihyanite, Thamudic, and Nabataean.

A Lihyanite inscription from Dedan (modern Al-ᶜUlā) in northwest Arabia reads: "Jašm son of Šahr and ʿAbd, governor of Dedan." This Jašm is identified by Frederick Winnett and William F. Albright with the biblical Geshem.[111]

In 1947 several silver vessels, some with Aramaic inscriptions dating to the late fifth century B.C., were discovered at Tell el-Maskhūta near Ismaila by the Suez Canal. One inscription bore the name "Geshem son of Shahar," and another "Qainu son of Geshem."[112] Because this also seems to refer to the biblical Geshem, the latter must have been in charge of a powerful north Arabian confederacy that controlled vast areas from northeast Egypt to northern Arabia and southern Palestine. Geshem may have been opposed to Nehemiah's development of an independent kingdom because he feared it might interfere with his lucrative trade in myrrh and frankincense.[113]

Some scholars conjectured that Geshem controlled the area south of Judah, using Lachish as a residence. But recent archaeological evidence

111. F. V. Winnett, *A Study of the Lihyanite and Thamudic Inscriptions* (Toronto: University of Toronto Press, 1937), pp. 50–51; W. F. Albright, "Dedan," in *Geschichte und Altes Testament* (Tübingen: J. C. B. Mohr, 1943), pp. 1–12.

112. J. D. Cooney, *Five Years of Collecting Egyptian Art (1951–56)* (Brooklyn: Brooklyn Museum, 1956), p. 43.

113. F. M. Cross, "Geshem the Arabian, Enemy of Nehemiah," *BA* 18 (1955): 46–47; I. Rabinowitz, "Aramaic Inscriptions of the Fifth Century BCE," *JNES* 15 (1956): 1–9; W. J. Dumbrell, "The Tell el-Maskhuṭa Bowls and the 'Kingdom' of Qedar in the Persian Period," *BASOR* 203 (1971): 33–44; A. K. Irvine, "The Arabs and Ethiopians," in *POT*, pp. 287–311; A. Lemaire, "Un nouveau roi arabe de Qedar dans l'inscription de l'autel à encens de Lakish," *RB* 81 (1974): 63–72; I.Ephʿal, *The Ancient Arabs: Nomads on the Borders of the Fertile Crescent 9th–5th Centuries B.C.* (Leiden: Brill, 1983).

indicates the Arabs were subordinate to Persian authority in this region also. Stern summarizes the data as follows:

> In recent excavations a number of military fortresses have been unearthed, for example, at Tell Jemmeh, Tell el-Faraʿ (south), Beersheba, Arad, Kadesh-Barnea, and Tell el-Kheleifeh. Ostraca found at some of these sites indicate the presence of garrison troops. Two ostraca from Arad even designate the unit by name, "degel" (standard), which is the name of a Persian military unit also mentioned in the Elephantine papyri.
>
> In the opinion of the present writer, this entire area was under the direct rule of a Persian governor, assisted perhaps by Arab soldiers.[114]

Rebuilding the Walls

Despite abortive attempts to rebuild them (Ezra 4:6–23), the walls of Jerusalem, which had been destroyed by Nebuchadnezzar in 586, had remained in ruins for almost a century and a half when Nehemiah arrived in Jerusalem. The first thing Nehemiah did was to make a nocturnal inspection of the walls (Neh. 2:11–15). Kathleen Kenyon's excavations from 1961 to 1967 on the eastern slopes of Ophel (the original hill of Jerusalem just south of the temple area) revealed the collapse of the terraces, possibly the "Millo" that David and Solomon had to keep repairing. Kenyon writes:

> The tumble of stones uncovered by our Trench 1 is a vivid sample of the ruinous state of the eastern side of Jerusalem that baulked Nehemiah's donkey. The event shows that the sight of this cascade of stones persuaded Nehemiah that he could not attempt to restore the quarter of Jerusalem on the eastern slope of the eastern ridge, or the wall that enclosed it.[115]

Kenyon found what she believes was part of Nehemiah's wall on the crest of the rock scarp higher up on the slope of Ophel. "It was solidly built, c. 2.75 metres thick, but its finish was rough, as might be expected in work executed so rapidly."[116]

On the crest of the Ophel Hill Robert Macalister discovered in 1923 to 1925 a complex including a wall, ramp, and a great tower that he ascribed to David and Solomon. Kenyon's excavations demonstrated

114. Stern, *CHJ*, p. 81; see also idem, "Province of Yehud," p. 12.

115. K. Kenyon, *Jerusalem* (London: Thames and Hudson, 1967), pp. 107–8.

116. Kenyon, *Jerusalem*, p. 111; idem, *Digging up Jerusalem* (London: Ernest Benn, 1974), pp. 183–84.

that the complex rests on the ruins of houses destroyed by Nebuchadnezzar in 586 and must, therefore, be more recent. Kenyon believed that the tower should be dated to the second century B.C.[117] On the other hand, Mazar believes that

> it is not possible to determine whether it is hellenistic, or whether it had already been erected in Persian times. In the latter case, it may possibly be identified with the "great projecting tower" described by Nehemiah (3:26–27).[118]

Excavations in 1978 at the base of the tower revealed "for the first time in Jerusalem a Persian-period ceramic layer within clear stratigraphical context—solid archaeological evidence for that resettlement of the Babylonian exiles in the City of David."[119] Yigal Shiloh, after excavations from 1978 to 1982, also dated the tower to the second century B.C., but reinterpreted the ramp as a stepped stone structure supporting the Davidic Ophel or central citadel area.[120]

From 1970 to 1971 Avigad, excavating in the Jewish Quarter of the walled city of Jerusalem, discovered 275 meters to the west of the temple area a seven-meter-thick wall and cleared it for some 440 meters. Avigad identified this with the "broad wall" (Hebrew *haḥōmâ hārᵉḥābâ*—Neh. 3:8) repaired by Nehemiah.[121] The phrase is usually understood to refer to a thick wall, but Rafi Grafman interprets it to mean a long, extensive wall.[122]

The wall is dated to the early seventh century and was probably built by Hezekiah (2 Chron. 32:5). Magen Broshi surmises that the great expansion to and beyond the broad wall, which caused a three- to fourfold expansion of the city, was occasioned by the influx of refugees from Samaria in 722.[123]

The discovery of this wall led to a heated debate between a maximalist and minimalist interpretation of the size of Jerusalem. The former assumes a continuation of the wall to have included the southwestern hill, today called Mount Zion; the latter assumes a circuit of the wall turning east to have excluded the southwestern hill.[124]

117. Kenyon, *Jerusalem*, p. 115.

118. B. Mazar, *The Mountain of the Lord* (Garden City: Doubleday, 1975), p. 198.

119. Y. Shiloh, "City of David: Excavation 1978," *BA* 42 (1979): 168.

120. See H. Shanks, "The City of David after Five Years of Digging," *BAR* 11 (1985): 27–29.

121. N. Avigad, "Excavations in the Jewish Quarter of the Old City, Jerusalem, 1970," *IEJ* 20 (1970): 129–40; idem, "Excavations . . . 1971," pp. 193–200.

122. R. Grafman, "Nehemiah's 'Broad Wall,' " *IEJ* 24 (1974): 50–51.

123. M. Broshi, "The Expansion of Jerusalem in the Reigns of Hezekiah and Manasseh," *IEJ* 24 (1974): 21–26.

124. For an orientation to the topography of Jerusalem, see I. W. J. Hopkins, *Jerusalem: A Study in*

The maximalist view, suggested by Josephus, has been adopted by a number of earlier scholars,[125] and, especially after Avigad's discovery of the "broad wall," by Israeli scholars.[126] The maximalist position has been criticized by Kenyon[127] and by her colleague, Douglas Tushingham.[128]

John Crowfoot's discovery of a gate on the western slope of the southeastern hill, which Albrecht Alt identified with the Valley Gate, led to the adoption of the minimalist position by Galling and others. The excavations of Kenyon from 1961 to 1967 seemed to demonstrate that the southwest hill was settled only in the Hellenistic period.[129]

Hugh Williamson, who adopts the minimalist view, concludes: "I have attempted to show on the basis of a number of archaeological and literary considerations that when Nehemiah rebuilt the walls of Jerusalem he did not follow the full extent of the late pre-exilic line but an earlier, shorter line which did not yet include the Mishneh on the western hill."[130] This interpretation of the archaeological evidence helps explain the rapidity with which the work was completed. In spite of opposition from without and dissension from within, Nehemiah was able to galvanize the people by his leadership so that they were able to complete the rebuilding in only fifty-two days (Neh. 6:15).

Nehemiah the Reformer[131]

The economic crisis faced by Nehemiah is described in chapter 5, placed in the middle of his major effort to rebuild the walls of Jerusalem. Many scholars have considered it unlikely that Nehemiah would have called a great assembly (5:7) in the midst of such a project. They

Urban Geography (Grand Rapids: Baker, 1970); E. Yamauchi, "Jerusalem," in *Young's Bible Dictionary,* ed. G. D. Young (Wheaton: Tyndale, 1984), pp. 333–40; W. H. Mare, *The Archeology of the Jerusalem Area* (Grand Rapids: Baker, 1987).

125. M. Burrows, "Nehemiah's Tour of Inspection," *BASOR* 64 (1936): 12; L–H. Vincent and A. M. Steve, *Jérusalem de l'Ancient Testament* (Paris: Gabalda, 1954), 1: 237–59.

126. Grafman, "Nehemiah's 'Broad Wall,' " pp. 50–51; H. Geva, "The Western Boundary of Jerusalem at the End of the Monarchy," *IEJ* 29 (1979): 84–91.

127. Kenyon, *Digging up Jerusalem,* p. 148.

128. A. D. Tushingham, "The Western Hill of Jerusalem: A Critique of the 'Maximalist' Position," *Levant* 19 (1987): 137–43.

129. Kenyon, *Jerusalem,* p. 107; idem, *Digging up Jerusalem,* pp. 146–47; compare Mazar, *Mountain of the Lord,* p. 193.

130. H. G. M. Williamson, "A Reconsideration of ʿzb II in Biblical Hebrew," *ZAW* 97 (1985): 78; idem, "Nehemiah's Wall Revisited," *PEQ* 116 (1984): 81–88.

131. For the comparison of Nehemiah's reforms with those of an earlier Greek reformer, see E. Yamauchi, "Two Reformers Compared: Solon of Athens and Nehemiah of Jerusalem," in *The Bible World: Essays in Honor of Cyrus H. Gordon,* eds. G. Rendsburg et al. (New York: KTAV, 1980), pp. 269–92.

suggest that the assembly was called only after the rebuilding of the wall.

On the other hand, the economic pressures created by the rebuilding program may have exposed problems that had long been simmering and needed attention before work could proceed. This is the position of E. Neufeld:

> The only obvious explanation is that Nehemiah follows in his narrative the chronological order of his diary, and that therefore his social reform took place in the course of his building activities. According to Neh. 6.15, the wall was completed on Elul 25. . . . The complaint of the debtors, therefore, was raised between these two dates, probably in the last week of Elul (Aug./Sept). . . . We are justified in assuming that the complaint came at a moment when the harvest of all important products of the soil had come to an end. That was the time when the creditors exacted their capital and interest.[132]

Among the classes affected were: the landless who were short of food (v. 2); the landowners who were compelled to mortgage their properties (v. 3); those forced to borrow money at exorbitant rates because of oppressive taxation (v. 4);[133] and those forced to sell their children into slavery (v. 5).

The gravity of the situation was underscored by the fact that the wives (v. 1) joined in the protest when they ran short of funds and supplies to feed their families. The workers evidently were not able to earn the subsistence wage of a silver shekel a month, which would have provided the six and a half bushels, and other items needed to feed a family for a month.[134] In times of dire need, the wealthy generally had enough stored up to feed themselves. It was the poor who suffered because of the huge rise in prices caused by scarcities.[135]

The imposition of taxes by the Persians affected the Jews as it did other subjects. Speaking of the province of Yehud, Stern observes:

> But the area where Persian influence is most conspicuous is that of taxation and money. In contrast to the liberal approach of the Persian rulers

132. E. Neufeld, "The Rate of Interest and the Text of Nehemiah 5:11," *JQR* 44 (1953–1954): 203–4.

133. The Hebrew of Neh. 5:4 reads: "We have borrowed money for the king's tax (*middâ*) our fields and vineyards." Most translations supply "on" before "our fields" to express the idea that the tax was on the lands.

134. M. Meuleau, "Mesopotamia under Persian Rule," in *The Greeks and the Persians*, ed. H. Bengtson (London: Weidenfeld and Nicolson, 1968), p. 374.

135. See K. S. Gapp, "The Universal Famine under Claudius," *HTR* 28 (1935): 261.

> towards the conquered people in matters of cult and administration, in questions of economy and taxation it was rather severe.[136]

It is estimated that the Persian kings collected the equivalent of twenty million darics a year in taxes. According to Herodotus (3.91), the fifth satrapy (which included *Eber Nahar,* "across the river,"[137] that is, Syria and Palestine) paid 350 talents, which was the smallest amount paid by the western satrapies. This represented but 2.5 percent of the treasury's total annual income of 14,560 talents. Salo Baron notes: "Moreover, Palestine seems to have been free from contributions in kind which, in many other satrapies, equaled or exceeded the monetary payments."[138] Nonetheless, the taxes were still a heavy burden on the Jews.

Incalculable wealth poured into the Persian coffers. As Olmstead observes: "Little of this vast sum was ever returned to the satrapies. It was the custom to melt down the gold and silver and to pour it into jars which were then broken and the bullion stored."[139] Maurice Meuleau notes:

> At Susa alone, Alexander acquired 9,000 talents of coined gold (about 270 tons), but 40,000 talents of silver (about 1,200 tons), were found uselessly heaped up in piles of ingots. The draining-away and disappearance of precious metals were such that men found greater and greater difficulty in paying the cash portion of their taxes, to the extent that excessive cash borrowing was a general plague.[140]

The recent study by Stolper of the Murashu Archive undermines the thesis that excessive taxation produced a scarcity of cash in the overall economy of Achaemenid Babylonia. But it did concentrate wealth in the hands of the royalty and of entrepreneurs like Murashu and Sons who could take advantage of the situation. Stolper concludes:

> The crown and members of the political elite profited: so did the Murashu firm; the small farmers—or at least small-scale rentiers—did not. Those feudatories who leased their property to the firm drew income only from cheap land. Their economic status was precarious and deteriorating.[141]

136. Stern, *CHJ,* p. 113.

137. A. F. Rainey, "The Satrapy 'Beyond the River,' " *Australian Journal of Biblical Archaeology* 1 (1969): 51–78.

138. S. W. Baron, *A Social and Religious History of the Jews,* 2d ed. (Philadelphia: Jewish Publication Society, 1952), 1: 162.

139. A. T. Olmstead, *History of the Persian Empire* (Chicago: University of Chicago Press, 1948), p. 298.

140. Meuleau, "Mesopotamia under Persian Rule," p. 370.

141. Stolper, *Entrepreneurs,* p. 151. Stolper (p. 154) observes: "In both these matters, tenure and

A study by Waldo Dubberstein reveals that under Darius I, Artaxerxes I, and the first years of Darius II, the price of dates doubled.[142] One of the reasons for this sharp inflation is explained by Muhammed Dandamayev as follows:

> It should also be borne in mind that large areas of fertile land had become property either of the Persians, or of military colonists. This resulted in a sharp increase in the quantity of people alienated from property and means of production, and probably served as one of the causes which brought about the 50% rise in prices for different articles of consumption noted by Dubberstein in Babylonia under the Persian rule.[143]

As a striking parallel to the dire economic conditions of Judah illustrated in Nehemiah 5, Dandamayev further observes:

> Documents from Babylonia show that many inhabitants of this satrapy too had to mortgage their fields and orchards to get silver for the payment of taxes to the king. In many cases they were unable to redeem their property, and became landless hired labourers; sometimes they were compelled to give away their children into slavery. According to some Egyptian data, the taxation was so heavy that the peasants escaped to the cities, but were arrested by the nomarchs and brought back by force.[144]

To pay the taxes and survive many of the poor had to borrow, often at exorbitant interest rates. In the Persian period the rates rose sharply from 20 percent under Cyrus and Cambyses up to 40 to 50 percent at the end of the fifth century B.C. Texts of the House of Murashu during this period indicate rates of about 40 percent.[145]

When Nehemiah rebuked the wealthy citizens of Jerusalem (Neh. 5:11), he charged them: "Give back to them . . . the usury you are charging them—the hundredth part of the money, grain, new wine and oil" (NIV). The Hebrew *mēʾâ* literally means the "hundred" pieces of silver but in the context must mean one percent, that is per month, or

---

commercial practice, Achaemenid administration put new faces on old patterns. The Murashu texts point to some results of this policy: a tendency toward concentration of wealth, and a tendency toward relative impoverishment at the lowest ranks of the state-controlled agricultural sector, despite indications of overall prosperity in the province."

142. W. H. Dubberstein, "Comparative Prices in Later Babylonia," *AJSL* 56 (1939): 20–43.

143. M. Dandamayev, "Achaemenid Babylonia," in *Ancient Mesopotamia*, ed. I. M. Diakonoff (Moscow: Nauka, 1969), p. 309.

144. Ibid., p. 308.

145. R. P. Maloney, "Usury and Restrictions on Interest-Taking in the Ancient Near East," *CBQ* 36 (1974): 1–20; see idem, "Usury in Greek, Roman and Rabbinic Thought," *Traditio* 27 (1971): 79–109.

as the Vulgate translates it *centesiman pecuniae.* But even this relatively low rate of 12 percent per annum could result in unpayable debts.

The Old Testament passages prohibiting the giving of loans at interest were not intended to prohibit commercial loans, but rather the charging of interest so as to make a profit from the helplessness of one's neighbors.[146] Josephus (*Antiquities* 4.266) explained:

> Let it not be permitted to lend upon usury to any Hebrew either meat or drink; for it is not just to draw a revenue from the misfortunes of a fellow-countryman. Rather, in succouring his distress, ye should reckon as gain the gratitude of such persons and the recompense which God has in store for an act of generosity.

Among the Elephantine papyri we find two loan contracts (dated 456 and 455 B.C.), in which Jews lend each other money at interest. There is also a letter from Makkibanit, which speaks of a loan without interest: "Give to him readily and have no regrets when you do so, for in return the Lord your God will bless you in all your deeds and in all your undertakings."[147] The later Jewish rabbis permitted loans at interest to Gentiles but condemned usury among fellow Jews as tantamount to denying God and to the shedding of blood. Moneylenders were classed together with gamblers, pigeon trainers, and Sabbath traders, and were excluded from serving as witnesses (Sanhedrin 3.3).[148]

Nehemiah (5:7) excoriated the wealthy: "You are exacting usury from your own countrymen!" He urged the cessation of such opportunistic "usury" (5:10). Moreover, he urged the return of the forfeited lands, houses, and money: "Give back to them immediately their fields, vineyards, olive groves and houses, and also the usury you are charging" (v. 11).

Nehemiah sacrificed what was rightfully his to help those in need. In verse 10 he reveals that he, his brothers, and his men had been "lending the people money and grain," presumably without interest. Nehemiah proclaims: "Moreover, from the twentieth year of King Artaxerxes, when I was appointed to be their governor in the land of Judah, until his thirty-second year—twelve years—neither I nor my brothers ate the food allotted to the governor" (v. 14).

146. E. Neufeld, "The Prohibition Against Loans at Interest in Ancient Hebrew Laws," *HUCA* 26 (1955): 355–412; J. Sutherland, "Usury: God's Forgotten Doctrine," *Crux* 18 (1982): 9–14.

147. Porten, *Archives,* p. 271.

148. It is one of the supreme ironies of medieval history that the Old Testament passages against usury were used by the church to prohibit Christians from loaning money, thus opening the door for Jews to become the moneylenders of Europe. See J. T. Noonan, "Authority, Usury and Contraception," *Insight* (1967): 29–42; B. Nelson, *The Idea of Usury* (Chicago: University of Chicago Press, 1969).

The tomb of Artaxerxes I. (The Oriental Institute, University of Chicago)

Provincial governors normally assessed the people in the provinces for their support. But Nehemiah bent over backwards; his course of action was exceptional. What was normal is outlined in verse 15: "But the earlier governors—those preceding me—placed a heavy burden on the people and took forty shekels of silver from them in addition to food and wine. Their assistants also lorded it over the people." The Hebrew text is not clear as to what period of time the forty shekels were for; most interpreters follow the Vulgate, which reads "daily."

Instead of taking the opportunities afforded by his position to acquire wealth, Nehemiah and his men dedicated themselves to public service (v. 16). Far from extorting food from his subjects, Nehemiah generously shared his own supplies with 150 officials and Jews (v. 17). Nehemiah was a model leader in many different ways.[149]

Death and Burial of Artaxerxes I

After a long reign of forty years, Artaxerxes I died of natural causes—a relative rarity among Achaemenid kings—in the winter of 425/424, probably in December 424. His wife, Damaspia, was said to have died the same day. He was buried at Naqsh-i Rustam, probably in the second tomb from the left.[150]

149. See E. Yamauchi, "Nehemiah, A Model Leader," in *A Spectrum of Thought: Essays in Honor of Dennis F. Kinlaw,* ed. M. L. Peterson (Wilmore, Ky.: Francis Asbury, 1982), pp. 171–80. See also C. J. Barber, *Nehemiah and the Dynamics of Effective Leadership* (Neptune, N.J.: Loizeaux Brothers, 1976); R. H. Seume, *Nehemiah: God's Builder* (Chicago: Moody, 1978); D. K. Campbell, *Nehemiah: Man in Charge* (Wheaton: Victor, 1979).

150. For the confused situation that followed Artaxerxes I, in which there were several rivals for the throne, see D. M. Lewis, *Sparta and Persia* (Leiden: Brill, 1977), pp. 70–78.

7

Susa

The Capital of Elam

Susa (Old Persian *Çūšā*, Elamite and Akkadian *šu-ša-an*, Hebrew *šūšan*, Greek *Sousa*) was the major city of Elam, the area of southwestern Iran. Susa was located in a fertile alluvial plain 150 miles north of the Persian Gulf. The region, which is called Khuzestan today, was the area known as Elam in antiquity. Elam covered an area of 42,000 square miles—about the size of Denmark. Susa was within easy access of southern Mesopotamia and its history was inextricably linked with that region.[1]

1. L. Le Breton, "The Early Periods at Susa, Mesopotamian Relations," *Iraq* 19 (1957): 79–124. For general accounts of Elam, see W. Hinz, *Das Reich Elam* (Stuttgart: W. Kohlhammer, 1964); idem, *The Lost World of Elam* (New York: New York University Press, 1972); P. Amiet, *Elam* (Auvers-sur-Oise: Archée Editeur, 1966); F. Vallat, *Suse et l'Elam* (Paris: Editions A.D.P.F., 1980). It should be noted that the only history of Persia that exists for the third and second millennia B.C. is that of Elam. The classic work, G. Cameron, *History of Early Iran* (Chicago: University of Chicago Press, 1936; Westport: Greenwood, 1968 reprint), has been superseded by the relevant chapters on early Elamite history in the revised *Cambridge Ancient History,* eds. I. E. S. Edwards, C. J. Gadd, and N. G. L. Hammond, rev. ed. (Cambridge: Cambridge University Press, 1971–1975). See W. Hinz, "Persia *c.* 2400–1800 B.C.," in *CAH,* vol. 1, part 2, chapter 23; idem, "Persia *c.* 1800–1550 B.C.," in *CAH,* vol. 2, part 1,

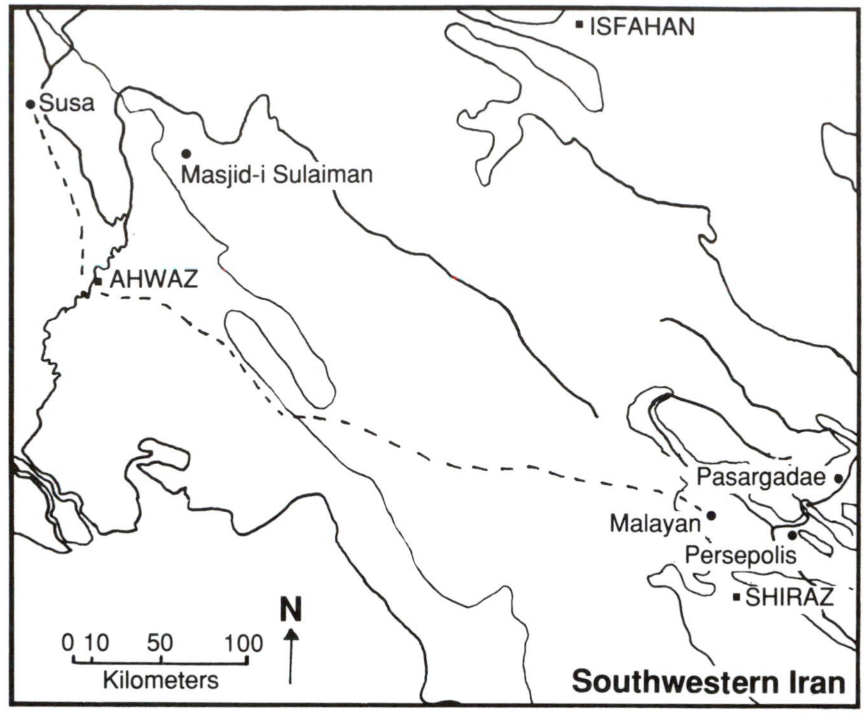

The area of Susa is watered by several rivers. The Kerkheh River flows west of Susa. The Assyrians called it *Uqnū* (lapis lazuli). The Greeks called it the Choaspes, and knew that Cyrus drank only from its waters (Herodotus 1.188). To the east of Susa flows the Ab-e-Diz, which has at times been linked to the Kerkheh by a channel. The Elamites and Assyrians called it the Idide; the Greeks named it the Koprates. Still further east is the Karun River into which the Ab-e-Diz flows. The Greeks called it the Pasitigris. The Karun River flows into the Persian Gulf. Susa itself is located on the east bank of the Shaᶜur. This channel was called the Ulai, the Eulaios in Greek.[2] At some point the name *Eulaios* was eventually extended to include the course of the Karun.[3]

During the winter the area is pleasant and Susa was used then as a residence by the Achaemenid kings. Rains in January and February cre-

chapter 7; R. Labat, "Elam *c.* 1600–1200 B.C.," in *CAH,* vol. 2, part 2, chapter 29; idem, "Elam and Western Persia/*c.*/1200–1000 B.C.," in *CAH,* vol. 2, part 2, chapter 32.

2. Hinz, *Das Reich Elam,* p. 16.

3. J. J. Finkelstein, "Mesopotamia," *JNES* 21 (1962): 89.

ate lush pastures for the shepherds. The area, however, is intolerably hot for six months of the year, particularly in July and August when temperatures reach 140 degrees Fahrenheit. Strabo (15.3.10) notes that snakes and lizards crossing the street at noon in the summer heat were roasted to death. The Elamite texts from Persepolis translated by Richard Hallock record only five references of travel to Susa from June through October, compared to forty-two references for the rest of the year.

Biblical References

Elam, the eponymous ancestor of the Elamites, is mentioned in Genesis 10:22 as a son of Shem, a reference that cannot mean the Elamites were Semites but only that there were Semites in the region. One of the kings of the east who attacked Palestine during Abraham's day was named Chedorlaomer, which is an Elamite name (Gen. 14:1).[4]

Elam is mentioned as a people who were used by Jehovah to chastise Babylon (Isa. 21:2) and Jerusalem (Isa. 22:6), but who were in turn punished by him (Jer. 25:25; 49:34–39; Ezek. 32:24).

Daniel (Dan. 8:2) saw himself in a vision in the citadel at Susa by the Ulai Canal; he also heard a man's voice from the Ulai (Dan. 8:16). Susa was the site of the story of Esther in the days of Ahasuerus (Xerxes). The Book of Esther contains numerous references to the *bīrâ* (citadel) of Susa (1:2, 5; 2:3, 5, 8; 3:15; 8:14; 9:6, 11, 12).

Ezra 4:9–10 refers to the men of Susa (KJV, "Susanchites") who were deported to Samaria by Ashurbanipal (KJV, "Asnappar"). Nehemiah (Neh. 1:1) was at Susa when he received news of the desolate state of Jerusalem's walls. Although Susa is not mentioned in the New Testament, some of the Jewish pilgrims on the day of Pentecost came to Jerusalem from Elam (Acts 2:9; compare Isa. 11:11).

Classical References

When the Ionians sought Spartan help during their rebellion against Darius they displayed a map, and pointed out: "therein, on the Choaspes (yonder it is), lies that Susa where lives the great king, and there are the storehouses of his wealth; take that city, and then you need not fear to challenge Zeus for riches" (Herodotus 5.49). Aeschylus (*Persai* 730) recounted at the news of Xerxes' defeat of Salamis: "Aye,

4. Hinz, *Das Reich Elam*, p. 9. The name means "the goddess Lagamar is a protectress." Compare E. A. Speiser, *Genesis* (Garden City: Doubleday, 1964), p. 107.

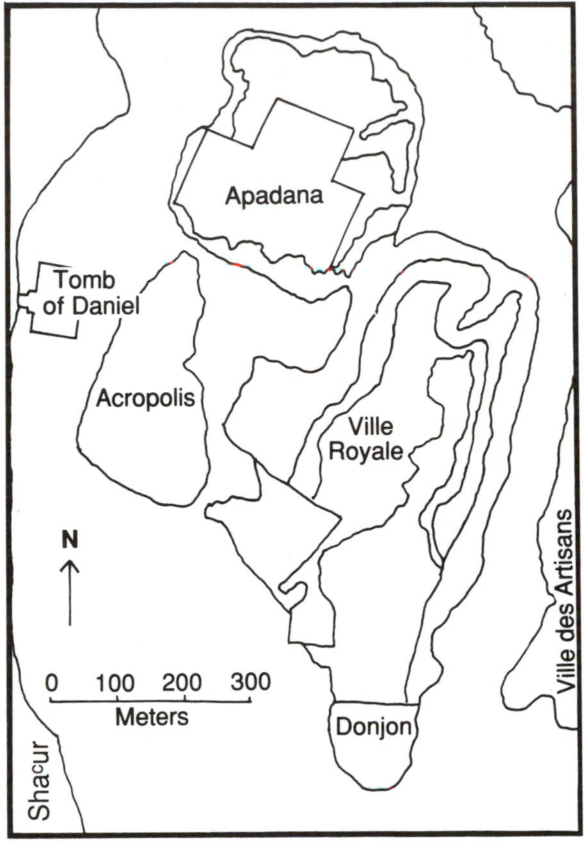

The mounds of Susa.
(After R. North,
Guide to Biblical Iran)

so that for this reason the whole city of Susa groans at its desolation." Strabo (15.3.3) reported that the Persians "adorned the palace at Susa more than any other."

Because Susa was the eastern terminal of the Royal Road from Sardis, many notable Greeks appeared at the Persian royal court of Susa, including Histiaeus of Miletus (Herodotus 5.30), Demaratus of Sparta (Herodotus 7.3), and Callias of Athens (Herodotus 7.151).

The Mounds

There are four major mounds at Susa, which the French excavators call Acropolis, Apadana, Ville Royale, and Ville des Artisans. The first three form a diamond-shaped area with sides about 1,000 meters (3,280 feet) long.

The Acropolis is the most important of the mounds for the earlier Elamite eras. It was settled at the earliest date, and has been the most extensively excavated. The Acropolis rises steeply at its highest point 38 meters above the waters of the Sha'ur. The southern part averages about 22 meters (72 feet) above the plain. The remains of stratified deposits are 25 meters (82 feet) deep. A castle built by French excavators in 1898 now stands on the northern point of the Acropolis.

North of the Acropolis is the Apadana, which is so called because the Achaemenids built their audience hall there. This was also the location of the palatial structures built by Darius and Xerxes.

To the east of the Acropolis and the Apadana is the long hill where merchants, artisans, and court functionaries lived. It covers an area of 550,000 square meters. At its southeastern corner is the area called the *Donjon* or "the keep." The fifteen strata of the Ville Royale extend from the Islamic to the Elamite eras.

To the east of the Ville Royale beyond the Tudela Valley is a hill where an Achaemenid village was excavated. This was an area inhabited by tradesmen.

Susa was occupied continuously from 3500 B.C. to the thirteenth century A.D. Today the modern village of Shush lies on the Sha'ur below the slopes of the Acropolis.

Aerial view of Susa. (Courtesy of The Oriental Institute, University of Chicago)

Apadana and the excavators' castle.

Excavations

The famous Jewish traveler Benjamin of Tudela (Spain) visited the site in A.D. 1165 and observed the Jewish community of Shush, noting that there were seven thousand Jews and fourteen synagogues there.

In 1850 the Englishmen Harry L. Churchill and William K. Loftus, who were on a commission to settle the boundary between the Ottoman Empire and Persia, visited the mounds of Shush. It was Loftus who correctly identified the site as ancient Susa. Opening up a trial trench in 1853/1854, Loftus uncovered the Apadana or hypostyle audience hall of the Achaemenid period.

Marcel and Jeanne Dieulafoy worked on the Apadana from 1884 to 1886, securing for the Louvre objects such as the archer frieze.[5] Jeanne Dieulafoy reported:

> Marcel would have set guards over the trenches, but the bravest of the workmen shut themselves up in the tomb of Daniel immediately after sunset and neither silver nor gold would tempt them to face the divas [demons], the fairies, the enchanters, and above all the thieves, who peopled the tumuli.[6]

In 1895 France concluded a treaty with the Persian Shah, Nasr-Eddin, which gave France exclusive excavation rights in Persia along

5. A. Parrot, *Le Musée du Louvre et la Bible* (Paris: Delachaux et Niestlé, 1957), pp. 125–35.
6. Cited by R. H. Dyson, "Early Work on the Acropolis at Susa," *Exped.* 10.4 (1968): 26.

with half of the finds. When the treaty was renewed in 1900 with the new Shah, Mozaffer-Eddin, the French were given the rights to all objects from the area of Susa. Later the provision for an equal division of objects was restored.

The French have sponsored annual excavations at Susa from 1897 to the present except for the periods of the World Wars.[7] The first director from 1897 to 1912 was Jacques de Morgan, a mining engineer. Almost immediately the expedition made one of its most famous discoveries; during the 1901/1902 season, in the southern part of the Acropolis, de Morgan found the eight-foot-high basalt stele of Hammurabi's Code. In the next season another fragment of the code was found. The code was promptly published by Vincent Scheil, who was to contribute over a dozen volumes on the texts from Susa.

De Morgan trenched a large area in the southwestern part of the Acropolis. He also discovered the Stele of Naram-Sin and the Obelisk of Manishtusu. Unfortunately de Morgan's object was to remove as much earth as possible to recover monuments for the Louvre. He cleared long parallel trenches, descending in steps 5 meters deep and wide, using 300 to 400 workers (once 1,200) at a time. He estimated he could remove a square meter of earth per man per day. According to Robert Dyson,

> During the first season, the expedition had available fifteen mine wagons and, according to de Morgan's estimate, moved a total of about 18,000 cubic meters of earth. By 1905, fifty-nine wagons and 3,000 meters of tracks had been assembled at Susa.[8]

Roland de Mecquenem, who began as an architect in 1903, succeeded Morgan as director from 1913 to 1939. From 1927 on he was joined by Jamsheji M. Unvala, the son of a Parsee priest from India. They cleared the palace on the Apadana from 1909 to 1923. Mecquenem uncovered large areas in the Ville Royale, including the site of the Donjon, and worked in the north, south, and central part of the Acropolis. In the center Mecquenem found the temple of Nin Harsag

7. The official excavation reports have been issued in about fifty folio volumes under a variety of names: *Mémoires de la Délégation en Perse* (1–13), *Mémoires de la Mission Archéologique de Susiane* (14), *Mission Archéologique de Perse* (15), *Mémoires de la Mission Archéologique de Perse, Mission en Susiane* (16–28), and *Mémoires de la Mission Archéologique en Iran, Mission de Susiane* (29–46). For a detailed summary of the contents up to volume 36 (1954) and of other works on Susa, see L. van den Berghe, *Archéologie de l'Iran ancien* (Leiden: Brill, 1959), pp. 165–74. See ibid., pp. 71–83, for a brief history of the excavations. Provisional reports of recent excavations have appeared in *Iran, Syria,* and in the annual *Cahiers de la Délégation Archéologique Française en Iran* (*CDAFI*). Since 1979 the Iranian revolution and then the war between Iran and Iraq have halted all excavations.

8. Cited by Dyson, "Early Work," p. 27.

and the large bronze statue of Queen Napir-Asu, weighing almost two tons.

During the early twentieth century the area of Susa was extremely dangerous, imperiled by fighting between the Seghevend and Lours tribes, and by brigands. The excavators' castle was often seized by armed forces, and much blood was shed around it.[9] It was Mecquenem's custom to leave France in December, arriving at Susa after a month's travel, and then to conduct excavations until April before the hot season began. It was only on his last visit in 1947 that he took a plane.

From 1945 the expedition was directed by Roman Ghirshman, who opened new areas. He began work in the northern part of the Ville Royale, uncovering settlements from the late third millennium B.C. to the Islamic period. In the early 1950s Ghirshman uncovered an Achaemenid village in the Ville des Artisans, and also an important cemetery dated 300 B.C. to A.D. 200.[10] While he was working at Susa, Ghirshman also cleared the important Middle Elamite site of Choga Zanbil (ancient Dur Untash), located thirty miles southeast of Susa. Even after his "official" retirement in 1967, Ghirshman returned to dig at Masjid-i Sulaiman.[11]

In the 1960s Marie-Joseph Stève and Hermann Gasche conducted extensive work on the west-central area of the Acropolis and uncovered important structures of the third millennium B.C.[12] In the 1970s Jean Perrot and his colleagues uncovered sensational finds from the Achaemenid period in the area of the Apadana.

The only exception to the work of the French has been a sondage in the southern part of the Acropolis by the American, Robert Dyson, in 1954.

Inscriptions

From approximately 3000 B.C. the Elamites wrote in a pictographic script known as Proto-Elamite. The latest of these texts dates to the time of Hammurabi. More than 1,400 such texts have been recovered

9. R. de Mecquenem, "Les fouilleurs de Suse," *IA* 15 (1980): 26, 30, 35. This is a fascinating account that was published decades after the author's death.

10. R. Ghirshman, *Village perse-achéménide, Mémoires* 36 (Paris: Presses Universitaires de France, 1954).

11. See P. Amiet, "Sommaire de l'activité du Prof. R. Ghirshman entre 1946 et 1967 à Suse et en Susiane," *IA* 15 (1980): 107–16; L. Vanden Berghe, "Roman Ghirshman (1895–1979)," *IA* 15 (1980): xi–xv.

12. M.-J Stève and H. Gasche, *L'Acropole de Suse,* Mémoires 46 (Leiden: Brill, 1971).

from Susa, nineteen from Tepe Sialk,[13] and six from Tepe Yahya, a site in southeast Iran.[14] The most important Proto-Elamite text is a treaty between the Elamite king Khita and Naram-Sin of Agade (2280 B.C.), which gives us a list of the Elamite gods. Despite attempts at decipherment by Walther Hinz and others, the Proto-Elamite script is imperfectly understood.[15]

The Elamite language was later written in a cuneiform script. Numerous inscriptions exist from the Middle Elamite era (thirteenth–twelfth centuries B.C.), including six thousand inscriptions on bricks from Choga-Zanbil. Then there is a blank period of four hundred years until the seventh century. The Achaemenids regularly used Elamite for their royal inscriptions and for accounting purposes as in the Persepolis Treasury and Fortification tablets (see chapter 5 on cuneiform sources). From the Neo-Babylonian period we have three hundred economic texts, twenty-five letters, and one astrological text in Elamite.[16]

The Third Millennium B.C.

The earliest pottery of the area is the Susiana A–E series from Djafferabad and Djowi north of Susa dating from 5000 B.C. The earliest pottery (3500 B.C.) from Susa itself comes from a depth of 11 meters (36 feet) on the Acropolis from a cemetery with over 2,000 burials. This is a brilliantly designed pottery decorated with the curved horns of an ibex and geometric patterns.[17]

The earliest excavators distinguished only between Susa I and Susa II (from 2800 B.C.) pottery. Much of the material from the earlier excavations could not be dated accurately. Louis Le Breton broke this down to a series from A to D: A dates to 3600 B.C., B to 3500, C to 3200, and D to 2800.[18] The earliest copper appears in 3000 B.C. From this period comes

13. R. Ghirshman, *Fouillès de Sialk prés de Kashan* (Paris: Geuthner, 1938–1939); E. Yamauchi, "Tepe Sialk," in *The New International Dictionary of Biblical Archaeology*, eds. E. M. Blaiklock and R. K. Harrison (Grand Rapids: Zondervan, 1983), p. 447.

14. C. C. Lamberg-Karlovsky, "The Proto-Elamite Settlement at Tepe Yaḥyā," *Iran* 10 (1971): 87–94; C. C. and Martha Lamberg-Karlovsky, "An Early City in Iran," *Scientific American* 224 (June 1971): 102–11.

15. W. Hinz, "Zur Entzifferung der elamischen Strichschrift," *IA* 2 (1962): 1–21; W. Brice, "The Writing System of the Proto-Elamite Account Tablets of Susa," *BJRL* 45 (1962): 15–39; P. Meriggi, *La Scrittura Proto-Elamica* (Rome: Accademia Nazionale dei Lincei, 1971).

16. H. H. Paper, *The Phonology and Morphology of Royal Achaemenid Elamite* (Ann Arbor: University of Michigan Press, 1955); E. Reiner, "The Elamite Language," *Handbuch der Orientalistik* (Leiden: Brill, 1969), 1 Abt., 2 Band, 1–2, pp. 54–67.

17. A. Parrot, *Sumer* (London: Thames and Hudson, 1960), pp. 60–63; Amiet, *Elam*, p. 41, fig. 13.

18. For the most recent analysis, see E. Carter, "The Susa Sequence—3000–2000 B.C.: Susa, "Ville Royale I," *AJA* 83 (1979): 451–54; idem, "Excavations in Ville Royale I at Susa: The Third Millennium B.C. Occupation," *CDAFI* 11 (1980): 11–134.

a masterpiece of a powerful, muscular lion-headed monster in white magnesite measuring only 8 centimeters (about 3 inches) high.[19]

In the third millennium B.C. the history of Susa and the area of Elam was inextricably connected with that of Sumer. Elam is first mentioned in Sumerian texts around 2700: Enmebaragisi of Kish "carried off the arms of the land of Elam as booty." This hostile action was to characterize relations between the areas. Eannatum of Lagash attacked Elam around 2400.

There were numerous contacts between Elam and Mesopotamia during the reigns of the Semitic Akkadian period of Sargon of Agade (2371–2316) and his successors Rimush (2315–2307), Manishtusu (2306–2292), Naram-Sin (2291–2255), and Shar-kali-sharri (2254–2230). Sargon conquered Susa, which under Akkadian influence became an important city. A copy of the treaty signed between Naram-Sin and Khita of Elam was found in Susa. Excavators have uncovered a granary on the Acropolis, dated to the reign of Shar-kali-sharri, similar to those of the Indus River civilization with which the Akkadians had numerous trade contacts.

Puzur-In-Shushinak, who was the governor of Susa as a vassal under Naram-Sin, showed increasing independence as Shar-kali-sharri was overwhelmed by the Gutian barbarians from the Zagros Mountains. His constructions on the Acropolis and numerous inscriptions in Akkadian and Proto-Elamite have been found.

Shulgi (2095–2048), the Sumerian king of Ur, conquered Susa in his twenty-eighth year and installed a non-Elamite governor there. But he placated the Elamites by building a temple for In-Shushinak (lord of Susa). The foundations of this building, and of a temple he built for Nin Harsag, have been traced in the center of the Acropolis. Ibbi-Sin (2029–2006), however, was attacked not only by the Amorites from the west but by the Elamites, who sacked the city of Ur.

In the early second millennium B.C. Elam was governed by the Simash Dynasty (until 1850), and then by the Eparti Dynasty. The period from 1850 to 1550 is known as the epoch of the Sukkal-makh (or grand regent), who was succeeded by his brother rather than by his son. The main documents of this period are eight hundred legal and commercial texts in Akkadian, mainly from Susa. The sole historical document from this period is an Elamite text of Siwe-palar-khuppak, who was defeated in 1764 by Hammurabi.

The most important remains at Susa from this period come from Ghirshman's work on the Ville Royale. From the period of Kutir-Nahhunte the excavators uncovered vast dwellings of an Elamite lord,

19. Parrot, *Sumer*, p. 79.

Temti-wartash.[20] This grandee received silver payments from Dilmun (the island of Bahrain in the Persian Gulf).[21] From the seventeenth century comes a large house with jars full of exercise tablets, indicating that it was used as a school. The most striking discoveries from the fourteenth century are figurines of nude goddesses and votive beads depicting nude couples promoting fertility through ritual copulation.[22]

The Kassites not only ended the Old Babylonian dynasty but must have also overrun Elam.[23] The Kassite king Kurigalzu II (circa 1330) conquered Susa. There is a blank in Elamite documents from 1500 to 1300 B.C.

The Middle Elamite Era

The apogee of Elamite culture was reached in the Middle Elamite period (1300–1100) with a succession of energetic kings: Untash-Gal (1266–1245), Shutruk-Nahhunte (fl. 1200), Kutir-Nahhunte (fl. 1150), and Shilkhak-In-Shushinak (fl. 1130).

Untash-Gal defeated the Kassite Kashtiliash III and carried off his protective deity to Susa. A broken, but still massive, bronze statue of his queen Napir-Asu was found in the center of the Acropolis. The four-foot-high monument weighs almost two tons and is the largest metal statue found in the Near East.[24]

Untash-Gal's greatest monument is the ziggurat that he erected at Choga-Zanbil. Excavated by Ghirshman, it is one of the best-preserved ziggurats with three of the original five stories intact.[25]

It was Shutruk-Nahhunte and his son Kutir-Nahhunte who around 1160 brought an end to Kassite rule in Babylonia. Shutruk-Nahhunte removed from Sippar the Stele of Naram-Sin and the Hammurabi Code, and probably removed from Kish the Obelisk of Manishtusu. He installed his son as ruler over Babylonia. To the Babylonians their worst crime was the removal of the god Marduk from Babylon to Susa.

Shilkhak-In-Shushinak was the most brilliant of these kings. His

20. Amiet, *Elam*, p. 325, fig. 244. For interpretations of the second-millennium strata, see M.-J. Stève, H. Gasche, and L. de Meyer, "La Susiane au deuxième millénaire," *IA* 15 (1980): 49–107.

21. See E. Yamauchi's review of S. H. Ali Al-Khalifa and M. Rice, eds., *Bahrain through the Ages*, in *NEASB* n.s. 28 (1987): 78–83.

22. Amiet, *Elam*, pp. 328–29. For the use of sexual coitus to promote fertility in sacred marriages or sacred prostitution, see S. N. Kramer, *The Sacred Marriage Rite* (Bloomington: Indiana University Press, 1969); E. Yamauchi, "Cultic Prostitution—A Case Study in Cultural Diffusion," in *Orient and Occident*, ed. H. Hoffner (Kevelaer: Butzon and Bercker, 1973), pp. 213–22.

23. See E. Yamauchi, "Kassites," in *NIDBA*, pp. 276–78.

24. Parrot, *Sumer*, pp. 61–64.

25. Ibid., pp. 398–99.

Female figurine from In-Shushinak's temple. (Metropolitan Museum of Art, Rogers Fund, 1951 [51.159])

conquests extended to the island of Bushire and to the interior area of Shiraz. Numerous inscriptions attest to his building activities on the Acropolis. A unique bronze object from his reign, the *Sit-Shamshi* (sunrise), depicts a ritual with two nude figures performing ablutions between two staged towers.[26]

Middle Elamite remains have also been found at Malyan, now identified by an inscription as the important site of Anshan.[27] This large site of five hundred acres is located twenty-seven miles west of Persepolis and twenty-nine miles north of Shiraz.

The collapse of the Elamites coincided with the rise of the energetic Babylonian ruler, Nebuchadnezzar I (1124–1103), who recovered the

26. Ibid., pp. 332–33.

27. E. Reiner, "Tall-i Malyān, Epigraphic Finds, 1971–72," *Iran* 12 (1974): 176–77. W. Sumner, "Excavations at Tall-i Malyan, 1971–72," *Iran* 12 (1974): 155–75; idem, "Excavations at Tall-i Malyan (Anshan) 1974," *Iran* 14 (1976): 103–13; idem, "Excavations at Tal-e Malyān: A Summary of Three Seasons' Results," in *Proceedings of the IIIrd Annual Symposium on Archaeological Research in Iran*, ed. F. Bagherzadeh (Tehran: Iranian Centre for Archaeological Research, 1975), pp. 157–61; E. Carter and M. Stolper, "Middle Elamite Malyan," *Exped.* 18/2 (1976): 38–42.

statue of Marduk from Susa. The Elamites disappear from historical sources until they are mentioned by the Assyrian king Shamshi-Adad V, three hundred years later.

The Neo-Elamite Era

There was a brief Elamite renaissance from 720 to 640, when Ashurbanipal brutally destroyed Susa. A small chapel on the southeast Acropolis built by Shutruk Nahhunte II (717–699), and dating to this renaissance period, has been uncovered.[28]

The imperialistic Assyrians were the dominant power in the Near East during the eighth and seventh centuries. During this era the Elamites generally supported the Chaldeans of southern Mesopotamia in their struggle to gain independence.[29]

The Elamites and the Chaldeans fought the Assyrians in the Battle of Der in 720 between the Tigris River and the Zagros Mountains. There are three versions of this battle. In one Sargon II, the Assyrian king, claimed victory; in a second version Merodach-Baladan, the Chaldean leader, claimed credit for the victory; and a third story, which is the relatively objective Babylonian Chronicle, gave the palm of victory to the Elamites.[30]

There was further conflict during the reign of Sennacherib (704–681). In 695 the Assyrian king sailed a fleet, manned with Phoenician and Cypriote sailors, down the Tigris River to the Persian Gulf and attacked Elamite territory. The Elamite king Hallushu counterattacked, took Sippar, and placed one of his followers on the throne of Babylon. In 689 the Elamites aided the Babylonians against the Assyrians at the Battle of Hallule on the Tigris.

Ashurbanipal's Destruction of Susa

Conflict between Elam and Assyria reached a climax during the reign of the last great Assyrian king, Ashurbanipal (668–627). At the

28. Amiet, *Elam*, p. 505, n. 380.

29. See E. Yamauchi, "Chaldea, Chaldeans," in *NIDBA*, pp. 123–25; R. Borger, "Der Aufstieg des Neubabylonischen Reiches," *JCS* 19 (1965): 59–77.

30. A. K. Grayson, "Problematical Battles in Mesopotamian History," in *Studies in Honor of Benno Landsberger*, eds. H. G. Güterbock and T. Jacobsen (Chicago: University of Chicago Press, 1965), pp. 340–41. For a general survey of Assyrian history, see H. W. F. Saggs, *The Might That Was Assyria* (London: Sidgwick and Jackson, 1984). This was the same Merodach-Baladan who sent a solicitous message to Hezekiah (Isa. 39:1; 2 Kings 20:12).

beginning of the latter's reign relations were amicable. In fact, the Assyrians sent grain to keep the Elamites from starving. But then in 653 B.C. a usurper (named *Tept-Humban* in Elamite, *Teumman* in Akkadian) seized power.[31] Five princes and sixty other members of the Elamite royal family fled to Ashurbanipal. After hunting down Teumman, Ashurbanipal had his head cut off, slashed it, spat on it, and had it hung as a gruesome trophy on a tree even while he and the queen enjoyed a banquet.[32]

When Ashurbanipal's brother Shamash-Shum-Ukin, the king of Babylon, revolted in 652, the Elamites aided the rebels. The rebellion was finally crushed in 648. When the puppet king of Elam later rebelled, Ashurbanipal decided to devastate Susa (640). An Assyrian army marched into Elam and wreaked havoc. "His soldiers trod the paths of secret groves into which no stranger had ever been permitted to enter, and set them on fire." In his inscription the king proclaimed:

> I broke their gods, appeasing the heart of the lord of lords. His gods, his goddesses, his goods, his property, the people small and great I carried off to Assyria. Sixty double-hours of ground within Elam I laid waste, scattering salt and tares thereon.[33]

The inhabitants of Susa who were deported were among those who were settled by Ashurbanipal in Samaria according to Ezra 4:9–10. The dead were cut up and fed to the dogs, the swine, the wolves, the vultures, and the fish of the deep. The Assyrians even opened the tombs, and took bones to Assyria. Ashurbanipal declared, "I put restlessness on their ghosts, I deprived them of food offerings and libations of water."

A statue of the goddess Nana, whom the Elamites had taken from Uruk, was returned to her home, and In-Shushinak, the god of Susa, and thirty-two royal statues, were taken to Mesopotamia. So thoroughly did the Assyrians dismantle the ziggurat of Susa that excavators only recently have recognized its location in the blank area on the Acropolis between the temple of In-Shushinak and the temple of Ninhursag.

Silence again envelopes Elamite history until the Neo-Babylonian

31. A. K. Grayson, "The Chronology of the Reign of Ashurbanipal," *ZA* 70 (1980): 233, 241. For Assyrian reliefs of their conflicts with the Elamites, see A. Parrot, *The Arts of Assyria* (New York: Golden, 1961), pp. 42–43; Y. Yadin, *The Art of Warfare in Biblical Lands* (London: Weidenfeld and Nicolson, 1963), pp. 442–49; Compare J. Reade, "Elam and Elamites in Assyrian Sculpture," *AMI* 9 (1976): 97–105.

32. Parrot, *Arts of Assyria*, pp. 51–52.

33. R. Campbell Thompson, *The Prisms of Esarhaddon and of Ashurbanipal* (London: British Museum, 1931), p. 34.

period, when we learn that the first recorded act of Nabopolassar was the restoration of the Elamite gods from Uruk to Susa.[34]

Achaemenid Susa

Excavations by Ghirshman revealed that there had been a Persian settlement on the Ville des Artisans since the end of the seventh century. Tablets from Susa also indicate the infiltration into the area of those with Old Persian names.[35] When Cyrus captured Babylon in 539, according to the Cyrus Cylinder, he returned additional Elamite gods to Susa (compare Ezra 1:1–4). We have three hundred Elamite texts dealing with revenues from his reign.

In 521 B.C. Susa regained its importance when Darius made it the administrative capital of the Persian Empire. Thus it remained throughout the Achaemenid period. Darius built a great defensive wall about the palace and the city, possibly surrounded by a moat filled with waters of the Shaʿur. He built up a terrace 15 meters (49 feet) high—made with gravel enclosed within brick walls—which covered an Elamite graveyard and perhaps even Elamite palaces. It must have taken two or three years to transport the more than a million cubic meters of earth, gravel, and bricks for the terrace.[36] The terrace covered an area of 14 hectares (35 acres), which was as large as the one at Persepolis. The entire city of Susa, circumscribed by Darius's walls, extended over 70 hectares.

The Apadana and the Palace

On the Apadana to the north of the palace was the audience hall. It covered an area of ten thousand square meters. Its central hall was a hypostyle structure, that is, it had columns distributed throughout in six rows of six each. This was surrounded by columned porticos on all sides but the south. The fluted stone columns were topped with capitals decorated with bulls' heads.[37] Although none of the columns remain standing, they were probably sixty-five feet high.

34. E. Yamauchi, "Nabopolassar," in *NIDBA*, pp. 326–27.

35. Vallat, *Suse et l'Elam*, pp. 7–8; P. Amiet, "Elamites et Perses en Susiane," *Archaeologia* 43 (1971): 6–13.

36. D. Canal, "Travaux à la terrasse haute de l'acropole de Suse," *CDAFI* 9 (1978): 11–93. See also R. De Mecquenem, "The Achaemenid and Later Remains at Susa," in *A Survey of Persian Art*, ed. A. U. Pope (London: Oxford University Press, 1938), 1: 321–29.

37. J. M. Unvala, "The Palace of Darius the Great and the Apadana of Artaxerxes II in Susa," *BSOAS* 5 (1928–1930): 229–32; R. Ghirshman, "L'Apadana," *IA* 3 (1963): 148–54.

Bull-shaped protome which topped a column.

There were a series of three courts connected by passageways as well as storerooms on the periphery. The palatial complex covered an area of forty thousand square meters.[38] The palace incorporated features of Babylonian palaces, such as Nebuchadnezzar's at Babylon.[39] Ghirshman also compares a room with four pilasters with Elamite prototypes at Choga-Zanbil.[40] The west court of the Susa palace in turn served as the model for the Persian "residency" uncovered at Lachish in Judea.[41]

The palace and Apadana were decorated with molded glazed brick panels colorfully depicting griffins, winged bulls, and lions. Ann Farkas observes:

38. P. Amiet, "Quelques observations sur le palais de Darius à Suse," *Syria* 51 (1974): 166–73.

39. D. J. Wiseman, *Nebuchadrezzar and Babylon* (London: Oxford University Press, 1985), chapter 2; E. Yamauchi, "Palaces in the Biblical World," *NEASB* n.s. 23 (1984): 35–67; idem, "Palace," in *The International Standard Bible Encyclopedia*, ed. G. W. Bromiley (Grand Rapids: Eerdmans, 1986), 3: 629–32.

40. R. Ghirshman, "L'architecture élamite et ses traditions," *IA* 5 (1965): 93–102.

41. See D. Ussishkin, "Lachish," in *Encyclopedia of Archaeological Excavations in the Holy Land*, eds. M. Avi-Yonah and E. Stern (Jerusalem: Israel Exploration Society, 1977), 3: 745–46. W. F. Albright, *The Archaeology of Palestine* (Harmondsworth: Penguin, 1960), pp. 144–45, failed to recognize the Achaemenian parallel but pointed to Parthian parallels.

Bell-shaped base of a column.

> The rows of gaily robed Susian guards themselves testify that the Persians liked richly patterned fabrics for their costumes. . . . That the Persian palace at Susa was adorned with wall hangings is suggested by a passage in Esther (1:6).[42]

She also notes that Elamite texts of the Persian period excavated at Susa demonstrate that this city was a center for textile production. She observes that the tablets refer to garments of various styles and colors, even to carpets and bed coverings. One extraordinary example of a Persian carpet was preserved in the frozen Scythian tomb at Pazyryk.[43]

Palatial Inscriptions

In 1953 Erich Schmidt wrote: "As to the palace compound, although there is no doubt that it was founded by Darius I, a study of the reports dealing with this complex structure reveals that none of its parts have been attributed with certainty to his reign or to the reigns of his successors."[44]

The inscription known as the "Charter of Foundation" notes that from 518 to 512 Darius built a palace on the Apadana by employing materials and workmen from every part of his realm. Hinz declares: "The trilingual inscription of Darius I (522–486) recording the building of his palace at Susa must be reckoned among the most important docu-

42. A. Farkas, "Is There Anything Persian in Persian Art?" in *Ancient Persia: The Art of an Empire,* ed. D. Schmandt-Besserat (Malibu, Calif.: Undena, 1980), p. 20.

43. E. Yamauchi, *Foes from the Northern Frontier* (Grand Rapids: Baker, 1982), pp. 118–20.

44. E. Schmidt, *Persepolis* (Chicago: University of Chicago Press, 1953), 1: 30.

Glazed palmette decoration. (Metropolitan Museum of Art, acquired by exchange, Tehran Museum, 1948 [48.98.20 a-c])

ments contributing to our knowledge of the history of ancient civilization."[45] The Old Persian version of this text (DSf) reads as follows:

> This palace which I built at Susa, from afar its ornamentation was brought. Downward the earth was dug, until I reached rock in the earth. When the excavation had been made, then rubble was packed down, some 40 cubits in depth, another (part) 20 cubits in depth. On that rubble the palace was constructed.
>
> And that the earth was dug downward, and that the rubble was packed down, and that the sun-dried brick was molded, the Babylonian people—it did (these tasks).
>
> The cedar timber, this—a mountain by name Lebanon—from there was brought. The Assyrian people, it brought it to Babylon; from Babylon the Carians and the Ionians brought it to Susa. The *yakā*-timber was brought from Gandhara and from Carmania.
>
> The gold was brought from Sardis and from Bactria, which here was wrought. The precious stone lapis-lazuli and carnelian which was wrought here, this was brought from Sogdiana. The precious stone turquois, this was brought from Chorasmia, which was wrought here.
>
> The silver and the ebony were brought from Egypt. The ornamentation with which the wall was adorned, that from Ionia was brought. The ivory which was wrought here, was brought from Ethiopia and from Sind and from Arachosia.
>
> The stone columns which were wrought, a village by name Abiradu, in Elam—from there were brought. The stone-cutters who wrought the stone, those were Ionians and Sardians.

45. W. Hinz, "The Elamite Version of the Record of Darius's Palace at Susa," *JNES* 9 (1950): 1.

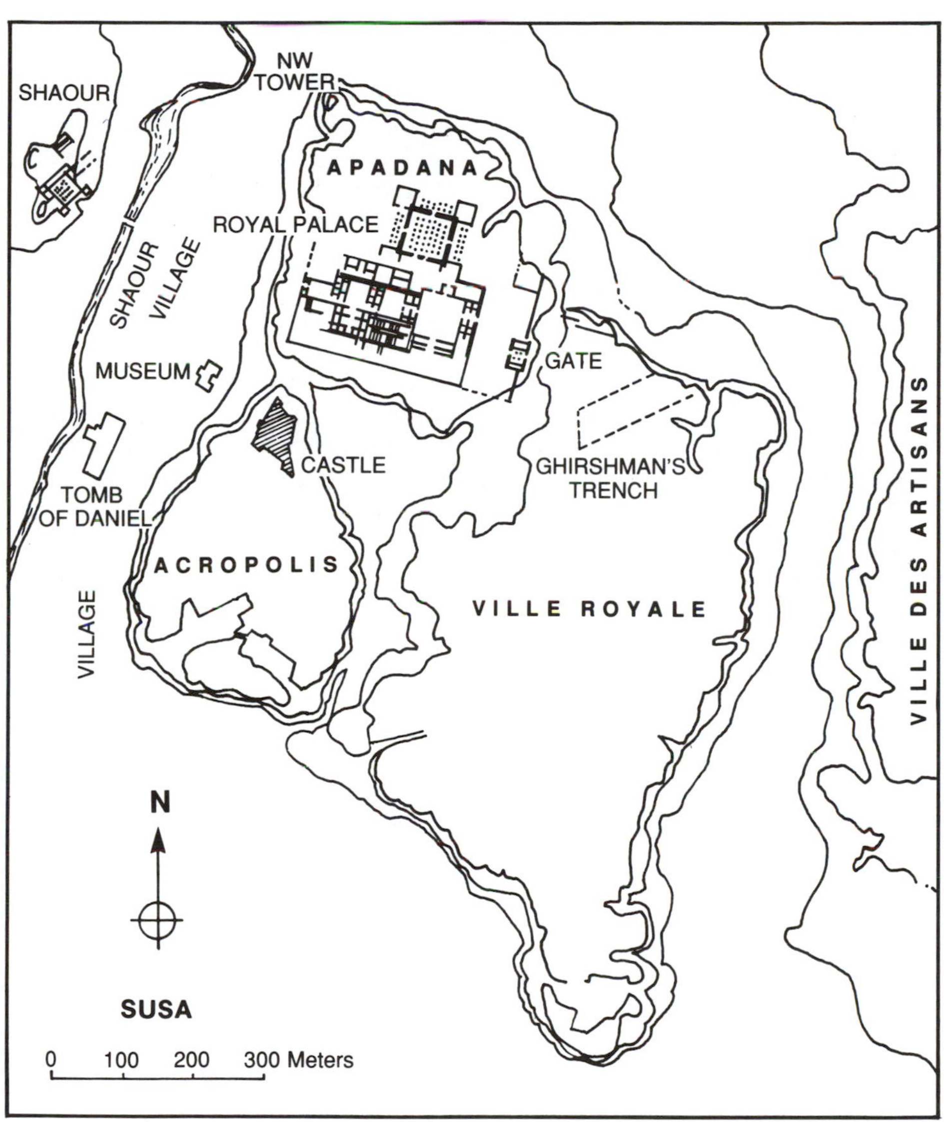

Structures cleared by the excavators. (Courtesy of F. Vallat, Centre National de la Recherche Scientifique)

The men who wrought the baked brick, those were Babylonians. The men who adorned the wall, those were Medes and Egyptians.

Saith Darius the King: At Susa a very excellent (work) was ordered, a

> very excellent (work) was (brought to completion). Me may Ahuramazda protect, and Hystaspes my father, and my country.[46]

The Old Persian copies of this inscription were not found in situ. But in 1970 two perfectly preserved stone tablets bearing copies of this text in Akkadian and in Elamite were discovered in place under the walls in the west court of the palace. The stones, measuring 33.6 by 33.6 by 8.7 centimeters (13 by 13 by 3½ inches), were inscribed on all six sides. The Elamite version (DSz) has fifty-six lines and the Akkadian version (DSaa) has forty lines.[47] These prove irrefutably that the palace and the Apadana to the north were conceived by Darius I.[48]

Minor differences indicate that the Old Persian version probably belonged to another building in the complex.[49] It also came from an earlier date when Darius's father Hystaspes was still alive; the new Akkadian and Elamite charters no longer mention him.[50] François Vallat would date the death of Hystaspes about 519/518.[51] He also observes that although DSf and DSz/DSaa were nearly contemporary, their lists of peoples who contributed to the building of Darius's palaces were not identical.

The Gate House

Ghirshman believed that the main entrance to the palace was to the west.[52] In spite of years of excavations in the area of the Apadana and palace it was not until the expeditions of the 1970s that a monumental gate house was uncovered 80 meters to the east of the palace.[53] The

46. R. G. Kent, *Old Persian*, 2d ed. (New Haven: American Oriental Society, 1953), p. 144; see also F. W. König, *Der Burgbau zu Susa nach dem Bauberichte des Königs Dareios I* (Leipzig: J. C. Hinrichs, 1930); R. G. Kent, "The Record of Darius's Palace at Susa," *JAOS* 53 (1933): 1–23.

47. F. Vallat, "Deux inscriptions élamites de Darius 1er (DSf et DSz)," *Studia Iranica* 1 (1972): 3–13; M.-J. Stève, "Inscriptions de Achéménides à Suse," *Studia Iranica* 3 (1974): 135–68, especially 146–49.

48. J. Perrot and D. Ladiray, "Travaux à l'Apadana (1969–1971)," *CDAFI* 2 (1972): 22.

49. Excavations in 1976 uncovered a new palace of Darius on the Ville Royale; the references in XSa (Kent, *OP*, p. 152) to palaces may refer to buildings located not on the Apadana but elsewhere in Susa.

50. F. Vallat, "Deux nouvelles 'Chartres de Fondation,' d'un palais de Darius Ier à Suse," *Syria* 48 (1971): 53–59.

51. F. Vallat, "Table accadienne de Darius Ier (*DSaa*)," in *Fragmenta Historiae Aelamicae*, M.-J. Stève Festschrift, eds. L. de Meyer, H. Gasche, and F. Vallat (Paris: Editions Recherche sur les Civilisations, 1986), p. 281.

52. R. Ghirshman, *The Arts of Ancient Iran* (New York: Golden, 1964), p. 139: "The main gate must have been located on the west side of the enclosure wall, opposite the west portico of the Apadana."

53. The area to the east of the palace on the Apadana had been subjected to years of excavation in 1851 by Loftus, 1884 to 1886 by Dieulafoy, 1900 by de Morgan, 1920 to 1938 by Mecquenem, and 1946 to 1967 by Ghirshman. This vividly illustrates the point I have made about the fragmentary nature of

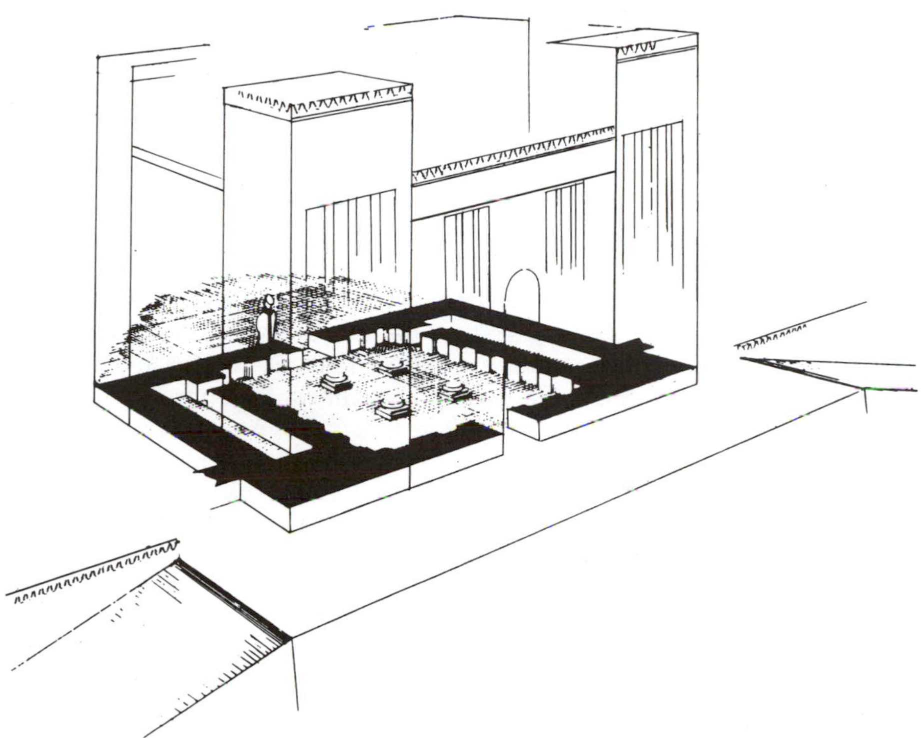

Artist's reconstruction of the gate. (Courtesy of F. Vallat, Centre National de la Recherche Scientifique)

width of the wall penetrated by the gate was 15 meters (49 feet) thick. There was probably a ramp that approached the gate from the east.

The gate was 40 by 28 meters (131 by 92 feet), covering about 1,200 square meters. Its central room was a square 21 meters (69 feet) at a side with four columns. There were two smaller rooms to the north and to the south, which were connected to the main hall by one-meter-wide doors. The height of the columns was probably about 12 to 13 meters (39 to 43 feet).[54]

---

our archaeological evidence, including the fraction that is examined on a tell. See E. Yamauchi, *The Stones and the Scriptures* (Grand Rapids: Baker, 1981), chapter 4, especially pp. 151–54.

54. J. Perrot and D. Ladiray, "La porte de Darius à Suse," *CDAFI* 4 (1974): 49; J. Perrot, "Le Palais de Darius le Grand à Suse," *Proceedings of the Second Annual Symposium on Archaeological Research in Iran, 1973,* ed. F. Bagherzadeh (Tehran: Iranian Centre for Archaeological Research, 1974), pp. 91–101.

In 1973 the excavators discovered two column bases with trilingual inscriptions of Xerxes, which declare: "Xerxes the King says, 'by the grace of Ahuramazda, this Gate, Darius the King made it, he who was my father."[55]

This was the gate area where Mordecai sat (Esther 2:19, 21; 5:9, 13; 6:10; see also 3:2, 3; 4:2; 6:12). The discovery of this gate and other features of the palace, such as the square before the gate (Esther 4:6), correspond well with the details of Ahasuerus's palace. In fact the French excavators are convinced that the author of Esther had accurate information about the royal palace complex at Susa. Perrot comments: "One today rereads with a renewed interest the Book of Esther, whose detailed description of the interior disposition of the palace of Xerxes is now in excellent accord with archaeological reality."[56] Perrot also adds: "Still other indications regarding the women's residences and the gardens tend to confirm the impression that the biblical narrative, whose historicity remains to be established, derives its source from the Achaemenid period from the milieu of those who were familiar with the great palace of Susa."[57]

As noted before in chapter 4 on Darius, in December 1972 the excavators discovered an oversized statue of Darius, minus its head, which had originally been set up at the west entrance of the gate. Some have argued that the present statue was probably a copy made by Egyptian artists of an original statue erected in Egypt. More probably the four-ton statue was transported by Xerxes from Egypt around 493. Heinz Luschey examined other fragments of royal statues found at Susa,[58] and concluded there were probably four or five similar statues set up before the gate on its inner and outer faces.[59]

55. J. Perrot, "Historique des recherches," *CDAFI* 4 (1974): 18–19; F. Vallat, "L'inscription trilingue de Xerxes à la porte de Darius," *CDAFI* 4 (1974): 178.

56. J. Perrot, "Historique des recherches," p. 20: "On relira aujourd'hui avec un intérêt renouvelé le livre d'Esther dont la description détaillée qui y est faite de la disposition intérieure du palais de Xerxès est en bon accord à présent avec la réalité archéologique."

57. Ibid., p. 20, n. 13: "D'autres indications encore concernant les maisons des femmes, les jardins, tendent à confirmer l'impression que le récit biblique, dont l'historicité reste à établir, a bien sa source à la période achéménide dans le milieu des familiers du grand palais de Suse." See also Vallat, "L'inscription trilingue de Xerxes," p. 176. For an earlier exposition, see A. Barucq, "Esther et la cour de Suse," *Bible et Terre Sainte* 39 (June 1961): 3–5.

58. One of the fragments of a face bears a king's chin, beard, mouth, and nose. See Ghirshman, *Arts of Ancient Iran*, p. 140, fig. 189.

59. H. Luschey, "Die Darius-Statuen aus Susa und ihre Rekonstruktion," in *Kunst, Kultur and Geschichte der Achämenidenzeit und ihr Fortleben*, eds. H. Koch and D. N. MacKenzie (Berlin: Dietrich Reimer, 1983), pp. 191–223; M. C. Root, *The King and Kingship in Achaemenid Art* (Leiden: Brill, 1979), pp. 110–12.

Xerxes and the Later Achaemenids

Xerxes, who destroyed Babylon when it revolted, made Susa his principal winter residence. It was to Susa that Xerxes retired from Sardis after his disastrous campaign in Greece in 480/479 (Herodotus 9.108). Over thirty stone vessels and sherds with Xerxes' name, often in quadrilingual inscriptions, have been found.[60] The inscriptions from the newly discovered gate indicate that Xerxes completed his father Darius's work at Susa as well as at Persepolis.[61]

During the reign of Artaxerxes I the Apadana burned to the ground. There are three great faults in the terrace; it is possible that an earthquake toppled lamps to set off the fire.[62] Although no inscription attests to the building activities of Artaxerxes I at Susa, he may have begun the small palace in the Donjon area of the Ville Royale. According to Ghirshman, a small hypostyle hall with a reception hall and living quarters were built there by Artaxerxes I and completed by his successor Darius II (423–405 B.C.).[63] From this small palace have come nearly all the fragments of stone bas-relief from Susa.

The Apadana was reconstructed by Artaxerxes II (404–359 B.C.), who faithfully reproduced Darius's structure. Artaxerxes II declared:

> This palace [*Apadana*] Darius my great-great-grandfather built; later under Artaxerxes [I] my grandfather it was burned; by the favor of Ahuramazda, Anaitis, and Mithras, this palace I built. May Ahuramazda, Anaitis, and Mithras protect me from all evil, and that which I have built may they not shatter nor harm.[64]

In 1969 bulldozers accidentally uncovered a new hypostyle hall, measuring 37.5 by 34.6 meters (123 by 114 feet), with eight rows of eight columns on the plain west of the Shaʿur. Additional buildings were excavated between 1970 and 1976.[65] Fragments of trilingual inscriptions on column bases have been found, indicating that the complex was the provisional palace of Artaxerxes II while he proceeded

60. Schmidt, *Persepolis*, vol. 1, p. 34; M. Mayrhofer, *Supplement zur Sammlung der altpersischen Inschriften* (Vienna: Österreichischen Akademie der Wissenschaften, 1978), p. 26.

61. Perrot and Ladiray, "La porte de Darius," p. 51.

62. Perrot and Ladiray, "Travaux à l'Apadana," p. 17 and plate V. D. L. Page, *The Santorini Volcano and the Destruction of Minoan Crete* (London: Society for the Promotion of Hellenic Studies, 1970), suggested that the earthquakes generated by the Santorini explosion may have toppled lamps, causing the fiery destruction of the Late Minoan palaces.

63. Ghirshman, *Arts of Ancient Iran*, p. 142.

64. Kent, *OP*, p. 154.

65. J. Perrot, "Le palais du Chaour et l'Apadana," *Iran* 9 (1971): 179–81; R. Boucharlat and A. Labrousse, "Le palais d'Artaxerxès II sur la rive droite du Chaour à Suse," *CDAFI* 10 (1979): 21–85.

The palace of Artaxerxes II by the Sha'ur.

with the reconstruction on the Apadana.[66] On these bases had been placed wooden columns painted blue. Pieces of colored plaster with multicolored plant and geometric reliefs have also been found.[67]

Alexander and His Successors

In 331 B.C. Alexander captured Susa and its enormous treasure without resistance. The classical sources (Arrian, Plutarch, Diodorus, Curtius) agree that the sum was between forty to fifty thousand talents, although they disagree on how much of this was in coins.[68] Leaving the satrap of Susa in his post, Alexander proceeded to Persepolis. In 324, after his return from campaigns in the east, Alexander celebrated the symbolic marriage of himself and eighty Macedonian officers to native brides at Susa.

Under the Seleucids Susa was renamed Seleucia-on-the-Eulaios. The city suffered destruction perhaps during the revolt of Molon against Antiochus III (223–187). Thereafter the area fell under the Parthians, who gave the Greek inhabitants of Susa considerable freedom. Greek inscriptions from this period include the manumission of slaves in the temple of Artemis (Nanaia) and poetic compositions.

66. F. Vallat, "Les inscriptions du palais d'Artaxerxès II," *CDAFI* 10 (1979): 145–50.

67. J. Perrot, "Suse 1974," in *Proceedings of the IIIrd Annual Symposium*, p. 215; J. Perrot, A. Lebrun, and A. Labrousse, "Recherches archéologiques à Suse et en Susiane en 1969 et en 1970," *Syria* 48 (1971): 36–40.

68. Arrian (3.16.7) says fifty thousand talents of silver; Plutarch, *Alexander* (36–37), says forty thousand talents of coined money; Diodorus (17.66) has forty thousand talents of uncoined silver; Quintus Curtius (5.6.3ff.) reports fifty thousand talents of uncoined wealth.

The Parthian, Sasanian, and Islamic Eras

Ghirshman excavated in the Ville des Artisans a necropolis of the Partho-Seleucid period (300 B.C. to A.D. 200).[69] Around A.D. 100 an interesting change in burial practices took place: the dead were laid on benches for their flesh to decay—a practice similar to that of the early magi and the later Zoroastrians.

From circa A.D. 250, under the Sasanids Ardashir I and Shapur I, Susa began to flourish. However, a revolt by the Christians was suppressed by the destruction of Susa by Shapur II (A.D. 309–379). Evidence of Christians buried with Nestorian crosses have been recovered from this period. Although rebuilt under the name *Eranshahr-Shapur* by later Sasanids, Susa never flourished again.

The Arabs captured Susa in A.D. 638. Abu Musa, the conqueror, was shown the coffin of a saint, whom some called Daniel and others called Darius or Khusrau.[70] The tradition of Daniel's tomb was reported by Benjamin of Tudela (twelfth century A.D.), and may go back to the eighth or even seventh centuries A.D. A mosque with its striking conical tower at the edge of the Shaʿur is venerated as the tomb of Daniel. This so-called tomb of Daniel has been on the same site at least since the twelfth century.[71]

Susa was finally abandoned in the thirteenth century, after over five millennia of habitation.[72]

69. R. Ghirshman, "The Town Which Three Hundred Elephants Razed to the Ground," *Illustrated London News* (Oct. 1950): 571–73.

70. P. Calmeyer, "The Persian King in the Lion's Den," *Iraq* 45 (1983): 138–39.

71. S. Matheson, *Persia: An Archaeological Guide,* rev. ed. (London: Faber and Faber, 1976), p. 151.

72. According to M. Charlesworth, "Preliminary Report on War-Damaged Cities and Sites in South-western and Western Iran," *Iran* 25 (1987): xv:

> In 1980–81, the front line was only 4 kms. away along the line of the river Karkheh. As a result, with its dominating position, the site suffered extensive damage from artillery and other fire. The castle has taken heavy external damage, although with surprisingly little internal damage. The mound is extensively cratered, and the Apadana has lost large chunks of its southern walls. The Museum building is relatively unscathed. Most of its contents were evacuated to Tehran in the early months of the war, but the heavier stone objects, including Achaemenid inscribed blocks, were perforce left behind and have consequently suffered some damage. The shrine of Daniel was about 70 per cent destroyed, but has now been restored to its former appearance.

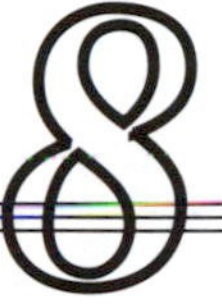

Ecbatana

The Capital of the Medes

Ecbatana (Old Persian *Hangmatana,* meaning "gathering place"; Elamite *Agamatanu;* Akkadian *Agmatānú;* Aramaic *'Aḥmᵉtā',* compare KJV, "Achmetha"; Greek *Agbátana,* also *Ecbátana*) was the capital city of Media in northwestern Iran. Its ancient name is still preserved in the name of the modern town, Hamadan, which rests over the ancient settlement.

The Location of Ecbatana

The city of Hamadan is 175 miles by air and 230 miles by road west-southwest of Tehran. Ecbatana was located at an altitude of 5,500 feet above sea level near the 11,000-foot-high Mount Elvend. It was on the main route between Mesopotamia and the Iranian highlands. Stuart C. Brown notes the advantages of its strategic location for the Medes:

> A chiefdom at Ecbatana, by virtue of its location, would have had a considerable advantage over any potential competitors in its ability to

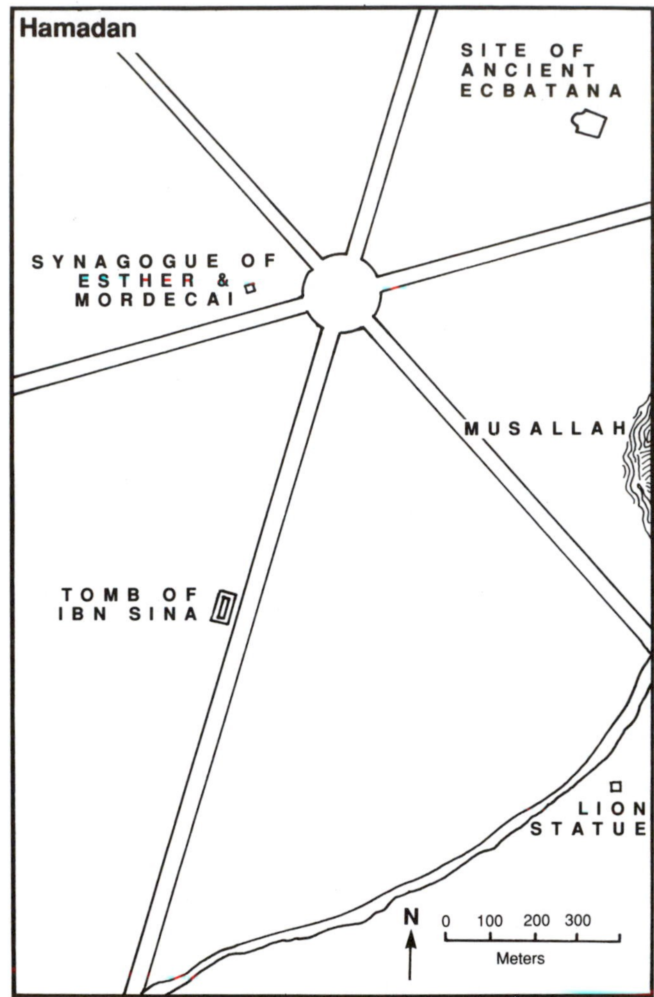

(Courtesy of Robert North and the Editrice Pontificio Istituto Biblico)

monopolize control over and profit from the east-west flow of long-distance trade and regional exchange that, of necessity, passed through its territory. In any situation of economic intensification in the central Zagros involving both regional exchange and long-distance trade, Ecbatana would have enjoyed a monopoly control on exchange enhanced by its freedom from Assyrian intervention and impositions of tribute and taxation.[1]

1. S. C. Brown, "Media and Secondary State Formation in the Neo-Assyrian Zagros," *JCS* 38 (1986): 116.

The ancient settlement was not on the prominent bare hill called *Musallah* in the southeastern section of the city of Hamadan. Rather it was located in the northeast section of the town as revealed by aerial photographs made by Erich Schmidt in 1937.[2] It was in this section that early travelers noted Achaemenian remains such as columns and capitals.[3] That this was the site of ancient Ecbatana was confirmed by the cutting of Ekbatan Street.[4]

Biblical and Apocryphal References

The sole reference to Ecbatana in the Old Testament is Ezra 6:2, where it is reported that Cyrus's decree granting the Jews permission to rebuild the temple was discovered there during the reign of Darius. There are a number of references in the Apocryphal books to Ecbatana. Judith 1:1–4 fancifully describes its construction with gates a hundred cubits high by an unknown king named Arphaxad. In Tobit (3:7; 7:1; 14:12) Tobias travels to Ecbatana to marry his cousin, Sarah, the daughter of Raguel. Maccabees (2 Macc. 9:1–3) describes the flight of Antiochus IV to Ecbatana just before his death.

Classical Descriptions

According to Herodotus (1.96ff.), Deioces, the first ruler to unite the Medes, founded Ecbatana at the end of the eighth century B.C. His description of seven colored, concentric walls seems to derive from the mythological castle Kangdiz.[5] Cyrus captured Ecbatana from his grandfather, Astyages, in 550. It was to Ecbatana that Cyrus brought the treasures of Croesus after he captured Sardis (Herodotus 1:153). According to Xenophon (*Cyropaedia* 8.6.22; compare *Anabasis* 3.5.15), Cyrus spent his summers there.

Alexander the Great captured Ecbatana in 330 B.C. Polybius (10.27)

2. E. Schmidt, *Flights over Ancient Cities of Iran* (Chicago: University of Chicago Press, 1940), pp. 74ff.

3. Nineteenth-century travelers, Flandin and Coste, also observed column bases two kilometers east of Hamadan, which led Herzfeld to locate the Median capital there. See E. Herzfeld, *Iran in the Ancient East* (Oxford: Oxford University Press, 1941), p. 290.

4. R. H. Dyson, "Iran 1956," *University Museum Bulletin* 21 (1957): 31–33.

5. E. Herzfeld, *Archaeological History of Iran* (London: British Academy, 1935), pp. 22–27; idem, *Iran in the Ancient East* (London: Oxford University Press, 1941), p. 200. Assyrian representations of Median cities found in the reliefs of Tiglath-pileser III at Nimrud and Sargon II at Khorsabad depict multiple walls surmounted by numerous towers. See A. Gunter, "Representations of Urartian and Western Iranian Fortress Architecture in the Assyrian Reliefs," *Iran* 20 (1982): 103–12.

Inscriptions at the base of Mount Elvend.

described the city at the time of Antiochus III (209 B.C.). His description of the splendid temple of Anias (the goddess Anahita) and woodwork plated with silver and gold is a credible account.

Achaemenid Inscriptions and Objects

There have been no excavations at Hamadan except for a brief dig by Charles Virolleaud and Charles Fossey in 1914, which according to Oscar Muscarella, yielded "a bronze vessel wth a curved spout terminating in a lion's head and with a plaque attachment at the rear of the vessel depicting a winged male figure" (ninth to seventh centuries B.C.).[6] When I visited the site in 1974 and 1975 the Department of Antiquities had expropriated the area of the ancient site and was clearing it for future excavation, but to my knowledge no excavations were actually conducted.[7] Chance finds of priceless objects and valuable inscriptions suggest that the excavation of the ancient site of Ecbatana could be most rewarding.

Some seven miles southwest of Hamadan on the face of a spur of Mount Elvend are two Achaemenid inscriptions of Darius and of Xerxes at a place known as Ganj-i-Nameh ("treasure book").[8] Xerxes made a slavish copy of Darius's text and simply inserted his name in place of his father's.

From Hamadan have come two gold tablets inscribed in Old Persian cuneiform purportedly by Ariaramnes and by Arsames, the great-grandfather and the grandfather of Darius.[9] Ernst Herzfeld has defended

6. O. W. Muscarella, "Median Art and Medizing Scholarship," *JNES* 46 (1987): 125. See also R. Ghirshman, *The Arts of Ancient Iran* (New York: Golden, 1964), pp. 94–95.

7. In the recent war between Iraq and Iran, rockets shot by Iraq have hit Hamadan on several occasions.

8. R. G. Kent, *Old Persian* (*OP*), rev. ed. (New Haven: American Oriental Society, 1953), pp. 14, 152.

9. Ibid., pp. 107, 116.

Inscriptions of Darius and Xerxes.

their authenticity, but Roland Kent and other scholars believe they were inscribed much later by Artaxerxes II.[10]

In 1923 gold and silver plates bearing trilingual inscriptions of Darius were found in a poor private house.[11] Probably from Hamadan are gold and silver bowls with the names of Darius and of Xerxes.[12] A gold tablet and two column bases with inscriptions of Artaxerxes II have been recovered from Hamadan.[13]

Chance finds at Hamadan have yielded magnificent examples of the goldsmith's art. These include two golden daggers (one in the Tehran Museum and the other in the Metropolitan Museum),[14] and two gold rhytons or drinking vessels in the form of winged lions (in the Tehran Museum and in the Metropolitan Museum).[15] Probably

10. R. G. Kent, "The Oldest Old Persian Inscriptions," *JAOS* 66 (1946): 206–12. For an extensive bibliography on these texts, see C. Nylander, "Clamps and Chronology," *IA* 6 (1966): 130, n. 1.

11. Kent, *OP*, p. 147.

12. Ghirshman, *Arts of Ancient Iran*, p. 257, fig. 310, and p. 256, fig. 309.

13. Kent, *OP*, pp. 114, 155.

14. C. K. Wilkinson, "Assyrian and Persian Art," *Bulletin of the Metropolitan Museum of Art* 13 (1955): 220–21; Ghirshman, *Arts of Ancient Iran*, p. 267, fig. 328; E. Porada, *The Art of Ancient Iran* (New York: Crown, 1965), p. 164, plate 47.

15. Ghirshman, *Arts of Ancient Iran*, p. 242, fig. 290, and pp. 252–53, fig. 306; Porada, *Art of Ancient Iran*, pp. 162–64, plate 47. It was only after Greek contact with the Persians that the Greeks developed their own rhyta. See H. Hoffmann, "The Persian Origin of Attic Rhyta," *Antike Kunst* 4 (1961): 21–26.

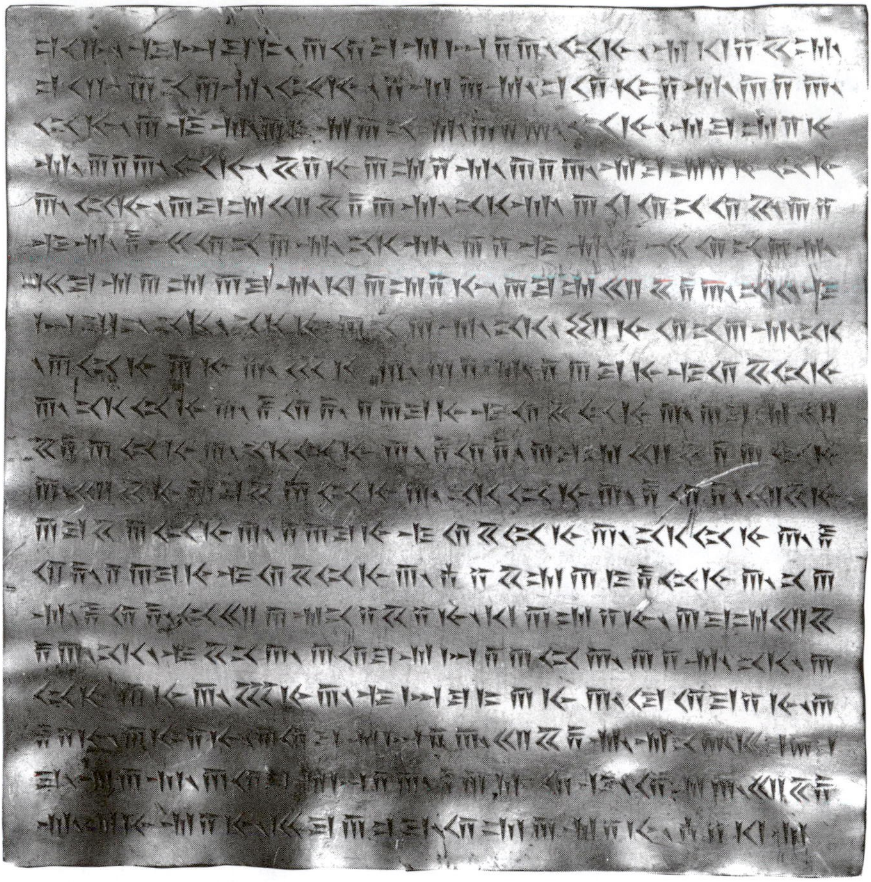

Gold plaque of Artaxerxes II. (Cincinnati Art Museum, purchase)

from Hamadan are a gold dish with an eagle design,[16] and an applique of a winged lion.[17]

A white marble head, presumably found at Hamadan, was purchased by the Louvre Museum and displayed as an Achaemenian masterpiece.[18] Although Pierre Amiet and André Parrot have accepted the

16. Ghirshman, *Arts of Ancient Iran*, p. 370, fig. 478.

17. Porada, *Art of Ancient Iran*, pp. 172–75, plate 52; Helene Kantor, "Achaemenid Jewelry in the Oriental Institute," *JNES* 16 (1957): 1–23. For Persian jewelry and the goldsmith's art, see also P. Amandry, "Orfèvrie achéménide," *Antike Kunst* 2 (1959): 8–22; idem, "Toreutique achéménide," *Antike Kunst* 2 (1959): 38–56.

18. A. Parrot, "Tête royale achéménide(?)," *Syria* 44 (1964): 247ff.

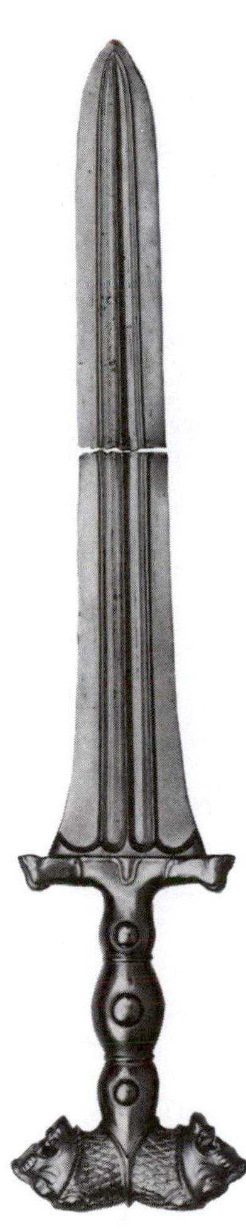

Gold dagger. (Metropolitan Museum of Art, Harris Brisbane Dick Fund, 1954 [54.3.4ab])

work as genuine and have suggested it may represent Astyages, Margaret Root and Heinz Luschey believe it is not an authentic Median work.[19]

19. M. C. Root, *The King and Kingship in Achaemenid Art* (Leiden: Brill, 1979), 114–16; H. Luschey, "Die Darius-Statuen aus Susa and ihre Rekonstruktion," in *Kunst, Kultur and Geschichte der Achämenidenzeit und ihr Fortleben*, eds. H. Koch and D. N. MacKenzie (Berlin: Dietrich Reimer, 1983), p. 194.

Gold rhyton. (Metropolitan Museum of Art, Harris Brisbane Dick Fund, 1954)

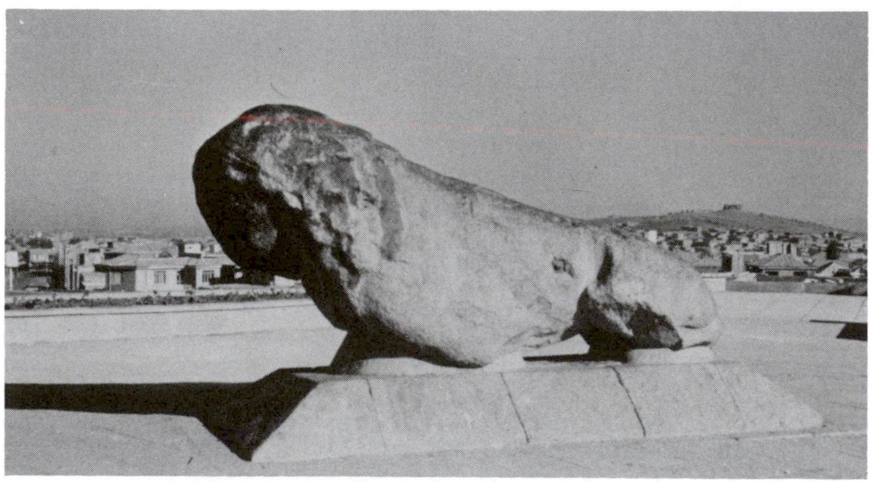

The Hellenistic lion.

The synagogue of Esther and Mordecai.

The Hellenistic Lion

On the southeast outskirts of Hamadan is the Sang-i-Shir, a mutilated lion statue, which once stood by a city gate. Although it has been described as a Median or Parthian work, it was probably erected by Alexander in honor of his general Hephaestion, who died at Ecbatana.[20] Clinton Scollard (1860–1932) recalls that of the glories of Alexander and other ancient worthies nothing remains

> Save a couchant lion lone,
> Mute memorial in stone
> Of three Empires overthrown—
> Median, Persian, Parthian—
> Round the walls of Hamadan.[21]

In the Islamic era the lion was regarded as a protector of the city and as a talisman against sickness. It has been split open by treasure hunters; its nose has been kissed smooth by women seeking husbands.[22]

20. H. Luschey, "Der Löwe von Ekbatana," *AMI* n.F. 1 (1968): 120–22.

21. Cited by Luschey, ibid., p. 117.

22. Ibid., p. 119. Compare G. Gropp, "Mittelalterliche Arabische Quellen zum Löwen von Hamadan-Ekbatana," *AMI* n.F. 1 (1968): 119–22.

Jewish and Muslim Monuments

The Synagogue of Esther and Mordecai in the center of Hamadan contains sarcophagi covered with brocaded cloth. One of the tombs may be that of the Jewish queen of the Sasanian ruler Yazdegird (A.D. 399–421).[23]

Hamadan is the city of the renowned Muslim philosopher, Ibn Sina, known to the West as Avicenna. Avicenna, who died at Ecbatana in A.D. 1037, exercised enormous influence on medieval Europe through his writings. He is commemorated by a striking, new tower.[24]

23. S. A. Matheson, *Persia: An Archaeological Guide,* rev. ed. (London: Faber and Faber, 1976), pp. 108–12.

24. For the later history of Hamadan, see B. Fragner, *Geschichte der Stadt Hamadān und ihrer Umgebung in den ersten sechs Jahrhunderten nach der Hiğra* (Vienna: Notring, 1972).

9

Pasargadae

The Capital of Cyrus

Pasargadae, the new capital of Cyrus the Great, had the same name as that of the noblest tribe of the Persians (Herodotus 1.125; 4.167). A later source, Quintus Curtius, gives the variant spelling, *Parsagada*. The etymology of the original Persian name is uncertain. Anaximenes of Lampsakos interpreted the name of the city as "camping ground of the Persians." Among the suggestions that scholars have made are: **Parsagarda* (settlement of the Persians), **Parsagadeh* (the throne of Parsa), **Parsagert* (the fortress of Parsa), **Pasragada* (those who wield strong clubs), and **Pathra-kata* (shelter home).[1]

1. D. Stronach, *Pasargadae* (Oxford: Clarendon, 1978), p. 280. Hallock suggests that the Elamite name of the site may have originally been Badrakata. See R. T. Hallock, *Persepolis Fortification Tablets* (Chicago: University of Chicago Press, 1969), p. 676. Compare W. Hinz, "Die elamischen Buchungstäfelchen der Darius-Zeit," *Or* 39 (1970): 425.

The Location of Pasargadae

Pasargadae is located in Fars (the province of ancient Persia in southwestern Iran), about fifty miles north of Persepolis. It lies in the Dasht-i Morghab (plain of the water bird) of the Pulvar River over six thousand feet above sea level. It is almost entirely surrounded by mountains. The area is bitterly cold in winter and hot in summer.

Classical Descriptions

Pasargadae became a major settlement after Cyrus chose it as his capital in 550 B.C.[2] Most of the buildings date from 546 to 530. According to Strabo (15.3.8): "Cyrus held Pasargadae in honor, because he there conquered Astyages the Mede in his last battle, transferred to himself the empire of Asia, founded a city, and constructed a palace as a memorial of his victory."

Even after Darius established his new capital at Persepolis, Pasargadae served as the religious center where Persian kings were crowned. Plutarch (*Artaxerxes* 3.1) tells us that the new Persian king was crowned at Pasargadae:

> A little while after the death of Darius [II], the new king [Artaxerxes II] made an expedition to Pasargadae, that he might receive the royal initiation at the hands of the Persian priests. Here there is a sanctuary of a warlike goddess whom one might conjecture to be Athena [that is, Anahita]. Into this sanctuary the candidate for initiation must pass, and after laying aside his own proper robe, must put on that which Cyrus the Elder used to wear before he became king; then he must eat of a cake of figs, chew some turpentine-wood, and drink a cup of sour milk. Whatever else is done besides this is unknown to outsiders.

In 330 B.C. Alexander the Great seized Pasargadae without fighting and removed from its treasury some six thousand talents of bullion. He paid his respects at the tomb of Cyrus, and upon his return from India in 325 was outraged to discover that the tomb had been looted in his absence (Arrian, *Anabasis* 6.29.1ff.).

2. R. Ghirshman, *The Art of Ancient Iran* (New York: Golden, 1964), p. 131, speculated that it was Cyrus's father, Cambyses I, who chose the site and built the terrace, but Stronach's excavations proved him wrong.

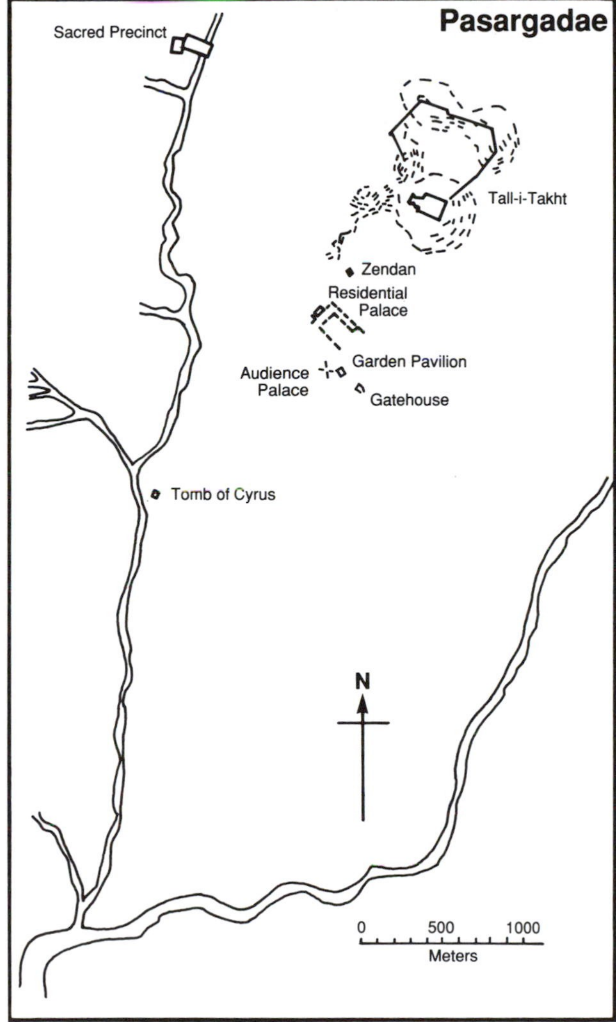

(Courtesy of the British Institute of Persian Studies and David Stronach)

Excavations

It was Robert Ker Porter in the early nineteenth century who was the first to identify the tomb at Pasargadae as that of Cyrus from classi-

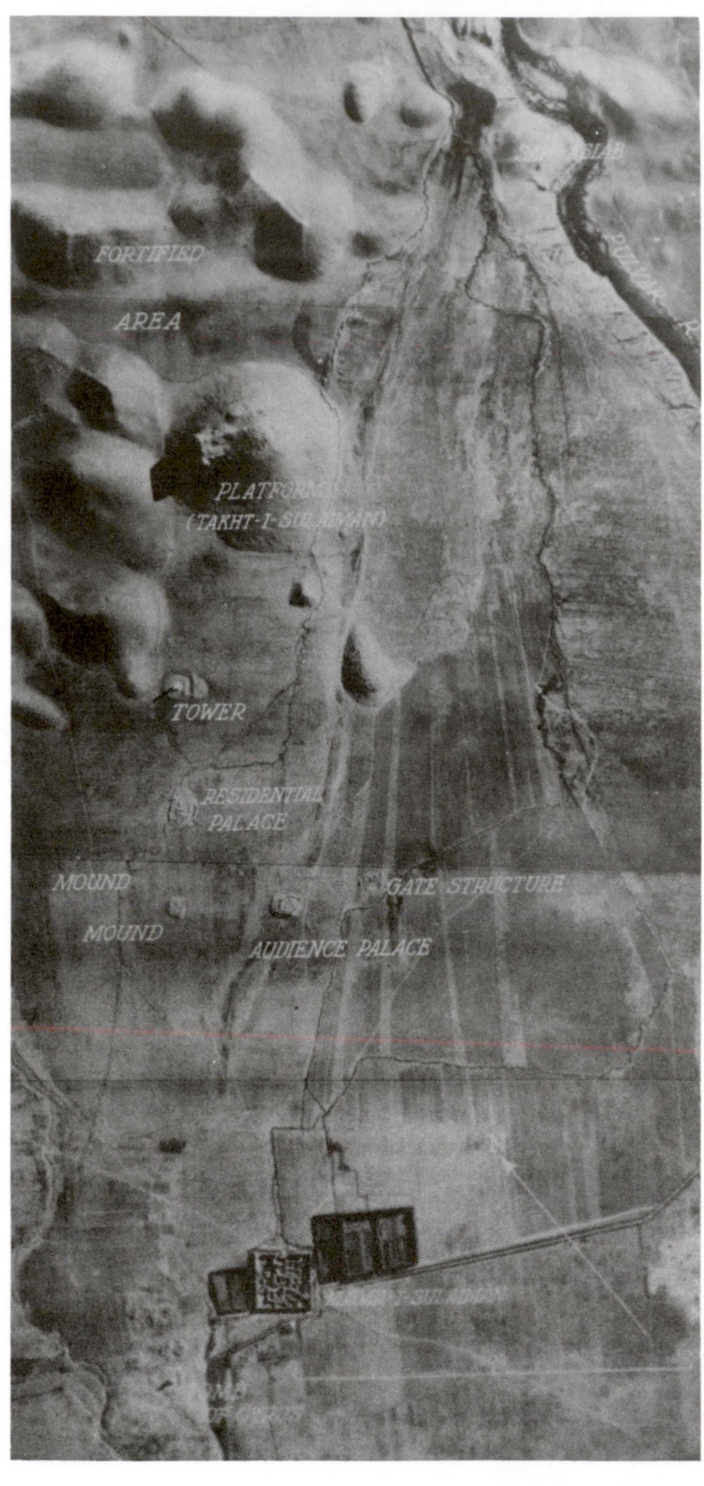

Aerial view of Pasargadae. (Courtesy of The Oriental Institute, University of Chicago)

cal descriptions.[3] The first excavations were begun in 1928 by Ernst Herzfeld.[4] He dug but four trenches, and did not publish all of his discoveries. Sir Aurel Stein, most noted for his extensive travels, conducted a brief excavation in 1934. Ali Sami, an Iranian scholar, worked at the site for five years beginning in 1949.[5]

David Stronach of the British Institute of Persian Studies excavated primarily in the citadel area from 1961 to 1963, and produced in 1978 a magisterial volume on all of the monuments at the site.[6] Stronach's investigations revealed three major occupational periods: period I, the original establishment of Cyrus; period II, from 500 to 280 B.C.; and period III, from 280 to 180 B.C. There was also a brief occupation during the last Sasanian or early Islamic period.

The monuments are widely scattered over a vast area. Henri Frankfort observed that Pasargadae still retained characteristics of a nomad chief's settlement: "Separate pavilions stood in a vast park surrounded by a wall thirteen feet thick."[7] The monuments are concentrated in four major areas: the sacred precinct to the northwest; the citadel nearly a mile to the southeast of the sacred precinct; the palace area 500 to 1,000 meters southwest of the citadel; and the tomb of Cyrus 1,500 meters southwest of the palace area.

The Sacred Precinct and Terrace

In the sacred precinct are two plinths or blocks of limestone. The south plinth is made up of two parts, an eight-step staircase and a white limestone block measuring 2.16 meters (7 feet) high and 2.43 meters (8 feet) square. It may have had a black limestone cap. Leo Trümpelmann suggests that this plinth was a platform that was originally decorated with crenelations.[8] The north plinth, which is 8 meters (26 feet) away, measures 2.10 meters (6 feet 10 inches) high and 2.8 meters (9 feet) square.

Albert T. Olmstead believes these were twin altars to Ahuramazda and Anahita.[9] Trümpelmann hypothesizes that the southern plinth may

3. See E. Herzfeld, "Pasargadae," *Klio* 8 (1908): 1–68.

4. E. Herzfeld, "Bericht über die Ausgrabungen von Pasargadae 1928," *AMI* 1 (1929–1930): 4–16.

5. A. Sami, *Pasargadae, the Oldest Imperial Capital of Iran* (Shiraz: Learned Society of Fars, 1956).

6. For preliminary reports, see D. Stronach, "Excavations at Pasargadae, First Preliminary Report," *Iran* 1 (1963): 19–42; idem, "Excavations at Pasargadae, Second Preliminary Report," *Iran* 2 (1964): 21–39; idem, "Excavations at Pasargadae, Third Preliminary Report," *Iran* 3 (1965): 9–40. A comprehensive report was published in 1978 (see n. 1).

7. H. Frankfort, *The Art and Architecture of the Ancient Orient* (Baltimore: Penguin, 1954), p. 216.

8. L. Trümpelmann, "Das Heiligtum von Pasargadae," *Studia Iranica* 6 (1977): 10, fig. 2.

9. A. T. Olmstead, *History of the Persian Empire* (Chicago: University of Chicago Press, 1948), p. 61.

Tall-i Takht.

have been used for various offering materials such as haoma (a sacred plant) for Anahita, whereas the northern plinth may have served to receive pieces of meat for Mithra.[10] On the basis of a relief showing Darius worshiping in this manner, Stronach suggests that Cyrus and his later successors probably mounted the southern plinth to worship before a portable fire altar on the northern plinth.[11] Three fragments of such fire altars made of stone have been found at Pasargadae.[12]

A terrace some 120 meters (about 400 feet) west of the plinths was built on a natural rock outcrop. This was actually a series of five ascending terraces ranging from about 75 by 50 meters (245 by 165 feet) to 20 by 15 meters (48 by 36 feet). The summit is 50.4 meters (120 feet) above the level of the plain. The terrace complex seems to be of a later construction than the altars, which date from Cyrus's original settlement. There is no evidence that the terrace served as a foundation for a temple. Stronach offers the following suggestions for the function of the site:

> It may have been built, in either Achaemenian or post-Achaemenian times, as a suitably distant vantage point for those who were privileged to witness the solemn ceremonies that were enacted at the two free-standing plinths; it may have been erected as an elevated stage for sacrificial rites; or, yet again, it may have been built to support further altars at a time when the changing patterns of Achaemenian belief, in or after the reign of Artaxerxes II, demanded additional religious appointments.[13]

10. Trümpelmann, "Das Heiligtum," p. 16.

11. Stronach, *Pasargadae,* p. 138; K. Erdmann, *Das iranische Feuerheiligtum* (Leipzig: J. C. Hinrichs, 1941), p. 13.

12. J. Duchesne-Guillemin, "Le dieu de Cyrus," *Commémoration Cyrus* (Leiden: Brill, 1974), 3: 12, points out that the cult of fire was an ancient trait of the religion of the Aryans and not just of the Zoroastrians.

13. Stronach, *Pasargadae,* p. 145.

The limestone blocks of the terrace were fitted together with metal clamps (most of which have been stolen).

The Citadel

The citadel called Takht-i Madar-i Sulaiman (the throne of the mother of Solomon) is an impressive terrace, built upon a hill, the Tall-i Takht, rising 50 meters (164 feet) above the plain. An aerial photograph by Erich Schmidt revealed a polygonal circuit of mudbrick walls about the citadel. The terrace proper was 14.5 meters (48 feet) high and is built of well-drafted limestone blocks fitted together with metal butterfly-shaped clamps over an inner core of sandstone blocks and limestone chips. There are up to twenty courses of limestone blocks. The impressive stone masonry betrays the influence of Lydian and Ionian masons, whom Cyrus must have brought back after his conquest of Lydia and Ionia in 547/546.[14] Stronach suggests:

> Indeed, limited as the evidence is, it is not unreasonable to suppose that Cyrus' own unfinished design for an elevated residential palace was based, in part at least on the signal model of the Lydian royal acropolis at Sardis and that many of his masons were brought directly to Pasargadae from the still unfinished temple of Artemis at Ephesus.[15]

Stronach uncovered a columned hall, 25 by 7 meters (82 by 23 feet), which had a row of eight column bases and a low plastered bench. He

14. For a thorough study of Ionian workmanship at the site, see C. Nylander, *Ionians in Pasargadae* (Uppsala: Almqvist and Wiksells, 1970).

15. Stronach, *Pasargadae,* p. 23; for the contemporary monuments at Sardis and Ephesus, see E. Yamauchi, *New Testament Cities in Western Asia Minor* (Grand Rapids: Baker, 1980), chapters 5 and 7.

The citadel terrace.

also discovered paved bathroom facilities and extensive drains. Neo-Babylonian booty found in the wall was probably from the capture of Babylon by Cyrus in 539.

The unfinished platform of Cyrus was transformed by Darius into a mudbrick citadel; Darius had his stone masons occupied with his new capital at Persepolis. A limestone cover over a drain in the citadel turned out to be a copy of Xerxes' Daiva inscription.

The citadel was probably the treasury surrendered to Alexander. Period II ended violently around 280 B.C., perhaps by a national revolution at the time of the death of Seleucus I, whose coins were discovered among two hoards.[16]

The Zendan

The Zendan-i Sulaiman, or "prison of Solomon," is a quadrangular tower 600 meters (2000 feet) southwest of the Tall-i Takht. All that stands today is one wall about 13 meters (43 feet) high with three rows of false windows. A staircase of 29 steps probably ascended to the chamber of the Zendan. Three rosettes, which are of Greek inspiration, once decorated the door to the chamber. A better-preserved and nearly identical structure is the Kaʿabah-i Zardusht (cube of Zoroaster) at Naqsh-i Rustam near Persepolis.

16. G. Jenkins, "Coin Hoards from Pasargadae," *Iran* 3 (1965): 41–52.

Remains of the Zendan and the palaces beyond it.

The function of these two towers is disputed because they are unique, although Stronach believes that possible prototypes were Urartian towers.[17] There are three theories. David Stronach, Walter Henning, and Max Mallowan believe they were repositories for archives or royal objects. Others (Walther Hinz, Roman Ghirshman, Robert Zaehner, and Jacques Duchesne-Guillemin) have suggested they were fire temples. Finally, it has also been proposed that they were tombs (by Marcel Dieulafoy, Ernst Herzfeld, Ali Sami, and Friedrich Krefter) or temporary repositories for the dead (André Godard and Bernard Goldman).[18]

Recently Helena Sancisi-Weerdenburg has discussed the nature of these structures. She argues that there are no likely candidates for their funerary function.[19] She believes the structures were used for the coronation of the Persian kings: "Quite literally the king had to become elevated and this was brought about somewhere between heaven and earth. We can imagine the king, after the ritual, appearing in full regalia on top of the stairs; an epiphany in a sense."[20] Sancisi-Weerdenburg suggests the doors may have been left open while the king was alive to permit his personal fire to burn.[21] As to the puzzling duplication of two quite similar structures, she speculates:

17. D. Stronach, "Urartian and Achaemenian Tower Temples," *JNES* 26 (1967): 278–88.

18. See B. Goldman, "Persian Fire Temples or Tombs?" *JNES* 24 (1965): 305–8.

19. M. Boyce, *A History of Zoroastrianism* (Leiden: Brill, 1982), 2: 59, 116–17, has suggested that the Zendan was built for Queen Cassandane and the Kaʿabah for Queen Atossa.

20. H. W. A. M. Sancisi-Weerdenburg, "The Zendan and the Kaʿbah," in *Kunst, Kultur und Geschichte der Achämenidenzeit,* eds. H. Koch and D. N. MacKenzie (Berlin: Dietrich Reimer, 1983), p. 147.

21. But one would doubt whether this would permit enough ventilation; there is no evidence of soot, smoke, or ash in the interiors.

The remaining wall of the Zendan.

> It is possible that both monuments were used contemporarily: the Zendan for the coronation itself and the Kaʿabah for the annual renewal of the coronation. It is, however, also possible that the Zendan was left temporarily as a relic of the past, to be used again only in the time of Artaxerxes II.[22]

A fragmentary inscription was recovered in 1952 from the ruins of the Zendan, and published by Ali Sami in 1956.[23] This fragment contains but two lines in Old Persian and one line in Elamite. The Elamite contains the relative pronoun, as does the second line of the Old Persian. Of the three signs in the Old Persian, the last two signs are clear: *u-ša.*

Carl Nylander prefers the reading [*Ku-ra*]-*u-ša,* the genitive form of Cyrus. He draws the rather far-fetched conclusion that this is the first known inscription of Cyrus's son, Cambyses.[24] But there is no other evidence to support the idea that Cambyses built at Pasargadae in the short period before he left to invade Egypt.

Stronach suggests that the probable reading [*Ku*]*u-ša,* which would ordinarily represent Kush (Nubia), is an error for *Kuruš* (Cyrus).[25] On

22. Sancisi-Weerdenburg, "Zendan," p. 151.

23. R. Borger and W. Hinz, "Eine Dareios-Inschrift aus Pasargadae," *ZDMG* 109 (1959): 126, reproduced a photo of this fragment.

24. C. Nylander, "Bemerkungen zu einem Inschriftfragment in Pasargadae," *Orientalia Suecana* 11 (1962): 121–25.

25. Stronach, *Pasargadae,* pp. 136–37.

the other hand, George Cameron believed this was a fragmentary inscription of one of Darius's texts that did mention Kush.[26]

What can be made of these suggestions? First, Nylander used the drawing of Ali Sami, which appears to have incorrectly rendered the fragmentary first sign. A recent drawing by Ann Britt Tilia, reproduced by Stronach, shows the first sign cannot represent a *ra* but was probably a *ku*. Second, Stronach's suggestion is implausible. Cameron's guess is possible, but the small size of the fragment makes any hypothesis uncertain.

The Residential Palace

The residential palace (Palace P) is located 300 meters (almost 1,000 feet) southwest of the Zendan. It is a structure measuring 76 by 42 meters (250 by 138 feet), which had a central hall with five rows of six columns. On one side of this hall is a long portico with two rows of twenty columns and on the other side a shorter portico with two rows of twelve columns. A projecting white throne in the longer portico has been interpreted as a "throne seat." Fragments discovered by Herzfeld indicate that the central hall was brilliantly decorated in blue, turquoise, green, red, and yellow. Two side rooms were probably used for domestic purposes, or less likely as gardens.

The horizontally fluted bases of the columns were due to Greek influence. Greek inspiration has also been detected in the fragmentary reliefs from this palace and in the exceptionally long porticoes.[27] One set of reliefs shows only the lower parts of a king and his attendant. Holes indicate that the relief was originally plated with gold. Margaret Root comments: "Finally, as concerns the CMc text inscribed on the royal robes of the Palace P reliefs, there is no reason to doubt that they were inscribed during the reign of Cyrus on reliefs carved during his reign."[28]

A lively debate has ensued as to whether these reliefs date from the reign of Cyrus or of Darius. Nylander favors the former position[29] as does Root.[30] Stronach favors the later date.[31] Hinz has offered a contro-

26. G. G. Cameron, "An Inscription of Darius from Pasargadae," *Iran* 5 (1967): 7–10.

27. Stronach, *Pasargadae*, p. 72.

28. M. C. Root, *The King and Kingship in Achaemenid Art* (Leiden: Brill, 1979), p. 55.

29. C. Nylander, "Old Persian and Greek Stonecutting and the Chronology of Achaemenian Monuments," *AJA* 69 (1965): 49–55.

30. Root, *King and Kingship*, p. 58.

31. Stronach, *Pasargadae*, p. 96; see also A. Farkas, *Achaemenid Sculpture* (Istanbul: Nederlands Historisch-Archaeologisch Instituut in het Nabije Oosten, 1974), pp. 23–25.

versial translation of an inscription (CMb or DMa) from Palace P to suggest that, although Cyrus built the palace, it was Darius who set up all the Old Persian inscriptions at Pasargadae:

> Saith Darius, the great [king, the son] of Hystaspes, the Achaemenian: "This [palace] has [king] Cyrus . . . erected for himself and also [this] relief, an inscription [*however he had not*] added. I have written my [inscription] on it."[32] (emphasis added)

Because of the fragmentary nature of this text and the questionable translation by Riekele Borger and Hinz, we still cannot be sure whether the fine reliefs of Palace P were installed by Cyrus or Darius, although at least some of the inscriptions may have been set up by Darius.

A sudden flood in 1971 revealed a new palace of Cyrus about thirty miles from the Persian Gulf near the highway between Borazjan and Bushire. Ali Akba Sarfaraz uncovered two rows of black column bases. The dimensions of these bases are similar to those of Pasargadae's Palace P.

The Palace of Audience

The palace of audience (Palace S) is located 300 meters south of the residential palace. It was 45 by 56 meters (148 by 184 feet), with a central hypostyle hall measuring 32.4 by 22 meters (106 by 72 feet), surrounded on all four sides by porticoes. The central hall had black stone bases for eight white columns. A solitary column still stands over 13 meters (43 feet) high. Three of the original eight antae or corner pillars remain. Until at least 1840 each of these antae bore a copy of a trilingual inscription; today one still bears this text: "I Cyrus, the King, an Achaemenian." Despite arguments by Hinz to the contrary, there should be little doubt that Cyrus was the one who inscribed these brief texts.

Fragmentary remains of the jambs reveal the lower parts of the reliefs of a bull man, a fish man,[33] a lion demon, and other figures with

32. Borger and Hinz, "Eine Dareios-Inschrift," p. 125. The insertion by Hinz of *jedoch nicht* ("however he had not") is gratuitous. The basis for reconstructing the name *Darius* is a fragmentary Akkadian text, which contains but the last syllable (*muš*) of Darius's name (ibid., p. 118).

33. These were either representations of priests wearing fish garb, or mythological man/fish creatures of Apsu. See A. Green, "A Note on the Assyrian 'Goat-Fish,' 'Fish-Man' and 'Fish-Woman,' " *Iraq* 48 (1986): 25; F. A. M. Wiggermann, *Babylonian Prophylactic Figures: The Ritual Texts* (Amsterdam: Free University, 1986), p. 153.

Jamb from the audience palace.

talons, drawn from Assyrian prototypes.[34] Richard Barnett suggests some of these jambs, which also have Urartian elements, may represent iconographically Cyrus's religious toleration.[35]

The Gatehouse

The gatehouse (Palace R) is a monumental entrance to the palace area 200 meters southeast of the audience palace. Measuring 28.5 by 25.5 meters (93½ by 83⅔ feet), it was a hypostyle hall with two rows of four columns on black stone bases, which had two main and two side entrances. According to the fragments that Herzfeld found, the outer entrance was guarded by two huge winged bulls and the inner entrance by human-headed bulls.[36] From the size of the column bases, it has been estimated that the columns were probably more than 16 meters (52 feet) high.[37]

One white limestone jamb still bears a bearded figure wearing a triple Egyptian Atef (or Hemhem) crown, four wings, and an Elamite garment.[38] As late as 1861 the figure was surmounted by the trilingual

34. Frankfort, *Art and Architecture,* p. 216; Farkas, *Achaemenid Sculpture,* p. 10; T. Kawami, "A Possible Source for the Sculptures of the Audience Hall, Pasargadae," *Iran* 10 (1972): 146–48.

35. R. Barnett, "'Anath, Ba'al, and Pasargadae," *Mélanges de l'Université Saint-Joseph* 45 (1969): 422.

36. P. Calmeyer, "Figürliche Fragmente aus Pasargadae nach Zeichnungen E. Herzfelds," *AMI* 14 (1981): 27–44.

37. Stronach, *Pasargadae,* p. 44.

38. Ghirshman, *Art of Ancient Iran,* p. 128. The garment is like that worn by King Teuman of Elam, who was killed by Ashurbanipal.

The gatehouse.

CMa inscription, "I, Cyrus, the King, an Achaemenian." Mallowan suggests this may represent the powers attributed to kings like Cyrus.[39] Barnett identified this figure with the Phoenician god Baal.[40] Stronach agrees with Herzfeld's interpretation of the figure as an apotropaic, protective spirit.[41] But Peter Calmeyer, noting that the figure faces inward, argues that it was not a figure that averted evil but one that blessed the ruler.[42] Root concludes:

> But—whether it represents a syncretic deity, some metaphorical vision of an abstract ideal of imperial domain, or a vision of Cyrus himself in a mythical aspect of ideal kingship—the Pasargadae "Genius" is an Achaemenid creation emerging from and responding to the demands of empire as Cyrus saw them.[43]

The Garden and the Bridge

Excavations by Stronach in 1963 uncovered two new structures. Between the palace of audience and the gatehouse he uncovered the remains of a bridge that had five rows of three stone columns about 2 meters (6½ feet) high. The superstructure may have been wooden.

39. M. Mallowan, "Cyrus the Great (558–529 B.C.)," *Iran* 10 (1972): 2.
40. Barnett, "ʿAnath, Baʿal," p. 420.
41. Stronach, *Pasargadae*, p. 53.
42. Calmeyer, "Figürliche Fragmente," p. 28.
43. Root, *King and Kingship*, p. 303.

The winged Genius from the gatehouse.

Stronach believes that this was either a late- or post-Achaemenian structure.[44]

Between the palace of audience and the residential palace Stronach also discovered two pavilions that were set in a paradise or park-like setting irrigated by an extensive set of water courses. In this area the excavators found a jar with thirty-seven different kinds of precious objects, including gold bracelets, earrings, bells, silver spoons, and coral and pearl beads. The objects, which date between 450 and 350 B.C., may have been hidden when Alexander approached.

The Tomb of Cyrus

The tomb of Cyrus, called the Qabr-i Madar-i Sulaiman or "the tomb of the mother of Solomon," was described by many classical writers.[45] They note that magi offered daily sacrifices of sheep and monthly sacrifices of horses at the tomb. Within the tomb Cyrus's golden coffin was placed. Arrian (*Anabasis* 6.29.8) reports that it bore the following inscription: "Mortal! I am Cyrus, son of Cambyses, who founded the Persian Empire, and was Lord of Asia. Grudge me not, then, my monument."[46]

44. Stronach, *Pasargadae*, p. 113.

45. Sami, *Pasargadae*, p. 18, believes that it was the ascription of the tomb to Solomon's mother that helped to preserve the structure. A mosque was built enclosing the tomb in the thirteenth century.

46. See also Strabo 15.3.7; Plutarch, *Alexander* 69.4. Stronach, *Pasargadae*, p. 26, doubts the accuracy of the inscription as reported by the classical writers.

Remains of the bridge.

Remains of a garden pavilion.

The tomb of white limestone, 5.5 meters high, rests upon a six-level base also 5.5 meters high, for a total height from the foundation level of about 11 meters (36 feet). The structure may have been patterned after a ziggurat like the one at Choga-Zanbil, but many of the features are Lydian and Ionian Greek in origin.[47]

According to Nylander:

> In short, there is much in this building that is undoubtedly Ionic and not a little that may well have the same background, although it is impossible to prove. There is, as far as I can see, little or nothing in the Cyrus Tomb that could not be Ionic, except the motif as a whole, with the six-

47. Ibid., pp. 42–43.

The tomb of Cyrus.

> tiered plinth probably taken from Mesopotamia and the steep roof from a traditional Iranian tomb and house.[48]

There is a small entrance to the inner chamber that once held the golden sarcophagus of Cyrus. The gabled roof is formed of five enormous stones arranged around a relieving hollow space, discovered by Ali Sami in 1951. In 1969 Stronach found the faint design of a rosette on the northwest pediment, which Stronach takes as a symbol of Ahuramazda.[49]

In 1950 a crude parallel to Cyrus's tomb was discovered in the Buzpar Valley sixty miles southwest of Kazerun in the Sar Mahshad region. The white limestone monument is called Gur-i Dokhtar (the tomb of the daughter). This was probably a late- or post-Achaemenian copy of Cyrus's tomb.[50] In Lydian Sardis in western Turkey a small stepped tomb, with some similarities to Cyrus's tomb, has been discovered.[51] This probably belonged to a Persian official stationed at Sardis after its conquest by Cyrus.

48. Nylander, *Ionians*, p. 102.

49. D. Stronach, "A Circular Symbol on the Tomb of Cyrus," *Iran* 9 (1971): 155–58. On the other hand, Duchesne-Guillemin, "Le dieu de Cyrus," p. 17, interprets this rosette as a symbol of Mithra.

50. Stronach, *Pasargadae*, p. 300; Mallowan, "Cyrus," p. 17, had viewed it as more rudimentary and primitive.

51. J. M. Cook and D. J. Blackman, "Archaeology in Western Asia Minor, 1965–70," *Archaeological Reports for 1970–71* (London: British School at Athens, 1971), p. 40.

Paradises

Although there were some antecedents among the Assyrians[52] and among the Neo-Babylonians such as the famed Hanging Gardens of Nebuchadnezzar built for his Median wife,[53] it was the Persians who were noted for developing the so-called paradise or royal park. For example, Arrian (*Anabasis* 6.29.4) comments: "The tomb of this Cyrus was in the territory of the Pasargadae, in the royal park (*paradeisos*); round it had been planted a grove of all sorts of trees; the grove was irrigated, and deep grass had grown in the meadow."

The Greek word *paradeisos* was borrowed from the Median word **paridaiza* (Old Persian **paridaida,* Avestan *paridaēza,* Elamite *partetaš*).[54] It literally meant "beyond the wall," hence "enclosure" or "park." It was borrowed as *pardēsu* in Akkadian and as *pardēs* in Hebrew.

After examining a number of Babylonian texts of the Achaemenid era, Muhammed Dandamayev writes: "We can conclude from the texts under consideration that in Babylonia there were at least three 'paradises' belonging to the Achaemenid kings, which were situated in the neighbourhood of Sippar, Uruk and Nippur."[55]

The Hebrew word *pardēs* occurs three times in the Old Testament: when Nehemiah sought timber from Asaph the keeper of the king's park or *pardēs* (NIV "forest"; see Neh. 2:8); "I made gardens and *parks* and planted all kinds of fruit trees in them" (Eccles. 2:5); "Your plants are an *orchard* of pomegranates with choice fruits, with henna and nard" (Song of Sol. 4:13).

The Greek writers have many comments to make about the Persian predilection for planting paradises. In Xenophon (*Oeconomicus* 4.13–14) the following dialogue is given:

> "Yet further," continued Socrates, "in all the districts he [the Persian king] resides in and visits he takes care that there are 'paradises,' as they call them, full of all the good and beautiful things that the soil will produce, and in this he himself spends most of his time, except when the season precludes it."
>
> "Then it is of course necessary, Socrates, to take care that these para-

52. D. J. Wiseman, "Mesopotamian Gardens," *Anatolian Studies* 33 (1983): 137–44.

53. D. J. Wiseman, *Nebuchadrezzar and Babylon* (London: Oxford University Press, 1985), pp. 56–60.

54. R. N. Frye, *The History of Ancient Iran* (Munich: C. H. Beck'sche Verlagsbuchhandlung, 1984), p. 78.

55. M. A. Dandamayev, "Royal *Paradeisoi* in Babylonia," in *Orientalia J. Duchesne-Guillemin Emerito Oblata* (Leiden: Brill), p. 117. P. Briant, *Rois, Tributs et Paysans* (Paris: Les Belles Lettres, 1982), pp. 20ff., believes that each satrapy had at least one "paradise."

dises in which the king spends his time shall contain a fine stock of trees and all other beautiful things that the soil produces."

Xenophon (*Anabasis* 1.2.7) describes the royal paradise of Cyrus the Younger at Celaenae in Phrygia (western Turkey) as "a large park full of wild animals, which he used to hunt on horseback whenever he wished to give himself and his horses exercise." There was also a "paradise" at the Persian satrapal capital at Daskyleion in northwest Turkey.[56] Plutarch (*Artaxerxes* 25), speaking of Artaxerxes II, notes his "admirable parks in elaborate cultivation, although the region round about was bare and treeless." Royal paradises were also established in Syria and Phoenicia.[57]

In the Hellenistic period the Septuagint translators of the Old Testament used the word *paradeisos* for the garden of Eden (Gen. 3:8–10). The concept of paradise as a garden full of fruitful trees and watered by a river is found in passages of the Pseudepigrapha in the intertestamental era, such as 2 Enoch 8 (A):[58]

> And they placed me in the midst of Paradise. And that place has an appearance of pleasantness that has never been seen. Every tree was in full flower. Every fruit was ripe, every food was in yield profusely; every fragrance was pleasant. And the four rivers were flowing past with gentle movement, with every kind of garden producing every kind of good food. And the tree of life is in that place, under which the Lord takes a rest when the Lord takes a walk in Paradise. And that tree is indescribable for pleasantness of fragrance.[59]

The concept of paradise as a garden occurs in about thirty passages of the Qur'an.[60] The Arabic loan-word from Persian, *firdaus,* occurs in two passages.[61]

> Surah 18.108 (Arabic 18.107)[62]
>
> Lo! those who believe and do good works, theirs are the Gardens of Paradise (*jannātul-firdausi*) for welcome.

56. A. R. Burn, "Persia and the Greeks," in *The Cambridge History of Iran II: The Median and Achaemenian Periods,* ed. I. Gershevitch (Cambridge: Cambridge University Press, 1985), p. 339.

57. C. Clermont-Ganneau, "Le paradeisos royal achéménide de Sidon," *RB* 30 (1921): 106–9.

58. J. H. Charlesworth, ed., *The Old Testament Pseudepigrapha* (Garden City: Doubleday, 1983), 1: xxxiii.

59. Ibid., p. 115. See also 1 Enoch 23–25.

60. S. Mahmood, "The Earthly Paradise: The Concept of Garden in Islam," *Muslim World League Journal* 11/7 (1984): 23–26.

61. In the Persian epic, *The Shâhnâme,* a derivative of the Old Persian word, *pâlêz,* is used for "park." See R. N. Frye, "Achaemenid Echoes in Sasanian Times," in *Kunst, Kultur,* pp. 247–52.

62. See M. M. Pickthall, trans., *The Meaning of the Glorious Koran* (New York: New American Library, 1953); G. Fluegel, *Corani Textus Arabicus* (Ridgewood, N.J.: Gregg, 1965 reprint of 1883

Surah 23.11
Those who will inherit Paradise (*firdausa*). There they will abide.

The more usual word used to express the concept of paradise is the word *jannātun* (gardens), as in the following passages:

Surah 2.25 (Arabic 2.23)
And give glad tidings (O Muhammad) unto those who believe and do good works; that theirs are Gardens (*jannātun*) underneath which rivers flow; as often as they are regaled with food of the fruit thereof, they say: This is what was given us aforetime; and it is given to them in resemblance. There for them are pure companions; there for ever they abide.

Surah 18.32 (Arabic 18.30)
As for such, theirs will be Gardens of Eden (*jannātu ʿadnin*), wherein rivers flow beneath them; therein they will be given armlets of gold and will wear green robes of finest silk and gold embroidery, reclining upon thrones therein. Blest the reward, and fair the resting-place!

Surah 37.43–48 (Arabic 37.42ff.)
In the Gardens (*jannāti*) of delight, on couches facing one another; a cup from a gushing spring is brought round for them, white, delicious to the drinkers, wherein there is no headache nor are they made mad thereby. And with them are those of modest gaze, with lovely eyes.

Hamilton Gibb summarizes the many Qur'anic passages on Paradise as follows:

> Then the blessed, the godfearing men and women, the humble and charitable, the forgiving, those who have suffered and been persecuted for God's sake, those who have fought in the way of God, shall be summoned to enter the Garden of Paradise, the Abode of Peace, the abiding mansion, where they shall dwell for ever by flowing rivers, praising God, reclining on silken couches, enjoying heavenly food and drink and the company of dark-eyed maidens and wives of perfect purity, and yet greater bliss which no soul knoweth.[63]

---

edition); G. Fluegel, *Concordantiae Corani Arabicae* (Ridgewood, N.J.: Gregg, 1965 reprint of 1842 edition).

63. M. Gibb, *Mohammedanism* (New York: Oxford University Press, 1962), p. 61. See also Surahs 22:23; 38:51–53 (Arabic 38:50ff.); 44:51–52.

10
Persepolis

The Capital of Darius and Xerxes

Persepolis seems to be a contraction of *Persia polis* (Persian city). Persepolis was probably called *Perseptolis* (destroyer of cities) by Aeschylus in *Persae* (65) as a reference to the burning of Athens by Xerxes. The Persians themselves called it *Parsa.*[1] The Persepolis texts refer to the site as the "fortress" (Old Persian *dīda,* Elamite *birta*). After around A.D. 300 the area was known as *Sat-Setūn* (hundred-column palace). The site today is known as *Takht-i Jamshid* (the throne of Jamshid), a legendary Persian hero.[2]

Persepolis is forty-eight miles south of Pasargadae and thirty-five miles northeast of the modern town of Shiraz. The famous site is located at the base of the Kuh-i Rahmat (mountain of mercy) in the Marv-i Dasht Plain at an altitude of 5,800 feet.

1. The name *Parsa* occurs about 350 times in the Elamite tablets from Persepolis. The workers' boom town or "Persepolis West" has been identified as Matezziš. See W. M. Sumner, "Achaemenid Settlement in the Persepolis Plain," *AJA* 90 (1986): 21. Sumner estimates that the plain, which contained thirty-nine habitation sites, had a population of 43,600 in the Achaemenid period.

2. A. S. Shahbazi, "From *Parsa* to *Taxt-e Jamshid,*" *AMI* n.F. 10 (1977): 197–200.

Classical References

There are no biblical references to Persepolis. Maccabees (2 Macc. 9:2) mentions the unsuccessful attempt of Antiochus Epiphanes IV to plunder the site before his death in 164 B.C.

Roman Ghirshman held that Ctesias, the Greek physician at the court of Artaxerxes II (404–359 B.C.), did not mention the city, and therefore concluded that "no foreigners were admitted to the city."[3] But it is probable that when Ctesias (*Persika* 28, 44–45) described the goal of the Achaemenid funeral processions as *Persa,* he was referring to Persepolis.[4]

Numerous Hellenistic and Roman sources discuss the sack of Persepolis by Alexander the Great (see below). According to Strabo (15.3.6), a Roman writer under Augustus: "Persepolis, next to Susa, was the most beautifully constructed city, and the largest, having a palace that was remarkable, particularly in respect to the high value of its treasures."

Travelers' Descriptions

The ruins of Persepolis were plundered in the pre-Islamic period. Three Achaemenian doorways were set up at the Sasanian site of Qaṣr-i-Abu Naṣr, located thirty-five miles from Persepolis and southeast of Shiraz.[5] The doorways have now been returned to Persepolis.

Muslims who saw the standing ruins misunderstood their significance. Ibn al-Balkhi, a writer of the twelfth century, commenting on the colossal winged bulls, remarked: "Further, there is to be seen here the figure of Buraq, . . . the face is as the face of a man . . . but the body, with the fore and hind legs, are those of a bull."[6] Buraq was the winged horse upon which Muhammad made his miraculous night journey to the al-Aqsah Mosque in Jerusalem.[7]

From the fourteenth century European travelers sent back descriptions of Persepolis. An early visitor was Josafa Barbaro who visited the site in 1474. Pietro della Valle, who was the first to bring to Europe

3. R. Ghirshman, *The Art of Ancient Iran* (New York: Golden, 1964), p. 154.

4. R. N. Frye, *The History of Ancient Iran* (Munich: C. H. Beck'sche, 1984), p. 125.

5. C. K. Wilkinson, "The Achaemenian Remains at Qaṣr-i-Abu Naṣr," *JNES* 24 (1965): 341–45.

6. Cited by D. N. Wilber, *Persepolis, Capital of Parsa* (New York: Thomas W. Crowell, 1969), p. 105.

7. A. Bevan, "Mohammed's Ascension to Heaven," *Beihefte zur ZAW* 27 (1914): 51–61; J. Porter, "Muhammad's Journey to Heaven," *Numen* 21 (1974): 64–80.

cuneiform inscriptions, saw Persepolis in 1621.[8] Carsten Niebuhr correctly identified the site as Persepolis in 1765. Noteworthy travelers in the nineteenth century included Robert Ker Porter (1817), Eugène Flandin and Pascal Coste (1840), and German photographers Friedrich Andreas and Franz Stolze in 1882.

Excavations

The first man to dig at Persepolis was Mo'tamed ad-Dawla Farhad Mirza, the governor of Fars. In 1876/1877 he worked with six hundred men in the area of the throne hall. Unfortunately we know nothing of what he recovered.

In 1924 the Iranian government asked Ernst Herzfeld of Berlin to prepare a report on the possibilities of clearing Persepolis. He grossly underestimated the time it would take to work at the site.

The first scientific excavations were conducted by Herzfeld from 1931 to 1934 for the Oriental Institute of Chicago. He was assisted by an architect, Fritz Krefter. In 1931 he cleared the area of the harem and then erected a structure on it for his staff. In 1932 he uncovered the Apadana, the gate of all nations, the central building, and palace G. In the final years he excavated the court between the Apadana and the throne hall. Although Herzfeld discussed his discoveries in a number of publications, he failed to publish a final report before his death in 1948.

In 1935 Erich Schmidt assumed the directorship and continued in that post until 1939. Schmidt was born in Germany and had been held as a prisoner in Siberia for four years during the First World War. He came to the United States, where he received his Ph.D. in anthropology. Schmidt worked primarily in the area of the treasury and recovered numerous Elamite tablets, Achaemenid inscriptions, and Aramaic texts. He produced comprehensive reports in two folio volumes.[9] A third folio volume was published posthumously in 1970 after Schmidt's death in 1964.[10]

Since 1939 the Iranian Archaeological Service under the direction of the French scholar, André Godard, and under the Iranians, Muhammad Mustafavi, Ali Sami, and A. Tajvidi, have conducted excavations. Be-

8. C. W. Ceram, *A Picture History of Archaeology* (London: Thames and Hudson, 1963), pp. 188–89.

9. E. F. Schmidt, *Persepolis I* (Chicago: University of Chicago Press, 1953); idem, *Persepolis II* (Chicago: University of Chicago Press, 1953).

10. E. F. Schmidt, *Persepolis III* (Chicago: University of Chicago Press, 1970).

Guest tents set up for the 1971 2500th anniversary celebration.

tween 1964 and 1969 the Italian scholars, Giuseppe and Ann Tilia, supervised ambitious restorations.[11]

In 1971 the refurbished site of Persepolis was the stage for the Shah's 2500th anniversary celebration of his nation at an estimated cost of over 100 million dollars. An emperor, nine kings, and sixteen presidents were in attendance. The guests were housed in air-conditioned tents below the terrace. They were served wine and meals catered by Maxim's of Paris. Iranians garbed in ancient costumes and armor paraded past in review.[12]

The History of the Site

Darius I (521–486 B.C.) began the construction of Persepolis some time after 520. A foundation document of Darius is dated circa 514 because of coins found with it. This led Fritz Krefter to believe that the preparatory work on the terrace took almost six years.[13] The buildings were completed only after sixty years of labor during the reigns of Xerxes (485–465) and Artaxerxes I (464–424).[14]

Darius was responsible for building the fortifications, the platform, the monumental stairway, the central building, his palace, the Apa-

11. A. and G. Tilia, *Studies and Restorations at Persepolis and Other Sites of Fārs* (Rome: Istituto Italiano per il Medio ed Estremo Oriente, 1972).

12. "Iran: The Show of Shows," *Time* (Oct. 25, 1971): 32–33; "The Shah's Princely Party," *Life* (Oct. 29, 1971): 22–30.

13. F. Krefter, *Persepolis-Rekonstruktion* (Berlin: Gebrüder Mann, 1971), p. 11.

14. Schmidt, *Persepolis I*, p. 39; A. Godard, "Les travaux de Persépolis," *Archaeologica Orientalia in Memoriam Ernst Herzfeld* (Locust Valley, N.Y.: J. J. Augustin, 1952), p. 122.

dana, and part of the treasury. Xerxes completed the Apadana, the gate of all nations, his palace, the harem, and the treasury. He began the throne hall, which was completed by Artaxerxes I. The Elamite tablets indicate that building activities largely ceased after the seventh year of this king. Artaxerxes III (358–337 B.C.) did add a staircase on the western side of Darius's palace, and built the facade of palace G.

Alexander the Great came to Persepolis in 330 B.C. According to Arrian (*Anabasis* 3.8.11) he destroyed the city as an act of vengeance for the destruction of Athens by Xerxes in 480.

> He set the Persian palace on fire, even though Parmenio urged him to save it, arguing that it was not right to destroy his own property. . . . But Alexander replied that he intended to punish the Persians for their invasion of Greece, the destruction of Athens, the burning of the temples, and all manner of terrible things done to the Greeks; because of these things, he was exacting revenge.

Other classical sources (Diodorus Siculus, Plutarch, Curtius, Cleitarchus) add that it was Thaïs, a courtesan from Attica, who urged the destruction of the site as a deed worthy of Alexander. While many scholars reject this embellishment as fictitious, Sir Mortimer Wheeler is inclined to accept it as credible.[15]

Archaeologists found vivid evidence of Alexander's conflagration, particularly in the areas of the throne hall and the treasury. In some areas Herzfeld discovered ash over a foot thick from the carbonized remains of cedar beams. In their haste the Macedonians left behind many valuable objects in the treasury. A silver coin, dated 340 to 330 B.C., may have been dropped by one of the looters.[16]

According to Diodorus Siculus (17.71.2) and Curtius (5.6.9), Alexander and his men removed 120,000 talents of bullion from Persepolis. Plutarch (*Alexander* 37.4) claims that a caravan of 20,000 mules and 5,000 camels was needed to haul the booty away.

The Function of Persepolis

Because of its isolation, Persepolis was clearly not designed as an administrative center. Many scholars believe it was intended primarily

15. M. Wheeler, *Flames over Persepolis* (New York: Reynal, 1968), pp. 23ff. See further J. R. Hamilton, *Plutarch, ALEXANDER, A Commentary* (Oxford: Clarendon, 1969), pp. 96–101; E. N. Borza, "Fire from Heaven: Alexander at Persepolis," *CP* 67 (1972): 233–45; J. M. Balcer, "Alexander's Burning of Persepolis," *IA* 13 (1978): 119–33.

16. Schmidt, *Persepolis I*, p. 192.

Relief of a lion devouring a bull.

as a religious shrine. They interpret the procession of representatives from every part of the empire as coming to Persepolis for the New Year at the time of the spring equinox, a festival later called the No Ruz.[17] The reliefs of the lion devouring the bull have been interpreted as having a seasonal significance, with the lion representing the summer heat and the bull the winter rains.[18] Arthur Pope interpreted the crenelated walls as representing mountains and the numerous columns as symbolic of the sacred forest.[19] This explanation of Persepolis as a ritual city has been widely accepted by many scholars.[20]

To provide details of such a New Year's rite at Persepolis, James Fennely recently drew upon Babylonian texts to develop a detailed step-by-step program.[21] But his arguments, such as his suggestion that

17. G. Widengren, *Les Religions de l'Iran* (Paris: Payot, 1968), pp. 58–67.

18. J. Hinnells, *Persian Mythology* (London: Hamlyn, 1973), p. 99.

19. A. Pope, "Persepolis as a Ritual City," *Arch* 10 (1957): 123–30.

20. Balcer, "Alexander's Burning of Persepolis," p. 128; K. Erdmann, "Persepolis: Daten und Deutungen," *MDOG* 92 (1960): 21–47; G. de Francovich, "Problems of Achaemenid Architecture," *EW* 16 (1966): 204; R. Ghirshman, "A propos de Persépolis," *Artibus Asiae* 20 (1957): 265ff.; idem, *Art of Ancient Iran*, pp. 154ff.; Krefter, *Persepolis-Rekonstruktion*, p. 96; I. Luschey-Schmeisser, "Nachleben und Wiederaufnahme achämenidischer Elemente in der späteren Kunst Irans," in *Kunst, Kultur und Geschichte der Achämenidenzeit*, eds. H. Koch and D. N. MacKenzie (Berlin: Dietrich Reimer, 1983), p. 279; M. C. Root, *The King and Kingship in Achaemenid Art* (Leiden: Brill, 1979), p. 278; G. Walser, *Die Völkerschaften auf den Reliefs von Persepolis* (Berlin: Gebrüder Mann, 1966), pp. 20, 23–24.

21. J. M. Fennely, "The Persepolis Ritual," *BA* 43 (1980): 135–62.

Darius's palace was actually a temple, are strained.[22] Wolfgang Lentz and his colleagues have offered the suggestion that Persepolis's siting was oriented according to astrological/astronomical factors—not so much the spring equinox but the summer solstice.[23] But these suggestions have been rejected as speculative by other scholars.[24]

Recently the conventional interpretation of Persepolis as solely a ritual city has been questioned by scholars. It seems that the original interpretation of the site as a setting for a New Year's rite came to Herzfeld as an inspiration when he was invited by the governor of Shiraz to celebrate the No Ruz rite at Persepolis.[25] Since we have no contemporary Old Persian texts describing such a rite, scholars have extrapolated backwards over a millennium, using data from an Arabic source (eleventh century A.D.) that describes No Ruz gifts presented to a Sasanian king by his subjects. But as Oscar Muscarella notes, "the conspicuous absence of a Persian delegation bearing gifts on the Apadana facade seems very much out of character with what we can surmise of the nature of the Persian No Ruz celebration during the Sasanian Period and later."[26] Muscarella therefore concludes: "It is, thus, perhaps more likely that the Apadana relief was intended to represent (albeit in concrete terms) a certain abstract vision of empire and of imperial harmony rather than an *illustration* of an *actual* No Ruz ceremony."[27]

Gerd Gropp believes that the concept of Persepolis as primarily the setting of a New Year's rite is too narrow. Persepolis was a residential palace as well. He observes a distinction between public area—those on platforms provided with building inscriptions—and the private area at Persepolis. He interprets the reliefs as a general proclamation of royal might over the peoples of the realm.[28]

22. See the letter of L. D. Levine, E. J. Keall, T. C. Young, Jr., and J. S. Holladay, Jr., in *BA* 44 (1981): 72–73.

23. W. Lentz and W. Schlosser, "Persepolis—Ein Beitrag zur Funktionsbestimmung," *ZDMG* Supplement 1 (1969) M: 957–83; W. Lentz, W. Schlosser, and G. Gropp, "Persepolis—weitere Beiträge zur Funktionsbestimmung," *ZDMG* 121 (1971): 254–68.

24. See the objections of W. Hinz and W. Eilers in Lentz and Schlosser, "Persepolis—Ein Beitrag zur Funktionsbestimmung," pp. 981–83; L. Trümpelmann, "Tore von Persepolis: Zur Bauplannung des Dareios," *AMI* n.F. 7 (1974): 163, 170.

25. C. Nylander, "Achaemenid Imperial Art," in *Power and Propaganda*, ed. M. T. Larsen (Copenhagen: Akademisk Forlag, 1979), p. 348. Herzfeld later suggested the celebrations depicted on the reliefs were reflections of the Mithrakana feast instead of the New Year's rite. See A. D. H. Bivar, "Religious Subjects on Achaemenid Seals," in *Mithraic Studies*, ed. J. Hinnells (Manchester: Manchester University Press, 1975), 1: 97.

26. O. Muscarella, review of G. Walser, *Die Völkerschaften*, in *JNES* 28 (1969): 278. P. Calmeyer, "Textual Sources for the Interpretation of Achaemenian Palace Decorations," *Iran* 18 (1980): 55–56, also raises questions about the New Year's interpretation.

27. Ibid., p. 279.

28. G. Gropp, "Beobachtungen in Persepolis," *AMI* n.F. 4 (1971): 48.

In a similar vein Bernard Goldman observes:

> The celebrations of the king's majesty take place under the ever-present symbol of Ahuramazda, but there is no overt sign that Persepolis was in any sense a sacred precinct or dedicated to the divine. Each of its buildings, in the sculpture and short inscriptions, is clearly marked as consecrated to the living, immortal state manifest in the corporeal presence of the reigning king.[29]

Carl Nylander comments: "It seems more promising today, to see Persepolis, the richest and most eloquent expression of Achaemenid power, in a political, dynastic context, an elaborate statement of kingship and empire."[30]

Peter Calmeyer also concludes:

> To sum up the results: all parallels to the reliefs drawn from contemporary sources point in the same direction; all reliefs are most easily explained as expressions of royalty; none of them has a special religious connection. In the interpretation of the texts they are neither confined to Persepolis nor to a certain time of the year, they are everyday kingship.[31]

The Terrace

In contrast with the few scattered buildings at Pasargadae, the buildings at Persepolis are concentrated on a great terrace, which is as long as the Athenian Acropolis but is four to five times as wide.[32] It is about 430 meters (1411 feet) long and 300 meters (984 feet) wide and covers 33 acres.[33] Its height of 12 meters (40 feet) was formed by stone blocks that were joined by iron staples.

The extensive drainage system within the terrace was prepared beforehand. The huge stone columns, thirty tons in weight, were cut out from nearby quarries, transported to the site, and then worked and

29. B. Goldman, "Political Realia on Persepolitan Sculpture," *Orientalia Lovaniensia Periodica* 5 (1974): 41.

30. Nylander, "Achaemenid Imperial Art," p. 348.

31. P. Calmeyer, "Textual Sources for the Interpretation of Achaemenian Palace Decorations," *Iran* 18 (1980): 61. M. Boyce, *A History of Zoroastrianism* (Leiden: Brill, 1982), 2: 108, concedes: "More knowledge of ancient Near Eastern antecedents for the sculptured motifs of Persepolis has made it, moreover, unnecessary to seek religious implications in them."

32. A. W. Lawrence, "The Acropolis and Persepolis," *JHS* 71 (1951): 111–19.

33. Since the terrace is not a perfect rectangle its sides are not equal: the east side is 430 meters, the west is 455 meters, the north is 300 meters, and the south is 290 meters.

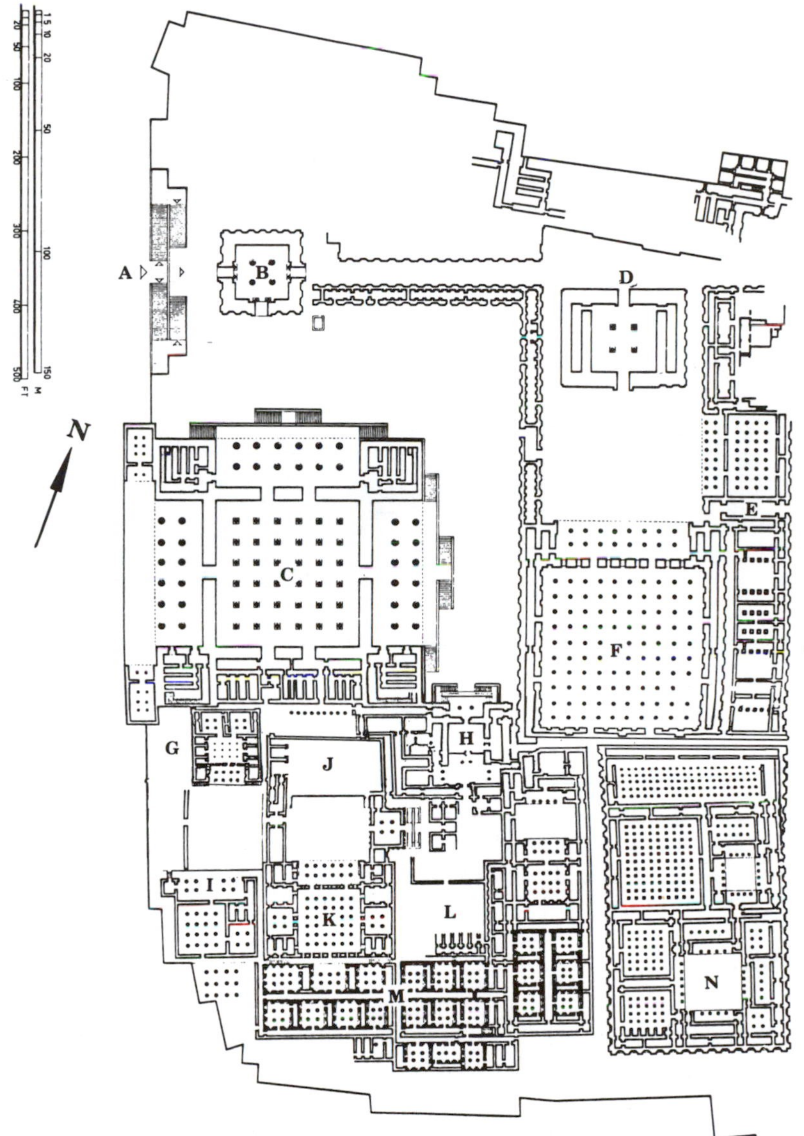

Plan of Persepolis.

(After E. Schmidt, University of Chicago)

A. **Stairway**
B. **Gate of All Nations**
C. **Apadana**
D. **Unfinished Gate**
E. **Barracks**
F. **Throne Hall**
G. **Darius' Palace**
H. **Central Building**
I. **Palace H**
J. **Palace G**
K. **Xerxes' Palace**
L. **Palace D**
M. **Harem**
N. **Treasury**

The great stairway leading up to the gate of all nations. (Courtesy of Gebrüder Mann Verlag)

polished in place. Artists sketched the designs on the surface of the stones, and sculptors then carved the reliefs.[34] The sculptors were among the lowest-paid workers at Persepolis.[35] Hundreds of masons' marks probably marked the organization of teams of workers.[36]

The Stairway

Access to the terrace is gained by a magnificent double stairway, which is 7.35 meters (24 feet) wide, with 111 steps. The steps, which rise only 10 centimeters high (4 inches), could be easily ascended by mounted horsemen. Herzfeld, who described these stairs as "perhaps the most perfect flight of steps ever built,"[37] believed they served as the only entrance. Schmidt suggested there were probably postern gates and service gates as well.[38]

34. P. Roos, "An Achaemenian Sketch Slab and the Ornaments of the Royal Dress at Persepolis," *EW* n.s. 20 (1970): 51–59.

35. M. Roaf, "Sculptures and Sculptors at Persepolis," *Iran* 21 (1983): 69.

36. C. Nylander, "Masons' Marks in Persepolis," *Akten des VII. Internationalen Kongresses für iranische Kunst und Archäologie, AMI* Ergänzungsband 6 (Berlin: Dietrich Reimer, 1979), pp. 236–39.

37. E. Herzfeld, *Iran in the Ancient East* (London: Oxford University Press, 1941), p. 225.

38. Schmidt, *Persepolis I*, p. 64.

The gate of all nations.

The Gate of All Nations

The imposing gate of all nations stands just above the grand stairway in the northwest corner of the terrace. The overall structure is 36 meters (118 feet) square. Its central room is square—25 meters (82 feet) on a side—with four columns that supported the roof. It contained a throne with a footstool. Visitors could wait upon black marble benches. The western and eastern portals of the gate were guarded by pairs of colossal winged and human-headed bulls. A trilingual inscription by Xerxes (XPa) declares:

> Saith Xerxes the King: By the favor of Ahuramazda, this Colonnade of All Lands I built. Much other (construction) was built within this (city)

Xerxes' throne hall and Darius's Apadana.

> Persepolis, which I built and which my father built. Whatever good construction is seen, all that by the favor of Ahuramazda we built.[39]

The Apadana

The great audience hall, begun by Darius and completed by Xerxes, was the largest and most impressive building on the site, measuring 120 meters (394 feet) square. Its tall columns—19 meters (62 feet) high—were capped by double bull protomes. The columns stood on a terrace 2.6 meters (8½ feet) high. The main hall was a square—60.5 meters (almost 200 feet) on a side—surrounded on all sides except the south with columned porticoes. There were 36 columns in the central hall and 36 in the three porticoes. Of the original 72 columns, 13 are still standing. The roof was supported by wooden beams. The walls were of sun-dried bricks with towers at each of the four corners. In the northeast and southeast corners stone boxes with gold and silver tablets inscribed by Darius were discovered.[40] Herzfeld estimated the Apadana could accommodate a crowd of 10,000.

39. R. G. Kent, *Old Persian*, rev. ed. (New Haven: American Oriental Society, 1953), p. 148.

40. DPh in Kent, *OP*, pp. 136–37. Inasmuch as these inscriptions do not mention Darius's conquest of the European Scythians, Schmidt concluded that the foundation of the Apadana was laid before that expedition, that is, before 513 B.C. See Schmidt, *Persepolis I*, p. 70.

An experimental griffin protome intended for the top of a column.

The Apadana Stairway Reliefs

Among the most important and impressive features of the Apadana are the reliefs on the northern and the eastern stairways.[41] Each staircase is about 84 meters (275 feet) long, and has two wings and a central stair. The northern stairway has been badly damaged by weather, Muslims, and tourists over the centuries. The eastern stairway, which was covered until excavations in 1932, is in an excellent state of preservation.

The northern part of the eastern staircase depicts alternating Persian and Median nobles conversing with each other. The most important section is the southern wing of the eastern staircase. It bears three registers of reliefs, each about .9 meters (3 feet) high, depicting twenty-three delegations bearing gifts or tribute. The envoys are set apart by reliefs of cypress (or pine) trees. More than eight hundred figures were carved on the Apadana reliefs.[42]

Scholars have tried to identify the ethnic backgrounds of the representatives by comparison with lists of peoples and other reliefs that are accompanied by inscriptions. About a dozen categories of such lists are

41. Five buildings have two decorated stairways each: the Apadana (north and east); Darius's palace (west and south); the central building (north and south); Xerxes' palace (west and east); and Artaxerxes' palace (northwest and northeast).

42. More than three thousand figures were carved at Persepolis. Root suggests that the Apadana reliefs may have inspired the Parthenon frieze. M. C. Root, "The Parthenon Frieze and the Apadana Reliefs at Persepolis: Reassessing a Programmatic Relationship," *AJA* 89 (1985): 103–20.

The Apadana according to Krefter's reconstruction. (Courtesy of Gebrüder Mann Verlag)

The Apadana viewed from the north. (Courtesy of Gebrüder Mann Verlag)

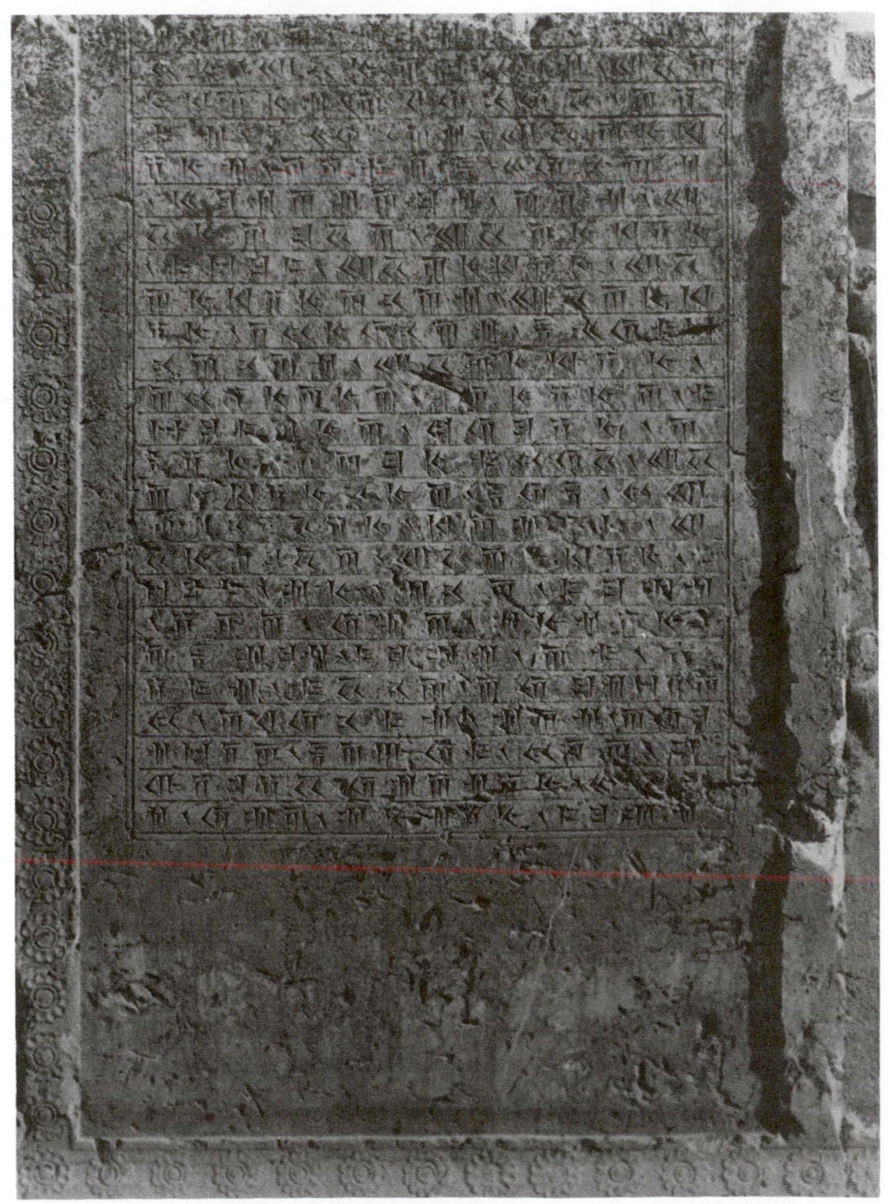

An inscription of Xerxes from the northern stairway of the Apadana. (Courtesy of The Oriental Institute, University of Chicago)

Eastern stairway of the Apadana.

Alternating Persians and Medes.

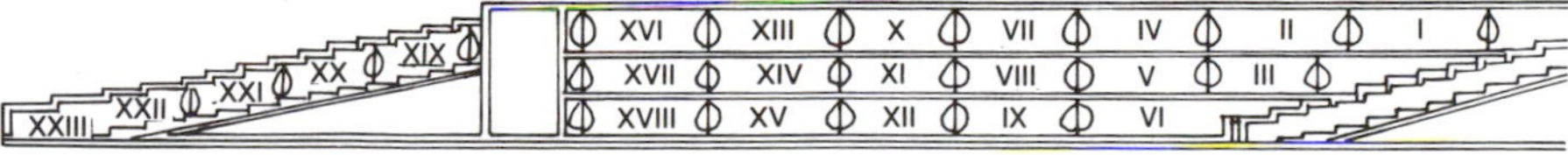

Diagram showing placement of delegations.

Delegations II. Elamites, III. Armenians.

V. Babylonians, VI. Lydians.

found in classical sources and Old Persian texts including groups who helped with the buildings at Susa (DSf, DSz, DSaa) and people who brought tribute (DPe, DSe, XPh).[43]

43. P. Calmeyer, "Zur Rechtfertigung einiger grossköniglicher Inschriften und Darstellungen: Die Yaunâ," in *Kunst, Kultur und Geschichte der Achamenidenzeit,* eds. H. Koch and D. N. MacKenzie, (Berlin: Dietrich Reimer, 1983), p. 162.

VIII. Assyrians, IX. Cappadocians.

X. Egyptians (destroyed), XI. Scythians.

The groups on the eastern Apadana stairway were numbered by Schmidt from top to bottom and from right to left: that is, number I is the group that is farthest to the right on the top row; number II is the next group below.[44] The following table compares ethnic groups portrayed in the reliefs: Richard Barnett (1957),[45] Gerold Walser

44. Schmidt, *Persepolis I*, pp. 85–90.
45. R. D. Barnett, "Persepolis," *Iraq* 19 (1957): 55–77.

XII. Ionians. (Courtesy of The Oriental Institute, University of Chicago)

XIV. Gandarans, XV. Bactrians or Parthians.

(1966),[46] Walter Hinz (1969),[47] Erich Schmidt (1970),[48] Bruno Jacobs (1982),[49] and Michael Roaf (1983).[50]

46. Walser, *Die Völkerschaften.* A. W. Muscarella in a review of this work in *JNES* 28 (1969): 280–85, expresses considerable scepticism about the possibility of identifying all the groups.

47. W. Hinz, "Die Völkerschaften der Persepolis-Reliefs," *Altiranische Funde und Forschungen* (Berlin: W. de Gruyter, 1969), pp. 95–114.

48. Schmidt, *Persepolis III,* pp. 143–58.

49. B. Jacobs, "Persepolisdelegation und Satrapienordnung," *Acta Praehistorica et Archaeologica* 13–14 (1982): 75–82.

50. Roaf, "Sculptures and Sculptors," pp. 50–51.

XVII. Sogdians, XVIII. Indians.

No.	Barnett	Walser	Hinz	Schmidt	Jacobs	Roaf
I.	Medes	Medes	Medes	Medes	Medes	Medes
II.	Elamites	Elamites	Elamites	Elamites	Elamites	Elamites
III.	Armenians	Armenians	Armenians	Armenians	Armenians	Armenians
IV.	Arians	Arians or Arachosians	Parthians	Arians?	Arians	Arians
V.	Babylonians	Babylonians	Babylonians	Babylonians	Babylonians	Babylonians
VI.	Lydians	Syrians	Lydians	Lydians	Lydians	Lydians
VII.	Arachosians	Arachosians or Arians	Arachosians or Drangians	Arachosians	Drangians	Drangians
VIII.	Sogdians	Cilicians	Syrians	Assyrians	Assyrians	Assyrians
IX.	Cappadocians	Cappadocians	Cappadocians	Cappadocians	Cappadocians	Cappadocians
X.	Egyptians	Egyptians	Egyptians	Egyptians	Egyptians	Egyptians
XI.	Saka tigrachauda	Scythians	Saka tigrachauda	Saka paradraya	Saka	Saka tigrachauda
XII.	Ionians	Lydians?	Ionians	Ionians	Indians	Ionians
XIII.	Parthians	Parthians	Bactrians	Bactrians	Bactrians	Bactrians
XIV.	Gandarans	Gandarans	Gandarans	Gandarans	Maka	Gandarans
XV.	Bactrians	Bactrians	Arians	Parthians	Arachosians	Parthians
XVI.	Sagartians	Sagartians	Sagartians	Sagartians	Chorasmians	Sagartians?
XVII.	Chorasmians	Sogdians	Sogdians or Chorasmians	Saka haumavarga	Sogdians	Sogdians or Chorasmians
XVIII.	Indians	Indians	Indians	Indians	Sattagydians	Indians
XIX.	Thracians	Thracians	Thracians	Thracians?	Thracians	??
XX.	Arabians	Arabians	Arabians	Arabians	Arabians	Arabians
XXI.	Drangians	Median tribe	Hyrcanians	??	Parthians	Carians?
XXII.	Libyans	Libyans	Punt	Libyans	Libyans	Libyans
XXIII.	Ethiopians	Ethiopians	Ethiopians	Ethiopians	Ethiopians	Ethiopians[51]

51. The Saka of groups XI and XVII are various Scythian groups. See my *Foes from the Northern Frontier* (Grand Rapids: Baker, 1982), pp. 100–101. The Ethiopians of XXIII were the Nubians south of Egypt.

Among the various gifts the delegations brought were the following:

Description of Gifts

I.	Bowls, bows, daggers, and a sword. The Medes wear a rounded hat, a tunic belted at the waist, and trousers.[52]
II.	A leashed lioness and cubs, daggers, and bows
III.	A precious vase and a stallion[53]
IV.	A feline skin and a camel[54]
V.	Bowls, fabric, and a humped bull
VI.	Vessels, bowls, and a two-horse chariot
VII.	Basins, lion skins, and a dromedary
VIII.	Sheep skins and a pair of rams
IX.	Garments and a horse
X.	Cloth and a bull
XI.	Jewelry and a horse
XII.	Skeins of wool and beehives(?)
XIII.	Cups and a camel
XIV.	Lances, a shield, and a humped bull
XV.	Bowls and a camel
XVI.	A horse and clothes
XVII.	Bracelets, axes, a sword, and a stallion
XVIII.	An ass, axes, and jars (with gold dust?)
XIX.	A horse, spears, and shields
XX.	Textiles and a dromedary
XXI.	A lance, a shield, and a long-horned bull
XXII.	A twisted-horn antelope
XXIII.	Ivory and a giraffe or an okapi[55]

Darius's Palace

The king's *tachara* or palace is located just south of the southwest corner of the Apadana. The inscriptions (DPa, DPc, DPd, DPe) reveal that although Darius began the building, Xerxes (XPc) completed it.[56]

52. G. Thompson, "Iranian Dress in the Achaemenian Period," *Iran* 3 (1965): 121–26. P. R. S. Moorey, "The Iranian Contribution to Achaemenid Material Culture," *Iran* 23 (1985): 24, notes that the Median costume of Persian warriors as depicted on the fourth-century B.C. "Alexander" sarcophagus was made of colored leather.

53. A. Afshar and J. Lerner, "The Horses of the Ancient Persian Empire at Persepolis," *Antiquity* 53 (1979): 44–47.

54. There are two kinds of camels depicted: (1) the *Camelus bactrianus* with two humps associated with the northeast delegations; and (2) the *Camelus dromedarius* with one hump brought by the Arabians. See A. Afshar, "Camels at Persepolis," *Antiquity* 52 (1978): 228–31.

55. A. Afshar, W. Dutz, and M. Taylor, "Giraffes at Persepolis," *Arch* 27 (1974): 114–17. According to a less probable recent conjecture it was a male Nilgai antelope, which was native to India. See R. Valdez and R. G. Tuck, "On the Identification of the Animals Accompanying the 'Ethiopian' Delegation in the Bas-reliefs of the Apadana at Persepolis," *Iran* 18 (1980): 156–57.

56. A. S. Shahbazi, ed., *Old Persian Inscriptions of the Persepolis Platform* (London: Lund Humphries, 1985), pp. 10–12. Shahbazi concludes, from the fact that identical figures on the south doorway of the Tachara are identified as Darius and Xerxes, that Darius shared power with his son Xerxes.

Darius's palace.

The palace is on a platform measuring 2.4 meters (about 8 feet) high. The building is 29 by 40 meters (95 by 131 feet) with its central room a square—15 meters (49 feet) on a side. It was furnished with 12 columns. The door jambs were decorated with reliefs depicting the king with one attendant carrying a parasol and another a scarf. Other stairway reliefs depict servants carrying animals and covered dishes for a banquet. Outstanding features of the structure include cavetto cornices derived from Egyptian prototypes and masonry polished like mirrors. Krefter suggests that south of Darius's palace there may have been a garden setting.[57]

The Central Building

The so-called central building or tripylon is a triple-chambered building to the southeast of the Apadana. It is 51 by 54 meters (167 by 177 feet) in dimensions. This was interpreted by Schmidt as a council hall because the northern stairway reliefs depict various dignitaries. But since the southern stairway reliefs show servants bearing food, another suggestion is that it served as a banquet hall.[58] Its central position serves as a gateway between the public and private sections

57. Krefter, *Persepolis-Rekonstruktion*, p. 19.
58. Schmidt, *Persepolis I*, p. 107.

of the terrace according to Krefter, who calls it the Tor der Könige (the gate of the kings). Most scholars believe the central building was built by Darius.[59] Others, however, have suggested it was built later under Xerxes.[60]

Fortifications

The fortifications of the terrace are best preserved on the eastern boundary abutting the hillside. A dry moat, together with a drainage tunnel, protected the mudbrick structures from the run-off of torrential rains. The enclosure wall is about 10 meters (33 feet) thick and is preserved for approximately two-thirds of its original height of about 20 meters (66 feet). The remains of towers are preserved in the south-east and northeast corners of the outer perimeter.

The sunbaked brick buildings in the northeast seem to have functioned as barracks and stables. An estimated three thousand soldiers were garrisoned here. In the debris of a southeastern room were uncovered seven stone slabs containing the important Daiva inscription of Xerxes.[61]

The Treasury

The vast complex of 93 rooms that occupies the entire southeastern section of the terrace was begun by Darius in two stages (511–507, 494–491 B.C.), and then completed by Xerxes.[62] In its final phase it covered an area 134 meters (440 feet) long and 78 meters (256 feet) wide. Although there is evidence of second stories, most of the structures were of a single story, perhaps 7 to 11 meters (23 to 36 feet) high.[63]

The great west hall (number 41) in the form of a square was built by Darius. It had nine rows of eleven slender wooden columns that rested on stone bases. The wooden cores were encased in mud and plaster and covered with a painted lozenge pattern. The columns were set on bases of dark gray limestone. Plaster fragments in red, white, and blue have been recovered.

Xerxes completed the great north hall (number 38), a rectangular

59. Root, *King and Kingship,* p. 95.

60. R. Nicholls and M. Roaf, "A Persepolis Relief in the Fitzwilliam Museum, Cambridge," *Iran* 15 (1977): 148.

61. Kent, *OP,* pp. 112, 150–52.

62. Schmidt, *Persepolis I,* p. 200.

63. Ibid., p. 156.

The treasury's 100-column hall; the tomb of Artaxerxes III in the background.

room with five rows of twenty columns. Ghirshman believes that the hall of ninety-nine columns was used as a provisional throne hall for Darius, and that the hall of one hundred columns served as a provisional throne hall for Xerxes.[64] Gropp believes guests were housed in the larger rooms and private audiences were given in room 17, where the treasury reliefs were found.[65]

The treasury area was devastated by fire when it was plundered by Alexander. In their haste the Macedonians left behind a remarkable number of valuable objects. Among these are forty-one prizes that the Persians had carried off as booty from areas they had conquered. These include: a granite vessel inscribed by Ashurbanipal, eyestone fragments of Nebuchadnezzar, alabaster objects inscribed with the names of pharaohs Necho and Amasis, and a number of Greek objects including the so-called Penelope statue.

Left behind were also royal tableware and works of art like the head of a prince made of "Egyptian blue," a glasslike material.[66] Most of the lances and javelins were carried off; only eight iron lance heads and four bronze javelin heads were found. Many arrows were left behind: 826 iron arrowheads and 3,858 bronze arrowheads were found. The carbonized remains of arrowshafts were also discovered.[67] The Persians

64. Ghirshman, "A propos de Persépolis," pp. 277–78.
65. Gropp, "Beobachtungen," p. 34.
66. A. Godard, *The Art of Iran* (New York: F. A. Praeger, 1965), pp. 160–61.
67. Schmidt, *Persepolis II*, p. 99.

The treasury relief.

did have scale armor for fragments have been recovered; such armor, however, was never depicted in the reliefs.[68] In fact there were so many valuable objects that Schmidt devoted only one page of his report to the usual product of most excavations—pottery.[69]

The most valuable discoveries were texts and inscribed objects. About 750 Elamite tablets and fragments were found mainly in room 33, located south of the north hall and east of the west hall. About three hundred mortars, pestles, and dishes of green chert, most of them with Aramaic texts, were found in the north hall[70] (see below).

The Treasury Reliefs

Two nearly identical bas-reliefs about six meters (20 feet) in length were discovered in 1936 in the treasury (see chapter 4, fig. 29). The better-preserved relief is now in the Tehran Museum, and the second is on display in the treasury area.[71] The king sits on a throne holding a staff in his right hand and a flower in his left. A Median official approaches with his hand to his mouth in a gesture of deference before two incense altars.[72] The identity of this figure is questionable: Schmidt believed he

68. Ibid., p. 100.
69. Ibid., p. 96, plate 7.
70. Ibid., p. 5.
71. Wilber, *Persepolis,* p. 84; Ghirshman, *Art of Ancient Iran,* pp. 205–6.
72. R. N. Frye, "Gestures of Deference to Royalty in Ancient Iran," *IA* 9 (1972): 102–7.

was the *hazarapatish* (Greek *chiliarch*) or commander of the king's bodyguard, Hinz thought he was the master of the royal household, and Ghirshman identified him as the grand master of ceremonies.[73]

Standing behind the seated king and the standing prince is an attendant with a folded towel. Schmidt suggested this servant may be the lord chamberlain or the royal cupbearer.[74] Furthermore, he believed this individual was beardless, and therefore a eunuch.[75] A. Shapur Shahbazi believed this individual was a eunuch, and suggests he was the royal chamberlain.[76] Behind the figure is a weapon bearer in Median dress who carries the royal axe.

Until recently all scholars identified the seated king as Darius and the crown prince standing behind him as Xerxes. Then Ann and Giuseppe Tilia discovered that the reliefs were originally set up on the central staircases of the Apadana and later removed to the treasury.[77] In their places were set the present reliefs of alternating Persian and Median guards. Ann Tilia, who supports the traditional identification of the king with Darius, suggested that it was Artaxerxes I who removed the reliefs because of a change in the New Year's ceremony.[78]

Richard Frye suggests the king was Xerxes, and the crown prince his oldest son Darius,[79] as does Shahbazi.[80] Xerxes was assassinated in 465 by a conspiracy that may have involved Darius, who hated Xerxes because his father had seduced his wife, Artaynte. Darius himself was killed by his brother Artaxerxes I. Frye reasons that the latter removed the reliefs because they were distasteful reminders of his brother.[81] Hubertus von Gall has argued that the king must have been Xerxes in that Darius always wore a dentate crown.[82] If the king was Xerxes, then

73. Tilia, *Studies,* p. 202.

74. Schmidt, *Persepolis I,* p. 169. For a cupbearer from Susa, see Ghirshman, *Art of Ancient Iran,* p. 144. See also E. Yamauchi, "Was Nehemiah the Cupbearer a Eunuch?" *ZAW* 92 (1980): 13–21.

75. Schmidt, *Persepolis I,* pp. 133, 169.

76. A. S. Shahbazi, "The Persepolis 'Treasury Reliefs' Once More," *AMI* n.F. 9 (1976): 153.

77. Tilia, *Studies,* pp. 191–208.

78. A. B. Tilia, "Persepolis Sculptures in the Light of New Discoveries," an appendix in A. Farkas, *Achaemenid Sculpture* (Istanbul: Nederlands Historisch-Archaeologisch Instituut in het Nabije Oosten, 1974), p. 129.

79. R. N. Frye, "Persepolis Again," *JNES* 33 (1974): 383–86.

80. Shahbazi, "Persepolis Treasury Reliefs," pp. 151–56.

81. If on the other hand Darius were innocent, then Artaxerxes I may have suffered remorse at having killed his brother.

82. H. von Gall, "Die Grosskönigliche Kopfbedeckung bei den Achämeniden," in *Proceedings of the IIIrd Annual Symposium on Archaeological Research in Iran,* ed. F. Bagherzadeh (Tehran: Iranian Centre for Archaeological Research, 1975), p. 222; see idem, "Die Kopfbedeckung des persischen Ornats bei den Achämeniden," *AMI* n.f. 7 (1974): 151. But Root, *King and Kingship,* p. 93, remarks: "I am not convinced of the validity of von Gall's theory on exclusive and distinctive crowns—intriguing and well presented though it is." A further problem with von Gall's theory is noted by Roaf, in "Sculptures and Sculptors," p. 131. Roaf points out that some headdresses may have once had crenellations added to them either in paint or as metal attachments. We do know that each of the later

The reconstructed harem building which serves as a museum.

the chamberlain could have been the very Aspamitres who led his relative, Artapanos, into the bedchamber to kill the king.[83]

Some questions remain with this new interpretation. If the prince was indeed the hated Darius, why did Artaxerxes not destroy these monuments? In their new locations in the treasury were the reliefs simply stored or were they still on public display?[84] Some scholars have, therefore, chosen to retain the traditional identification of the king with Darius and the prince with Xerxes.[85]

The Harem

The western extension of the treasury area built by Darius was leveled so that Xerxes could build a series of rooms, which Herzfeld labeled the harem. On the other hand, Leo Trümpelmann suggests that the twenty-two apartments served as guest houses for high officials.[86]

Sasanid kings adopted a new crown. See E. Yarshater, ed., *The Cambridge History of Iran III.1: The Seleucid, Parthian and Sasanian Periods* (Cambridge: Cambridge University Press, 1983), p. 135; G. Azarpy, "Crowns and Some Royal Insignia in Early Iran," *IA* 9 (1972): 108–15.

83. Shahbazi, "Persepolis 'Treasury Reliefs,' " p. 153.

84. For example, Krefter, *Persepolis-Rekonstruktion*, Beilage 32, has the reliefs on display in an audience hall in the treasury. Cahill objects to the interpretations of Frye and Shahbazi: "Nor would this hypothesis explain why the reliefs were installed so prominently in the main courtyard of the Treasury." He suggests that broad changes in the ceremony or the cessation of the ceremony led to the transferal of the reliefs. See N. Cahill, "The Treasury at Persepolis: Gift-Giving at the City of the Persians," *AJA* 89 (1985): 386.

85. See Root, *King and Kingship*, pp. 94–95; Farkas, *Achaemenid Sculpture*, pp. 53, 117. See further E. Porada, "Some Thoughts on the Audience Reliefs of Persepolis," in *Studies in Classical Art and Archaeology in Honour of P. H. von Blankenhagen*, eds. G. Kopcke and M. B. Moore (Locust Valley, N.J.: J. J. Augustin, 1979), pp. 37–43.

86. L. Trümpelmann, "Zu den Gebäuden von Persepolis und ihrer Funktion," in Koch and McKenzie, *Kunst, Kultur und Geschichte der Achämenidenzeit*, p. 236.

The excavators built their living quarters here. At the site of the main hall a building in ancient Achaemenian style now serves as a museum.

During Alexander's conquest the harem was not subject to a general conflagration, but separate fires were methodically set to burn up combustible items. According to Schmidt: "The modest finds leave doubt whether the western apartments of the west wing were occupied at the time of the conquest of Persepolis."[87] Since no articles of adornment were found here, it is possible the structure functioned as a storehouse rather than as a harem.[88]

Xerxes' Palace

The palace of Xerxes, called a *hadish,* is in the southwest area of the terrace. It extends 41 by 57 meters (135 by 187 feet) and is thus about double that of Darius's in size. Its central hall, 27 meters (89 feet) square, had six rows of six columns. A number of trilingual inscriptions of Xerxes were found on various parts of the building.[89] Krefter believes that this functioned as a royal banquet hall.[90] Because it was located on the highest level of the terrace, Xerxes' palace has suffered severely from looters and from the ravages of the elements.

The Throne Hall

Xerxes' audience hall, located to the east of Darius' Apadana, is, next to the latter, the largest single structure on the terrace. It is not quite a square, measuring 88.5 by 96 meters (290 by 315 feet). Its central hall is a square, 68.6 meters (225 feet) long, which is even larger than the central hall of the Apadana. The ten rows of ten columns of the central hall, none of which is still standing, may have been about 11.3 meters (37 feet) high, or about half to two-thirds the height of the Apadana columns. The ashes indicate that the roof was made of cedar beams. On the north there was an open portico with sixteen columns, flanked by towers or guard rooms.

There were two entrances on each of the four sides, with reliefs carved on the stone jambs. The king is depicted seated on his throne

87. Schmidt, *Persepolis I,* p. 263.
88. Wilber, *Persepolis,* p. 73.
89. XPd, XPe in Kent, *OP,* pp. 112, 149.
90. Krefter, *Persepolis-Rekonstruktion,* pp. 18, 98.

Xerxes' throne hall.

under a baldachin with a servant with a fly switch standing behind him. The enthroned king, who is supported on two reliefs by representatives of twenty-eight nations, is probably Artaxerxes I. In the southeast corner a stone foundation slab was found, which had been inscribed by Artaxerxes I. He claimed he completed the building begun by Xerxes.

The building has been called the throne hall because of the reliefs of the king on a throne. But the purpose of a second audience hall is puzzling. Schmidt comments: "It appears senseless to us that the second hall should have been intended for the same purpose as the first."[91] Schmidt, therefore, suggested that the structure was really an extension of the treasury: "The Throne Hall was without doubt the 'palace museum' of Persepolis, erected for the storage, and, above all, for the exhibition of the greatest royal treasures."[92] The badly scorched column bases reveal that the throne hall bore the brunt of the conflagration set by Alexander. Because the site was plundered by Farhad Mirza in 1877 we are ignorant of the objects that may have been left behind.

Unlike Schmidt, both André Godard and Krefter suggest that Xerxes' building was a hall of honor for the army.[93] To the north of the throne hall and to the east of the gate of all nations is a large unfinished gate, 38 by 56 meters (125 by 184 feet), which Krefter has called the gate of

91. Schmidt, *Persepolis, I,* p. 129.
92. Ibid., p. 42.
93. Godard, "Les travaux de Persépolis," pp. 126ff.; Krefter, *Persepolis-Rekonstruktion,* p. 15.

the army.[94] Between the unfinished gate and the throne hall is a large court that may have served as the parade ground of the army.

Palace D

The large area, 39 by 45 meters (128 by 148 feet), between the palace of Xerxes and the harem area was designated by Schmidt as palace D. Today all that remains is a high hill. Its attribution is uncertain. The excavators found only incoherent remains and masses of stone chips and fragments, perhaps from the ruined palace of Xerxes.[95] Following the lead of Sami, Géza de Francovich believes that this area was a garden.[96] His conjecture unfortunately was based on the mistaken views of Robert Koldewey about the hanging garden of Babylon. Krefter interprets the site as a banquet hall for the army.[97]

Palace G

The large empty site east of Darius's palace, 33 by 52 meters (108 by 171 feet), was designated by Schmidt as palace G.[98] On the south side rows of foundation stones were discovered. Building G is probably from the time of Xerxes and Artaxerxes I. Herzfeld guessed that the site of palace G was a cult place.[99] Francovich suggested that both sites G and D were gardens, a view rejected by Krefter, who suggests that the site was another banquet hall.[100] It appears that the facade of a palace of Artaxerxes III, which was found at site H, originally came from site G.

Palace H

An Akkadian inscription of Artaxerxes I was found in the facade of palace H, just to the west of Xerxes' palace. Since site H was made of used material, Schmidt considered it might be the palace of Artaxerxes III or even a post-Achaemenid building.[101] The stairway of Artaxerxes

94. Ibid., p. 17.
95. Schmidt, *Persepolis I,* p. 269.
96 Francovich, "Problems of Achaemenid Architecture," pp. 209–13.
97. Krefter, *Persepolis-Rekonstruktion,* p. 73.
98. Schmidt, *Persepolis I,* pp. 274–75.
99. He is followed in this view by Trümpelmann, "Zu den Gebäuden," p. 227.
100. Krefter, *Persepolis-Rekonstruktion,* pp. 71–72.
101. Schmidt, *Persepolis I,* pp. 279–81.

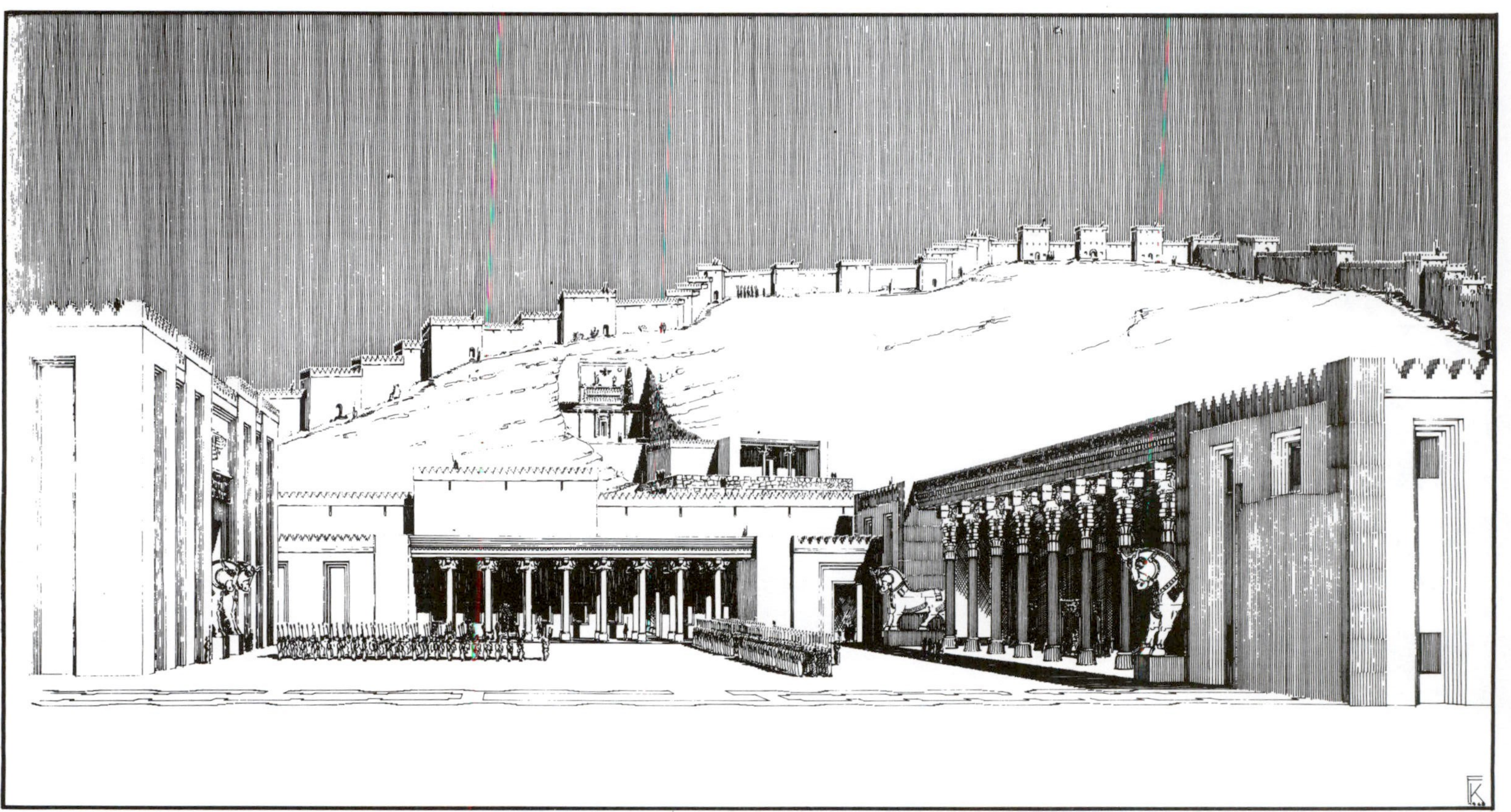

The throne hall according to Krefter's reconstruction. (Courtesy of Gebrüder Mann Verlag)

Servants carrying food for a banquet. (Metropolitan Museum of Art, Harris Brisbane Dick Fund, 1934)

Facade of the tomb of Artaxerxes III.

III was apparently moved to this site in post-Achaemenid times from palace G.[102]

Recent studies have demonstrated that site H was actually the site of Artaxerxes I's palace. Tilia in 1973 discovered 130 blocks and fragments decorated with reliefs.[103] Made of black limestone, these originally represented twenty-four delegations. According to Tilia,

> The number of delegates and accompanying ushers on this façade must have been some 300 against 138 on the eastern Apadāna façade and the total length of the tribute procession some 90 m. against 63.32 m. including the separating pine-trees on the Apadāna façades.[104]

Structures of the Later Achaemenids

We have nothing from Darius II (423–405 B.C.) at Persepolis. His tomb may be one of those at Naqsh-i Rustam.

Artaxerxes II (404–359 B.C.), who had the longest reign of all the Achaemenids, was probably buried in the southern tomb on the Kuh-i Rahmat slopes. A relief on the facade of the tomb depicts the king before a fire altar. An inscription identifies the representatives of different nations that are also depicted.[105]

Artaxerxes III (358–338 B.C.) may have built at site G.[106] Four copies of this ruler's inscription were found on the west side of Darius's pal-

102. Root, *King and Kingship*, pp. 108–9.

103. Tilia, *Studies*, p. 266; A. B. Tilia, "Discoveries at Persepolis 1972–1973," in *Proceedings of the IInd Annual Symposium on Archaeological Research in Iran*, ed. F. Bagherzadeh (Tehran: Iranian Centre for Archaeological Research, 1974), pp. 241–42; A. B. Tilia, "Recent Discoveries at Persepolis," *AJA* 81 (1977): 67–77; Farkas, *Achaemenid Sculpture*, pp. 127–30.

104. Tilia, "Persepolis Sculptures," p. 132.

105. A?P in Kent, *OP*, pp. 114, 155–56.

106. Godard, "Les travaux de Persépolis," p. 127.

The unfinished tomb. (Courtesy of The Oriental Institute, University of Chicago)

ace, so he may have completed the facade of this building.[107] The northern tomb on Kuh-i Rahmat is now identified as that of Artaxerxes III.[108]

There are no monuments from the brief reign of Arses (337–336 B.C.).

The unfinished tomb, about five hundred meters south of the terrace, has been ascribed to the last Achaemenid, Darius III (335–330 B.C.), the king who was conquered by Alexander. A recent study by Calmeyer, however, disputes this. It appears that the tomb was unfinished be-

107. A^{3}Pa,b,c,d in Kent, *OP,* pp. 114, 156.
108. Schmidt, *Persepolis III,* pp. 99–107.

cause of cracks that developed in the cliff face. The tomb belongs stylistically between the latest tomb of Naqsh-i Rustam and the earliest tomb of the Kuh-i Rahmat.[109]

Architectural and Decorative Elements

Although the superstructures have been destroyed, some elements can be reconstructed from the debris and from written sources. An analysis of the ashes indicates the roof of the Apadana was made with cedar beams (compare 1 Kings 7:2–4). No doubt there were elaborate curtains decorating the walls (Esther 1:6). We read of wooden doors covered with gold. The texts speak of wooden sculptures but none has been preserved.[110] Gold-plated bronze nails have been recovered from the throne hall. As at Susa, there were probably multicolored tile decorations.

Traces of color have been found on various stone fragments. Some traces of red paint remain on the lips, nostrils, and eyes of the Persian guards on the central building.[111] A limestone relief of the god Ahuramazda from the throne hall, acquired by the Fogg Art Museum in 1943, was cleansed in 1965 of a layer of calcium carbonate, revealing traces of red, green, and yellow. Judith Lerner has reconstructed the original color scheme of this relief.[112]

The Persepolis Tablets

As noted earlier (chapter 5) thousands of important Elamite tablets were discovered both in the fortification (PF) and in the treasury (PT) from the reigns of Darius, Xerxes, and Artaxerxes I.

These tablets speak about payments made to sculptors and other workmen at Persepolis.[113] They also mention such workers as "stone removers" and "road counters" who were concerned with the improve-

109. P. Calmeyer, "Das unvollendete achaemenidische Felsgrab bei Persepolis," *AMI* n.F. 8 (1975): 81–98.

110. Roaf, "Sculptures and Sculptors," p. 69.

111. Ibid., p. 8.

112. J. A. Lerner, "A Painted Relief from Persepolis," *Arch* 26 (1973): 116–22. See also F. Krefter, "Zur Steinmetztechnik von Persepolis," in *Festschrift für Wilhelm Eilers* (Wiesbaden: Harrassowitz, 1967), p. 440; P. Naster, "Indices de peinture des reliefs à Persepolis," *Orientalia Lovaniensia Periodica* 5 (1974): 47–51; Wilber, *Persepolis,* p. 79.

113. M. Roaf, "Texts about the Sculptures and Sculptors at Persepolis," *Iran* 18 (1980): 65–74.

ment of roads.[114] Most of the texts are about the distribution of food, including grain, oil, and sheep.[115]

Silver was paid during times of commodity shortages, but normal payments were in grain. Monthly payments ranged from a minimum of five quarts of grain (presumably barley) to boys and girls, up to fifty quarts to chief workers. The average payment of thirty quarts was made in 83 percent of the cases. In 20 percent of the disbursements wine or beer was also dispensed. PF 6 mentions a shipment of 30,000 quarts of grain to Persepolis. PF 2007 itemizes 16,843 sheep; another text lists 435 camels. Rewards were given for the bearing of children: "Those who bear boys receive 10 quarts of wine or beer, or 20 quarts of flour, barley or other cereals; while those who bear girls receive half as much."[116]

In addition to commodities, silver was disbursed as supplementary payments from a quarter-shekel up to eight shekels. A sheep cost three shekels, and ten quarts of wine could be bought with a shekel. While it has been suggested that the payments in fractions of shekels indicate weights of silver rather than coins,[117] others believe the payments were in coins.

The treasury tablets list large numbers of craftsmen. Among the specialized personnel are masons, vine workers, and beer brewers. About 30,000 workmen from over 100 localities were employed at Persepolis. These individuals were called *kur-tash.* Of these 37.5 percent were men, 39.8 percent women, 12.7 percent boys, and 10 percent girls. Their status is disputed among scholars; Igor Dyakonov believes that most were slaves or captives, George Cameron that they were free workers, and Janos Harmatta that half were free. A study by Muhammed Dandamayev reveals that although they were not well paid under Darius, their remuneration rose handsomely under Xerxes.[118]

While the Jews were too insignificant a nation to be represented among the official delegations on the Apadana reliefs, a number of them have been identified among the proper names found in the Persepolis tablets:

114. R. T. Hallock, "Selected Fortification Texts," *CDAFI* 8 (1978): 114–15.

115. P. Briant, "L'élevage ovin dans l'empire achéménide," *JESHO* 22 (1979): 136–61.

116. R. T. Hallock, "The Evidence of the Persepolis Tablets;" in *The Cambridge History of Iran II: The Median and Achaemenian Periods,* ed. I. Gershevitch (Cambridge: Cambridge University Press, 1985), p. 606. See H. Koch, "Zu den Lohnverhältnissen der Dareioszeit in Persien," in Koch and MacKenzie, *Kunst, Kultur und Gerschichte der Achämenidenzeit,* pp. 19–50.

117. P. Naster, "Were the Labourers of Persepolis Paid by Means of Coined Money?" *Ancient Society* 1 (1970): 129–34.

118. M. A. Dandamayev, "Forced Labour in the Palace Economy in Achaemenid Iran, *Altorientalische Forschungen* 2 (1975): 78.

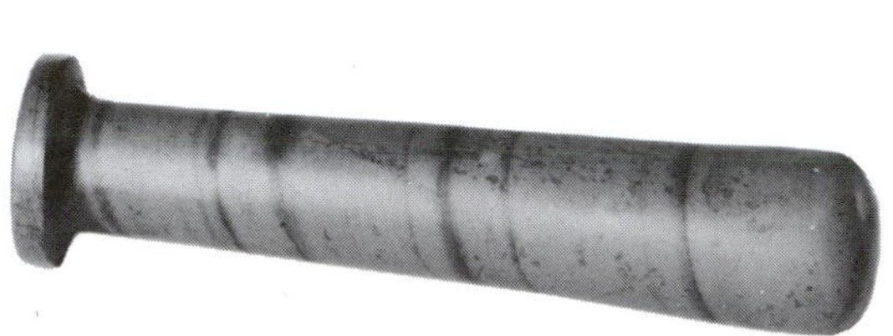

Mortar and pestle. (Courtesy of The Oriental Institute, University of Chicago)

Abīyāw, spelled Ab-pi-ia-ma (PF 700:9); compare Abijah (Neh. 10:7)

Abīya, spelled Ab-pi-ia (PF 2075:3); a hypocoristicon or shortened form of the above

Barūk(a), spelled Bar-ru-uk-qa (PF 50:3-4), Ba-ru-uk-qa (PF 379:2); compare Baruch (Neh. 3:20)

Zakariya, spelled Da-qa-ri-ia (PF 1627:3-4); compare Zechariah

Ḥazaqī, spelled *ḥzqy* in an Aramaic gloss (PF 173); compare Hezekiah

Nutaniya, spelled Nu-tan-nu-ia (PF 1827:13; PT 2:23); compare Nethaniah (Jer. 40:14)

Shabbatay, spelled *ša-ab-ba-at-d*[a] (PF 2033:3), "born on the Sabbath"[119]

Aramaic Inscriptions

From 1936 to 1938 the excavators found about 300 mortars, pestles, and plates of a flinty green stone in hall 38 of the treasury. Dating from the reigns of Xerxes and Artaxerxes I (479–435 B.C.), a number of them bear Aramaic inscriptions, including 68 mortars, 57 pestles, 37 plates, and one tray. Raymond Bowman published these texts in 1970.[120] Schmidt called these ritual vessels because they seem to correspond to a mortar and a pestle on a seal, which also depicts 2 priests and a fire

119. E. Lipiński, "Western Semites in Persepolis," *Acta Antiqua* 25 (1977): 101–12.

120. R. A. Bowman, *Aramaic Ritual Texts from Persepolis* (Chicago: University of Chicago Press, 1970).

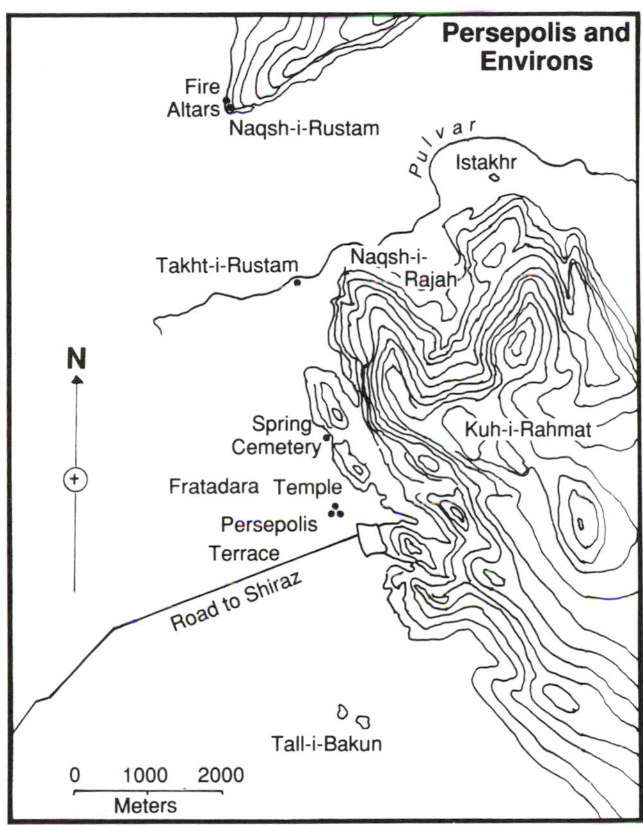

altar.[121] Bowman believes these vessels were used in the preparation of the haoma (compare Vedic *soma*), an intoxicating drink that was used by the Persians but was denounced by Zoroaster. The identification of the haoma/soma plant is unknown. A recent suggestion, made by Gordon Wasson, is that it was the hallucinogenic Fly Agaric mushroom (see chapter 12).[122]

Since the Aramaic inscriptions refer to officials with theophoric names compounded with Mithra, such as Dāta-Mithra,[123] Bowman concluded: "In the light of all facts at our disposal, it seems likely that in the green stone ritual vessels bearing Aramaic texts from Persepolis,

121. Schmidt, *Persepolis II*, p. 53 and plate 7.

122. R. G. Wasson, "The Soma of the Rig Veda: What Was It?" *JAOS* 91 (1971): 169–87; idem, *Soma: Divine Mushroom of Immortality* (New York: Harcourt, Brace, Jovanovich, 1973); I. Gershevitch, "An Iranianist's View of the Soma Controversy," in *Mémorial Jean de Menasce*, eds. P. Gignoux and A. Tafazzoli (Louvain: Imprimerie Orientaliste, 1974), pp. 45–75.

123. Compare the name *Mithredath* in Ezra 4:7.

Tomb of Darius I at Naqsh-i Rustam.

we see evidence that already in Achaemenid times a proto-Mithraic cult was actively operative in the Persian army."[124]

Reviewers, however, have unanimously rejected Bowman's translations. Joseph Naveh and Shaul Shaked write: "It may be stated right away that we consider Cameron's secular interpretation more acceptable than Bowman's ritualistic one."[125] According to Baruch Levine: "We conclude that they are administrative notations, recording the names of the objects on which the texts are inscribed."[126] That is, although the vessels may have been used in rituals the inscriptions are no more than prosaic dedications.[127]

Extramural Discoveries

In 1952 a structure with inscribed column bases identifying it as the *tachara* of Xerxes was cleared below the terrace. The palace seems to

124. Bowman, *Aramaic Ritual Texts*, p. 15.

125. J. Naveh and S. Shaked, "Ritual Texts or Treasury Documents?" *Or* 42 (1973): 446.

126. B. Levine, "Aramaic Texts from Persepolis," *JAOS* 92 (1972): 70.

127. See further P. Bernard, "Les mortiers et pilons inscrits de Persépolis," *Studia Iranica* 1 (1972): 165–76; J. A. Delaunay, "A propos des *Aramaic Ritual Texts from Persepolis* de R. A. Bowman," *Commémoration Cyrus* (Leiden: Brill,) 3: 193–217; W. Hinz, "Zu den Mörsern und Stösseln aus Persepolis," *Acta Iranica* 4 (1975): 371–85; K. Kamioka, "Philological Observations on the Aramaic Texts from Persepolis," *Or* 11 (1975): 45–66.

have been located in a large garden with an ornamental lake. In 1967 a farmer plowing 1,700 meters north-northwest of Persepolis uncovered an inscribed stone tablet in pillow form dating to the reign of Xerxes.[128] In a mountain recess 1,200 meters north-northwest of the terrace, Schmidt uncovered a cemetery by a spring. The graves are from either the late Achaemenid or the Seleucid period.[129]

In 1923 Herzfeld discovered post-Achaemenid reliefs in the plain three hundred meters northwest of the terrace. When he cleared the site in 1932 he uncovered the remains of a temple of the Fratadara era, dating to the early third century B.C. After the Seleucid rule at Persepolis between 323 and 300 B.C., the Fratadara (keeper of the fire) rulers reigned from 300 to 150 B.C. before the takeover of the area by the Parthians.

Naqsh-i Rustam

Naqsh-i Rustam is a rock cliff three and a half miles north of Persepolis where there are four Achaemenid tombs. Only the third tomb from the left is identified by inscriptions as the tomb of Darius I. It is believed the other tombs are, from left to right, those of Darius II, Artaxerxes I, and, on the extreme right, the tomb of Xerxes.[130] On the cliff face are earlier Elamite bas-reliefs as well as later Sasanian reliefs of Ardashir and Shapur I (third century A.D.).

Like the other tombs the facade of Darius I's tomb is cut in the form of a large cross, 23 meters (75 feet) high and 11 meters (36 feet) wide. The top section bears a relief, originally painted, depicting the king before the winged symbol and the sacred fire. The king's throne is upheld by two tiers of representatives from thirty nations whose identities are given in an inscription (DNa).[131] Within the tomb were three vaults and nine cists.

In front of the tomb of Darius is the Kaʿabah-i Zardusht, a rectangular tower built of sandstone with three rows of blind windows. It is about 11 meters (36 feet) high and 7 meters (23 feet) wide. As in the case of its twin, the poorly preserved Zendan at Pasargadae (see chapter 9), the function of the Kaʿabah is in dispute.

On the lower walls of the Kaʿabah are important Middle Persian inscriptions of Kartir, the high priest of the Sasanian king Shapur (A.D.

128. Hinz, *Altiranische Funde*, p. 45.

129. Schmidt, *Persepolis II*, p. 123. See further W. Kleiss, "Beobachtungen in der Umgebung von Persepolis und Naqš-i Rustam," *AMI* n.F. (1976): 131–50.

130. Schmidt, *Persepolis III*, pp. 90–93.

131. Kent, *OP*, pp. 137–40.

Ka‘abah-i Zardusht. (Courtesy of The Oriental Institute, University of Chicago)

240–272).[132] Kartir's inscriptions are also found on the cliffs at Naqsh-i Rustam and also at Naqsh-i Rajab at the base of the Kuh-i Rahmat Mountain. Kartir was such an ardent Zoroastrian that he persecuted Hindus, Buddhists, Jews, Christians, and Nazoreans (who were probably Mandaeans).[133] He was also responsible for the death of Mani.[134]

To the west of the Naqsh-i Rustam tombs are two fire altars that Louis Vanden Berghe assigned to the Achaemenid period.[135] Ghirshman, however, believed that these were Sasanian (third–sixth century A.D.).[136] The discovery in 1965 by David Stronach of a striking parallel in a single fire altar at Sang-i Sanduki, about twenty-five miles northwest of Naqsh-i Rustam, strengthens the case for the Sasanian origins of all these altars.[137]

The site of the capital of the Sasanids at Istakhr, two and a half miles east of Naqsh-i Rustam, was excavated to a very limited extent by Schmidt in the 1930s.[138]

132. M. Sprengling, *Third Century Iran: Sapor and Kartir* (Chicago: University of Chicago Press, 1953); R. N. Frye, *The Heritage of Persia* (Cleveland: World, 1963), pp. 209–10.

133. On the Mandaeans, see E. S. Drower, *The Mandaeans of Iraq and Iran* (Leiden: Brill, 1962); K. Rudolph, *Die Mandäer* (Göttingen: Vandenhoeck and Ruprecht, 1960–1961), vols. 1 and 2; idem, *Gnosis* (San Francisco: Harper and Row, 1983); E. Yamauchi, *Gnostic Ethics and Mandaean Origins* (Cambridge: Harvard University Press, 1970); idem, "Mandaeism," in *The Interpreter's Dictionary of the Bible, Supplementary Volume*, eds. V. Furnish et al. (Nashville: Abingdon, 1976), p. 563.

134. On Mani, see G. Widengren, *Mani and Manichaeism* (New York: Holt, Rinehart and Winston, 1965); L. J. R. Ort, *Mani* (Leiden: Brill, 1967); E. Yamauchi, "The Manichaeans," in *Handbook of Christian History*, ed. T. Dowley (Grand Rapids: Eerdmans, 1977), pp. 48–49.

135. See Schmidt, *Persepolis III*, p. 12.

136. Ghirshman, *Art of Ancient Iran*, p. 227.

137. D. Stronach, "The Kūh-i-Sharak Fire Altar," *JNES* 25 (1966): 217–27.

138. S. Matheson, *Persia: An Archaeological Guide*, rev. ed. (London: Faber and Faber, 1976), pp. 220–21.

11
Persia and the Greeks

The Greek Words in Daniel

As expressed long ago in 1897 by Samuel Driver, the Greek loan-words in the Aramaic of Daniel have been regarded as objective proof for the late date of Daniel.[1] This has been restated by Peter Coxon: "Of

1. Problems concerning the date of Daniel cannot be addressed here, but see E. Yamauchi, "Hermeneutical Issues in the Book of Daniel," *JETS* 23 (1980): 13–21; idem, "The Archaeological Background of Daniel," *BS* 137 (1980): 3–16.

On Nebuchadnezzar, see D. J. Wiseman, "Some Historical Problems in the Book of Daniel," in *Notes on Some Problems in the Book of Daniel*, eds. D. J. Wiseman et al. (London: Tyndale, 1965), pp. 9–18; idem, *Nebuchadrezzar and Babylon* (London: Oxford University Press, 1985).

On the term *Chaldeans*, see A. R. Millard, "Daniel 1–6 and History,"*EQ* 49 (1977): 67–68.

On Belshazzar and Nabonidus, see E. Yamauchi, "Nabonidus," in *The International Standard Bible Encyclopedia*, ed. G. W. Bromiley (Grand Rapids: Eerdmans, 1986), 3: 468–70.

On the Qumran Nabonidus document, see E. Yamauchi, "Magic or Miracle? Diseases, Demons and Exorcisms," in *Gospel Perspectives VI: The Miracles of Jesus*, eds. D. Wenham and C. Blomberg (Sheffield: JSOT, 1986), pp. 121, 169–70.

all the linguistic arguments which have been used in the debate concerning the age of the Aramaic sections of *Daniel* and the date of the composition of the book, the Greek loans seem to provide the strongest evidence in favour of the second century B.C."[2] Such recent commentaries as the volume on Daniel by Louis Hartmann and Alexander Di Lella continue to repeat the conventional critical position: "The Greek names for the musical instruments in 3:5 probably do not antedate the reign of Alexander the Great (336–323 B.C.)."[3] The widespread view of a Hellenistic date for the Book of Daniel is based in part on the mistaken impression that it was only after the conquest of Alexander that there were widespread contacts with the Greeks in the Near East. It is worthwhile, therefore, to review some of the recent evidence of early contacts between the Greeks and the Near East.[4]

Harold Rowley, in his review of Kenneth Kitchen's essay on the Aramaic of Daniel,[5] still maintained that these Greek words were proof of the late date of Daniel's Aramaic.[6] Edward Kutscher, however, was persuaded of the cogency of Kitchen's argument and agreed that such musical terms could have been borrowed from the Greek of Ionia or the islands prior to Alexander.[7] Coxon pointed out that the form of *qaytᵉrōs* indicates the word was borrowed from Ionic *kitharis* rather than Attic *kithara.*[8]

It is significant that the three Greek words in Daniel 3:5 are all musical terms.[9] They are:

On Darius the Mede, see chapter 6.

On the correspondence with events of the second century B.C., see D. W. Gooding, "The Literary Structure of the Book of Daniel and Its Implications," *TB* 32 (1981): 43–80.

2. P. W. Coxon, "Greek Loan-Words and Alleged Greek Loan Translations in the Book of Daniel," *Glasgow University Oriental Society Transactions* 25 (1973–1974): 24.

3. L. F. Hartman and A. Di Lella, *The Book of Daniel* (Garden City: Doubleday, 1978), p. 13.

4. For my previous studies on this subject, see E. Yamauchi, *Greece and Babylon* (Grand Rapids: Baker, 1967); idem, "The Greek Words in Daniel in the Light of Greek Influence in the Near East," in *New Perspectives on the Old Testament,* ed. J. B. Payne (Waco: Word, 1970), pp. 170–200; idem, "Daniel and Contacts Between the Aegean and the Near East before Alexander," *EQ* 53 (1981): 37–47.

5. K. A. Kitchen, "The Aramaic of Daniel," in his review of *Notes on Some Problems in the Book of Daniel* (see n. 1 above).

6. H. H. Rowley, *JSS* 11 (1966): 112–16.

7. E. Y. Kutscher, "Aramaic," in *Current Trends in Linguistics,* ed. T. A. Sebeok (The Hague: Mouton, 1970), 6: 401–2. See also P. W. Coxon, "The Distribution of Synonyms in the Light of Official Aramaic and the Aramaic of Qumran," *RQ* 9 (1978): 497–512, who criticizes some of Rowley's arguments.

8. Coxon, "Greek Loan-Words," p. 31.

9. See T. C. Mitchell and R. Joyce, "The Musical Instruments in Nebuchadrezzar's Orchestra," in *Notes on Some Problems,* pp. 19–27.

qayt^{e}rōs (Greek *kitharis*)
p^{e}santērîn (Greek *psaltērion*)
sumpōn^{e}yâ (Greek *sumphōnia*)

The first word signifies a kind of lyre; the second a harplike instrument. Alfred Sendry suggests that the latter was one of a number of musical instruments originally imported from the East, improved by the Greeks, and reexported to the East.[10] The rendering of the third word as "bagpipe" in the King James Version is based on late rabbinical views.[11] The earliest meaning of the Greek word *sumphōnia* was "sounding together," that is, the simultaneous playing of instruments or voices producing a concord. Jerome, commenting on Luke 15:25 where the word occurs, noted: "The *symphonia* is not a kind of instrument, as some Latin writers think, but it means concordant harmony. It is expressed in Latin by *consonantia.*"[12] Coxon agrees with Jerome's view: "We have tried to show that the use of *sumphōnia* in Dan. 3 accords with its older meaning and not, as in the later classical sources, with an individual musical instrument."[13]

As I have shown elsewhere, foreign musicians and their musical instruments played a prominent role at royal courts among the Egyptians, Kassites, Assyrians, Babylonians, and Persians as indicated by both textual and iconographic evidence.[14] It is also likely that foreign mercenaries brought their own musical instruments with them.

There is considerable evidence that music transcended national bounds. Mesopotamian influence on Greek music exists in both the form of the lyre and the modes or scales of tones.[15] Friedrich Ellermeier made a detailed study of the distribution of the Near Eastern double flute (or oboe), which was used in Mesopotamia, Syria, Palestine, Egypt, Cyprus, Crete, and Greece. He notes that the Syrian *embūbu* passed into Latin as *ambubaiae,* a word that designated both the instrument and the Syrian girls who played it.[16]

10. A. Sendry, *Music in Ancient Israel* (New York: Philosophical Library, 1969), p. 297.

11. It is surprising that Hartman and Di Lella, *Book of Daniel,* p. 157, revert to the discredited view that this was a "bagpipe."

12. Cited by Sendry, *Music in Ancient Israel,* pp. 325–33, who devotes a long discussion to this word.

13. Coxon, "Greek Loan-Words," p. 36.

14. Yamauchi, *Greece and Babylon,* pp. 19–24; idem, "Greek Words," pp. 176–77.

15. M. Duchesne-Guillemin, "Survivance orientale dans la désignation des cordes de la lyre en Grèce," *Syria* 44 (1967): 233–46; idem, "L'animal sur la cithare: nouvelle lumière sur l'origine sumérienne de la cithare grecque," in *Orientalia J. Duchesne-Guillemin Emerito Oblata* (Leiden: Brill, 1984), pp. 129–41.

16. F. Ellermeier, *Sibyllen, Musikanten, Haremsfrauen* (Herzberger am Harz: Junger, 1970), pp. 12–19.

Among the Semitic loan-words in Greek are the following musical instruments: *nablas* ("harp") (compare Hebrew *nēbel*),[17] *pandoura* ("lute"[18]), *sambukē* ("small triangular harp") (compare Aramaic *sabkâ'* in Dan. 3:5[19]), and *tumpanon* ("tambourine") (compare Hebrew *tuppîm*).[20]

The converse of Greek words in Semitic dialects is the phenomenon of Semitic and other Near Eastern words in Greek from as early as the Mycenaean Linear B texts.[21] A symposium edited by Wilhelm Krause listed forty Akkadian words in European languages, including six in Greek.[22] Emily Vermeule accepts Canaanite etymologies for the following Greek words: *phoinix* ("palmtree or griffin"), *chrusos* ("gold"), *chitōn* ("tunic"), *sēsamē* ("sesame"), and *amōmos* ("blameless"[23]). In his monograph, Emilia Masson lists numerous other early Semitic loans in Greek.[24] The presence of such foreign loans—including Persian words—in Greek is evidence of considerable contact between the Greeks and the Near East long before the invasion of Alexander.[25] In addition to such linguistic evidence there is also textual and artifactual evidence of early contacts.

Ionia/Yawan

After the Dorian invasions, refugees from Mycenaean sites such as Pylos migrated to the west coast of Turkey in an area that came to be known as Ionia.[26] The Hebrew word for the Greeks, *Yawan* (Vulgate *Javan*), is derived from the Greek 'Ιαονες or 'ΙαϜονες (compare Linear

17. E. Masson, *Recherches sur les plus anciens emprunts sémitiques en grec* (Paris: C. Klincksieck, 1967), pp. 67–69.

18. Ibid., pp. 90–91.

19. Ibid., pp. 91–93.

20. Ibid., pp. 94–95.

21. Yamauchi, *Greece and Babylon*, p. 33.

22. W. Krause, "Griechische-orientalische Lehnwortbeziehungen," in *Festschrift für Karl Vretska* (Heidelberg: C. Winter, 1970), p. 89.

23. E. Vermeule, *Greece in the Bronze Age* (Chicago: University of Chicago Press, 1972), pp. 71–72.

24. Masson, *Recherches*, pp. 19–67.

25. See further E. Benveniste, "Relations lexicales entre la Perse et la Grèce ancienne," in *La Persia e il Greco-Romano* (Rome: Accademia Nazionale dei Lincei, 1966), pp. 479–87; R. Schmitt, " 'Méconnaissance' altiranischen Sprachgutes im Griechischen," *Glotta* 49 (1971): 95–110; O. Szemerényi, "The Origins of the Greek Lexicon: *Ex Oriente Lux*," *JHS* 94 (1974): 144–57; T. F. R. G. Braun, "The Greeks in the Near East," in *The Cambridge Ancient History: The Expansion of the Greek World, Eighth to Sixth Centuries B.C.*, eds. J. Boardman and N. G. L. Hammond, 2d ed. (Cambridge: Cambridge University Press, 1982), vol. 3, pt. 3, pp. 25–26.

26. See J. M. Cook, *The Greeks in Ionia and the East* (New York: Praeger, 1963).

B, *I-ya-wo-ne*), because the Hebrews' first contacts were with the Greeks from the settlements of Ionia. The word appears in the table of nations (Gen. 10:4), where the sons of Javan are listed, according to the New International Version, as Elishah, Tarshish, the Kittim, and the Rodanim.

Elishah is the same as the name *Alashiya* found in Egyptian, Hittite, and Ugaritic texts. Most scholars identify it as the name for Cyprus.[27] Tarshish is based on a Phoenician word that means "smeltery," and was the name of many sites, including Tartessus in Spain.[28] In this context, it no doubt means Tarsus in Cilicia, the home of Paul. The word *Kittim* is derived from Kition, a Mycenaean settlement on Cyprus.[29] In the Old Testament and in the Arad ostraca, it is used for the Greeks. In the Dead Sea Scrolls, however, the term has come to mean the Romans.[30] Although the Masoretic Text in Genesis 10:4 has Dodanim, the correct reading is no doubt Rodanim (as in 1 Chron. 1:7), signifying the inhabitants of the large island of Rhodes, where there were Minoan and Mycenaean colonies.

Poul Riis, speaking as a classical archaeologist rather than a biblical exegete, makes this important comment on Genesis 10:4:

> So the genealogical list of the Old Testament apparently contains some truth as far as the ethnic relations of Yawan, Tarsos, Alašiya, Kition, and Rhodes are concerned. If Yawan originally meant Ionians it must have been adopted by the Semitic languages in the period before the destruction of Alašiya about 1000 B.C., before the establishment of a Phoenician rule over Kition in the 10th century B.C. and before the Dorians' coming to Rhodes at the same time.[31]

Ezekiel (27:13) speaks of Tyre's trade with Greece (*Yawan*). The Hebrews were accused of selling their kinsmen as slaves to the Greeks (*Yawanim*) in Joel 3:6 (Heb. 4:6), a work that Jacob Myers believes to be preexilic in date.[32] A related word for "Ionian" also appears in cuneiform texts from the time of Sargon II (722–705 B.C.):

27. Y. L. Holmes, "The Location of Alashiya," *JAOS* 91 (1971): 426–29.

28. W. F. Albright, "The Role of the Canaanites in the History of Civilization," in *The Bible and the Ancient Near East*, ed. G. E. Wright (Garden City: Doubleday, 1961), pp. 347, 361.

29. V. Karageorghis, *Kition: Mycenaean and Phoenician* (London: Oxford University Press, 1973).

30. F. M. Cross, *The Ancient Library of Qumran*, rev. ed. (Garden City: Doubleday, 1961), p. 124.

31. P. J. Riis, *Sūkās I: The North-East Sanctuary and the First Settling of Greeks in Syria and Palestine* (Copenhagen: Munksgaard, 1970), p. 134.

32. J. M. Myers, "Some Considerations Bearing on the Date of Joel," *ZAW* 74 (1962): 177–95. On the other hand, a study of astronomical data on eclipses (Joel 2:31), has Stephenson dating the book circa 350 B.C. See F. R. Stephenson, "The Date of the Book of Joel," *VT* 19 (1969): 224–29.

Akkadian	*Yaman*[33]
Old Persian	*Yaunā*
Elamite	*Yauna*[34]

Greeks in the East Mediterranean

There were contacts between the Aegean and the Near East in the Middle Bronze period through the Minoans. Extensive trade developed in the Late Bronze age as attested by the widespread distribution of Mycenaean pottery in the Levant and Egypt.[35] After the disruption of the Dorian invasion and the dislocation of the Sea Peoples around 1200 B.C., the Aegean entered a Dark Age that saw a great diminution, if not a complete cessation, of trade. A Protogeometric hydria from the early part of this era (eleventh–tenth centuries B.C.) was discovered at Shiqmona near Mount Carmel in 1970.[36]

In his important study that surveys Greek imported ware along the Levant, Riis notes the extensive importation of Protogeometric cups (ninth century B.C.) at many sites along the coast (such as Sukas, Abu Hawam, and Askalon), at inland sites (such as Tayinat and Hama), and even into Mesopotamia in the Habur Valley, Halaf, and Nineveh.[37] Riis dates the renewed influx of Greeks into the Near East from about 850 B.C. based on the following data:

> I may recapitulate that Tall Ābū Hawam III, Megiddo IV, and Samaria V were the earliest strata to yield Greek Geometric ware, but that there is no unanimity about the dates of these deposits. Nevertheless it seems beyond doubt that Tall Ābū Hawam III belongs to a time before about 815 B.C., Megiddo IV to one before about 750 B.C. and Samaria V before about

33. For a list of occurrences, see S. Parpola, *Neo-Assyrian Toponyms* (Kevelaer: Butzon und Bercker, 1970), under "Jawan." P. R. Helm, *"Greeks" in the Neo-Assyrian Levant and "Assyria" in Early Greek Writers,* University of Pennsylvania, Ph.D. diss. (Ann Arbor: University Microfilms International, 1987), pp. 138–39, 162–63, 166. Helm restricts the sense of the Akkadian term *Yaman* to Cypriotes by taking this term as synonymous with *Yadnana.* He fails, however, to explain how one can dissociate Yaman from Greek *Iaones* (**Iawones*).

34. W. Röllig, "Griechische Eigennamen in Texten der babylonischen Spätzeit," *Or* 29 (1960); 383. In the Persian Empire *Yaunā* was a designation for Greeks, especially those of the seventh satrapy, which included the west and south coasts of Anatolia. See Riis, *Sūkās I,* p. 133; Braun, "Greeks in the Near East," pp. 1, 3.

35. V. Hankey, "Mycenaean Pottery in the Middle East: Notes of Finds Since 1951," *Annual of the British School at Athens* 62 (1967): 107–42; idem, "Mycenaean Trade with the South-Eastern Mediterranean," *Mélanges des l'Université Saint-Joseph* 46 (1970–1971): 11–30; H. Buchholz and V. Karageorghis, "Ägäische Funde und Kultureinflüsse in den Randgebieten des Mittelmeers," *AA* 89 (1974): 325–460; E. Cline, "Amenhotep III and the Aegean," *Or* 56 (1987): 1–36.

36. J. Elgavish, archaeological report on Shiqmona, *IEJ* 20 (1970): 230.

37. Riis, *Sūkās I,* pp. 142ff.

735 B.C., and the lowest proposed beginnings of the said strata are about 980, 850, and 750 B.C. respectively.[38]

Although Greeks were in the area by the ninth century, it was only around 675 B.C. that a Greek temple was built at Sukas. The first Greek inscription comes from a still later stratum: "a spindle-whorl of local clay, but of a Greek 8th–6th century type was inscribed about 600 B.C. in a Greek dialect and in Greek characters betraying an Insular origin of the owner."[39]

From Palestine itself excavations, particularly along the coast, have added to the list of imported Greek ware, particularly from the seventh through the fifth centuries B.C. In the seventh and sixth centuries it was primarily Eastern Greek (Ionian) and Cypriote ware; from the fifth century it was primarily Attic ware from Athens.[40]

Greek pottery of the seventh century has been found at Ashdod, Tell Abu Hawam, Ascalon, and Tell Jemmeh.[41] More recently in the remains of an Assyrian palace at Shari'a dating to the seventh century and located ten miles northwest of Beersheba, excavators have found Greek wine amphorae, a Corinthian aryballos, and the head of a Greek figurine.[42]

There is striking evidence that some Greek mercenaries, probably from Egypt, found employment during the seventh and sixth centuries in Palestine. In 1960, between Ashdod and Jaffa at Meṣad Ḥashavyahu, a fortress covering 1½ acres was excavated. East Greek ware in large quantities dating to the end of the seventh century was found here. The site was established by Greeks about 650 to 625.[43]

Farther inland, just west of the Dead Sea at Arad, inscribed ostraca were discovered from the fortress that was destroyed in Nebuchadnezzar's first campaign (circa 600–598). These ostraca come from the archive of Eliashib, who was in charge of distributing supplies to the Kittim. Yohanon Aharoni concluded that the Kittim mentioned in the

38. Ibid., p. 162. For evidence of Greek ware at other sites along the Levant such as Al Mina, see Yamauchi, *Greece and Babylon*, pp. 54–57; Helm, *"Greeks" in the Neo-Assyrian Levant*, pp. 79ff.

39. Ibid., p. 158. As opposed to earlier scholars (Woolley, Boardman, Riis), Helm, *"Greeks" in the Neo-Assyrian Levant*, pp. 95, 101, 314–15, does not believe that substantial Greek settlement was possible until the collapse of the Neo-Assyrian Empire around 610 B.C.

40. D. Auscher, "Les relations entre le Grèce et la Palestine avant la conquête d'Alexandre," *VT* 17 (1967): 8–30.

41. M. Dothan, archaeological report on Tel Ashdod, *IEJ* 18 (1968): 254.

42. E. D. Oren, "Esh-Shari'a, Tell," in *Encyclopedia of Archaeological Excavations in the Holy Land*, eds. M. Avi-Yonah and E. Stern (Jerusalem: Massada, 1978), 4: 1062.

43. J. Naveh, "The Excavations at Meṣad Ḥashavyahu—Preliminary Report," *IEJ* 12 (1962): 89–113; Braun, "Greeks in the Near East," p. 21, suggests that the Greek mercenaries may have been employed by Judah.

ostraca were Greek mercenaries serving in the remote forts of Judah.[44] Some of the personal names in the ostraca are apparently Greek.[45] East Greek ware has been found at nearby Tel Malḥata.[46]

Ephraim Stern wrote a dissertation analyzing the archaeological evidence of the Persian period in Israel. In an article summarizing his findings, he concluded: "This fits the picture of life in the area as portrayed both by the sources and by the archaeological finds, namely of expanding Greek trade at the end of the 8th century and mainly in the 7th century."[47]

Concerning the great increase of Greek pottery in the sixth and fifth centuries, Stern says:

> In the Persian period imported ware streamed into Palestine from East Greece (mainly Rhodes), Cyprus and especially Athens, according to which of the various areas of Greece dominated the international trade at the time. At the end of the seventh and the sixth century B.C., the East-Greek and Cypriot wares were predominant in Palestine.[48]

Greeks and the Neo-Assyrians

One might well concede contacts between the Aegean and the Levant, but question whether Greek objects and words could have penetrated into Mesopotamia. The archaeological and textual data demonstrate that Aegean influence did penetrate the interior at an early date.

The Assyrians came into direct contact with Greeks in Cilicia and Cyprus during the eighth century. In 713 seven Greek kings of Cyprus came to do homage to Sargon II at Babylon.[49] In 712 Sargon was forced to act against Yamani—the Greek (Cypriote?)[50]—who had rebelled after being enthroned by the people of the Philistine city of Ashdod.[51] Greek

44. Y. Aharoni, "Hebrew Ostraca from Tel Arad," *IEJ* 16 (1966): 4; Braun, "Greeks in the Near East," p. 22.

45. Y. Aharoni, "Arad: Its Inscriptions and Temple," *BA* 31 (1968): 11.

46. M. Kochavi, "Notes and News," *IEJ* 17 (1967): 273.

47. E. Stern, "Israel at the Close of the Period of the Monarchy: An Archaeological Survey," *BA* 38 (1975): 53.

48. E. Stern, *Material Culture of the Land of the Bible in the Persian Period 538–332 B.C.* (Warminster: Aris and Phillips, 1982), p. 232. He also notes that Greek coins began to appear in Palestine by the end of the sixth century.

49. Braun, "Greeks in the Near East," p. 15, cites a Nimrud letter published by Saggs dating the first contact between the Assyrians and the Greeks earlier in the reign of Tiglath-pileser III (738). But this letter about a raid of the Yawan along the coast has been dated to Sargon II by Helm, *"Greeks" in the Neo-Assyrian Levant*, pp. 179–80, 210, n. 107.

50. H. Saggs, "The Nimrud Letters," *Iraq* 25 (1963): 77–78.

51. D. W. Thomas, ed., *Documents from Old Testament Times* (New York: Harper and Brothers,

fibulae were found in Sargon's palace in Assyria.[52]

In 696 B.C. Sennacherib (705–682 B.C.), Sargon's successor, had to contend with a revolt in Cilicia, led by Kirua, the Assyrian governor of Illubri. Kirua was supported by Greeks from Ingira (Greek *Anchiale*) and Tarsus.[53] Sennacherib ruthlessly suppressed the revolt and transported the captives to Mesopotamia. According to Leonard King:

> The deportation of considerable bodies of these [Ionian] men to Nineveh, where they were employed upon the royal palace then in course of construction, may well have had important effects, in certain directions, on contemporary Assyrian work.[54]

Memories of this conflict were preserved by Berossus, a Babylonian who wrote a Greek account in the third century B.C.

About the same time Sennacherib assembled a navy built by Phoenicians to hunt down the ambitious Babylonian king Merodach-Baladan. The ships were staffed by Tyrians, Sidonians, and Ionian Greeks.[55] German excavators found at Babylon, in the area of Merkes, cremation burials, which they ascribed to Greeks. These were found in the levels before the destruction of the city by Sennacherib, that is, in the very early seventh century B.C.[56]

Esarhaddon (681–670) took up residence at Nineveh and at the beginning of his reign undertook the construction of buildings in a new suburb. He turned to the west for the materials. The list of contributors included ten rulers from Cyprus, most of whose names are Greek.[57] Greek Geometric ware has been found at Nineveh.[58]

At the Aegean end of the trade route, some Assyrian glazed pottery has been found in recent excavations at Sardis in Lydia, an area just east of Ionia.[59] What is most remarkable is the evidence of Iranian

---

1968), pp. 62–63.

52. G. Loud, *The Palace of Sargon II* (Chicago: University of Chicago Press, 1938), plate 59.

53. A. T. Olmstead, *A History of Assyria* (Chicago: University of Chicago Press, 1964), p. 290; compare J. Boardman, "Tarsus, Al Mina, and Greek Chronology," *JHS* 85 (1965): 5–15.

54. L. W. King, "Sennacherib and the Ionians," *JHS* 30 (1910): 331. For the tradition of this conflict as preserved in the later Greek account of Berossus, see Helm, *"Greeks" in the Neo-Assyrian Levant*, pp. 192–93, 319–26.

55. Olmstead, *History of Assyria*, p. 290; Braun, "Greeks in the Near East," p. 19.

56. E. Schmidt, "Die Griechen in Babylon und das weiterleben ihren Kultur," *Jahrbuch des Deutschen Archäologischen Instituts* 56 (1941): 797.

57. Olmstead, *History of Assyria*, pp. 368–69; Helm, *"Greeks" in the Neo-Assyrian Levant*, p. 164.

58. J. Boardman, *The Greeks Overseas*, rev. ed. (London: Thames and Hudson, 1980), p. 45.

59. G. M. A. Hanfmann and N. H. Ramage, *Sculpture from Sardis* (Cambridge: Harvard University Press, 1978), p. 14.

objects, transported via Assyria and Syria, to the west from the ninth to seventh centuries.[60]

The Greeks and the Neo-Babylonians

We know that Antimenidas, the brother of the famous Greek poet Alcaeus, fought for Nebuchadnezzar as a mercenary against Ascalon in 604.[61] Nebuchadnezzar no doubt employed Greek craftsmen because Neo-Babylonian texts record twice a group of eight and twice a group of seven Ionian craftsmen.[62] The throne room of Nebuchadnezzar at Babylon also indicates Greek influence.[63] Seton Lloyd comments: "A tall panel recovered from a wall outside the throne-room is of special interest, in that classical motifs are adapted to the design, suggesting that some contact now existed between Babylon and Greece."[64]

Greeks, probably Cypriotes, were well known to Nabonidus, the father of Belshazzar. His annals record that iron was imported to Babylonia from Yamana.[65] Leo Oppenheim published two Neo-Babylonian texts from Uruk (YOS 6.168; TCL 12.84) that detail trade between Mesopotamia and Greek centers (Yamana) in copper and iron.[66] He notes that "even before Cyrus occupied Babylon in 539 B.C., the economic texts from the great sanctuaries in Sippar, Babylon, and Uruk offer evidence of trade relations that reached to the Mediterranean (Cilician iron) and even as far as Greece."[67]

Greek pottery is represented in Babylonia at the earliest by one Mycenaean sherd.[68] After the Greek Dark Ages, imports began again

60. O. W. Muscarella, "The Archaeological Evidence for Relations Between Greece and Iran in the First Millennium B.C.," *JANE* 9 (1977): 31–57; Helm, *"Greeks" in the Neo-Assyrian Levant,* p. 111.

61. J. Quinn, "Alcaeus 48 (B16) and the Fall of Ascalon (604 B.C.)," *BASOR* 164 (1961): 19–20; D. Page, *Sappho and Alcaeus* (Oxford: Clarendon, 1955), pp. 223ff.

62. E. Weidner, "Jojachin, König von Juda, in babylonischen Keilschrifttexten," in *Mélanges syriens offerts à M. René Dussaud* (Paris: Paul Geuthner, 1939), 2: 923–35; W. F. Albright, "Cilicia and Babylonia under the Chaldaean Kings," *BASOR* 120 (1950): 25; J. Pritchard, ed., *Ancient Near Eastern Texts Relating to the Old Testament,* rev. ed. (Princeton: Princeton University Press, 1955), p. 308. Boardman, *Greeks Overseas,* p. 52, comments: "At Babylon there is inscriptional evidence for the presence of 'Ionian' craftsmen, but perhaps only from Lycia or Cilicia, to judge from their names, and some mid-sixth-century Athenian pottery."

63. Yamauchi, *Greece and Babylon,* pp. 14, 68–69.

64. S. Lloyd, *The Archaeology of Mesopotamia* (New York: Thames and Hudson, 1978), p. 228.

65. C. Roebuck, *Ionian Trade and Colonization* (New York: Archaeological Institute of America, 1959), p. 102.

66. A. L. Oppenheim, "Essay on Overland Trade in the First Millennium B.C.," *JCS* 21 (1969): 236–54.

67. A. L. Oppenheim, *Ancient Mesopotamia* (Chicago: University of Chicago Press, 1964), p. 65.

68. O. Deubner, "Die griechischen Scherben von Babylon," in *Das Babylon der Spätzeit,* by F. Wetzel et al. (Berlin: Gebrüder Mann, 1957), p. 52.

with red-figure ware (after 530 B.C.). Sherds of nine Greek vessels dating to the sixth century were found in homes, the palace, and temples.[69] Among two fine painted pieces were those by the painter Sotades (fl. 460–450 B.C.). Our knowledge of Greek pottery in Mesopotamia is incomplete. Christoph Clairmont's survey of Greek pottery in the Near East did not include such major collections as those in Berlin, the British Museum, and Baghdad. Clairmont refers to numerous black-glazed Attic pottery in the Iraq Museum, noting that "as a whole they have never been published."[70]

The Greeks and Persians

According to Daniel 5, Daniel himself witnessed the overthrow of Babylon by Cyrus in 539. First-hand Persian contact with the Ionian Greeks came some time before this with the conquest by Cyrus of Lydia and Ionia in 547/546. While one must not reduce Persian art to a branch of Greek art and must remember that the Greeks were but one of numerous elements in the Persian Empire, it cannot be denied that the Greek presence and contributions to the Persians in the late sixth and early fifth centuries were substantial.[71]

The Greeks under Cyrus

At his new capital at Pasargadae Cyrus employed Ionian craftsmen. Carl Nylander examined the evidence of Ionian stone masons at Pasargadae.[72] At first he concluded the Greek toothed chisel was initially introduced into Persia during the reign of Darius,[73] but then observed limited use of this tool at Pasargadae from the reign of Cyrus.[74] Other technical features ascribed to the Greeks by Nylander include the marking of stone blocks by red color and the use of certain

69. Schmidt, "Die Griechen in Babylon," p. 794.

70. C. Clairmont, "Greek Pottery from the Near East, II," *Berytus* 12 (1956–1957): 3. See Boardman, *Greeks Overseas,* p. 54.

71. See the seminal article of G. M. A. Richter, "Greeks in Persia," *AJA* 50 (1946): 15–30. For further studies of Greek and other elements in Persian art, see A. Farkas, "Is There Anything Persian in Persian Art?" in *Ancient Persia: The Art of an Empire,* ed. D. Schmandt-Besserat (Malibu: Undena, 1980), pp. 15–21; E. D. Francis, "Greeks and Persians: The Art of Hazard and Triumph," in *Ancient Persia,* ed. Schmandt-Besserat, pp. 53–86.

72. C. Nylander, *Ionians in Pasargadae* (Lund: Universitetsbiblioteke Uppsala, 1970).

73. C. Nylander, "Old Persian and Greek Stonecutting and the Chronology of Achaemenian Monuments," *AJA* 69 (1965): 54–55.

74. C. Nylander, "The Toothed Chisel in Pasargadae: Further Notes on Old Persian Stonecutting," *AJA* 70 (1966): 376.

forms of metal clamps.[75] Speaking of the various elements in the art of Pasargadae, Nylander concludes:

> And there is Ionia in the numerous soaring columns, fluted or plain, sometimes on bases of Greek type, in the extensive, stoa-like porticoes, and there is a Greek feel over the little naos-like tomb chamber of the Cyrus monument and over much of the sculpture.[76]

Ann Farkas, who is also impressed by the Greek contribution at Pasargadae, comments: "The Greek features in the architecture of Cyrus, the placement of the upper arm within the body contours of the genie on the gate house relief, and the scarcity of native sculptors trained in monumental stone carving, are all factors in favor of the presence of Greek sculptors at Pasargadae."[77] Among other possible evidence of their technique was the practice of adding metal decorations to stone reliefs.[78] Géza de Francovich also notes the following Greek features at Cyrus's capital: "These bases are clearly meant to imitate the tori of the Ionian buildings as, for instance, those of the first temple of Samos and of the Artemision of Ephesus, both of which can be referred to 560–550 B.C."[79] He observes:

> Even in the so-called Audience Hall as in the Residential Palace echoes of Ionian architecture are evident—in the very accurate trimming of limestone blocks, in the diffused dichromatism of structures, and in the proportions of the high column still surviving and belonging to the Palace of Audience. The proportions are very similar to those of the columns of Ionian temples of the 6th century as, for example, the columns of the Artemision of Ephesus.[80]

The long porticoes of palace P may have been inspired by Greek stoas.[81] The rosettes from a Zendan fragment have their clearest parallels in Ionia.[82] One of the features of Persian sculpture at Pasargadae

75. C. Nylander, "Clamps and Chronology," *IA* 6 (1966): 139 n.

76. C. Nylander, "Achaemenid Imperial Art," in *Power and Propaganda,* ed. M. T. Larsen (Copenhagen: Akademisk Forlag, 1979), p. 348.

77. A. Farkas, *Achaemenid Sculpture* (Istanbul: Nederlands Historisch-Archeologisch Instituut in het Nabije Oosten, 1974), p. 109.

78. Ibid., p. 94.

79. G. de Francovich, "Problems of Achaemenid Architecture," *EW* 16 (1966): 235. See also J. Boardman, "Chian and Early Ionic Architecture," *Antiquaries Journal* 39 (1959): 216; G. Goossens and J. J. Guepin, "On the Position of Greek Artists under Achaemenid Rule," *Persica* 1 (1963–1964): 42; E. Porada, *The Art of Ancient Iran* (New York: Crown, 1965), p. 145; G. M. A. Hanfmann, *From Croesus to Constantine* (Ann Arbor: University of Michigan Press, 1975), p. 15.

80. De Francovich, "Problems," p. 239.

81. D. Stronach, *Pasargadae* (New York: Oxford University Press, 1978), p. 72.

82. Nylander, *Ionians,* p. 140.

and elsewhere, which a number of scholars have cited as evidence of Greek technique, is the manner in which the folds of garments are depicted.[83] There are, however, some scholars who believe that the reliefs were based on actual pleated Persian robes rather than on a Greek artistic convention.[84]

The Greeks under Darius and Xerxes

After the Ionian revolt was suppressed in 494 Darius deported Milesians from Ionia to Susa and settled them in Mesopotamia (Herodotus 6.20). In 490 his forces captured the city of Eretria, an ally of Athens, and also deported the Eretrians and settled them nearby (Herodotus 6.119). Darius's famous building charter describing the erection of his palace at Susa explicitly names Ionian workmen.[85] Some Greek ware has been found at Susa.[86]

The new capital of Darius at Persepolis provides clearly dated evidence for the presence of Greeks. The Persepolis Fortification tablets, which are dated from 509 to 494 B.C., have several references to the *Yauna* (or *Yaunā*), that is, "Ionians."[87] Tablet PF 1224 lists twenty-three Ionian mothers and the rations they received, two quarts for bearing boys and one quart for bearing girls.[88] Tablet PF 2072 mentions a group of sixteen (or seventeen) Ionian workmen.[89] Ionians are also mentioned among the workers listed in the Persepolis Treasury Tablets (dated 492 to 458 B.C.), for example, in PT 15.[90] An Ionian is noted as the giver of a receipt to a treasury official in PT 21.[91] Among the names

83. Richter, "Greeks in Persia," pp. 17–18; Farkas, *Achaemenid Sculpture*, p. 25; S. Casson, "Achaemenid Sculpture," in *A Survey of Persian Art*, ed. A. U. Pope (London: Oxford University Press, 1938), 1: 358–60; H. Luschey, "Die Darius-Statuen aus Susa und ihre Rekonstruktion," in *Kunst, Kultur und Geschichte der Achämenidenzeit*, eds. H. Koch and D. N. MacKenzie (Berlin: Dietrich Reimer, 1983), p. 192.

84. A. Roes, "The Achaemenid Robe," *BiOr* 8.4 (1951): 141; B. Goldman, "Origin of the Persian Robe," *IA* 4 (1964): 133–52.

85. R. G. Kent, *Old Persian*, rev. ed. (New Haven: American Oriental Society, 1953), p. 144. Kent thinks that "Babylonians" in 1.53 are "Ionians resident in Babylonia" on the basis of the Akkadian version (p. 143, n.).

86. G. Goossens, "Artistes et artisans étrangers en Perse sous les Achéménides," *La Nouvelle Clio* 1 (1949): 35; K. De Vries, "Attic Pottery in the Achaemenid Empire," *AJA* 81 (1977): 546.

87. R. T. Hallock, *Persepolis Fortification Tablets* (Chicago: University of Chicago Press, 1969), p. 772.

88. Ibid., p. 349. See also C. W. Fornara, ed., *Archaic Times to the End of the Peloponnesian War* (Baltimore: Johns Hopkins University Press, 1977), #45, pp. 45–46.

89. Hallock, *Persepolis Fortification Tablets*, p. 644.

90. G. Cameron, *Persepolis Treasury Tablets* (Chicago: University of Chicago Press, 1948), p. 110.

91. Ibid., p. 119.

at Persepolis is one *Yaunaparza,* which Ilya Gershevitch analyzes as **yauna-b(a)rǰa,* "he who welcomes Greeks."[92]

There is even one tablet (PF 1771) written in Greek: *oinos duro maris tebēt* ("two marrish of wine. Tebet").[93] One tablet (PF 3821) is sealed with the impression of an Athenian coin.[94] In the foundation of the Apadana (built between 517 and 514) were found four Lydian gold and four Greek silver coins.[95] Several Greek graffiti were incised in the quarries near Persepolis. The Pytharchos graffito is dated to circa 500 by Giovanni Carratelli.[96] Another graffito is dated to the beginning of the fifth century B.C.

The Persians developed an admiration for Greek art. They sent back a number of masterpieces including the bronze statue of Harmodius and Aristogeiton from Athens, a statue of Artemis from Brauron, and a statue of Apollo from Didyma. A seated Greek statue of Penelope (or Demeter) was found in the treasury at Persepolis.[97]

The Persians sponsored artists such as Telephanes, who worked in the studios of Xerxes and Darius according to Pliny the Elder (*N.H.* 34.68).[98] It is too speculative to consider Telephanes "the grand master of the Persepolis friezes" as does John Cook.[99] Among the discoveries at Persepolis was the drawing of a human head on a limestone fragment by a Greek artist, which has been dated by Gisela Richter to 510 to 500 B.C.[100] A fragment of a Heracles-like figure was found by Erich Schmidt in the treasury at Persepolis. This was lost when the ship carrying it was torpedoed by a German submarine. Further fragments from the same scene were recently discovered by Giuseppe Tilia in a storeroom at Persepolis. Michael Roaf and John Boardman have reconstructed the panel as a scene with Heracles and Apollo.[101]

92. I. Gershevitch, "Amber at Persepolis," in *Studia Classica et Orientalia Antonino Pagliaro Oblata* (Rome: Istituto di Glottologia dell'Universita de Roma, 1969), 2: 246.

93. Hallock, *Persepolis Fortification Tablets,* p. 2.

94. See C. Starr, "A Sixth Century Athenian Tetradrachm Used to Seal a Clay Tablet from Persepolis," *Numismatic Chronicle* 16 (1976): 219–22.

95. M. Dandamayev, "Politische und wirtschaftliche Geschichte," in *Beiträge zur Achämenidengeschichte,* ed. G. Walser (Wiesbaden: Franz Steiner, 1972), p. 45.

96. G. P. Carratelli, "Greek Inscriptions of the Middle East," *EW* n.s. 16 (1966): 31; see also Fornara, *Archaic Times,* no. 46, p. 46.

97. C. M. Olmstead, "A Greek Lady from Persepolis," *AJA* 54 (1950): 10–18. See also T. S. Kawami, "Greek Art and Persian Taste: Some Animal Sculptures from Persepolis," *AJA* 90 (1986): 259–67.

98. Goossens and Guepin, "On the Position," p. 41, have suggested that he worked under Xerxes II and Darius II instead of under Xerxes I and Darius I, but this is unlikely. Xerxes II reigned for only forty-five days in 424 B.C.

99. Cook, *Greeks in Ionia and the East,* p. 127.

100. Richter, "Greeks in Persia," fig. 26, p. 29; Goossens and Guepin, "On the Position," p. 35, date the sketch thirty years later.

101. M. Roaf and J. Boardman, "A Greek Painting at Persepolis," *JHS* 100 (1980): 204–6.

Other Greeks at the Persian Court

In an important dissertation A. Wiedersich catalogued some three hundred Greeks who came to or lived at the Persian court in the period between Cyrus and Alexander.[102] These included such outstanding leaders as Demaratus, king of Sparta; Hippias, tyrant of Athens; and Themistocles.[103] Some of these Greeks were numbered among the "friends" and "benefactors" of the Great King.[104]

One hundred of the Greeks at the Persian court were military personnel. Although most of the Greek mercenaries were employed by the Persians after 450, some served before this (Herodotus 8.26).[105] When Cambyses invaded Egypt in 525, Greek mercenaries were fighting both with and against the Persians as Phanes defected to the side of the invaders (Herodotus 3.4).

Among the Greeks who served the Persian king were at least two dozen Greek sculptors, architects, artists, doctors, philosophers, and courtesans.[106] These notables included Democedes, a physician at the court of Darius (Herodotus 3.125, 129–37), the first of a long line of physicians at the Persian court, and Mandrocles of Samos, an engineer who built the bridges across the Hellespont for Xerxes. Needless to say, the number of Greeks involved in the Near East with the Persians kept multiplying in the late fifth and the early fourth centuries before Alexander's invasion.[107]

Some twenty years ago I wrote:

102. "Prosopographie der Griechen beim Perserkönig," (Breslau, 1922). See J. Hofstetter, "Zu den griechischen Gesandtschaften nach Persien," in Walser, *Beiträge zur Achämenidengeschichte*, p. 95; J. Hofstetter, *Die Griechen in Persien* (Berlin: Dietrich Reimer, 1978).

103. G. Walser, "Griechen am Hofe des Grosskönigs," in *Festgabe Hans von Greverz*, ed. E. Walder (Bern: H. Lang, 1967), pp. 189–202.

104. J. Wiesehöfer, "Die 'Freunde' und 'Wohltäter' des Grosskönigs," *Studia Iranica* 9 (1980): 7–21.

105. G. F. Seibt, *Griechische Söldner im Achaimenidenreich* (Bonn: Rudolf Habelt, 1977), p. 15.

106. J. M. Balcer, *Sparda by the Bitter Sea* (Chico: Scholars, 1984), pp. 180–81.

107. See A. Andrewes, "Thucydides and the Persians," *Historia* 10 (1961):1–18; E. Badian, "The Peace of Callias," *JHS* 107 (1987): 1–39; M. S. Goldstein, "Athenian-Persian Peace Treaties: Thuc. 8.56.4 and 8.58.2," *CSCA* 7 (1975): 155–64; S. W. Hirsch, *The Friendship of the Barbarians* (Hanover: University Press of New England, 1985); I. Kleeman, *Der Satrapen-Sarkophag aus Sidon* (Berlin: Gebrüder Mann, 1958); D. M. Lewis, *Sparta and Persia* (Leiden: Brill, 1977); C. Mossé, "Les rapports entre la Grèce et la Perse au IVème siècle avant Jesus-Christ," in *La Persia e il Mondo Greco-Romano*, pp. 177–82; A. E. Raubitschek, "The Treaties Between Persia and Athens," *GRBS* 5 (1964): 151–59; G. Richter, "Greek Subjects on 'Graeco-Persian' Seal Stones," *Archaeologica Orientalia in Memoriam Ernst Herzfeld* (Locust Valley: J. J. Augustin, 1952), pp. 189–94; R. Schmitt, "Achaimenidisches bei Thukydides," in Koch, *Kultur*, pp. 69–86; C. G. Starr, "Greeks and Persians in the Fourth Century B.C.," *IA* 11 (1975): 44–60; *IA* 12 (1977): 49–116; D. L. Stockton, "The Peace of Callias," *Historia* 8 (1959): 61–79.

> In conclusion, we may safely say that the presence of Greek words in an Old Testament book is not a proof of Hellenistic date, in view of the abundant opportunities for contacts between the Aegean and the Near East before Alexander. The evidence which I have presented is but a small fraction, which no doubt will be amplified many times by future discoveries.[108]

This conclusion, I believe, remains irrefutable.

108. Yamauchi, "Greek Words," p. 192.

12
Zoroastrianism

Historical Epochs

Early Iranian Migrations

The Medes and Persians were Indo-European tribes who migrated into the Iranian plateau from southern Russia, first into the area southeast of the Caspian Sea perhaps as early as the thirteenth century B.C., and then into western Iran around 1000 B.C. The Medes became unified around the early seventh century B.C. and at first dominated the Persians.

The Achaemenid Dynasty

The Persians achieved supremacy under Cyrus (550–530), who expanded the Persian Empire to incorporate Media, Lydia, and Babylonia. His son, Cambyses, conquered Egypt in 525. A usurper, Gaumata, seized the throne for seven months in 522, until he was overthrown by Darius (522–486). Darius was succeeded by his son Xerxes, the Ahasuerus of the Book of Esther (485–465). Both Ezra and Nehemiah served under Artaxerxes I (464–424). The later Achaemenids included Darius II (423–404), Artaxerxes II (403–359), Artaxerxes III (358–337), and finally Darius III (336–30), who was conquered by Alexander.

The Seleucid Era

The descendants of Seleucus, one of Alexander's generals, ruled Persia for a brief period (323–247) after Alexander's death. They left a lasting legacy of Hellenistic culture to the next Persian rulers.

The Parthian Era

Parthians from southeast of the Caspian Sea established a new dynasty under Arsaces in 247 B.C. Henceforth the Arsacids ruled Persia until A.D. 224. Unfortunately almost no texts from Iran have been recovered from this crucial epoch. Classical writers were interested mainly in Roman-Parthian conflicts. Robert Zaehner comments: "Of the fortunes of the Zoroastrians during the centuries of Seleucid and Parthian dominion we know practically nothing."[1] Roman Ghirshman also laments: "We know nothing, or practically nothing, about how far the Parthians adopted the religion practiced in Iran."[2]

In view of this lack of evidence, scholars have taken different views of the religious situation in Iran during this period. Jacob Neusner concludes: "Though Zoroastrianism as we know it from Sasanid times may have taken shape in the Arsacid period, we have no way to trace its development."[3] The archaeological evidence suggests a strongly Hellenized polytheism. Persian deities were identified with Greek gods and were portrayed in their likenesses. For example, Verethraghna was identified with Herakles.[4] Therefore some scholars, such as Zaehner,

1. R. C. Zaehner, *The Dawn and Twilight of Zoroastrianism* (New York: G. P. Putnam's Sons, 1961), p. 22. The title of his book is significant: the author says virtually nothing of what should have been the "midday" of Zoroastrianism.

2. R. Ghirshman, *Iran* (Harmondsworth: Penguin, 1954), p. 268. In reviewing E. Yarshater, ed., *The Cambridge History of Iran III: The Seleucid, Parthian and Sasanian Period* [*CHI*] (Cambridge: Cambridge University Press, 1983) for the *American Historical Review* 89 (1984): 1055–56, I was struck by repeated remarks about the lack of evidence for this period. The editor, E. Yarshater, comments: "In fact, not a single book survives from pre-Islamic Iran" (p. xx). M. Boyce likewise notes: "No Parthian literature survives from the Parthian period in its original form" (p. 1151). See also C. J. Bleeker, "Wer war Zarathustra?" *Persica* 7 (1978): 32; D. A. Fox, "Darkness and Light: The Zoroastrian View," *JAAR* 35 (1967): 134; A. Hultgard, "Das Judentum in der hellenstisch-römischen Zeit und die iranische Religion—ein religionsgeschichtliches Problem," *ANRW* II.19.1 (1979): 518–19; J. Neusner, *A History of the Jews in Babylonia: I. The Parthian Period* (Leiden: Brill, 1969), pp. X–XI.

3. Neusner, *Parthian Period*, p. 19.

4. M. Boyce, "Iconoclasm among Zoroastrians," in *Christianity, Judaism, and Other Greco-*

believe the Parthians were indifferent to Zoroastrianism.[5]

Other scholars, however, are convinced the Iranians in the Parthian period must have been Zoroastrians to explain the reemergence of Zoroastrianism during the Sasanian period.[6] The kings' names, the ostraca from Nisa, and the fire temples are given as evidence for the Zoroastrianism of this period.[7] Outside of Iran areas where Persian and/or Zoroastrian influence can be attested include Armenia and Asia Minor.[8]

The Sasanian Era

Ardashir I, who came from the area of Fars near the Persian Gulf, established the new Sasanian dynasty in A.D. 224. Zoroastrianism became the state religion and its adherents persecuted Christians, Jews, Manichaeans, Mandaeans, Buddhists, and Brahmins, as indicated by the important inscriptions of Kartir, who served under five kings (Ardashir I, Shapur I, Hormizd I, Bahram I, and Bahram II).[9] The Sasanids ruled until the Islamic conquest in 651. The religious developments of this era are reflected in the ninth-century Zoroastrian compilations.

The Post-Islamic Era

The larger part of the Zoroastrian community fled Iran in the tenth century and settled in the area of Bombay, India.[10] There they were called Parsis (Parsees) or "Persians."

The Zoroastrians left in Iran have been contemptuously named

Roman Cults, M. Smith Festschrift, ed. J. Neusner (Leiden: Brill, 1975), 4: 99.

5. Zaehner, *Dawn,* p. 22. For the artistic and archaeological remains, see M. A. R. Colledge, *The Parthians* (New York: Praeger, 1967); C. Hopkins, "The Parthian Temple," *Berytus* 7 (1942): 1–18; R. Ghirshman, *Iran: Parthians and Sassanians* (London: Thames and Hudson, 1962).

6. M. Boyce, "On Mithra's Part in Zoroastrianism," *BSOAS* 32 (1969): 31; C. Colpe, "Parthische Religion und parthische Kunst," *Kairos* 17 (1975): 119. For a balanced survey, see J. Duchesne-Guillemin, "Zoroastrian Religion," chapter 20 in Yarshater, *CHI* III.2. G. Widengren has labored to reconstruct Iranian religion and influence during the Parthian era. See G. Widengren, "Quelques rapports entre juifs et iraniens à l'époque des Parthes," *Supplement to VT* 4 (1957): 197–242; idem, *Iranisch-semitische Kulturbegegnung in parthischer Zeit* (Cologne: Westdeutscher Verlag, 1960); idem, "Iran and Israel in Parthian Times with Special Regard to the Ethiopic *Book of Enoch,*" *Temenos* 2 (1966): 139–77, reprinted in B. A. Pearson, ed., *Religious Syncretism in Antiquity* (Missoula: Scholars, 1975), pp. 85–129.

7. J. R. Hinnells, "Zoroastrian Influence on the Judaeo-Christian Tradition," *Journal of the K. R. Cama Oriental Institute* 45 (1976): 15.

8. G. Widengren, *Les religions de l'Iran* (Paris: Payot, 1968), p. 201.

9. M. Sprengling, "Kartīr, Founder of Sasanian Zoroastrianism," *AJSL* 57 (1940): 197–228.

10. Some sources claim that the flight began even earlier in the eighth century.

A mountain shrine of Iranian Zoroastrians. (Courtesy of Professor Mary Boyce)

Gabars or "unbelievers" by the Muslims. They were not permitted to ride horses, and could not veil their women. In 1960 there were only 10,000 to 15,000 Gabars in Iran including 6,500 in Tehran, 3,700 in Kirman, and 700 in Yazd. The continuity of their faith is threatened by the diminishing pool of priests; in the 1930s there were some 200 priests in Yazd, but not even 10 in 1964.[11]

In India most of the Parsis continue to live in Bombay. Their numbers have been declining. In 1951 there were 116,000 Parsis; in 1975 only 85,000—a loss of 31,000 in twenty-four years.

Under the influence of Western scholars and Christian missionaries, some Parsis have tried to reform their religion by rejecting all the Avestan scriptures except the Gathas and by emphasizing ethics rather than ritual and rules of purity.[12] They have interpreted Zoroastrianism as an unqualified monotheism. Jivanji J. Modi, a distinguished Parsi scholar, allegorized the catechism to remove all traces of dualism.[13]

The Parsis prospered under British rule. Their women were educated

11. M. Boyce, *A Persian Stronghold of Zoroastrianism* (New York: Oxford University Press, 1977), p. 14.

12. E. Kulke, *The Parsees in India* (Munich: Weltforum, 1974), p. 97.

13. J. Duchesne-Guillemin, *Symbols and Values in Zoroastrianism* (New York: Harper and Row, 1966), pp. 17–18.

in larger numbers than Hindu women. Although a tiny minority in India (.016 percent), their influence is out of proportion to their numbers. They constitute the wealthiest and best-educated minority in India. Parsis started India's first textile mill and Air India. Most of the charitable institutions in Bombay were established by them.[14]

Other small Zoroastrian minorities include 5,000 in Pakistan, and about 3,000 each in Britain, Canada, and the United States. One famous Parsi émigré to the United States is the conductor, Zubin Mehta.

Sources

Sanskrit

The oldest of the Hindu scriptures, the Sanskrit Rig Veda, preserves traditions of the Indo-Aryans who invaded the Indus River Valley (now in Pakistan) around 1500 B.C. The close affinities between the Vedic texts and the oldest Avestan scriptures from Iran enable us to reconstruct the pantheon of the pre-Zoroastrian religion.

The earliest attestation of the Vedic gods is in a famous treaty between the Hittite king Suppiluliuma (1375–1345 B.C.) and the Mitannian king Mattiwaza. This mentions the gods Indra, Varuna, Mithra, and the Nasatyas.[15] The Rig Veda was transmitted orally for centuries, and was written down only after the coming of European scholars to India. The date of the original composition of the songs of the Rig Veda has been placed in 1700 B.C.,[16] 1500 to 1400,[17] and before 1000 B.C.[18]

Old Persian

Important royal inscriptions in three cuneiform versions (Old Persian, Elamite, and Akkadian) exist from the Achaemenids. The most

14. See further J. Whitehurst, "The Zoroastrian Response to Westernization: A Case Study of the Parsis of Bombay," *JAAR* 37 (1969): 224–36; M. Boyce, *Zoroastrians* (London: Routledge and Kegan Paul, 1979); S. S. Hartman, *Parsism: The Religion of Zoroaster* (Leiden: Brill, 1980); P. Axelrod, "Myth and Identity in the Indian Zoroastrian Community," *JMS* 3 (1980): 150–65; J. R. Hinnells, "The Parsis: A Bibliographical Survey," *JMS* 3 (1980): 100–49; idem, *Zoroastrianism and the Parsis* (London: Ward Lock Educational, 1981).

15. R. T. O'Callaghan, *Aram Naharaim* (Rome: Pontificium Institutum Biblicum, 1948), p. 63; P. Thieme, "The Aryan Gods of the Mitanni Treaties," *JAOS* 80 (1960): 301–17.

16. M. Boyce, *A History of Zoroastrianism I: The Early Period* (Leiden: Brill, 1975), p. 3.

17. S. Pigott, *Prehistoric India* (Harmondsworth: Penguin, 1961), p. 255.

18. W. H. Maurer, *Pinnacles of India's Past* (Amsterdam: John Benjamins, 1986), p. 5. See W. D. O'Flaherty, trans., *The Rig Veda* (Harmondsworth: Penguin, 1981), pp. 301–4, for a basic bibliography.

extensive text is Darius's famous inscription carved on a cliff at Behistun. Also significant is the Daiva inscription of Xerxes.

Elamite

Tablets from the treasury and the fortification of Persepolis, the capital built by Darius and Xerxes, deal mainly with provisions for workers but include some incidental information on religion. These texts are dated from the thirtieth year of Darius I to the seventh year of Artaxerxes I (492–458 B.C.).

Greek and Latin

Our main Greek source is Herodotus, who describes the conflict between the Persians and the Greeks during the fifth century B.C. Although he does not mention Zoroaster, he tells about the customs of the Persians and especially of the priestly tribe of the magi. (See chapter 13.) The Persians offered sacrifices to Zeus (Ahuramazda), the sun, moon, earth, fire, water, winds, and a goddess called Mitra (1.131). As Mithra was a god, Herodotus has mistaken him for the goddess Anahita. The Persians denounced lying and would not pollute water by urinating or defecating in it (1.138). The magi chanted a sacred text (1.132), killed noxious creatures like ants and snakes, and exposed human corpses to be mangled by "bird or dog" (1.140). Many of these practices correspond to those found in later Zoroastrian texts.[19]

A contemporary of Herodotus, Xanthos of Lydia, was the first Westerner to mention Zoroaster. Pliny the Elder (*N.H.* 30.1.3) cites Eudoxos of Cnidus, a disciple of Plato, for the view that Zoroaster lived six thousand years before. By the end of the fourth and beginning of the third centuries B.C., Zoroaster was known to the Greeks as a magos and an ancient lawgiver of the Iranian people.

Strabo (63 B.C.–A.D. 19) has an extensive passage (15.3.13–14) on Persian religion:

> Now the Persians do not erect statues or altars, but offer sacrifice on a high place, regarding the heavens as Zeus; and they also worship Helius [the Sun], whom they call Mithras, and Selenē [the Moon] and Aphrodite,

19. M. Molé, *Culte, mythe et cosmologie dans l'Iran ancien* (Paris: Presses Universitaires de France, 1963), p. 78; M. Boyce, *A History of Zoroastrianism II: Under the Achaemenids* [*History II*] (Leiden: Brill, 1982), p. 183: "In general Herodotus' comments on the religion of the Persians accord very well with Zoroastrian beliefs and practices as these would have been apprehended by an intelligent and inquiring observer, who did not seek to penetrate far into doctrine or priestly acts of worship, but was content to record what he saw himself and what his friends could tell him."

and fire and earth and winds and water; and with earnest prayer they offer sacrifice in a purified place, presenting the victim crowned; and when the Magus, who directs the sacrifice, has divided the meat the people go away with their shares, . . . ; but still, according to some writers, they place a small portion of the caul upon the fire.

But it is especially to fire and water that they offer sacrifice. To fire they offer sacrifice by adding dry wood without the bark and by placing fat on top of it; and then they pour oil upon it and light it below, not blowing with their breath, but fanning it; and those who blow the fire with their breath or put anything dead or filthy upon it are put to death.

Plutarch (second century A.D.), in his essay on Isis and Osiris (chapter 46), maintains the following:

For some believe that there are two gods who are rivals, as it were, in art, the one being the creator of good, the other of evil; others call the better of these a god and his rival a daemon, as, for example, Zoroaster the Magian, who lived, so they record, five thousand years before the Siege of Troy. He used to call the one Horomazes and the other Areimanius, and showed also that the former was especially akin, among objects of perception, to light, and the latter, on the contrary, to darkness and ignorance, while in between the two was Mithrēs; and this is why the Persians call Mithrēs the Mediator. He also taught that votive- and thank-offerings should be made to Horomazes, but gloomy offerings to Areimanius, and those intended to avert evil. For they pound a certain herb called *omōmi* in a mortar, invoking Hades and darkness, and then after mixing with it the blood of a slain wolf, they take it out to a sunless spot and throw it away. They believe that among plants too, some belong to the good god and others to the evil daemon, and that among animals some, such as dogs, birds and land hedgehogs, belong to the good god, whereas water-rats belong to the bad deity, and for this reason they regard as happy whoever kills a great number of them.[20]

Other Texts

Soviet scholars have published some of the three thousand Parthian ostraca found at Nisa in southern Turkmenistan. Dated from 100 to 29 B.C., these prosaic records of the delivery of wine document the oldest use of the Zoroastrian calendar. Armenian sources inform us about Zurvanism, the Zoroastrian heresy. Syriac sources preserve legends

20. J. G. Griffiths, *Plutarch's De Iside et Osiride* (Cardiff: University of Wales Press, 1970), pp. 191, 193. See D. C. Hood, *Plutarch and the Persians* (Ann Arbor: University Microfilms, 1981), pp. 124–31. In general, see E. Benveniste, *The Persian Religion According to the Chief Greek Texts* (Paris: Paul Geuthner, 1929).

about the magi. Arabic sources such as Tabari (d. A.D. 923) retain various traditions about Zoroaster.[21]

Archaeology

Until the 1960s we had no archaeological information on the Medes except for a few rock-cut tombs. Excavations by David Stronach begun in 1967 at Tepe Nush-i Jan, forty miles south of Hamadan, revealed a Median temple with a fire altar. Because the ash indicates that the fire consumed more than fat or special woods, this altar was not similar to that used by the Zoroastrians.[22]

Excavations have been conducted at Susa since the late nineteenth century, at Persepolis by the University of Chicago from 1931 to 1939, and at Pasargadae by Stronach from 1961 to 1963. Objects of religious significance uncovered include altars, tombs, reliefs, pestles, and mortars. Some scholars have interpreted the two similar towered structures, known as the Zendan-i Sulaiman and the Kaʿaba-i Zardusht, as fire temples.[23] (See chapters 9 and 10 on Pasargadae and Persepolis.)

The oldest Zoroastrian temple may be the one excavated at Susa, probably dated to the reign of Artaxerxes II.[24] Numerous religious structures, including fire temples from the Parthian and Sasanian eras, have been identified.[25] Mary Boyce has suggested that many of the fire temples were introduced by orthodox Zoroastrians in reaction to the image temples introduced by Artaxerxes II.[26]

An extraordinary Achaemenian temple was excavated from 1962 to 1965 by the Italian archaeologist Umberto Scerrato at Dahan-i Ghulman (ancient Zarin) in the province of Drangiana in eastern Iran near its borders with Afghanistan and Pakistan. He found a square building (53 by 54 meters or 174 by 177 feet) that was equipped with ovens and, in its

21. See J. R. Russell, *Zoroastrianism in Armenia* (Cambridge: Harvard University Press, 1987), R. J. H. Gottheil, "References to Zoroaster in Syriac and Arabic Literature," in *Classical Studies in Honour of H. Drisler* (New York: Macmillan, 1894), pp. 24–51.

22. Boyce, *History I*, p. 191.

23. See B. Goldman, "Persian Fire Temples or Tombs," *JNES* 24 (1965): 305–8. Boyce, *History II*, pp. 57–59, offers the unlikely suggestion that the Zendan was built by Cyrus as a mausoleum for members of his royal family.

24. Boyce, "Iconoclasm," p. 95. S. Wikander, *Feuerpriester in Kleinasien und Iran* (Lund: C. W. K. Gleerup, 1946), p. 68, suggests that the Susa fire temple was dedicated to Anahita.

25. K. Erdmann, *Das iranische Feuerheiligtum* (Leipzig: J. C. Hinrichs, 1941); K. Schippmann, *Die iranischen Feuerheiligtümer* (Berlin: W. de Gruyter, 1971); E. J. Keall, "Archaeology and the Fire Temple," in *Iranian Civilization and Culture*, ed. C. J. Adams (Montreal: McGill University Press, 1972), pp. 15–22; I. N. Khlopin, "Archäologische Materialen zur Enstehung des altiranischen Feuerkultes," *Klio* 57 (1975): 53–71; W. Kleiss, "Bemerkungen zu achaemenidischen Feueraltären," *AMI* n.F. 14 (1981): 61–64.

26. M. Boyce, "On the Zoroastrian Temple Cult of Fire," *JAOS* 95 (1975): 454–65.

second phase, with three central altars. There was an immense quantity of ash and crushed bones, providing evidence of animal sacrifices.[27] Scerrato believes the altars were dedicated to the triad of gods—Ahuramazda, Mithra, and Anahita—honored by Artaxerxes II. The excavator dates the building to the late sixth and early fifth centuries.[28] Stronach, however, prefers to date the structure to the first half of the fifth century B.C.[29]

Zoroastrian Sacred Texts

The Zoroastrian texts are rather disparate and, with one exception, relatively late. They are limited and difficult sources to utilize for a reconstruction of Persian religion. Richard Frye compares an Iranologist's task to a situation where a student of Judaism has only the Psalms, fragments of the Talmud, and later writings as sources for reconstructing the history of ancient Jewish religion.[30]

The Gathas

Our oldest and most important texts are the sixteen Gathas of Zoroaster himself now incorporated in the Yasna (chapters 28–34, 43–51), the main Zoroastrian liturgy. A seventeenth text (Y. 53), a marriage liturgy for Zoroaster's daughter, is sometimes associated with this group.[31] The Gathas are admittedly very difficult to translate and interpret.[32] According to William Malandra: "the Gāthās are perhaps the

27. Boyce, *History II*, p. 130, comments: "What, however, is wholly unZoroastrian is the mingling of animal bones in the embers of fire."

28. U. Scerrato, "L'edificio sacro di Dahan-i Ghulaman (Sistan)," in *La Persa e il mondo grecoromano* (Rome: Accademia Nazionale dei Lincei, 1965), pp. 457–70; idem, "Excavations at Dahan-i Ghulaman (Seistan-Iran), First Preliminary Report (1962–1963)," *EW* 16 (1966): 9–30; idem, "Religious Life at Dahan-e Ghulaman," in *South Asian Archaeology*, ed. M. Taddei (Naples: Istituto Universitario Orientale, 1979), 2: 709–35.

29. D. Stronach, "On the Evolution of the Early Iranian Fire Temple," in *Papers in Honour of Professor Mary Boyce*, eds. A. D. H. Bivar and J. R. Hinnells (Leiden: Brill, 1985), p. 610.

30. R. N. Frye, "Iran and Israel," in *Festschrift für Wilhelm Eilers* (Wiesbaden: O. Harrassowitz, 1967), p. 75.

31. W. Hinz, *Zarathustra* (Stuttgart: W. Kohlhammer, 1961), p. 19. Hinz observes that the 16 Gathas comprise altogether 859 lines. One of the few scholars who does not assign all the Gathas to Zarathushtra is V. Lesný, "Zarathuštra's Leben und Zeit im Lichte der Gāthāüberlieferung," *AO* 2 (1920): 95–107.

32. English translations include: L. H. Mills, *The Zend-Avesta*, Sacred Books of the East 31 (Oxford: Clarendon, 1887; reprint Delhi: Motilal Banarsidass, 1965); F. A. Bode and P. Nanavutty, *Songs of Zarathushtra* (London: George Allen and Unwin, 1952); J. Duchesne-Guillemin, *The Hymns of Zarathustra* (Boston: Beacon, 1963); S. Insler, *The Gāthās of Zarathustra* (Leiden: Brill, 1975). A superior German translation is H. Humbach, *Die Gathas des Zarathustra*, 2 vols. (Heidelberg: Carl Winter, 1959); see also H. Lommel, *Die Gathas des Zarathustra* (Basel: Schwabe, 1971).

most obscure and ambiguous compositions of all oriental religious literature. Almost every Gāthic passage is capable of multiple interpretations."[33] The date of the Gathas depends upon the date that is assigned to Zoroaster (see below).

How can Zarathushtra's many references expressing a concern and even reverence for the cow be interpreted? Are these to be taken literally as in the reverence for the cow in Hinduism?[34] Or, as George Cameron has argued, are they to be taken as metaphors for the righteous people who accepted the prophet's teaching in the sense that sheep in the Bible are a metaphor for the people of God?[35] Malandra regards the question as an open one.[36]

One other text—the *Yasna Haptanhaiti* or "Yasna of seven chapters" (chapters 35–41 of the Yasna)—is in the same ancient dialect as the Gathas. It originally may have been devoted to fire and water, but in its present form is a text devoted to the Bounteous Immortals. The text, which was written by a priest, reflects both Zoroaster's teachings and pre-Zoroastrian concepts.

The Younger Avesta

The main body of Zoroastrian scriptures is known as the Avesta (Middle Persian *Awastag* or "tradition"). These texts are known as the Younger Avesta since they were composed in an eastern Iranian dialect called Avestan (abbreviated Av.) a long time after Zoroaster. This collection of numerous works was never combined in a single book. Only those portions preserved in a liturgical context remain. Of the twenty-one *nasks* or volumes known from the Denkard, only one entire nask and portions of others are preserved. It is estimated that no more than one-fourth of the original Avesta has survived. No doubt much was destroyed with the Islamic conquest of Iran in A.D. 651.

From the Achaemenian era the various sources of the Avesta circulated orally for centuries. Ilya Gershevitch guesses that the composi-

33. W. W. Malandra, ed., *An Introduction to Ancient Iranian Religion* (Minneapolis: University of Minnesota Press, 1983), p. vi.

34. This was the view held by earlier scholars such as J. H. Moulton, H. Lommel, H. Nyberg, E. Herzfeld, H. Humbach, and J. Duchesne-Guillemin.

35. G. G. Cameron, "Zoroaster the Herdsman," *IIJ* 10 (1968): 261–81. The metaphorical interpretation of the "cow" in the Gathas is also adopted by Hinz, *Zarathustra*, p. 121; Insler, *Gāthās*, p. 141; J. P. Asmussen, "Die Verkundigung Zarathustras im Lichte der Religionsgeschichte," *Temenos* 6 (1970): 29–30; H.-P. Schmidt, *Zarathustra's Religion and His Pastoral Imagery* (Leiden: Universitaire Pers, 1975); idem, "Old and New Perspectives in the Study of the Gathas of Zarathustra," *IIJ* 21 (1979): 89, 107; G. L. Windfuhr, "*Vohu Manah:* A Key to the Zoroastrian Word-Formula," in *Michigan Oriental Studies in Honor of George G. Cameron*, ed. L. L. Orlin (Ann Arbor: University of Michigan Press, 1976), pp. 269–310.

36. Malandra, *Introduction*, p. 35.

tion of the Avesta began around 425 B.C.[37] When these texts were put into writing is unknown. Late Zoroastrian traditions in the Denkard blamed Alexander for the wanton destruction of the Avesta, which had supposedly been written in gold ink on twelve thousand hides and stored near Persepolis. But this is clearly a story without historical foundation.[38]

Some scholars have interpreted a remark of Mani's *Kephalaia* and references in the Denkard to Vologases I (A.D. 51–77) to support a Parthian date for a written Avesta.[39] But this remains highly speculative. There is evidence for a compilation into writing of oral traditions under Shapur I (A.D. 240–270). But the contemporary Zoroastrian high priest Kartir cited no Avestan text in his proclamations.[40]

It is, therefore, possible that the Avesta was not put into writing until as late as the reign of Khusrau I (531–579).[41] Boyce notes: "The tradition of a *written* Arsacid Avesta is now rejected by most."[42] She herself maintains: "It is possible that some part of the Avesta was written down in the late Parthian period, but the fixed canon was not established until the Sasanian era, apparently as late as the 6th century A.C."[43] It may have been in rivalry with Christians and Manichaeans, who had their own Scriptures, that the Zoroastrians felt compelled to have their own traditions in written form.[44] But evidently there were very few copies available, as Muslims did not classify Zoroastrians as *Ahl al-Kitab* or "people of the book." As late as the tenth century a priest was known to have memorized the entire Avesta by heart.[45]

The Avesta was written down and translated into a Middle Iranian dialect in a script known as Book Pahlavi ("Parthian"). This was a very

37. I. Gershevitch, "Zoroaster's Own Contribution," *JNES* 23 (1964): 14.

38. Contrary to the view of S. K. Eddy, *The King Is Dead* (Lincoln: University of Nebraska Press, 1961), p. 14. E. Herzfeld, *Archaeological History of Iran* (London: British Academy, 1935), pp. 52–53, made the unlikely suggestion that there was an initial attempt to fix the Avesta in writing as early as A.D. 50 under Vologases I.

39. Widengren, *Les Religions*, p. 226; G. Widengren, "The Problem of the Sassanid Avesta," in *Holy Book and Holy Tradition*, eds. F. F. Bruce and E. G. Rupp (Manchester: Manchester University Press, 1968), p. 40. Compare F. Altheim and R. Stiehl, *Geschichte Mittelasiens im Altertum* (Berlin: W. de Gruyter, 1970), pp. 100–101; J. Duchesne-Guillemin, *The Religion of Ancient Iran* (Bombay: Tata, 1973), p. 30.

40. Wikander, *Feuerpriester*, p. 134.

41. K. Barr, "Die Religion der alten Iraner," in *Handbuch der Religionsgeschichte*, eds. J. P. Asmussen and J. P. Laessøe (Göttingen: Vandenhoeck and Ruprecht, 1972), p. 302.

42. M. Boyce, "Middle Persian Literature," *Handbuch der Orientalistik* (Leiden: Brill, 1968), IV.1.2.1, p. 33. So also H. Nyberg, "Stand der Forschung zum Zoroastrismus," *AMI* n.F. 1 (1968): 41.

43. Boyce, *History I*, p. 20.

44. J. W. Boyd, "Zoroastrianism: Avestan Scripture and Rite," in *The Holy Book in Comparative Perspective*, eds. F. M. Denny and R. L. Taylor (Columbia: University of South Carolina Press, 1985), p. 110.

45. M. Molé, "Le problème des sectes zoroastriennes dans les sources pehlevis," *Oriens* 13/14 (1960–1961): 6. Molé prefers to regard the Avesta as the name of a living tradition rather than as a book. Boyd, "Zoroastrianism," also regards the Avesta as a collection of ritual texts.

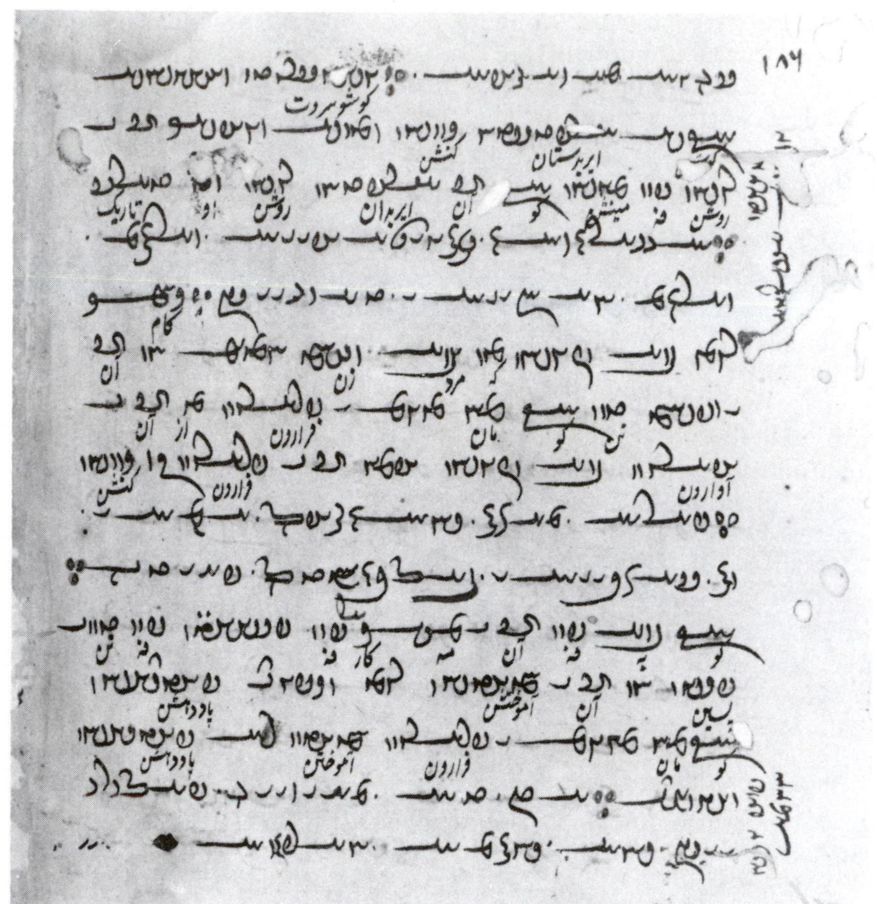

An Avestan manuscript with an interlinear Pahlavi translation. (Courtesy of the Bodleian Library, Oxford)

confusing script because the twenty-two letters of the Aramaic alphabet had been reduced to fourteen letters, resulting in many ambiguous readings, particularly of ligatures, places where two letters were joined. This was replaced by a special alphabet with forty-eight signs developed from the Pahlavi script of the late Sasanid era. By the Sasanid era Avestan was known only imperfectly as a learned language. Our oldest manuscript of the Avesta, which comes from India, is dated to 1323.[46] The following are the main components of the Avesta:

46. M. Schwartz, "The Religion of Achaemenian Iran," in *The Cambridge History of Iran II: The Median and Achaemenian Periods*, ed. I. Gershevitch (Cambridge: Cambridge University Press, 1985), p. 665.

Yasna [Y.] ("sacrifice")

The Yasna contains in seventy-two chapters the texts that priests recite in the central ritual of the pressing of the haoma plant.

Visparad [Vr.] ("all protective powers")

This is a collection of twenty-four chapters of invocations to protectors of living beings, which are recited at the end of the Yasna especially during the feasts for the various seasons.

Vendidad [Vd.]

(This name is a corruption of the Pahlavi *Videvdad* from Avestan *vidaevo data* "the law directed against demons.") This is the only one of the twenty-one nasks of the Sasanid Avesta that has been preserved. The Vendidad may have been compiled from older material during the Parthian period. According to Claas Bleeker, it was begun under the Arsacid Vologeses III (A.D. 148–191) and completed under the Sasanian Chosroes I (531–579).[47] The twenty-two chapters reveal how the Evil Spirit created sins, plagues, and death. Chapter 2 contains the myth of Yima, the good lord who sinned. Ceremonies and formulae deal with repentance and purification for sins and protection against the 99,999 diseases created by the Evil Spirit.

Yashts [Yt.] ("prayers")

Although later in composition than the Gathas, the Yashts preserve much older pre-Zoroastrian myths and legends.[48] Gershevitch dates their composition to about 430 to 420 B.C.[49] These are twenty-one ritual hymns in honor of the pre-Zoroastrian *yazatas,* beings who deserve reverence.[50] On the status of these divinities, Boyce comments:

> Since his [Ahuramazda's] creation included all beneficent lesser divinities, they, the *yazatas* of Zoroastrianism, cannot properly be called "gods," for this word suggests the independent divine beings of a pagan pantheon. . . . On the other hand the origin of most of the *yazatas* as pagan divinities, and their position still as beings worthy of worship in their own right, makes them more than the angels with which other monotheisms have bridged the gulf between man and the Deity.[51]

47. Bleeker, "Wer war Zarathustra," p. 31; Boyce, *History I,* p. 95.

48. H. Lommel, *Die Yašt's des Awesta* (Göttingen: Vandenhoeck and Ruprecht, 1927). The Yashts also contain post-Zoroaster materials such as a litany of praise to Zoroaster in Yasht 13.87–95.

49. I. Gershevitch, *The Avestan Hymn to Mithra* (Cambridge: Cambridge University Press, 1959), p. 22.

50. The term is absent from the Gathas but appears in the Yasna of the Seven Chapters.

51. Boyce, *History I,* p. 196. Modern Parsis compare the yazatas with Christian saints or angels.

Among the yazatas who are honored are Ahuramazda (Yt. 1), Anahita (Yt. 5), Khvar Khshaeta (Yt. 6), Mah (Yt. 7), Tishtrya (Yt. 8), Mithra (Yt. 10), Sraosha (Yt. 11), the Fravashis (Yt. 13), Verethraghna (Yt. 14), Vayu (Yt. 15), Ashi (Yt. 17), Khvarenah (Yt. 19), and Haoma (Yt. 20).

Ahuramazda is the supreme god of Zoroastrianism (see below). But in the Yashts he is depicted as venerating the other yazatas and asking for their help. Anahita is the goddess of water and fertility. The Avestan word *anahita* means "immaculate," and was the appellative of the goddess Ardvi.[52] She is depicted as a beautiful maiden, clothed in beaver skins and driving a chariot pulled by wind, rain, cloud, and sleet. Her cult was strongly influenced by the Babylonian goddess Ishtar. Like the latter she was identified with the planet Venus. She later became popular under her Greek name *Anaitis* in Anatolia. At Zela, cultic prostitution was practiced in her honor according to Strabo (12.3.37).[53] Fire temples were also maintained in conjunction with her cult.

Khvar Khshaeta is the sun, Mah the moon, and Tishtrya the star Sirius. Mithra is one of the most important Indo-Iranian gods.[54] He was to become the center of a mystery religion during the time of the Roman Empire (see chapter 14). Sraosha is obedience personified. He later served as the protector and guide for righteous souls after death.[55]

Fravashis are the protective spirits of the pious. They represent ancestor spirits, guardian spirits, and the spiritual elements of the human personality. Verethraghna is the god of victory. He manifested himself in various incarnations as a bull or a boar. He was later identified, for example, at Commagene, with Herakles.[56] Vayu is the wind-god. Ashi is the goddess of luck. She is the yazata invoked more often than any divinity by modern Parsis.[57] Khvarenah is the divine charisma or grace given to those favored by the gods. Haoma is the sacred plant (see below).[58]

52. H. Weller, *Anahita* (Stuttgart: W. Kohlhammer, 1938), p. 77; H. Lommel, "Anahita-Sarasvati," in *Asiatica*, eds. J. Schubert and U. Schneider (Leipzig: O. Harrassowitz, 1954), pp. 405–13.

53. J. Duchesne-Guillemin, "Zoroastrian Religion," p. 873; compare E. Yamauchi, "Cultic Prostitution," in *Orient and Occident*, ed. H. Hoffner (Kevelaer: Butzon and Bercker, 1973), pp. 213–22.

54. Gershevitch, *Avestan Hymn to Mithra.*

55. G. Kreyenbroek, *Sraoša in the Zoroastrian Tradition* (Leiden: Brill, 1985).

56. J. R. Hinnells, *Persian Mythology* (London: Hamlyn, 1973), pp. 33–36.

57. Boyce, *History I*, p. 225.

58. Most scholars, for example, Zaehner, *Dawn*, pp. 80–81, have viewed these yazatas as pagan gods who were reinstated after Zoroaster passed from the scene. Most of these yazatas, although important in the Younger Avesta, became less significant in the later Pahlavi texts.

Khorda Avesta ("little Avesta")

This collection of hymns was compiled by Aderpad Marespand during the reign of Shapur II (309–379). It serves as a prayer book for daily use.

The Pahlavi Texts

In the post-Islamic era Zoroastrian scholars translated the Avesta and attached to it a commentary known as the Zand ("elucidation") in the Middle Persian dialect. These scholars misunderstood much of the Avesta. In addition to translations and commentaries on the Avesta, we have other Pahlavi texts dealing with such important themes as cosmology and eschatology, which were not composed until the ninth to tenth centuries A.D.[59] These texts mainly reflect developments of the Sasanian era.[60]

How much they preserve earlier materials is a matter of debate. Boyce and others believe that much may be pre-Sasanian.[61] Frye, however, warns against the facile retrojection of materials in these late texts back into antiquity.[62] Because of their late date Malandra also cautions: "For this reason, they must be used with extreme care as evidence for the earlier forms of the religion."[63]

Of the fifty-five Pahlavi texts, the most important are:

Bundahishn [Bd.] ("creation")

This important treatise, which was composed in the ninth century, relates how Ohrmazd (Pahl. for Av. Ahuramazda) and Ahriman (Pahl. for Av. Angra Mainyu) came into being. It narrates their nine-thousand-year-long conflict. The Bundahishn represents a priestly compilation on various themes (including apocalyptic ones). It recounts the legendary history of the so-called Kayanian kings.[64] There exist both a major Iranian and an Indian version of the Bundahishn.

59. See H. W. Bailey, *Zoroastrian Problems in the Ninth-Century Books* (Oxford: Clarendon, 1943).

60. Hartman, *Parsism*, p. 7.

61. Boyce, *History I*, pp. xii–xiii; Widengren, "Problem," p. 44.

62. R. N. Frye, "Methodology in Iranian History," in *Neue Methodologie in der Iranistik*, ed. R. N. Frye (Wiesbaden: O. Harrassowitz, 1974), p. 59.

63. Malandra, *Introduction*, p. vi; see also G. Gnoli, "Considerazioni sulla religione degli Achemenidi alla luce di una recente teoria," *SMSR* 35 (1964): 245.

64. G. Messina, "Mito, leggenda e storia nella tradizione iranica," *Or* 4 (1935): 269–90.

Denkard [Dk.] ("acts of religion")

This is a huge encyclopedia of 169,000 words, compiled in the ninth century.[65] The first two of its original nine books have been lost. Book 6 contains an exposition of ethical wisdom.[66] The seventh book contains a legendary biography of Zoroaster, which was paraphrased in the later *Zardush Nameh.* The eighth book contains an important summary of the original twenty-one nasks of the Avesta.

Arda Wiraz Namag [A.W.]

This recounts the vision of Arda Wiraz who visited heaven and hell while he was in a dream-trance for seven days and nights. It was composed in the post-Islamic era and redacted during the ninth to tenth centuries. This is the most popular of all Zoroastrian works.

The Counsel of Zartusht

This a short treatise that sums up what every young Parsi must know before he or she is invested with the sacred cord.[67]

Pre-Zoroastrian Religion

Although the Medes and Persians are not mentioned until Assyrian texts of the ninth century B.C. and although there are no Persian texts prior to the sixth century B.C., we can reconstruct the earliest Iranian religion through an analysis of the parallel Vedic texts from India and from pre-Zoroastrian elements preserved especially in the Yashts.

Early Iranian religion was very similar to Indo-Aryan religion. Both were polytheistic. In the earliest parts of the Rig Veda we have deities known as *asuras* and *devas.* In Hinduism the devas continued to be worshiped as heavenly creatures whereas the asuras were demoted to the status of demons. The reverse development took place in Iranian religion. The *ahuras* were the deities; the *daēvas* became the demons.[68]

65. J.-P. de Menasce, *Une encyclopédie mazdéene: Le Dênkart* (Paris: Presses Universitaires de France, 1958).

66. S. Shaked, trans., *The Wisdom of the Sasanian Sages (Dēnkard VI) by Aturpāt-i Emētān* (Boulder: Westview, 1979).

67. R. C. Zaehner, *The Teachings of the Magi* (New York: Oxford University Press, 1976), contains a brief selection of the Pahlavi texts.

68. Compare Arabic *dīv;* Greek *theos;* Latin *deus.* Boyce, *History I,* p. 23; J. P. Asmussen, "A Zoroastrian 'De-Demonization' in Judeo-Persian," in *Irano-Judaica,* ed. S. Shaked (Jerusalem: Ben-Zvi Institute, 1982), pp. 112–21; E. Yamauchi, *Mandaic Incantation Texts* (New Haven: American Oriental Society, 1967), pp. 30–31.

The earliest written attestation of the Indo-Aryan gods is found in a treaty between the Hittite king Suppiluliuma and Mattiwaza of Mitanni (fourteenth century B.C.). This text mentions the important Vedic gods Indra and Nasatya, who were demoted to the demons Indra and Naghathya in the Vendidad. Mitra (Avestan Mithra), who also appears in this text, was worshiped by both the Iranians and Indians. In both communities the god was associated with the sun.[69]

While Indra is mentioned in Avestan texts, the other great Vedic god, Varuna, is not mentioned by name. The Old Persian *baga* or "god" (Vedic *bhaga*) appears in many proper names such as Bagadata, "given by Baga" (Greek *Megabates*). Baga has been identified by many scholars as Mithra. But since a Sogdian text distinguishes between Baga and Mithra, Boyce has suggested that Baga must be identified with the otherwise missing Varuna.[70]

Some scholars, for example Jacques Duchesne-Guillemin, also believe that early Avestan society reflected the tripartite division into classes of priests, warriors, and commoners known from the Indo-Aryans and posited for Indo-Europeans in general by Georges Dumézil.[71]

Zoroaster

The Quest for the Historical Zoroaster

The English spelling, *Zoroaster,* is derived from the Greek spelling *Zōroastēr,* which incorporates the word *astēr* or "star," probably because of the later identification of the prophet as the source of astrological knowledge. His Avestan name, *Zarathushtra,* may have meant "he who can manage camels."[72] Another possible etymology is "having yellow camels"[73] or "having old camels."[74] The Old Persian form of his

69. G. Dumézil, "The Vedic Mitra," *JMS* 1 (1976): 26–35.

70. M. Boyce, "Varuna the Baga," in *Monumentum Georg Morgenstierne,* ed. J. Duchesne-Guillemin (Leiden: Brill, 1981), 1: 59–73. For a critique of her attempted reconstruction of * *Vouruna,* see P. Gignoux, "Des structures imaginaires du panthéon pré-zoroastrien à l'existence de Baga," in *Iranica,* by G. Gnoli and A. V. Rosi (Naples: Istituto Universitario Orientale, 1979), pp. 366–67. For a detailed attempt to reconstruct a full pantheon of gods from Vedic materials, see H. W. Bailey, "The Second Stratum of the Indo-Iranian Gods," in *Mithraic Studies,* ed. J. Hinnells (Manchester: Manchester University Press, 1975), 1: 1–20.

71. See J. Duchesne-Guillemin, *The Western Response to Zoroaster* (Oxford: Clarendon, 1958), pp. 33–34. For a critique, see R. N. Frye, "Georges Dumézil and the Translators of the Avesta," *Numen* 7 (1960): 161–71.

72. Boyce, *History I,* p. 182; M. Schwartz, "The Old Eastern Iranian World View According to the Avesta," in Gershevitch, *CHI* I, p. 660.

73. W. Eilers, "The Name of Cyrus," *Acta Iranica* 3 (1974): 3; F. M. Kotwal and J. W. Boyd, *A Guide to Zoroastrian Religion* (Chico: Scholars, 1982), p. 11.

74. M. Mayrhofer, "Zarathustra und kein Ende?" *AAH* 25 (1977): 89.

name would have been **Zaraushtra,* and the Median form **Zaratushtra,* which produced the Avestan *Zarathushtra* and the Pahlavi *Zardusht.*

The difficult nature of the sources about Zoroaster has permitted the proliferation of wildly differing interpretations. The earliest synthesis, Thomas Hyde's *De vetere religione Persarum* (1700), viewed Zoroaster as one who had taught Pythagoras and who had prophesied about Christ.[75] In the eighteenth century Voltaire sought to use Zoroaster to prove truth could be found outside of Christianity. In the late nineteenth century Friedrich Nietzsche also used Zoroaster in his celebrated work, *Also sprach Zarathustra,* as a mouthpiece in his attempt to emancipate humanity from Christianity.[76] James Darmesteter's work, *Ormazd et Ahriman* (1877), viewed Zoroaster as a personification of thunder. He held that the Gathas were forgeries composed under the influence of Philo.

In the twentieth century Henrik Nyberg, a Swedish scholar, cast Zoroaster as a kind of hemp-intoxicated shaman; in his view it is no wonder that the Gathas are unintelligible gibberish![77] A later Swedish scholar, Geo Widengren, has sought to retain some elements of the ecstatic nature of Nyberg's interpretation.[78]

At the other extreme, the archaeologist Ernst Herzfeld developed a detailed reconstruction of Zoroaster's life as set at the Achaemenid court. According to Herzfeld, Zoroaster was the grandson of the last Median king and a brother-in-law of both Cambyses and Darius. The Vishtaspa, whom Zoroaster converted, was Hystaspes, the father of Darius. He then supposed that Zoroaster had been convicted of a crime by Gaumata. When Gaumata usurped the throne in 522, Zoroaster incited Darius to kill the imposter.[79] In a brief but incisive critique, Walter Henning criticized both Nyberg and Herzfeld and offered a balanced view of Zoroaster as a prophet.[80]

Since the Gathas are the only authentic source, there is little trustworthy data on the life of Zoroaster.[81] Most of the information from the

75. Duchesne-Guillemin, *Western Response,* p. 10.

76. "Thus Spake Zoroaster," inspired Richard Strauss's work of the same name, which was used as the theme song for the movie, "2001 a Space Odyssey."

77. H. S. Nyberg, *Die Religionen des alten Iran* (Leipzig: J. C. Hinrichs, 1938; Osnabrück: O. Zeller, 1966 reprint).

78. Widengren, *Les religions,* pp. 91–92; G. Widengren, "Révélation et prédication dans les Gāthās," in *Iranica,* by Gnoli and Rossi, pp. 352, 362.

79. E. E. Herzfeld, *Zoroaster and His World,* 2 vols. (Princeton: Princeton University Press, 1947), 1: 205–10.

80. W. B. Henning, *Zoroaster, Politician or Witch Doctor?* (London: Oxford University Press, 1951).

81. G. Gnoli, "Problems and Prospects of the Studies of Persian Religion," in *Problems and Methods of the History of Religion,* eds. U. Bianchi, C. J. Bleeker, and A. Bausani (Leiden: Brill, 1972), p. 67.

Avesta, such as in the Yashts (13.88–95) and the even later Pahlavi sources (such as the Denkard and the Zatspram), are legendary.[82] The *Zardusht Name*, a Persian text written in A.D. 1278, is the main source of popular Parsi tradition about Zoroaster. According to William Darrow's analysis: "In fact, the tradition itself came to conceive Zoroaster on the prophetic model in the face of the overwhelming authority of the Islamic version of that model in the Muslim period."[83]

Zoroaster's Date

Greek sources place Zoroaster thousands of years in the past. Diogenes Laertius (A.D. 230) reported that Xanthus of Lydia (circa 450 B.C.) placed Zoroaster six thousand years before the invasion of Xerxes in 480 B.C.[84] Pliny the Elder (d. A.D. 79) said that Eudoxus (fourth century B.C.) dated Zoroaster six thousand years before the death of Plato. Hermodoros, however, set Zoroaster five thousand years before the Trojan War.[85] Some modern Parsis have been influenced by these statements and believe that Zoroaster lived about 6000 B.C.[86]

Many scholars (for example, Franz Altheim, Jes Asmussen, A. D. H. Bivar, Carsten Colpe, Muhammed Dandamayev, Jacques Duchesne-Guillemin, Ilya Gershevitch, Walter Henning, Ernst Herzfeld, Walther Hinz, Abraham Jackson, Manfred Mayrhofer, William Tisdall, Robert Zaehner) have been led to adopt a "late" date for Zoroaster (seventh to sixth centuries B.C.) or at the time of the early Achaemenids on the basis of chronological data preserved in Pahlavi and Arabic sources.

The Bundahishn (36.8) gives a list of kings, whose reigns total 258 years, in the period between Zoroaster and Alexander. Arabic traditions (Mas'udi and al-Biruni) also place Zoroaster's appearance 258 years before Alexander. The precise date of Zoroaster depends on what is meant by "before Alexander" and "the appearance of Zoroaster." The era of Alexander may mean his invasion in 330 B.C. or the Seleucid era (312 B.C.); the appearance of Zoroaster may mean either his birth or

82. J. H. Moulton, *The Treasure of the Magi* (London: Oxford University Press, 1917), pp. 115–16, cites M. Dhalla's remark: "In the Later Avesta he [Zoroaster] is surrounded by an aureole, and becomes superhuman; but in the Pahlavi works his personality is enshrouded by miracles, and he is transformed into a myth." See M. Molé, *La légende de Zoroaster selon les textes pehlevi* (Paris, 1964); J. P. de Menasce, "Zoroastrian Pahlavi Writings," in Yarshater, *CHI* III.2, pp. 1172–73.

83. W. R. Darrow, "Zoroaster Amalgamated: Notes on Iranian Prophetology," *HR* 27 (1987): 111; see his 1981 Harvard Ph.D. diss., "The Zoroaster Legend: Its Historical and Religious Significance."

84. Some Greek manuscripts have the reading 600, which would yield a date of 1080 B.C.

85. K. Rudolph, "Zarathuštra—Priester und Prophet," *Numen* 8 (1961): 84.

86. Hartman, *Parsism*, p. 15. Many scholars believe that the Greek sources reflect the Zoroastrian millennial cycle of history and eschatology.

his encounter with Ahuramazda. By assuming the traditional age of Zoroaster at his death, seventy-seven, one can place his lifetime in the seventh and sixth centuries.[87]

But the figure 258 does not appear to be trustworthy, because it is based on the reigns of wholly fictional kings.[88] Earlier scholars placed Zoroaster early in the first millennium B.C.: Christian Bartholomae (at least 900), Edward Meyer (at latest around 1000), Otto von Wesendonk (tenth–ninth centuries B.C.), Hans Schaeder (not later than 1000), and George Gray (1000).[89] Recent scholars who have argued for similar dates include Gernot Windfuhr (eleventh–ninth centuries),[90] Gherardo Gnoli, who favors a period about 1000,[91] and Kurt Rudolph, who prefers the ninth to eighth centuries.[92] Shahpur Shahbazi cites the Arabic writer Al-Biruni to arrive at a date of 1080.[93]

The earliest possible dates have been advocated by Boyce in her many publications. These suggestions fluctuate between 1700 and 1000 B.C. In a work published in 1975 she concluded: "in the absence of any sound external evidence, therefore, it seems natural to conclude that the prophet lived sometime between, say, 1400 and 1000 B.C., at a time when his people were perhaps still dwelling in north Central Asia, before moving south in their turn to fix their abode in Khwarezm."[94] In 1977 she wrote: "one has to remember that Zoroaster lived a very long time ago, possibly about 1500 B.C. or even earlier."[95] In another publication issued in 1979, she dated Zoroaster between 1700 and 1500 B.C.[96] In 1982 she placed him before 1200 B.C.[97] Most recently she has writ-

87. Some suggested possibilities are 630–553, 628–551, 618–541, 600–523, 599–522, and 570–493. See F. Altheim, *Zarathustra und Alexander* (Frankfurt am Main: Fischer Bücherei, 1960), p. 18; F. Altheim and R. Stiehl, *Geschichte Mittelasiens im Altertum* (Berlin: W. de Gruyter, 1970), pp. 15–17; C. Colpe, "Zarathustra und der frühe Zoroastrismus," in *Handbuch der Religionsgeschichte,* eds. J. P. Asmussen and J. Laessøe (Göttingen: Vandenhoeck and Ruprecht, 1972), 2: 320; M. Dandamayev, "La politique religieuse des Achéménides," *Acta Iranica* 4 (1975): 217; Henning, *Zoroaster,* p. 41; Malandra, *Introduction,* p. 17; A. D. Nock, "The Problem of Zoroaster," *AJA* 53 (1949): 272–85; C. F. Whitley, "The Date and Teaching of Zarathustra," *Numen* 4 (1957): 215–27; Zaehner, *Dawn,* p. 33.

88. J. Kellens, "L'Avesta comme source historique: La liste des Kayanides," *AAH* 24 (1976): 37–49; A. S. Shahbazi, "The 'Traditional Date of Zoroaster' Explained," *BSOAS* 40 (1977): 25–35.

89. E. Herzfeld, "The Iranian Religion at the Time of Darius and Xerxes," *Religions* 15 (1936): 20; G. B. Gray, "Religion," in *The Cambridge Ancient History,* eds. J. B. Bury, S. A. Cook, and F. E. Adcock (Cambridge: Cambridge University Press, 1964), 4: 207.

90. G. Windfuhr, "The Word in Zoroastrianism," *Journal of Indo-European Studies* 12 (1984): 133.

91. G. Gnoli, *Zoroaster's Time and Homeland* (Naples: Istituto Universitario Orientale, 1980).

92. Rudolph, "Zarathuštra," p. 88; O. Klíma, "The Date of Zoroaster," *AO* 27 (1959): 556–64, also places Zoroaster in the eighth century B.C.

93. Shahbazi, "Traditional Date," p. 34.

94. Boyce, *History I,* p. 190.

95. Boyce, *Persian Stronghold,* p. 16.

96. Boyce, *Zoroastrians,* p. 2.

97. Boyce, *History II,* p. 3.

ten: "The most likely date would therefore seem to be between 1400 and 1200 B.C."[98]

Boyce's arguments are based on the linguistic affinities of the Gathas with the Rig Veda, and on the cultural milieu reflected in the Gathas. For example, while cattle are very prominent, there are no similes drawn from agriculture in the Gathas.[99]

But dialects may develop at different rates. Asmussen comments: "The close relationship and resemblances between the Avestan and Vedic languages surely need not imply chronological concurrence—witness for example Icelandic/Danish vis à vis Old Norse."[100] Frye cautions: "Boyce's 'about 1500 B.C., or even earlier,' places perhaps too much weight on the hoary antiquity of both the Gathic dialect and on archaic rites and the contents of the hymns."[101]

Zoroaster's Homeland

The evidence of the Avestan dialect of the Gathas places the prophet in the area of northeastern Iran or its environs. The three areas that have been suggested are: Chorasmia or Margiana in the Soviet Union; Areia in eastern Iran; and Bactria in Afghanistan. Chorasmia (OP Khuvarazmish; Pahl. Khwarazm) is the area bordering the Oxus River, which flows into the Aral Sea, today in Uzbek and Turkmen S.S.R. Margiana (OP Margush; Pahl. Marv) is further south. Areia (OP Haraiva; Pahl. Harev) is further south in eastern Iran.[102]

The suggestion that Zoroaster was active in Bactria (OP Bakhtrish) is based on late references to the prophet's activities in the city of Balkh (Bactra) in Bactria, which is the area east of northeastern Iran.[103] This suggestion has been disproved by recently discovered inscriptions from Bactria, which indicate that the Avestan language was quite different from Bactrian.[104]

The late Arabic traditions place the prophet in Azerbaijan in northwestern Iran. Al-Biruni (A.D. 973–1048) reported: "Zarathustra went

98. M. Boyce, "On the Antiquity of Zoroastrian Apocalyptic," *BSOAS* 47 (1984): 75. See also M. Boyce, *Textual Sources for the Study of Zoroastrianism* (Manchester: Manchester University Press, 1984), pp. 11, 22.

99. Boyce, *History I*, p. 14. See also C. Rempis, "Die Zeit Zarathuštras," *WO* 6 (1971): 238.

100. J. P. Asmussen's review of Boyce, *History I* in *JMS* 2 (1978): 232.

101. R. N. Frye, *The History of Ancient Iran* (Munich: C. H. Beck'sche, 1984), p. 58.

102. Ibid., p. 57; Gnoli, "Problems," p. 87; Rudolph, "Zarathuštra," p. 88; I. M. Diakonoff, "Media," in *CHI* II, pp. 131–32. The suggestion that Zoroaster came from a region south of Haraiva in Seistan (OP Zranka, Pahl. Sagistan) is based on the late tradition that Zoroaster's seed was preserved in Lake Helmand on the border between Iran and Afghanistan.

103. See E. Yamauchi, "Bactria," in *The New International Dictionary of Biblical Archaeology*, eds. E. M. Blaiklock and R. K. Harrison (Grand Rapids: Zondervan, 1983), pp. 87–90.

104. Frye, *History of Ancient Iran*, p. 61; Diakonoff, "Media," p. 130.

forth from Adharbaijan and preached Magism in Balkh." Some earlier scholars (such as Karl Geldner, Bartholomae, Jackson, and Herzfeld) took this tradition as trustworthy. The northwest location can be explained as Zoroaster's later appropriation by the magi whose home was in that area.[105] Other traditions placed Zoroaster's birthplace in Ragha. If this were the same as the later city, Ray, this would place Zoroaster in the vicinity of Tehran.[106] But this is a dubious assumption.

Zoroaster's Family

Zoroaster was born into the Spitama clan (Y. 29.8; 46.13). Avestan tradition gives us the name of his father—Pourushaspa, "with grey horses" (Yt. 5.18; Vd. 19)—and the name of his mother—Dughdhova, "who milked cows."

The legendary account of the Denkard describes Zoroaster as the only infant to laugh at the moment of his birth. His mother conceived him by drinking the sacred haoma. Demons plotted to kill him by having him placed in fire, laid in the path of stampeding cattle, and left in the den of a she wolf; he was miraculously saved each time.[107]

According to various traditions Zoroaster was married three times and had three sons and three daughters. His first wife bore him a son and three daughters, including Pouruchista (Y. 53.3), who was married to Jamaspa (Dk. 9.45). His second wife bore him two sons. His third wife, named Hvovi (Yt. 13), had no children.[108]

Zoroaster's Ministry

According to the Gathas, Zoroaster came from a background of cattle herders, menaced by nomads who stole and slaughtered cattle. Zoroaster himself speaks of his own weakness and lack of cattle and men (Y. 46.2). Even the Soul of the Cow complains about Zoroaster's weakness (Y. 29.9). For his reward he asked for "ten mares with a stallion and a camel" (Y. 44.18, translated by Duchesne-Guillemin).

Zoroaster identified himself as a *zaotar* (Vedic *hotar*) or priest (33.6) and as a *manthran* or one who produced sacred utterances (Y. 51.8).[109] As he began to preach his new message of the worship of Ahuramazda,

105. Boyce, *Zoroastrians*, p. 93.

106. Kotwal and Boyd, *Guide*, p. 13; Zaehner, *Dawn*, p. 33.

107. See Molé, *La légende de Zoroaster*, pp. 23ff. These tales are as of little value as the stories about Jesus found in the apocryphal infancy gospels. See E. Yamauchi, "Apocryphal Gospels," in *The International Standard Bible Encyclopedia*, ed. G. W. Bromiley, rev. ed. (Grand Rapids: Eerdmans, 1979) 1: 181–88.

108. Boyce, *History I*, p. 188.

109. M. Boyce, "Zoroaster the Priest," *BSOAS* 33 (1970): 22–38.

A young Parsi woman in India placing a garland on the portrait of Zoroaster. (Courtesy of Paul Popper, Ltd.)

he faced opposition from the secular and priestly nobles. Zoroaster taught his followers to be like himself, an enemy to the wicked (Y. 43.8). He recalls one humiliating winter evening when he and his beasts were left out in the cold (Y. 51.12). At one point he felt he had to flee (Y. 46.1).

According to the account of his life in the Denkard, Zoroaster at the age of thirty received the first of eight visions of Ahuramazda and the Immortals (see below). For ten years he had no converts except his cousin. He then converted his wife's uncle. Two years later, when he was forty-two, he gained his most notable convert, the ruler Vishtaspa and his queen Hutaosa.

Zoroaster's Teachings

Zoroaster preached the worship of Ahuramazda, "the wise lord." Whether this was a new or old god is a matter of dispute.[110] Whether Zoroaster also preached a monotheism, a henotheism—that is, the exaltation of one god over other gods—or a dualism is also disputed (see

110. See E. Herzfeld, "Die Religion der Achaemeniden," *RHR* 113 (1936): 22; Rudolph, "Zarathuštra," p. 102, remarks that the preexistence of Ahuramazda has been often assumed but not proven.

below). It is certain that he preached an ethical dualism, teaching that each man must choose between righteousness and the Lie.[111]

In numerous passages (Y. 32.12 and 14, Y. 44.20, Y. 48.10, Y. 51.14) Zoroaster protested the violent, orgiastic, and bloody sacrifices of the cattle by the daeva worshipers. In Yasna 29 the Soul of the Cow lamented her treatment. Zoroaster condemned the primeval Yima, possibly because he had given men flesh to eat (Y. 32.8).

In the past scholars interpreted these passages to mean that Zoroaster had proscribed bloody animal sacrifices.[112] But recently other scholars have concluded that Zoroaster was not opposed to animal sacrifice as such, but sought a more humane method of killing the creatures, perhaps by stunning them first.[113] Boyce observes:

> The former, almost universally held conviction among scholars that Zoroaster was passionately opposed to animal sacrifice arose partly, it seems from a preconception (that such sacrifices could not form part of a lofty ethical faith), partly from a wilful assumption that the blood offering was never made by his followers.[114]

A similar controversy has arisen over Zoroaster's attitude toward the sacred haoma plant, which later became the focus of the central yasna ceremony of Zoroastrianism. The haoma plant is not explicitly mentioned in the Gathas, but there are two possible allusions to it. In a difficult passage Zoroaster calls out to his god: "when will you smite the *mūthra* of this intoxicant?" (Y. 48.10). The word *mūthra* means either filth or urine. The other possible reference to it is Yasna 32.14, where an epithet of haoma, *duraoša* ("averting death"), is used.

The traditional interpretation of the first passage is that this is a condemnation of the intoxicating haoma rite by Zoroaster.[115] But in view of haoma's positive epithet, "averting death," and the fact that it has been a central rite in later Zoroastrianism, some scholars argue that Zoroaster may not have condemned the haoma rite itself but certain abuses of it.[116] Boyce represents this point of view: "Zoroaster's supposed denunciation of this cult, and also of animal sacrifice, has

111. Ibid., pp. 134–35. There was also a similar contrast between Asha and Drug in the Vedic texts. See Gnoli, "Problems," p. 81.

112. Zaehner, *Teachings of the Magi*, pp. 15, 17.

113. Colpe, "Zarathustra," p. 333; Malandra, *Introduction*, p. 21.

114. Boyce, *History I*, p. 214; see also Boyce, *Zoroastrians*, p. 31.

115. See Cameron, "Zoroaster the Herdsman," p. 279; Widengren, *Les religions*, p. 85; H. Smith, "Wasson's *Soma*," *JAAR* 40 (1972): 497; G. Gnoli, "Zoroastrianism," in *Encyclopedia of Religion*, ed. M. Eliade (New York: Macmillan, 1986), 15: 581.

116. Gnoli, "Problems," p. 74; see also G. Cameron, *Persepolis Treasury Tablets* (Chicago: University of Chicago Press, 1948), p. 8, who concedes this possibility.

been deduced partly from certain obscure passages of the Gāthas, which may well, however, represent an attack by the prophet on abuses of cult, linked with daēva-worship, rather than on the observances themselves."[117]

Zoroaster's Death

According to the Arabic writer Al-Biruni (A.D. 973–1048) Zoroaster was killed at the age of seventy-seven by invading Turanians (White Huns). According to Firdausi, Zoroaster was killed while praying in the fire temple at Balkh.[118] His work, *The Shah Namah* or "the epic of the kings" (circa A.D. 1000), describes the event as follows:

> And all before the Fire the Turkmans slew
> And swept that cult away. The Fire, that erst
> Zardusht had litten, of their blood did die;
> Who slew that priest himself I know not.[119]

Another tradition identifies Zoroaster's murderer as a hostile priest of the ancient religion.[120]

The Achaemenids and Zoroastrianism

Were the Achaemenids Zoroastrians or Not?

The question of whether the Achaemenids were Zoroastrians is a hotly debated issue.[121] Information on the religious orientation of the earliest Achaemenids, Cyrus and Cambyses, is incomplete. The inscriptions of Darius and Xerxes exalt Ahuramazda, the god of Zoroaster, and also stress the conflict between Truth and the Lie.[122]

At the same time there are some omissions and discrepancies between the Achaemenid inscriptions and our other sources: Herodotus

117. Boyce, "On Mithra's Part," p. 13; see also Boyce, *History I*, pp. 216–17.

118. Bode and Nanavutty, *Songs of Zarathustra*, p. 19. See Boyce, *History I*, p. 191.

119. Cited by J. Finegan, *The Archeology of World Religions I: The Background of Primitivism, Zoroastrianism, Hinduism, Jainism* (Princeton: Princeton University Press, 1952), p. 88.

120. Hinnells, *Zoroastrianism*, p. 10. Zoroaster's age of seventy-seven is also preserved in the Denkard and Zatspram. The commander of the invading army is called Arjasp, and the killer Bradrokresh. See Darrow, "Legend of Zoroaster," pp. 419–20.

121. See S. A. Nigosian, "The Religions in Achaemenid Persia," *Studies in Religion* 4 (1974–1975): 378–86; J. Duchesne-Guillemin, "Religion et politique de Cyrus à Xerxès," *Persica* 3 (1967–1968): 1–9; idem, "La religion des Achéménides," in *Beiträge zur Achämenidengeschichte*, ed. G. Walser (Wiesbaden: F. Steiner, 1972), pp. 59–82.

122. Zaehner, *Dawn*, pp. 156–61.

does not mention Zoroaster in connection with the Achaemenids; neither Zoroaster nor Angra Mainyu are found in the inscriptions; with the exception of *Arta* ("Truth") none of the key concepts of the Gathas is found in them; there are no references to Zoroaster's Bounteous Immortals.[123]

The vocabulary in the Achaemenid texts and the Zoroastrian sources differs. For "gods" the former uses the word *baga* rather than *yazata;* the Old Persian word for priest, *magu,* appears but once in the Avesta; the Gathic word for priest is *zaotar.* Even the same words are used in different senses: in Old Persian *fraša* means "excellent," whereas in the Avesta it is used as a technical term for the final restoration; Old Persian *xsaça* means a territorial kingdom, Avestan *xšathra* means "power."[124] With three exceptions the personal names found in the Achaemenid texts are of a non-Zoroastrian type.[125] The Zoroastrian texts do not seem to recall the Achaemenids except in a most garbled fashion. The Achaemenids buried their kings instead of exposing them in contrast with the ancient magi and the modern Parsis.[126]

Scholars Who Deny the Zoroastrianism of the Achaemenids

There are almost as many scholars who question as scholars who affirm the Zoroastrianism of the Achaemenids. Among the former are Emile Benveniste, Bleeker, Arthur Christensen, Colpe, Dandamayev, Duchesne-Guillemin, Ghirshman, Gnoli, Sven Hartman, Jackson, Malandra, Marian Molé, Nyberg, Justin Prášek, V. Strouve, Widengren, and Ehsan Yarshater.

Benveniste, for example, declares: "All the positive elements which seemed to supply evidence for a comparison between the Achemenid religion and that of Zoroaster, show themselves, one by one, to be different and irreconcilable."[127] Bleeker concludes that the Achaemenian inscriptions betray no clear Zoroastrian character.[128] Duchesne-

123. Widengren, *Les religions,* pp. 166ff.; Duchesne-Guillemin, *Western Response,* pp. 53ff.

124. Gnoli, "Considerazioni," p. 246; G. Gnoli, "Politique religieuse et conception de la royauté sous les Achéménides," in *Commémoration Cyrus* (Tehran-Liège: Bibliothèque Pahlavi, 1974), 2: 177. See also J. Kellens, "Trois réflexions sur la religion des Achéménides," *Studien zur Indologie und Iranistik* 2 (1976): 115–17.

125. E. Benveniste, *Titres et noms propres en Iranien ancien* (Paris: C. Klincksieck, 1966), pp. 97–98.

126. R. Ghirshman, *The Art of Ancient Iran* (New York: Golden, 1964), p. 230: "The Achaemenids were not Zoroastrians, for the monarchs were buried, from the time of Darius in the cliffs of Naqsh-i-Rustam."

127. Benveniste, *Persian Religion,* p. 43.

128. Bleeker, "Wer war Zarathustra?" p. 34. Compare Gnoli, "Problems," p. 79.

Guillemin comments: "Nevertheless, it would seem easier to think that the Achemenids had never heard of Zoroaster and his reform."[129]

Molé holds that in spite of certain analogies, the perspective of the Achaemenid and Gathic systems was quite different. The former centered around the concept of royalty, and the latter around the concept of fertility.[130] Strouve believes the Avesta does not mention the Achaemenids because they were not considered true Zoroastrians.[131] He concludes:

> To sum up, it can definitely be asserted that the absence of Zarathustra's name in the inscriptions of Darius and Xerxes, and also in the works of Herodotus, Xenophon and Strabo, is not accidental: the religious system of the first Achaemenids was devoid of Zoroaster, the prophet of Ahuramazda; he was supplanted by the king.[132]

Strouve explains away the common points such as the worship of Ahuramazda and the prohibition of the daeva cult as derived from their same source, "the religion of ancient Armenia and Azerbaijan."[133]

Widengren is almost certain that the Achaemenians were not Zoroastrians, although he concedes that some Zoroastrian ideas had a vague impact upon the Persians.[134] Yarshater agrees: "The present writer is of the opinion that this question has not found a truly satisfactory answer and is inclined to believe that the Zoroastrian tradition had evolved and taken shape prior to the rise of Cyrus, so that the advent of the Achaemenians was neither reflected in it nor did it affect that tradition."[135]

Scholars Who Affirm the Zoroastrianism of the Achaemenids

There is an equally impressive list of scholars who find echoes of Zoroastrian teachings and practices in the Achaemenid inscriptions

129. Duchesne-Guillemin, *Western Response,* p. 54.; see J. Duchesne-Guillemin, *Zoroastre* (Paris: G. P. Maisonneuve, 1948), pp. 120ff.; J. Duchesne-Guillemin, "Die Religion der Achämeniden," *AAH* 19 (1971): 25–35.

130. Molé, *Culte,* p. 30.

131. V. V. Strouve, "The Religion of the Achaemenids and Zoroastrianism," *Cahiers d'histoire mondiale* 5 (1959–1960): 537–38. Dandamayev, "La politique religieuse des Achéménides," p. 229: "Therefore the Achaemenids cannot be considered as followers of Zoroastrianism in any real sense of this word." See also Hartman, *Parsism,* p. 7.

132. Strouve, "Religion," p. 541.

133. Ibid., p. 543.

134. Widengren, *Les religions,* p. 174; G. Widengren, *Die Religionen Irans* (Stuttgart: W. Kohlhammer, 1965), p. 166.

135. E. Yarshater, "Iranian National History," in Yarshater, *CHI* III.1, p. 439.

and in the classical sources: Kaj Barr, Boyce, Cameron, Carl Clemen, Igor Diakonov, Wladyslaw Duleba, Geldner, Gershevitch, Herzfeld, John Hinnells, Roland Kent, Heidemarie Koch, Meyer, James Moulton, Albert T. Olmstead, and Josef Wiesehöfer.

Herzfeld maintained that the names of Darius, Xerxes, and Artaxerxes reveal Gathic concepts, with the name of Darius "almost a quotation" from a Gatha (Y. 31.7). According to Herzfeld: "They mark their owners as Zarathustrians. . . . But they reveal still more: these three kings were the only Zarathustrians."[136]

Boyce, on the other hand, believes that "the whole Achaemenian dynasty was indeed Zoroastrian."[137] As to the omission of Zoroaster's name in the royal inscriptions she notes: "The same curious omission is found in the royal inscriptions of the later Sasanians, and even in those of their great high priest, Kirder."[138] That is, since no one doubts that the Sasanians were Zoroastrians the omission of Zoroaster's name in the inscriptions does not prove that the Achaemenids were not Zoroastrians.

As to the fact that the Achaemenids were buried and not exposed as required in later Zoroastrianism, Boyce believes that the custom of exposure was adopted only gradually and that in any case the Achaemenid kings sought to avoid contaminating the sacred elements in their burials.[139]

Cyrus

Many scholars (Christensen, Herzfeld, Nyberg, and Jackson) believe that Cyrus was an Iranian polytheist. Jackson, for example, states: "Cyrus seems to me to have been a daevasyanian, not a mazdayasnian."[140] That is, Cyrus was a worshiper of daevas and not of Ahuramazda. Others (Boyce, Hinz, Anton Jirku, Hildegard Lewy, Max Mallowan, Morton Smith, and Sidney Smith) assume that Cyrus was a Zoroastrian.

While we have only brief Old Persian texts from Cyrus, Akkadian and Hebrew texts indicate he acknowledged non-Persian deities such as Marduk and Yahweh. Ezra (1:1–4) has Cyrus claiming Yahweh ordered the Persian king to build him a house in Jerusalem. At Cyrus's capital city of Pasargadae (see chapter 9) we have such religious struc-

136. Herzfeld, *Archaeological History*, p. 40; see Herzfeld, "Iranian Religion," p. 20.

137. Boyce, *History II*, p. xi.

138. Boyce, *Zoroastrians*, p. 57.

139. Boyce, *History II*, pp. 54ff.

140. A. V. W. Jackson, "The Religion of the Achaemenian Kings," *JAOS* 21 (1901): 178.

tures as the Zendan, the terrace, and two altars.[141] The decorative elements in his palace have been interpreted as revealing Cyrus's tolerance for other religions.

As to his burial Stronach suggests:

> On a strictly speculative note, if Cyrus should have been a Zoroastrian or, more probably, an adherent of a pre-Zoroastrian Iranian faith with many of the prescriptions of the later, reformed religion, this condition could have brought him to reject the idea of tumulus burial; far from wishing to cover his tomb with a mound of earth he may have elected to raise it above the earth in order not to defile this sacred element.[142]

Boyce claims that "Cyrus built himself a tomb in which his embalmed body was subsequently laid in defiance of the religious laws demanding the swift destruction of corrupting flesh; but he had the tomb made in such a way that there was not the smallest danger that his corpse could pollute the elements."[143]

A faint rosette on Cyrus's tomb has been interpreted by Stronach as the symbol of Ahuramazda.[144] Duchesne-Guillemin, on the other hand, has interpreted this rosette as a symbol of Mithra, whom he considers the main god worshiped by Cyrus.[145] Dandamayev also believes both Cyrus and Cambyses worshiped Mithra as their great god.[146] Clarisse Herrenschmidt maintains that Darius replaced Mithra with Ahuramazda.[147]

The belief that Cyrus's god was Mithra is based on two disputable assumptions: that the unnamed Baga "god" was Mithra, and Duchesne-Guillemin's interpretation that the rosette on Cyrus's tomb was a symbol of Mithra. The first assumption has been undermined by Boyce's argument that the Baga was Varuna. The second assumption was based on Duchesne-Guillemin's interpretation of a lotus symbol on a late monument at Taq-e Bostan. That view has now been refuted,[148] and Duchesne-Guillemin has revised his interpretation of the Pasargadae flower as a rose, the symbol of the sun.[149]

141. For example, L. Trümpelmann, "Das Heiligtum von *Pasargadae*," *Studia Iranica* 6 (1977): 16. Trümpelmann interprets the two altars as set up for Anahita and Mithra.

142. D. Stronach, *Pasargadae* (New York: Oxford University Press, 1978), p. 43, n. 75.

143. Boyce, *History II*, p. 56.

144. D. Stronach, "A Circular Symbol on the Tomb of Cyrus," *Iran* 9 (1971): 155–58.

145. J. Duchesne-Guillemin, "Le dieu de Cyrus," in *Commémoration Cyrus*, 3: 17.

146. Dandamayev, "La Politique religieuse," pp. 200ff.

147. C. Herrenschmidt, "La religion des Achéménides: état de la question," *Studia Iranica* 9 (1980): 328.

148. M. L. Carter, "Mithra on the Lotus," in *Monumentum Georg Morgenstierne*, 1: 74ff.

149. J. Duchesne-Guillemin, "Sonnenkönigtum und Mazdareligion," in *Kunst, Kultur und Geschichte der Achämenidenzeit und ihr Fortleben*, eds. H. Koch and D. N. MacKenzie (Berlin: Dietrich Reimer, 1983), p. 136.

In view of the lack of texts from Cyrus himself and the subjectivity involved in interpreting his monuments, we cannot be certain of Cyrus's religious convictions.[150]

Cambyses

In contradiction to Herodotus's account of Cambyses's desecration of the Egyptian Apis bull, Egyptian texts reveal that Cambyses honored the Apis, the incarnation of the god Ptah, and also the god Neith of Sais.[151] (See chapter 3.) Amelie Kuhrt comments:

> Quite apart from the fact that there is *no* hint whatever during the reign of Cyrus and Cambyses of Zoroastrianism being practised by or influencing the Persian kings (it may, indeed, have been entirely unknown until the reign of Darius I and even that is debatable), this adoption of local traditions and procedure formed a standard part of both Cyrus' and Cambyses' conquest policy.[152]

Darius

The strongest case for a Zoroastrian background can be made in the case of Darius.[153] But what kind of Zoroastrianism was espoused by Darius and what kind of religion was practiced by the Persian people under his reign? Fortunately there are extensive texts from his reign, including both royal inscriptions and mundane accounts.

In his extensive inscriptions Darius mentions only Ahuramazda by name. In the Behistun inscription the god is mentioned sixty-nine times in 420 lines. Darius claims thirty-four times that he was under the protection of Ahuramazda. It is important to note Darius does not claim Ahuramazda is the only god.[154] Rather he is "the greatest of

150. R. Mayer, "Monotheismus in Israel und in der Religion Zarathustras," *BZ* n.F. 1 (1957): 56.

151. This convinces Jackson, "Religion," p. 179, that Cambyses was not a Zoroastrian.

152. A. Kuhrt, "The Cyrus Cylinder and Achaemenid Imperial Policy," *JSOT* 25 (1983): 89.

153. A. R. Burn, *Persia and the Greeks* (New York: St. Martin's, 1962), 118; W. Duleba, "Was Darius a Zoroastrian?" *Folia Orientalia* 18 (1977): 205–9; Gershevitch, *Avestan Hymn,* p. 15; Gershevitch, "Zoroaster's Own Contribution," p. 16; H. Koch, *Die religiösen Verhältnisse der Dariuszeit* (Wiesbaden: O. Harrassowitz, 1977), p. 176; D. Wilber, *Persepolis* (New York: Thomas Y. Crowell, 1969), p. 36. This can be argued without identifying Darius's father, Hystaspes, with the Vištaspa converted by Zoroaster as did Herzfeld, "Iranian Religion," p. 20, or arguing with A. Shahbazi, "An Achaemenid Symbol II: Farnah '(God Given) Fortune' Symbolized," *AMI* n.F. 13 (1980): 125, that the depiction of Darius's six helpers on his tomb was a conscious attempt to represent Zoroaster's six Holy Immortals.

154. M. Schwartz, "Religion of Achaemenian Iran," p. 685: "Such passages make it possible that Darius was a monotheist. But Darius may merely have been a henotheist," that is, someone who exalted Ahuramazda over the other gods.

gods" (*mathišta bagānām*).[155] Darius also mentions "other gods" (*aniyāha bāgha*).[156] Darius does not refer to the great adversary Angra Mainyu but condemns *Drauga*, "the Lie."

Darius mentions (DB I.63) the *ayadana*, which he restored after Gaumata had destroyed them.[157] It is unclear what these were or why they were destroyed (see chapter 4). Ghirshman suggests they were podiums on which altars for the sacred fires were placed like the terraces that he discovered at Bard-i Nechandeh and Masjid-i Solaiman.[158]

In Darius's tomb at Naqsh-i Rustam, the king is depicted on a pedestal facing a fire altar beneath a winged figure.[159] Boyce interprets the scene as follows: "This is the earliest known representation of the fire-holder with burning fire, which was to be the most generally used Zoroastrian symbol down the ages. . . . by this carving Darius was making a strong visual affirmation of his faith."[160]

The Fortification Tablets from Persepolis, which date from the thirteenth to the twenty-eighth year of Darius, however, as well as the non-Persian texts from his reign present a picture of popular Persian religion that differs markedly from the royal proclamations.[161] According to Richard Hallock, in these texts "the Elamite Humban and Šimut occur alongside Ahuramazda and Mithra, the Semitic Adad, and certain gods otherwise unknown. Any appearance of religious syncretism may be illusory; but the texts do testify that the economic administration treated the gods equally."[162]

Ahuramazda (Elamite *Uramasda*) is attested only four times (PF 337–39, 771). In the first three cases Ahuramazda is mentioned before the other gods, and in the last case he is mentioned alone. "The great god" is mentioned in PF 353 and 354.[163] Humban the Elamite god is named fourteen times (PF 339–51, 2029), more frequently than any other god, which is not surprising since the tablets were written by

155. DB 4.61, 63, DPd 1f., DPh 9, DSf 9, DSp 1, and DH 7.

156. DB 4.61, 62f., DSe 50f., and DSt 8. See R. Schmitt, "Zur babylonischen Version der Bīsutūn-Inschrift," *AfO* 27 (1980): 119.

157. The Akkadian version has *bītāti ša ilāni* "houses of gods," and the Elamite has *siyan* "temple."

158. R. Ghirshman, "La religion de l'Iran du VIII siècle avant notre ère à l'Islam," in *Le plateau iranien et Asie Centrale des origines à la conquête islamique* (Paris: Centre National de la Recherche Scientifique, 1977), pp. 344–45.

159. E. Schmidt, *Persepolis III: The Royal Tombs and Other Monuments* (Chicago: University of Chicago Press, 1970), p. 80.

160. Boyce, *History II*, p. 113.

161. W. Hinz, "Die elamischen Buchungstäfelchen der Darius-Zeit," *Or* 39 (1970): 422–40; H. Koch, "Götter und ihre Verehrung im achämenidischen Persien," *ZA* 77 (1987): 239–78; idem, *Die religiösen Verhältnisse der Dariuszeit*.

162. R. T. Hallock, *Persepolis Fortification Tablets* (Chicago: University of Chicago Press, 1969), p. 5.

163. Boyce, *History II*, p. 139, suggests that the Great God was probably Varuna.

Elamite scribes. In PF 339 Humban is offered almost three times as much wine as Ahuramazda. Adad appears three times (PF 351–53); Mithra (Elamite Miše) once (PF 338). Many other less well-known gods appear such as Shimut and Mišduši. The Elamite gods were served by priests with Elamite names. The offerings were vegetable or drink offerings rather than meat sacrifices. Lacking are any references to Anahita or to the haoma ceremony.

If Darius was a Zoroastrian, as it appears likely, it seems clear that he adapted and modified Zoroastrianism to serve his royal policies. Any rebellion against him was also a rebellion against Ahuramazda. He was not a Zoroastrian after the mold of the intolerant Sasanid high priest Kartir. As Frye observes: "All of the Achaemenid rulers, it would appear from their inscriptions, recognized the existence of other deities, even if they themselves did not worship them."[164] Boyce muses:

> Perhaps it was possible for Zoroastrian theologians to regard the benevolent gods worshipped by non-Iranians as, remotely, also the evocations of Ahuramazda; but whatever doctrinal justification was found, the Achaemenids in general showed a positive benevolence towards the established religions of their subject peoples.[165]

Xerxes

In his famous Daiva text, Xerxes condemned the daivas who were associated with the Lie. Cameron has called it "perhaps the most important religious document discovered at Persepolis."[166] Two copies in Old Persian, one in Akkadian, and one in Elamite were discovered in the southeastern quarter of Persepolis. Another copy was discovered by Stronach at Pasargadae.[167] Herzfeld originally dated it to between 486 and 480, then later to 478.[168]

The key passage reads:

> And among these countries there was (a place) where previously false gods [*daivā*] were worshipped. Afterwards, by the favor of Ahuramazda, I destroyed that sanctuary of the demons [*daivadāna*] and I made proclamation, "The demons shall not be worshipped!" Where previously the

164. R. N. Frye, "Religion in Fars under the Achaemenids," in *Orientalia J. Duchesne-Guillemin Emerito Oblata* (Leiden: Brill, 1984), p. 172.

165. M. Boyce, "Persian Religion in the Achaemenid Age," in *The Cambridge History of Judaism I: Introduction; The Persian Period*, by W. D. Davies and L. Finkelstein (Cambridge: Cambridge University Press, 1984), p. 288.

166. G. G. Cameron, "The 'Daiva' Inscription of Xerxes: In Elamite," *WO* 2 (1959): 470.

167. D. Stronach, "Excavation at Pasargadae: A Third Preliminary Report," *Iran* 3 (1965): 19.

168. E. Herzfeld, *The Persian Empire* (Wiesbaden: F. Steiner, 1968), p. 351.

> demons were worshipped, there I worshipped Ahuramazda and Arta reverent[ly].[169]

In the Gathas the word *daiva* can designate gods as opposed to men (Y. 29.4), or it can mean spirits who incite men to violence and oppose prosperity (Y. 1.5).[170] Questions remain as to the identity of the daivas whose worship Xerxes interdicted. Was it in one region or more than one?[171]

The gods of various areas have been suggested. Isidore Levy believed Xerxes was referring to the destruction of the Athenian temples (Herodotus 8.54).[172] But in the same passage Herodotus (8.133–35) orders the Greek exiles to sacrifice to their gods. Another improbable suggestion is that they were the gods of the rebellious Egyptians.[173] Many scholars have interpreted the daivas as the gods of Babylonia and the daivadana as the temple of Marduk, destroyed by Xerxes after the Babylonians rebelled.[174]

Other scholars have placed the banned daiva worship within Iran itself. Herzfeld assumed the daivas were the gods of a rebellious Media.[175] Olmstead thought of the gods of eastern Iran or Bactria.[176] According to Frye:

> Xerxes' act in suppressing *daiva* worship presumably had a special significance for the homeland, Persis. Therefore, in my opinion, either cults in Kirman or elsewhere in the east, or more likely Elamite cults in Fars and western Iran were the target of Xerxes, and his decree was a definite act in the Iranicization of Fars, culturally and religiously.[177]

Some scholars have suggested that the daivas must have been the old Iranian gods who were displaced by Ahuramazda, such as Indra.[178] According to Boyce, "the natural interpretation of Xerxes' words is

169. R. G. Kent, *Old Persian*, rev. ed. (New Haven: American Oriental Society, 1953), p. 151.

170. Molé, *Culte*, p. 18. The word is derived from Indo-European **deiuós*; in Avestan it became *daēva*, in Pahlavi *dēv*. See W. Th. in der Smitten, "Xerxes und die Daeva," *BO* 30 (1973): 369.

171. Dandamayev, "La politique religieuse," p. 195, points out that the Akkadian version indicates that a plurality of places was condemned.

172. I. Levy, "L'inscription triomphale de Xerxès," *Revue Historique* 185 (1939): 117–22.

173. Ibid., pp. 109–11; C. Hignett, *Xerxes' Invasion of Greece* (Oxford: Clarendon, 1963), p. 89, n. 5.

174. Duchesne-Guillemin, "Le dieu de Cyrus," p. 13; Herrenschmidt, "La religion," p. 326; Widengren, *Die Religionen Irans*, p. 138; idem, *Les religions*, p. 163.

175. Herzfeld, "Iranian Religion," p. 27.

176. A. T. Olmstead, *History of the Persian Empire* (Chicago: University of Chicago Press, 1948), pp. 231–32.

177. Frye, "Religion in Fars," p. 174; see also Frye, *History of Ancient Iran*, p. 121.

178. U. Bianchi, "L'inscription 'des daivas' et le Zoroastrisme des Achéménides," *RHR* 192 (1977): 3–30; Asmussen, "Zoroastrian 'De-Demonization,' " p. 113; Schwartz, "Religion," p. 691; J. Balcer, *Sparda by the Bitter Sea* (Chico: Scholars, 1984), p. 253.

that, as a Zoroastrian, he was recording the destruction of an Iranian sanctuary devoted to the worship of those warlike beings condemned by the prophet as having 'rushed to Fury, with whom they have afflicted the world and mankind.' "[179]

But as Martin Schwartz has observed: "It is difficult to believe that Xerxes was motivated by monotheistic considerations."[180] It is highly unlikely that Xerxes was banning the worship of all other gods but Ahuramazda. Even under the reign of so devoted a follower of Ahuramazda as Darius, the Persepolis tablets prove that other gods were tolerated. All that we know about the policies of Cyrus, Cambyses, Darius, and Xerxes indicates they generally supported the worship of other gods where it suited their political policies and only destroyed sanctuaries of those who rebelled against them.

Artaxerxes I

Some eighty pestles and ninety-seven mortars found at Persepolis bear Aramaic inscriptions that date from the seventh year of Xerxes to the twenty-ninth year of Artaxerxes I (see chapter 10). Raymond Bowman attempted to interpret these inscriptions as directions for the haoma ritual in a Mithraic cult. All other scholars who translated the texts interpret them as simple dedications.

Bowman's controversial translations included his rendering *prkn* as the "(haoma) crushing ceremony," *srk* as "ritual," *hst* as an Iranian expression for the haoma ceremony, and *škr* as an "intoxicant." Other scholars have interpreted these words as place-names connected with Arachosia, the source of the stone for the mortars and pestles.[181] That these may have been used in religious ceremonies is indicated by a seal depicting two priests, a fire altar, a mortar, and a pestle.[182]

It has been widely claimed, on the basis of calculations by Seyyed Taqizadeh, that the so-called Zoroastrian calendar was adopted in 441 B.C. during the reign of Artaxerxes I.[183] According to this calendar each day and month had a religious name. Numerous scholars have used this datum as a basis for the certain Zoroastrianism of Artaxerxes I.[184]

179. Boyce, *History II*, p. 175.

180. Schwartz, "Religion," *CHI* II, p. 691.

181. W. Hinz, "Zu den Mörsern und Stösseln aus Persepolis," in *Monumentum H. S. Nyberg* (Tehran-Liège: Bibliothèque Pahlavi, 1975), 1: 371.

182. E. Schmidt, *Persepolis II* (Chicago: University of Chicago Press, 1953), table 7, number 20.

183. S. H. Taqizadeh, *Old Iranian Calendars* (London: Royal Asiatic Society, 1938), pp. 13, 33.

184. For example, Burn, *Persia and the Greeks*, p. 118; W. Culican, *The Medes and Persians* (New York: Praeger, 1965), p. 174; Duchesne-Guillemin, *Western Response*, p. 54; R. N. Frye, *The Heritage of Persia* (Cleveland: World, 1963), p. 115; Gershevitch, *Avestan Hymn*, p. 18; idem, "Zoroaster's Own Contribution," p. 21.

For example, Cameron called this new religious calendar "the oldest datable record of Zoroastrianism in western Iran."[185]

Elias Bickerman, however, has analyzed Taqizadeh's conclusions to show how subjective his arguments were. Taqizadeh counted backwards from A.D. 399, a date under Yazdagird I. Bickerman comments: "I must confess, however, that the idea of intercalations carried on each 120 years during a millennium from the Achaemenids to the Sassanids, does not strike me as a probable conjecture."[186] Furthermore Bickerman demonstrated that the Achaemenids used the Babylonian luni-solar calendar in the fifth century B.C. The first certain use of the Zoroastrian calendar is found in the Nisa ostraca dated to 90 B.C.[187] The only possibly earlier evidence is a damaged Aramaic inscription from Naqsh-i Rustam dated to the Seleucid era.[188]

Artaxerxes II

The Old Persian inscriptions of Artaxerxes II introduce by name gods other than Ahuramazda. The king's texts from Susa and Ecbatana (Hamadan) mention Ahuramazda, Anahita, and Mithra; a text from Ecbatana mentions only Mithra; another text from Ecbatana mentions Ahuramazda alone.[189]

An important passage from the Babylonian priest Berossus (third century B.C.) reports:

> Later, however, after many years they began to worship statues in human form as Berossus reports in the third book of his Chaldaean history. Artaxerxes, the son of Darius, the son of Ochus, introduced this practice. He was the first to set up an image of Aphrodite Anaitis in Babylon and to require such worship from the Susians, Ecbatanians, Persians and Bactrians and from Damascus and Sardis.[190]

The explicit reference to Anahita and Mithra under Artaxerxes II can be considered the introduction of new gods or something that was

185. Cameron, *Persepolis Treasury Tablets,* p. 9.

186. E. Bickerman, "The 'Zoroastrian Calendar,' " *AO* 35 (1967): 203. Frye, *Ancient History of Iran,* p. 133, points out that the date rests on conjecture. According to Gnoli, "Politique," p. 143, Bickerman has shown that Taqizadeh's thesis is unsupportable.

187. Ibid., p. 207. See also J. Duchesne-Guillemin, "The Religion of Ancient Iran," in *Historia Religionum,* ed. C. J. Bleeker (Leiden: Brill, 1969), 1: 326; E. Bickerman, "Time-Reckoning," in Yarshater, *CHI* III.2, p. 788; M. Boyce, "Parthian Writings and Literature," in idem, p. 1152.

188. Duchesne-Guillemin, "Sonnenkönigtum," pp. 137–38.

189. Kent, *Old Persian,* pp. 154–55.

190. S. Burstein, *The BABYLONIACA of Berossus* (Malibu: Undena, 1978), p. 29. The temple of Anahita in Ecbatana was later pillaged by Antiochus III in 209 B.C. See Boyce, "Iconoclasm," p. 100.

implicit in Darius's earlier phrase *all the gods.*[191] According to Herzfeld: "The notice of Berossos, confirmed by the inscriptions of Artaxerxes II, gives us the exact date at which the original polytheism, the *daivayasnian* religion was re-introduced in 400 B.C."[192] Gershevitch also believes this king's reign marks the change from the monotheism of the Gathas, reflected in Darius's inscription, to the polytheism of the Younger Avesta.[193] On the other hand, Frye cautions, "the oft mentioned change in the religion of the Achaemenids from the time of Darius to Artaxerxes II, on the basis of the appearance of Mithra and Anahita in the royal inscriptions, may be more apparent than real."[194]

The Winged Figure

Hovering over the king in many Achaemenid reliefs is a winged figure inside a circle, sometimes with the tail and wings of a bird. Originally this was a motif associated with Horus in Egypt, which was borrowed by the Assyrians as a symbol of Ashur, and then adopted by the Persians.

Darius first used this figure on his Behistun inscription. A noteworthy depiction of this figure is found in a pair of earrings, inlaid with lapis lazuli, carnelian, and turquoise, which date circa 400 B.C. Around the central winged figure are six smaller, similar figures.[195] Shahbazi interpreted the earrings as reflecting the Zoroastrian doctrine of the "king of the seven climes" (*šah-i haft kišvar*).[196]

The Parsis interpret the winged symbol as the king's *fravashi* or spirit. They deny that it could represent their god, citing Herodotus (1.132), who reports the Persians did not make statues of their gods.[197] Prior to 1974 Western scholars generally agreed the winged symbol represented Ahuramazda.

This consensus was independently challenged in articles published in 1974 and 1980 by Shahbazi[198] and in 1979 by Peter Calmeyer.[199]

191. Molé, *Culte*, p. 33. Gnoli, "Considerazioni," pp. 248–49, has argued that the Iranian triad of Ahuramazda, Anahita, and Mithra has been influenced by the Mesopotamian triad of Anu, Ishtar, and Nebo.

192. Herzfeld, "Iranian Religion," p. 26.

193. Gershevitch, "Zoroaster's Own Contribution," p. 16.

194. Frye, *Ancient History of Iran*, p. 133.

195. J. F. X. McKeon, "Achaemenian Cloisonné-Inlay Jewelry: An Important New Example," in *Orient and Occident*, pp. 109–18.

196. A. S. Shahbazi, "Darius' 'haft kišvar,' " in *Kunst*, pp. 242–43.

197. Hartman, *Parsism*, p. 6.

198. A. S. Shahbazi, "An Achaemenid Symbol I: A Farewell to 'Fravahr' and Ahuramazda," *AMI* n.F. 7 (1974): 135–44; idem, "An Achaemenid Symbol II: Farnah '(God Given) Fortune,' " *AMI* n.F. 13 (1980): 119–47.

199. P. Calmeyer, "Fortuna-Tyche-Khvarnah," *Jahrbuch des Deutschen Archäologischen Instituts* 94 (1979): 346–65.

An Achaemenid winged figure thought to represent Ahuramazda. (Courtesy of The Oriental Institute, University of Chicago)

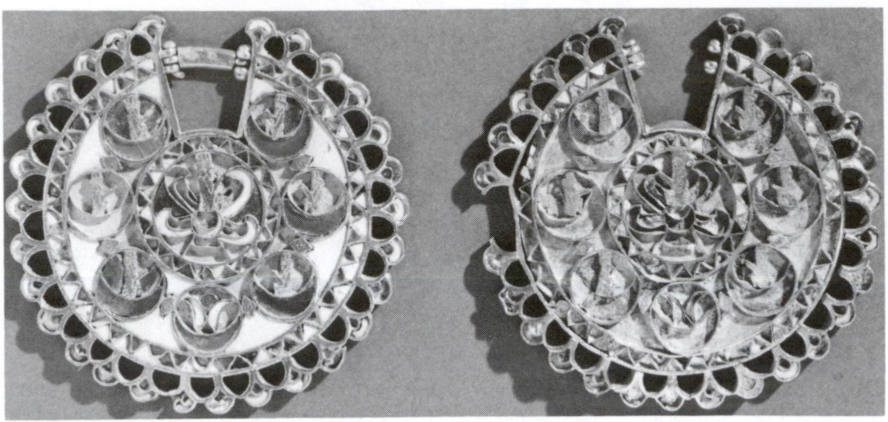

Achaemenid earrings with the winged figure. (Edward J. and Mary S. Holmes Fund, Courtesy, Museum of Fine Arts, Boston)

Shahbazi and Calmeyer agreed that the winged symbol represented Avestan Khvarenah (Median Farnah), the divine charisma given to kings. Calmeyer compared the latter concept with the Semitic Gad, the Greek Tychē, and the Latin Fortuna. Shahbazi noted that the winged symbol was linked to each king in a personal way as indicated by the details of their crowns. This new interpretation has been accepted by Boyce and other scholars.[200]

One glaring problem with this explanation is the absence of the Old Persian equivalent of *xvarenah* in the Achaemenid inscriptions, although the Median *farnah* occurs in numerous names. Duchesne-Guillemin explains its absence by positing a tension between the old Indo-Iranian concept of the king as the son of the sun associated with *xvarenah* and the Zoroastrian teaching of Ahuramazda as all-powerful.[201] Gnoli, however, argues that its absence indicates this concept did not play an important role among the Achaemenids.[202]

Many scholars have remained unconvinced of the revisionist interpretation of the winged figure.[203] John Cook argues: "In favour of the view that it represents Ahura Mazda are the fact that it seems to appear on independent satrapal coins (as of Datames) and above all the postures: the King is raising his hand as though in adoration to a superior being."[204] A detailed refutation of the views of Shahbazi and Calmeyer

200. Boyce, *History II*, pp. 103–5; see Frye, "Religion in Fars," p. 177.

201. Duchesne-Guillemin, "Sonnenkönigtum," pp. 138–39.

202. Gnoli, "Politique religieuse," p. 171.

203. M. Roaf, "Sculptures and Sculptors at Persepolis," *Iran* 21 (1983): 133, n. 116: "His [Shahbazi's] interpretation . . . I do not find convincing." See also M. C. Root, *The King and Kingship in Achaemenid Art* (Leiden: Brill, 1979), pp. 169–72.

204. J. M. Cook, *The Persian Empire* (New York: Schocken, 1983), p. 149.

has been presented by Pierre Lecoq, who shows the only plausible identification of the winged figure is the traditional one of Ahuramazda.[205] Gnoli also concludes: "We can state with certainty that the winged disk represents Ahura Mazdā despite the divergent opinions of some scholars and some Parsis, the latter concerned about preserving the aniconic coherence of their religion."[206]

Conclusions

There is no unanimity on the question of the Achaemenids' religion. Our evidence does not permit a definitive decision as to the religion of Cyrus and Cambyses. The worship of Ahuramazda by Darius and Xerxes can be explained away as the worship of an Iranian deity, but it is hardly likely this can be plausibly separated from the revelation of Ahuramazda to Zoroaster. Since Zoroaster evidently lived long before and far away from the Achaemenids, his teachings were mediated in a modified manner and in turn adapted by the kings as a royal ideology.[207] It is anachronistic to attempt to attribute to these kings Zoroastrian beliefs from the later texts.[208]

Discontinuity or Continuity?

Devolution

Most scholars have understood the change from the Gathas to the Younger Avesta, and from the exaltation of Ahuramazda under Darius to the polytheism of Artaxerxes II as a process of devolution. For example, Gershevitch, in a seminal article, proposed the various stages be designated as follows: the religion of the Gathas was Zarathustrianism;

205. P. Lecoq, "Un problème de religion achéménide: Ahura Mazda ou Xvarnah?" in *Orientalia J. Duchesne-Guillemin Emerito Oblata*, pp. 301–26.

206. Gnoli, "Zoroastrianism," p. 587.

207. Cf. Cameron, *Persepolis Treasury Tablets*, p. 9: "In short, the religion of the early Achaemenids would seem to have been basically untouched by Zoroaster's work and the particular beliefs of his community; the real foundation of that religious world appears to have been the old Aryan religion, reshaped to its own ends because it was a political religion proceeding from an old aristocratic and war religion, created by and for great kings." Compare J. Wisehöfer, *Der Aufstand Gaumātas und die Anfänge Dareios I* (Bonn: Rudolf Habelt, 1978), pp. 130, 167.

208. Frye, "Religion in Fars," p. 176, concludes: "for the Achaemenid period, however, it is clear that there was neither a 'fixed,' 'orthodox' religion of the Iranians, nor was there an elaborate priestly hierarchy, and one can hardly speak of the 'Zoroastrianism' or 'non-Zoroastrianism' of the Achaemenids since there was no fixed body of doctrines and rites which could be called 'Zoroastrian,' in the sense of much later developments in the Near East."

the religion of the Younger Avesta was Zarathustricism; and the religion of the later Sasanian period was Zoroastrianism.

According to Gershevitch the so-called monotheism of the Gathas was contaminated with the polytheism of the Avesta: "This polytheistic attitude is of course a travesty of Zarathuštra's intentions, even though the pious authors expressly ascribe it to him."[209] Later this pagan polytheism of the Avesta is virtually abandoned for the dualism of the Sasanian period.

Zaehner's designations for these three phases are simpler. They are: primitive Zoroastrianism for the message of the prophet; catholic Zoroastrianism for the repaganization of his message; and reformed Zoroastrianism for the dualist orthodoxy of Sasanian times.[210] Zaehner laments: "Never has a great religious thinker been more grossly travestied—travestied by his own followers."[211] According to Cameron:

> It nevertheless is a sad but demonstrable fact that Zoroaster's own immediate followers misunderstood those same allusions; though seeking to retain his inspiration, they made—as he did not—a semi-sacred animal of the barnyard cow. . . . and the prophet's Gathas, which were never intended for ritualistic purposes, were recited at the very sacrifices which the prophet abhorred.[212]

In Gnoli's summary: "The original Zoroastrian message, however, was profoundly transformed by the first generations of the prophet's disciples. Later, elaborations by the clergy even went so far as to allow various aspects of the old polytheistic and ritualistic practices to reemerge, albeit with some limitations."[213] The view of a devolution from the prophet's lofty ethical message to a reemergent paganism is held by many other scholars such as Duchesne-Guillemin,[214] Frye,[215] and Schwartz.[216]

209. Gershevitch, "Zoroaster's Own Contribution," p. 14. See Bleeker, "Wer war Zarathustra," p. 26; see also Gershevitch, *Avestan Hymn*, pp. 9, 13.

210. Zaehner, *Dawn*, p. 18.

211. Ibid., p. 19; see Zaehner, *Teachings of the Magi*, p. 15.

212. Cameron, "Zoroaster the Herdsman," p. 272.

213. Gnoli, "Zoroastrianism," p. 581; see also Gnoli, "Politique religieuse," p. 186; Gnoli, "Problems," pp. 67, 71.

214. See Duchesne-Guillemin, "Religion," p. 327; Duchesne-Guillemin, *Religion of Ancient Iran*, pp. 147ff.

215. Frye, "Georges Dumézil," p. 169. See n. 71 above.

216. Schwartz, "Religion of Achaemenid Iran," p. 664. According to Kotwal and Boyd, *Guide*, p. xxvii, Parsi scholars, however, assume the basic continuity of Zoroastrian teachings and consider the Younger Avesta an accurate record of the early disciples of Zoroaster.

Continuity

Against the majority of Zoroastrian scholars, Boyce has almost single-handedly emphasized the continuity between Zoroaster's teachings and later Zoroastrian doctrines and practices. Her six-month stay among Iranian Zoroastrians in 1963/1964 sensitized her to the believers' viewpoint. She came to appreciate the role of Zoroaster as a priest and the significance of ritual among the Parsis. "In general, she has argued for substantial continuity between the beliefs of Zoroaster, and those of both his forebears, and of his followers."[217]

Boyce holds that theological utterances, which survive only in works compiled in the Sasanian period, go back essentially to Zoroaster. She states:

> The writer finds it impossible to agree with those scholars who interpret this great faith as the product of compromise and confusion. On the contrary, the fundamental doctrines taught by Zoroaster appear to have been maintained with admirable strictness by his followers down to the 19th century, when the sudden impact of European ideas and modern science had a cataclysmic effect on their theology.[218]

For example, Boyce does not believe there was a contradiction between Zoroaster's proclamation of Ahuramazda and the honoring of other yazatas in the Yashts:

> Thus, despite the statements of generations of Western scholars (which by now have had their influence upon the Parsis), there is not the smallest piece of evidence to suggest that his proclamation of one original Godhead led him to deny the present existence of other *yazatas,* lesser created beings according to his revelation, the servants of the Lord, to whom veneration should be duly accorded.[219]

Boyce does not believe Zoroaster's failure to mention Mithra meant any hostility to him. She holds that Zoroaster did not condemn animal sacrifice and the haoma drink as such, but only certain abuses of these practices.

As already noted, Boyce believes all the Achaemenids were Zoroas-

217. A. D. H. Bivar and J. R. Hinnells, "Professor Mary Boyce," *Papers in Honour of Professor Mary Boyce,* p. xvii. For example, Boyce, *History I,* p. 229: "Probably, therefore, one should attribute to Zoroaster himself the full doctrine so well known from the later theological works of his faith, that everything living has a pre-existence."

218. Boyce, "Iconoclasm," p. 109, n. 81. See idem, *History I,* chapters 8 and 9; idem, *Persian Stronghold,* p. 18, n. 37; idem, "On Mithra's Part," p. 34.

219. Boyce, *History I,* p. 225.

trians. Despite the lack of any explicit evidence from the Seleucid-Parthian period, Boyce also maintains Zoroastrian orthodoxy preceded the Sasanian era: "The present writer finds it impossible to subscribe to the commonly held opinion that Zoroastrianism managed to exist for hundreds of years (becoming during them the dominant religion throughout Iran) without possessing an orthodoxy before the rise of the Sasanians in the 3rd century A.D."[220]

Boyce has persuaded a number of other scholars, including Windfuhr[221] and G. Kreyenbroek,[222] of the correctness of her views. But her opinions have also been criticized as being too credulous about Zoroastrian claims, as reading too much into the evidence, and as maintaining too static a development of Zoroastrian religion. Gnoli objects: "The idea that the Zoroastrian religion was handed down over the centuries in a fairly compact manner from its pre-Achaemenian origins down to the Sassanians and afterwards, without being substantially affected by profound and radical changes, seems to me to be historically untenable."[223]

Zoroastrian Doctrines and Practices

Ahuramazda

The supreme god preached by Zoroaster and exalted by Darius and Xerxes was (Av.) Ahuramazda, "the wise lord." Ahura means "lord," and Mazda, "wise." The name appears in Old Persian as Auramazda (Elamite *Uramasda,* Pahl. *Ohrmazd*). Scholars disagree on whether such a god was known before Zoroaster. According to Boyce: "It is probable that, even before the coming of Zoroastrianism, Ahura Mazdā had been acknowledged by the Medes and Persians as their chief divinity."[224] Others such as Shaul Shaked believe that Zoroaster preached a new god.[225] In the Gathas the name *Mazda* occurs 116

220. Boyce, "On the Zoroastrian Temple Cult of Fire," p. 456.

221. Windfuhr, "Word," p. 134.

222. Kreyenbroek, *Sraoša,* p. 1.

223. B. Schlerath, "Zàrathustra im Awesta," in *Festgabe deutscher Iranisten zur 2500 Jahrfeier Irans,* ed. W. Eilers (Stuttgart: Hochwacht Druck, 1971), pp. 133–40, criticizes her views about Zoroaster and the haoma cult.

224. Boyce, *History I,* p. 39. Agreeing with her position is F. B. J. Kuiper, "*Ahura Mazda* 'Lord Wisdom'?" *IIJ* 18 (1976): 25–42.

225. S. Shaked, "First Man, First King," in *Gilgul,* Zvi Werblowsky Festschrift, eds. S. Shaked, D. Shulman, G. G. Stroumsa (Leiden: Brill, 1987), p. 239: "The structure of this divine name serves, I believe, as a powerful argument in favour of the Zoroastrian origin of this deity, although the issue is still disputed." R. Kent, "The Name Ahuramazda," in *Oriental Studies in Honour of Cursetji Erachji Pavry* (London: Oxford University Press, 1933), pp. 200–208, also believes that Ahuramazda originated with Zoroaster.

times, *Ahura* 64 times, *Mazda Ahura* 28 times, and *Ahura Mazda* only 6 times.[226]

Monotheism?

Some interpreters and modern Parsis maintain that Zoroaster preached the monotheistic worship of Ahuramazda, citing for example, Yasna 32.3–5: "But you gods all are a manifestation of evil thinking, and he who so much worships you [is a manifestation] of falsehood and dissent." In this view the daevas or other gods have no ontological reality.

But Zoroaster's message was not an unqualified monotheism. Douglas Fox points out: "In no single coherent statement does the prophet unambiguously proclaim monotheism."[227] Duchesne-Guillemin speaks of the "rudiments of monotheism" in the Gathas and in Darius's inscriptions.[228] According to Boyce: "The character of every known Old Iranian religion appears polytheistic; and no declaration of the existence of one God, and one God alone, can be found in any source, not even in the utterances of Zoroaster."[229] In Malandra's view Zoroaster's theology exalted Ahuramazda: "It is a status that falls short of absolute monotheism, yet may be rightly called 'qualified' monotheism, in that Zarathushtra recognizes a plurality of 'Wise Lords' (Y. 30.9, 31.4) as well as the so-called Entities or aspects of Ahura Mazdā's personality."[230]

A problem facing the monotheistic interpretation of Ahuramazda is the question of the source of evil, specifically the Evil Spirit. According to the monotheistic view Ahuramazda created both Spenta Mainyu ("the holy spirit") and Angra Mainyu ("the fiendish spirit").[231] Gnoli suggests these spirits acquired their respective character by their choice between Asha and Druj.[232] According to Widengren, Ahuramazda is an all-powerful god who bears in himself the contradiction of good and evil, as Zoroaster has combined elements of monism and dualism.[233] Fox comments: "This form of Zoroastrianism, then, hardly

226. S. S. Hartman, "Der Name Ahura Mazdāh," in *Synkretismus im syrisch-persischen Kulturgebiet*, ed. A. Dietrich (Göttingen: Vandenhoeck and Ruprecht, 1975), pp. 170.

227. Fox, "Darkness and Light," p. 132.

228. Duchesne-Guillemin, "Religion," p. 335.

229. Boyce, "On Mithra's Part," p. 18.

230. Malandra, *Introduction*, p. 19.

231. Windfuhr, "*Vohu Manah*", p. 271; Duchesne-Guillemin, *Religion of Ancient Iran*, p. 105; J. W. Boyd and D. F. Crosby, "Is Zoroastrianism Dualistic or Monotheistic?" *JAAR* 47 (1979): 565.

232. G. Gnoli, "L'évolution du dualisme iranien et le problème zurvanite," *RHR* 201 (1984): 118.

233. Widengren, *Les religions*, pp. 94–95; W. G. Oxtoby, "Interpretations of Iranian Dualism," in *Iranian Civilization and Culture*, ed. C. J. Adams (Montreal: McGill University Press, 1972), p. 64:

escapes imputing evil ultimately to God himself, and in a way which the Bible avoids."[234]

The Bounteous Immortals

Associated with Ahuramazda were six Amesha Spentas (Pahl. Amshaspands) or "Bounteous Immortals," who are conceived as semi-personal manifestations of the supreme god: *Asha* = Righteousness; *Vohu Manah* = Good Mind; *Khshathra* = Power; *Armaiti* = Suitable Disposition; *Haurvatat* = Health; and *Ameretat* = Immortality.[235] These appear to be personified abstractions. But they were more than abstractions because they were venerated by Zoroaster.[236]

The concept of the Immortals is one of the most important and original doctrines of Zoroaster. They are prominent in the Gathas, which state explicitly that Ahuramazda created the first four Immortals. Each of the Immortals is associated with some aspect of creation: Vohu Manah with animals, Asha with fire, Khshathra with metals, Armaiti with earth, Haurvatat with water, and Ameretat with plants. In later times the Amesha Spentas were transformed into male and female deities. Armaiti became the spouse of Ahuramazda. The Parsis now regard the Immortals as archangels.[237]

Dualism

Many leading scholars believe Zoroaster taught not a monotheism, but a dualism, with two primordial uncreated Spirits, a Good Spirit (that is, God) and an Evil Spirit. Willard Oxtoby defines dualism as "a conception of the universe which postulates two ultimate principles, seen as opposed to each other and more or less evenly matched."[238] A key text is Yasna 30.3: "Now these two spirits, which are twins, revealed themselves at first in a vision." This interpretation follows only if Ahuramazda is equated with Spenta Mainyu (Y. 30.5).[239] According to Boyce: "together with Ahura Mazdā in the beginning, and likewise uncreated was another being who was opposed to him, the Hostile

---

"Now, on the whole, the *Avesta* is neither explicitly dualistic nor explicitly monotheistic." Oxtoby ("Interpretations," p. 66) concludes: "I do not think that the religion of Zoroaster was either a thoroughgoing, thought-out monotheism *or* a systematized dualism."

234. Fox, "Darkness and Light," p. 136.

235. Widengren, *Les religions*, pp. 98–99; Zaehner, *Dawn*, p. 45; J. Narten, *Die Aməša Spəṇtas im Avesta* (Wiesbaden: O. Harrassowitz, 1982).

236. Boyce, *History I*, p. 202.

237. Moulton, *Treasure of the Magi*, p. 21.

238. Oxtoby, "Interpretations," p. 59.

239. Fox, "Darkness and Light," p. 133.

Spirit, Angra Mainyu."[240] In the dualistic view God is wholly good while all evil comes from the Evil Spirit. But God is not all-powerful. Only with the help of men who choose his side will God triumph over the Evil One in the end.[241] Fox observes: "Is it not men who, by choosing in sufficient numbers one of these gods in a way that gives him sovereignty, actually save their god?"[242]

The Evil Spirit, called Angra Mainyu (Pahl. Ahriman, Greek Areimanios), occurs but once in the Gathas, apparently as an epithet (Y. 45.2): "Yes, I shall speak of the two fundamental spirits of existence, of which the virtuous one would have thus spoken to the evil one" (Insler trans.).[243] He appears in the Yashts (3.14, and 13.76–78), and notably in the Vendidad (chapter 22) as the author of 99,999 diseases.

According to Gnoli the Avesta as a whole does not reflect a pronounced dualism.[244] In contrast to Boyce, he and other scholars believe the ethical dualism of Zoroaster developed into an ontological dualism only in the Sasanian period,[245] although the dualistic doctrine of the Zoroastrians is attested already in the *Peri Philosophias* of Aristotle (fourth century B.C.).

The classical dualist position is especially expounded in the Pahlavi Bundahishn. All things in creation belong either to one sphere or another: aligned with the Good Spirit are light, fire, summer, water, fertile land, health, growth, and domestic animals, especially the dog. Aligned with the Evil Spirit are darkness, night, winter, drought, infertile land, vermin, sickness, and death.

Foremost among the maleficent demons is Aeshma, "Wrath." A number of the other demons are also personified abstractions. The Denkard (6.23) speaks of "one who makes battle against the nonmaterial demons, whatever they may be, and in particular does not let these five demons into his body: Greed, Envy, Lust, Wrath and Shame."[246] Other demons are demoted Indo-Aryan devas such as Indra; still others are demons of disaster, such as Apaosha the demon of drought. One of the most feared is Nasu, the demon of decay

240. Boyce, *History I*, p. 192; see also Yarshater, "Iranian Common Beliefs," in *CHI* III.1, p. 347. But according to Moulton, *Treasure of the Magi*, p. 27: "It does not seem probable that he would have favoured any interpretation which made Ahura Mazda either twin or parent of the evil principle! It is best to assume that the word 'Twin' is thrown out for a momentary purpose without thought of logical developments."

241. Boyd and Crosby, "Is Zoroastrianism Dualistic?" p. 558.

242. Fox, "Darkness and Light," p. 136.

243. Moulton, *Treasure of the Magi*, p. 9. The more characteristic term for evil in the Gathas is *Drug*, "The Lie" or "Evil" (for example, Y. 30.10).

244. G. Gnoli, "Ahura Mazdā and Angra Mainyu," in Eliade, *Encyclopedia*, 1: 157–58.

245. Asmussen, "Zoroastrian 'De-Demonization,' " p. 112.

246. Shaked, *Wisdom*, p. 11.

inhabiting corpses, which comes as a loathsome fly from the North (Vd. 7.2–4).[247]

Menog and *Getig*

The dualism of the two states, *menog* and *getig*, is another Zoroastrian concept found only in the late sources that Boyce proposes to retroject back to Zoroaster himself.[248] But these concepts are not found in the Avesta but in such Pahlavi texts as the Denkard and Dadistan-i Denig.[249]

The *menog* state is nonmaterial and ideal whereas the *getig* state is material and earthly. According to Shaked: "Only Ohrmazd and his creations 'really' exist in getig, while Ahreman and the demons have no getig at all, and they only participate in the life of getig in a secondary way, parasitically as it were."[250] In contrast to Gnostic dualism, which regarded the material world as evil, the dualism of *menog/getig* regards the material world as good and evil as having no material form of its own.

Zurvanism

A special form of Zoroastrianism, which developed in the late Achaemenid era and flourished in the Sasanid era, was Zurvanism. Zurvanism considered *Zurvan* or "time" to be the father of the twins Ohrmazd and Ahriman. The nature of Zurvanism is controversial because the fullest sources are both late and non-Zoroastrian. Greek sources (fourth century B.C.), such as Eudemus of Rhodes, seem to refer to Zurvanite beliefs.[251] But our most complete sources include the fifth-century A.D. Armenian writer Eznik and the Arabic author Sharistani (twelfth century). The Avestan and Pahlavi texts are silent except for passages that refer to a "road created by Zurvan" (Vd. 19.29) and refer to Zurvanism as a demon-inspired heresy (Dk. 9.30.4). Some scholars maintain that references to this "heresy" were suppressed by orthodox Zoroastrianism; other scholars believe they can recover Zurvanite materials from the Avesta.

The name *Zurvan* appears as Avestan *Zrvan* and Pahlavi *Zurwan*. Swedish scholars, such as Nyberg, claimed that Zurvan was a pre-

247. Schwartz, "Religion of Achaemenian Iran," pp. 682–83; Boyce, *History I*, chapter 3.

248. Boyce, *History I*, p. 229.

249. H.-P. Hasenfratz, "Iran und der Dualismus," *Numen* 30 (1983): 38.

250. S. Shaked, "The Notions *menog* and *getig* in the Pahlavi Texts and Their Relation to Eschatology," *Acta Orientalia* 33 (1971): 71.

251. On the assumption that Damascius is dependent on Theopompus.

Silver Luristan plaque interpreted by R. Ghirshman to represent Zurvan and the twins Ohrmazd and Ahriman. (Cincinnati Art Museum, purchase)

Zoroastrian Median god. They further suggested that Mithraism and Manichaeism developed from Zurvanism. All of this is extremely speculative.[252] Also highly subjective is Ghirshman's interpretation of a silver Luristan plaque as depicting the triad Zurvan, Ohrmazd, and Ahriman.[253]

Zurvan as infinite time is a depersonalized abstraction. The reasoning that led to his exaltation resulted from an interpretation of the twin spirits of Yasna 30.3. The Zurvanites assumed the twins were Ohrmazd and Ahriman, and concluded they must have had a father, namely Zurvan.[254] Zurvanism seems to have gained its fatalistic outlook from astrology.

Since all of the sources are late, the bare existence of Zurvanism in the late Achaemenid period is inferred rather than proven.[255] Its existence during the Parthian era is likewise assumed.[256] Some scholars believe Zurvanism was a philosophical movement dominant during the Sasanian period.[257] Others, however, postulate that Zurvanism was the religion of the populace during this period as opposed to the official Mazdaism of the court.[258] Boyce believes Zurvanism was dominant in southwestern Iran, while Mazdaism was popular among the Parthians in the northeast.[259] Frye observes, "we do not have any evidence that

252. R. Frye, "Zurvanism Again," *HTR* 52 (1959): 63–74. The view of the Uppsala School was followed by R. C. Zaehner in *Zurvan: A Zoroastrian Dilemma* (Oxford: Oxford University Press, 1955), but rejected in *The Dawn and Twilight of Zoroastrianism* (1961).

253. Ghirshman, *Art of Ancient Iran*, p. 52; Duchesne-Guillemin, *Symbols*, p. 42.

254. Boyce, *History I*, p. 193.

255. Boyce, *Zoroastrians*, p. 68; idem, *History II*, p. 240.

256. Duchesne-Guillemin, "Zoroastrian Religion," p. 899; Widengren, *Les religions*, p. 249.

257. Duchesne-Guillemin, "Religion," p. 349; Gnoli, "Zurvanism," in *Encyclopedia*, 15: 595–96.

258. Duchesne-Guillemin, *Western Response*, p. 18.

259. M. Boyce, "Some Reflections on Zurvanism," *BSOAS* 19 (1957): 308.

Zurvanism ever had separate rites, a special rite, a special priesthood and different places of worship or gathering."[260] He adds: "In conclusion, I feel that the separate existence of a Zurvanite religion and church is more the creation of European scholars than a true picture of what existed in Sassanian times."[261]

Cosmology

No detailed cosmology is outlined in the Gathas. Ahuramazda created the Immortals and through them the cosmos. In Yasna 44.3–7 Zoroaster, after asking rhetorically who created the sun, stars, and moon, the water and the plants, light and darkness, morning, noon, and night, acknowledges that Ahuramazda is the creator of all things. The Two Spirits created life and death (Y. 30.4). Ahuramazda gave a body to the soul of life and created deeds and words that man might decide freely (Y. 31.11).

The most complete cosmology is found in the Bundahishn (1.23–28; 25.1–2). The world is planned by Ohrmazd as a means of overcoming Ahriman in the *getig* or material state, since both are invincible in the *menog* or spiritual state.[262] The world was made in six stages: First the sky was made of stone and rock crystal, a second stage produced the water, and a third stage formed the earth. From the surface of the latter grew mountains, the greatest of which was Hara Berezaiti or "High Hara" (Pahlavi Harburz, the Alburz Mountains near Tehran). The earth was divided into seven circular continents, only one of which, Xhvaniratha, was to be inhabited by man. The fourth stage came with the creation of vegetation, and the fifth stage was animal life. The latter included a uniquely created bull, who was killed by Ahriman. From the bull's seed were born all kinds of beneficent animals, and from his limbs sprang a variety of plants including twelve kinds of medicinal herbs.[263] As the primal bull died, fifty-five species of corn and twelve species of medicinal herbs grew from its limbs. In the sixth and final stage, man was created. Ahriman was responsible for the creation of evil evidenced in darkness, night, winter, drought, infertile land, vermin, sickness, and death.[264]

260. Frye, "Zurvanism Again," p. 67.

261. Ibid., p. 73.

262. Shaked, "First Man, First King," p. 248. For the text and translation of the Bundahishn, see F. Justi, *Der Bundehesh* (Hidesheim: Georg Olms, 1976, reprint of 1868 edition).

263. Boyce, *History I*, chapter 5; Hinnells, *Zoroastrianism and the Parsis*, p. 59.

264. Hasenfratz, "Iran und der Dualismus," pp. 41–42.

Anthropology

Zoroastrian mythology has two important primal figures. The first is Yima (later called Jamshid), the first king. He is a semidivine figure with a flaw.[265] The second figure is the first just man, Gaya Maretan ("mortal Life" [Yt. 13.87]; Pahl. Gayomart [Bd. ch. 15]). Ahriman kills Gayomart, whose corpse produces different kinds of metals.[266] Gayomart's semen was preserved and produced a single rhubarb stalk, which after forty years developed into the first human couple, Mashya and Mashyānag.[267] Ahriman so confused them they thought that he was their creator. After they produced offspring they devoured them, until Ahuramazda took away their taste for children.[268]

First of all man has a *tan* or body, and in addition four invisible aspects: *jan*, "life" or "vitality"; *urvan*, "soul"; *bod*, "light"; and *frawahr* or *fravashi*, "spirit" (see Yt. 13.74 and 149).[269] Man does not inherit a sinful nature, but becomes just or sinful by using his free will to choose between good and evil.

Soteriology

Zoroaster taught that man would be judged by whether his good deeds outweighed his evil deeds (Y. 31.20, 33.1, 49.4).[270] According to Zoroaster, "salvation depended upon works alone, and there could be no intervention, whether compassionate or capricious, by an omnipotent Being to alter their consequence."[271] Not only do men save themselves by their good deeds, but in effect they save Ahuramazda also! According to Shaked:

> Man in the actual world is thus presented as the main battleground for the spirits. The outcome of the battle is in fact entirely dependent on man, the ultimate victory is effected by man's ability to vanquish the demons within himself.[272]

265. Shaked, "First Man, First King," pp. 240–41.
266. Duchesne-Guillemin, "Religion of Ancient Iran," p. 366.
267. Boyce, *History I*, pp. 97–98.
268. Hinnells, *Zoroastrianism and the Parsis*, p. 60.
269. Darrow, "Zoroaster Amalgamated," p. 128.
270. Boyce, *History I*, p. 237; G. Widengren, "Salvation in Iranian Religion," in *Man and His Salvation*, S. G. F. Brandon Festschrift, eds. E. Sharp and J. Hinnells (Manchester: Manchester University Press, 1973), pp. 315ff.
271. Ibid., p. 246; see Kotwal and Boyd, *Guide*, p. 98; R. Masani, *Zoroastrianism* (New York: Collier, 1962), p. 72.
272. Shaked, "Notions," p. 83.

Later Zoroastrianism developed rites of repentance and expiation (Av. *paitita*, Pahl. *patīt*).[273] Boyce comments: "None of these activities can be logically reconciled with Zoroaster's fundamental teaching that each man must achieve his own salvation, and that the only way to do so is through good thoughts, words, and acts."[274]

Saoshyants

The word *saoshyant* is sometimes translated "redeemer," but this is no savior from sin and guilt. The word is a future active participle from the verb *to benefit* and means "he who will bring benefit," that is, a "benefactor."[275] In the Gathas it is used three times in the singular. Some believe Zoroaster was obliquely referring to himself by this term.[276]

Others believe that in the Gathas the term was used of those future benefactors who would help bring about the final renovation.[277] Zoroaster may have hoped to be one of them.[278] According to Duchesne-Guillemin:

> Zoroaster did not give himself out to be the redeemer. When his prayers call the redeemer who is to renew existence, he means the prince who shall accept his doctrine and realize the Dominion of Righteousness and Good Mind. He even allows the role of redeemer to any man, provided he practices righteousness.[279]

The doctrine of a future redeemer who will drive out the Lie from the world of truth is developed in the Yashts (19.86–96).[280] The still later Pahlavi texts teach the future coming of three world saviors born of the seed of Zoroaster preserved in a lake in eastern Iran. These saviors would smite demons, resurrect the dead, and bring about the restoration of the primeval paradise.[281] Boyce offers the unprovable

273. Boyce, *History I*, p. 319.

274. Boyce, *Persian Stronghold*, p. 156; see idem, *History I*, p. 328; Kreyenbroek, *Sraoša*, p. 151.

275. J. R. Hinnells, "Zoroastrian Saviour Imagery and Its Influence on the New Testament," *Numen* 16 (1969): 164.

276. Boyce, *History I*, p. 234; S. S. Hartman, "Der grosse Zarathustra," *Orientalia Suecana* 14/15 (1965–1966): 106.

277. E. Yarshater, "Iranian Common Beliefs," in Yarshater, *CHI* III.1, p. 356.

278. Duchesne-Guillemin, "Religion of Ancient Iran," p. 367.

279. Duchesne-Guillemin, *Hymns*, p. 19.

280. Yarshater, "Iranian Common Beliefs," p. 356.

281. C. Colpe, "Development of Religious Thought," in *CHI* III.2, p. 859; W. G. Oxtoby, "Reflections on the Idea of Salvation," in *Man and His Salvation*, p. 23.

suggestion that this later doctrine had its origins in the Achaemenian period.[282]

Duties

Zoroastrians are to destroy such noxious creatures as ants and snakes (compare Herodotus 1.140).[283] They are to cultivate *humat* ("good thoughts"), *hukht* ("good words"), and *huvarsth* ("good deeds"). Among the latter are agriculture, industry, and marriage. A Pahlavi creed has the Zoroastrian acknowledging:

> My first (duty) on earth is to confess the Religion, to practice it, and to take part in its worship and to be steadfast in it.
> My second (duty) is to take a wife and to procreate earthly offspring, and to be strenuous and steadfast in this.[284]
> My third (duty) is to cultivate and till the soil.
> My fourth to treat all livestock justly.[285]

Zoroastrians have steadfastly opposed asceticism, celibacy, abortion, and homosexuality.

Among the most important duties are those of a ritualistic character. Every child must undergo the *Naojote* or initiation ceremony, generally between twelve to fourteen years of age.[286] During this rite each child is invested with the sacred *kusti* and *sudre* by a priest. The *sudre* is a cotton undershirt that has a pocket symbolizing a purse, which should be full of good thoughts, words, and deeds. The *kusti* is a long woven belt made of seventy-two threads of white lamb's wool, which is wrapped three times around the waist and tied before and behind with a fourfold knot.[287] It represents the armor of God against evil. Except at the time of bathing a Parsi must always wear the *kusti* and *sudre.* The *kusti* must be retied after leaving the bed in the morning, after a call of nature, before prayers, at the time of bathing, and before meals. A modern Parsi scholar goes so far as to aver: "The *sudre* and *kusti* are the foundation of our religion. If one believes in God, and the

282. Boyce, *Zoroastrians,* p. 74; idem, "On the Antiquity," p. 75.

283. Boyce, *History II,* p. 182; Shaked, *Wisdom,* p. 217.

284. According to Parsi texts, a childless person cannot cross the Chinvat Bridge even if he has performed many good deeds. He must have an adopted son; if he died before he could adopt, his relatives must appoint an adopted son for him. See J. D. C. Pavry, *The Zoroastrian Doctrine of a Future Life,* 2d ed. (New York: Columbia University Press, 1929; New York: AMS, 1965 reprint), p. 109.

285. Zaehner, *Teachings of the Magi,* p. 22.

286. Boyce, *Persian Stronghold,* pp. 12–15; but Duchesne-Guillemin, "Zoroastrian Religion," p. 897, writing of the age for the initiation says: "The exact age is unknown, but since it is now about 7 in India and 10 in Iran it seems safe to put it somewhere between these two figures."

287. Boyce, *History I,* p. 257.

The initiation of a young Zoroastrian girl with the sacred *kusti* and *sudre*. (Courtesy of Professor Mary Boyce)

Avesta as the word of God, but does not wear *sudre* and *kusti,* he is not a Zoroastrian."[288]

Prayers must be said five times a day: at sunrise, at the midday meal, in the afternoon, at dusk, and between midnight and sunrise. Prayers must be made standing before a fire[289] or facing the sun, untying and retying the *kusti.* The mouth must be covered to keep the breath from contaminating the sacred fire. The Parsi not only prays to Ohrmazd, but also execrates Ahriman.[290] Prayers are not spontaneous but are recitations of scriptural texts. As Moulton observes:

> We notice how very prominent is the conception of prayer as the due repetition of formulae. The Gathas are now *manthra,* sacred spells of ineffable power, to be repeated without a flaw, by men who may or may not understand them.[291]

288. Kotwal and Boyd, *Guide,* p. 40.

289. Boyce, *History II,* p. 51, attributes this custom to Zoroaster himself: "The great innovation made in this ancient cult by Zoroaster had been to appoint fire as the symbol of righteousness, before which every member of his community should pray five times a day."

290. Boyce, *Zoroastrians,* p. 32.

291. Moulton, *Treasure of the Magi,* p. 89.

Fire

Fire was used by non-Zoroastrian Iranians and others in cultic contexts such as at the Median site of Tepe Nush-i Jan. Whether or not non-Zoroastrians had a cult of perpetual fire is a matter of dispute.[292] In the Gathas Zoroaster associated fire with Asha as in Yasna 34.4: "Thy fire, O Lord, mighty through Righteousness, swift and powerful" (trans. Duchesne-Guillemin).[293] Fire is venerated in Yasht 62.

Darius is shown in reliefs before a fire altar. Whether the quadrangular towers at Pasargadae and Naqsh-i Rustam were used as fire temples is uncertain (see chapters 9 and 10). Under Artaxerxes II (404–359 B.C.) temples with cult statues of Anahita were established. Boyce has proposed that it was at this time that the orthodox Zoroastrians established fire temples as a countermeasure.[294]

Because fire is considered the symbol of Ahuramazda, it is protected from even the rays of the sun and from the gaze of unbelievers in the inner sanctuary of fire temples. Eckehard Kulke comments: "Fire stands at the center of the Zoroastrian cult; no ceremony can take place without fire being present. Of course, fire is only the symbol for Ahura Mazda, the light and the truth. . . . It is therefore incorrect to speak of the Zoroastrians as 'fire worshippers.' "[295] A Pahlavi text advises: "Go three times a day to the Fire Temple and do homage to the Fire; for he who makes a habit of going to the Fire Temple and of doing homage to the Fire, will be blessed with a greater share of both worldly wealth and of holiness."[296]

Priests

Atharvans, "fire priests," reciting from memory verses of the Avesta, carefully feed the perpetual fire with sandalwood. They have their mouths covered with the *paiti-dhana,* a cloth to prevent polluting the

292. This is affirmed by Wikander, *Feuerpriester,* pp. 56ff., but is denied by Boyce, "Iconoclasm," p. 93.

293. Boyce, *History I,* p. 212.

294. Boyce, "On the Zoroastrian Temple Cult of Fire," pp. 455ff.; idem, *History II,* p. 221.

295. Kulke, *Parsees in India,* p. 20. J. W. Boyd and F. W. Kotwal, "Worship in a Zoroastrian Fire Temple," *IIJ* 26 (1983): 293, declare: "A properly consecrated and fueled fire is believed to be a spark of the endless light which is the abode of the infinite, a physical epiphany of the realm of Ahura Mazda Himself. . . . In addition to being a concrete embodiment of the light of the infinite, fire also epitomizes the principle of cosmic order for Zoroastrians."

296. Zaehner, *Teachings of the Magi,* p. 26. According to Hinnells, *Zoroastrianism,* p. 60, the Parsis had only one fire temple until the seventeenth century; today they have 8 cathedral fire temples and 180 ordinary temples. For photos of fire temples, see Hartman, *Parsism,* plates 7–13. See also M. Boyce, "On the Sacred Fires of the Zoroastrians," *BSOAS* 31 (1968): 52–68.

fire. Another name for priest is *mobed,* "he who understands much"; the chief *mobed* is called the *dastur.*[297]

The training of priests begins at the age of seven.[298] The priest must learn to recite all seventy-two chapters of the Yasna liturgy and other texts from memory.[299] In accordance with their high regard for marriage, Zoroastrian priests must be married. As in the case of Mandaeanism in Iran and Iraq, the dearth of candidates for the priesthood among the Parsis today threatens the survival of Zoroastrianism.[300]

Animal Sacrifices

Under the Achaemenids animal sacrifices were offered, as illustrated on a number of cylinder seals.[301] Earlier scholars interpreted Zoroaster's preaching in the Gathas as a condemnation of cattle sacrifices. Other scholars have concluded that he did not condemn animal sacrifices as such, but only certain abuses of the daiva worshipers.[302] Boyce argued that in an imperfect world, corrupted by Ahriman, Zoroastrians must kill, "but they must limit the wrong which they thus do to animals by slaying them as mercifully as possible, and always consecrating them first."[303] The sacrifice of bulls is mentioned in the Avesta. In the Yasna (11.4–5) the god Haoma is offered a tongue and a left eye, evidently of the sacrificial bull. Today milk represents the *gav* or cow in the Yasna ceremony.

Haoma

The most important daily ceremony involves the pressing of the sacred haoma (compare Vedic *soma,* Pahl. *hōm*). The etymology of the word indicates it was a substance that was pressed or crushed.[304] Today the Parsis substitute the ephedra plant for the original haoma. The identity of the haoma is one of the most disputed issues in Iranian studies.

297. Kotwal and Boyd, *Guide,* p. 184.

298. Boyce, "Zoroaster the Priest," p. 23.

299. Boyd, "Zoroastrianism," p. 115.

300. E. Yamauchi, "The Present Status of Mandaean Studies," *JNES* 25 (1966): 88.

301. P. R. S. Moorey, "Aspects of Worship and Ritual on Achaemenid Seals," in *Akten des VII Internationalen Kongresses für iranische Kunst und Archäologie* (Berlin: Dietrich Reimer, 1979), pp. 218–26.

302. Duchesne-Guillemin, *La religion,* pp. 99–103; Duchesne-Guillemin, "Religion," p. 353; Scerrato, "Excavations," p. 16.

303. Boyce, *Persian Stronghold,* p. 244; Boyce, "Zoroaster the Priest," p. 31.

304. Boyce, *History I,* p. 157.

Over one hundred different plants have been suggested, including ephedra,[305] grapes, hemp,[306] rhubarb,[307] harmaline,[308] and ginseng.[309]

The most controversial suggestion for the identity of the soma/haoma plant is Robert G. Wasson's suggestion that it was the Fly Agaric (*Amanita muscaria*) mushroom.[310] This is a hallucinogenic mushroom.[311] Siberian shamans eat it and then swallow their urine to concentrate its effectiveness. Although some scholars have accepted Wasson's suggestion,[312] others have objected because the mushroom is red, whereas haoma is described as green or yellow.[313] Most scholars believe the centrality of the haoma ritual was the result of the same devolution that restored the pre-Zoroastrian gods as yazatas.[314] Noting the conservatism of Zoroastrian ritual, however, Boyce has maintained that Zoroaster must have condemned certain abuses but not the haoma cult itself.[315]

The Yasna Ceremony

The most important Zoroastrian ritual is the Yasna ("veneration" or "worship") ceremony. The current form of the rite was probably established by liturgical reform during Sasanian times.[316] The Yasna rite reproduces the primordial offering that brought plants into existence and anticipates the eschatological coming of Zoroaster's three saoshyant sons. The Dadistan-i Denig (chapter 48) maintains the rite makes

305. Boyce, *Zoroastrians,* p. 5.

306. A. H. Godbey, "Incense and Poison Ordeals in the Ancient Orient," *AJSL* 46 (1930): 221.

307. Colpe, "Zarathustra," p. 333.

308. Schwartz, "Old Eastern Iranian World View," p. 653; D. S. Flattery and M. Schwartz, *Haoma and Harmaline* (Berkeley: University of California Press, 1984).

309. G. L. Windfuhr, "Haoma/Soma: The Plant," in *Papers in Honour of Professor Mary Boyce,* pp. 699–726.

310. R. G. Wasson, "The Soma of the Rig Veda: What Was It?" *JAOS* 91 (1971): 169–87; idem, *Soma and the Fly-Agaric: Mr. Wasson's Rejoinder to Professor Brough* (Cambridge: Botanical Museum of Harvard University, 1972); idem, *Soma: Divine Mushroom of Immortality* (New York: Harcourt, Brace, Jovanovich, 1973). For an attempt to explain certain aspects of Greek religion on the basis of this mushroom, see R. G. Wasson, S. Kramrisch, J. Ott, and C. A. P. Ruck, *Persephone's Quest: Entheogens and the Origins of Religion* (New Haven: Yale University Press, 1986).

311. This mushroom was the focus for J. M. Allegro's *Sacred Mushroom and the Cross* (London: Hodder and Stroughton, 1970), an outrageous attempt to explain away Judaism and Christianity as disguised fertility cults.

312. See Smith, "Wasson's *SOMA*," pp. 480–500.

313. J. Brough, "Soma and *Amanita muscaria,*" *BSOAS* 34 (1971): 331–62; I. Gershevitch, "An Iranianist's View of the Soma Controversy," in *Mémorial Jean de Menasche,* eds. P. Gignoux and A. Tafazzoli (Louvain: Imprimerie Orientaliste, 1974), pp. 45–75; Malandra, *Introduction,* p. 151.

314. Gershevitch, "Zoroaster's Own Contribution," p. 54; Gnoli, "Zoroastrianism," p. 586.

315. Boyce, *History I,* pp. 217–19.

316. Boyce, *Zoroastrians,* p. 125.

the yazatas rejoice and vexes the demons.[317] During the ritual the seventy-two chapters of the Yasna liturgy are recited from memory. These include the Gathas of Zoroaster, a Yasht to Hom (chapters 9–11), a creed (chapter 12), various prayers, and invocations.[318]

The Yasna ceremony is performed in a special room of the fire temple. The room is demarcated by *pavis* or channels of water.[319] The ceremony is performed by two priests, a *zotar,* and his assistant, a *raspi.* Among the objects employed are the mortar and pestle, various vessels, and metal rods, which have replaced the plant twigs of the original barsom. Goat's milk called *jiwam* ("life") serves as a substitute for an original animal sacrifice.

The first part of the ceremony is called the *paragna.*[320] This is followed by a second pressing of the elements. The *zohr* or hom drink is made of a mixture of pressings from ephedra and pomegranate twigs mixed with milk. This is filtered through a special *waras* ring made from the hairs of a pure white bull.[321] The *dron* or sacred bread is a wheaten cake on which is placed some clarified butter. The hom drink is the first liquid given to a Parsi baby; it is the last drink given to a dying Parsi.

Marriage

Zoroastrians have regarded marriage as a sacred duty. At one stage they also advocated incestuous marriage—a practice that is denied by Parsis.[322] The practice was known as *khvaetvadatha,* "Next-of-Kin" marriage. A father could marry his daughter, and a man could marry his sister, daughter, or even his mother.[323] This bizarre practice was noted by Greek, Latin, Armenian, and Syriac writers. For example, Minucius Felix (*Octavius* 31.3) observed *ius est apud Persas misceri cum matribus* ("among Persians it is proper to marry [their] mothers").

Xvaevadatha is not mentioned in the Gathas; it appears five times in the Avesta, including a reference in the Fravarane, the profession of faith recited by new converts (Y. 12.9; compare Dk. 7.1, Vr. 3.3). The

317. E. W. West, trans., *Pahlavi Texts: Part II,* S.B.E. XVIII (Delhi: Motilal Banarsidass, 1965 reprint of 1882 edition), pp. 159ff.

318. L. H. Mills, trans., *The Zend-Avesta: Part III,* S.B.E. XXXI (Delhi: Motilal Banarsidass, 1965 reprint of 1887 edition), pp. 195–332.

319. E. S. Drower, *Water into Wine* (London: John Murray, 1956), p. 200.

320. F. M. Kotwal and J. W. Boyd, "The Zoroastrian *paragna* Ritual," *JMS* 2 (1977): 18–52.

321. See Drower, *Water into Wine,* chapter 15 for a description of the Yasna rite; for illustrations, see Hartman, *Parsism,* plates 24, 32–38.

322. J. Katrak, *Marriage in Ancient Iran* (Bombay: Katrak, 1965).

323. Boyce, *History II,* p. 75; O. Klíma, "Zur problematik der Ehe-Institution im alten Iran," *AO* 34 (66): 554–69.

Pahlavi texts warmly recommended the practice. Schwartz comments: "It is important to realize that incestuous marriages were not merely tolerated, but indeed regarded as acts of piety and great merit, and even efficacious against the demonic forces."[324] To make these marriages was a religious duty for king and commoner, layman and priest.[325]

Conversion

Modern Parsis do not believe in proselytizing. Their priests will not even initiate children of intermarriages.[326] This is based on the conviction that one must be born into a Parsi family in order to keep the stringent purity laws.[327] Although the Denkard proclaims that the revelation to Zoroaster was meant for all the people of the world, Firoze Kotwal, a Parsi scholar, comments:

> Insofar as Zoroastrian practices are concerned, therefore, it is the Parsi and Irani people who possess the indigenous tradition. Hence, although everyone can advantageously follow the ethical principles, not everyone can become a part and parcel of this ethnic group.[328]

Some American Parsis have objected that this policy is contrary to the teachings of Zoroaster and is suicidal as far as the survival of Parsism is concerned.[329]

Impurity and Purity

As with many other religious communities, the Zoroastrians developed elaborate concepts of purity and impurity that separated them from all others.[330] Anything that leaves the body is impure including one's spittle, which is why the priests wear a veil over their mouths.[331]

324. Schwartz, "Old Eastern Iranian World," p. 656.

325. Duchesne-Guillemin, "Religion," p. 359. In this regard they were different from the consanguineous marriages in Egypt, which were practiced by the pharaohs and Ptolemies. See J. Černy, "Consanguineous Marriages in Pharaonic Egypt," *JEA* 40 (1954): 23–29; H. Bell, "Brother and Sister Marriage in Graeco-Roman Egypt," *Revue Internationale des Droits de L'Antiquité,* 2d ser. (1949): 83–92.

326. Hinnells, *Zoroastrianism,* p. 51; idem, "Parsis," p. 132; Boyd, "Zoroastrianism," p. 113; Axelrod, "Myth and Identity," p. 161.

327. Boyce, *History I,* p. 295.

328. Kotwal and Boyd, *Guide,* p. 25.

329. For example, K. Antia, *The Argument for Acceptance* (Chicago: Parsiana, 1985).

330. See E. Yamauchi, "*ṭāhēr,* be pure, clean," and "*ṭāmē',* become unclean," in *Theological Wordbook of the Old Testament,* eds. R. L. Harris, G. L. Archer, and B. K. Waltke (Chicago: Moody, 1980), 1: 343–45, 349–51.

331. Boyce, *Persian Stronghold,* p. 99.

According to the Vendidad (6.29) one should not defile the water by casting into it bones, hair, flesh, urine, or blood. Nail parings and hair trimmings are considered defiling[332] and must be buried during a special ceremony.[333] Menstruating women are considered especially impure (Vd. 16). Among Irani Zoroastrians such a woman was kept isolated in places "where she could not see sky or water, earth, plants or animals, men or fire."[334] Noxious creatures of Ahriman such as beetles, tarantulas, and wasps are unclean. A scrupulous Zoroastrian will not readily touch a dead fly with his bare hand. Death is, of course, the greatest impurity.

Ritual pollutions are purified by the application of *gomez* or urine from a bull or cow; *nirang* or consecrated bull's urine is drunk for inward cleansing.[335] For major pollutions a nine-day purificatory rite called the *bareshnum* is required. This includes a seven-hour recitation of the Vendidad to consecrate the bull's urine.[336]

One of the requirements of the *bareshnum* is the presence of a "four-eyed" dog, that is, one with two spots under its eyes.[337] The dog is considered to be the creature closest to man. In pious Zoroastrian families the dog is fed even before the humans.[338] Food thus given to the dog is believed to nourish the souls of the dead.[339] When a Parsi dies, his body should be shown to a dog as his gaze drives away demons.[340]

Death and Exposure

Kreyenbroek observes: "There is probably no occasion when the forces of evil and pollution manifest themselves so uncompromisingly, and have to be confronted so directly, as the death of a believer."[341] When death comes, the Zoroastrians must try to dispose of the polluting corpse within a day if possible.[342] The body is washed in *gomez*.

To bury a man or a dog in the earth was to be guilty of defiling the earth (Vd. 3.36–41, 6.3; Y. 65.8). Nor should one defile water or fire with the dead. This is the rationale for exposing the dead to vultures.

332. Hinnells, *Zoroastrianism*, p. 56.
333. K. Jamaspasa, "The Ritual of Hair-Trimming and Nail-Paring in Zoroastrianism," in *Monumentum Georg Morgenstierne*, pp. 316–32.
334. Boyce, *Persian Stronghold*, p. 100.
335. Boyce, *History I*, pp. 296–97, 311–12; Boyce, *Persian Stronghold*, pp. 92–93; Hinnells, *Zoroastrianism*, p. 56.
336. Hartman, *Parsism*, pp. 22–23, plates 28–30.
337. Duchesne-Guillemin, "Religion," p. 356.
338. Boyce, *Persian Stronghold*, p. 143.
339. Boyce, *History I*, p. 163.
340. Ibid., p. 303; Kotwal and Boyd, *Guide*, pp. 76–77.
341. Kreyenbroek, *Sraoša*, p. 150.
342. Boyce, *Persian Stronghold*, p. 138.

The Vendidad (6.46) prescribes: "In this way the dead should be taken near the corpse-eating birds." This is to be done as soon as possible lest a foul wind exuding from the corpse bring harm to others.[343]

The exposure of the dead was a custom attested by Herodotus (1.140) for the magi and was also practiced in Central Asia (see Strabo 11.11.3).[344] Exposure of the dead was not followed by the Achaemenids and is not found in the oldest parts of the Avesta. The oldest archaeological evidence for the practice may be either Median tombs (chapter 1) or a Lycian tomb that has an inscription explicitly identifying an *astodana* or an ossuary for the deposit of bones after the flesh has been removed.[345]

Parsis in Bombay still dispose of their dead in *dakhmas* or "towers of silence."[346] The corpse is stripped by vultures within a half-hour. The sun-bleached bones are eventually cast into a pit. Where there are no vultures, Parsis now dispose of their dead by burial in concrete vaults or even by cremation![347]

The Chinvat Bridge

Zoroaster spoke of the judgment of individuals at the *Chinvato Peretu* or "the Bridge of the separator" (Y. 46.10, 51.13), which he anticipated crossing with his followers. The Vendidad (19.30) sets the beginning of this bridge leading over hell to paradise on the heights of Mount Alburz. The later Bundahishn (30.1, 9–13) gives an elaborate account of the nature of the bridge. If the soul is righteous the bridge becomes broad, but if the soul is wicked the bridge stands on its edge and shrinks to a razor's edge.

Each man's deeds are weighed carefully on scales of hair's-breadth precision before Mithra, Sraosha, and Rashnu. If his good deeds outweigh his evil deeds, he will be saved. Three days after his death he will meet his own *daena* or "conscience" personified. According to the Denkard (9.19) this will be a beautiful female figure if he has been righteous, and a hideous hag if he has been wicked. The former figure is described in more detail in the Hadokht Nask: "There appears to him his own Conscience in the form of a Maiden, beautiful, radiant, white-

343. Kotwal and Boyd, *Guide*, p. 76.

344. Frye, "Religion in Fars," p. 175. Y. A. Rapoport, "Some Aspects of the Evolution of Zoroastrian Funeral Rites," in *XXVth International Congress of Orientalists* (Moscow: Oriental Literature, 1960), p. 3; E. Benveniste, "Coutumes funéraires de l'Arachosie ancienne," in *A Locust's Leg*, S. H. Taqizadeh Festschrift, eds. W. B. Henning and E. Yarshater (London: Lund Humphries, 1962), pp. 39–43.

345. Boyce, *Zoroastrians*, p. 59; Boyce, *History II*, p. 210.

346. Hartman, *Parsism*, plates 14–15.

347. Whitehurst, "Zoroastrian Response," p. 279; Hinnells, *Zoroastrianism*, p. 61.

armed, robust, fair-faced, erect, high-breasted, of stately form, noble-born, of glorious lineage, fifteen years old in appearance, as beautiful in form as the most beautiful of creatures."[348] The latter figure is described in the Arda Wiraz Namag: "It beheld that which was its own Conscience and deeds, as a whore, naked and decrepit, with exposed thighs in front and buttocks behind, with endless spots . . . like the most noxious creatures."[349]

Heaven, Hell, and Hamestagan

The dwelling-place of the righteous is described in the Gathas as the house of Ahuramazda or the house of Vohu Manah (Y. 32.13). There are numerous descriptions of a paradisical realm in the Yashts (9.9–10, 15.16–17, 17.29–30, 19.32–33) as "a realm without heat or cold, snow or rain; without cares or suffering, tears or pain; a realm without darkness, sickness, old age, or death; a realm where labor and want are equally unknown."[350] A Pahlavi Rivayat proclaims that in paradise, "there is sexual satisfaction without procreation."[351] According to some texts the soul ascends through three stages[352] or through seven stages[353] such as the region of the stars, the moon, and the sun to the paradise of infinite lights.

The fate of the wicked is described by Zoroaster as follows: "Long-lasting darkness, ill food, and wailing—to such an existence shall your conscience lead you by your own deeds, O wicked ones" (Y. 31.20, trans. Duchesne-Guillemin). Hell is also called the "house of worst purpose" (Y. 32.13).

The Pahlavi text Menok-i Khrat declares:

> Then they bring him poison and venom, snakes and scorpions and other noxious reptiles (that flourish) in Hell, and they serve him with these to eat. . . . And the food that he must for the most part eat there is all, as it were, putrid and like unto blood.[354]

The Gathas mention those "whose false [things] and what are just balance" (Y. 33.1) as well as those who are righteous and those who are wicked. Later Pahlavi texts assigned an intermediate state (*Hames-*

348. Pavry, *Zoroastrian Doctrine,* p. 34.

349. Ibid., p. 41.

350. B. Lincoln, "On the Imagery of Paradise," *Indogermanische Forschungen* 85 (1980): 159. See the end of chapter 9.

351. Cited by Shaked, "On the Notions," p. 86.

352. Duchesne-Guillemin, "Religion," p. 366.

353. Kotwal and Boyd, *Guide,* p. 144.

354. Zaehner, *Teachings,* p. 138.

tagan) between earth and the sphere of the stars, for those whose good deeds and wicked deeds exactly balanced. There they suffered only the pains of heat and cold.[355]

The End of the Ages

Zoroastrian texts speak of various millennial epochs of six, nine, and twelve thousand years. Boyce suggests that the shortest scheme was original.[356] The eschatological periodization of twelve millennia was established in the Bundahishn (chapter 34).[357] The latter chronology was divided into four epochs of three millennia each.

The first epoch (0–3000) was characterized by Ohrmazd's original creation in the *menog* or spiritual state. Yarshater summarizes this period as follows:

> For 3,000 years the world remained in this state, without movement, thought, or tangible substance. The time was fixed at noon, and peace and serenity prevailed. Ahriman, rising from his abyss of total darkness, caught sight of the Light and the luminous nature of Ohrmazd's world. True to his destructive nature, he invaded it. But faced with the valor and fortitude of Ohrmazd, he rushed back to his abyss and fashioned . . . many demons (dīvs) and death-dealers, then rose for battle.[358]

Ohrmazd and Ahriman agreed upon nine thousand years as the length of the conflict between them.

The second epoch (3000–6000) is the period during which Ohrmazd transforms the *menog* state to the visible, material *getig* state, while Ahriman is incapacitated. Within a single year Ohrmazd created in succession the sky, water, earth, plants, beneficial animals, and fire as a defense against Ahriman.

The third epoch (6000–9000) is the era of *Gumezishn* or "mixture" during which Ahriman and his evil forces attack. The seventh millennium was at first a time of bliss under the primordial Yima before the attack of Ahriman. During the eighth millennium life worsened under the domination of the evil Ashi Dahaka. The era ends with the reign of the Kayanian kings and the Indo-Turanian wars.

The final epoch of *Wizarishn* or "separation" (9000–12,000) begins with the revelation of Ohrmazd to Zoroaster. Zoroaster's sperm was

355. Ibid., pp. 131–32; P. Gignoux, "L'enfer et le paradis d'après les sources pehlevies," *JA* 256 (1968): 225–27.

356. Boyce, *History I*, p. 286.

357. Messina, "Mito," pp. 269ff.

358. Yarshater, "Iranian Common Beliefs," in *CHI* III.1, p. 354.

preserved in Lake Kasaoya in Seistan in eastern Iran. Virgins bathing in this lake would give birth to three saoshyants or saviors. The first of these was to be born 1,000 years after the death of Zoroaster, the second in 11,000, and the third at the end of history in 12,000.[359]

The first savior named Ushedar will renew Zoroaster's message and defeat the forces of evil. After a period of decline, the second savior named Ushedarmah will renew another golden age. The third savior, Asvatereta, will overcome all disease and death. He will usher in the final victory of Ohrmazd over Ahriman.[360]

Resurrection

There is no certain affirmation of a belief in a resurrection by Zoroaster in the Gathas.[361] Yasna 34.14 is sometimes cited for such a belief, but this clearly refers to bodily prosperity in this life. Some scholars have argued that Yasna 30.7, where Armaiti gives body and breath to endure the ordeal of molten metal, may provide an implicit basis for the later developed teaching of the resurrection.[362]

The concept of the resurrection does not appear in the Yasna Haptanghaiti, and appears relatively sparsely in the Younger Avesta. Yashts 19.11 declares that Ahuramazda made the creatures

> so that they may restore the world, which will [thenceforth] never grow old and never die, never decaying and never rotting, ever living and ever increasing, and master of its wish, when the dead will rise, when life and immortality will come, and the world will be restored at its wish.[363]

Some infer the resurrection from Yasna 33.10: "Raise up the bodily life of man to the height of bliss through Vohu Mana, Xshathra and Asha."

The fullest account of the resurrection appears in the Pahlavi

359. Boyce, *History II,* pp. 242–43.

360. Boyce, "On the Antiquity," p. 68, believes that the scheme of three saviors was developed in the third century B.C.; and that the concept of a world year of twelve millennia began circa 400 B.C. (p. 75).

361. Bode and Nanavutty, *Songs of Zarathustra,* p. 24; Hultgard, "Das Judenthum," p. 543; F. König, *Zarathustras Jenseitsvorstellungen und das Alte Testament* (Vienna: Herder, 1964), p. 279; P. L. Suarez, "Escatologia personal en los antiquos Persos," *Semana Biblica Española* 15 (1954): 19.

362. For example, Boyce, *History II,* p. 198: "the resurrection of the dead, alluded to, it seems, in Y. 30.7"; R. Mayer, "Der Auferstehungsglaube in der iranischen Religion," *Kairos* 7 (1965): 195–98.

363. J. Darmesteter, trans., *The Zend-Avesta; Part II,* S.B.E. XXIII (Delhi: Motilal Banarsidass, 1965 reprint of 1883 edition), p. 290. Theopompus (fourth century B.C.) attributes a belief in an *anastasis* ("resurrection") to the Persians. Herodotus's (3.62) statement attributed to Prexaspes—"If then the dead can rise, you may look to see Astyages the Mede rise up against you; but if nature's order be not changed, assuredly no harm to you will arise from Smerdis"—seems to indicate a lack of a belief in a resurrection among the Persians in the fifth century B.C.

Bundahishn (chapter 30). After Gayomart and the first human pair are raised, then the rest of mankind will arise with the coming of the final saoshyant to be subject to the fiery judgment.

The Fiery Ordeal and the Final Restoration

Zoroaster spoke of a judgment by molten metal (Y.30.7; 32.7; 51.9), apparently referring to an ordeal in which molten metal was poured on an accused person.[364] As developed in the Bundahishn, the *Frashkert* or final restoration will be introduced by a fiery ordeal: "Then the divine Airyaman and Fire will melt all the metal in the hills and mountains and will cause all souls, both righteous and wicked to go through an ordeal by fire and molten metal for their purification."[365] "The sins of the damned will be burnt away by the ordeal and the wicked will be purged."[366]

It appears that contrary to Zoroaster's own teaching[367] a universalistic doctrine developed in post-Sasanian times. This taught the ultimate abolition of hell so that all men will be cleansed and enter the kingdom of God.[368] The world will then be restored to the paradise-like days of Gayomart. Zoroastrian theologians disagreed as to whether Ahriman was destroyed or was rendered eternally helpless.

Influences of Zoroastrianism

On Greek Philosophy

A myriad of works circulated under the name of Zoroaster in the Hellenistic world. Greek sources made Zoroaster the teacher of Pythagoras. A fragment of Aristotle's *Peri philosophias* associated Plato's teaching with the dualism of the magi.[369]

A few scholars such as Robert Eisler (1910) and Richard Reitzenstein (1924) accepted these traditions at face value.[370] Jacques Duchesne-

364. Boyce, *History I*, p. 35.

365. Menasce, *Une Encyclopédie*, p. 21; Pavry, *Zoroastrian Doctrine*, p. 2.

366. Yarshater, "Iranian Common Beliefs," p. 357.

367. Moulton, *Treasure of the Magi*, p. 157: "It does not appear, however, that in Zarathustra's own thought the annihilation of evil and evil beings was contemplated. For him the 'House of the Lie' is to be the permanent abode of those who choose here to follow the Lie."

368. Boyce, *History I*, p. 242.

369. Duchesne-Guillemin, *Western Response*, p. 4.

370. Ibid., p. 70. See R. Afnan, *Zoroaster's Influence on Greek Thought* (New York: Philosophical Library, 1965); idem, *Zoroaster's Influence on Anaxagoras, the Greek Tragedians, and Socrates* (New York: Philosophical Library, 1969).

Guillemin has argued that Heraclitus, an early pre-Socratic philosopher, may have been inspired by Iranian ideas on fire and truth.[371]

But most scholars are sceptical about such traditions. As Frye observes:

> Further the Zoroastrian origin of Plato's dualism is most unlikely since any ethical dualism in Plato should be based on his metaphysical dualism, and an Ahriman has no place in Plato's thought. In my opinion it is now convincingly established that Classical opinions of the Iranian origin of Platonic, or for that matter other Greek, philosophy are based on a later Hellenistic construction, perhaps all to be traced to Aristoxenos [fl. 318 B.C.], who made Pythagoras a student of Zoroaster. We must never forget that, surmises aside, there is no evidence for schools of philosophy, or even a fixed Zoroastrian orthodoxy with scholasticism in Iran before the late Parthian-Sassanian period.[372]

On Judaism

Since the initial suggestion of Count Constantin in 1791, numerous scholars have assumed that Zoroastrianism influenced Judaism. This point of view was vigorously promoted at the beginning of this century by the History of Religions School.[373] Especially influential was Wilhelm Bousset's *Die Religion des Judentums in späthellenistischen Zeitalter* (1902; 3d ed., 1926). Other early scholars who affirmed a strong Iranian influence on Judaism included Nathan Söderblom (1901) and Alfred Bertholet (1916).[374]

Currently many important scholars maintain the thesis of Zoroastrian influence on Judaism. These include Duchesne-Guillemin,[375] Gnoli,[376] Hinnells,[377] Anders Hultgard,[378] Joseph Kitagawa,[379] Shaked,[380] and David Winston.[381] The foremost champion of Persian

371. J. Duchesne-Guillemin, "Heraclitus and Iran," *HR* 3 (1963): 34–49; idem, "D'Anaximandre à Empédocle," in *La Persia e il Mondo Greco-Romano* (Rome: Accademia Nazionale dei Lincei, 1966), p. 425.

372. R. N. Frye, "Reitzenstein and Qumran Revisited by an Iranian," *HTR* 55 (1962): 265. See also the criticisms of A. D. Nock, "Iranian Influences in Greek Thought," *JHS* 49 (1929): 111–16.

373. E. Yamauchi, "History-of-Religions School," in *New Dictionary of Theology*, eds. S. B. Ferguson and D. F. Wright (Leicester: Inter-Varsity, 1988), pp. 308–9.

374. Duchesne-Guillemin, *Western Response*, chapter 6.

375. Duchesne-Guillemin, "Religion," p. 369.

376. Gnoli, "L'evolution," p. 137.

377. Hinnells, *Zoroastrianism*, p. 7.

378. Hultgard, "Das Judentum," pp. 516–17.

379. J. Kitagawa, "Religious Visions of the End of the World," in S. Shaked et al., *Gilgul*, p. 129.

380. S. Shaked, "Qumran and Iran: Further Considerations," *Israel Oriental Studies* 2 (1972): 444.

381. D. Winston, "The Iranian Component in the Bible, Apocrypha, and Qumran," *HR* 5 (1966): 210–13.

priority is Boyce, who maintains that the Achaemenid period was the age in which Zoroastrianism exerted its influence upon the Jews.[382]

The doctrinal areas where Persian inspiration are claimed include teachings on Satan, demonology, angelology, and especially eschatological beliefs such as judgment, resurrection, apocalypticism, a fiery trial, heaven, and hell. To this list Boyce would also add the doctrines of creation and purity.[383] To sustain such claims one must assume: the chronological priority of the Iranian beliefs; late dates for the Old Testament texts; a close parallelism between the beliefs; and reasons for dependence. A detailed analysis of some of these claims is necessary.

Boyce's position that the Hebrew doctrine of creation was influenced by Zoroaster's teachings is buttressed by the analysis of Isaiah 40–45 by Morton Smith and others as a reflection of Gathic texts (Y. 44–45).[384] But such a claim is based on a disputable interpretation of the Isaianic text[385] and ignores the creation account of Genesis.

Her claim that Zoroastrian rules of purity inspired Jewish practices centers on the role of Nehemiah. She surmises:

> After years of necessary keeping of the Zoroastrian purity code . . . it is hardly surprising that Nehemiah, although a layman, should have concerned himself in Jerusalem with questions of purity among the Jews. Nor does it seem overbold to suppose that it was Zoroastrian example, visible throughout the Empire, which led to the gradual transformation of the Jewish purity code from regulations concerning cultic matters to laws whose observance was demanded of every individual in his daily life. . . .[386]

Such a claim not only ignores the earlier levitical regulations, but requires several dubious assumptions such as the supposition that Artaxerxes I was a rigorous Zoroastrian who required his Jewish cupbearer to maintain the purity restrictions known from later Zoroastrian texts.[387]

The development of the Old Testament Satan, "the accuser" (Job 1:6; Zech. 3:1–2; 1 Chron. 21:1), into the postexilic devil is often

382. Boyce, *History II*, p. xii.

383. Boyce, *Zoroastrians*, pp. 76–77. Compare A. Kashani, *Iranian Influence in Judaism and Christianity* (Tehran: Kayhan, 1970), pp. 48–61, 74–85.

384. Boyce, *History II*, pp. 44–47; M. Smith, "II Isaiah and the Persians," *JAOS* 83 (1963): 415–21.

385. See the criticisms of Nock, "Problem of Zoroaster," p. 284; Duchesne-Guillemin, "Religion et politique," p. 3.

386. Boyce, *History II*, p. 190.

387. J. Barr, "The Question of Religious Influence: The Case of Zoroastrianism, Judaism, and Christianity," *JAAR* 53 (1985): 229, n. 47. Upon summarizing this particular proposal, Barr remarks: "As the reader of this article will have realized, Professor Boyce's reconstructions of what may have happened on the Jewish side are often highly adventurous."

attributed to Iranian influence.[388] But the Jewish devil, who is subordinate to Yahweh, is not like the primordial Ahriman, who is equal in power to Ohrmazd.[389] The strongest evidence for an Iranian influence upon Jewish religion is the probable derivation of the demon Asmodeus in the book of Tobit from the Iranian *Aeshma daeva.*[390] This etymology is favored by most scholars despite some reservations about the phonological equivalents and the difference in character between the two.[391]

With respect to the development of angelology, Boyce states:

> Further, as the Jews came to venerate Yahweh as the all-powerful Creator, they appear to have felt an increasing need to acknowledge lesser immortal beings, his servants, who would bridge the vast gulf that now opened between him and his worshippers. The earliest reference to such a belief appears to be in Isaiah 24.21: "the host of heaven in heaven." It is generally held that Jewish angelology, which became highly developed, reflects to a large extent Zoroastrian belief in the yazatas, with the "seven angels that stand in the presence of God" (Rev. 8.2) corresponding to the Ameša Spentas themselves.[392]

But such a claim ignores the host of pre-Isaianic references to angels, and disregards the differences in character between the Iranian Bounteous Immortals and yazatas who were worshiped and the Hebrew angels who were but servants of the Lord.

It is commonly acknowledged that references to a resurrection hope appear in only a few of the later Old Testament books (Ezek. 37:1–14; Isa. 26:19; Dan. 12:1–2).[393] This is the reason that the Sadducees, who accepted only the Torah (the Pentateuch) as Scripture, rejected the doctrine of the resurrection.[394]

Boyce and other scholars have suggested that the Hebrew doctrine of

388. Duchesne-Guillemin, "Religion," p. 370; Hasenfratz, "Iran und der Dualismus," p. 41. A. Lods, "Les origines de la figure de Satan . . . ," *Mélanges syriens offerts à M. R. Dussaud* (Paris: Geuthner, 1939), 2: 649–66. Lods suggested Satan's origin in the accusatory espionage system of the Persian king.

389. Contrary to the impression left by Boyce, *History II*, p. 195.

390. Schwartz, "Religion of Achaemenid Iran," p. 682; S. Shaked, "Iranian Influence on Judaism," in Davies and Finkelstein, *Cambridge History of Judaism*, p. 318.

391. Reservations are expressed by Barr, "Question," pp. 215–17. On ancient demonology, see E. Yamauchi, "Magic or Miracles? Diseases, Demons and Exorcisms," in *Gospel Perspectives VI: The Miracles of Jesus*, eds. D. Wenham and C. Blomberg (Sheffield: JSOT, 1986), pp. 89–183.

392. Boyce, *History II*, p. 195.

393. K. Schubert, "Die Entwicklung der Auferstehungslehre von der nachexilischen bis zur frührabbinischen Zeit," *BZ* 6 (1962): 177–214.

394. H. C. C. Cavallin, *Life after Death I: . . . An Enquiry into the Jewish Background* (Lund: C. W. K. Gleerup, 1974), p. 23.

a resurrection was based on Zoroastrian beliefs.[395] Hans-Peter Hasenfratz maintains that Ezekiel must have come into contact with Zoroastrian concepts for his vision of the dry bones.[396] Zaehner, however, is more cautious: "We cannot say with any certainty whether the Jews borrowed from the Zoroastrians or the Zoroastrians from the Jews or whether either in fact borrowed from the other."[397]

The answer depends first on the antiquity of the Zoroastrian belief in the resurrection. Boyce believes that Zoroaster's Gathas (Y. 30.7) allude to this belief. But as we have seen, most scholars disagree. The monographic study by Franz König on this subject concludes that the earliest attestation of a Zoroastrian belief in a resurrection cannot be dated before the fourth century B.C.[398]

Furthermore, there are fundamental differences in how the Jews and the Persians conceived of the resurrection. This has been noted by many scholars, for example, by Robert H. Charles.[399] The Jewish dead, who are buried, rise from the dust of the earth, whereas the Persian dead, who are exposed, must be recreated from the elements.[400] In Zoroastrianism the resurrection is linked with the fiery ordeal and the renewal,[401] whereas in Judaism the resurrection hope means life beyond the grave with Yahweh.[402] Walther Eichrodt therefore concludes: "As these differences indicate, the idea that the eschatological resurrection hope, in the form attested in the Old Testament, was influenced by Persian conceptions can be shown by any reasonably detailed comparison to be inadmissible."[403]

Finally, an investigation of the background of Israelite belief demonstrates that the doctrine of the resurrection can be explained on inner-Israelite grounds without the intervention of external inspiration. Bernhardus Alfrink observes: "We have seen how the idea of the resurrection is very solidly and very profoundly rooted in the very ancient Israelite

395. Ibid., p. 24; Boyce, *History II*, p. 193.

396. Hasenfratz, "Iran und der Dualismus," p. 44.

397. Zaehner, *Dawn*, pp. 57–58.

398. König, *Zarathustras Jenseitsvorstellungen.*

399. R. H. Charles, *Eschatology, The Doctrine of a Future Life* (New York: Schocken, 1963 reprint of 1913 edition), pp. 139–140.

400. D. S. Russell, *The Method and Message of Jewish Apocalyptic* (Philadelphia: Westminster, 1964), p. 385.

401. Hultgard, "Das Judentum," p. 544.

402. R. Mayer, "Der Auferstehungsglaube in der iranischen Religion," *Kairos* 7 (1965): 207.

403. W. Eichrodt, *Theology of the Old Testament*, 4th ed. (Philadelphia: Westminster, 1961), 2: 517. Other scholars who have come to a negative concusion about the role of Persian influence for the development of the Jewish doctrine of resurrection include F. Nötscher, *Altorientalischer und alttestamentlicher Auferstehungsglaube* (Würzburg: C. J. Becker, 1926), p. 195; O. Schilling, *Der Jenseitsgedanke im Alten Testament* (Mainz: Rheingold, 1951), p. 104; König, *Zarathustras Jenseitsvorstellungen*, p. 282.

beliefs. It is, in the first place, the doctrine of retribution, formulated in the Old Testament for a long time as the antithesis of death and life."[404]

The genre of apocalypse, such as Daniel in which a revelation is made of eschatological events, has been attributed by some to Persian influences.[405] Boyce has attempted to argue for the antiquity of the Zoroastrian apocalyptic tradition, tracing its inspiration back to the prophet himself.[406] But the Persian apocalyptic texts such as the Bahman Yasht, the Zat-Sparam, and the Ardaf Viraf date only to the ninth century A.D.[407]

Classical sources (as early as the fourth century B.C.) indicate an awareness of the millennial periodization of Persian eschatology. The popular Oracles of Hystaspes, which may have been based on oral Iranian tradition, may be dated to 200 or 100 B.C.[408] This text predicts the coming of a savior who will end the lawlessness of the Romans.

Recent study of the inner development of the apocalyptic genre in Old Testament texts has shown that the hypothesis of a Persian stimulus is not convincing. The so-called Isaianic apocalypse should be dated to no later than the sixth century B.C.[409] Paul Hanson concludes:

> But the important fact is that, already at the end of the sixth century, the basic schema of apocalyptic eschatology has evolved in Israel and that the whole development is perfectly comprehensible within the history of Israel's own community and cult. Hasty recourse to late Persian influence is therefore unnecessary and unjustifiable in the search for the origins of the basic eschatology of Jewish apocalyptic.[410]

The judgment by fire found in numerous Old Testament passages

404. B. Alfrink, "L'idée de résurrection d'après Daniel XII, 1–2," *Biblica* 40 (1959): 369; Hultgard, "Das Judentum," p. 544; König, *Zarathustras Jenseitsvorstellungen*, p. 284.

405. We must also reckon with the earlier Akkadian apocalypses. See W. W. Hallo, "Akkadian Apocalypses," *IEJ* 16 (1966): 231–42; H. Hunger and S. A. Kaufman, "A New Akkadian Prophecy Text," *JAOS* 95 (1975): 371–75; E. Yamauchi, "Hermeneutical Issues in Daniel," *JETS* 23 (1980): 15–16.

406. Boyce, "On the Antiquity," pp. 57–75.

407. J. J. Collins, "Persian Apocalypses," *Semeia* 14 (79): 212. P. Gignoux, "L'apocalyptique iranienne est-elle vraiment la source d'autre apocalypses?" *AAH* 31 (1988): 67–78, believes that the so-called Iranian apocalyptic tradition is a very late development based upon myth and Sasanid figures, and cannot be a source of Jewish apocalypses.

408. Widengren, "Iran and Israel," p. 144; idem, "The Problem of the Sassanid Avesta," pp. 228, 233; Colpe, "Development," p. 831; D. E. Aune, *Prophecy in Early Christianity* (Grand Rapids: Eerdmans, 1983), p. 43; J. R. Hinnells, "The Zoroastrian Doctrine of Salvation in the Roman World," in Sharp and Hinnells, *Man and His Salvation*, pp. 125–48. D. Flusser, "Hystaspes and John of Patmos," in Shaked, *Irano-Judaica*, pp. 12–17. Flusser has tried to argue that the Oracles of Hystaspes was a Jewish work based on Zoroastrian material that served as the basis of Rev. 11.

409. W. Miller, *Isaiah 24–27 and the Origin of Apocalyptic* (Missoula: Scholars, 1976).

410. P. D. Hanson, *The Dawn of Apocalyptic* (Philadelphia: Fortress, 1975), p. 160; see idem, "Jewish Apocalyptic Against Its Near Eastern Environment," *RB* 78 (1971): 54.

has sometimes been linked with the Zoroastrian fiery ordeal. This concept is found in such texts as Isaiah 5:24, 30:27; Joel 2:3; Zephaniah 1:18, 3:8; and Zechariah 12:6. But this judgment by fire is an expression of Yahweh's wrath, and differs from the purifying fire of the Iranian ordeal as demonstrated in a thorough study of the subject by Rudolf Mayer.[411]

A careful study of the postexilic Old Testament books (Daniel, Esther, Ezra, Nehemiah) by James Barr reveals that although there are many Persian loan-words, almost all of these are about administration and court ceremonial, not about religion.[412] Barr concludes: "Thus the evidence of loanwords, for what it is worth, seems to show no strong evidence of Jewish awareness of the Iranian religious structures."[413] He notes that the Elephantine papyri also betray little influence of Persian religion: "To summarize: the Jewish evidence lacks any indication of curiosity about the distinctive character of Persian religion."[414]

If any case of Persian influence upon Judaism can be made, it falls in the intertestamental or Hellenistic era.[415] Hinnells has departed from the position of his mentor, Boyce, in this regard. He concludes: "The period of influence is placed much later than that assumed by most scholars. The detailed parallels appear during the Parthian and not during the Achaemenid era."[416]

The Dead Sea Scrolls from Qumran, which come from the intertestamental era, have been cited as providing evidence for Persian influence upon Judaism, particularly with respect to the dualism found in these texts. A key text is from the Manual of Discipline (1QS 3.17–18): "He created man to rule the world, appointing for him two

411. R. Mayer, *Die biblische Vorstellung vom Welten Brand* (Bonn: Orientalisches Seminar der Universität Bonn, 1956), p. 135.

412. Barr, "Question," pp. 209–11. On the Persian loan-words in biblical Aramaic, see F. Rosenthal, *A Grammar of Biblical Aramaic* (Wiesbaden: O. Harrossowitz, 1961), pp. 58–59; M. Wagner, *Die lexikalischen und grammatikalischen Aramaismen im alttestamentlichen Hebräisch* (Berlin: A. Töpelmann, 1966), pp. 152–53. About the only Persian words with religious significance are *dath* ("law") and *raz* ("secret"). But these are very common words. Frye, "Qumran and Iran," in Neusner, *Christianity, Judaism and Other Greco-Roman Cults,* 3: 169, remarks: "Much has been made of the word *rāz* 'secret, alone', but since the word not only occurs in Sogdian and other Iranian languages, but also in Syriac and Mandaean, as well as in the Book of Daniel, I confess to a lack of enthusiasm for the word as an important proof of religious borrowing between Iran and Qumran." On the Old Testament concept of *raz,* see R. E. Brown, "The Semitic Background of the New Testament *Mysterion,*" *Biblica* 39 (1958): 426–48; 40 (1959): 70–87.

413. Barr, "Question," p. 212.

414. Ibid., p. 218.

415. Hultgard, "Das Judentum," p. 582.

416. Hinnells, "Zoroastrian Influence," p. 14. See W. F. Albright, *From the Stone Age to Christianity* (Garden City: Doubleday, 1957), pp. 363–64: "From the foregoing paragraphs it appears that Iranian conceptions did not begin to influence Judaism until the last two pre-Christian centuries, and even then exerted no effect except where the ground was already fully prepared."

spirits in which to walk until the time of His visitation—the spirits of truth and deceit." Parallels with Iranian texts were first pointed out by Karl Kuhn.[417] He has been followed by other scholars who have accepted the thesis of a Zoroastrian or Zurvanite background for Qumranian dualism.[418]

Some scholars, however, are having second thoughts. In 1957 Preben Wernberg-Møller accepted the Zoroastrian background of 1QS 3.17–18.[419] But four years later he became aware of closer parallels between the Qumran text and the Testament of the Twelve Patriarchs. He then concluded:

> One of the points of the above article has been to show that, on purely internal grounds, the "Zoroastrian" theory concerning the provenance of 1QS III, 13–IV,26 is difficult to uphold, and that both the strict dualism and the double predestination which are supposed to be found there, and which have been taken for granted by many scholars, must be abandoned.[420]

Barr points out that the antithesis of "truth" and "lie" in the scrolls is relatively rare; the "lie" at Qumran is not a quasi-metaphysical entity as in Zoroastrianism. He writes: "Taking the question as a whole, with openness towards either possibility, one is inclined to conclude that the dualism of the Two Spirits at Qumran, with the accompanying paraphernalia of light and darkness, truth and iniquity, could have evolved from inner-Jewish developments."[421] Frye remarks: "It seems to me that the study of Iranian words in the Qumran texts has not brought proof of Iranian influence."[422]

The argument of Iranian influence upon Judaism is undercut by the necessity of relying upon the extremely late Pahlavi texts, which are

417. K. G. Kuhn, "Die in Palāstina gefunden hebräischen Texte und das Neue Testament," *ZTK* 47 (1950): 211; idem, "Die Sektenschrift und die iranische Religion," *ZTK* 49 (1952): 296–314.

418. Hultgard, "Das Judentum," p. 561; H. Wildberger, "Der Dualismus in den Qumranschriften," *Asiatische Studien* 8 (1954): 163–77; H. Michaud, "Un mythe zervanite dans un des manuscrits de Qumrān," *RQ* 5 (1955): 137–47; J. Duchesne-Guillemin, "Le zervanisme et les manuscrits de la Mer Morte," *IIJ* 1 (1957): 96–99; H. W. Huppenbauer, *Der Mensch zwischen zwei Welten* (Zurich: Zwingli, 1959); R. G. Jones, "The Manual of Discipline (1QS), Persian Religion, and the Old Testament," in *The Teacher's Yoke,* ed. E. J. Vardaman (Waco: Baylor University Press, 1964), pp. 94–108; M. Hengel, *Judaism and Hellenism* (Philadelphia: Fortress, 1974), 1: 230.

419. P. Wernberg-Møller, *The Manual of Discipline* (Grand Rapids: Eerdmans, 1957), p. 70.

420. P. Wernberg-Møller, "A Reconsideration of the Two Spirits in the *Rule of the Community* (I Q. Serek III,13–IV,26)," *RQ* 3 (1961): 441.

421. Barr, "Question," p. 226.

422. Frye, "Qumran and Iran," p. 170. See F. Nötscher, "Heiligkeit in den Qumranschriften," *RQ* 2 (1959–1960): 343.

our major sources for the eschatological views of Zoroastrianism.[423] Unfortunately the Achaemenid texts are not very informative and Parthian texts are almost wholly lacking.[424] Even Shaked, who believes that Iranian influence was present at Qumran, admits: "All arguments about possible contacts between Israel and Iran come to the stumbling block of the problem of chronology. All detailed accounts of any aspect of Zoroastrian theology exist no earlier than in books compiled during the Sasanian period or later, after the Arab conquest of Iran."[425] Frye notes: "In other words, the basic Iranian sources for deriving influences are the ninth century A.D. Pahlavi books, the syncretic nature of which can easily be imagined."[426] Zaehner concludes:

> The case for a Judaeo-Christian dependence on Zoroastrianism in its purely eschatological thinking is quite different and not at all convincing, for apart from a few hints in the *Gathas* . . . and a short passage in *Yasht* 19.89–90 in which a deathless existence in body and soul at the end of time is affirmed, we have no evidence as to what eschatological ideas the Zoroastrians had in the last four centuries before Christ. The eschatologies of the Pahlavi books, though agreeing in their broad outlines, differ very considerably in detail and emphasis; they do not correspond at all closely to the eschatological writings of the intertestamentary period nor to those of St. Paul and the Apocalypse of St. John.[427]

Neusner, the scholar with the greatest knowledge of the Jews under the Parthians and the Sasanians, is not impressed with the actual Jewish evidence for the thesis of Zoroastrian influence upon Judaism. He writes:

> If we must make premature hypotheses, let me here hypothecate that Iranian "influences" on the culture and religion of Babylonian Jewry, and all the more so of Palestinian Jewry, have been for the most part exaggerated and overrated. Examining just what the Talmudic rabbis actually knew about Iranian culture, we can hardly be impressed by the depth of their knowledge.[428]

423. Suarez, "Escatologia personal," p. 20; König, *Zarathustras Jenseitsvorstellungen*, pp. 268–69.

424. J. Neusner, "The Rabbi and Magus in Third-Century Sasanian Babylonia," *HR* 6 (1967): 177.

425. Shaked, "Qumran and Iran," p. 443.

426. Frye, "Reitzenstein and Qumrân," p. 262.

427. Zaehner, *Dawn*, p. 57.

428. J. Neusner, "Jews and Judaism under Iranian Rule: Bibliographical Reflections," *HR* 8 (1968): 162; idem, *A History of the Jews in Babylonia* (Leiden: Brill, 1969), 4: 424; see also idem, "How Much Iranian in Jewish Babylonia?" in *Talmudic Judaism in Sasanian Babylonia* (Leiden: Brill, 1976), pp. 134–49.

In view of questions about the date of the Zoroastrian materials, the differences between Jewish and Persian concepts, and the probability of independent developments, not a few scholars have concluded that the earlier claims for the decisive influence of Persian beliefs upon Judaism have been overvalued.[429]

429. Barr, "Question," p. 225; B. Reicke, "Iranische Religion, Judentum und Urchristentum," in *Die Religion in Geschichte und Gegenwart*, eds. H. von Campenhausen et al. (Tübingen: J. C. B. Mohr, 1959), vol. 3, col. 883; J. Maier, *Geschichte der jüdischen Religion* (Berlin: W. de Gruyter, 1972), p. 42.

13
The Magi

The Original Magi

According to Herodotus (1.101), the magi (Greek *magos,* plural *magoi*) were originally one of the tribes of the Medes who functioned as priests and diviners under the Achaemenian Persians (sixth–fourth centuries B.C.).[1] Herodotus (1.132) wrote that "no sacrifice can be offered without a Magian." The magi also interpreted dreams (Herodotus 1.107, 120, 128). Other classical writers knew that the magi served before fire altars (Strabo 15.3.15; Xenophon, *Cyropedia* 4.5.14; 7.5.57) and offered libations (Strabo 15.3.14).[2]

Herodotus reports that a magos named Bardiya/Smerdis seized power

1. According to M. Boyce, *A History of Zoroastrianism II* [hereafter *History II*] (Leiden: Brill, 1982), p. 19: "The original meaning of the term, it has been suggested, was perhaps 'member of the tribe' (as in Av. *moghu*), given a special sense among the Medes as 'member of the priestly tribe.' " Herodotus's view that the magi were originally a Median tribe is supported by E. Benveniste, *Les mages dans l'ancien Iran* (Paris: G.-P. Maisonneuve, 1938), p. 11, but is questioned by G. Messina, *Der Ursprung der Magier und die zarathuštrische Religion* (Rome: Pontificio Istituto Biblico, 1930), p. 77.

2. See E. Benveniste, *The Persian Religion According to the Chief Greek Texts* (Paris: Paul Geuthner, 1929). For a list of studies on the Greek word *magos,* see E. D. Francis, "Greeks and

for seven months, posing as the brother of Cambyses, before Darius gained power in the fall of 522 B.C.[3] The Old Persian version of Darius's Behistun inscription calls this imposter, also known as Gaumata, a *maguš*.[4] The corresponding Elamite version calls him a *ma-ku-iš*, but the Akkadian version uses the term *LU KUR ma-da-*[*a-a*], that is, "Median man"[5] (see chapter 4).

The Persians continued to use derivations from the word *maguš* as a word for "priest" down to the end of the Sasanian era around A.D. 650. An ordinary priest was called *mog*, and the chief priest *magupat*, "master of the magi,"[6] or even *magupat magupatan*, "chief priest of chief priests."[7]

The relationship of the magi to Zoroaster and his teachings is a complex and controversial issue. The magi are strikingly absent from the Avesta with one possible exception.[8] The Zoroastrians and magi were probably initially in conflict for two reasons: the magi appear to have been polytheistic (Xenophon, *Cyropedia* 3.3.22; 8.3.11–12), whereas Zoroaster's own teachings about Ahuramazda were either monotheistic or dualistic; and Zoroaster was from the northeast and the magi were established in northwestern Iran. According to Mary Boyce: "It is reasonable, however, to suppose that the existence of this hereditary priesthood [i.e. the magi], with its own traditions and forms of worship, was a major factor in western Iranian resistance to Zoroastrian proselytizing."[9]

The religion of the magi under the Achaemenian kings is another

Persians: The Art of Hazard and Triumph," in *Ancient Persia: The Art of an Empire*, ed. D. Schmandt-Besserat (Malibu: Undena, 1980), p. 58, n. 27.

3. See chapter 4; J. Wiesehöfer, *Der Aufstand Gaumatas und die Anfänge Dareios I* (Bonn: Rudolf Habelt, 1978).

4. The etymology of the Old Persian word is uncertain. Pokorny suggests a relation to the Proto-Indo-European root *magh-*, "to be able." J. Pokorny, *Indogermanisches etymologisches Wörterbuch*, 8th ed. (Bern: A. Francke, 1954), p. 695.

5. On the role of the magi under the Achaemenians, see M. A. Dandamayev, *Persien unter den ersten Achämeniden*, trans. H.-D. Pohl (Wiesbaden: Ludwig Reichert, 1976), pp. 238–40; J. M. Cook, *The Persian Empire* (New York: Schocken, 1983), pp. 154–55; R. N. Frye, *The History of Ancient Iran* (München: C. H. Beck'sche, 1984), pp. 120–24; M. Schwartz, "The Religion of Achaemenian Iran," in *The Cambridge History of Iran II: The Median and Achaemenian Periods*, ed. I. Gershevitch (Cambridge: Cambridge University Press, 1985), pp. 696–97.

6. M. Boyce, *Zoroastrians* (London: Routledge, 1979), p. 102.

7. V. G. Lukonin, "Political, Social and Administrative Institutions: Taxes and Trade," *CHI* III.2 (1983), p. 689.

8. See F. Altheim and R. Stiehl, *Geschichte Mittelasiens im Altertum* (Berlin: W. de Gruyter, 1970), p. 54. This makes untenable G. Messina's thesis that the magi were priests of purely Zoroastrian origin.

9. M. Boyce, *A History of Zoroastrianism I: The Early Period* (Leiden: Brill, 1975), p. 21.

area of controversy. Arthur Darby Nock's judgment on this matter is cautiously stated:

> The balance of probability seems to me to indicate that Zoroaster's *Gathas* had been accepted by *some* of the Magi as inspired and that their phraseology and ideas had exercised *some* influence on them and through them on the language of Xerxes at least.[10]

A recent reconstruction of the history of the magi by Papatheophanes, which is admittedly inferential in nature, suggests that the Median magi defected to Cyrus, who presumably worshiped Mithras. When the Median magi supported the revolt of Gaumata the magos, Darius punished them and replaced them with Persian magi who accepted Zoroastrianism.[11] Some magi are mentioned in association with the cult of Ahuramazda in the Elamite tablets from Darius's reign.[12] Papatheophanes speculates that some of the Median magi may have fled to Ephesus, where they were observed by Heraclitus.[13] The earliest preserved occurrence of the Greek word *magos* is found in a passage of Heraclitus.[14]

With the conquest of Asia Minor by the Persian army under Cyrus in 546 B.C. came the settlement of many Medes and Persians accompanied by their magi.[15] A famous relief from the satrapal capital of Dascylion in northwest Asia Minor depicts a pair of magi with the barsom twigs and sacrificial animals.[16] Their mouths and noses are covered to keep them from contaminating the sacred fire.[17]

In any case the classical writers Plato, Pliny the Elder, and Plutarch maintained that Zoroaster himself was a magos and that the magi were his followers.[18] For example, Plutarch (*Moralia* 5.369 E–F) relates: "The Magian Zoroaster . . . called the one (god) Oromazes and the other

10. A. D. Nock, "The Problem of Zoroaster," *AJA* 53 (1949): 277, reprinted in his *Essays on Religion and the Ancient World,* ed. Z. Stewart (Cambridge: Harvard University Press, 1972), p. 690.

11. M. Papatheophanes, "Heraclitus of Ephesus, the Magi, and the Achaemenids," *IA* 20 (1985): 153.

12. H. Koch, *Die religiösen Verhältnisse der Dariuszeit* (Wiesbaden: O. Harrassowitz, 1977), p. 158.

13. Papatheophanes, "Heraclitus," p. 155.

14. Ibid., p. 102.

15. J. Bidez and F. Cumont, *Les mages hellénisés* (Paris: "Les Belles Lettres," 1938), pp. 90–92; F. Cumont, *Oriental Religions in Roman Paganism* (New York: Dover, 1956 reprint of the 1911 edition), pp. 139–41.

16. T. Macridy, "Reliefs gréco-perses de la région de Dascylion," *BCH* 37 (1913): 340–58; E. Akurgal, "Griechisch-persische Reliefs aus Daskyleion," *IA* 6 (1966): 147–56; P. Bernard, "Les bas-reliefs gréco-perses de Dascylion à la lumière de nouvelles découvertes," *RA* 125 (1969): 17–28.

17. See our discussion under "Fire" in chapter 12.

18. Boyce, *History II,* p. 261; J. H. Moulton, *Early Zoroastrianism: The Origins, the Prophet, the Magi* (Amsterdam: Philo, 1972 reprint of the 1913 edition), p. 197.

A relief of two Persian magi from Dascylium in northwest Anatolia. (Courtesy of the Istanbul Archaeological Museum, Turkey)

Areimanius." When Apuleius was on trial for magic, he argued that *magus* meant "priest" in Persia and cited Plato to indicate that the Persian princes studied the "*mageia* of Zoroaster, son of Oromazos."

The Magi and Magic

Although the Medo-Persian magi were rarely associated with spells (except at Herodotus 7.191), by the fifth century B.C. the word in some cases seems to have become synonymous with the Greek word *goēs* ("wizard, sorcerer"[19]). In Sophocles' play, *Oedipus the King,* Oedipus berates the blind seer Teiresias:

> The trusty Creon, my familiar friend,
> Hath lain in wait to oust me and suborned
> This mountebank (*magon*), this juggling charlatan,
> This tricksy beggar-priest, for gain alone.[20]

By the Roman era (for example, Tacitus, *Annals* 2.27; 12.22, 59) the magi and their arts were associated with sorcery. We derive our word *magic* from the Latin *magicus,* which in turn is a loan from the Greek *magikos.*[21] Because of the association of the magi with Zoroaster, Pliny the Elder (30.2) asserted: "Without doubt magic arose in Persia with Zoroaster."

It is in the sense of *magos* as "magician" that we read of the activities of Simon from Samaria, who "practiced sorcery" (*mageuōn* [Acts 8:9]) and amazed the people with his "magic" (*mageiais* [Acts 8:11]).[22] The Apocryphal Acts of Peter describes how Simon astounded the crowds at Rome by his "magical" flights until Peter prayed that he might crash to the ground.[23] While the Book of Acts describes Simon simply as a magician, the early church fathers came to regard Simon as the fountainhead of all the Gnostic heresies.[24]

19. See G. Delling, "*goēs,*" in *Theological Dictionary of the New Testament,* eds. G. Kittel and G. Friedrich (Grand Rapids: Eerdmans, 1964), 1: 737–38; also idem, "*magos,*" in *Theological Dictionary* (1967), 4: 356–59.

20. *Sophocles,* trans. F. Storr (London: Heinemann, 1928), pp. 38–39, lines 385–88.

21. On the definition of magic and its diffusion in the ancient world, see E. Yamauchi, *Mandaic Incantation Texts* (New Haven: American Oriental Society, 1967), pp. 12–61; idem, "Magic in the Biblical World," *TB* 34 (1983): 169–200.

22. C. S. Mann, "Epiphany—Wise Men or Charlatans?" *Theology* 61 (1958): 459–500. Mann makes the improbable suggestion that even the Christmas Magi belonged to this class of charlatans.

23. W. Schneemelcher, ed., *New Testament Apocrypha* (Philadelphia: Westminster, 1965), 2: 289–316.

24. R. P. Casey, "Simon Magus," in *The Beginnings of Christianity,* eds. F. J. Foakes Jackson and K. Lake (Grand Rapids: Baker, 1966 reprint), 5: 151–63; W. Meeks, "Simon Magus in Recent Re-

Elsewhere in Acts (13:6, 8) we read of a Jewish sorcerer, a *magos* named Elymas Bar-Jesus, who was influential at the court of Sergius Paulus, the proconsul of Cyprus. From Josephus (*Antiquities* 20.142) we learn of another Jewish *magos* from Cyprus named Atomus, through whose arts Felix, the governor of Judea, gained the hand of Drusilla (compare Acts 24:24–25).

By the New Testament era most of the occurrences of the word *magos* were in the pejorative sense of "magic."[25] According to John Hull: "The apostolic fathers always used the word *mágos* in a bad sense. The apologists used *mágos* and its cognates about sixteen times and always in the bad sense."[26] Harold Remus likewise concludes, "in the second century use of *mágos, mageía,* and derivative or related words is almost uniformly negative in the extant Christian sources."[27]

The Magi and Astrology

Among the functions of the Persian magi was their work as diviners. In the Hellenistic age magi in the West continued to have a reputation for foretelling the future. Cicero (*De divinatione* 1.47; followed by Plutarch, *Alexander* 3.2) records that when Alexander was born the magi interpreted a spontaneous fire in the temple of Artemis at Ephesus as a sign that a great calamity for Asia had been born.[28]

From the fourth century B.C. on the magi were increasingly associated with the Chaldeans as astrologers.[29] The name *Chaldean* assumed different meanings at different periods. In the Neo-Assyrian and Neo-Babylonian periods it meant an inhabitant of lower Mesopotamia.[30] In

search," *Religious Studies Review* 3 (1977): 137–42; E. Yamauchi, *Pre-Christian Gnosticism,* 2d ed. (Grand Rapids: Baker, 1983), pp. 58–65, 201–3; J. D. M. Derrett, "Simon Magus (Acts: 8:9–24)," *ZAW* 33 (1982): 52–68.

25. See A. F. Segal, "Hellenistic Magic: Some Questions of Definition," in *Studies in Gnosticism and Hellenistic Religions,* Gilles Quispel Festschrift, eds. R. Van Den Broek and M. J. Vermaseren (Leiden: Brill, 1981), pp. 349–75.

26. J. M. Hull, *Hellenistic Magic and the Synoptic Tradition* (London: SCM, 1974), p. 124.

27. H. Remus, " 'Magic or Miracle'? Some Second Century Instances," *Second Century* 2 (1982): 130; E. Yamauchi, "Magic or Miracle?" in *Gospel Perspectives VI: The Miracles of Jesus,* eds. D. Wenham and C. Blomberg (Sheffield: JSOT, 1986), pp. 89–91.

28. J. R. Hamilton, *Plutarch, Alexander, A Commentary* (Oxford: Clarendon, 1969), p. 8.

29. Bidez and Cumont, *Les mages hellénisés,* 1: 33–36.

30. E. Yamauchi, "Chaldea, Chaldeans," in *The New International Dictionary of Biblical Archaeology,* eds. E. M. Blaiklock and R. K. Harrison (Grand Rapids: Zondervan, 1983), pp. 123–25. The use of "Chaldean" in Dan. 2:10; 4:7; 5:7, 11, in the sense of "astrologer" has been regarded as a clear case of anachronism. A. R. Millard, "Daniel 1–6 and History," *EvO* 49 (1977): 70, however, points out that there is as yet no known example of "Chaldean" as either an ethnic or professional term from Neo-Babylonian texts.

the Hellenistic age it could mean a Babylonian priest or scholar versed in astrology, or a Greek who had studied such lore. In the Roman and early Christian eras it came to signify an astrologer. According to Strabo (16.1.6), "in Babylon a settlement is set apart for the local philosophers, the Chaldeans, as they are called, who are concerned mostly with astronomy." Strabo was also aware of a tribe of Chaldeans.

The development of "Chaldeans" in a professional as well as an ethnic sense derived from the interest in astronomy/astrology developed by priestly scholars among the Chaldeans of Mesopotamia. An interesting Greek text of Pseudo-Berossus asserts:

> From the time of Nabonassar (747–734 B.C.), the Chaldeans accurately recorded the times of the motion of the stars. The polymaths among the Greeks learned from the Chaldeans that—as Alexander (Polyhistor) and Berossus, men versed in Chaldean antiquities, say—Nabonassar gathered together (the accounts of) the deeds of the kings before him and did away with them so that the reckoning of the Chaldean kings would begin with him.[31]

Although there were considerable contacts between the Aegean and the Near East before Alexander as we have noted (chapter 11), it was after his capture of the area that a flood of Greeks visited, and in some cases settled in, Mesopotamia.[32] There some of them acquired a knowledge of Chaldean astrology.[33] According to Wilhelm Eilers:

> It is not for nothing that astrologers were called "Chaldeans," for their true home was in Aramaean southern Babylon, in Uruk which, especially in the Seleucid-Parthian period, was the center of ancient astronomy and interpretation of the stars. The latest dated cuneiform texts include clay tablets from this place containing astronomical observations; these texts come from the first century A.D.[34]

In the Hellenistic age Chaldeans also traveled west, where they practiced their divinatory arts. The most famous example of a Chaldean priest who left Babylon to teach astrology to the Greeks on the island of Cos some time after 281 B.C. was Berossus. His famous

31. Cited by J. A. Brinkman, *A Political History of Post-Kassite Babylonia 1158–722 B.C.* (Rome: Pontificium Institutum Biblicum, 1968), p. 227.

32. E. Yamauchi, *Greece and Babylon* (Grand Rapids: Baker, 1967); and chapter 11.

33. See J. Bidez, "Les écoles chaldéennes sous Alexandre et les Séleucides," *Annuaire de l'institut de philologie et d'histoire orientales* 3 (1935): 41–89.

34. W. Eilers, "Iran and Mesopotamia," in *CHI* III.1, p. 501.

Babyloniaca, written in Greek, contains invaluable traditions on astrological matters.[35]

A factor that may have contributed to the identification of the magi with the Chaldeans and astrologers is their association with Zoroaster. The Greek spelling of Zoroaster's name, *Zoroástres,* was first recorded by Xanthos of Lydia.[36] The Greeks saw in this name the word *astēr* ("star"). Hermodorus, a pupil of Plato, explained Zoroaster's name as *astrothútes* ("star worshiper"[37]). Because of these associations a mass of astrological matter circulated under the name of Zoroaster.[38]

Zodiacal Astrology

The development of astrology as we know it today was made possible by the discovery of the Zodiac, that is, the realization that the sun in passing through its path, the ecliptic, goes through twelve constellations, each "ruling" a thirty-degree section of the circle.[39] This made possible the casting of horoscopes based on the position of the planets and stars at the moment of one's birth. Otto Neugebauer points out the differences between the earlier astral omens and the later astrology:

> The (Assyrian) predictions concern the king and the country as a whole and are based on observed astronomical appearances, not on computation and not on the moment of birth. . . . Hellenistic horoscopes, however, concern a specific person and depend upon the computed position of the seven celestial bodies and of the zodiacal signs in their relation to the given horizon, for a given moment, the moment of birth.[40]

The Zodiacal constellations are first mentioned about 700 B.C. according to Bartel Van der Waerden,[41] but not until around 400 B.C.

35. S. M. Burstein, *The BABYLONIACA of Berossus* (Malibu: Undena, 1978), pp. 31–32.

36. Boyce, *History II,* p. 183.

37. Ibid., p. 260.

38. W. and H. G. Gundel, *Astrologumena: Die astrologische Literatur in der Antike und ihre Geschichte* (Wiesbaden: Sudhoffs Archiv, 1966), pp. 40–51, 60–66. Astrological lore is found in the ninth-century-A.D. Zoroastrian text, the Bundahišn. See D. N. MacKenzie, "Zoroastrian Astrology in the Bundahišn," *BSOAS* 27 (1964): 511–29.

39. For the early history of astronomy-astrology, see Bartel L. Van der Waerden, *Science Awakening II: The Birth of Astronomy* (Leyden: Noordhoff; New York: Oxford University Press, 1974).

40. O. Neugebauer, *The Exact Sciences in Antiquity* (New York: Harper and Brothers, 1962), p. 170.

41. Van der Waerden, *Science,* p. 92; B. L. Van der Waerden, "History of the Zodiac," *AfO* 16 (1953): 216–18; B. O. Long, "Astrology," in *Supplementary Volume, The Interpreter's Dictionary of the Bible,* eds. V. Furnish et al. (Nashville: Abingdon, 1976), p. 76.

according to Neugebauer.[42] In any case the earliest known cuneiform horoscope comes from the latter date.[43] Four examples are known from the third century B.C.[44]

The Diffusion of Astrology to the West

The first depiction of the Zodiac in Egypt comes from a temple at Esna from the third or second century B.C.[45] The famous circular Zodiac from the Dendera temple dates from 30 B.C.[46] Its Mesopotamian origin is betrayed by the design of each sign. While acknowledging key contributions of the Babylonians, such as their sexagesimal reckoning and carefully recorded ephemeridae,[47] Neugebauer stresses the independent Hellenistic (Ptolemaic) contributions:

> The roots of astrology are undoubtedly to be found in Mesopotamia, emerging from the general omen literature. Yet, we know much less about the history of Babylonian astrology than is generally assumed. Only that much seems clear that it was a far less developed doctrine than we find in Greek astrological literature. The real center of ancient astrology, from which it spread over the whole world, is undoubtedly Hellenistic Alexandria.[48]

With their victories over the Greeks in the second century B.C., the Romans were inundated with Greek influence in many fields, including

42. Neugebauer, *Exact Sciences,* pp. 102, 140, prefers to speak of such constellations as "ecliptical constellations" until we have evidence of their use in casting horoscopes. See D. R. Dicks, *Early Greek Astronomy to Aristotle* (Ithaca: Cornell University Press, 1970), p. 172; R. R. Newton, "Astronomy in Ancient Literate Societies," in *The Place of Astronomy in the Ancient World,* eds. D. G. Kendall et al. (London: British Academy, 1974), p. 13.

43. See A. Sachs, "Babylonian Horoscopes," *JCS* 6 (1952): 49–75. For other examples, see P. Hilaire de Wynghene, *Les présages astrologiques* (Rome: Pontificio Istituto Biblico, 1932).

44. Van der Waerden, *Science,* p. 181. Compare O. Neugebauer and H. B. Van Hoesen, *Greek Horoscopes* (Philadelphia: American Philosophical Society, 1959). The six known Greek horoscopes are from the reign of Augustus.

45. R. A. Parker, "Ancient Egyptian Astronomy," in Kendall, *Place of Astronomy,* p. 61.

46. J. N. Lockyer, *The Dawn of Astronomy* (Cambridge: MIT, 1964 reprint of 1894 edition), pp. 134, 146.

47. O. Neugebauer, ed., *Astronomical Cuneiform Texts: Babylonian Ephemeridae of the Seleucid Period,* 3 vols. (London: Lund Humphries, 1955).

48. O. Neugebauer, *A History of Mathematical Astronomy* (New York: Springer, 1975), 1: 5; idem, "On Some Aspects of Early Greek Astronomy," *Proceedings of the American Philosophical Society* 116 (1972): 251. M. P. Nilsson, *The Rise of Astrology in the Hellenistic Age* (Lund: Observatory, 1943), p. 5, also declares: "Because of this naive character of Babylonian astrology, it is permitted to doubt the correctness of the common opinion that the Babylonians created the great astrological system. . . . It can be proved that this is an achievement of the Greeks." F. Rochberg-Halton, "New Evidence for the History of Astrology," *JNES* 43 (1984): 115–40, while conceding the Greek innovations, points out new evidence for Babylonian antecedents of the later astrology.

philosophy and astrology. Astrology was given great prestige among the Romans by its support by Stoic philosophers. In the last century of the Roman Republic astrology was widely accepted by the elite as *the* scientific method of divination with the exception of a few sceptics like Cicero. Cicero's two learned friends, Nigidius Figulus and Terentius Varro, were believers in astrology.[49]

But the growing influence of astrologers was considered dangerous to the state. In 139 B.C. Cornelius Scipio Hispalus expelled astrologers from Rome. In the early Roman Empire such expulsions were ordered repeatedly:

> Accordingly, first in 33 B.C. by action of the aedile Agrippa, later by senatorial decree, and after 52 by imperial edict, the city or all Italy was repeatedly cleared of *mathematici, Chaldaei, astrologi, magi, góetes,* or however they were called, perhaps ten times over the period 33 B.C. to A.D. 93, and possibly once more under Marcus Aurelius.[50]

Although a satirist like Juvenal might poke fun at astrologers (*Satire* 6.585–86), historians like Suetonius and Dio Cassius were persuaded by the efficacy of astrology. Almost all the Julio-Claudian and Flavian emperors of the first century believed in the potency of astrology. Samuel Dill observes:

> It is not hard to see why the emperors at once believed in these black arts and profoundly distrusted their professors. They wished to keep a monopoly of that awful lore, lest it might excite dangerous hopes in possible pretenders. To consult a Chaldaean seer on the fate of the prince, or to possess his horoscope, was always suspicious, and might often be fatal.[51]

On the day of Augustus's birth, Nigidius Figulus allegedly prophesied a notable destiny for the future ruler from a knowledge of the hour of his birth (Suetonius, *Augustus* 94.5; Dio Cassius 45.1.3–5). At Apollonia the astrologer Theogenes cast a horoscope for Augustus (Suetonius, *Augustus* 94.12): "From that time on Augustus had such faith in his destiny, that he made his horoscope public and issued a silver coin stamped with the sign of the constellation Capricornus, under which he was born." Manilius, a poet who lived during Augustus's reign,

49. F. H. Cramer, *Astrology in Roman Law and Politics* (Philadelphia: American Philosophical Society, 1954), pp. 58–74.

50. R. MacMullen, *Enemies of the Roman Order* (Cambridge: Harvard University Press, 1966), pp. 132–33. See also F. H. Cramer, "Expulsion of Astrologers from Ancient Rome," *Classica et Mediaevalai* 12 (1951): 9–50.

51. S. Dill, *Roman Society from Nero to Marcus Aurelius* (New York: Meridian, 1956 reprint of 1904 edition), p. 447.

wrote an extant work on the stars,[52] which is cited in the great *Mathesis* of Firmicus Maternus (fourth century A.D.).[53] In A.D. 11 Augustus passed a law making it a crime to consult astrologers about the fate of the emperor.[54]

Suetonius's life of Tiberius (A.D. 14–37) is filled with references to astrologers. Because he feared their potential for his enemies, "he banished the astrologers as well, but pardoned such as begged for indulgence and promised to give up their art" (*Tibierius* 36). Juvenal made fun of the emperor's "herd of Chaldean astrologers" surrounding him in his retirement at Capri (*Satire* 10.94).[55]

Claudius (A.D. 41–54) tried to revive the ancient order of augurs, but banished astrologers (Tacitus, *Annals* 12.52). His wife, Agrippina the Younger, and her son Nero were devotees of astrology.[56] Nero (A.D. 54–68) delayed his coronation on the advice of his Chaldeans.[57] To avert the dangers portended by a comet, Nero determined to put to death some distinguished men (Suetonius, *Nero* 36).

Although Vespasian (A.D. 69–79) banished astrologers, he retained the most skillful for his own guidance (Dio Cassius 66.10.9). Titus (A.D. 79–81), according to Suetonius (*Titus* 9), inquired into horoscopes. Domitian (A.D. 81–96) put Mettius Pompusianus to death because he had an imperial horoscope (Suetonius, *Domitian* 10). Just before his assassination Domitian put to death the astrologer Ascletarion, who correctly predicted that dogs would attack his own corpse after his death (*Domitian* 15).

Astrology among the Jews

While Jewish interest in astrology during the Middle Ages has never been doubted, as evidenced in the Kabbalah,[58] there has been some question as to how wide and early this interest was. Both in the Sasanian and Parthian eras rabbis in Mesopotamia did not question the

52. *M. Manilii Astronomicon*, ed. A. E. Housman, 2d ed. (London: Cambridge University Press, 1937). See W. Hübner, "Manilius als Astrologe und Dichter," *ANRW* II.32.1 (1986): 126–320.

53. Firmicus Maternus, *Ancient Astrology, Theory and Practice*, trans. J. R. Bram (Park Ridge: Noyes, 1975).

54. MacMullen, *Enemies of the Roman Order*, p. 132.

55. There are a number of demotic horoscopes on ostraca from Egypt from the reigns of Augustus and Tiberius. See O. Neugebauer, "Demotic Horoscopes," *JAOS* 63 (1943): 115–26.

56. M. Grant, *Nero: Emperor in Revolt* (New York: American Heritage, 1970), p. 148.

57. Astral influence was admitted by Seneca, Nero's Stoic tutor. See Cramer, *Astrology in Roman Law*, pp. 118–21.

58. S. Gandz, *Studies in Hebrew Astronomy and Mathematics*, ed. S. Sternberg (New York: KTAV, 1970); A. Altman, "Astrology," in *Encyclopaedia Judaica* (Jerusalem: Encyclopaedia Judaica, 1971), 3: cols. 788–95; G. Scholem, *Kabbalah* (New York: New American Library, 1974), pp. 186–87.

validity of astrology but only whether it applied to Israel.[59] There are numerous references to astrology in the Talmud (for example, *b. Sabb.* 156a–b), reporting the teaching of R. Hanina Bar Hama (early third century A.D.), who thought that the constellation at the hour of one's birth determined one's character. Many rabbis held that "Israel is not subject to planetary influences" (literally "Israel has no star"), but R. Hanina disagreed.

The recently published Jewish magical text, the *Sepher ha-Razim,* holds that Noah learned "to master the investigation of the strata of the heavens, to go about in all that is in their seven abodes, to observe all the astrological signs, to examine the course of the sun, to explain the observations of the moon, and to know the paths of the Great Bear, Orion, and the Pleiades. . . ."[60] This work dates from after the third century A.D.[61]

Jewish knowledge of the Zodiac is attested during the first century A.D., for example, by Josephus (*War* 5.217–18) when he makes the following comparison of the sacred elements in the temple: "The seven lamps . . . represented the planets; the loaves on the table, twelve in number, the circle of the Zodiac and the year." Furthermore, a clay tablet with zodiacal signs was found in a Hellenistic stratum at Gezer.[62]

Indisputable early evidence of Jewish interest in astrology has now been provided by the publication of important documents from the Dead Sea Scrolls of Qumran.[63] The first of these documents (4Q Cryp-

59. J. Neusner, *A History of the Jews in Babylonia II: The Early Sasanian Period* (Leiden: Brill, 1966), pp. 84–85; idem, *A History of the Jews in Babylonia I: The Parthian Period* (Leiden: Brill, 1969), p. 171; L. Wächter, "Astrologie und Schicksalsglaube im rabbinischen Judentums," *Kairo* 11 (1969): 181–200; R. A. Rosenberg, "The 'Star of the Messiah' Reconsidered," *Bib* 53 (1972): 105–9; J. H. Charlesworth, "Jewish Astrology in the Talmud, Pseudepigrapha, the Dead Sea Scrolls, and Early Palestinian Synagogues, *HTR* 70 (1977): 183–200.

60. M. Morgan, trans., *Sepher Ha-Razim: The Book of Mysteries* (Chico: Scholars, 1983), p. 17.

61. M. Margalioth, *Sepher Ha-Razim* (Jerusalem: American Academy for Jewish Research, 1966). Margalioth dated the work to the third century. Morgan, *Sepher Ha-Razim,* p. 8, also suggests the third or fourth century. I. Gruenwald, "Knowledge and Vision," *Israel Oriental Studies* 3 (1973): 71, prefers a fifth- to sixth-century date.

62. M. Delcor, "Recherches sur un horoscope en langue hébraïque provenant de Qumran," *RevQ* 6 (1966): 536. Byzantine synagogues in Galilee had mosaics decorated with the Zodiac motif. See I. Sonne, "The Zodiac Theme in Ancient Synagogues and in Hebrew Printed Books," *Studies in Bibliography and Booklore* 1 (1953): 3–13; R. Wischnitzer, "The Beth Alpha Mosaic: A New Interpretation," *Jewish Social Studies* 17 (1955): 133–44; G. Stemberger, "Die Bedeutung des Tierkreises auf Mosaikfussböden Spätantiker Synagogen," *Kairos* 17 (1975): 11–56; R. Hachlili, "The Zodiac in Ancient Jewish Art: Representation and Significance," *BASOR* 228 (1977): 61–77. For Christian adaptations of the Zodiac motif, see W. Huebner, *Zodiacus Christianus* (Königstein: Hain, 1983). I owe many of the above references to my doctoral student, Lester Ness, who is writing his dissertation on the subject of the Zodiac synagogue mosaics.

63. Balaam's famous prophecy of the star (Num. 24:17) is frequently cited in the Dead Sea Scrolls. See P. Prigent, "Quelques testimonia messianiques," *Theologische Zeitschrift* 15 (1959): 419–30.

tic; formerly 4Q 186) was written in a strange amalgam of proto-Hebrew, Greek, and cryptic signs. It was first published by John Allegro in 1964.[64] In Allegro's translation it reads:

> His thighs are long and thin, and his toes
> are thin and long, and he is of the Second Vault.
> He has six (parts) spirit, and three in the Pit
> of Darkness. And this is the time of birth on which he is
> brought forth—on the festival of Taurus. He will be poor;
> and this is his beast: Taurus. (Col. II.5–9)

The text reflects the idea that the body and spirit are determined by the zodiacal sign at birth; the ratio of the man's spirit in light or darkness depends on the relative length of the days.

Another Aramaic text from cave 4, originally published by Jean Starcky in 1964,[65] seems to be the horoscope of a new Solomon, whose hair would be red. During his youth he would be like a lion.[66] Both of these texts have provoked considerable discussion.[67]

Also from cave 4 are fragments from an unpublished brontologion, which gives the signs of the Zodiac and then makes predictions on the basis of thunder:[68] "If it thunders in the sign of the Twins, terror and distress caused by foreigners. . . ." The closest parallel is a brontologion ascribed to Zoroaster in the *Geoponica* 1.1.[69]

Attitudes toward astrology are not uniformly represented in the

64. J. M. Allegro, "An Astrological Cryptic Document from Qumran," *JSS* 9 (1964): 291–94; J. M. Allegro, *Qumrân Cave IV.1*, Discoveries in the Judaean Desert V (Oxford: Clarendon, 1968), pp. 88–91.

65. J. Starcky, "Un texte messianique araméen de la grotte 4 de Qumrân," in *Memorial du cinquantenaire de l'Ecole des Langues Orientales Anciennes de l'Institut Catholique de Paris* (Paris: Bloud et Gay, 1964), pp. 51–66.

66. J. Carmignac, "Les Horoscopes de Qumran," *RQ* 5 (1965): 216.

67. Delcor, "Recherches sur un horoscope"; A. Dupont-Sommer, "Deux documents horoscopiques esséniens découverts à Qoumrân près de la Mer Morte," *CRAIBL* (1965): 239–53; idem, "La secte des Esséniens et les horoscopes de Qumran," *Archaeologia* 15 (1967): 24–31; F. Sen, "Los horóscopos de Qumrán," *Cultura Biblica* 23 (1966): 366–67; J. Fitzmyer, "A Bibliographical Aid to the Study of the Qumran Cave IV Texts," *CBQ* 31 (1969): 70–71; M. Hengel, *Judaism and Hellenism* (Philadelphia: Fortress, 1974), 1: 236–37; 2: 158–59; M. R. Lehmann, "New Light on Astrology in Qumran and the Talmud," *RQ* 14 (1975): 599–602.

68. Divination by thunder and lightning was especially practiced by the Etruscans and Romans. See O.-W. Von Vacano, *The Etruscans in the Ancient World* (Bloomington: Indiana University Press, 1965), pp. 19–23; R. Bloch, "La divination en Etrurie et à Rome," in *La Divination*, eds. A. Caquot and M. Leibovici (Paris: Presses Universitaires de France, 1968), 1: 197–232.

69. J. T. Milik, *Ten Years of Discovery in the Wilderness of Judaea* (Naperville, Ill.: Alec R. Allenson, 1959), p. 42; Charlesworth, "Jewish Astrology," 192, n. 28: "Unfortunately the two fragmentary columns of another scroll are unpublished, although J. T. Milik mentioned them twenty years ago."

Pseudepigrapha (200 B.C.–A.D. 200).[70] Astrology is condemned in a number of works, as James Charlesworth notes:

> According to the author of *1 Enoch* 8.3 (probably early second century B.C.), astrology is an evil and demonic idea since it was taught to men by one of the fallen angels, Baraqiyal. The third book of the *Sibylline Oracles* (second century B.C.) in lines 220–36 praises righteous men who neither search the mystical meaning of the movements of the heavenly bodies nor are deceived by the predictions of Chaldean astrology.[71]

In a similar fashion, Jubilees (12:17) has Abraham coming to himself after observing the stars at night: "And a word came into his heart, saying: 'All of the signs of the stars, and the signs of the sun and the moon are all in the hand of the Lord. Why am I seeking?' "[72]

On the other hand, parts of 1 Enoch such as 72:1–37 incorporate numerous zodiacal ideas. First Enoch (80:2–8) attributes the disorders of the planets to the sons of men.[73] Second Enoch, which dates to the late first century A.D., has Enoch declaring: "And I saw the eighth heaven, which is called in the Hebrew language Muzaloth, the changer of the season, of dry and of wet, and the 12 zodiacs, which are above the seventh heaven. And I saw the ninth heaven, which in the Hebrew language is called Kukhavim, where the heavenly houses of the 12 zodiacs are."[74]

Charlesworth has recently published a Syriac manuscript called the Treatise of Shem, which is the only Jewish pseudepigraphon that consistently advocates astrology.[75] It is a calendologion, that is, it seeks to determine the character of a year according to the zodiacal sign in which it begins. According to Charlesworth's analysis, the document was composed by an Alexandrian Jew shortly after the Battle of Actium in 31 B.C. Charlesworth concludes: "The recovery of the Treatise of Shem, coupled with the indisputable fact of a 'most unusual celestial display' near the time of Jesus' birth, by no means prove that Matthew ii preserves reliable historical information; but it is now more difficult to claim that Matthew's star was created purely out of a myth."[76]

70. J. H. Charlesworth, ed., *The Old Testament Pseudepigrapha*, 2 vols. (Garden City: Doubleday, 1983, 1985).

71. Charlesworth, "Astrology," p. 188. See also J. H. Charlesworth, "Jewish Interest in Astrology during the Hellenistic and Roman Period," *ANRW* (1987): II.20.2, pp. 926–50.

72. Charlesworth, *Old Testament Pseudepigrapha*, 2: 81.

73. No fewer than eleven manuscripts of Enoch were found at Qumran. See J. T. Milik, *The Books of Enoch: Aramaic Fragments of Qumrân Cave 4* (Oxford: Clarendon, 1976).

74. Charlesworth, *Old Testament Pseudepigrapha*, 1: 136.

75. Ibid., pp. 473–80.

76. J. H. Charlesworth, "Rylands Syriac MS 44 and a New Addition to the Pseudepigrapha: The Treatise of Shem," *BJRL* 60 (1977–1978): 394. On the attempts to explain away the Magi story as a

The Christmas Magi

Gherardo Gnoli asserts: "The Zoroastrian doctrine of the Savior of the Future (Saoshyant) was the basis for the story of the coming of the Magi of Bethlehem in the *Gospel of Matthew* (2:1–12)."[77] The argument for this unlikely thesis has been developed by Giuseppe Messina.[78] Messina first denies that the magi were a Median priestly caste. He views them as adherents of Zoroaster, who came into conflict with Darius for this reason! To suggest that the Christmas Magi were Zoroastrians who were responding to Zoroastrian apocalyptic prophecy, Messina cites such sources as the Oracle of Hystaspes, the Arabic infancy gospel,[79] Theodore Bar Konai (eighth century), and Bar Hebraeus (thirteenth century).[80] He is assuming that the Zoroastrian doctrine of the Saoshyant inspired Matthew.[81] This overlooks the profound differences in the concepts of savior and salvation in Zoroastrianism and Christianity.

Despite the fact that some of the church fathers (for example, Clement of Alexandria) believed the Christmas Magi were Zoroastrians, it is clear from the history of the Magi and the biblical context that they were astrologers[82] who were probably from Mesopotamia.[83]

---

midrash based on either Tiridates' trip to meet Nero, on Balaam's prophecy of the star, or on the Lucan shepherd story, see my "The Episode of the Magi," *Chronos, Kairos, and Christos,* eds. J. Vardaman and E. Yamauchi, Jack Finegan Festschrift (Winona Lake, Ind.: Eisenbrauns, 1989), pp. 15–39.

77. G. Gnoli, "The Magi," in *The Encyclopedia of Religion,* ed. M. Eliade (New York: Macmillan, 1986), 9: 81.

78. G. Messina, *Der Ursprung der Magier* (Rome: Pontificio Istituto Biblico, 1930); idem, "Una profezia di Zoroastro sulla venuta del Messia," *Biblica* 14 (1933): 170–98; idem, *I. Magi a Betlemme e una Profezia di Zoroastro* (Rome: Pontificio Istituto Biblico, 1933); idem, "Ecce *Magi* ab Oriente venerunt," *Verbum Domini* 14 (1934): 7–19.

79. This late work asserts that "some magi came to Jerusalem according to the prediction of Zoroaster."

80. Bar Hebraeus declared: "In those days (of Cyrus) came Zardosht, chief of the Magian sect. It is reported that he was one of Elijah's disciples, and he informed the Persians of the sign of the birth of Christ and that they should bring him gifts."

81. Compare J. R. Hinnells, "Zoroastrian Saviour Imagery and Its Influence on the New Testament," *Numen* 16 (1969): 161–85.

82. David Hughes, *The Star of Bethlehem* (New York: Walker, 1979), p. 193. Hughes tries to maintain that the Magi were both Zoroastrian priests and astrologers, but this is untenable. D. Pingree, "Astronomy and Astrology in India and Iran," *Isis* 54 (1963): 240–41, points out: "In fact, virtually nothing is known of the astronomy and astrology of pre-Sasanian Iran. There was indeed a Greek astrological text of the second century B.C. ascribed to Zoroaster of which fragments are preserved by Proclus and the Geoponica; the material with which it deals is overwhelmingly Babylonian. . . . However, trustworthy knowledge of Iranian astronomy and astrology is non-existent before the reign of Shâpûr I (240–270)."

83. E. Bishop, "Some Reflections on Justin Martyr and the Nativity Narratives," *EQ* 39 (1967): 33. Bishop observes: "Origen, who knew the Palestine of his day, and Jerome, who lived in Bethlehem, considered favourably the claims of Babylonian astrologers, as did St. Augustine of Hippo; and it must be admitted that the consensus of three such scholars is formidable."

The Christmas Star

There are over five hundred books, articles, and reviews on the subject of the "star," offering a variety of explanations of the celestial light that guided the Magi.[84] Some have suggested the idea of a nova—a star that suddenly increases in brightness.[85] Chinese records indicate that a nova was visible near the star Alpha Aquilae for seventy days in 5 B.C.[86] Others have suggested the possibility of a comet. Some have focused on Halley's Comet, which appeared in 12 B.C.[87] On the basis of Chinese records, Jack Finegan suggested that the comets (or novae) of 5 or 4 B.C. could have started the Magi on their journey, and that the comet of April 4 B.C., could have been shining when they reached Judea.[88] Comets, however, were usually–though not always—believed to be unfavorable portents.[89]

Johannes Kepler, the great astronomer of the seventeenth century, calculated that the triple conjunction of Jupiter and Saturn, which took place before the supernova of 1604, must have also taken place in 7 B.C. in the constellation Pisces.[90] David Hughes argued this triple conjunction of Saturn and Jupiter was the Christmas star.[91] Some have interpreted Pisces as the constellation of the Jews, Saturn as associated with

84. For a nearly comprehensive bibliography, see R. S. Freitag, *The Star of Bethlehem: A List of References* (Washington, D.C.: Library of Congress, 1979). See also A. Strobel, "Weltenjahr, grosse Konjunktion und Mesiasstern," *ANRW* II.20.2 (1987): 988–1187.

85. C. P. Richards, "The Star of Bethlehem," *Sky and Telescope* 16 (Dec. 1956): 66–67; P. and L. Murdin, *The New Astronomy* (New York: Crowell, 1978), pp. 21–24.

86. D. H. Clark, J. H. Parkinson, and F. R. Stephenson, "An Astronomical Re-Appraisal of the Star of Bethlehem—A Nova in 5 B.C.," *Quarterly Journal of the Royal Astronomical Society* 18 (1977): 443; compare A. J. Morehouse, "The Christmas Star as a Supernova in Aquila," *Journal of the Royal Astronomical Society of Canada* 72 (1978): 65.

87. A. C. Stentzel, *Jesus Christus und sein Stern,* 2 vols. (Hamburg: H. Christian, 1928); J. E. Bruns, "The Magi Episode in Matthew 2," *CBQ* 23 (1961): 51–54; Ho Peng Yoke, "Ancient and Medieval Observations of Comets and Novae in Chinese Sources," *Vistas in Astronomy* (Oxford: Pergamon, 1962), 5: 127–226. For an advocacy of Halley's Comet, see J. Vardaman, *The Year of the Nativity* (Mississippi State: Cobb Institute of Archaeology, 1983); idem, "Jesus' Life: A New Chronology," in Vardaman and Yamauchi, *Chronos,* pp. 66, 78. Nikos, Kokkinos, "Crucifixion in A.D. 36: The Keystone for Dating the Birth of Jesus," in Vardaman and Yamauchi, *Chronos,* pp. 159–62.

88. J. Finegan, *Handbook of Biblical Chronology* (Princeton: Princeton University Press, 1964), p. 248. Compare J. and M. W. Seymour, "The Historicity of the Gospels and Astronomical Events Concerning the Birth of Christ," *Quarterly Journal of the Royal Astronomical Society* 19 (1978): 194–97.

89. Cramer, *Astrology in Roman Law and Politics,* p. 78: "The traditional interpretation of the significance of comets was overwhelmingly unfavorable." Augustus, however, persuaded the people that the comet of 44 B.C. represented the deification of Julius Caesar in the heavens. For a critique of the nova and comet hypotheses, see Hughes, *Star,* pp. 145–57.

90. Johannes Kepler, *De Stella Nova in Pede Serpentarii* (Prague: Pauli Sessi, 1606).

91. Hughes, *Star,* p. xii.

Saturday (the Sabbath), and Jupiter as the planet of royalty (called in Hebrew *Tsedeq*).[92] But this interpretation of Pisces seems to be based on late interpretations such as Abarbanel's commentary on Daniel (fourteenth century). Ptolemy (second century A.D.), the astrologer, associated Aries with the Jews.[93]

Contrary to the view of many interpreters, Kepler did not interpret the conjunction of planets as analogous to the Christmas star, but rather the nova that appeared at the time as the triple conjunction.[94] Jupiter and Saturn passed each other at a distance equal to twice the moon's diameter so they could not have been mistaken as a single object. The Greek word *astēr* is used for an individual star or planet.[95] While the extant Babylonian almanac for 7/6 B.C. covers the period of such a conjunction, it takes no special note of it.[96]

Ernest Martin has favored identifying Jupiter with the Bethlehem star.[97] The identification with Jupiter has been advocated by Konradin Ferrari d'Ochieppo, the former chair of the Department of Theoretical Astronomy at the University of Vienna.[98] He is, however, critical of other aspects of Martin's theory.[99] Still other planets such as Saturn,[100] Mars,[101] and even Uranus[102] have been suggested.

Finally, the difficulty of explaining the guidance of the Magi to the place where the Christ child lay has persuaded others that the passage

92. F. L. Filas, "The Star of the Magi," *IER* 85 (1956): 432–33; H. W. van der Vaart Smit, *Born in Bethlehem* (Bethlehem: Helicon, 1963), pp. 79–113; Adler Planetarium and Astronomical Museum, Chicago, "What Was the Star of Bethlehem?" *Christianity Today* 9 (Dec. 18, 1964): 277–80; R. A. Rosenberg, "Star of Bethlehem," in *IDBS*, p. 842; J. F. Farquharson, "The Star of Bethlehem," *Journal of the British Astronomical Association* 89 (Dec. 1978): 8–20.

93. O. Gingerich, "More on the Star of Bethlehem," *Harvard Magazine* (Sept. 1975): 4–5.

94. A. J. Sachs and C. B. F. Walker, "Kepler's View of the Star of Bethlehem and the Babylonian Almanac for 7/6 B.C.," *Iraq* 46 (1984): 44.

95. W. Foerster, "*astēr*," and "*astron*," in *TDNT* I, p. 501. See F. Boll, "Der Stern des Weisen," *ZNW* 18 (1917–1918): 40–43.

96. Sachs and Walker, "Kepler's View," p. 45.

97. E. L. Martin, "The Celestial Pageantry Dating Christ's Birth," *Christianity Today* 21 (Dec. 3, 1976): 16–18, 21–22; idem, *New Star over Bethlehem* (Pasadena: Foundation for Biblical Research, 1980), pp. 9–11.

98. K. Ferrari-d'Occhieppo, *Der Stern der Weisen—Geschichte oder Legende*, 2d ed. (Vienna: Herold, 1977); idem, "The Star of Bethlehem," *Quarterly Journal of the Royal Astronomical Society* 19 (1978): 517; idem, "The Star of the Magi and Babylonian Astronomy," chapter 3 in Vardaman and Yamauchi, *Chronos*, pp. 41–53.

99. K. Ferrari-d'Occhieppo, "Weitere Erwägungen zum Stern von Bethlehem," *Sterne und Weltraum* 20 (June–July 1981): 209–10.

100. F. Zinniker, *Probleme der sogenannten Kindheitsgeschichte bei Mattäus* (Freiburg: Paulus, 1972), p. 115.

101. J. K. Fotheringham, "The Star of Bethlehem," *JTS* 10 (1908): 116–19.

102. J. E. Ciotti, "The Magi's Star: Misconceptions and New Suggestions," *Griffith Observer* 42 (Dec. 1978): 2–11.

in Matthew was intended to describe a supernatural and not a natural phenomenon.[103]

Our current system of dating was devised by a monk, Dionysus Exiguus, in the sixth century A.D. He miscalculated the date of Augustus—an error that was discovered only in the seventeenth century. Those scholars who would identify the Christmas star with Halley's Comet, which appeared in 12 B.C., date Jesus' birth accordingly.[104] At the other extreme, Martin has suggested a lowering of the date of Herod's death to 1 B.C. and consequently of Jesus' birth to 2 B.C.[105] Hughes follows Timothy Barnes in dating Herod's death to 5 B.C., and because he identifies the star with the triple conjunction of Jupiter and Saturn, he arrives at the date of 7 B.C.[106] Most scholars have dated Herod's death in the spring of 4 B.C., because an eclipse that is mentioned by Josephus is believed to have occurred at that time. This would place the birth of Jesus in 5 or possibly 6 B.C.[107]

The Magi in the Church Fathers

The Magi's gifts of gold, myrrh, and frankincense recall Psalm 72:10: "The kings of Tarshish and of distant shores will bring tribute to him; the kings of Sheba and Seba will present him gifts." This association helped to facilitate the metamorphosis of the Magi into kings. According to Tertullian (*Adversus Marcion* 3.13): "The East considers the Magi almost as kings."

103. P. Iohannes Schaumberger, "Textus cuneiformis de stella Magorum?" *Biblica* 6 (1925): 448–49; B. Ramm, *The Christian View of Science and Scripture* (Grand Rapids: Eerdmans, 1954), pp. 163–167; B. Davidheiser, *Science and the Bible* (Grand Rapids: Baker, 1971), pp. 103–5; W. White, "Star of the Magi," in *The Pictorial Encyclopedia of the Bible*, ed. M. G. Tenney (Grand Rapids: Zondervan, 1975), 5: 512–14; K. Boa and W. Proctor, *The Return of the Star of Bethlehem* (Garden City: Doubleday, 1980); J. A. Moore, *Astronomy in the Bible* (Nashville: Abingdon, 1981), pp. 146–54.

104. See n. 87 above.

105. E. L. Martin, *The Birth of Christ Recalculated*, 2d ed. (Pasadena: Foundation for Biblical Research, 1980), pp. 4–25; idem, "The Nativity and Herod's Death," in Vardaman and Yamauchi, *Chronos*, pp. 85–92. See also P. Gaecherter, "Die Magierperikope," *Zeitschrift für katholische Theologie* 90 (1968): 257–95; J. Mosely, "When Was That Christmas Star?" *Griffith Observer* 44 (Dec. 1980): 2–9; J. Thorley, "When Was Jesus Born?" *Greece and Rome* 28 (1981): 81–89.

106. Hughes, *Star*, p. 200; T. D. Barnes, "The Date of Herod's Death," *JTS* 19 (1968): 204–9.

107. See Finegan, *Handbook of Biblical Chronology*, pp. 231–33; D. Johnson, "The Star of Bethlehem Reconsidered," *Planetarian* 10 (1981): 14–16; idem, "When the Star of Bethlehem Appeared," *Planetarian* 10 (1981): 20–23; idem, " 'They Went Eight Stades toward Herodeion,' " pp. 93–99; H. W. Hoehner, "The Date of the Death of Herod the Great," pp. 101–11 and P. L. Maier, "The Date of the Nativity and the Chronology of Jesus' Life," pp. 113–30, in Vardaman and Yamauchi, *Chronos*. H. W. Hoehner, *Chronological Aspects of the Life of Christ* (Grand Rapids: Zondervan, 1977), pp. 11–25.

Myrrh and frankincense were precious aromatic spices obtained from the exudation of short trees that grew only in two parts of the world, Somaliland in east Africa and Yemen in southwest Arabia (biblical Sheba).[108] Knowledge that these substances came from Arabia may have influenced Justin Martyr in his *Dialogue with Trypho* (78) to assert that the Magi came from Arabia.[109] He was followed in this view by Tertullian and Epiphanius. The vast majority of church fathers, however, believed that the Magi came from Persia (for example, Clement of Alexandria, Cyril of Alexandria, Chrysostom, Origen, Ephraem Syrus).[110]

The notion that God apparently used astrology to guide the Magi troubled the church fathers. Tertullian (*On Idolatry* 9) declared: "What then? Shall therefore the religion of those Magi act as patron now also to astrologers? . . . But, however, that science has been allowed until the Gospel, in order that after Christ's birth no one should thenceforward interpret any one's nativity by the heavens."

Ignatius (*Ephesians* 19.3) declared that when the star shone, "thence was destroyed all magic, and every bond vanished."[111] Justin Martyr in his *Dialogue with Trypho* (78) declared: "For the Magi, who were held in bondage for the commission of all evil deeds through the power of that demon, by coming to worship Christ, show that they have revolted from the dominion which held them captive." Other church fathers maintained that the Magi were not mere astrologers like the Chaldeans but were learned followers of Zoroaster. Origen (*Contra Celsum* 1.58–60) took Celsus to task for failing to distinguish between the Chaldeans and the Magi. He believed the Magi knew the prophecy of Balaam, and were inspired on their quest when they found their magic declining in power.

108. Gus W. Van Beek, "Frankincense and Myrrh," *BA* 23 (1960): 70–95; Nigel Groom, *Frankincense and Myrrh* (London: Longman, 1981); G. Ryckmans, "De l'or(?), de l'encens et de la myrrhe," *RB* 58 (1951): 372–76. Ryckmans makes the unlikely suggestion that the Gospel writer misunderstood the Semitic word for gold, which was really a third type of aromatic substance.

109. The few modern scholars to follow this orientation include H. J. Richards, "The Three Kings," *Scripture* 8 (1956): 23–28; R. North, *Guide to Biblical Iran* (Rome: Pontifical Institute of Biblical Archaeology, 1956), p. 56; F. Salvoni, "La visita dei Magi e la fuga in Egitto," *Ricerche bibliche e religiose* 14 (1979): 22.

110. Messina, "Ecce," p. 11; Hughes, *Star,* p. 36.

111. W. R. Schoedel, *Ignatius of Antioch* (Philadelphia: Fortress, 1985), p. 88. Schoedel comments: "It is presumably the heavenly bodies that are here said to lose their grip on humankind."

Monument to Severa depicting the three Magi.

The Magi in the Apocryphal Gospels

The episode of the Magi was expanded in the infancy gospels from the second century on.[112] In the earliest of these, *The Protevangelium of James* (circa A.D. 150), we read:

> And the wise men said: "We saw a very great star shining among those stars and dimming them so that the stars appeared not: and thereby knew we that a king was born unto Israel, and we came to worship him." . . . And lo, the star which they saw in the east went before them until they entered the cave: and it stood over the head of the cave.[113]

The sixth-century Syriac *Cave of Treasures* gives the names of the Magi as Hormizdah, king of Persia; Yazdegerd, king of Saba; and Perozadh, king of Sheba (compare Ps. 72:10).[114] The first references to the traditional names of the Magi—Melchior, Balthasar, and Gaspar[115]—occur in the *Excerpta Latina Barbari,* a Latin translation of a sixth-century Greek chronicle. *The Armenian Infancy Gospel,* which was based on an early Syriac composition, specifies that Melqon (Melchior) came from Persia, Balthasar from Arabia, and Gaspar from India.[116]

112. See my article, "Apocryphal Gospels," in *The International Standard Bible Encyclopedia,* ed. G. W. Bromiley, rev. ed. (Grand Rapids: Eerdmans, 1979), 1: 181–88.

113. M. R. James, *The Apocryphal New Testament* (Oxford: Clarendon, 1960 reprint), p. 47. Compare W. Schneemelcher, ed., *New Testament Apocrypha* (Philadelphia: Westminster, 1963), 1: 386. See also Alois Kehl, "Der Stern der Magier," *JBAChr* 18 (1975): 115–26.

114. B. M. Metzger, "Names for the Nameless in the New Testament," in *Kyriakon,* J. Quasten Festschrift, eds. P. Granfield and J. Jungmann (Münster: Aschendorff, 1970), 1: 82.

115. The name *Melchior* means "my king is light"; *Balthasar* was probably derived from "Belteshazzar," the Babylonian name given to Daniel; and *Gaspar* may come from the Indian name *Gundaphorus.* See Metzger, "Names for the Nameless," p. 85; M. V. Scheil, "Melchior, Gaspar, Balthasar," in *Melchior de Vogüé, Florilegium ou receuil de travaux d'érudition* (Paris: Imprimerie Nationale, 1909), pp. 551–54.

116. James, *Apocryphal New Testament,* p. 83.

Mosaic of the three Magi from the Church of S. Vitale in Ravenna (6th cent.). (Alinari/Editorial Photocolor Archives)

The *Excerpta et Collectanea* gives us further details:

> Melchior, an old man with white hair and a long beard . . . who offered gold to the Lord as to a king. The second, Gaspar by name, young and beardless and ruddy complexioned . . . honored him as God by his gift of incense, an oblation worthy of divinity. The third, black-skinned and heavily bearded, named Balthasar . . . by his gift of myrrh testified to the Son of Man who was to die.[117]

The Magi in Art

The adoration of the Magi was one of the most popular motifs in early Christian art,[118] appearing already in the catacomb of Santa Pris-

117. Cited by R. E. Brown, *The Birth of the Messiah* (Garden City: Doubleday, 1977), p. 199. R. E. McNally, "The Three Kings in Early Irish Latin Writing," in *Kyriakon*, 2: 669, comments on this work as follows: "This curious compilation, if not actually of Irish provenance, certainly reflects and parallels early Irish thinking. Largely a collection of disparate pieces of different character and origin, it was probably put together about the middle of the eighth century, possibly somewhat later."

118. See H. Kehrer, *Die heiligen drei Könige in Literatur und Kunst*, 2 vols. (Leipzig: Seemann, 1908–1909); J. C. Marsh-Edwards, "The Magi in Tradition and Art," *Irish Ecclesiastical Review* 85 (1956): 1–9.

The Church of the Nativity in Bethlehem. (Courtesy of Palphot)

cilla two centuries before the representation of shepherds adoring the Christ child.[119] The number of Magi varied from two to four but eventually stabilized at three.[120] The three Magi, dressed in Persian garb, were usually depicted presenting gifts to the infant Jesus resting on the lap of his mother, as in the famous epitaph of Severa.[121]

The three Magi appear in the famous sixth-century mosaic from the church of St. Apollinaris Nuovo in Ravenna. Above their figures are inscribed the names: SCS. (= *Sanctus* "Saint") Balthassar, SCS. Melchior, and SCS. Gaspar. The purple mantle of the empress Theodora on the Church of San Vitale in Ravenna is embroidered with the figures of the Magi.[122]

The Magi were customarily portrayed in Persian dress with belted tunics, full sleeves, trousers, and peaked hats. Franz Cumont suggests that Christian artists adopted the Roman representation of Persians presenting tributes to the emperors.[123] When the Persian army under Chosroes invaded Palestine in 614, his soldiers destroyed the churches

119. Brown, *Birth of the Messiah*, p. 197.

120. C. R. Morey, *Early Christian Art* (Princeton: Princeton University Press, 1953), p. 68; André Grabar, *Christian Iconography* (Princeton: Princeton University Press, 1968), fig. 26; Pierre du Bourguet, *Early Christian Art* (New York: William Morrow, 1971), p. 46.

121. In the illustrated epitaph of Severa (dated to 330), a star looms above the Magi and the Madonna. The figure behind her pointing to the star has been interpreted as Balaam or as a personification of the Holy Spirit. See J. P. O'Neill et al., eds., *The Vatican Collections: The Papacy and Art* (New York: Metropolitan Museum of Art, 1983), p. 221, no. 136.

122. Morey, *Early Christian Art*, p. 167; Grabar, *Christian Iconography*, fig. 252.

123. F. Cumont, "L'adoration des mages et l'art triomphal de Rome," *Atti di Pontificia Accademia di Archeologia*, ser. 11A, Memorie 111 (1932): 82–105.

The adoration of the Magi on a clay torta. (Courtesy of the Detroit Institute of Art)

of Jerusalem but spared the Church of the Holy Nativity in Bethlehem when they saw that a mosaic of the church depicted Magi in Persian dress.[124]

This mosaic of the Magi may have been reproduced in some of the *eulogiae,* souvenirs brought back from the Holy Land by pilgrims. These were of two types. The first were *ampullae,* small bottles of lead in which the pilgrims brought back from the Holy Land water or holy oil from the lamps that burned at the shrines. Among the famous Monza ampullae given by Pope Gregory the Great to the Lombard queen (circa 600) are examples that depict the Virgin in a frontal pose, flanked by Magi on one side and shepherds on the other.[125]

The other rare type of souvenirs were *tortae,* tokens made of clay or earth stamped with images of the shrines. As these were intended to be ground into powder, then dissolved in water and drunk for their curative powers, very few have survived. Recently two sixth-century examples, now in Istanbul, were published. These depict three bearded Magi wearing peaked hats and bearing gifts as they advance toward the Christ child held by the seated Virgin. A later example is owned by the Detroit Institute of Art.[126]

From the sixth century on, the Magi were often depicted as being of different ages: a youth, an adult, and an older man. Leonardo Olschki suggested this trimorphism was inspired by the threefold manifesta-

124. This story was reported at the Synod of Jerusalem in 836. See Jack Finegan, *The Archeology of the New Testament* (Princeton: Princeton University Press, 1969), p. 26; Messina, "Ecce," p. 7.

125. Morey, *Early Christian Art,* p. 123; Grabar, *Christian Iconography,* fig. 209; J. Daoust, "Les ampoules de Monza," *BTS* 170 (Apr. 1975): 1–8.

126. L. Y. Rahmani, "The Adoration of the Magi on Two Sixth-Century C.E. *Eulogia* Tokens," *IEJ* 29 (1979): 34–36.

The adoration of the Magi by Botticelli (15th cent.). (Courtesy of the National Gallery of Art, Washington, D.C.)

tion of the god Zurvan.[127] In a series of studies Jacques Duchesne-Guillemin suggested this differentiation stemmed from the Hellenistic cult of Aion.[128]

Artists began depicting the "wise men" from the east as kings first during the twelfth century. Between the years 1360 and 1420 one of the three kings was first represented as a black.[129]

The Relics of the Magi

When Marco Polo traveled in Persia in the late thirteenth century, he was shown the tombs of the Magi fifty miles southwest of Tehran:

> In Persia is the city called Saveh, from which the three Magi set out when they came to worship Jesus Christ. Here, too, they lie buried in three sepulchres of great size and beauty. . . . Their bodies are still whole, and they have hair and beards. One was named Beltasar, the second Gaspar, and the third Melchior. . . . The inhabitants declare that in days gone by three kings of this country went to worship a new-born prophet and took with them three offerings—gold, frankincense, and myrrh—so as to discover whether this prophet was a god, or an earthly king or a healer.[130]

In competition with the Persian claim that the relics of the Magi were preserved in their homeland, the West came to believe the relics of the Magi were recovered from Hadramaut in South Arabia by the Emperor Zeno in 490. From Constantinople they were then taken to Milan.

When Frederick Barbarossa, the German Holy Roman emperor, vanquished the city of Milan, Reinald von Dassel, the emperor's chancellor, obtained the precious relics for his native city of Cologne. The relics were received with great jubilation in 1164 and became the prized treasure of the great Gothic cathedral built at Cologne.[131]

127. L. Olschki, "The Wise Men of the East," in *Oriental Traditions . . . Presented to William Popper*, ed. W. J. Fischel (Berkeley: University of California Press, 1951), pp. 375–95.

128. J. Duchesne-Guillemin, "Die drei Weisen aus dem Morgenlande," *Antaios* (1965): 234–53; idem, "Jesus' Trimorphism and the Differentiation of the Magi," in *Man and His Salvation*, S. G. F. Brandon Festschrift, eds. E. Sharpe and J. Hinnells (Manchester: Manchester University Press, 1974), pp. 91–98; idem, "The Wise Men from the East in the Western Tradition," in *Papers in Honour of Mary Boyce*, eds. A. D. H. Bivar and J. Hinnells (Leiden: Brill, 1985), pp. 149–57.

129. J. Vercoutter, J. Leclant, F. M. Snowden, and J. Desanges, *The Image of the Black in Western Art* (New York: William Morrow, 1976), 1: 24.

130. *The Travels of Marco Polo*, trans. R. Latham (Harmondsworth: Penguin, 1958), pp. 58–59. See A. V. W. Jackson, "The Magi in Marco Polo and the Cities in Persia from which They Came to Worship the Infant Christ," *JAOS* 26 (1905): 79–83.

131. Duchesne-Guillemin, "Wise Men from the East," p. 157.

14
Mithraism

Mitra/Mithra/Mithras

The Vedic *Mitra,* the Avestan *Mithra,* and the Roman *Mithras* were manifestations of a god whose worship extended over the millennia from India to England. The earliest attestation of the god occurs in the famous treaty between the Hittite king Suppiluliuma (1375–1345 B.C.) and the king of Mitanni.[1] In the Hindu scriptures, the Rig Veda, the god Mitra is mentioned more than two hundred times. He was the first among the triad of gods—Mitra, Varuna, and Indra.[2]

Mithra does not appear in the earliest Zoroastrian scriptures—the Gathas of Zoroaster. Some scholars interpret this silence as an indication of Zoroaster's hostility toward Mithras, but others believe this is an unwarranted conclusion.[3] Mithra is the subject of Yasht 10 in the

1. P. Thieme, "The Aryan Gods of the Mitanni Treaties," *JAOS* 80 (1960): 301–17.

2. G. Dumézil, "The Vedic Mitra," *JMS* 1 (1976): 26–35; P. Thieme, "The Concept of Mitra in Aryan Belief," in *Mithraic Studies,* ed. J. Hinnells (Manchester: Manchester University Press, 1975), 1: 21–39; J. Gonda, "Mitra in India," *MS* 1, pp. 40–52; idem, *The Vedic God Mitra* (Leiden: Brill, 1972).

3. R. C. Zaehner, *The Dawn and Twilight of Zoroastrianism* (New York: G. P. Putnam's Sons, 1961), p. 69; M. Boyce, "On Mithra's Part in Zoroastrianism," *BSOAS* 32 (1969): 10–34.

Younger Avesta[4] (see chapter 12). There he is depicted as an omniscient warrior god, who blessed his followers but who also inflicted horrible calamities on his foes.[5] The Avestan Mithra was associated with the sun, but was not identified with it. He was especially known as "the lord of wide pastures," a phrase that occurs 111 times.[6] Ali Akbar Jafarey believes the epithet reflects Mithra's origin as the god of the green grass of the Russian steppes, the homeland of the Persians before they migrated to the Iranian plateau.[7]

Some scholars such as Jacques Duchesne-Guillemin have speculated that Mithra was the god of Cyrus.[8] But there is no solid evidence to support this suggestion. Mithra, however, does appear along with Anahita in the texts of Artaxerxes II.[9] In the Parthian era Mithra was identified with the Greek god Helios at Commagene in eastern Turkey. Mithra played a role in the Manichaean pantheon.[10] The late ninth-century Pahlavi texts "take comparatively little interest in Mithra, and add little to what is known of him from older sources."[11] Today Mithra is still the center of one of two great Zoroastrian festivals—the Mihragān, "festival of Mithra," which falls on the day of Mihr in the month of Mihr (Oct.).[12]

Mithraism

The central question in Mithraic studies today is the relationship between the Persian Mithra and the Roman Mithras, who became the center of an important mystery religion called Mithraism.[13] This flourished in the Roman Empire as a rival of Christianity. Some scholars have even suggested it influenced early Christianity.

Mithraism was one of many popular mystery religions from the

4. I. Gershevitch, *The Avestan Hymn to Mithra* (Cambridge: Cambridge University Press, 1959).

5. P. Thieme, "Mithra in the Avesta," in *Études Mithriaques* [*EM*], ed. J. Duchesne-Guillemin (Tehran-Liège: Bibliothèque Pahlavi, 1978), pp. 501–10.

6. E. Benveniste, "Mithra aux vaste pâturages," *JA* 248 (1960): 421–29.

7. A. Jafarey, "Mithra, Lord of Lands," *MS,* 1: 54–61.

8. J. Duchesne-Guillemin, "Le Dieu de Cyrus," in *Commémoration Cyrus* [*CC*] (Tehran-Liège: Bibliothèque Pahlavi, 1974), 3: 11–21.

9. R. G. Kent, *Old Persian,* rev. ed. (New Haven: American Oriental Society, 1953), p. 203.

10. W. Sundermann, "Some More Remarks on Mithra in the Manichaean Pantheon," *EM,* pp. 485–99.

11. Gershevitch, *Avestan Hymn,* p. 3.

12. M. Boyce, "Mithragān among the Irani-Zoroastrians," *MS,* 1: 106–18; idem, *Zoroastrians* (London: Routledge and Kegan Paul, 1987), pp. 72–73.

13. Popular introductions to the subject are F. Cumont, *The Mysteries of Mithra* (New York: Dover, 1956 reprint of 1903 edition); M. J. Vermaseren, *Mithras, The Secret God* (London: Chatto and Windus, 1963).

eastern Mediterranean area.[14] As a mystery religion its members were initiated and pledged to secrecy.[15] It is because their teachings were closely guarded secrets that so little is known about the mystery religions. Whereas there are extensive texts (Rig Veda, Avesta) about Mitra/Mithra in pre-Roman times, few sources provide information about Mithras in the Roman period apart from incidental passages in pagan and Christian writers, dedicatory inscriptions, and some enigmatic graffiti. On the other hand, there is an abundance of archaeological evidence from the *mithraea,* or cave-like sanctuaries, such as statues, reliefs, and frescoes. But there is much controversy about the interpretation of such mute evidence.

The Tauroctony

The central cult image of Mithraism was the statue of the tauroctony or depiction of Mithras slaying the bull. Mithras is depicted on the back of a crouching bull as he pulls its head back with his left hand and thrusts a sword between its shoulders with his right hand. A raven hovers above, while a snake glides on the ground; a dog leaps at the bull's wound, and a scorpion attacks the bull's genitals. The tip of the bull's tail ends in an ear of wheat.

Over five hundred representations of Mithras slaying the bull have been found. One of the earliest datable reliefs (circa A.D. 160–70) is displayed in the Cincinnati Art Museum.[16] An ambitious attempt to analyze all of these tauroctonies in a systematic manner has been undertaken by Leroy A. Campbell.[17] Unfortunately his study has been flawed by the adoption of untenable presuppositions. Richard L. Gordon is harshly critical:

> At the moment the study of Mithraic art labours, or hovers on the brink of labouring, under one of the most ill-conceived of formal typologies, that of L. A. Campbell. . . . Founded upon a tangle of indefensible assumptions and executed in a cloud of errors, it deserves simply to be ignored.[18]

14. See F. Cumont, *Oriental Religions in Roman Paganism* (New York: Dover, 1956 reprint of the 1911 edition); J. Ferguson, *The Religions of the Roman Empire* (Ithaca: Cornell University Press, 1970), pp. 99–122; E. Yamauchi, *Harper's World of the New Testament* (San Francisco: Harper and Row, 1981), pp. 55–62; J. Godwin, *Mystery Religions in the Ancient World* (San Francisco: Harper and Row, 1981).

15. The oath of secrecy was called a *sacramentum* in Latin.

16. R. L. Gordon, "A New Mithraic Relief from Rome," *JMS* 1 (1976): 166–86.

17. L. A. Campbell, "Typology of Mithraic Tauroctones," *Berytus* 11 (1954): 1–60; idem, *Mithraic Iconography and Ideology* (Leiden: Brill, 1968).

18. R. L. Gordon, "Panelled Complications," *JMS* 3 (1980): 201.

The Tauroctony. (The Cincinnati Art Museum, gift of Mr. and Mrs. Fletcher E. Nyce)

John Hinnells comments: "The most serious criticism of all, however, is that at no point does Campbell note that the Zoroastrian theology he urges lies behind Mithraism is derived wholly from the Pahlavi texts whose final redaction dates from the ninth century A.D. and even later."[19]

Depicted on either side of the tauroctony are two standing human figures: Cautes holding his torch up and Cautopates holding his torch down. Franz Cumont interpreted these two figures as the representations of the morning rising sun and of the evening setting sun. Roger Beck prefers to associate Cautes with the sun as it travels northward in the spring and Cautopates with the sun as it travels southward in the autumn. "If this hypothesis is correct," he concludes, "then the torchbearers are not, as Cumont was inclined to think . . . , the spring and autumn *manifestation* of Mithras as the sun god, but rather his seasonal *companions* at those two times of the year."[20]

19. J. R. Hinnells, "Method and Message in Mithraism," *Religion* 1 (1971): 70.

20. R. Beck, "Cautes and Cautopates: Some Astronomical Considerations," *JMS* 2 (1977): 7. For the variations, see J. R. Hinnells, "The Iconography of Cautes and Cautopates I: The Data," *JMS* 1 (1976): 36–67.

The Tauroctony with Cautes and Cautopates. (Courtesy of the Museum of London)

The Lion-Headed Image

An enigmatic figure associated with Mithraism is a lion-headed statue whose body is entwined with a snake. The lion-headed figure is usually depicted having four wings and holding two keys. It sometimes stands on a globe. There is also a variant of this figure with a man's head. Zodiacal signs appear at times on the figure.

The image's identity has been greatly debated. It has been identified with Aion, Kronos, Chronos, and Zurvan.[21] The last identification was advocated especially by Cumont. On the basis of an inscription associated with an example in York, England, some scholars identified the

21. H. Von Gall, "The Lion-Headed and the Human-Headed God in the Mithraic Mysteries," *EM*, pp. 511–25.

figure as Arimanius (Ahriman), the evil god of Zoroastrianism.[22] Stanley Insler writes: "Furthermore, I would endorse the identification of the lion-headed god of the cult with Arimanius (Ahriman) in light of the daëvic nature of winter found in the Iranian texts."[23] But most scholars, even those who accept the idea that this god was named Arimanius, view the figure as a benevolent, rather than malevolent, deity.

Maarten Vermaseren argues that the figure symbolized eternity.[24] Howard Jackson concludes: "The leontocephaline, as the distillation of celestial power, cannot, then, have been an irredeemably oppressive force but, as it embodied souls, so it might aid—by initiation and not by compulsion—in freeing them from that embodiment."[25] After a thorough study of various examples of the lion-headed figure, Hinnells came to the following conclusion: "The interpretation of the lion-headed figure here offered is that it represents a being who presided over the soul's ascent of the planetary ladder; a cosmic power which ruled over man's passage through the gates to the higher spiritual life."[26]

Other Images

Around the central tauroctony are often panels representing various aspects of the myth of Mithras.[27] A frequent motif is of the rock birth, which shows the young Mithras emerging from a rock, holding a dagger and a torch.[28] In an example from the Housesteads temple at Hadrian's Wall in northern England, Mithras is shown being born from an egg as was the Orphic Phanes.[29] The egg-shaped frame is decorated with zodiacal signs.

22. Zaehner, *Dawn*, pp. 129–30. The name *Arimanius*, which occurs in only six other Mithraic inscriptions, may, however, have been simply a person's name.

23. S. Insler, "A New Interpretation of the Bull-Slaying Motif," in *Hommages à Maarten J. Vermaseren*, eds. M. B. de Boer and T. A. Edridge (Leiden: Brill, 1978), 2: 529.

24. M. J. Vermaseren, "A Magical Time God," *MS*, 2: 446–56.

25. H. M. Jackson, "The Meaning and Function of the Leontocephaline in Roman Mithraism," *Numen* 32 (1985): 23.

26. J. R. Hinnells, "The Lion-Headed Figure in Mithraism," *Acta Iranica* 4 (1975): 364. Quite speculative is J. Hansman's article, "A Suggested Interpretation of the Mithraic Lion-man Figure," *EM*, pp. 215–17, which proposes that the figure is the visual reproduction of Plato's tripartite structure of the human soul (*Republic* 588B–589B).

27. Vermaseren, *Mithras, The Secret God*, chapter 10, "The Legend of Mithras"; Gordon, "Panelled Complications."

28. M. J. Vermaseren, "The Miraculous Birth of Mithras," *Studia Archaeologica Gerardo van Hoorn Oblata* (Leiden: Brill, 1951), pp. 93–109.

29. E. and J. R. Harris, *The Oriental Cults in Roman Britain* (Leiden: Brill, 1965), p. 34; C. M. Daniels, "The Role of the Roman Army in the Spread and Practice of Mithraism," *MS*, 2: 269.

The symbolism of the rock birth has been taken to mean that Mithras was born from the stone as fire from the flint or as the sun rises from behind a mountain. Shepherds are also shown on the scene of the young naked god's emergence.[30]

Other panels show Mithras battling a wild bull and carrying it into a cave. Mithras is seen on horseback, at times with a bow and arrow. Numerous scenes portray Mithras in relationship to Sol or Helios (the sun-god). In one typical scene Sol kneels before Mithras. In another scene Mithras is depicted dining with Sol. Vermaseren comments: "The divine meal is more frequently portrayed than any other scene except the bull-slaying and sometimes the latter appears on the front of a relief which portrays the meal on its reverse."[31] Mithras also rides a chariot that ascends to the heavens.

Other divine figures associated with Mithras include Kronos-Saturn and Jupiter.[32] Very prominent are numerous astrological symbols including the symbols of the zodiacal constellations.[33]

The Church Fathers and Mithraism

The church fathers were aware that this "Persian" religion was a rival to Christianity. The most important references are found in Justin Martyr (circa 100–65), Tertullian (circa 160–220), Origen (circa 185–254), and Jerome (circa 345–419).

After relating the tradition that Jesus was born in a cave, Justin wrote: "those who presided over the mysteries of Mithras were stirred up by the devil to say that in a place, called among them a cave, they were initiated by him" (*Dialogue* 78). Earlier he had written: "And when those who record the mysteries of Mithras say that he was begotten of a rock and call the place where those who believe in him are initiated a cave, do I not perceive here that the utterance of Daniel (2:34), that a stone without hands was cut out of a great mountain, has been imitated by them?"

In an important passage describing the communion service for the newly baptized, Justin contended: "the wicked devils have imitated in the mysteries of Mithras, commanding the same thing to be done. For, that bread and a cup of water are placed with certain incantations in

30. Vermaseren, *Mithras, The Secret God,* pp. 75–79.

31. Ibid., p. 99.

32. Ibid., pp. 106–11.

33. R. Beck, "Interpreting the Ponza Zodiac I," *JMS* 1 (1976): 1–19; idem, "Interpreting the Ponza Zodiac II," *JMS* 2 (1978): 87–147; idem, *Planetary Gods and Planetary Orders in the Mysteries of Mithras* (Leiden: Brill, 1988).

the mystic rites of one who is being initiated, you either know or can learn" (*I Apology* 66).

Tertullian challenged Christians by pointing out the dedication of the Mithraists:

> Are you not ashamed, fellow soldiers of Christ, that you will be condemned, not by Christ, but by some soldier of Mithras? At the initiation, deep in a cavern, in the very camp of darkness (*vere castra tenebrarum*), a crown is presented to the candidate at the point of a sword, as if in mimicry of martyrdom, and put upon his head; then he is admonished to resist and throw it off and possibly slip it on the shoulder of the god, saying: "Mithras is my crown." (*De corona* 15)

In another work (*De praescriptione haereticorum* 40) Tertullian alludes to the marking of the Mithraic *milites* or "soldiers" with some kind of symbol. There are major problems, however, with this text and its interpretation. Which word is the subject of the clauses in sections 3 to 5 is questioned. It can be read according to certain manuscripts, *Mithra signat illic in frontibus milites suos, celebrat et panis oblationem* ("Mithras puts his mark on the foreheads of his own soldiers and celebrates his own oblation of bread") or, with some manuscripts, *diabolus . . . si adhuc memini Mithrae signat illic in frontibus milites suos* ("if I am right in my memory of Mithras . . . in that cult the devil puts his mark on the foreheads of his own soldiers"). According to J. P. Kane: "It is then open to personal interpretation whether one refers the following clause (*celebrat et panis oblationem*) to the mysteries of Mithras or to some other pagan god."[34]

Although many scholars (Franz Cumont, Geo Widengren, Carl Vollgraff) have interpreted this passage as referring to a branding of the Mithraists, Per Beskow, after a careful examination of the evidence, concludes: "The nature of this sign is unknown. There is no evidence for branding or tattooing, nor for crosses or X-marks applied to the bodies of the initiates, nor any indication that such marks were considered to symbolize the sun in the mysteries."[35]

Whether Tertullian's remark that *imaginem resurrectionis inducit* meant the Mithraists believed in a resurrection[36] is disputable.[37] Tertullian's further comment that the Mithraic cult also had *virgines et*

34. J. P. Kane, "The Mithraic Cult Meal in Its Greek and Roman Environment," in *MS*, 2: 317. One editor, Kroyman, removes the word *Mithra(e)* from Tertullian's text.

35. P. Beskow, "Branding in the Mysteries of Mithras," in *Mysteria Mithrae* [*MM*], ed. U. Bianchi (Leiden: Brill, 1979), p. 499.

36. Vermaseren, *Mithras, The Secret God*, p. 103.

37. R. L. Gordon, "Franz Cumont and the Doctrines of Mithraism," *MS*, 1: 236.

continentes, continent women as well as men, has received no confirmation.[38]

Origen, in his refutation of Celsus (*Contra Celsum* 6.2), described the Mithraic *klimax heptapylos* ("ladder of seven gates") through which the initiate progressed:

> After this from a desire to parade his erudition in his attack on us Celsus also describes some Persian mysteries, where he says: These truths are obscurely represented by the teaching of the Persians and by the mystery of Mithras which is of Persian origin. For in the latter there is a symbol of the two orbits in heaven, the one being that of the fixed stars and the other that assigned to the planets, and of the soul's passage through these. The symbol is this. There is a ladder with seven gates and its top an eighth gate.[39]

Each of the gates was associated with the "planets": Kronos, Aphrodite, Zeus, Hermes, Ares, the moon, and the sun. This passage may be compared with one in Porphyry (*De antro nympharum* 24) as a key passage for the astrological interpretation of Mithraic monuments.[40]

In one of Jerome's letters (*Epistula ad Laetam*) the seven grades of the Mithraic initiates are listed:

> A few years ago did not your neighbor Gracchus, whose name echoes patrician nobility, when a prefect of the city, overturn, demolish and throw out all the portentious masks with which the Corax, Nymphus, Miles, Leo, Perses, Heliodromus, and Pater are initiated, and when these had been dispatched in advance like hostages did he not enforce Christian baptism?[41]

Firmicus Maternus (fourth century), in his *Error of the Pagan Religions* (5.2), declared:

38. This places into question the view expressed by A. D. Nock, *Early Gentile Christianity and Its Hellenistic Background* (New York: Harper and Row, 1964 reprint of 1928 edition), p. 61, that Tertullian himself might once have been a Mithraist.

39. H. Chadwick, *Origen, Contra Celsum* (Cambridge: Cambridge University Press, 1980), p. 334.

40. B. Lincoln, "Mithra(s) as Sun and Savior," *MM*, p. 506.

41. *Ante paucos annos propinquus uester Gracchus nobilitatem patriciam nomine sonans, cum praefecturam regeret urbanam, nonne specu Mithrae et omnia portentuosa simulacra, quibus corax, nymphus, miles, leo, Perses, heliodromus, pater initiantur subuertit, fregit, exussit et his quasi obsidibus ante praemissis impetrauit baptismum Christi?* B. M. Metzger, "St. Jerome's Testimony Concerning the Second Grade of Mithraic Initiation," *AJP* 66 (1945): 225–33. Metzger has pointed out how I. Hilberg (1912) and editors as recently as 1942 emended the text against all the manuscript evidence to replace *nymphus* with *cryphius* on the basis of two Mithraic inscriptions published by Cumont. That *nymphus* was the correct name for the grade was confirmed by the discovery of the Dura Europos mithraeum. *Nymphus* was derived by adding a masculine ending to the word for "bride."

> Him they call Mithra, and his cult they carry on in hidden caves, so that they may be forever plunged in the gloomy squalor of darkness and thus shun the grace of light resplendent and serene. O true consecration of a divinity! O repulsive inventions of a barbaric code! . . . So you who declare it proper for the cult of the Magi to be carried on by the Persian rite in these cave temples, why do you praise only this among the Persian customs?[42]

Hypotheses of Franz Cumont

Mithraic studies were established at the turn of the century by the Belgian scholar, Franz Cumont, who gathered the first comprehensive collection of Mithraic monuments.[43] His interpretation of these monuments was to remain dominant through most of this century.[44]

Cumont believed Mithraism developed directly from Persian Zoroastrianism through the agency of the magi in Asia Minor.[45] After all, the church fathers believed Mithraism was a Persian religion, Mithras was a Persian god, and a number of words (Perses, Cautes, Cautopates, Nama) in the cult have an Iranian background.

Cumont interpreted the central cult image, the tauroctony, against the background of Zoroastrian dualism. On the basis of the late Zoroastrian creation account in the Bundahishn,[46] Cumont interpreted the slaying of the bull by Mithras as an act of creation.[47] The snake and scorpion were viewed by Cumont as evil creatures.

He took Plutarch's reference (*Pompey* 24) to Pompey's encounter with Cilician pirates who "celebrated secret rites or mysteries, among which were those of Mithras," as the means by which Mithraism was introduced into Italy around 65 B.C.[48]

42. For a summary of the patristic data, see C. Colpe, "Die Mithrasmysterien und die Kirchenväter," in *Romanitas et Christianitas,* eds. W. Den Boer and others (Amsterdam: North Holland, 1973), pp. 29–43.

43. F. Cumont, *Textes et monuments figurés relatifs aux mystères de Mithra,* 2 vols. (Brussels: H. Lamertin, 1896, 1899).

44. Cumont, *Mysteries of Mithra.*

45. F. Cumont, "Mithra en Asie Mineure," in *Anatolian Studies Presented to William Hepburn Buckler* (Manchester: Manchester University Press, 1939), pp. 67–76.

46. On the problems of Zoroastrian sources, see chapter 12.

47. Cumont, *Mysteries of Mithra,* pp. 135–36. But in the Persian texts it was Ahriman, the evil god, who killed the primordial bull. No Persian text speaks of Mithras killing the bull. See Gershevitch, *Avestan Hymn to Mithra,* p. 62.

48. Cumont, *Mysteries of Mithra,* p. 37. Cumont's interpretation of this passage has been followed uncritically by Vermaseren, *Mithras, The Secret God,* pp. 8–9; S. G. F. Brandon, "Mithraism and Its Challenge to Christianity," *Hibbert Journal* 53 (1955): 110; S. Laeuchli, "Urban Mithraism," *BA* 31 (1968): 73–99.

The History of Religions School

On the basis of Cumont's view of Mithraism as a pre-Christian phenomenon, scholars of the History of Religions School[49] and others speculated about the influence of Mithraism upon nascent Christianity.[50] Richard Reitzenstein thought he could detect the presence of Iranian myths in the New Testament milieu. He suggested the sacrifice of Christ aligned itself on the doctrine of salvation represented by the immolation of the Mithraic bull.[51] Reitzenstein and others relied heavily upon Albrecht Dietrich's interpretation of part of the magical papyri as a so-called Mithraic liturgy.[52]

A scholar who continues to support Cumont's view of Mithraism as an essentially Persian phenomenon is Geo Widengren.[53] In his latest study he cites parallels with a movement in northwestern Iran and the border of Armenia and Caucasus, "the very regions where we may suppose that the origin of that type of Mithra religion is to be looked for, from which Mithraic mysteries developed."[54] This movement, however, is from the ninth century A.D.! Widengren understands the Christian tradition of Jesus' birth in a cave as derived from an earlier Iranian/Mithraic tradition.[55] Some scholars even thought such a tradition had been stricken out of Matthew's Gospel.[56]

49. C. Colpe, *Die religionsgeschichtliche Schule* (Göttingen: Vandenhoeck and Ruprecht, 1961); E. Yamauchi, "History-of-Religions School," in *New Dictionary of Christian Theology*, eds. S. B. Ferguson and D. F. Wright (Leicester: Inter-Varsity, 1988), pp. 308–9.

50. For a thorough critique of this tendency, see G. Wagner, *Pauline Baptism and the Pagan Mysteries* (Edinburgh: Oliver and Boyd, 1967).

51. R. Reitzenstein, *Die hellenistischen Mysterienreligionen* (Darmstadt: Wissenschaftliche Buchgesellschaft, 1966 reprint of the 1926 edition); J. E. Steely, trans., *Hellenistic Mystery-Religions* (Pittsburgh: Pickwick, 1978). See E. Yamauchi, *Pre-Christian Gnosticism*, 2d ed. (Grand Rapids: Baker, 1983), pp. 21–24, 178–81; J. Ries, "Mithriacisme et Christianisme à la lumière des recherches anciennes et récentes," in *Orientalia J. Duchesne-Guillemin Emerito Oblata* (Leiden: Brill, 1984), p. 444.

52. A. Dietrich, *Eine Mithrasliturgie* (Darmstadt: Wissenschaftliche Buchgesellschaft, 1966 reprint of the 1923 edition). This interpretation was rejected by Cumont. Many scholars now question whether this text was either a liturgy or Mithraic. See Wagner, *Pauline Baptism*, p. 68. M. J. Vermaseren, "Sotériologie dans les Papyri Graecae Magicae," in *La Soteriologia dei Culti Orientali nell' Impero Romano*, eds. U. Bianchi and M. J. Vermaseren [*SCO*] (Leiden: Brill, 1982), p. 25. Vermaseren speculates that it might be a document of "Egyptian Mithraism." See also M. W. Meyer, *The "Mithras Liturgy"* (Missoula: Scholars, 1976), p. viii.

53. G. Widengren, "The Mithraic Mysteries in the Greco-Roman World with Special Regard to Their Iranian Background," *La Persia e il Mondo Greco-Romano* (Rome: Accademia Nazionale dei Lincei, 1966), pp. 433–55. He labored under the illusion that a mithraeum had been identified at Uruk in Mesopotamia. Ibid., p. 436.

54. G. Widengren, "Bâbakîyah and the Mithraic Mysteries," *MM*, p. 694.

55. G. Widengren, "Stand und Aufgaben der iranischen Religionsgeschichte," *Numen* 2 (1955): 106. Widengren's views are based upon very late sources such as an apocryphal Armenian gospel and the Syrian Chronicle of Zuqnin. They have been refuted by J. Duchesne-Guillemin, "Die Magier in Bethlehem und Mithras als Erlöser?" *ZDMG* 111 (1961): 469–75; idem, "Die drei Weisen aus dem Morgenlande," *Antaios* (1965): 234–52. See R. Beck, "Mithraism since Franz Cumont," *ANRW* II.17.4 (1984): 2070.

56. See E. Benz, "Die Heilige Höhle in der alten Christenheit und in der östlich-orthodoxen Kirche," *Eranos Jahrbuch* 22 (1953): 380–81.

John Hinnells, though he has been critical of Cumont and the earlier theories of the History of Religions School,[57] has advanced the possibility of Iranian or Mithraic influence upon the Old and the New Testaments. He claims that Mithraism "is the very one which can be shown, not only to be the oldest (mystery religion), but also the one to have come into frequent and direct contact with the Jews from the time of Cyrus to the time of Christ, both in the Diaspora, and in Palestine itself."[58] He further claims that "it will be shown that the Mithraic worship was to be met in Syria, and even Palestine, in the first century B.C., and that it spread to Asia Minor long before the arrival of Christianity there."[59]

Discovery of Mithraea and Mithraic Monuments

Some three thousand Mithraic monuments and inscriptions have now been discovered, many of them dedicated by soldiers in frontier areas.[60] When Cumont wrote at the beginning of the century, he was aware of only four mithraea at Ostia.[61] We now know of fourteen at this site.[62]

Mithraea have been found as far west as Hadrian's Wall in northern England. The Housesteads mithraeum at the wall yielded an unusual Mithras-Phanes figure. The Carrawburgh mithraeum, also at the wall, had an altar of Mithras with a radiate halo pierced for illumination.[63] These two mithraea date to the third century A.D. The Walbrook mithraeum in London (second century A.D.) yielded extremely fine marble heads of Mithras and Serapis.[64]

57. J. R. Hinnells, "The Iranian Background of Mithraic Iconography," in *CC,* 1: 242–50.

58. J. R. Hinnells, "Christianity and the Mystery Cults," *Theology* 71 (1968): 20.

59. Ibid., p. 61. See J. R. Hinnells, "Zoroastrian Saviour Imagery and Its Influence on the New Testament," *Numen* 16 (1969): 161–85; idem, "Iranian Influence upon the New Testament," in *CC,* 2: 271–84. See J. Ferguson, "More about Mithras," *Hibbert Journal* 53 (1955): 323.

60. See especially M. J. Vermaseren, *Corpus Inscriptionum et Monumentorum Religionis Mithriacae,* 2 vols. (The Hague: Martinus Nijhoff, 1956, 1960).

61. Cumont, *Mysteries of Mithra,* p. 38.

62. Beck, "Mithraism since Franz Cumont," pp. 2021–22.

63. I. A. Richmond and J. P. Gillam, *The Temple of Mithras at Carrawburgh* (Newcastle upon Tyne: Society of Antiquaries, 1951); Harris, *Oriental Cults,* p. 17.

64. M. J. Vermaseren, "A Mithraic Temple in London," *Numen* 2 (1955): 139–45; J. M. C. Toynbee, *The Roman Art Treasures from the Temple of Mithras* (London: Middlesex Archaeological Society, 1986).

The rock birth of Mithras from the Housesteads mithraeum at Hadrian's Wall. (Courtesy of the Museum of Antiquities, University of Newcastle)

The Carrawburgh mithraeum at Hadrian's Wall.

The richest areas for Mithraic monuments have been Italy and the Rhine–Danube frontier regions. Of all Mithraic inscriptions 31 percent were found in Italy (18 percent in Rome) and 49 percent in the Rhine–Danube area.[65] Very little has been recovered from Egypt, Greece, and Anatolia. Persia itself has produced no monuments of Mithraism. To date no tauroctony, the central icon of the Mithraic mysteries, has been found in Iran.[66]

65. R. L. Gordon, "Mithraism and Roman Society," *Religion* 2 (1972): 102.
66. R. N. Frye, "Mithra in Iranian Archaeology," in *EM*, p. 205.

Altar to the "Unconquered God" Mithras from the Carrawburgh mithraeum. (Courtesy of the Museum of Antiquities, University of Newcastle)

Richard N. Frye, who is normally cautious, has declared: "Admitted there is sparse evidence of a Mithra cult in Persepolis, but there is nothing to contradict the assumption that primarily the soldiers stationed in Persepolis had their own cult of Mithra, which could have been something similar to the Knights of Malta in Christianity."[67] This speculation is based upon Raymond Bowman's translation of Aramaic inscriptions on stone mortars, pestles, and plates of the Achaemenid period. Bowman concluded: "In the light of all facts at our disposal, it seems likely that in the green stone ritual vessels bearing Aramaic texts from Persepolis, we see evidence that already in Achaemenid

67. R. N. Frye, "Mithra in Iranian History," in *MS,* 1: 64.

The head of Mithras from the Walbrook mithraeum in London. (Courtesy of the Museum of London)

times a proto-Mithraic cult was actively operative in the Persian army."[68] Unfortunately for this hypothesis, all other Aramaic scholars who have examined the texts conclude that the inscriptions are simply administrative notations rather than ritual texts.[69]

68. R. A. Bowman, *Aramaic Ritual Texts from Persepolis* (Chicago: University of Chicago Press, 1970), p. 15.

69. P. Bernard, "Les mortiers et pilons inscrits de Persépolis," *Studia Iranica* 1 (1972): 165–76; J. A. Delaunay, "A propos des Aramaic *Ritual Texts from Persepolis* de R. A. Bowman," *Acta Iranica* 2 (1974): 193–217; K. Kamioka, "Philological Observations on the Aramaic Texts from Persepolis," *Orient* 11 (1975): 45–66; B. A. Levine, "Aramaic Texts from Persepolis," *JAOS* 92 (1975): 70–79; J. Naveh and S. Shaked, "Ritual Texts or Treasury Documents?" *Orientalia* 42 (1973): 445–57. See J. R. Hinnells, "Religion at Persepolis," *Religion* 3 (1973): 157–60.

The Role of Anatolia

The development of the cult of Mithras in the Hellenistic/Parthian period is still shrouded in obscurity. The origins of the Mithraic mysteries are thought to have been in Hellenistic Anatolia. The kings of Cappadocia, Commagene, and Armenia bear the name *Mithradates,* "the gift of Mithras" (compare Ezra 4:7). Cumont took the occurrence of these names as evidence of Mithras worship in these areas.[70] Hinnells, however, cautions: "Indeed it may be questioned whether any significance can be attached to the use of theophoric names; they may represent convention and not a person's own faith."[71] From Commagene we have first-century-B.C. texts that identify Mithras with Helios. But as Vermaseren notes, "the inscriptions do not say anything about a secret cult of Mithras; the god simply takes his place beside the acknowledged state gods."[72]

Cumont recognized an embarrassing lack of Mithraic monuments from Asia Minor,[73] a situation that has not improved in the decades since Cumont wrote. Israel Roll comments:

> But he (Cumont) continued to believe that the lack of documentation was primarily the result of insufficient archaeological excavations. But his hopes have not been fulfilled. . . . As a matter of fact, no new evidence of major importance related to the mysteries has been discovered in Anatolia in the past thirty years or so.[74]

The genuine Mithraic monuments from Asia Minor are but four,[75] and none date before A.D. 150.[76]

Plutarch speaks of the pirates' worship of Mithras and of their resettlement (*Pompey* 28; 24). Most of these pirates probably came from Cilicia Tracheia, that is, "rough" Cilicia to the west of Tarsus, a mountainous and forested region. Plutarch reveals that most of twenty thousand prisoners were settled at Dyme in Achaea in Greece, which has yielded almost no Mithraic monuments.[77]

70. Cumont, *Oriental Religions,* p. 143. D. M. Winston, "The Iranian Component in the Bible, Apocrypha and Qumran," *HR* 5 (1966): 209–10. Winston goes so far as to speculate that the diffusion of Mithraism in Asia Minor was the source of the Iranian elements found in the Dead Sea Scrolls!

71. Hinnells, "Religion at Persepolis," p. 158.

72. Vermaseren, *Mithras, The Secret God,* p. 29. Compare H. Waldmann, *Die Kommagenischen Kultreformen unter König Mithradates I* (Leiden: Brill, 1973), p. 111.

73. Cumont, *Mysteries of Mithra,* p. 29.

74. I. Roll, "The Mysteries of Mithras in the Roman Orient," *JMS* 2 (1977): 58.

75. Beck, "Mithraism since Franz Cumont," p. 2018.

76. Gordon, "Franz Cumont and the Doctrines of Mithraism," p. 217.

77. Beck, "Mithraism since Franz Cumont," p. 2047–48: "It has long been a notorious fact about the Mysteries that, for reasons we can only guess at, they by-passed Greece proper. Research this century has not changed that perception, though a few isolated discoveries have been made."

Many scholars have drawn unwarranted conclusions from Plutarch's text. A careful analysis of the passage does not justify the idea that a fully developed Mithraism was introduced into Italy during the first century B.C. by the instrumentality of these pirates. Plutarch provides no information about the nature of the pirates' Mithras cult.[78] Gary Lease comments: "Note well that Plutarch does not speak of an introduction of Mithraic ties to the West; this text cannot support an early appearance of Mithraism in the Western Mediterranean."[79] This negative conclusion has been effectively demonstrated by E. David Francis.[80]

Mithras and Mithraism in the Roman Empire

The first public recognition of the Persian god Mithras in Rome was the occasion of the state visit of Tiridates, the king of Armenia, in A.D. 66. According to Dio Cassius (63.1–7), Tiridates addressed Nero with these words: "And I have come to thee, my god, to worship thee as I do Mithras." Pliny (*Natural History* 30.6.17) says that Tiridates had brought "magi with him, had initiated Nero into their banquets." It is going beyond the evidence to assert that this means Nero became an initiate in the Mithraic mysteries.[81] This conclusion can only be based on Cumont's assumption that these magi were already practitioners of the Mithraic mysteries.[82] As Kane observes of Pliny's statement: "There is no mention of Mithras, and whether *magicis cenis* means '*Magian* banquets' (i.e. *Persico ritu*) or '*magical* banquets' is a matter of personal interpretation."[83]

It is significant that no Mithraic monuments have been discovered from either Herculaneum[84] or Pompeii[85]—both of which were de-

78. Roll, "Mysteries of Mithras," p. 58.

79. G. Lease, "Mithraism and Christianity: Borrowings and Transformations," *ANRW* II.23.2 (1980): 1310, n. 29.

80. E. D. Francis, "Plutarch's Mithraic Pirates," in *MS*, 1: 207–14. See also J. M. C. Toynbee, "Still More about Mithras," *Hibbert Journal* 54 (1956): 109; E. Yamauchi, "The Apocalypse of Adam, Mithraism, and Pre-Christian Gnosticism," *EM*, pp. 553–54.

81. As asserted by A. Schütze, *Mithras-Mysterien und UrChristentum* (Stuttgart: Urachhaus, 1972), p. 17. Even Reitzenstein, *Hellenistic Mystery-Religions*, p. 154, n. 4, expressed reservations: "On the other hand, I cannot share Cumont's confidence in connecting with the actual Mitras-mysteries the report of the elder Pliny (XXX 17) that Tiridates had initiated Nero through *magicae cenae.*"

82. Cumont, *Mysteries of Mithra*, p. 85; see Vermaseren, *Mithras, The Secret God*, p. 24.

83. J. P. Kane, "The Mithraic Cult Meal in Its Greek and Roman Environment," in *MS*, 2: 317. See also Beck, "Mithraism since Franz Cumont," p. 2073.

84. J. J. Deiss, *Herculaneum: Italy's Buried Treasure* (New York: Harper and Row, 1985).

85. M. Grant, *Cities of Vesuvius* (New York: Macmillan, 1971).

stroyed by the eruption of Mount Vesuvius in A.D. 79. There is thus a gap of about 150 years between Pompey's encounter with the Cilician pirates and the earliest literary reference to the Mithraic myth.

The poet Statius (circa A.D. 80) in his *Thebaid* has the following line: "Mithras, that beneath the rocky Persian cave strains at the reluctant-following horns" (*seu Persei sub rupibus antri indignata sequi torquentem cornua Mithram*). Campbell takes this as evidence for "a tauroctone relief of the rustic cave type" of Mithraism.[86] On the other hand, Gordon concedes that this may be evidence for a Mithraic cult but not for Mithraism. He dates the establishment of the Mithraic mysteries to the reign of Hadrian (117–138) or Antoninus Pius (138–161).[87]

The earliest dated Mithraic inscription in the West is a statue of Alcimus, the servant of T. Claudius Livianus, who was a prefect under Trajan in A.D. 101.[88] There are a handful of inscriptions that date to the early second century, but the vast majority of texts date after A.D. 140. Gordon maintains:

> The first evidence for Mithraea is around 140–50 A.C. In contrast to the situation in Christianity, the building of the Mithraic mysteries is important in cultic and symbolic terms. It is therefore reasonable to argue that Western Mithraism did not exist until the mid-second century A.C., at least in a developed sense, since there certainly is some earlier scattered evidence for a cult or cults of Mithras in the West. The question is whether this earlier evidence actually relates to the mysteries, and, if so, how.[89]

Mithraic Texts

A total of fifty-five mithraea have been excavated, twenty-five in Italy, the majority of these in Ostia. The fourteen mithraea at Ostia date between A.D. 150 and 260.[90] On the basis of fragmentary evidence and projections, scholars have offered widely differing estimates for the number of possible mithraea in ancient Rome. Vermaseren believes there

86. Campbell, "Typology," p. 96.

87. Gordon, "Franz Cumont," pp. 245–46, n. 119. Other scholars date the spread of Mithraism to the reigns of the Flavians—Vespasian (69–79), Titus (79–81), and Domitian (81–96). See Ferguson, *Religions of the Roman Empire*, p. 48.

88. Vermaseren, *Mithras, The Secret God*, p. 29; see *CIMRM* 1: 594.

89. R. Gordon, "Second Plenary Discussion," in *MS* 2: 352; see Gordon, "Mithraism and Roman Society," p. 93. V. Tran Tam Tinh, *Le culte des divinités orientales en Campanie* (Leiden: Brill, 1972). Tran Tam Tinh notes that evidence for Mithraism in Campania for the late first century is quite vague and dates the expansion of Mithraism in this area to the second century, especially from the Antonines.

90. S. Laeuchli, ed., *Mithraism in Ostia* (Evanston: Northwestern University Press, 1967).

were about one hundred.[91] Filippo Coarelli lists forty actual or possible mithraea, but calculates there may have been close to seven hundred mithraea at one time![92] The most important mithraea are: the mithraeum at Capua, which provides illustrations of the initiation ceremonies; the Felicissimus mithraeum at Ostia, which lists the grades of initiates; and the Santa Prisca mithraeum at Rome, which provides texts. Vermaseren accepts an early second-century date for the mithraeum at Capua,[93] but Francis suggests a late second-century date.[94] The Santa Prisca mithraeum is dated to the late second century.[95]

The mosaic at the Felicissimus mithraeum depicts the symbols of the grades mentioned by Jerome, from the lowest to the highest: Corax = raven; Nymphus = bridegroom; Miles = soldier; Leo = lion; Perses = Persian; Heliodromus = courier of the sun; and Pater = father. The scenes of the mithraeum at Capua show a naked and blindfolded initiate groping with outstretched hands. In another scene he kneels with his hands tied before the mystagogus, who is clothed in a red tunic. Farther on we see him kneeling but with his hands no longer bound.[96]

Vermaseren comments that until the excavation of the Capua mithraeum in 1924 the only evidence for the Mithraic initiation rite was the church fathers. A scene showing the initiate being offered bread and a cup confirms Justin Martyr's observation. The Capua scenes also vividly confirm the text of the fourth-century writer Ambrosiaster:

> Their eyes are blindfolded that they may not refuse to be foully abused; some moreover beat their wings together as birds do, and croak like ravens, and others roar like lions; and yet others are pushed across ditches filled with water: their hands have previously been tied with the intestines of a chicken, and then somebody comes up and cuts these intestines (he calls himself their "liberator").[97]

Perhaps the single most important Mithraic sanctuary is the Santa Prisca mithraeum, discovered in 1935, because of the important texts that are depicted on its walls.[98] The site was excavated in 1952/1953,

91. Vermaseren, *Mithras, The Secret God*, p. 36.

92. Cited in Beck, "Mithraism since Franz Cumont," p. 2026.

93. M. J. Vermaseren, *Mithriaca I: The Mithraeum at S. Maria Capua Vetere* (Leiden: Brill, 1971), pp. 1, 49.

94. Review of the above by E. D. Francis in *Mithras* 1 (1972): 6.

95. Vermaseren, *Mithras, The Secret God*, p. 44.

96. Vermaseren, *Mithriaca I*, pp. 26–36; Vermaseren, *Mithras, The Secret God*, pp. 129–37.

97. *Alii autem ligatis manibus intestinis pullinis projiciuntur super foveas aqua plenas, accedente quodam cum gladio et inrumpente intestina supra dicta qui se liberatorem appellet.* Cited by R. L. Gordon, "Reality, Evocation and Boundary in the Mystery of Mithras," *JMS* 3 (1980): 24.

98. See H. Betz, "The Mithras Inscriptions of Santa Prisca and the New Testament," *NT* 10 (1968): 52–80.

and the resulting study published in 1965.[99] Among the interesting sayings that read like mottos or slogans are the following:

Nubila per ritum ducatis tempora cuncti, "together you must sustain clouded times through service"

Dulcia sunt ficata avium sed cura gubernat, "sweet are the livers of birds, but pain governs"

Primus et hic aries restrictius ordine currit, "here also the Ram walks in front, strictly in line"

Nama leonibus novis et multis annis, "hail, Lions, for new and many years"

Accipe thuricremos pater, accipe sancte leones, per quos thuradamus, per quos consumimur ipsi, "father, receive those who burn incense, holy one, receive the Lions, through whom we offer the incense, through whom we are ourselves consumed"

The most important and widely quoted text, which for the first time appears to give an explicit statement of Mithraic soteriology, is:[100]

Et nos servasti eternali sanguine fuso, "us too you have saved after having shed the eternal blood"

The blood is without doubt the blood of the slain bull. Following the suggestion of Alfred Loisy, who was influenced by Christian soteriology, Vermaseren entertained the suggestion that the bull was an incarnation of Mithras himself, although he correctly notes there is no evidence for this identification.[101]

In 1978 during the International Seminar on Mithraism at Rome a restudy of the Santa Prisca texts was undertaken by Silvio Panciera. This has now cast doubt on the original reading of this text.[102] The *et nos* given by Vermaseren is not very visible today. Ugo Bianchi doubts that *servasti* was visible even at the time of the earlier study. The "s" is lost. The word *eternali* has some serious problems. Only the phrase *sanguine fuso* is relatively secure.[103] Beck therefore concludes that this

99. M. J. Vermaseren and C. C. Van Essen, *The Excavations in the Mithraeum of the Church of Santa Prisca in Rome* (Leiden: Brill, 1965).

100. See R. Turcan, "Salut mithriaque et sotériologie néoplatonicienne," in *SCO*, pp. 1173–91.

101. Vermaseren and Van Essen, *Santa Prisca in Rome*, p. 220; Vermaseren, *Mithras, The Secret God*, p. 103.

102. S. Panciera, "Il materiale epigrafico dallo scavo del mitreo di S. Stefano Rotondo," in *MM*, pp. 87–112, especially 103–5.

103. U. Bianchi, "Prolegomena," in *MM*, p. 53.

text, "which has perhaps been the principal warrant for the interpretation of Mithras' bull-killing as a salvific act effective because it transcends time, can no longer carry the weight placed upon it."[104]

The Taurobolium

A sanguinary rite that has been connected by some scholars with Mithraism is the sacrifice of the bull called the *taurobolium*. But this rite was practiced by Mithraists only in exceptional cases.[105] It was associated almost entirely with the cult of the Magna Mater or Cybele, another mystery religion.[106] In its developed phase, an initiate went into a pit and was drenched with the blood of a bull that was sacrificed on a grate above him according to Prudentius (circa A.D. 400).

Loisy (d. 1940) interpreted Christianity as a mystery religion. For him Christ was "a savior-god, after the manner of an Osiris, an Attis, a Mithra."[107] Following Reitzenstein's lead, he suggested this rite was the basis of the idea of Christ's redemption by blood. He cited a particular taurobolic inscription (CIL 6.510), which speaks of *in aeternum renatus* ("reborn for eternity"), as a parallel to the Christian concept of rebirth as proof of his thesis.[108]

The fatal flaw of the History of Religions School and scholars who were influenced by it was their disregard of the dates of the sources they cited and the implications of these dates for the possibility of influence. We have 155 taurobolium or criobolium (ram sacrifice) inscriptions, which have been studied by Robert Duthoy.[109] Almost all of these inscriptions come from the west: from Africa, Italy, and above all France. The taurobolium in the Attis cult is first attested only about A.D. 160. It is only in the fourth century that the sacrifice of the bull develops into the blood-bath described by Prudentius. The *renatus* inscription is dated after A.D. 375. Another *renatus* inscription, dated to about the same time, is only good for twenty years.

Apparently in this case it was Christianity that influenced a mystery religion. Duthoy concludes, "the phrase '*in aeternum renatus*' that occurs in one inscription shows that in a few exceptional cases the influence of Christianity was even more marked."[110] According to Bruce Metzger:

104. Beck, "Mithraism since Franz Cumont," p. 2028.
105. Ferguson, *Religions of the Roman Empire*, p. 112.
106. J. B. Rutter, "The Three Phases of the Taurobolium," *Phoenix* 22 (1968): 231.
107. A. Loisy, "The Christian Mystery," *Hibbert Journal* 10 (1911–1912): 51.
108. H. Willoughby, *Pagan Regeneration* (Chicago: University of Chicago Press, 1929), p. 132.
109. R. Duthoy, *The Taurobolium: Its Evolution and Terminology* (Leiden: Brill, 1969).
110. Ibid., p. 121.

Thus, for example, one must doubtless interpret the change in the efficacy attributed to the rite of the taurobolium. In competing with Christianity, which promised eternal life to its adherents, the cult of Cybele officially or unofficially raised the efficacy of the blood bath from twenty years to eternity.[111]

Eastern Mithraea

On the question raised by the History of Religions School of possible Mithraic influence on Christianity, only the evidence from the eastern Roman Empire is relevant. Since evidence for Mithraism in Egypt, Greece, and Anatolia is negligible, evidence for Mithraism in Syria and Palestine must be examined.

There are Mithraic monuments from five sites in Syria and one in Palestine. In Syria we have evidence from Sidon, from Si, from the coast near Lattakieh, from Arsha-wa-Qibar, and most significantly from Dura-Europos. The Sidon mithraeum is dated either to A.D. 188 according to Campbell,[112] or to A.D. 389 according to Ernest Will.[113] The two bas-reliefs from Si can hardly be dated to the first century, as Frothingham suggested,[114] but should be dated to the second century according to Will.[115] The fragmentary head found near Lattakieh is dated to the first half of the second century.[116]

The most important mithraeum in the East is that from Dura-Europos on the Euphrates River, a site that also yielded a synagogue and a church. Using the first typewritten report by Henry Pearson, Campbell argued the cult of Mithra may have existed at Dura as early as A.D. 80 or 85.[117] But the official report and other scholars date the first mithraeum in A.D. 168 (or 165) on the basis of inscriptional evidence.[118] This mithraeum was established by a contingent from Pal-

111. B. Metzger, "Methodology in the Study of the Mystery Religions and Early Christianity," in his *Historical and Literary Studies: Pagan, Jewish and Christian* (Grand Rapids: Eerdmans, 1968), p. 11. For other examples of Christianity's influence upon the mystery religions of Attis and Adonis, see P. Lambrechts, "Les fêtes 'phrygiennes' de Cybèle et d'Attis," *Bulletin de l'Institut Historique Belge de Rome* 27 (1952): 141–70; idem, "La 'résurrection d'Adonis'," in *Mélanges Isidore Levy* (Brussels: L'Institut de Philologie et d'Histoire Orientales, 1955), pp. 214–40; E. Yamauchi, "Easter—Myth, Hallucination, or History?" *Christianity Today* 18 (Mar. 15, 1974): 12–14, 16.

112. Campbell, "Typology," pp. 26–27.

113. E. Will, "La date du mithréum du Sidon," *Syria* 37 (1950): 261.

114. A. Frothingham, "A New Mithraic Relief from Syria," *AJA* (1918): 61.

115. E. Will, "Nouveaux monuments sacrés de la Syrie romaine," *Syria* 29 (1952): 71.

116. *CIMRM* I, p. 90.

117. Campbell, "Typology," p. 31.

118. *CIMRM* I, p. 57. See E. D. Francis, "Mithraic Graffiti from Dura-Europos," in *MS*, 2: 424.

One of the magos figures from the Dura Europos mithraeum. (Courtesy of the Yale University Art Gallery)

myra, although extensive excavations at that Syrian site have yielded no Mithraic monuments.[119]

The texts from Dura mention six of the seven Mithraic grades. Por-

119. Will, "Nouveaux monuments," p. 69; S. B. Downey, "Syrian Images of Mithras Tauroctonos," in *EM*, p. 86.

traits of two magos figures, seated and carrying scrolls and canes, were identified by Cumont as Zoroaster and Otanes.[120] They were probably the *patres* of the community. In view of Cumont's stress on the magi as bearers of the Mithraic teachings, it is surprising to learn that only Dura had a Mithraic inscription with the word *magos,* "[N]ama Maximus Magus" (inscription 859). The only other text that contains a derivative is a graffito found at Rome in 1940 and published by Margherita Guarducci in 1979.[121] It is an acclamation to a Mithraist who entered into the arts of the magi.

An analysis of all Mithraic evidence from Syria undercuts Cumont's view of a transmission of Mithraic traditions from Anatolia to Syria, because all of these monuments reflect Roman Mithraic iconography.[122] Roll concludes: "Our group of Syrian monuments provides no real support for the hypothesis of an Oriental origin for the mysteries of Mithras."[123]

Earlier speculations about mithraea in Palestine were founded on the basis of stories recounted by rabbis of a cave in Galilee and of readings of Egyptian hieroglyphs![124] In 1973 a mithraeum was discovered by Robert Bull at Caesarea, built in the vault of a warehouse by the shore. This yielded a tauroctone medallion and poorly preserved frescoes.[125] In any case, this mithraeum is very late, dated to the third or probably the fourth century A.D.[126]

Revised Interpretations

With few exceptions Cumont's theory of Mithraism as a Roman expression of Zoroastrianism remained unchallenged until the First International Mithraic Congress at Manchester in 1971.[127] Further criticisms were raised at the Second International Mithraic Congress at Tehran in 1975[128] and in the short-lived *Journal of Mithraic Studies,* both sponsored by the late Shah of Iran. The "paradigm shift" in

120. F. Cumont, "The Dura Mithraeum," in *MS,* 1: 183–84. This is a posthumously published essay.

121. M. Guarducci, "Ricordo della 'magia' in un graffito del mitreo del Circo Massimo," in *MM,* pp. 153–70.

122. Downey, "Syrian Images," in *EM,* pp. 148–49.

123. Roll, "Mysteries of Mithras," p. 62.

124. R. Eisler, "Ein Mithräum in Galiläa," *OLZ* (1909): 425–27; W. Müller, "Der Gott Mithra in Palestina," *OLZ* (1912): 252–54; F. Pfister, "Das angebliche Mithräum in Galiläa und Alexanders Besuch in der Götterhöhle," *OLZ* (1913): 402–3.

125. R. Bull, "A Mithraic Medallion from Caesarea," *IEJ* 24 (1974): 187–90.

126. R. Bull, "The Mithraeum at Caesarea Maritima," in *EM,* pp. 75–89; L. M. Hopfe and G. Lease, "The Caesarea Mithraeum," *BA* 38 (1975): 2–10.

127. Edited by J. Hinnells as *Mithraic Studies* (1975).

128. Edited by J. Duchesne-Guillemin as *Études Mithriaques* (1978). The *Journal of Mithraic Studies* ended after three volumes in 1980, as the 1979 overthrow of the Shah deprived it of funding.

Mithraic studies has been described in detail by Beck,[129] a study that has been summarized by David Ulansey.[130]

Cumont's interpretations have been analyzed and rejected on all major points. Gordon concludes that "Cumont simply assumed at every critical point that the Magian evidence was relevant, and proceeded to argue as though this were an established fact and not merely a working hypothesis."[131] Hinnells demonstrated Cumont's dualistic interpretation of the tauroctony has no basis in either Iranian or Roman evidence.

> Since Cumont's reconstruction of the theology underlying the reliefs in terms of the Zoroastrian myth of creation depends upon the symbolic expression of the conflict of good and evil, we must now conclude that his reconstruction simply will not stand. It receives no support from the Iranian material and is in fact in conflict with the ideas of that tradition as they are represented in the extant texts. Above all, it is a theoretical reconstruction which does not accord with the actual Roman iconography.[132]

His interpretation of the Mithraic meal as a "sacramental meal" is an unwarranted extrapolation from Justin Martyr's text, which only describes bread and water given to initiates. Francis comments: "Cumont's systematic description of Mithraic liturgy in Christian terms is now seen to be misleading, not to say mischievous. In particular, his description of the Mithraic meal as 'communion' has been called in question."[133] After a detailed examination of the subject, Kane concluded:

> But once again I remind the reader that in all this we have not yet found a cult meal, a meal in which *all the initiates* can participate. . . . On the other hand I have found no support for a "haoma ceremony," the existence of which is the basic assumption of Cumont's theory of a *sacramental* Mithraic meal. Nor can I find any support for Vermaseren's assumption that Mithraic initiates ate the flesh of a bull and drank its blood so as to be born again, whether from Mithraic iconography and archaeology, Avestan texts, or the Greek and Graeco-Roman milieu.[134]

129. Beck, "Mithraism since Franz Cumont," pp. 2002–15.

130. D. Ulansey, "Mithraic Studies: A Paradigm Shift?" *RSR* 13 (1987): 104–10.

131. Gordon, "Franz Cumont and the Doctrines of Mithraism," p. 221.

132. J. R. Hinnells, "Reflections on the Bull-Slaying Scene," in *MS*, 2: 303.

133. E. D. Francis, "Two Notes on Mithraic Liturgy," *Mithras* 1 (1972): 5.

134. Kane, "Mithraic Cult Meal," pp. 348, 351. See M. Meslin, "Convivialité ou communion sacramentelle? Repas mithraïque et eucharistie chrétienne," *Paganisme, Judaïsme, Christianisme* (Paris: E. de Boccard, 1978), pp. 295–305.

Beck and a number of other scholars have concluded that the key to understanding the mysteries lies in the identification of the various icons with astrological bodies; for example, the bull would represent Taurus and the scorpion Scorpio.[135] Michael Speidel identifies Mithras as the constellation Orion.[136] David Ulansey connects Mithras with Perseus.[137] While all of these scholars agree that astrology is the key, they do not agree on what that astrological interpretation ought to be.

As to Hinnells' claim that Mithraism could have influenced the Old and New Testaments, this is based on a failure to distinguish between the worship of Mithras and Mithraism, and reliance upon very late Zoroastrian texts. For example, Hinnells' suggestion that the Parthians who invaded Palestine in 40 B.C. under the banner of Mithras were welcomed by the Jews—just as Cyrus had marched under the aegis of Mithras—is irresponsible.[138] He writes, "perhaps it is only speculation, but it is reasonable speculation, to say that this would present Mithra to the Jews in a most favourable light."[139] His further suggestion that "one might reasonably conclude that the development in the Judeo-Christian saviour imagery is indebted to Iranian influence" is based on the saoshyant concept found in very late Persian texts.[140] Hinnells uses this idea to interpret the tauroctony. Insler remarks, "in identifying Mithra's divine act of the slaughter of the bull with the later Zoroastrian legend concerning the Savior, Hinnells commits the same type of error for which he blames Cumont in the latter's identification of the bull-slaying scene with the legend involving the Evil Spirit."[141]

Most scholars conclude that Mithraism, which developed at the earliest late in the first century A.D., could not have influenced nascent Christianity. After an analysis of the evidence, Lease concludes: "To be specific, it is clear that the few scattered remarks in Christian polemical literature against Mithraism, together with the scanty archeological remains of the Mithraic religion, simply do not bear out a direct influence of the one religion upon the other."[142]

135. R. Beck, "A Note on the Scorpion on the Tauroctony," *JMS* 1 (1976): 208–9.

136. M. P. Speidel, *Mithras-Orion, Greek Hero and Roman Army God* (Leiden: Brill, 1980).

137. D. Ulansey, "Mithras and Perseus," *Helios* 13 (1986): 33–62.

138. We are uncertain of the religion of Cyrus.

139. Hinnells, "Christianity and the Mystery Cults," p. 24.

140. The saoshyant is no redeemer from sin and guilt. He is more correctly a "benefactor." The teaching of the coming of three world saviors is found in ninth-century A.D. Pahlavi texts. See chapter 12.

141. Insler, "New Interpretation of the Bull-Slaying Motif," p. 521.

142. Lease, "Mithraism and Christianity," p. 1328.

Later Emperors, Mithras, and Sol Invictus

Although some emperors, such as Commodus (A.D. 180–192), were privately initiated into the mysteries of Mithras, it was only in the late empire that Mithras worship flourished because the god was linked with the cult of the sun. The emperor Elagabalus (A.D. 218–222) from Syria introduced the sun-god of his native town of Emesa (Homs) as the supreme god of the empire. But he was despised for his decadence and was killed by the praetorian guard. Then in A.D. 274 the cult of Sol Invictus, "the unconquerable sun," was made popular by Aurelian, the Roman emperor who conquered Zenobia, queen of Palmyra.

The close identification of Mithras with the sun is seen in his titulature, *Deo Soli Invicto Mithrae,* and its variations.[143] Gaston Halsberghe, in his study of Sol Invictus, however, has stressed the need to distinguish between the two cults. They had different ceremonies and priests. The worship of Mithras was secretive; the worship of Sol Invictus was public.[144]

While Mithras was closely identified with Sol Invictus, it was the latter that was formally recognized and not the former. Mithras never appears on imperial coins.[145] The sole public example of imperial devotion to Mithras is the dedication by Diocletian at Carnuntum in 307.

Mithraism was a competitor of Christianity. Sometimes a mithraeum was located next to a church, as at the Santa Prisca mithraeum in Rome. But Mithraism was not as potent a rival as the cult of Sol Invictus. The fact that Mithraism excluded women and consisted of small congregations of initiates[146] indicate that Ernest Renan's often-quoted statement ("if Christianity had been checked in its growth by some deadly disease, the world would have become Mithraic"[147]) was completely off the mark.[148] Arthur Darby Nock's judgment was: "There was, if anything, less chance of the Roman Empire turning

143. D. W. MacDowall, "Sol Invictus and Mithra: Some Evidence from the Mint of Rome," in *MM,* p. 561.

144. G. H. Halsberghe, *The Cult of Sol Invictus* (Leiden: Brill, 1972), pp. 117–21.

145. J. Ries, "Mithriacisme et Christianisme," p. 450; M. Simon, "Mithra et les empereurs," in *MM,* p. 419.

146. The average Ostian mithraeum was 30 to 40 feet long and 13 to 18 feet wide.

147. E. Renan, *Marc-Aurèle et la fin du monde antique* (Paris: Calmann Lévy, 1883), p. 579: "Si le christianisme eût été arrêté dans sa croissance par quelque maladie mortelle, le monde eût été mithraiste."

148. Ferguson, *Religions of the Roman Empire,* p. 49: "But Mithraism scarcely touched the civil population; it was gross exaggeration by Renan to suggest in his celebrated epigram that if some mortal malady had afflicted the Christian Church the world would have been Mithraist." Compare Beck, "Mithraism since Franz Cumont," p. 2095; M. Simon, "Mithra, Rival du Christ?" in *EM,* p. 477: "Il est difficile en définitive . . . d'admettre que Mithra ait été le rival le plus redoutable du Christ" ("It is difficult to concede definitively that Mithra was the most formidable rival of Christ").

Mithraic than of seventeenth-century England turning Quaker. To say this is not to under-estimate Mithraism or Quakerism."[149]

December 25

Aurelian celebrated the *dies natalis Solis Invicti* ("birthday of Sol Invictus") on December 25.[150] Whether this festival was celebrated earlier than the third century is unknown.[151] Nor is it certain that December 25 was the birthday of Mithras as well as of Sol Invictus.[152] This has not prevented many scholars from assuming that Mithraic influence upon Christianity was involved in the adoption of this date for Christmas.

We do not know the exact date of Jesus' birth.[153] Notwithstanding the sheep out in the fields, a winter date is not excluded.[154] Roger Beckwith concludes that "a date in the depths of winter (January–February) is therefore one of the two possibilities; and it may be that Clement, and through him Hippolytus, were in possession of a genuine historical tradition to this effect, which in the course of time had been mistakenly narrowed down to a particular day."[155]

Clement of Alexandria (circa 200) in his *Stromateis* (1.146) noted that Gnostic Basilidians in Egypt celebrated Jesus' baptism either on January 10 or January 6.[156] By the early fourth century Christians in the East were celebrating Jesus' birth on January 6. Ephraem of Syria (306–373) praised January 6 as the most sublime day that celebrates Christ's birth. The following day was devoted to the epiphany ("manifestation") of the Magi, with the Christians singing Ephraem's hymn: "The whole creation proclaims, the Magi proclaim, the Star proclaims: Behold the king's son is here."

149. A. D. Nock, "The Genius of Mithraism," *JRS* 27 (1937): 113.

150. J. Noiville, "Origines du Natalis Invicti," *REA* 38 (1936): 174. Noiville notes this was the date of the dedication of Aurelian's temple on the Campus Martius.

151. J. Duchesne-Guillemin, "Die Magier in Bethlehem," p. 471.

152. As Cumont, *Mysteries of Mithra,* p. 196, and J. Duchesne-Guillemin, "Jesus' Trimorphism and the Differentiation of the Magi," in *Man and His Salvation,* eds. E. J. Sharpe and J. R. Hinnells (Manchester: Manchester University Press, 1973), pp. 93–94, and other scholars have assumed. For a criticism of this assumption, see Beck, "Mithraism and Christianity," p. 2071, n. 102.

153. Most scholars would date the birth of Jesus before 4 B.C., although some scholars would prefer an earlier or a later date. See J. Vardaman and E. Yamauchi, eds., *Chronos, Kairos, Christos,* Festschrift for Jack Finegan (Winona Lake, Ind.: Eisenbrauns, 1989). The anonymous *De Pascha computus* (A.D. 243) dated Jesus' birth to March 28. See F. J. Dölger, "Das Sonnengleichnis in einer Weihnachtspredigt des Bischofs Zeno von Verona," *Antike und Christentum* 6 (1940): 24.

154. H. W. Hoehner, *Chronological Aspects of the Life of Christ* (Grand Rapids: Zondervan, 1977), pp. 25–26.

155. R. Beckwith, "St. Luke, the Date of Christmas and the Priestly Courses at Qumran," *RQ* 9 (1977): 94.

156. Duchesne-Guillemin, "Jesus' Trimorphism," p. 95, believes that the Jan. 6 date was derived from the birthday festival of the time-god, Aion, in Egypt.

Apart from a problematic passage in Hippolytus's (d. 236) *Commentary on Daniel* (4.23),[157] the first attestation of December 25 as the date for Christmas is found in the *Depositio Martyrum* in the Roman Chronograph of 354. This was composed in 336, and declared: VIII KAL. IAN. NATUS CRISTUS IN BETLEEM IUDEAE ("on the eighth day before the Kalends of January [Dec. 25] Christ was born in Bethlehem of Judea").[158] The date of 336 was a year before the death of Constantine, the first Roman emperor to embrace Christianity.

Before his conversion to Christianity Constantine was a devoted adherent of Sol Invictus.[159] He accepted the aid of Christ in his victory at the Milvian Bridge in 312. In the following year with his colleague Licinius he issued the famous Edict of Toleration at Milan. The symbols of the Deus Sol Invictus continued to appear on his coins until 323.[160]

In 321 Constantine declared that Sunday was to be a holiday: "All the judges, the city folk and the handicraftsmen shall cease work on the venerable day of the sun."[161] Oscar Cullmann therefore suggests, "the analogy of Sunday, which certainly became the official holy day under Constantine, seems to make it probable that it was as early as Constantine, and through his influence, that the festival of Christ's birth was now linked up with the sun on December 25th in the same way as his resurrection with Sunday (the day of the sun)."[162]

Hermann Dörries concludes: "The monument of the victory of Christ over the sun is Christmas. Constantine himself did not institute it, but the Church did in his time."[163] Others credit Ambrose, bishop of Milan (d. 397), as the one who provided the impetus to substitute the birth of Christ for the birth of the sun.[164]

When Jerome came from Rome to Bethlehem in 386, he tried to get the Palestinian Christians to change their celebration of Christmas from January 6 to December 25. But it was not until the sixth century that the Palestinian Christians accepted this date. January 6 is still celebrated as the date of the nativity by the Armenians but is regarded by most churches as the epiphany of the Magi.

157. Beckwith, "St. Luke," p. 74.

158. D. Hughes, *The Star of Bethlehem* (New York: Walker, 1979), p. 85.

159. Halsberghe, *Cult of Sol Invictus,* pp. 167–68.

160. Ibid., p. 169.

161. H. Dörries, *Constantine the Great* (New York: Harper and Row, 1972), p. 121. See also T. D. Barnes, *Constantine and Eusebius* (Cambridge: Harvard University Press, 1981), pp. 51–52.

162. O. Cullmann, "The Origin of Christmas," in his *The Early Church* (London: SCM, 1956), p. 32. See also his *Weihnachten in der alten Kirche* (Basel: Heinrich Majer, 1977).

163. Dörries, *Constantine the Great,* p. 181.

164. See H. Frank, "Frühgeschichte und Ursprung des römischen Weihnachtsfestes im Lichte neuerer Forschung," *Archiv für Liturgiewissenschaft* 2 (1952): 1–24; Lease, "Mithraism and Christianity," pp. 1322–23.

Appendix

When Alexander conquered Egypt he sacrificed especially to the Apis (Arrian, *Alexander* 3.1.4). His successor, Ptolemy I, made use of the popularity of Apis to promote the deity Serapis (Sarapis) to help unite his Greek and Egyptian subjects.

In typical Egyptian fashion Osiris and Apis were identified as Usar-Hapi (Greek *Osorapis*), hence the name *Serapis.* An indigenous god of Rhacotis or Memphis may have been the basis of the cult, although classical tradition speaks of the importation of a god from Sinope on the north coast of Turkey.[1] The main cult centers of Serapis were Memphis and Alexandria. Serapis was depicted in Hellenistic-Roman art as a bearded man rather like Zeus. Figurines of both Serapis and the

1. H. Kees, *Ancient Egypt* (Chicago: University of Chicago Press, 1961), pp. 142–43; S. Morenz, *Egyptian Religion* (Ithaca: Cornell University Press, 1973), for the merging of different Egyptian gods. On the origins of the Serapis cult, see K. Sethe, "Zur Herkunft des Sarapis," in *Festschrift zu C. F. Lehmann-Haupts sechzigstem Geburtstage*, eds. K. Regling and H. Reich (Vienna: W. Braumüller, 1921), pp. 207–13; R. Stiehl, "The Origin of the Cult of Sarapis," *History of Religions* 3 (1963): 21–33; J. E. Stambaugh, *Sarapis under the Early Ptolemies* (Leiden: Brill, 1972).

Apis bull were widely distributed in the Hellenistic and Roman periods, even as far away as Britain.[2]

The cult of Serapis, and his even more popular consort, Isis, became widespread, especially in the period of Ptolemaic power.[3] The cult of Isis understandably appealed to women.[4] The earliest inscriptional evidence for the cult of Serapis at Athens is dated to 215/214 B.C.[5]

Apparently the cult of Serapis and Isis was established at Corinth and its harbor of Kenchreai when Paul ministered there. We have not only the references of Pausanias (2.4.6),[6] but also numismatic and iconographic evidence.[7] While the evidence is circumstantial, Robert Scranton believes that a Roman temple on the southwest mole of Kenchreai may have been an Iseum.[8]

The cults of the Egyptian deities continued to flourish in the Late Roman Empire well into the third and fourth centuries.[9] Papyri of the second to third centuries A.D. record prayers before "my lord Apis."[10] The last Apis bull was hailed during the reign of Julian the Apostate (361–363).[11] The emperor Theodosius ordered the closing of the temples of Isis in 384. Christians destroyed the Serapeum at Alexandria in 391. The temple of Isis on the island of Philae near Aswan continued for a half-century longer as the last bastion of Egyptian paganism.

2. T. A. Brady, "A Head of Serapis from Corinth," *Athenian Studies Presented to William S. Ferguson* (Cambridge: Harvard University Press, 1940), pp. 61–69; W. Horbostel, *Sarapis* (Leiden: Brill, 1973); G. Kater-Sibbes, *Preliminary Catalogue of Sarapis Monuments* (Leiden: Brill, 1973). See also R. Salditt-Trappman, *Tempel der ägyptischen Götter in Griechenland und an der Westküste Kleinasiens* (Leiden: Brill, 1970); L. Vidman, *Isis and Sarapis bei den Griechen und Romern* (Berlin: W. de Gruyter, 1970).

3. R. E. Witt, *Isis in the Graeco-Roman World* (Ithaca: Cornell University Press, 1971); J. Leclant and G. Clerc, *Inventaire bibliographique des Isiaca* (Leiden: Brill, 1974); F. Solmsen, *Isis among the Greeks and Romans* (Cambridge: Harvard University Press, 1980).

4. S. Heyob, *The Cult of Isis among Women in the Graeco-Roman World* (Leiden: Brill, 1975).

5. S. Dow, "The Egyptian Cults at Athens," *HTR* 30 (1937): 188–97.

6. Apuleius set his novel, *The Golden Ass*, written around A.D. 170, in part at Kenchreai, where Isis changed Lucius from an ass into a human. See J. G. Griffiths, *Apuleius: The Isis Book* (Leiden: Brill, 1975).

7. C. H. Morgan, "Excavations at Corinth, 1936–37," *AJA* 41 (1937): 539; J. H. Kent, ed., *Corinth* (Princeton: American School of Classical Studies at Athens, 1966), 8.3, p. 33; D. Smith, "The Egyptian Cults at Corinth," *Numina Aegea* 2 (1975): 4, 15; J. G. McMahon, "Cults at Corinth" (unpublished M.A. thesis, Oxford: Miami University, 1979), chapter 4; J. Murphy-O'Connor, *St. Paul's Corinth* (Wilmington: Michael Glazier, 1983), pp. 17, 21.

8. R. L. Scranton, L. Ibrahim, R. Brill, and J. W. Shaw, *Kenchreai: Eastern Port of Corinth* (Leiden: Brill, 1976), 1: 70–73; ibid., 2: 252. On the alleged influence of the Isis/Serapis mystery religion on the New Testament, see G. Wagner, *Pauline Baptism and the Pagan Mysteries* (Edinburgh: Oliver and Boyd, 1967).

9. Stambaugh, *Sarapis*, pp. 65–66; R. E. Witt, "The Importance of Isis for the Fathers," *Studia Patristica VIII*, series: Texte und Untersuchungen 93 (Berlin: Akademie Verlag, 1966), pp. 135–45.

10. E. G. Turner, "My Lord Apis," *Recherches de Papyrologie* 2 (1962): 117–21; idem, "My Lord Apis—A Further Instance," *Studien zur Papyrologie und Antiken . . . Fr. Oertel* (Bonn: Habelt, 1964), pp. 32–33.

11. A. Hermann, "Der letzte Apisstier," *JAC* 3 (1960): 42.

Select Bibliography

Ackroyd, P. R. *Exile and Restoration.* Philadelphia: Westminster, 1968.

———. *Israel under Babylon and Persia.* London: Oxford University Press, 1970.

Adams, C. J., ed. *Iranian Civilization and Culture.* Montreal: McGill University Press, 1972.

Afnan, R. M. *Zoroaster's Influence on Greek Thought.* New York: Philosophical Library, 1965.

Akten des VII. Internationalen Kongresses für iranische Kunst und Archäologie. Berlin: Dietrich Reimer, 1979.

Akurgal, E. "Griechisch-persische Reliefs aus Daskyleion." *IA* 6 (1966): 147–56.

Altheim, F. *Zarathustra und Alexander.* Frankfurt: Fischer, 1960.

Altheim, F., and R. Stiehl. *Die aramäische Sprache unter den Achämeniden.* Frankfurt: V. Klostermann, 1960.

Amiet, P. *Elam.* Auvers-sur-Oise: Archée Editeur, 1966.

———. "Quelques observations sur le palais de Darius à Suse." *Syria* 51 (1974): 65–73.

Andrewes, A. "Thucydides and the Persians." *Historia* 10 (1961): 1–18.

Arberry, A. J., ed. *The Legacy of Persia.* Oxford: Clarendon, 1953.

Asmussen, J. P. "Die Verkundigung Zarathustras im Lichte der Religionsgeschichte." *Temenos* 6 (1970): 20–35.

Avigad, N. *Bullae and Seals from a Post-Exilic Judean Archive.* Jerusalem: Hebrew University Press, 1975.

Avi-Yonah, M. *The Holy Land.* Grand Rapids: Baker, 1966.

Badian, E. "The Peace of Callias." *JHS* 107 (1987): 1–39.

Bagharzadeh, F., ed. *Proceedings of the IInd Annual Symposium on Archaeological Research in Iran.* Tehran: Iranian Centre for Archaeological Research, 1974.

———, ed. *Proceedings of the IIIrd Annual Symposium on Archaeological Research in Iran.* Tehran: Iranian Centre for Archaeological Research, 1975.

Bailey, H. W. *Zoroastrian Problems in the Ninth Century Books.* Oxford: Clarendon, 1943.

Balcer, J. "Alexander's Burning of Persepolis." *IA* 13 (1978): 119–34.

———. *Herodotus & Bisitun.* Stuttgart: Franz Steiner, 1987.

———. *Sparda by the Bitter Sea.* Chico: Scholars, 1984.

Baldwin, J. G. *Daniel.* Leicester: Inter-Varsity, 1978.

———. *Esther.* Leicester: Inter-Varsity, 1984.

———. *Haggai, Zechariah, Malachi.* Leicester: Inter-Varsity, 1972.

Barnett, R. D. "Persepolis." *Iraq* 19 (1957): 55–77.

Barr, J. "The Question of Religious Influence: The Case of Zoroastrianism, Judaism, and Christianity." *JAAR* 53 (1985): 201–33.

Barr, K. "Die Religion der alten Iraner." In *Handbuch der Religionsgeschichte,* edited by J. P. Asmussen and J. P. Laessøe, pp. 265–318. Göttingen: Vandenhoeck and Ruprecht, 1972.

Barucq, A. "Esther et le cour de Suse." *Bible et Terre Sainte* 39 (1961): 3–5.

Beck, R. "Mithraism since Franz Cumont." *ANRW* II.17.4 (1984): 2002–115.

———. *Planetary Gods and Planetary Orders.* Leiden: Brill, 1988.

Beckwith, R. T. "St. Luke, the Date of Christmas and the Priestly Courses of Qumran." *RQ* 9 (1977): 73–96.

Bengtson, H., et al. *The Greeks and the Persians.* London: Weidenfeld and Nicolson, 1970.

Ben-Sasson, H. H., ed. *A History of the Jewish People.* Cambridge: Harvard University Press, 1976.

Benveniste, E. *The Persian Religion According to the Chief Greek Texts.* Paris: Paul Geuthner, 1929.

———. *Titres et noms propres en Iranien ancien.* Paris: Klincksieck, 1966.

Berg, S. B. *The Book of Esther.* Missoula: Scholars, 1979.

Betz, H. "The Mithras Inscriptions of Santa Prisca and New Testament." *NT* 10 (1968): 52–80.

Bianchi, U. "L'inscription 'des daivas' et le Zoroastrisme des Achéménides." *RHR* 192 (1977): 3–30.

———, ed. *Mysteria Mithrae.* Leiden: Brill, 1979.

Bianchi, U., C. J. Bleeker, and A. Bausani, eds. *Problems and Methods of the History of Religions.* Leiden: Brill, 1972.

Bianchi, U., and M. J. Vermaseren, eds. *La Soteriologia dei Culti Orientali nell' Impero Romano.* Leiden: Brill, 1982.

Bickerman, E. J. "The Edict of Cyrus in Ezra 1." *JBL* 65 (1946): 249–75.

———. *From Ezra to the Last of the Maccabees.* New York: Schocken, 1962.

———. "The 'Zoroastrian Calendar.' " *AO* 35 (1967): 197–207.

Bidez, J. and F. Cumont. *Les mages hellénisés.* 2 vols. Paris: Les Belles Lettres, 1938.

Bigwood, J. M. "Ctesias as Historian of the Persian Wars." *Phoenix* 32 (1978): 19–34.

Bishop, E. F. F. "Some Reflections on Justin Martyr and the Nativity Narratives." *EQ* 39 (1967): 30–39.

Bivar, A. D. H., and J. R. Hinnells, eds. *Papers in Honour of Professor Mary Boyce.* 2 vols. Leiden: Brill, 1985.

Blaiklock, E. M., and R. K. Harrison. *The New International Dictionary of Biblical Archaeology.* Grand Rapids: Zondervan, 1983.

Blamire, A. "Pausanias and Persia." *GRBS* 11 (1970): 295–305.

Bleeker, C. J. "Wer war Zarathustra?" *Persica* 7 (1978): 25–41.

Boa, K., and W. Proctor. *The Return of the Star of Bethlehem.* Garden City: Doubleday, 1980.

Boardman, J. *The Greeks Overseas.* 2d ed. London: Thames and Hudson, 1973.

Boardman, J., and N. G. L. Hammond. *The Cambridge Ancient History III.3: The Expansion of the Greek World.* Cambridge: Cambridge University Press, 1982.

Bode, F. A., and P. Nanavutty. *Songs of Zarathushtra.* London: George Allen and Unwin, 1952.

Borger, R. *Die Chronologie des Darius-Denkmals am Behistun-Felsen.* Göttingen: Vandenhoeck and Ruprecht, 1982.

Bowman, J., ed. *Samaritan Documents.* Pittsburgh: Pickwick, 1977.

Bowman, R. A. *Aramaic Ritual Texts from Persepolis.* Chicago: University of Chicago Press, 1968.

Boyce, M. "On the Antiquity of Zoroastrian Apocalyptic." *BSOAS* 47 (1984): 57–75.

———. "On the Calendar of Zoroastrian Feasts." *BSOAS* 23 (1970): 513–38.

———. *A History of Zoroastrianism.* 2 vols. Leiden: Brill, 1975, 1982.

———. "On Mithra's Part in Zoroastrianism." *BSOAS* 32 (1969): 10–34.

———. *A Persian Stronghold of Zoroastrianism.* New York: Oxford University Press, 1977.

———. "On the Sacred Fires of the Zoroastrians." *BSOAS* 31 (1968): 52–68.

———. "Some Reflections on Zurvanism." *BSOAS* 19 (1957): 304–16.

———. *Textual Sources for the Study of Zoroastrianism.* Manchester: University of Manchester Press, 1984.

———. "Zoroaster the Priest." *BSOAS* 33 (1970): 22–38.

———. "On the Zoroastrian Temple Cult of Fire." *JAOS* 95 (1975): 454–65.

———. *Zoroastrians.* London: Routledge and Kegan Paul, 1979.

Boyce, M., and I. Gershevitch, eds. *W. B. Henning Memorial Volume.* London: Lund Humphries, 1970.

Boyd, J. W. "Zoroastrianism: Avestan Scripture and Rite." In *The Holy Book in Comparative Perspective,* edited by F. M. Denny and R. L. Taylor. University of South Carolina Press, 1985.

Boyd, J. W., and D. F. Crosby. "Is Zoroastrianism Dualistic or Monotheistic?" *JAAR* 47 (1979): 557–86.

Boyd, J. W., and F. M. Kotwal. "Worship in a Zoroastrian Fire Temple." *IIJ* 26 (1983): 293–318.

Boyle, J. A., ed. *Persia: History and Heritage.* London: Allen and Unwin, 1978.

Bradford, E. *The Year of Thermopylae.* London: Macmillan, 1980.

Brandenstein, W., and M. Mayrhofer. *Handbuch des Altpersischen.* Wiesbaden: Harrassowitz, 1964.

Brandon, S. G. F. "Mithraism and Its Challenge to Christianity." *HJ* 53 (1955): 107–14.

Breasted, J. H. *Ancient Records of Egypt.* 4 vols. Chicago: University of Chicago Press, 1906–1907.

Briant, P. "L'élévage ovin dans l'empire Achéménide." *JESHO* 22 (1979): 136–61.

———. "La Perse avant l'empire." *IA* 19 (1984): 71–118.

———. *Rois, Tributs et Paysans.* Paris: Les Belles Lettres, 1982.

Bright, J. "The Date of Ezra's Mission to Jerusalem." In *Yehezkel Kaufmann Jubilee Volume,* edited by M. Haran, pp. 70–87. Jerusalem: Magnes, 1960.

———. *A History of Israel.* 3d ed. Philadelphia: Westminster, 1981.

Brindle, W. A. "The Origin and History of the Samaritans." *Grace Theological Journal* 5 (1984): 47–75.

Broadhead, H. D. *The Persae of Aeschylus.* Cambridge: Cambridge University Press, 1960.

Brockington, L. H. *Ezra, Nehemiah and Esther.* London: Nelson, 1969.

Brough, J. "Soma and *amanita muscaria.*" *BSOAS* 34 (1971): 331–62.

Brown, R. E. *The Birth of the Messiah.* Garden City: Doubleday, 1977.

———. "The Meaning of the Magi and the Significance of the Star." *Worship* 49 (1975): 574–82.

Bruns, J. E. "The Magi Episode in Matthew 2." *CBQ* 23 (1961): 51–54.

Bull, R. "A Mithraic Medallion from Caesarea." *IEJ* 24 (1974): 187–90.

Burn, A. R. *Persia and the Greeks.* New York: St. Martin's, 1962.

———. "Thermopylai Revisited and Some Topographical Notes on Marathon and Plataiai." In *Greece and the Eastern Mediterranean in Ancient History and Prehistory,* edited by K. H. Kinzl, pp. 89–105. Berlin: W. de Gruyter, 1977.

Burstein, S. M. *The BABYLONIACA of Berossus.* Malibu: Undena, 1978.

Cagni, L., G. Giovinazzo, and S. Graziani. "Typology and Structure of Mesopotamian Documentation during the Achaemenid Period." *Annali Istituto Universitario Orientale* 45 (1985): 547–83.

Cahill, N. "The Treasury at Persepolis." *AJA* 89 (1985): 373–89.

Calmeyer, P. "Fortuna-Tyche-Khvarnah." *Jahrbuch des Deutschen Archäologischen Instituts* 94 (1979): 347–65.

———. "Textual Sources for the Interpretation of Achaemenian Palace Decorations." *Iran* 18 (1980): 55–64.

Cameron, G. "The 'Daiva' Inscription of Xerxes in Elamite." *WO* 2 (1959): 470–76.

———. "Darius and Xerxes in Babylonia." *AJSL* 58 (1941): 314–25.

———. *History of Early Iran.* New York: Greenwood, 1968 reprint of 1936 edition.

———. "An Inscription of Darius from Pasargadae." *Iran* 5 (1967): 7–10.

———. "New Tablets from the Persepolis Treasury." *JNES* 24 (1965): 167–92.

———. *Persepolis Treasury Tablets.* Chicago: University of Chicago Press, 1948.

———. "Persepolis Treasury Tablets Old and New." *JNES* 17 (1958): 161–76.

———. "The Persian Satrapies and Related Matters." *JNES* 32 (1973): 47–56.

———. "Zoroaster the Herdsman." *IIJ* 10 (1968): 261–81.

Campbell, L. A. *Mithraic Iconography and Ideology.* Leiden: Brill, 1968.

———. "Typology of Mithraic Tauroctones." *Berytus* 11 (1954): 1–60.

Cargill, J. "The Nabonidus Chronicle and the Fall of Lydia." *AJAH* 2 (1977): 97–116.

Carmignac, J. "Les horoscopes de Qumran." *RQ* 5 (1965): 199–217.

Carratelli, G. P. "Greek Inscriptions of the Middle East." *EW* 16 (1966): 31–36.

Carter, E., and M. W. Stolper. *Elam.* Berkeley: University of California Press, 1985.

Cary, M., and E. H. Warmington. *Ancient Explorers.* Baltimore: Penguin, 1963.

Cavallin, H. C. C. "Leben nach dem Tode im Spätjudentum und im frühen Christentum I: Spätjudentum." *ANRW* II.19.1 (1979): 240–345.

———. *Life after Death I: An Enquiry into the Jewish Background.* Uppsala: C. W. K. Gleerup, 1974.

Chambers, M. "The Authenticity of the Themistocles Decree." *AHR* (1961–1962): 306–16.

———. "The Significance of the Themistocles Decree." *Philologus* 111 (1967): 159–69.

Champdor, A. *Cyrus.* Paris: Michel, 1952.

Charlesworth, J. H. "Jewish Astrology in the Talmud, Pseudepigrapha, the Dead Sea Scrolls, and Early Palestinian Synagogues." *HTR* 70 (1977): 183–200.

———. "Jewish Interest in Astrology during the Hellenistic and Roman Period." *ANRW* II.20.2 (1987): 926–50.

———. "Rylands Syriac MS 44 and a New Addition to the Pseudepigrapha: The Treatise of Shem." *BJRL* 60 (1978): 376–403.

Chattopadhyaya, S. *The Achaemenids and India.* New Delhi: Munshiram Manoharlal, 1974.

Clines, D. J. *The Esther Scroll.* Sheffield: University of Sheffield Press, 1984.

———. *Ezra, Nehemiah, Esther.* Grand Rapids: Eerdmans, 1984.

Coggins, R. J. *The Books of Ezra and Nehemiah.* New York: Cambridge University Press, 1976.

———. *Samaritans and Jews.* Atlanta: John Knox, 1975.

Colledge, M. *The Parthians.* New York: Praeger, 1967.

Collins, J. J. "Persian Apocalypses." *Semeia* 14 (1979): 207–17.

Colpe, C. "Die Mithrasmysterien und die Kirchenväter." In *Romanitas et Christianitas,* J. H. Waszink Festschrift, edited by W. den Boer, et al., pp. 29–43. Amsterdam: North Holland, 1973.

———. "Parthische Religion und parthische Kunst." *Kairos* 2 (1975): 118–23.

———. *Die religionsgeschichtliche Schule.* Göttingen: Vandenhoeck and Ruprecht, 1961.

Commémoration Cyrus. 3 vols. Teheran/Liège: Bibliothèque Pahlavi, 1974.

Coogan, M. D. *West Semitic Personal Names in the Murašû Documents.* Missoula: Scholar's, 1975.

Cook, J. M. *The Persian Empire.* New York: Schocken, 1983.

Coulson, W. D. E., and A. Leonard, Jr. *Cities of the Delta, Part I: Naukratis.* Malibu: Undena, 1982.

Cowley, A. E. *Aramaic Papyri of the Fifth Century.* Oxford: Clarendon, 1923.

Cross, F. M. "Aspects of Samaritan and Jewish History in Late Persian and Hellenistic Times." *HTR* 59 (1966): 201–11.

———. "The Discovery of the Samaria Papyri." *BA* 26 (1963): 110–20.

———. "A Reconstruction of the Judean Restoration." *JBL* 94 (1975): 4–18.

Culican, W. *The Medes and Persians.* New York: Praeger, 1965.

Cumont, F. *The Mysteries of Mithra.* New York: Dover, 1956 reprint of 1903 edition.

———. *Oriental Religions in Roman Paganism.* New York: Dover, 1956 reprint of 1911 edition.

Dandamayev, M. A. "Achaemenid Babylonia." In *Ancient Mesopotamia,* by J. M. Diakonov, et al., pp. 296–311. Moscow: Nauka, 1969.

———. *Persien unter den ersten Achämeniden.* Translated by H.-D. Pohl. Wiesbaden: Ludwig Reichert, 1976.

Daniélou, J. *Infancy Narratives.* New York: Herder and Herder, 1968.

Darrow, W. R. "Keeping the Waters Dry: The Semiotics of Fire and Water in the Zoroastrian *Yasna.*" *JAAR* 56 (1988): 417–42.

———. "Zoroaster Amalgamated: Notes on Iranian Prophetology." *HR* 27 (1987): 109–32.

———. "The Zoroaster Legend: Its Historical and Religious Significance." Unpublished Ph.D. dissertation. Cambridge: Harvard University Press, 1981.

Davies, W. D., and L. Finkelstein, eds. *The Cambridge History of Judaism I: Introduction: The Persian Period.* Cambridge: Cambridge University Press, 1984.

Delcor, M. "Recherches sur un horoscope en langue hébraïque provenant de Qumran." *RQ* 5 (1966): 521–42.

Derrett, J. D. M. "Further Light on the Narratives of the Nativity." *NT* 17 (1975): 81–109.

Dietrich, A., ed. *Synkretismus im syrisch-persischen Kulturgebiet.* Göttingen: Vandenhoeck and Ruprecht, 1975.

Drews, R. "The Fall of Astyages and Herodotus' Chronology of the Eastern Kingdoms." *Historia* 18 (1969): 1–11.

———. *The Greek Accounts of Eastern History.* Cambridge: Harvard University Press, 1973.

Drioton, E., and J. Vandier. *L'Égypte.* Paris: Presses Universitaires de France, 1952.

Driver, G. R. *Aramaic Documents of the Fifth Century B.C.* Oxford: Clarendon, 1954.

Drower, E. S. *Water into Wine.* London: John Murray, 1956.

Duchesne-Guillemin, J. "Die drei Weisen aus dem Morgenlande." *Antaios* (1965): 234–52.

———. "L'étude de l'Iranien ancien au vingtième siècle." *Kratylos* 7 (1962): 1–44.

———, ed. *Études Mithriaques.* Teheran/Liège: Bibliothèque Pahlavi, 1978.

———. "Heraclitus and Iran." *HR* 3 (1963): 34–49.

———. *The Hymns of Zarathustra.* Boston: Beacon, 1963.

———. "Die Magier in Bethlehem and Mithras als Erlöser?" *ZDMG* 111 (1961): 469–75.

———, ed. *Monumentum Georg Morgenstierne.* Leiden: Brill, 1981.

———. "Die Religion der Achämeniden." *AAH* 19 (1971): 25–35.

———. *La religion de l'Iran ancien.* Paris: Presses Universitaires de France, 1962.

———. "Religion et politique de Cyrus à Xerxès." *Persica* 3 (1967–1968): 1–9.

———. "The Religion of Ancient Iran." In *Historia Religionum,* edited by C. J. Bleeker, 1: 323–76. Leiden: Brill, 1969.

———. *The Religion of Ancient Iran.* Bombay: Tata, 1973.

———. *Symbols and Values in Zoroastrianism.* New York: Harper and Row, 1966.

———. *The Western Response to Zoroaster.* Oxford: Clarendon, 1958.

———. "Le zervanisme et les manuscrits de la Mer Morte." *IIJ* 1 (1957): 96–99.

———. *Zoroastre.* Paris: G. P. Maisonneuve, 1948.

Duleba, W. "Was Darius a Zoroastrian?" *Folia Orientalia* 18 (1977): 205–9.

Dumbrell, W. J. "The Tell el-Maskhuta Bowls and the 'Kingdom' of Qedar in the Persian Period." *BASOR* 203 (1971): 33–44.

Duthoy, R. *The Taurobolium, Its Evolution and Terminology.* Leiden: Brill, 1969.

Dyson, R. H. "Early Work on the Acropolis at Susa, The Beginning of Prehistory in Iraq and Iran." *Exped* 10.4 (1968): 21–33.

———. "Ninth Century Men in Western Iran." *Arch* 17 (1964): 3–11.

———. "Problems of Protohistoric Iran as Seen from Hasanlu." *JNES* 24 (1965): 193–217.

Eilers, W. *Iranische Beamtennamen in der keilschriftlichen Überlieferung.* Leipzig: Brockhaus, 1940.

———, ed. *Festgabe deutscher Iranisten zur 2500-Jahrfeier Irans.* Stuttgart: Hochwacht, 1971.

Elayi, J. "The Phoenician Cities in the Persian Period." *JANE* 12 (1980): 13–28.

———. "Le rôle de l'oracle de Delphes dans le conflit gréco-perse d'après 'Les Histoires' d'Hérodote." *IA* 14 (1979): 67–150.

English, P. W. "The Origin and Spread of Qanats in the Old World." *PAPS* 112 (1968): 170–81.

Erdmann, K. *Das iranische Feuerheiligtum.* Leipzig: J. C. Hinrichs, 1941.

———. "Persepolis: Daten and Deutungen." *MDOG* 92 (1960): 21–47.

Evans, J. A. S. *Herodotus.* Boston: Twayne, 1982.

———. "The Final Problem at Thermopylae." *GRBS* 5 (1964): 231–37.

———. "Notes on Thermopylae and Artemisium." *Historia* 18 (1969): 389–406.

Farkas, A. *Achaemenid Sculpture.* Istanbul: Nederlands Historische-Archaeologisch Instituut in het Nabije Oosten, 1974.

Fensham, F. C. *The Books of Ezra and Nehemiah.* Grand Rapids: Eerdmans, 1982.

Ferrari-d'Occhieppo, K. *Der Stern der Weisen: Geschichte oder Legende?* Vienna: Herold, 1969.

Fine, J. V. A. *The Ancient Greeks.* Cambridge: Harvard University Press, 1983.

Fisher, W. B., ed. *The Cambridge History of Iran I: The Land of Iran.* Cambridge: Cambridge University Press, 1968.

Fontenrose, J. *The Delphic Oracle.* Berkeley: University of California Press, 1981.

Forbes, R. J. "Petroleum and Bitumen in Antiquity." *Journal of the Institute of Petroleum* 25 (1939): 19–23.

Fornara, C. W., ed. *Archaic Times to the End of the Peloponnesian War.* Baltimore: Johns Hopkins University Press, 1977.

Forrest, W. G. *A History of Sparta 950–192 B.C.* New York: W. W. Norton, 1968.

Fox, D. A. "Darkness and Light: The Zoroastrian View." *JAAR* 35 (1967): 129–37.

France, R. T. "Herod and the Children of Bethlehem." *NT* 21 (1979): 98–120.

Francis, E. D. "Two Notes on Mithraic Liturgy." *Mithras* 1 (1972): 3–5.

Francovich, G. de. "Problems of Achaemenid Architecture." *EW* 16 (1966): 201–60.

Frankfort, H. *Ancient Egyptian Religion.* New York: Harper, 1961.

Frei, P., and K. Koch. *Reichsidee und Reichsorganisation im Perserreich.* Göttingen: Vandenhoeck and Ruprecht, 1984.

Freitag, R. S. *The Star of Bethlehem.* Washington, D. C.: Library of Congress, 1979.

Frost, F. J. *Plutarch's Themistocles.* Princeton: Princeton University Press, 1980.

Frye, R. N. "The Charisma of Kingship in Ancient Iran." *IA* 6 (1964): 36–56.

———. "Gestures of Deference to Royalty in Ancient Iran." *IA* 9 (1972): 102–7.

———. *The Heritage of Persia.* Cleveland: World, 1963.

———. *The History of Ancient Iran.* Munich: C. H. Beckische, 1984.

———. "Iran and Israel in Antiquity." *Journal of the K. R. Cama Oriental Institute* 44 (1973): 71–75.

———, ed. *Neue Methodologie in der Iranistik.* Wolfgang Lentz Festschrift. Wiesbaden: Harrassowitz, 1974.

———. "Persepolis Again." *JNES* 33 (1974): 383–86.

———. "Problems in the Study of Iranian Religions." In *Religions of Antiquity,* edited by J. Neusner, pp. 583–89. Leiden: Brill, 1968.

———. "Qumran and Iran." In *Christianity, Judaism and Other Greco-Roman Cults,* M. Smith Festschrift, edited by J. Neusner, 3: 167–73. Leiden: Brill, 1975.

———. "Reitzenstein and Qumran Revisited by an Iranian." *HTR* 55 (1962): 261–68.

———. "Zurvanism Again." *HTR* 52 (1959): 63–74.

Gadd, C. J. *The Fall of Nineveh.* London: British Museum, 1923.

Galling, K. *Studien zur Geschichte Israels im persische Zeitalter.* Tübingen: J. C. B. Mohr, 1964.

Gammie, J. G. "Herodotus on Kings and Tyrants." *JNES* 45 (1986): 171–95.

Gardiner, A. *Egypt of the Pharaohs.* London: Oxford University Press, 1961.

Georges, P. B. "Saving Herodotus' Phenomena: The Oracles and the Events of 480 B.C." *Classical Antiquity* 5 (1986): 14–59.

Gershevitch, I. "Amber at Persepolis." In *Studia Classica et Orientalia Antonino Pagliaro Oblata,* 2: 167–251. Rome: Istituto di Glottologia dell'Universita di Roma, 1969.

———. *The Avestan Hymn to Mithra.* Cambridge: Cambridge University Press, 1959.

———. "An Iranianist's View of the Soma Controversy." In *Mémorial Jean de Menasche,* edited by P. Gignoux and A. Tafazzoli, pp. 45–75. Louvain: Imprimerie Orientaliste, 1974.

———. "Zoroaster's Own Contribution." *JNES* 23 (1964): 12–38.

———, ed. *The Cambridge History of Iran II: The Median and Achaemenian Periods.* Cambridge: Cambridge University Press, 1985.

Gharib, B. "A Newly Found Old Persian Inscription." *IA* 8 (1968): 54–69.

Ghirshman, R. "L'Apadana de Suse." *IA* 3 (1963): 148–54.

———. "L'architecture élamite et ses traditions." *IA* 5 (1965): 93–98.

———. *Cinq campagnes des fouilles à Suse, 1946–51.* Paris: Presses Universitaires de France, 1952.

———. *The Art of Ancient Iran.* New York: Golden, 1964.

———. "Les Daivadâna." *AAH* 24 (1976): 3–14.

———. *Iran.* Baltimore: Penguin, 1954.

———. *L'Iran et la migration des Indo-Aryens et des Iraniens.* Leiden: Brill, 1977.

———. *L'Iran des origines à l'Islam.* Paris: Albin Michel, 1976.

———. *Iran: Parthians and Sassanians.* London: Thames and Hudson, 1962.

———. "Notes iraniennes VII: à propos de Persépolis." *Artibus Asiae* 20 (1957): 265–78.

———. *Village perse-achéménide.* Paris: Presses Universitaires de France, 1954.

Gibson, McG., and R. D. Biggs, eds. *Seals and Sealing in the Ancient Near East.* Malibu: Undena, 1977.

Gignoux, P. "L'enfer et le paradis d'après les sources pehlevies." *JA* 256 (1968): 219–45.

Gignoux, P., and A. Tafazzoli, eds. *Mémo-*

rial Jean de Menasce. Louvain: Imprimerie Orientaliste, 1974.

Gillis, D. *Collaboration with the Persians.* Wiesbaden: Franz Steiner, 1979.

Gnoli, G. "L'évolution du dualisme iranien et le problème zurvanite." *RHR* 201 (1984): 115–38.

———. "Problems and Prospects of the Studies of Persian Religion." In *Problems and Methods of the History of Religion,* edited by U. Bianchi, C. J. Bleeker, and A. Bausani, pp. 67–101. Leiden: Brill, 1972.

———. *Zoroaster's Time and Homeland.* Naples: Istituto Universitario Orientale, 1980.

Gnoli, G., and A. V. Rossi, eds. *Iranica.* Naples: Istituto Universitario Orientale, 1979.

Godard, A. *The Art of Iran.* New York: Praeger, 1965.

———. "Persepolis, le Tatchara." *Syria* 28 (1951): 62–69.

———. "Les travaux de Persépolis." In *Archaeologica Orientalia in Memoriam Ernst Herzfeld,* pp. 119–28. Locust Valley: J. J. Augustin, 1952.

Godwin, J. *Mystery Religions in the Ancient World.* San Francisco: Harper and Row, 1981.

Goldman, B. "Origin of the Persian Robe." *IA* 4 (1964): 133–52.

———. "Persian Fire Temples or Tombs?" *JNES* 24 (1965): 305–8.

Goldstein, M. S. "Athenian-Persian Peace Treaties." *CSCA* 7 (1975): 155–64.

Gonda, J. *The Vedic God Mitra.* Leiden: Brill, 1972.

Goosens, G., and J. J. Guepin. "On the Position of Greek Artists under Achaemenid Rule." *Persica* 1 (1963–1964): 34–52.

Gordon, R. L. "Franz Cumont and the Doctrines of Mithraism." In *Mithraic Studies,* edited by J. R. Hinnells, 1: 215–48. Manchester: Manchester University Press, 1975.

———. "Mithraism and Roman Society." *Religion* 2 (1972): 92–121.

———. "Reality, Evocation and Boundary in the Mystery of Mithras." *JMS* 3 (1980): 19–99.

———. "The Sacred Geography of a Mithraeum: The Example of Sette Sfere." *JMS* 1 (1976): 119–65.

Graf, D. "Greek Tyrants and Achaemenid Politics." In *The Craft of the Ancient Historian,* edited by J. W. Eadie and J. Ober, pp. 79–123. Lanham: University Press of America, 1985.

———. "Medism: The Origin and Significance of the Term." *JHS* 104 (1984): 15–30.

Grayson, A. K. *Assyrian and Babylonian Chronicles.* Locust Valley: J. J. Augustin, 1975.

———. *Babylonian Historical-Literary Texts.* Toronto: University of Toronto Press, 1975.

Green, P. *Xerxes at Salamis.* New York: Praeger, 1970.

Greenfield, J. C., and B. Porten. *The Bisitun Inscription of Darius the Great: Aramaic Version.* London: Lund Humphries, 1982.

Grelot, P. *Documents araméens d'Egypte.* Paris: Cerf, 1972.

Groom, N. *Frankincense and Myrrh.* London: Longman, 1981.

Grundy, G. B. *The Great Persian War and Its Preliminaries.* New York: AMS, 1969 reprint of 1901 edition.

Gschnitzer, F. *Die sieben Perser und das Königtum des Dareios.* Heidelberg: Carl Winter, 1977.

Gundry, R. H. *Matthew.* Grand Rapids: Eerdmans, 1982.

Gyles, M. F. *Pharaonic Policies and Administration 663–323 B.C.* Chapel Hill: University of North Carolina Press, 1959.

Hallock, R. T. *The Evidence of the Persepolis Tablets.* Cambridge: Middle East Centre, 1971.

———. "New Light from Persepolis." *JNES* 9 (1950): 237–52.

———. "On the Old Persian Signs." *JNES* 29 (1970): 52–55.

———. *Persepolis Fortification Tablets.* Chicago: University of Chicago Press, 1969.

———. "Selected Fortification Texts." *CDAFI* 8 (1978): 109–35.

Halsberghe, G. H. *The Cult of Sol Invictus*. Leiden: Brill, 1972.

Hammond, N. G. L. "The Battle of Salamis." *JHS* 76 (1956): 32–54.

———. *A History of Greece to 322 B.C.* Oxford: Clarendon, 1959.

———. "The Narrative of Herodotus VII and the Decree of Themistocles at Troezen." *JHS* 102 (1982): 75–93.

Hands, A. R. "On Strategy and Oracles, 480/79." *JHS* 85 (1965): 56–61.

Hanfmann, G. M. A., and W. E. Mierse, eds. *Sardis from Prehistoric to Roman Times*. Cambridge: Harvard University Press, 1983.

Hansman, J. "Elamites, Achaemenians and Anshan." *Iran* 10 (1972): 101–25.

Harris, E. and J. R. *The Oriental Cults in Roman Britain*. Leiden: Brill, 1965.

Hart, J. *Herodotus and Greek History*. New York: St. Martin's, 1982.

Hartman, L. F., and A. A. Di Lella. *The Book of Daniel*. Garden City: Doubleday, 1978.

Hartman, S. S. "Der grosse Zarathustra." *Orientalia Suecana* 14–15 (1965–1966): 99–117.

———. *Parsism, The Religion of Zoroaster*. Leiden: Brill, 1980.

Hasenfratz, H.-P. "Iran und der Dualismus." *Numen* 30 (1983): 35–52.

Hauben, H. "The Chief Commanders of the Persian Fleet in 480 B.C." *Ancient Society* 4 (1973): 24–37.

Hayes, H., and J. M. Miller, eds. *Israelite and Judaean History*. Philadelphia: Westminster, 1977.

Helm, R. R. "Herodotus' *Medikos Logos* and Median History." *Iran* 19 (1981): 85–90.

Hengel, M., and H. Merkel. "Die Magier aus dem Osten und die Flucht nach Ägypten (Mt 2) im Rahmen der antiken Religionsgeschichte und der Theologie des Matthäus." In *Orientierung an Jesus*, Josef Schmid Festschrift, edited by P. Hoffmann, pp. 139–69. Freiburg: Herder, 1973.

Henning, W. B. *Zoroaster, Politician or Witch Doctor?* London: Oxford University Press, 1951.

Hensley, C. "The Official Persian Documents in the Book of Ezra." Unpublished Ph.D. dissertation. Liverpool: University of Liverpool, 1977.

Herrenschmidt, C. "Les créations d'Ahuramazda." *Studia Iranica* 6 (1977): 17–58.

———. "La religion des Achéménides: état de la question." *Studia Iranica* 9 (1980): 325–39.

Herzfeld, E. *Archaeological History of Iran*. London: Oxford University Press, 1935.

———. *Iran in the Ancient East*. Oxford: Oxford University Press, 1941.

———. "The Iranian Religion at the Time of Darius and Xerxes." *Religions* 15 (1936): 20–28.

———. "Pasargadae." *Klio* 8 (1908): 1–68.

———. *The Persian Empire: Studies in the Geography and Ethnography of the Ancient Near East*. Wiesbaden: F. Steiner, 1968.

———. *Zoroaster and His World*. 2 vols. Princeton: Princeton University Press, 1947.

Heygi, D. "Historical Authenticity of Herodotus in the Persian 'Logoi.' " *AAH* 21 (1973): 73–87.

Hicks, J. *The Persians*. New York: Time-Life, 1975.

Hignett, C. *Xerxes' Invasion of Greece*. Oxford: Clarendon, 1963.

Hinnells, J. R. "Christianity and the Mystery Cults." *Theology* 71 (1968): 20–25.

———. "The Iconography of Cautes and Cautopates I: The Data." *JMS* 1 (1976): 36–67.

———. "Iranian Influence upon the New Testament." In *Commémoration Cyrus*, 3: 271–84. Leiden: Brill, 1974.

———. "Method and Message in Mithraism." *Religion* 1 (1971): 66–71.

———, ed. *Mithraic Studies*. 2 vols. Manchester: Manchester University Press, 1975.

———. "The Parsis: A Bibliographical Survey I." *JMS* 3 (1980): 100–49.

———. *Persian Mythology.* London: Hamlyn, 1973.

———. "Zoroastrian Influence on the Judaeo-Christian Tradition." *Journal of the K. R. Cama Oriental Institute* 45 (1976): 1–23.

———. "Zoroastrian Saviour Imagery and Its Influence on the New Testament." *Numen* 16 (1969): 161–85.

———. *Zoroastrianism and the Parsis.* London: Ward Lock Educational, 1981.

Hinz, W. "Achämenidische Hofverwaltung." *ZA* 61 (1971): 260–311.

———. "Zur achämenidischen Hofverwaltung." *ZDMG* 108 (1958): 126–32.

———, ed. *Altiranische Funde und Forschungen.* Berlin: W. de Gruyter, 1969.

———. "Die elamischen Buchungstäfelchen der Darius-Zeit." *Or* 39 (1970): 422–40.

———. "The Elamite Version of the Record of Darius's Palace at Susa." *JNES* 9 (1950): 1–7.

———. *The Lost World of Elam.* New York: New York University Press, 1972.

———. *Neue Wege im Altpersischen.* Wiesbaden: Harrassowitz, 1973.

———. *Darius und die Perser.* 2 vols. Baden-Baden: Holle, 1976, 1979.

———. *Zarathustra.* Stuttgart: W. Kohlhammer, 1961.

Hirsch, S. W. *The Friendship of the Barbarians: Xenophon and the Persian Empire.* Hanover: University Press of New England, 1985.

Hofmann, I., and A. Vorbichler, *Der Äthiopenlogos des Herodot.* Vienna: Institut für Afrikanistik und Ägyptologie, 1979.

Hofstetter, J. *Die Griechen in Persien.* Berlin: Dietrich Reimer, 1978.

Hole, F., ed. *The Archaeology of Western Iran.* Washington, D.C.: Smithsonian Institute, 1987.

How, W. W. "Arms, Tactics and Strategy in the Persian War." *JHS* 43 (1923): 117–32.

How, W. W., and J. Wells. *A Commentary on Herodotus.* 2 vols. Oxford: Clarendon, 1957 and 1961 reprint of 1928 edition.

Huart, C. *Ancient Persia and Iranian Civilization.* New York: A. A. Knopf, 1927.

Hughes, D. W. *The Star of Bethlehem.* New York: Walker, 1979.

Hultgard, A. "Das Judentum in der hellenistisch-römischen Zeit und die iranische Religion." *ANRW* II.19.1 (1979): 512–90.

Humbach, H. *Die Gathas des Zarathustra,* 2 vols. Heidelberg: Carl Winter, 1959.

Huot, J.-L. *Persia I: From the Origins to the Achaemenids.* Cleveland: World, 1965.

Huxley, G. H. *Interaction of Greek and Babylonian Astronomy.* Oxford: Vincent, 1960.

Insler, S. *The Gāthās of Zoroaster.* Tehran/Liège: Bibliothèque Pahlavi, 1975.

———. "A New Interpretation of the Bull-Slaying Motif." In *Hommages à Maarten J. Vermaseren,* edited by M. B. de Boer and T. A. Eldridge, 2:519–38. Leiden: Brill, 1978.

Jackson, A. V. W. "The Magi in Marco Polo and the Cities in Persia from which They Came to Worship the Infant Christ." *JAOS* 26 (1905): 79–83.

———. *Persia Past and Present.* London: Macmillan, 1906.

———. "The Religion of the Achaemenian Kings." *JAOS* 21 (1901): 160–84.

———. *Zoroaster: The Prophet of Ancient Iran.* New York: Columbia University Press, 1899.

Jackson, H. M. "The Meaning and Function of the Leontocephaline in Roman Mithraism." *JMS* 32 (1985): 17–45.

Jacobs, B. "Persepolisdelegation und Satrapienordnung." *Acta Praehistorica et Archaeologica* 13–14 (1982): 75–82.

Jameson, M. H. "A Decree of Themistokles from Troizen." *Hesperia* 29 (1960): 198–223.

———. "How Themistocles Planned the Battle of Salamis." *Scientific American* 204 (1961): 111–18, 120.

———. "A Revised Text of the Decree of Themistokles from Troizen." *Hesperia* 31 (1962): 310–15.

———. "Waiting for the Barbarian." *Greece and Rome* 8 (1961): 5–18.

Janssen, E. *Juda in der Exilzeit.* Göttingen: Vandenhoeck and Ruprecht, 1956.

Jones, R. G. "The Manual of Discipline (1QS), Persian Religion, and the Old Testament." In *The Teacher's Yoke,* edited by E. J. Vardaman, pp. 94–108. Waco: Baylor University Press, 1964.

Jordan, B. *The Athenian Navy in the Classical Period.* Berkeley: University of California Press, 1974.

Justi, F. *Der Bundehesn.* Hildesheim: Georg Olms, 1976 reprint of 1868 edition.

Kane, J. P. "The Mithraic Cult Meal in Its Greek and Roman Environment." In *Mithraic Studies,* edited by J. R. Hinnells, 2: 313–51. Manchester: Manchester University Press, 1975.

Kashani, A. *Iranian Influence in Judaism and Christianity.* Teheran: Kayhan, 1973.

Katrak, J. *Marriage in Ancient Iran.* Bombay: Katrak, 1965.

Kawami, T. "Greek Art and Persian Taste: Some Animal Sculptures from Persepolis." *AJA* 90 (1986): 259–67.

———. "A Possible Source for the Sculptures of the Audience Hall, Pasargadae." *Iran* 10 (1972): 146–48.

Keall, E. J. "Archaeology and the Fire Temple." In *Iranian Civilization & Culture,* edited by C. J. Adams, pp. 15–22. Montreal: McGill University Press, 1972.

Kellens, J. "L'Avesta comme source historique: la liste des Kayanides." *AAH* 24 (1976): 37–49.

———. "Trois réflections sur la religion des Achéménides." *Studien zur Indologie und Iranistik* 2 (1976): 115–17.

Kellermann, U. *Nehemia Quellen Überlieferung und Geschichte.* Berlin: A. Töpelmann, 1967.

Kent, R. G. "The Name Ahuramazda." In *Oriental Studies in Honour of Cursetji Erachji Pavry,* pp. 200–208. London: Oxford University Press, 1933.

———. *Old Persian.* 2d ed. New Haven: American Oriental Society, 1953.

———. "The Record of Darius's Palace at Susa." *JAOS* 53 (1933): 1–23.

Kenyon, K. M. *Digging up Jerusalem.* London: Benn, 1974.

———. *Jerusalem.* London: Thames and Hudson, 1967.

———. *Royal Cities of the Old Testament.* New York: Schocken, 1971.

Khlopin, I. N. "Archäologische Materialen zur Entstehung des altiranischen Feuerkultes." *Klio* 57 (1975): 53–71.

Kidner, D. *Ezra & Nehemiah.* Leicester: Inter-Varsity, 1979.

Kienitz, F. K. *Die politische Geschichte Ägyptens vom 7. bis zum 4. Jahrhundert vor der Zeitwende.* Berlin: Akademie Verlag, 1953.

King, L. W., and R. C. Thompson. *The Sculptures and Inscriptions of Darius the Great on the Rock of Behistun in Persia.* London: British Museum, 1907.

Kitchen, K. A. *The Third Intermediate Period in Egypt.* Warminster: Aris and Phillips, 1973.

Klasens, A. "Cambyses en Egypte." *Ex Oriente Lux* 10 (1945–1948): 339–49.

Klein, R. W. *Israel in Exile.* Philadelphia: Fortress, 1979.

Kleiss, W. "Bemerkungen zu achaemenidischen Feueraltären." *AMI* n.F. 14 (1981): 61–64.

———. "Zur Entwicklung der achaemenidischen Palastarchitektur." *IA* 15 (1980): 199–211.

Klíma, O. "The Date of Zoroaster." *AO* 27 (1959): 556–64.

———. "Zur Problematik der Ehe-Institution im alten Iran." *AO* 34 (1966): 554–69.

Koch, H. "Götter und ihre Verehrung im achämenidischen Persien." *ZA* 77 (1987): 239–78.

———. *Der religiösen Verhältnisse der Dariuszeit.* Wiesbaden: Harrassowitz, 1977.

———. "Steuern in der achämenidischen Persis?" *ZA* 70 (1981): 105–37.

Koch, H., and D. N. MacKenzie, eds. *Kunst, Kultur und Geschichte der Achämenidenzeit.* Berlin: Dietrich Reimer, 1983.

Koch, K. "Ezra and the Origins of Judaism." *JSS* 19 (1974): 173–97.

Kohl, P. L. "Carved Chlorite Vessels." *Exped* 18 (1975): 18–31.

König, F. *Zarathustras Jenseitsvorstellungen und das Alte Testament.* Vienna: Herder, 1964.

———. *Der Burgbau zu Susa nach dem Bauberichte des Königs Dareios I.* Leipzig: J. C. Hinrichs, 1930.

———. *Die Persika des Ktesias von Knidos.* Graz: Archiv für Orientforschung, 1972.

Kotwal, F. M., and J. W. Boyd. *A Guide to Zoroastrian Religion.* Chico: Scholars, 1982.

———. "The Zoroastrian *paragna* Ritual." *JMS* 2 (1977): 18–52.

Kraeling, E. *The Brooklyn Aramaic Papyri.* New Haven: Yale University Press, 1953.

Krefter, F. *Persepolis-Rekonstructionen.* Berlin: Gebrüder Mann, 1971.

Kreissig, H. *Die sozialökonomische Situation in Juda zur Achämenidenzeit.* Berlin: Akademie, 1973.

Kreyenbroek, G. *Sraoša in the Zoroastrian Tradition.* Leiden: Brill, 1985.

Kuhn, K. G. "Die Sektenschrift und die iranische Religion." *ZTK* 49 (1952): 296–314.

Kuhrt, A. "The Cyrus Cylinder and Achaemenid Imperial Policy." *JSOT* 25 (1983): 83–94.

Kuiper, F. B. J. "Ahura Mazdā 'Lord Wisdom'?" *IIJ* 18 (1976): 25–42.

Kulke, E. *The Parsees in India.* Munich: Weltforum, 1974.

Laeuchli, S. *Mithraism in Ostia.* Chicago: Northwestern University Press, 1967.

———. "Urban Mithraism." *BA* 31 (1968): 73–99.

Lamberg-Karlovsky, C. C. *Excavations at Tepe Yahya, Iran, 1967–69.* Cambridge: Peabody Museum, 1970.

Lamberg-Karlovsky, C. C. and M. "An Early City in Iran." *Scientific American* 224 (June 1971): 102–11.

Lattimore, R. "Aeschylus on the Defeat of Xerxes." In *Classical Studies in Honor of W. A. Oldfather,* pp. 82–93. Urbana: University of Illinois Press, 1943.

Lawrence, A. W. "The Acropolis and Persepolis." *JHS* 71 (1951): 111–19.

Lazenby, J. F. *Spartan Army.* Chicago: Bolchazy-Carducci, 1986.

Lease, G. "Mithraism and Christianity: Borrowings and Transformations." *ANRW* II.23.2 (1980): 1306–32.

Lecoq, P. "Un problème de religion achéménide: Ahura Mazda ou Xvarnah?" In *Orientalia J. Duchesne-Guillemin Emerito Oblata,* pp. 301–26. Leiden: Brill, 1984.

Lehmann, M. R. "New Light on Astrology in Qumran and the Talmud." *RQ* 14 (1975): 599–602.

Lenardon, R. J. *Saga of Themistocles.* London: Thames and Hudson, 1978.

Lentz, W., and W. Schlosser. "Persepolis—Ein Beitrag zur Funktionsbestimmung." *ZDMG suppl.* 1 (1969): 957–83.

Lentz, W., W. Schlosser, and G. Gropp. "Persepolis—weiter Beiträge zur Funktionsbestimmung." *ZDMG* 121 (1971): 254–68.

Lerner, J. A. "A Painted Relief from Persepolis." *Arch* 26 (1973): 116–22.

Levine, L. D., and T. C. Young, Jr., eds. *Mountains and Lowlands.* Malibu: Undena, 1977.

Lewis, D. M. *Sparta and Persia.* Leiden: Brill, 1977.

Lincoln, B. "On the Imagery of Paradise." *Indogermanische Forschungen* 85 (1980): 151–64.

Lipínski, E. "Western Semites in Persepolis." *AAH* 25 (1977): 101–12.

Lipke, P. "Trials of the Trireme." *Arch* 41.2 (1988): 22–29.

Lloyd, A. *Marathon.* New York: Mentor, 1973.

Lloyd, A. B. *Herodotus Book II.* Leiden: Brill, 1976.

Lockhart, L. "Iranian Petroleum in Ancient and Medieval Times." *Journal of the Institute of Petroleum* 25, no. 183 (1939): 1–18.

Lommel, H. "Anahita-Sarasvati." In *Asiatica,* F. Weller Festschrift, edited by J.

Schubert and U. Schneider, pp. 405–13. Leipzig: Harrassowitz, 1954.

———. *Die Yašt's des Awesta.* Göttingen: Vandenhoeck and Ruprecht, 1927.

Luckenbill, D. D. *Ancient Records of Assyria and Babylonia.* 2 vols. Chicago: University of Chicago Press, 1927.

Luschey, H. "Iran und der Westen von Kyros bis Khosrow." *AMI* n.F. 1 (1968): 15–37.

MacDonald, J. "The Discovery of Samaritan Religion." *Religion* 2 (1972): 141–53.

———. *Theology of the Samaritans.* Philadelphia: Westminster, 1964.

Macridy, T. "Reliefs gréco-perses de la région de Dascylion." *BCH* 37 (1913): 340–58.

Majidzadeh, Y. "The Land of Aratta." *JNES* 35 (1976): 105–13.

Maier, P. *The First Christmas.* New York: Harper and Row, 1971.

Malandra, W. W., ed. *An Introduction to Ancient Iranian Religion.* Minneapolis: University of Minnesota Press, 1983.

Mallowan, M. E. L. "Cyrus the Great (558–529 B.C.)." *Iran* 10 (1972): 1–17.

———. *Early Mesopotamia and Iran.* New York: McGraw-Hill, 1965.

———. *Nimrud and Its Remains.* 2 vols. London: Collins, 1966.

Marsh-Edwards, J. C. "The Magi in Tradition and Art." *Irish Ecclesiastical Record* 85 (1956): 1–9.

Martin, E. L. *The Birth of Christ Recalculated.* 2d ed. Pasadena: Foundation for Biblical Research, 1980.

Masani, R. *Zoroastrianism.* New York: Collier, 1962.

Masson, V. M., and V. I. Sarianidi. *Central Asia: Turkmenia before the Achaemenids.* London: Thames and Hudson, 1972.

Matheson, S. *Persia: An Archaeological Guide.* 2d ed. London: Faber and Faber, 1976.

Mattingly, H. "The Peace of Kallias." *Historia* 14 (1965): 273–81.

Maurice, F. "The Size of the Army of Xerxes in the Invasion of Greece, 480 B.C." *JHS* 50 (1930): 210–35.

Mayer, L. A. *Bibliography of the Samaritans.* Leiden: Brill, 1964.

Mayer, R. "Der Auferstehungsglaube in der iranischen Religion." *Kairos* 7 (1965): 194–207.

———. *Die biblische Vorstellung vom Weltenbrand.* Bonn: Orientalisches Seminar der Universität Bonn, 1956.

———. "Monotheismus in Israel und in der Religion Zarathustras." *BZ* 1 (1957): 23–58.

Mayrhofer, M. *Nachlese altpersischer Inschriften.* Innsbruck: Innsbrucker Beiträge zur Sprachwissenschaft, 1978.

———. "Neuere Forschungen zum Altpersischen." In *Donum Indogermanicum,* Anton Scherer Festschrift, pp. 41–66. Heidelberg: Carl Winter, 1971.

———. *Supplement zur Sammlung der altpersischen Inschriften.* Vienna: Österreichische Akademie der Wissenschaften, 1978.

———. "Xerxes König der Könige." *Almanach der Österreichische Akademie der Wissenschaften* 119 (1969): 158–70.

———, ed. *Iranisches Personennamenbuch.* Vienna: Österreichische Akademie der Wissenschaften, 1977.

Mazar, B. *The Mountain of the Lord.* Garden City: Doubleday, 1975.

McEvenue, S. E. "The Political Structure in Judah from Cyrus to Nehemiah." *CBQ* 43 (1981): 353–64.

McKeon, J. F. X. "Achaemenian Cloisonné-Inlay Jewellery." In *Orient and Occident,* C. H. Gordon Festschrift, edited by H. A. Hoffner, pp. 109–19. Kevelaer: Butzon and Bercker, 1973.

Mecquenem, R. de. "Les fouilleurs de Suse." *IA* 15 (1980): 1–48.

Meiggs, R., and D. Lewis. *A Selection of Greek Historical Inscriptions to the End of the Fifth Century B.C.* Oxford: Clarendon, 1969.

Menasche, J.-P. de. *Une Encyclopédie Mazdéene, Le Dēnkart.* Paris: Presses Universitaires de France, 1958.

Meriggi, P. *La Scrittura Proto-Elamica.*

Rome: Accademia Nazionale dei Lincei, 1971.

Meslin, M. "Convivialité ou communion sacramentelle? Repas mithraïque et eucharistie chrétienne." In *Paganisme, Judaïsme, Christianisme,* pp. 295–305. Paris: E. de Boccard, 1978.

Messina, G. *I Magi a Betlemme e una profezia di Zoroastro.* Rome: Pontificium Institutum Biblicum, 1933.

———. "Una profezia di Zoroastro sulla venuta del Messia." *Biblica* 14 (1933): 170–98.

———. *Der Ursprung der Magier und die zarathuštrische Religion.* Rome: Pontificio Istituto Biblico, 1930.

Metzger, B. M. "Names for the Nameless in the New Testament." In *Kyriakon,* Johannes Quasten Festschrift, edited by P. Granfield and J. A. Jungmann, 1: 79–99. Münster: Aschendorff, 1970.

Meyer, L. de, H. Gasche, and F. Vallat, eds. *Fragmenta Historiae Aelamicae,* M.-J. Steve Festschrift. Paris: Editions Recherche sur les Civilisations, 1986.

Meyer, M. W., tr. *The "Mithras Liturgy."* Missoula: Scholars, 1976.

Michaud, H. "Un mythe Zervanite dans un des manuscrits de Qumrân." *VT* 5 (1955): 137–47.

Miguens, M. "The Infancy Narratives and Critical Biblical Method." *Communio* 7 (1980): 24–54.

Molé, M. *Culte, mythe et cosmologie dans l'Iran ancien.* Paris: Presses Universitaires de France, 1963.

———. *La légende de Zoroaster selon les textes pehlevis.* Paris: C. Klincksieck, 1967.

———. "Le problème des sectes zoroastriennes dans les sources pehlevis." *Oriens* 13–14 (1960–61): 1–28.

———. "Le problème zurvanite." *JA* 247 (1959): 431–69.

Montefiore, H. W. "Josephus and the New Testament." *NT* 4 (1960): 139–60.

Moore, C. A. "Archaeology and the Book of Esther." *BA* 38 (1975): 62–79.

———. *Daniel, Esther and Jeremiah: The Additions.* Garden City: Doubleday, 1977.

———. *Esther.* Garden City: Doubleday, 1971.

———. "Esther Revisited Again." *Hebrew Annual Review* 7 (1983): 169–86.

Moorey, P. R. S. *Ancient Iran.* Cambridge: Ashmolean Museum, n.d.

———. *Catalogue of Ancient Persian Bronzes in the Ashmolean Museum.* Oxford: Clarendon, 1971.

———. "The Iranian Contribution to Achaemenid Western Culture." *Iran* 23 (1985): 21–37.

———. "Iranian Troops at Deve Hüyük in Syria in the Earlier Fifth Century B.C." *Levant* 7 (1975): 108–17.

———. "Metal Wine-Sets in the Ancient Near East." *IA* 15 (1980): 181–97.

Morrison, J. S., and R. T. Williams. *Greek Oared Ships, 900–322 B.C.* Cambridge: Cambridge University Press, 1968.

Moulton, J. H. *Early Zoroastrianism.* Amsterdam: Philo, 1972 reprint of 1913 edition.

———. *The Treasure of the Magi.* London: Oxford University Press, 1917.

Mowinckel, S. *Studien zu dem Buche Ezra-Nehemia.* 3 vols. Oslo: Universitetsforlaget, 1964–1965.

Muscarella, O. W. "The Archaeological Evidence for Relations between Greece and Iran in the First Millennium B.C." *JANE* 9 (1977): 31–57.

Myers, J. *Ezra–Nehemiah.* Garden City: Doubleday, 1965.

———. *The World of the Restoration.* Englewood Cliffs: Prentice-Hall, 1968.

Myres, J. L. "Persia, Greece and Israel." *PEQ* 85 (1953): 8–22.

Naster, P. "Were the Labourers of Persepolis Paid by Means of Coined Money?" *Ancient Society* 1 (1970): 129–34.

Negahban, E. O. "Notes on Some Objects from Marlik." *JNES* 24 (1965): 309–27.

———. *A Preliminary Report on Marlik Excavation.* Tehran: Iranian Archaeological Service, 1964.

Neuffer, J. "The Accession of Artaxerxes I." *AUSS* 6 (1968): 60–87.

Neugebauer, O. "Demotic Horoscopes." *JAOS* 63 (1943): 115–26.

———. *The Exact Sciences in Antiquity.* New York: Harper and Brothers, 1962.

Neusner, J. *A History of the Jews in Babylonia.* 5 vols. Leiden: Brill, 1965–1970.

———. "Jews and Judaism under Iranian Rule: Bibliographical Reflections." *HR* 8 (1968): 159–77.

———. *Judaism, Christianity and Zoroastrianism in Talmudic Babylon.* Lanham: University Press of America, 1986.

———. *Talmudic Judaism in Sasanian Babylonia.* Leiden: Brill, 1976.

———. "A Zoroastrian Critique of Judaism." *JAOS* 83 (1963): 283–94.

Nigosian, S. "Religions in Achaemenid Persia." *Studies in Religion* 4 (1974–1975): 378–86.

Nock, A. D. "The Genius of Mithraism." *JRS* 27 (1937): 108–13.

———. "Iranian Influences in Greek Thought." *JHS* 49 (1929): 111–16.

———. "The Problem of Zoroaster." *AJA* 53 (1949): 272–85.

Nötscher, F. *Altorientalischer und alttestamentlicher Auferstehungsglaube.* Würzburg: C. J. Becker, 1926.

North, R. "Civil Authority in Ezra." In *Studi in onore di Edoardo Volterra,* pp. 377–404. Milan: A. Giuffrè, 1971.

———. *Guide to Biblical Iran.* Rome: PIBA, 1956.

Nyberg, H. S. *Der Reich der Achämeniden.* Bern: Francke, 1954.

———. *Die Religionen des alten Iran.* Leipzig: J. C. Hinrichs, 1938.

———. "Stand der Forschung zum Zoroastrianismus." *AMI* n.F. 1 (1968): 39–48.

Nylander, C. "Achaemenid Imperial Art." In *Power and Propaganda,* edited by M. T. Larsen, pp. 345–59. Copenhagen: Akademisk Forlag, 1979.

———. *Ionians in Pasargadae.* Lund: Almqvist and Wiksells, 1970.

———. "Old Persian and Greek Stonecutting and the Chronology of Achaemenian Monuments." *AJA* 69 (1965): 49–55.

———. "The Toothed Chisel in Pasargadae." *AJA* 70 (1966): 373–76.

———. "Who Wrote the Inscriptions at Pasargadae?" *Orientalia Suecana* 16 (1967): 135–78.

Oelsner, J. "Zwischen Xerxes und Alexander." *WO* 8 (1976): 310–18.

O'Flaherty, W. D. *The Rig Veda.* Harmondsworth: Penguin, 1981.

Olmstead, A. T. *History of the Persian Empire.* Chicago: University of Chicago Press, 1948.

———. "Persia and the Greek Frontier Problem." *CP* 34 (1939): 305–22.

———. "A Persian Letter in Thucydides." *AJSL* 49 (1933): 156–61.

Olmstead, C. M. "A Greek Lady from Persepolis." *AJA* 54 (1950): 10–18.

Olschki, L. "The Wise Men of the East." In *Oriental Traditions, Semitic and Oriental Studies,* William Popper Festschrift, edited by W. J. Fishel, pp. 375–95. Berkeley: University of California Press, 1951.

Orientalia J. Duchesne-Guillemin Emerito Oblata. Leiden: Brill, 1984.

Orlin, L. L. "Athens and Persia ca. 507 B.C.: A Neglected Perspective." In *Michigan Oriental Studies in Honor of George G. Cameron,* edited by L. L. Orlin, pp. 255–66. Ann Arbor: University of Michigan Press, 1976.

Oxtoby, W. G. *Ancient Iran and Zoroastrianism in Festschriften.* Waterloo: Council on the Study of Religion, 1973.

———. "Interpretations of Iranian Dualism." In *Iranian Civilizations and Culture,* edited by C. J. Adams, pp. 59–70. Montreal: McGill University Press, 1972.

Papatheophanes, M. "Heraclitus of Ephesus, the Magi, and the Achaemenids." *IA* 20 (1985): 101–61.

Paper, H. H. *The Phonology and Morphology of Royal Achaemenid Elamite.* Ann Arbor: University of Michigan Press, 1955.

Parke, H. W. *Greek Oracles.* London: Hutchinson University Library, 1972.

Parker, R. A., and W. H. Dubberstein. *Babylonian Chronology 626 B.C.–A.D.*

75. Providence: Brown University Press, 1956.

Parpola, S. *Neo-Assyrian Toponyms.* Kevalaer: Butzon and Bercker, 1970.

Parrot, A. *Le Musée du Louvre et la Bible.* Paris: Delachaux et Niestlé, 1957.

Pattullo, S. J. "Additions to the Selected Bibliography for the Art of Ancient Iran." *JANE* 10 (1978): 109–12.

Pavry, J. D. C. *The Zoroastrian Doctrine of a Future Life.* New York: AMS, 1965 reprint of 1929 edition.

Pearson, J. D. *A Bibliography of Pre-Islamic Persia.* London: Mansell, 1975.

Perrot, J. "Historique des recherches." *CDAFI* 4 (1974): 15–20.

———. "Récents découvertes de l'époche achéménide à Suse." *Archeologia* 39 (1971): 7–17.

Perrot, J., and D. Ladiray. "Travaux à l'Apadana." *CDAFI* 2 (1972): 13–60.

———. "La Porte de Darius à Suse." *CDAFI* 4 (1974): 43–56.

La Persia e il Mondo Greco-Romano. Rome: Accademia Nazionale dei Lincei, 1966.

Podlecki, A. J. *The Life of Themistocles.* Montreal: McGill-Queen's University Press, 1975.

———. *The Political Background of Aeschylean Tragedy.* Ann Arbor: University of Michigan Press, 1966.

———, tr. *The Persians by Aeschylus.* Englewood Cliffs: Prentice-Hall, 1970.

Pope, A. U. "Persepolis as a Ritual City." *Arch* 10 (1957): 123–30.

Porada, E. *The Art of Ancient Iran.* New York: Crown, 1965.

———. "Bibliography for the Art of Ancient Iran." *JANE* 9 (1977): 67–84.

———. "Iranian Art and Archaeology." *Arch* 22 (1969): 54–65.

———. "Some Thoughts on the Audience Reliefs of Persepolis." In *Studies in Classical Art and Archaeology in Honour of P. H. Von Blankenhagen,* edited by G. Kopcke and M. B. Moore, pp. 37–43. Locust Valley: J. J. Augustin, 1979.

Porten, B. *Archives from Elephantine.* Berkeley: University of California Press, 1968.

———. "Aramaic Papyri and Parchments: A New Look." *BA* 42 (1979): 74–104.

———. "The Religion of the Jews of Elephantine in Light of the Hermopolis Papyri." *JNES* 28 (1969): 116–21.

Porten, B., and J. C. Greenfield. *Jews of Elephantine and Arameans of Syene.* Jerusalem: Academon, 1976.

Posener, G. *La première domination perse en Egypte.* Cairo: L'Institut Français d'Archéologie Orientale, 1936.

Prášek, J. *Kambyses.* Leipzig: J. C. Hinrichs, 1912.

Pritchett, W. K. *The Greek State at War I.* Berkeley: University of California Press, 1971.

———. *The Greek State at War II.* Berkeley: University of California Press, 1974.

———. *The Greek State at War III.* Berkeley: University of California Press, 1979.

———. *The Greek State at War IV.* Berkeley: University of California Press, 1985.

———. "Herodotus and the Themistokles Decree." *AJA* 66 (1962): 43–47.

———. *Marathon.* Berkeley: University of California Press, 1960.

———. "New Light on Plataia." *AJA* 61 (1957): 9–28.

———. "New Light on Thermopylae." *AJA* 62 (1958): 202–13.

———. *Studies in Ancient Greek Topography.* Berkeley: University of California Press, 1965.

———. *Studies in Ancient Greek Topography II.* Berkeley: University of California Press, 1969.

———. *Studies in Ancient Greek Topography III.* Berkeley: University of California Press, 1982.

———. "Towards a Restudy of the Battle of Salamis." *AJA* 63 (1959): 251–62.

———. "Xerxes' Route over Mount Olympos." *AJA* 65 (1961): 369–75.

Pummer, R. "The Present State of Samaritan Studies." *JSS* 21 (1976): 39–61; 22 (1977): 27–47.

Purvis, J. D. *The Samaritan Pentateuch and the Origin of the Samaritan Sect.*

Cambridge: Harvard University Press, 1968.

———. "Samaritans." In *IDBS,* pp. 776–77.

Rahmani, L. Y. "The Adoration of the Magi on Two Sixth-Century C.E. *Eulogia* Tokens." *IEJ* 29 (1979): 34–36.

Rainey, A. F. "The Satrapy 'Beyond the River.' " *Australian Journey of Biblical Archaeology* 1 (1969): 51–78.

Raubitschek, A. E. "The Treaties between Persia and Athens." *GRBS* 5 (1964): 151–59.

Reade, J. "Elam and Elamites in Assyrian Sculpture." *AMI* n.F. 9 (1976): 97–105.

Rempis, C. "Die Zeit Zarathuštras." *WO* 6 (1971): 234–39.

Richter, G. "Greeks in Persia." *AJA* 50 (1946): 15–30.

Ries, J. "Mithriacisme et Christianisme à la lumière des recherches anciennes et récentes." In *Orientalia J. Duchesne-Guillemin Emerito Oblata,"* pp. 439–57. Leiden: Brill, 1984.

Roaf, M. "The Subject Peoples on the Base of the Statue of Darius." *CDAFI* 4 (1974): 73–160.

———. "Texts about the Scriptures and Sculptors at Persepolis." *Iran* 18 (1980): 65–74.

———. "Sculptures and Sculptors at Persepolis." *Iran* 21 (1983): 1–164.

Roaf, M., and J. Boardman. "A Greek Painting at Persepolis." *JHS* 100 (1980): 204–6.

Robertson, N. "The True Meaning of the 'Wooden Wall.' " *Classical Philology* 82 (1987): 1–20.

Roes, A. "The Achaemenid Robe." *BO* 8 (1951): 137–41.

Roll, I. "The Mysteries of Mithras in the Roman Orient." *JMS* 2 (1977): 53–68.

Root, M. C. *The King and Kingship in Achaemenid Art.* Leiden: Brill, 1979.

———. "The Parthenon Frieze and the Apadana Reliefs at Persepolis." *AJA* 89 (1985): 103–20.

Rosenberg, R. A. "The 'Star of the Messiah' Reconsidered." *Biblica* 53 (1972): 105–9.

Rowley, H. H. *Men of God.* London: Thomas Nelson and Sons, 1963.

———. "Nehemiah's Mission and Its Background." *BJRL* 37 (1955): 528–51.

———. "The Samaritan Schism in Legend and History." In *Israel's Prophetic Heritage,* James Muilenburg Festschrift, edited by B. W. Anderson and W. Harrelson, pp. 208–22. New York: Harper & Brothers, 1962.

———. *The Servant of the Lord and Other Essays on the Old Testament.* London: Lutterworth, 1952.

Rudolph, K. "Zarathuštra—Priester und Prophet." *Numen* 8 (1961): 81–116.

Rudolph, W. *Esra und Nehemia.* Tübingen: J. C. B. Mohr, 1949.

Russell, D. S. *The Method and Message of Jewish Apocalyptic.* Philadelphia: Westminster, 1964.

Russell, J. R. *Zoroastrianism in Armenia.* Cambridge: Harvard University Press, 1987.

Sachs, A. J. "Achaemenid Royal Names in Babylonian Astronomical Texts." *AJAH* 2 (1977): 129–48.

———. "Babylonian Horoscopes." *JCS* 6 (1952): 49–75.

Sachs, A. J., and C. B. F. Walker. "Kepler's View of the Star of Bethlehem and the Babylonian Almanac for 7/6 B.C." *Iraq* 46 (1984): 43–55.

Saley, R. J. "The Date of Nehemiah Reconsidered." In *Biblical & Near Eastern Studies,* W. S. LaSor Festschrift, edited by G. A. Tuttle, pp. 151–65. Grand Rapids: Eerdmans, 1978.

Sami, A. *Pasargadae: The Oldest Imperial Capital of Iran.* Shiraz: Learned Society of Fars, 1956.

Scerrato, U. "Excavations at Dahan-i Ghulaman (Seistan-Iran)." *EW* 16 (1966): 9–30.

———. "Religious Life at Dahan-e Ghulaman." In *South Asian Archaeology,* edited by M. Taddei, 2: 709–35. Naples: Istituto Universitario Orientale, 1979.

Schaeder, H. H. *Esra der Schreiber.* Tübingen: J. C. B. Mohr, 1930.

Schaumberger, P. I. "Textus Cuneiformis

de Stella Magorum?" *Biblica* 6 (1925): 444–49.

Schippmann, K. *Die iranischen Feuerheiligtümer.* Berlin: W. de Gruyter, 1971.

Schlerath, B., ed. *Zarathustra.* Darmstadt: Wissenschaftliche Buchgesellschaft, 1970.

Schmandt-Besserat, D., ed. *Ancient Persia.* Malibu: Undena, 1980.

Schmidt, E. *Flights over Ancient Cities of Iran.* Chicago: University of Chicago Press, 1940.

———. *Persepolis I.* Chicago: University of Chicago Press, 1953.

———. *Persepolis II.* Chicago: University of Chicago Press, 1953.

———. *Persepolis III.* Chicago: University of Chicago Press, 1970.

Schmidt, H.-P. "Old and New Perspectives in the Study of the Gathas." *IIJ* 21 (1979): 83–115.

———. *Zarathustra's Religion and His Pastoral Imagery.* Leiden: Universitaire Pers, 1975.

Schmitt, R. "Achaemenid Throne-Names." *Annali Istituto Orientale di Napoli* 42 (1982): 83–95.

———. "Die achaimenidische Satrapie TAYAIY DRAYAHYA." *Historia* 21 (1972): 522–27.

———. "Zur babylonischen Version der Bīsutūn-Inschrift." *AfO* 27 (1980): 106–26.

———. "The Medo-Persian Names of Herodotus in the Light of the New Evidence from Persepolis." *AAH* 24 (1976): 25–35.

———. "Perser und Persisches in der Attischen Komödie." In *Orientalia J. Duchesne-Guillemin Emerito Oblata,* pp. 459–72. Leiden: Brill, 1984.

Schneider, U. *Persepolis und Ancient Iran.* Chicago: University of Chicago Press, 1976.

Schubert, K. "Die Entwicklung der Auferstehungslehre von der nachexilischen bis zur frührabbinischen Zeit." *BZ* 6 (1962): 177–214.

Schultz, C. "The Political Tensions Reflected in Ezra-Nehemiah." In *Scripture in Context,* edited by C. Evans, W. Hallo, and J. White, pp. 221–44. Pittsburgh: Pickwick, 1980.

Seibt, G. F. *Griechische Söldner im Achaimenidenreich.* Bonn: Rudolf Habelt, 1977.

Seymour, J. and M. W. "The Historicity of the Gospels and Astronomical Events Concerning the Birth of Christ." *Quarterly Journal of the Royal Astronomical Society* 19 (1978): 194–97.

Shahbazi, A. S. "An Achaemenid Symbol I: A Farewell to 'Fravahr' and Ahuramazda." *AMI* n.F. 7 (1974): 135–44.

———. "An Achaemenid Symbol II: Farnah '(God Given) Fortune' Symbolized." *AMI* n.F. 13 (1980): 119–47.

———, ed. *Corpus Inscriptionum Iranicarum I: The Old Persian Inscriptions.* London: Lund Humphries, 1985.

———. "From Parsa to Taxt-e Jamshid." *AMI* n.F. 10 (1977): 197–207.

———. "The Persepolis 'Treasury Reliefs' Once More." *AMI* n.F. 9 (1976): 151–56.

———. "The 'Traditional Date of Zoroaster' Explained." *BSOAS* 40 (1977): 25–35.

Shaked, S. "The Notions *menog* and *getig* in the Pahlavi Texts and Their Relation to Eschatology." *Acta Orientalia* 33 (1971): 59–107.

———. "Qumran and Iran—Further Considerations." *Israel Oriental Studies* 2 (1972): 433–46.

———. *The Wisdom of the Sasanian Sages (Dēnkard VI).* Boulder: Westview, 1979.

———, ed. *Irano-Judaica: Studies Relating to Jewish Contacts with Persian Culture Throughout the Ages.* Jerusalem: Ben-Zvi Institute, 1982.

Shaked, S., D. Shulman, and G. Stroumsa, eds. *Gilgul,* Zvi Werblowsky Festschrift. Leiden: Brill, 1987.

Shea, W. H. "Esther and History." *AUSS* 14 (1976): 227–46.

Silverman, M. H. "Hebrew Name-Types in the Elephantine Documents." *Or* 39 (1970): 465–91.

Smith, H. "Wasson's *SOMA.*" *JAAR* 4 (1972): 480–500.

Smith, M. *Palestinian Parties and Politics*

That Shaped the Old Testament. New York: Columbia University Press, 1971.

———. "II Isaiah and the Persians." *JAOS* 83 (1963): 415–20.

Smith, S. *Babylonian Historical Texts.* London: Methuen, 1924.

Smitten, W. Th. in der. "Xerxes und die Daeva." *BO* 30 (1973): 368–69.

Snodgrass, A. *Arms and Armour of the Greeks.* London: Thames and Hudson, 1967.

Speidel, M. P. *Mithras-Orion, Greek Hero and Roman Army God.* Leiden: Brill, 1980.

Sprengling, M. "Kartīr, Founder of Sasanian Zoroastrianism." *AJSL* 57 (1940): 197–228.

Spronk, K. *Beatific Afterlife in Ancient Israel and in the Ancient Near East.* Kevelaer: Butzon and Bercker, 1986.

Starr, C. G. "Greeks and Persians in the Fourth Century B.C." *IA* 11 (1975): 44–99; *IA* 12 (1977): 49–116.

———. "Why Did the Greeks Defeat the Persians?" *Parola del Passato* 17 (1962): 321–29.

Stern, E. "Achaemenid Clay Rhyta from Palestine." *IEJ* 32 (1982): 36–43.

———. "Israel at the Close of the Period of the Monarchy." *BA* 38 (1975): 26–54.

———. *Material Culture of the Land of the Bible in the Persian Period 538–332 B.C.* Warminster: Aris and Phillips, 1982.

———. "The Province of Yehud: The Vision and the Reality." In *Jerusalem Cathedra,* 1: 9–21. Detroit: Wayne State University Press, 1981.

———. "Seal Impressions in the Achaemenid Style in the Province of Judah." *BASOR* 202 (1971): 6–16.

Steve, M.-J. "Inscriptions de Achéménides à Suse." *Studia Iranica* 3 (1974): 7–28, 135–69.

Steve, M.-J., and H. Gasche. *L'acropole de Suse.* Leiden: Brill, 1971.

Steve, M.-J., H. Gasche, and L. de Meyer. "La Susiane au deuxième millénaire." *IA* 15 (1980): 49–107.

Stolper, M. W. *Entrepreneurs and Empire.* Leiden: Nederlands Historisch-Archaeologisch Instituut te Istanbul, 1985.

Strobel, A. "Weltenjahr, grosse Konjunktion und Mesiasstern." *ANRW* II.20.2 (1987): 988–1187.

Stronach, D. "A Circular Symbol on the Tomb of Cyrus." *Iran* 9 (1971): 155–58.

———. "Cyrus the Great." *Revue d'archéologie et d'art iraniens* 7–8 (1971): 4–21.

———. *Pasargadae.* New York: Oxford University Press, 1978.

Strouve, V. V. "The Religion of the Achaemenids and Zoroastrianism." *Cahiers d'histoire mondiale* 5 (1959–1960): 529–45.

Suarez, P. L. "Escatologia personal en los antiquos persos." *Semana Biblica Espanõla* 15 (1954): 1–20.

Sumner, W. M. "Achaemenid Settlement in the Persepolis Plain." *AJA* 90 (1986): 3–31.

Sundermann, W. "Some More Remarks on Mithra in the Manichaean Pantheon." In *Études Mithriaques,* edited by J. Duchesne-Guillemin, pp. 485–99. Teheran-Liège: Bibliothèque Pahlavi, 1978.

Sykes, P. *A History of Persia.* 2 vols. London: Macmillan, 1951.

Tadmor, H. "Some Aspects of the History of Samaria during the Biblical Period." In *Jerusalem Cathedra,* 3: 1–11. Detroit: Wayne State University Press, 1983.

Tadmor, M. "Fragments of an Achaemenid Throne from Samaria." *IEJ* 24 (1974): 37–43.

Talmon, S. "Ezra and Nehemiah." In *IDBS,* pp. 317–28.

———. "The Samaritans." *Scientific American* 236 (1977): 100–8.

Taqizadeh, S. H. *Old Iranian Calendars.* London: Royal Asiatic Society, 1938.

Tarn, W. W. "The Fleet of Xerxes." *JHS* 28 (1908): 202–33.

Thieme, P. "The Aryan Gods of the Mitanni Treaties." *JAOS* 80 (1960): 301–17.

Thomas, D. W. "The Sixth Century B.C.: A Creative Epoch in the History of Israel." *JSS* 6 (1961): 33–46.

———, ed. *Documents from Old Testa-*

ment Times. New York: Harper and Brothers, 1968.

Thompson, G. "Iranian Dress in the Achaemenian Period." *Iran* 3 (1965): 121–26.

Thorley, J. "When Was Jesus Born?" *Greece and Rome* 28 (1981): 81–89.

Tilia, A. B. "Recent Discoveries at Persepolis." *AJA* 81 (1977): 67–77.

A. B. and G. Tilia. *Studies and Restorations at Persepolis and Other Sites of Fārs.* Rome: Istituto Italiano per il Medio ed Estremo Oriente, 1972.

Torrey, C. C. *Ezra Studies,* edited by W. F. Stinespring. New York: KTAV, 1970.

Trümpelmann, L. "Das Heiligtum von *Pasargadae.*" *Studia Iranica* 6 (1977): 7–16.

———. "Tore von Persepolis: zur Bauplanung des Dareios." *AMI* n.F. 7 (1974): 163–72.

Tushingham, A. D. "The Western Hill of Jerusalem: A Critique of the 'Maximalist' Position." *Levant* 19 (1987): 137–43.

Ulansey, D. "Mithraic Studies: A Paradigm Shift? *RSR* 13 (1987): 104–10.

———. "Mithras and Perseus." *Helios* 13 (1986): 33–62.

Unvala, J. M. "The Palace of Darius the Great and the Apadana of Artaxerxes II at Susa." *BSOAS* 5 (1928–1930): 229–32.

———. "Religious and Commercial History of Susa." *Indo-Iranica* 5 (1951): 1–15.

Vallat, F. "Deux inscriptions élamites de Darius? (DSf et DSz)." *Studia Iranica* 1 (1972): 3–13.

———. "Deux nouvelles 'chartes de fondation' d'un palais de Darius Ier à Suse." *Syria* 48 (1971): 53–59.

———. L'inscription trilingue de Xerxes à la porte de Darius." *CDAFI* 4 (1974): 171–80.

———. "L'inscription cunéiforme trilingue (DSab)." *JA* 260 (1972): 247–52.

———. *Suse et l'Elam.* Paris: Editions ADPF, 1980.

———. "Table élamite de Darius Ier." *RA* 64 (1971): 149–60.

———. "Les textes cunéiformes de la statue de Darius." *CDAFI* 4 (1974): 161–70.

———. "La triple inscription cunéiforme de la statue de Darius Ier." *RA* 68 (1974): 157–66.

Vanden Berghe, L. *Archéologie de l'Irān ancien.* Leiden: Brill, 1959.

———. *Bibliographie analytique de l'archéologie de l'Irān antique.* Leiden: Brill, 1979.

———. *Bibliographie analytique de l'archéologie de l'Irān antique ancien, Supplement I, 1978–1980.* Leiden: Brill, 1981.

Vandier, J. *La religion égyptienne.* Paris: Presses Universitaires de France, 1949.

Vardaman, J., and E. Yamauchi, eds. *Chronos, Kairos, and Christos,* Jack Finegan Festschrift. Winona Lake, Ind.: Eisenbrauns, 1989.

Vaux, R. de. *The Bible and the Ancient Near East.* Garden City: Doubleday, 1971.

Vermaseren, M. J. *Mithriaca I: The Mithraeum at S. Maria Capua Vetere.* Leiden: Brill, 1971.

———. *Mithriaca II: The Mithraeum at Ponza.* Leiden: Brill, 1974.

———. *Mithras, The Secret God.* London: Chatto and Windus, 1963.

Vermaseren, M. J., ed. *Corpus Inscriptionum et Monumentorum Religionis Mithriacae.* 2 vols. The Hague: Martinus Nijhoff, 1956, 1960.

Vermaseren, M. J., and C. C. Van Essen. *The Excavations in the Mithraeum of the Church of Santa Prisca in Rome.* Leiden: Brill, 1965.

Vogt, H. C. *Studien zur nachexilischen Gemeinde in Esra-Nehemiah.* Werl: Dietrich-Coelde, 1966.

Voigtlander, E. von. *The Bisitun Inscription of Darius the Great.* London: Lund Humphries, 1978.

Wächter, L. "Astrologie und Schicksalsglaube im rabbinischen Judentum." *Kairos* 11 (1969): 181–200.

Waerden, B. L. van der. *Science Awakening II: The Birth of Astronomy.* New York: Oxford University Press, 1974.

Wagner, G. *Pauline Baptism and the Pa-*

gan Mysteries. Edinburgh: Oliver and Boyd, 1967.

Wallis, G. "Jüdische Bürger in Babylonien während der Achämeniden-Zeit." *Persica* 9 (1980): 129–88.

Walser, G. *Die Völkerschaften auf den Reliefs von Persepolis.* Berlin: Gebrüder Mann, 1966.

———, ed. *Beiträge zur Achämenidengeschichte.* Wiesbaden: Franz Steiner, 1972.

Waltke, B. "The Samaritan Pentateuch and the Text of the Old Testament." In *New Perspectives on the Old Testament,* edited by J. B. Payne, pp. 219–39. Waco: Word, 1970.

Walvoord, J. F. *Daniel: The Key to Prophetic Revelation.* Chicago: Moody, 1971.

Wasson, R. G. "The Soma of the Rig Veda: What Was It?" *JAOS* 91 (1971): 169–87.

———. *Soma, Divine Mushroom of Immortality.* New York: Harcourt Brace Jovanovich, 1973.

Waters, K. H. *Herodotus on Tyrants and Despots.* Wiesbaden: F. Steiner, 1971.

Watkin, H. J. "The Cypriote Surrender to Persia." *JHS* 107 (1987): 154–63.

Wardman, A. E. "Herodotus on the Cause of the Greco-Persian Wars." *AJP* 82 (1961): 133–50.

———. "Tactics and the Tradition of the Persian Wars." *Historia* 8 (1959): 49–60.

Weinberg, J. P. "Demographische Notizen zur Geschichte der nachexilischen Gemeinde in Juda." *Klio* 54 (1972): 45–59.

Weisberg, D. B. *Guild Structure and Political Allegiance in Early Achaemenid Mesopotamia.* New Haven: Yale University Press, 1967.

———. *Texts from the Time of Nebuchadnezzar.* New Haven: Yale University Press, 1980.

Weller, H. *Anahita.* Stuttgart: W. Kohlhammer, 1938.

Wells, J. "The Persian Friends of Herodotus." *JHS* 27 (1907): 37–47.

Wernberg-Møller, P. "A Reconsideration of the Two Spirits in the *Rule of the Community* (I Q. Serek III,13–IV,26)." *RQ* 3 (1961): 413–41.

West, W. C. "The Trophies of the Persian Wars." *CP* 64 (1969): 7–19.

Wheeler, M. *Flames over Persepolis.* New York: Reynal, 1968.

Whitehurst, J. "The Zoroastrian Response to Westernization: A Case Study of the Parsis of Bombay." *JAAR* 37 (1969): 224–36.

Whitcomb, J. C. *Daniel.* Chicago: Moody, 1985.

———. *Esther.* Chicago: Moody, 1979.

Whitley, C. F. "The Date and Teaching of Zarathustra." *Numen* 4 (1957): 215–27.

———. *The Exilic Age.* Philadelphia: Westminster, 1957.

Widengren, G. "Iran and Israel in Parthian Times with Special Regard to the Ethiopic Book of Enoch." *Temenos* 2 (1966): 139–77.

———. *Iranisch-semitische Kulturbegegnung in parthischer Zeit.* Cologne: Westdeutscher Verlag, 1960.

———. "The Mithraic Mysteries in the Greco-Roman World with Special Regard to Their Iranian Background." In *La Persia e il mondo greco-Roman,* pp. 433–55. Rome: Academia Nazionale dei Lincei, 1966.

———. "The Problem of the Sassanid Avesta." In *Holy Book and Holy Tradition,* edited by F. F. Bruce and E. G. Rupp, pp. 36–53. Manchester: Manchester University Press, 1968.

———. "Quelques rapports enter juifs et iraniens à l'ępoque des Parthes." *Supplement to VT* 4 (1957): 197–241.

———. *Les religions de l'Iran.* Paris: Payot, 1968.

Wiesehöfer. *Der Aufstand Gaumātas und die Anfänge Dareios' I.* Bonn: Rudolf Habelt, 1978.

———. "Die 'Freunde' und 'Wohltäter' des Grosskönigs." *Studia Iranica* 9 (1980): 7–21.

Wikander, S. *Feuerpriester in Kleinasien und Iran.* Lund: C. W. K. Gleerup, 1946.

Wilber, D. N. *Iran: Past and Present.* 5th ed. Princeton: Princeton University Press, 1963.

———. *Persepolis, Capital of Parsa.* New York: Thomas Y. Crowell, 1969.

Williamson, H. G. M. *Ezra, Nehemiah.* Waco: Word, 1985.

———. "The Historical Value of Josephus' Antiquities XI.297–301." *JTS* 28 (1977): 49–66.

———. *Israel in the Book of Chronicles.* Cambridge: Cambridge University Press, 1977.

———. "Nehemiah's Wall Revisited." *PEQ* 116 (1984): 81–88.

Windfuhr, G. "Notes on the Old Persian Signs." *IIJ* 12 (1970): 121–25.

———. "The Word in Zoroastrianism." *Journal of Indo-European Studies* 12 (1984): 133–78.

Winston, D. "The Iranian Component in the Bible, Apocrypha, and Qumran." *HR* 5 (1966): 183–216.

Wiseman, D. J. *Chronicles of Chaldaean Kings (626–556* B.C.*).* London: British Museum, 1956.

———. *Nebuchadrezzar and Babylon.* London: Oxford University Press, 1985.

Wiseman, D. J., et al. *Notes on Some Problems in the Book of Daniel.* London: Tyndale, 1965.

———, ed. *Peoples of Old Testament Times.* Oxford: Clarendon, 1973.

Wood, L. *A Commentary on Daniel.* Grand Rapids: Zondervan, 1973.

Wright, G. E. "The Samaritans at Shechem." *HTR* 55 (1962): 357–66.

Wright, J. S. *The Building of the Second Temple.* London: Tyndale, 1958.

———. *The Date of Ezra's Coming to Jerusalem.* London: Tyndale, 1958.

———. "The Historicity of the Book of Esther." In *New Perspectives on the Old Testament,* edited by J. B. Payne, pp. 37–47. Waco: Word, 1970.

Wulff, H. "The Qanats of Iran." *Scientific American* 218.4 (1968): 94–105.

Wynghene, P. H. de. *Les présages astrologiques.* Rome: Pontificio Istituto Biblico, 1932.

Yamauchi, E. "The Achaemenid Capitals." *NEASB* no. 8 (1976): 5–81.

———. "The Apocalypse of Adam, Mithraism and Pre-Christian Gnosticism." In *Études Mithriaques,* edited by J. Duchesne-Guillemin, pp. 537–63. Teheran-Liège: Bibliothèque Pahlavi, 1978.

———. "The Archaeological Background of Daniel." *BS* 137 (1980): 3–16.

———. "The Archaeological Background of Esther." *BS* 137 (1980): 99–117.

———. "The Archaeological Background of Ezra." *BS* 137 (1980): 195–211.

———. "The Archaeological Background of Nehemiah." *BS* 137 (1980): 291–309.

———. *Composition and Corroboration in Classical and Biblical Studies.* Philadelphia: Presbyterian and Reformed, 1966.

———. "Ezra, Nehemiah." In *The Expositor's Bible Commentary,* edited by F. Gaebelein, 4: 563–771. Grand Rapids: Zondervan, 1988.

———. *Foes from the Northern Frontier.* Grand Rapids: Baker, 1982.

———. *Greece and Babylon.* Grand Rapids: Baker, 1967.

———. "Josephus and the Scriptures." *Fides et Historia* 13 (1980): 42–63.

———. *New Testament Cities in Western Asia Minor.* Grand Rapids: Baker, 1980.

———. *Pre-Christian Gnosticism.* 2d ed. Grand Rapids: Baker, 1981.

———. "Religions of the Biblical World: Persia." In *The International Standard Bible Encyclopedia,* edited by G. W. Bromiley, 4: 123–29. Rev. ed. Grand Rapids: Eerdmans, 1988.

———. "The Reverse Order of Ezra/Nehemiah Reconsidered." *Themelios* 5 (1980): 13–21.

———. "Two Reformers Compared: Solon of Athens and Nehemiah of Jerusalem." In *The Bible World: Essays in Honor of Cyrus H. Gordon,* edited by G. Rendsburg, et al., pp. 269–92. New York: KTAV, 1980.

———. "Was Nehemiah the Cupbearer a Eunuch?" *ZAW* 92 (1980): 132–42.

Yarshater, E., ed. *The Cambridge History of Iran III: The Seleucid, Parthian and Sasanian Periods.* 2 vols. Cambridge: Cambridge University Press, 1983.

Young, T. C., Jr. "480/479 B.C.—A Persian Perspective." *IA* 15 (1980): 213–39.

Zadok, R. *The Jews in Babylonia during the Chaldean and Achaemenian Periods.* Haifa: University of Haifa Press, 1979.

———. "Notes on the Biblical and Extra-Biblical Onomasticon." *JQR* 71 (1980): 107–17.

———. *On West Semites in Babylonia during the Chaldean and Achaemenian Periods.* Jerusalem: Waanarta, 1977.

Zaehner, R. C. *The Dawn and Twilight of Zoroastrianism.* New York: G. P. Putnam's Sons, 1961.

———. *The Teachings of the Magi.* New York: Oxford University Press, 1956.

———. *Zurvan: A Zoroastrian Dilemma.* Oxford: Oxford University Press, 1955.

Zinniker, F. *Probleme der sogenannten Kindheitsgeschichte bei Mattäus.* Freiburg: Paulus, 1972.

Index of Subjects

Index of Places

Index of Authors

Index of Scripture References

List of Maps and Illustrations

Maps

Illustrations